DATE DUE

HIGHSMITH 45-220

Children

HOLT, RINEHART AND WINSTON
New York · Chicago · San Francisco
Toronto · London

Children

and Adolescents

BEHAVIOR AND

DEVELOPMENT

and

Adolescents

BEHAVIOR AND

DEVELOPMENT

BY BOYD R. McCANDLESS

EMORY UNIVERSITY

To

ELINORE, BETH, MARK, AND CHRISTINE.

During the writing of this text, they have been

very patient with husband and father,

and their generally benign influence should be evident,

in both subtle and obvious ways,

throughout the book.

PREFACE

AT THE time of writing, it is impossible for a child psychologist to embrace (either in his own mind, or in one volume) *all* the research and *all* the theory that have been amassed about the development and behavior of children and adolescents. This volume, then, is selective: I have tried to stress the general principles—the theory—and the research that I have found particularly helpful in understanding children and young people as they *function* in society.

This is why I have not included the usual chapter on prenatal development: there are many excellent treatments of the subject, and I have nothing new to add to them; nor does the subject matter, although certainly of great scientific and practical value in its own right, seem to me to contribute greatly to *psychological* understanding of and work with children, or to predicting their behavior. Neither are the conventional sections on adolescence included in chapters specifically labeled "Adolescence." I believe that the principles of behavior relevant to the psychology and development of the child of 11 hold equally well for the child who has turned 14, with the possible exception of those phenomena and social considerations related to sexual maturity. These latter are treated in the chapters dealing with physical growth. Where relevant to understanding child development and personality, I have drawn freely on research employing adolescents (or adults or animals, for that matter) as subjects. I realize, of course, that the social forces bearing on adolescents are very different from those influencing younger children.

I have given more attention than is usually given in child psychology books to the child's life in school, because I believe that his school life is second in importance only to his life in the family setting. However, this book makes no pretense at being an educational psychology; it merely seeks to give teachers and schools their just due (and responsibility) in the developmental process.

Norms of child development are not stressed much in this book; consequently, a broad treatment of social attitudes is omitted. Instead, I have tried to give intensive treatment to one major, socially crucial, set of personal-social attitudes: prejudice, ethnocentrism, and authoritarianism. These are employed to exemplify the development of other attitudes and personality variables.

Throughout the book, the importance of learning is emphasized. Since some students come into a course in child and adolescent psychology untrained in learning theory, some elements of theory are treated in Chapter 4. Similarly, many students approach psychology courses unable to evaluate research critically. Some help is given them in Chapter 2.

Neither in child nor in general psychology are our data complete enough to provide us with (at the very best) anything more than general guide lines for understanding and working with children. Much of our practical interaction with them must be conducted "from the seat of our pants," as the early airplane pilots said. Hence, some sections of this book are frankly subjective and "clinical." I have drawn the material for these sections from my clinical work with children and from the experiences of my colleagues. I have incorporated observations of my children, the children of my friends, and the many youngsters with whom I have become acquainted as they attended schools with which I worked.

Regardless of how a title page reads, no author produces a book alone. It is impossible to say "who helped most." Equally important are colleagues, who keep you on your toes, support you, and, if necessary, cut you down to size; students, who serve much the same function, and who are ordinarily very good about letting you develop and test your ideas on them; professional readers and editors, who do their best to force an author to organize logically and write coherently; and family, who put up with prolonged preoccupations and irascibility.

Assiduous critical readings of major sections of this volume, which have resulted in broadening my own horizons as well as in extensive revisions of the manuscript, have been provided by Willard Hartup, Frances Horowitz, June Hoyt, Elinore McCandless, Howard Meredith, and Charles Spiker. Very helpful guidance for smaller sections of the manuscript has come from Jerry Alpern, Eleanore Luckey, John McDavid, and Siegmar Muehl. James Van Toor originally persuaded me to begin writing the book.

Blanche Knox and Dorothy Robinson and their assistants (particularly Maridon Estes) have given patient and detailed attention to the manuscript; Louis Price has been a clever detective on bibliography; and Elinore McCandless has done yeoman's service on "final assembly" at one time and another. I appreciate the help of Barbara Fumagalli, who did the line drawings illustrating physical growth.

January 1961   B. R. McC.
Iowa City, Iowa

TABLE OF CONTENTS

Culture and Human Organism

It's A BOY" or "It's a girl"; these simple declarations of "existence" and gender are usually the first bits of a complicated chain of information parents acquire about their child. Once begun, parent-child interactions change the parents profoundly and probably have more influence than anything else on the direction and type of the child's development.

The small, complex, yet primitive organism—the baby—arrives equipped with a head, arms, legs, torso; and with a set of sense organs that puts him in touch with the world around him. What this world transmits to him—through his eyes, ears, and sense of touch—will modify and shape the course of his development, just as will the sturdiness of his physique, the state of his health, his sex, and his physical appearance.

This chapter presents a brief sketch of the culture to which United States children are exposed and suggests some of the ways in which this culture may affect personality. Finally, it describes the sensory or "culture-receptive" equipment and functioning of the normal baby.

CULTURE AND HUMAN BEHAVIOR

The way in which a child *grows,* using the term broadly, is affected at least as much by the way life treats him, by the opportunities he has for learning, and by the richness and emotional health of his environment as it is by his sensory and muscular equipment. It is, however, logically and practically impossible to separate emotional, intellectual, and physical development. The best emotional environment cannot prevent difficulties for deaf, blind, or physically handicapped children. On the other hand, infants with rugged and efficient muscular and sensory equipment can go far in overcoming unfavorable environments.

Around us we see an infinite variety of people, young and old. Some are tall and thin, some short and fat, some medium and muscular. They may be happy or depressed, passive or active. Some are bright, some dull. Some have money, others are poor. Some are gregarious and others shun people.

Aside from such factors as weight, height, bone structure, eye color, and curliness of hair, the differences so apparent even to a casual observer are due largely to the intellectual, social, and emotional learning opportuni-

3

ties that have been available to these people. The broad, general term used
to describe these learning opportunities is *culture*. To a degree, each community, each section of this country, and each separate country has a unique
culture, insofar as it has customs more or less peculiar to it.

Sectional differences within the United States are easily discernible.
The man from Maine and the man from Louisiana differ. The San Diego
girl, in some respects, is a different person from the western Kansas farm
girl. Still more widely different, one from another, are the natives of different countries and widely different cultures. To the Andaman Islander,
tears may have a meaning entirely different from the meaning they have in
Texas (Murphy, Murphy, and Newcomb, 1937). The sexual attitudes and
behaviors of the native of New Guinea are very different from those of the
boy who was born and brought up in a Presbyterian home in Edinburgh.
The youngster from an impoverished family does not react to money in the
same way as the child who has never known what it is to be without a dime
or a dollar for his pleasure or his needs.

The influence of culture on so basic a process as perception is vividly
illustrated in an experiment by Allport and Pettigrew (1957).[1] The experiment uses a device called the Ames window (Fig. 1.1), which is so propor-
tioned that, as it rotates, the length of the longer edge is always greater on
the retina than the length of the shorter edge. By children and adults in the
United States, the rotation of this window is usually perceived as a sway,
back and forth in an arc. The experimenters appended to the window a cube
and rod, whose rotation was obvious, so that the whole illusion contrasted
the sway of the Ames window with the apparent detachment of the cube
from the window. According to Allport and Pettigrew, the cube was "usually seen to detach itself and swing without support in a ghostly fashion in
front of the window. . . . Similarly, the rod bends, twists or 'cuts through'
the mullions in order to accommodate itself to the phenomenal oscillation.
The observer finds the bizarre effect both amusing and inexplicable."
(p. 105)

This illusion would ordinarily be ascribed to the native or intrinsic
structure and function of the human eye. The prediction would be that,
regardless of culture, it would occur with equal frequency among normal
people who had made ordinary use of their eyes.

Allport and Pettigrew observed that the tribal Zulus of Africa grow up
in a circular culture: their houses are round, their *kraals* are round, and
their language does not even include a word for *square*. They predicted that
the more "native" the ten- to fourteen-year-old boys they used as subjects
(i.e., the less their experience with cities, windows, and squares), the less
frequently they would perceive the illusion. Their findings supported the
hypothesis. The youngsters with the least exposure to a culture other than
that of the tribe least frequently reported the illusion. There was no differ-
_____
[1] Complete citations will be found in the list of references on pages 486–510.

ence between *urban* European and *urban* African boys in the frequency
with which the illusion was reported.

The sciences concerned with the development of man are in general
agreement that differences between people from different cultures are to a
greater degree due to the learning opportunities provided by these cultures

FIG. 1.1.   The Ames window, with cube and rod attached, is
likely, in rotation, to produce the illusion of sway. (Courtesy of Dr.
Hadley Cantril.)

than they are to basic differences in, for example, sense modalities, brain
size, or potentiality for intellectual, social, and emotional development.
Many tentative conclusions, which might almost be called hunches, have
been set forth concerning the influence of culture on personality; much has
been written about this influence; many different cultures have been studied, some with good and some with poor scientific methods; and a few
sound scientific studies have appeared. Where the methods of science have
been applied to the field of culture and personality, the results have been
rewarding.

Definition of Culture

As it is usually employed, the term *culture* is a loose one. It refers to the total way in which a group of people organizes its life from the cradle to the grave. The term takes into account the major group methods of dealing with common life problems. For most people in the United States the culture includes a two-party political system and a reasonably formal set of religious behaviors, usually involving affiliation with a Protestant, Catholic, or Jewish religious group. Certain methods of handling childbirth are agreed upon by the majority; most start their children in school at kindergarten age if the community has a kindergarten, or at about 6 years of age in the first grade. Almost everyone agrees that a high-school education is a desirable minimum for all children. College is highly regarded by the majority, although a minority actually attends.

Most parents begin to turn loose the reins of authority as their children get well into adolescence, and most of them complain about their adolescents' irresponsibility and inability to handle this independence. The average parent expects his children to become self-supporting by the time they are between 17 or 18 and 23 or 24 years of age, depending on what the child is attempting to do with his life vocationally. People are expected to marry somewhere between approximately 20 and 27 or 28 years, although the age varies from region to region within the United States and from one group to another in a given region. Boys are expected to work consistently and to become good providers for their families. Women may work before marriage but are expected to stay at home and care for the house and children after marriage, although this expectation is not as strong as it once was. It is commonly held that grown children should maintain some ties with their parents, although it is not universal for the adult to assume responsibility for his parents. Old age is treated with reasonable consideration. Death is a very sober occasion, accompanied by elaborate funeral arrangements held, almost always, according to the rituals of the appropriate religious denomination.

It is almost taken for granted that there is corruption in politics, but that even the least important person in the community has his rights. It is general to feel prejudice against some "race" or "races," although most deny such feelings: antidemocratic though he may be in practice, the average American has been brought up religiously, within the framework of a democratic ideal, and on the principles of the Constitution and Thomas Jefferson. This upbringing does not make him consistently democratic in his behavior, either toward his fellow men, toward his subordinates or bosses, toward his spouse, or toward his dog, but in the long run he seems to do reasonably well at democracy.

Young people expect to be successful in their careers, to make more money and to have more prestige than their parents had. They in turn pass on similar expectations to their children. Men are nominally the heads of families, but women are actually responsible for more of the total management of the children, the social life of the family, and the spending of money.

It is of such stuff as this that a culture is made. It consists in part of the *formal* organization of the particular country or community, including the church and the political system, and in part of the commonly accepted standards of behavior in such areas as marriage and sex, work, cooperation versus competition, parenthood, and friendship, by which people *informally* regulate infinite complexities of daily life. Folklore—and, to a degree, science—attributes a different culture to each country and to each definable group or tribe or community within that country. The Italian has a culture different from that of the German; the northern Italian a culture different from that of the southern Italian; and the Sicilian a different culture still. The Ubangi differs from the Zulu; the Brahmin from the Untouchable. The Zuni differs culturally from the Sioux; and the Sioux from the Nez Perce.

Cultures can be clearly differentiated to the degree that the group in question is isolated geographically and educationally from other groups. The mountaineer culture of eastern Tennessee is therefore easier to specify than the urban culture of New York City or Detroit: residents of New York or Detroit are more likely to be in communication with people from all over the United States and the world than are the inhabitants of eastern Tennessee. Because of their educational opportunities, they are more likely to be aware of cultural differences, world events, and so on, and to have had a wider variety of socializing experiences. Thus, their culture is likely to be more variable and less easily defined.

Although certain broad practices and expectations apply to all members of a given group, the *effective* culture is never precisely the same for any two individuals or families in even the simplest, smallest tribal community. In so large and complex a community as the United States, one is hard put to find any single factor that applies even to a majority of the population. The loose description of United States culture given a few paragraphs ago probably never applies in all respects to any single person. However, it provides a recognizable pattern and gives the setting within which the American child is born and to which he reacts—the pattern that makes him, as an "average," different from the "average" child within any other culture, regardless of his social class.

Culture, then, consists of the *major institutional and social patterns followed by a larger or smaller, but definable, group of persons.* The term may be used broadly, in relation to a relatively large social group, or more narrowly, to define the usages of specific subgroups. The culture of the Middle West is often contrasted with that of the East or West Coast; the culture of the Old South is contrasted with that north of the Mason-Dixon line; that of the mandated islands with that of the mainland. Each of these cultures provides a roughly agreed-upon pattern of learning for the children born into it—a pattern different from that of other cultures or subcultures.

Illustrations of Cultural Variation

The vast range of cultural patterns can be clearly exemplified by diverse customs relating to marriage, since mate-taking is a universal custom. The following examples have been randomly selected from observation and anthropological accounts, and range from those common in a Western European culture to practices among the Bushmen of Australia.

1. Boy proposes, girl accepts; they cooperate in getting a marriage license, go with two witnesses to a justice of the peace, and are married without further ado. (*United States, informal.*)

2. Boy proposes, girl tentatively accepts, girl's father is approached. Diamond is bestowed and engagement announced. Waiting period intervenes while bride buys trousseau, selects bridesmaids and wedding guests; boy chooses ushers. Church is reserved, flowers are ordered, guests are invited; wedding ensues. Reception is held, during which bride changes from white satin and lace to traveling clothes, groom from morning coat to business suit. Newlyweds rush out front door, pelted by shoes, rice, and confetti, and go on honeymoon. (*United States, formal.*)

3. Father decides daughter of other father is appropriate for his son. Seeks intermediary, who approaches girl's father. Financial arrangements—dowry for girl, financial prospects for boy—are discussed; agreement is reached. Time—often years—is allowed for boy and girl, who have never seen each other, to grow up. When the time comes, formal wedding is celebrated with a feast. On wedding night, bride and groom may see each other for first time. (*Among others, traditional Chinese.*)

4. Boy meets and likes girl, courts and wins her. After she has proved she is capable of bearing a sound and healthy child, wedding arrangements are completed between boy's relatives and girl's relatives. Payment is made sometimes by the girl's, sometimes by the boy's family. (*Certain African tribes.*)

5. Boy meets and is attracted by girl. Their relationship is kept secret, because the adult members of the tribe would pronounce a sentence of death were love interest or matrimonial plans suspected. At an agreed-upon time, boy and girl elope in full flight, pursued by adults of the group. Amnesty is granted the fleeing couple if they reach a particular island. They are reprieved from sentence of death when they return to the tribe, provided they have managed to have a child by that time. (*Australian Bush tribe.*)

No universal pattern exists for handling any of the major tasks involved in human living. The infinite variety of human custom applies just as much to having a baby and caring for him as it does to getting married, worshipping a deity, growing old, and dying.

Social Class

So far in this chapter, variations in culture have been discussed largely in geographic terms. Another refinement of culture is often postulated: culture as it is affected by *social class*. According to Davis and Dollard (1940), *class* is a term that refers to the group with which one "visits, intermarries, and co-belongs . . . to organizations pitched primarily at the social level." Many sociologists separate the United States population into three classes: (1) the *upper*—reasonably free of narrow conventions, but in general law-abiding; conscious to a greater or lesser degree of their own superiority, but secure enough not to need to call it to anyone's attention and secure enough to be reasonably free from acting in any self-conscious manner; (2) the *middle*—ambitious, law-abiding, community-conscious, rather self-conscious; valuing education highly and having a hearty respect, by and large, for the status quo; and (3) the *lower,* where most of life's experiences are frustrating; where insecurity is the established pattern; where there is reasonably little hope of social or vocational climbing or of obtaining college degrees or professional status; where violence often occurs; and where sexual behavior is much more forthright and accepted than it is in the other two classes.

The terms *upper, middle,* and *lower,* perhaps irritating to the average democratically-minded American, may have been poorly chosen, but they seem to have validity as far as describing culture within a given community is concerned.

There are several different ways of defining social class, and many problems in measuring it. Some define it by parents' educational level (Kinsey, Pomeroy, and Martin, 1948): the higher the educational level, the higher the social-class rating. Others use level of father's occupation as a guide to social class (Sears, Maccoby, and Levin, 1957): professional men, such as doctors or lawyers, for example, are given the highest ranking; unskilled laborers, the lowest classification. A psychological definition of social class has been advanced by Centers (1950, 1951). The concept or social class has been criticized (e.g., Loevinger, 1940) as being vague, or false, or useless.

Nonetheless, social class, however defined, has been shown to be associated with important differences in the types of learning experience to which a given child is exposed, the degree of economic security he possesses, the way he is introduced to school, and the way in which fighting and sexuality are introduced to him. It probably plays a large part in the way he is fed and trained to go to the toilet, as well as in the way he is disciplined. His social class, finally, is thought to have much to do with the goals he eventually includes in his life pattern: goals of marriage, vocation, and parenthood.

The Family

The relation of *family* to *culture* is complex. Although the culture dictates the family form or pattern, the family is the immediate "in-group" or small subunit on the basis of which the culture is built and through which it is transmitted to the child. In the United States, the typical or average family is made up of the father (the titular head of the house); the mother (the "mainstay" of the home); one or more children; and a more or less loosely connected set of uncles, aunts, and grandparents. A large number of families together, subscribing in general to the same customs, makes up a culture; but within a given family, variability is less than between families, so that each family unit in effect constitutes a subculture. No two families interpret the general culture in precisely the same way to their children.

MOTHERHOOD AND INFANT CARE

For about seven out of eight United States couples, marriage is sooner or later followed by the birth of a child. On the basis of interviews with a large number of suburban mothers, Sears, Maccoby, and Levin (1957) rated 62 percent of the mothers of first-born children as *delighted* when they learned that they were pregnant, while another 19 percent were *generally pleased*. Fewer than one fifth had *mixed feelings* or were *displeased*. Mothers of later children were delighted less frequently than mothers of first children (in 34 percent of the cases) and had mixed feelings or were displeased more often (34 percent). The age of the next-older child markedly affected the sentiments of the mother: For example, when the next-older brother or sister was 21 months of age or less when the child who was the focus of the Sears, Maccoby, and Levin study was born, only 9 percent of the mothers were delighted; but when the next-older child was 55 months or more of age, 52 percent of the mothers expressed delight. Comparable figures for mixed feelings and displeasure were 68 and 32 percent.

Pregnancy

In the United States, women vary widely in their physical response to pregnancy, just as they do in their psychological response. During the early months of pregnancy, many will experience nausea (morning sickness). For a few, nausea persists throughout the pregnancy. Periods of faintness, food cravings, and moodiness are also frequent. Many modern obstetricians, particularly those with a psychiatric point of view, believe that such symptoms are due in part to the woman's culturally conditioned anxiety; women fear pregnancy; they *expect* a difficult time; hence, they *have* a difficult time. Some case-history material suggests that women who genuinely and deeply desire a child, and who have few fears about their ability to bear it and care for it after birth, are less disturbed in health during pregnancy than women who are fearful or ambivalent about having a baby. But this point has not been definitely established.

In other words, culture may affect so apparently physical a condition as the mother's well-being when she is carrying a child. The idea that the early stages of pregnancy are usually accompanied by illness is part of United States folklore, although many women experience nothing but well-being from conception to delivery. For most of those who are uneasy early in pregnancy, the frequency and intensity of their symptoms abate after the child quickens, at about four months after conception.

SOME INFLUENCES ON PRENATAL DEVELOPMENT

The baby at birth is largely the result of the combination of his father's and mother's genes; but environmental influences have also affected him. It is known that mothers who have good diets during pregnancy suffer less from illness, and that they threaten to or actually miscarry less frequently than women who have poor diets. Children born to well-nourished mothers have better health records during their first two weeks of life, and fewer major diseases afflict them in their first six months (e.g., Burke, *et al.,* 1943; Ebbs, *et al.,* 1942 *a, b*).

Maternal smoking speeds up fetal heart rate, although nothing is known concerning the significance of this speeding up for either fetal or later life development (Sontag and Wallace, 1935). X-ray treatment, especially heavy doses during early pregnancy, may produce disorders of the central nervous system, deformation, blindness, or microcephaly (Murphy, 1929, 1947).

Diseases such as syphilis may affect the fetus devastatingly. The mild disease *rubella,* or German measles, particularly when it occurs during the first trimester of pregnancy, may result in the birth of a child who is deaf, visually defective, mentally defective (including microcephalic), or afflicted with a pathological heart condition. Combinations of these defects may also occur.

Incompatibility in blood type between mother and infant, where the mother is Rh-negative and the child Rh-positive, may result in brain damage and/or death to the child. This incompatibility affects first-born children less often than it does those born later. With each pregnancy by an Rh-positive father, the Rh-negative mother produces more antibodies, and these antibodies interfere with oxygen distribution in the fetus or newborn. Modern medical techniques, including total replacement of the infant's blood supply immediately or soon after birth, have reduced the danger to the Rh-damaged baby. All couples should be informed about their Rh blood type, since possession of information concerning possible danger helps the specialist avoid the danger.

There is only one definitely known relation between age of the mother and condition of the child, and this relation is slight. Older mothers are more likely to have babies who fall into the category of the Mongolian mental defective (Malzberg, 1950). It has been estimated that two thirds of such babies are born to mothers older than 35. Mongolism is less likely to occur in a first pregnancy than it is in a later one. Of course, the older mother is the one more likely to have had several children, so that it cannot be said definitely whether the significant variable is age or number of pregnancies. There is a tendency for Mongolian mental defectives to be born to mothers who have had repeated pregnancy difficulties; but this too relates to the age of the mother and the number of children she has had. In any event, Mongolian mental deficiency is rare, occurring in a ratio of about 1 in 1,500 live births.

Until fairly recently, the effect of the mother's emotional state on the development of the fetus has been minimized. Old wives' tales about "marking the baby" do not, of course, hold up. Yet recent evidence exists to show that maternal emotional stress, unhappiness in marriage, and extreme rejection of a pregnancy, all predispose women to uneasy pregnancies, premature births, and possibly miscarriages, and to the production of tense, hyperactive, hard-to-live-with babies (see, e.g., Lakin, 1957; Howe, in personal communication, has also provided evidence for this from the Kaui pregnancy study).

Childbirth

Aside from the medical-physiological, little evidence exists concerning the effects of the birth process on the later adjustment of the baby. Prematurity poses psychological as well as physical perils, and is discussed in Chapter 3. Little is known about the effects of "severe" versus "mild" delivery, or "long" as contrasted with "moderate" or "short" times of delivery.

The medical aspects of childbirth are of only incidental interest here. Since World War II, the handling of childbirth seems to have become steadily more "natural" and "sensible." There is increasing regard for childbirth as a *natural* phenomenon, shared by all mammals; the conviction is growing that mothers may not *need* to be heavily anesthetized during delivery; and there is generally good agreement that prolonged hospitalization following childbirth is unnecessary. In general, also, fewer restrictions are placed on the activities of the new mother after her return home.

Patterns of Child Care

For a majority of American couples, the birth of their first child is what they expect it to be: a time of mature and deep enjoyment. Parenthood is inevitably larded with troubles and cares, illness, financial stresses, and personal annoyances; but by and large it is also a deeply satisfying experience. There are, of course, couples too immature to accept children; too sheltered or "spoiled" themselves to assume full, ungrudging responsibility for their children; or too rigid and dominating to allow their children freedom to grow. But within the limits of their personal make-up and knowledge, almost all do the best thing they can for the welfare of their children. Their practices are influenced by their personalities, singly and together, by the happiness of their marriage, by their intelligence, and by their understanding of child development. But there are few or no ill-meaning parents. This point is one often ignored or forgotten by teachers, child psychologists and psychiatrists, social workers, and all the host of persons who write, lecture, teach, and counsel on child-rearing methods and parent-child relationships.

Patterns of parental behavior begin when the infant enters the home. He enters it, literally, with a bang. As the authors of one monograph have aptly put it:

> With the arrival of the first baby, the parents are at once plunged into a new situation which is vastly different from preparental marital life. The child's coming into the household automatically sets up a more complex social structure and a different kind of relationship by introducing into the family a completely dependent organism for whose continued existence and happiness the parents are largely responsible. The advent of the baby necessitates many changes in the family schedule; regardless of his virtues, a baby is a far from ideal roomer—he is dirty, noisy, and addicted to highly irregular hours. His presence may restrict the social life of his parents, and his expensive taste for hospitals, doctors, and new clothes may cause them financial embarrassment.[2]

Countless books, pamphlets, and articles have been written advising parents how to handle this "far from ideal roomer." New parents are understandably insecure, faced as they are with an organism whose grip on life seems at best precarious, who cannot tell them either what ails him or what is right with him, who is both unscheduled and unreasonable, yet who possesses the germ of ultimate humanity.

Two theories about the development of this organism, the baby, have been particularly influential in the United States. The originator of one, the behaviorist Watson (1924, 1928), postulated, in a literal and narrow sense, that a child would become what he was taught to be. If he were fed regularly, he would learn to be regular in his habits. If he were picked up or fondled when he cried, he would soon become spoiled and cry simply because he wanted to be picked up, not because he was hungry or in pain. If he were toilet-trained early, he would learn to be neat, cleanly, and regular, not only in eliminative but in *all* habits.

The second theory has been constructed by his followers from the revolutionary psychoanalytic doctrines of Sigmund Freud. As early behaviorism emphasized the mechanistic learning capabilities of the baby, psychoanalytic thought stressed his instinctual-animal qualities. One of the most extreme of Freudian disciples, Ribble (1943), seems to advocate a return of child-rearing practices to the primitive. The baby, she indicates, should be endlessly cradled, should sleep with the mother, be breast-fed well into the second year, and be toilet-trained very late indeed—perhaps not until he decides voluntarily to become continent.

[2] Reprinted with permission from the American Psychological Association and A. L. Baldwin, from Baldwin, Kalhorn, and Breese, 1945.

These two theories represent two extremes of viewing the child. The first advocates socializing the child early (so that he will no longer "bother" the adult?). Extreme forms of the second consider the child to be the center of the family universe, advocating that all practices minister to his comfort and minimize his anxiety. Implicit in the first theory is a failure to appreciate the slow development from primitive, nonsymbolic organism to complex, symbol-using older child. This gradual process necessitates gratifying instincts and primitive needs in the preverbal infant. Implicit in the extremes of the second theory is a failure to understand the intricate demands of modern existence, where parents have legitimate, even urgent, needs that may conflict with the demands of parenthood. If their needs as adults are ignored, they may accumulate enough tension and anxiety so that the baby is worse off than if he had been tended less exhaustively but in a more relaxed fashion. Contributing to the anxiety of parents is the explicit and implicit assumption of both schools of thought that the child is what the parents make him. If he turns out well, they may take the credit; if ill, they are to blame.

Few United States child-rearing practices fit either of these extreme schools of thought. Most parents realize that babies do not run by clockwork, and love them, cuddle them, and make few demands on them (gratify, to a substantial degree, their instincts and primitive needs). On the other hand, parents in the United States tend to start socialization of their child before he is ready, before the child really understands what is happening to him: one has only to shop for groceries to see mothers punishing their children for infringements of property rights, such as "lifting' a package of cookies, long before the child can possibly have any idea of what is "mine" and what is "his." For the average child, toilet-training is started at about 11 months of age (Sears, Maccoby, and Levin, 1957), probably before sphincter control is complete, and certainly before the average child has enough understanding of words to know what it is that his parents are demanding of him.

SENSORY EQUIPMENT AND DEVELOPMENT

Introduction

In the first part of this chapter, emphasis was put more on the influence of the environment, or *setting for learning*, than on *equipment* for learning. But an environment has no influence unless it affects the individual. Its impact on babies is made through their sense organs. In the beginning of life, sense organs receive stimulation from the environment, and the organism responds to this stimulation, in a relatively simple fashion. No *meaning*, as older children and adults know it, is attached to stimuli. Light rays strike the eye, register on the retina, and are transmitted to the appropriate areas of the brain. The infant's reaction is simple: In bright light, his pupil contracts and some of the stimulation is shut out; in dim light, the pupil expands, and more light registers on the retina. Soon, the baby blinks as stimuli approach his eye rapidly; later, more complex responses are made to visual stimuli.

Simple reactions, such as pupil dilation and contraction and the blink reflex, persist through life; but meaning is progressively added to visual stimuli (and all others). Presently, a three-sided figure comes to be distinguished from a circle. Eventually it is labeled as a triangle. A certain face becomes "mother." A given configuration of distance and contrast is recognized as "a place I may fall off," and so on.

By *perception*, then, is meant *awareness of sensory stimuli, attention to them,* and *attachment of meaning to them.*

When the matter is reduced to its simplest elements, it may be said that an adult functions well or poorly—succeeds or fails—depending on the way he manages his behavior in terms of his perception of himself and the world around him, and on how his perceptions fit with those of the people among whom he lives. His sense organs and the meanings he gives to the sensations he receives determine this consonance or dissonance.

Such a statement, of course, begs the important question of how he comes to give a certain meaning, or make a certain response, to the stimuli that impinge on him. The elements of this fundamental process are discussed in Chapter 4.

The bodily equipment by which an infant receives stimulation (his sense modalities) has been classified in different ways, but the following scheme is one commonly used:

1. Vision
2. Hearing, or audition
3. Smell, or olfaction
4. Taste, or gustation
5. Touch, or pressure and contact
6. Touch, or movement (kinesthesis)
7. Pain[3]
8. Temperature, or thermal sensitivity

Until recently, studies of infants have been devoted in large part to determining the nature and function of the sensory equipment with which they came into the world. There are elaborate and highly controlled studies of what and how a baby sees, hears, tastes, and so on. No discussion of infancy can ignore the child's sensory equipment, because it is basic to everything that happens to him for the duration of his life. It has been mentioned that the absence of a sensory mode, as in deafness or blindness, leads to problems of living very different from those encountered by normal children.

The sweep of sensory development from infancy to adulthood, or even to the age of 2, is staggering. At birth, the child sees dimly, if indeed he sees at all in any adult sense of the word. He has no notion of what he sees, or of what his reaction to it should be. But as an adult, he reacts to the rainy sky, or the slippery pavement; while driving, he attends to the tentative be-

[3] It should be noted that excessive stimulation in any modality may produce pain.

havior of a pedestrian two blocks away; to the difference in texture between velvet and satin; and to the meaning of the printed page. On the basis of visual stimuli and the experiences he has had with them, he determines his behavior. The rainy sky suggests a raincoat; the slippery pavement, taking the bus to work. The errant pedestrian causes him to reduce his driving speed; the perception of velvet or satin leads to different sewing responses, or to a different set of expectations about touching or feeling. The printed page provokes thought, irritation, sympathy, amusement, or some other well-differentiated response.

Although increasing maturity of the sense organs is partly responsible for this increased acuity of perception, most of it is due to the learning opportunities afforded the older child or adult—opportunities that the infant has not yet encountered.

Vision

Normal older children and adults react to such characteristics of light as color or hue, brightness, saturation (how much of the hue is present), and length of exposure time. They use these dimensions in discriminative reactions and combine them with stimulation received from the eye muscles in order to judge distance, size, distortion, and so on. Additional information is gained by fusing the separate images received by the two eyes.

The infant has little more than the ability to react by pupillary reaction to different intensities of light, although some believe that the ability to distinguish figure from ground—to perceive primitive contrast—is present (Hebb, 1949). During the developmental process following birth, *size* and *shape constancy* are developed. An older child knows that he can blot out the image of a mountain in the distance by holding his hand a few inches from his eyes, or by holding his thumb close to one eye when the other is closed. But he knows that this does not mean that his hand or thumb is larger than the mountain. He has also gained the ability to recognize a circle as a circle, even though it is tilted so that the actual sensory image is one of an oval. The infant has not yet learned clues such as these, which help the older child or adult maintain order in his world.

At birth, normal babies possess organically complete visual equipment. Further visual development and differentiation, particularly around the fovea (the center of direct vision) goes on for about 16 weeks after birth (Zubek and Solberg, 1954). Zubek and Solberg describe an investigation of the electrical reaction patterns of the infant eye. Not until about 6 months of age did the 35 normal infants studied begin to show reactions to flashes of light rather similar to those of adults. At birth, little reaction was present to either moderate or bright light. Three-month-olds showed a slight reaction.

Much evidence exists to show that the infant's use of visual equipment is rudimentary. The following factors probably enter into the inadequate use he makes of vision for the first few days to weeks of his life: birth may be accompanied by mild injury (trauma) to the eye; the shape of the infant eyeball is not well adapted to adult-type vision—in all probability, infants are very nearsighted; accommodation—the bulging of the lens for close, and thinning or attenuation for distant, stimuli—seems to be present to only a meager degree; and, finally, the infant's eyes do not track well. When the left eye of an adult meets a stimulus, the right eye swings to fix on it. The eyes move in a parallel and coordinated way. Observation of the newborn shows imperfect coordination: the right eye does not necessarily follow the course of the left. The eyes of many infants pursue a relatively uncoordinated course, to the discomfort and surprise of the uninformed adult observer, unaccustomed to seeing a left eye going north, a right eye west or south.

An organism can obviously do nothing about a stimulus until it can, in some degree, adapt and attend to it. It follows from this that the first useful visual development should be adapting to and fixating on a source of light. Research indicates that this is the case with the human infant. There is some disagreement about when he can accomplish this (Sherman and Sherman, 1925; Gesell and Thompson, 1934), but convincing evidence exists (Sherman and Sherman, 1925) to show that the pupillary reflex comes into play two or three hours after birth. The pupillary reflex—the contraction of the pupil in strong light, its dilation in weak light—may be thought of as a protective, adaptive reflex. In response to flashes of light, infants may also show startle responses (a flexion response, not voluntary), Moro reflexes (a tensing of the body, flailing out and retracting of the arms, with roughly coordinated leg movements—a primitive extension response), and the eye-neck response (a throwing back of the head).

Equally good evidence indicates that an infant can fixate at least one eye on a source of light within a few hours after birth, and that by the time he is 2 or 3 days old, he can bring both eyes together to fixate on a light source (Zubek and Solberg, 1954). Efficiency in this fixation, and ability to fixate one thing after another, appear around the fourth week (Gesell and Thompson, 1934).

Ability to follow a moving stimulus—called *ocular pursuit* or *tracking*—is the next development in vision. This ability is of obvious biological usefulness, since it is the basis for later crucial avoidance and approach reactions. Although there is lively disagreement about the time at which tracking appears (Pratt, 1954), there is agreement that infants first follow a stimulus that is moving horizontally. When this new skill is fairly well established, the ability to follow a vertically moving stimulus appears. Only later can the infant follow a rotating stimulus. The ages at which these skills appear have been set at 4½, 9, and 10 weeks by one of the more careful investigators in the field (Shirley, 1931). Most studies indicate that some tracking occurs within the first week after birth, but that early tracking movements are jerky and frequently broken up by reversals of direction (McGinnis, 1930).

There is good agreement that infants react to color (Munn, 1938). To arrive at this conclusion, however, different colored and noncolored stimuli must be equated for brightness. This equation must be done by *adult* standards, since infants are not able to tell us whether something is brighter or darker than something else; hence there is always some question about color vision and color preferences in infancy. One experimenter (Smith, 1936) has found that the responses of boy babies to colored stimuli differ from those of girls very soon after birth. Others have found different reactions to colored and to uncolored light by as early as 15 days of age (Chase, 1937). It seems almost certain that by 6 weeks of age the average baby is making some sort of differential response to color.

Studies of babies' color preferences are numerous (see summaries by Munn, 1938; Pratt, 1954; and Zubek and Solberg, 1954). The "preference" is ordinarily judged by fixation time: if a baby stares longer at one color than another, it is assumed that he prefers it. According to this criterion, babies prefer yellows and reds at first; yellows lose some of their potency later; older children move toward the adult pattern obtaining for our culture, with blues and greens preferred.

Infants respond differently to different intensities of light. In contrast to the behavior of older children and adults, infants are most active in rather dim light, least active in moderate-to-bright light. This tendency to quiet down rather than grow active under conditions of moderate light stimulation may account for the common observation that "babies have their nights and days mixed up." This preference is a matter of considerable inconvenience to the average household. Learning to fit his schedule into that of the adults around him is one of the earliest learning tasks of the child and one for which his original sensory equipment and patterns of behavior equip him poorly.

One possible explanation of the frustrating reversal of nights and days manifested by infants has been provided indirectly by Hebb (1949, 1955). He and his students and co-workers have amassed evidence indicating that the human organism can become "stimulus hungry." College students, placed in soundproof darkness, touching as little as possible, and smelling nothing, soon grow exceedingly disturbed, even experiencing visual and auditory hallucinations (Bexton, *et al.*, 1954; Heron *et al.*, 1956). After release from such experiences of extreme sensory deprivation, their work efficiency suffers for some time. Perhaps the infant's exasperating relaxation during the day—full of sights, sounds, and smells—is due to a surfeit of stimulation. But, during the quiet, dark night, he grows stimulus-hungry and comes briskly to, seeking stimulation or providing it for himself.

During the four months following early infancy, visual perception and response become much more acute, and enormous amounts of learning occur. The six-month-old child can apparently distinguish between his father and mother, between familiar and strange adults, and between expressions of pleasure and disapproval. He forms clear images, reaches for things and grasps them with moderate accuracy. He definitely possesses the ability to distinguish colors; his judgment of distance is fair, although he makes determined efforts to reach things outside his normal grasp when he sees them and registers the seeing. He has probably outgrown his baby tendency to be least active in the light, most active in the dark. He recognizes certain toys as favorites; he often shows a degree of alarm when placed in strange situations. In general, he has become an exceedingly complicated visual receptor and reactor.

Scientists as well as parents have long puzzled over what the world *really* looks like to infants. No one can ever answer this question directly, of course, since no baby can tell us. One of the great early psychologist-philosophers, William James, has suggested that the infant's world is a "big, booming, buzzing confusion." Indirect evidence about the infant's visual perception of his world has been gleaned from observations and reports of people who, after a lifetime of blindness, have had their sight suddenly restored; this evidence supports James's position. Von Senden's observations on a number of such cases have been reported by Hebb (1949).

These newly sighted people cannot discriminate cubes from squares, nor squares from triangles, without handling them patiently, checking and rechecking their visual images with the touch modality to which they have become accustomed. While in the hospital following surgery, some learned color names that they retained eleven months later, whereas they forgot the names of geometric forms. They were shown an egg, a potato, and a cube of sugar until they could name them promptly; but when these objects were put into colored light, they were not recognized. A cube of sugar could be named easily when placed on a table or in another person's hand, but not when it was hung by a thread with a change in background.

For normal older children and adults, the perception and differentiation of squares, cubes, circles, and so forth, is so prompt that we think of this ability as automatic or inborn. This does not seem to be the case. Hebb believes that recognition of such common figures is the result of perceptual learning; that they can be recognized and identified only after a gradual process during which contrast, or the figure-ground relation, dominates perception first; then, separate and laborious attention is given to each part of the figure; until finally, with increasing speed and accuracy, the whole is identified as a whole. The baby, according to Hebb, comes into the world with only a "primitive, sensorily determined unity." This unity is simply the figure-ground relation (the infant can see a solid blot of ink on an indefinite white background, but ascribes no formal characteristics either to the figure or to the ground). Later the human organism perceives "nonsensory unities" such as the corner of a room, the middle of a rope, or the foreground of a scene; and finally he arrives at "identity," which involves seeing both the similarities and differences of a given thing in relation to other things.

Observation of the development of a baby in his first year suggests that he is attempting to become acquainted with all of his environment with all of his senses: he pokes, fondles, clutches, tastes, rubs, smells, manipulates with both hands and feet, stares long and quietly, observes things from far away, brings them near. It is as though he were trying to coordinate each sense with every other and with reference to all the objects he can encompass with his senses.

Hearing (Audition)

Adults and older children distinguish the pitch of sounds (whether they are low or high), loudness, or intensity; quality, or timbre; and duration. But there is some disagreement about whether the infant responds to sound at all immediately after birth. The fact that some have been observed to do so, as well as our knowledge that the hearing structures are reasonably complete at birth, leads us to believe that the newborn can respond to sound. It may be that he is relatively insensitive to auditory stimuli for the first few days after birth, probably because the ear cavities are filled with amniotic fluid. This fluid drains off after the first few hours or days of life, and from that time on reactions to sounds may be observed with increasing frequency.

There are well-controlled studies (Sontag and Richards, 1938; and Bernard and Sontag, 1947) which indicate that babies respond to sound before birth, and that this response is independent of physical vibration (i.e., the response is made to sound, not mechanical vibration). Loud, sharp sounds produce a reaction from birth in most infants; and the range of responses increases rapidly during the first two weeks as the ears clear (Pratt *et al.*, 1930). There appears to be little reaction to the human voice until the fourth week (Hetzer and Tudor-Hart, 1927).

Experiments by Stubbs (1934) have demonstrated that the very young infant reacts principally to loudness and duration of sounds. Tuning forks, pure-tone whistles, and other types of stimuli have been used to study infants' reactions to both pitch and intensity, No differential reactions to high and low tones have been conclusively shown, although some investigators (see Pratt, 1954) claim that high tones excite, low tones soothe very young children. The common-sense lore of the lullaby may be based on such a concept.

Short, intense noises disturb children. A study by Haller (1932) indicates that a noise of ten seconds' duration produces less response at its tenth than at its first second; but another study, by Stubbs (1934), suggests that it takes more than a minimum of 15 seconds to produce such an adaptation (increasing indifference or lack of response). The short, intense sound stimulus affects the child in much the same way that the short, intense visual stimulus does. The Moro, or the startle, reflex may occur; pulse-rate increases and blinking responses occur; crying may result. It was originally believed that fear of loud noises was a basic, inborn emotional response, although practical experience with infants and experimental results demonstrate that no two children react in precisely the same way to any stimulus, including sudden sounds (see Pratt, 1954). Where one child may show what we judge to be real terror, another may sleep unperturbed through al most any degree of intense noise.

Prolonged mild sounds actually seem to quiet the child (Weiss, 1934). It is probably this, rather than a differential response to pitch, which accounts for the soothing effects of lullabies. A combination of light and sound, as contrasted with dark and quiet, seems to be most effective in quieting the very young infant. This fact, as discussed in the section on vision, probably accounts for the confusion of night and day that so many babies show: the day is noisy as well as light; the night is dark as well as quiet.

The auditory pattern from the end of the first few weeks of the child's life—a period that might well be called one of sensory stabilization—to the sixth month is not essentially different from that described for vision. Ability to localize sound, absent in the newborn but obviously of as much biological importance as the ability to fixate and follow moving visual stimuli, comes into play at about the twentieth week (Gesell, 1925). At first inefficient and halting, this ability improves steadily and is moderately accurate by 6 months. By the end of his first half year, the baby reacts with pleasure to the parental voice; can apparently distinguish scolding or threatening sounds from comforting or loving and protective sounds; frequently exhibits pleasure in music; demonstrates by moving his head that he can follow a sound stimulus, such as a ticking watch, as it is moved in his immediate vicinity; may react to street noises, such as fire sirens or dogs barking; and, in general, has begun to develop a method of differential sound response similar to that of the adult. He may pitch his own voice differently as different pitches of sound are produced for him, although not until much later does the average child attempt to reproduce a melody.

Smell (Olfaction)

Partly because in our twentieth-century culture the sense of smell is of relatively little survival value for man, and partly because he makes less use of smell than of his other senses, there is considerably less research on infants' olfactory development than there is on visual and auditory development.

Research on the sense of smell in isolation from the sense of taste is very difficult. The mouth and nose are intimately connected. Hence, stimuli applied to the nostrils are likely to enter the mouth and affect taste organs. The same difficulty obviously confounds attempts to investigate taste independently. Intense olfactory stimuli, such as ammonia, are also likely to result in pain and sneeze stimulation, thus making the problem of research still more difficult.

However, newborn babies have at one time or another been subjected experimentally to stimulation with such varied substances as ammonia, acetic acid, oil of cloves, anise, essence of lavender, valerian, turpentine, lemon, and many others (Pratt *et al.*, 1930; Disher, 1934). Conclusions have been conflicting because it is not always known whether the responses observed—cataloged as approaching, withdrawing, sucking, smiling, and so on—were due to direct nerve stimulation or to the more indirect neural stimulation commonly thought of as the sense of smell.

Highly pungent odors, such as those of ammonia or acetic acid, seem to produce vigorous responses of withdrawal or "displeasure." According to one investigator (see Pratt, 1954), some substances, such as anise oil, seem to produce "pleasure."

In short, in the very young infant there seems to be a crude reaction to at least certain pungent or penetrating odors, perhaps due more to pain than to smell. More refined reactions, which have been likened to pleasure or displeasure, accompany other odors. Whether the sense of smell is acting independently is doubtful, and at present we can only conclude that the sense of smell in the newborn is, for practical purposes, nonfunctional.

The transition from relatively unlearned to learned, acculturated, methods of responding to odors is less easily mapped than it is for vision and hearing. Presumably the same process of increasingly refined discrimination and reaction occurs, although the less prominent place of odor in our culture appears to prevent a high-level development of responses. Certainly, as we move up the phylogenetic or evolutionary scale from the primitive vertebrates to the higher mammals and man, an increasingly smaller proportion of the brain is devoted to the rhinencephalon, or small brain; and in man this comprises only a small patch on the brain's undersurface (Zubek and Solberg, 1954). There are, of course, species variations in this progression.

Although the proportion of man's brain devoted to smell is relatively small, he possesses a good, although customarily underdeveloped, sense of smell—better than that of many of the lower species—and, if we are to believe the folklore about trackers and hunters of the so-called primitive tribes, he can use it acutely when necessary.

Despite the lack of scientific knowledge about the development and role of the sense of smell, ordinary observation indicates that odors have deep cultural and emotional significance, and that learning has produced this significance. To those who have grown up in a Western European culture, such as that of the United States, the odor of human feces and urine produces reactions that range from mild distaste to nausea. But human urine is valued as a hairdressing among the Eskimos. Certain perfumes are commonly advertised (and cartooned) as arousing erotic reactions in the human male; perspiration odors are considered to evoke withdrawal reactions. The odors of spring incite pleasure, relaxation, "thoughts of love." We react negatively to stuffy smells, positively to fresh ones. These responses to smells are learned in early childhood in conjunction with major training, pleasure, and pain situations. They appear to be primitive in that they are more often emotional and physical than intellectual and logical, and they seem to be remarkably resistant to change or retraining.

Research and theory about learning, as discussed in Chapter 4, include suggestions about how the sense of smell enters into emotionally tinged responses that affect, for example, much of our social, sexual, and food-choice behavior. Some of these responses are adaptive, or helpful; others are maladaptive. For example, it is not helpful to an elementary-school teacher if she becomes nauseated when one of her charges throws up.

Although we know little about the development of the sense of smell from the time of birth, when it is apparently nonfunctional, to adulthood, when its influence is pervasive, its effect on behavior is such that more thinking and research in this area are clearly required.

Taste (Gustation)

Adult taste sensations have been analyzed into four basic tastes: sweet, sour, bitter, and salt. The complex and subtle "tastes" we experience—numbering at least into the hundreds—are partially due to the sense of smell. The difficulty of studying taste independently of smell and pain has been discussed in the preceding section. Little research on taste has been done with people beyond the age of early infancy, and this little has concerned itself principally with the acuity of the sense of taste and the frequency of taste buds. The indications are that the acuity of this sense lessens with maturity and old age, and that there is an actual decrease in the number of taste buds, possibly starting at birth.

As is true of the sense of smell, taste is considered of relatively minor importance in learning compared with sight or hearing, and it has been studied less adequately. Certain findings are, however, agreed upon by most investigators. The preferred taste sensation for infants is sweetness, as in sugar or saccharine solutions. Preference has been judged by presence or amount of sucking and other approach reactions. Even in the very early days after birth, children have shown increased sucking responses to sugar solutions (see Pratt, 1954), and have manifested what adult observers believed were signs of pleasure. These same taste sensations disturb the pulse and breathing rate less than any of the other taste sensations. Sour stimuli seem to be next favored by infants and are also responded to by sucking, although the sucking is less vigorous than with a sweet stimulus. The infant's breathing and circulation are disturbed more by sour solutions than they are by sweet or salt. Salt solutions cause considerable breathing and circulation disturbance, as do bitter solutions, and interrupt the infant's sucking. Babies definitely avoid bitter solutions, and some observers maintain that infants make grimaces characteristic of dislike and disgust when they are offered solutions of quinine (see Pratt, 1954).

Babies in the first few weeks of life show avoidance of certain foods. Whether this is due to the taste, smell, or texture of the foods is not known, but each of the three factors probably enters into the reaction. Many foods will be rejected at the first feeding, apparently without any prior learning.

Of course, in many such instances, the child has formed certain associations to given types of food or stimulation and merely transfers similar patterns of response to the new food.

The sense of taste is central in the adjustment of the older child and the adult, but is so interwoven with the sense of smell and food texture that it is difficult to say just which sense modality is associated with later food preferences or rejections. Studies of adults suggest a relationship between good personal adjustment and lack of food dislikes: people who have few dislikes for certain reasonably common and basic foods show better personal adjustment than those with many food dislikes. Such a finding, of course, holds for groups but not necessarily for any given individual.

Poorly adjusted adults and older children, as is well known, frequently attach their symptoms of maladjustment to physical life processes—they develop psychosomatic symptoms. Peculiar taste preferences, digestive disorders, breathing difficulties, heart "flutters," and so forth, are often symptoms of emotional problems. Since food is essential to life, and since the senses of taste and smell are inextricably bound up with eating, it is important to build up predominantly pleasant associations with these senses and with the entire process of eating.

Touch (*Pressure or Contact*)

Studies of pressure independent of contact are difficult to carry out with infants, because it is difficult to separate touch or pressure from pain or taste, for example. Even casual observation indicates that the infant reacts in some fashion or another to various types of pressure on most surfaces of his body. Reactions to touch have been observed by the third month of fetal life. Touch sensitivity follows the cephalocaudal course of development: it seems to begin in the lip-nose area and move downward.

With increase in the length of fetal as well as infant life, reactions to touch become increasingly more specific. Different parts of the body are differentially sensitive, as each of us knows from experience with his own body; but systematic explorations of the sensitivity of the entire body are lacking.

Stimulation of the sole of the foot produces a reflex response called the Babinski or plantar response. Some investigators (Zubek and Solberg, 1954) think of these as separate responses. The Babinski can be demonstrated by drawing the convex nail of the little or ring finger lightly from the infant's heel in the direction of his toes. In very early infancy this reflex is ordinarily a fanning or extension of the toes; toward the sixth month it becomes a curling or flexion of the toes for most infants (the plantar phase), and deviation from the normal course of development is used as an indicator of possible neural damage.

Stimulation of the facial areas leads to head-turning in the direction of the contact, markedly so when the infant is awake and hungry, less so when awake and replete, little or not at all when he is asleep. The closer the touch is to the lip area, the more likely it is that head-turning and sucking will occur. Infants apparently do not respond to tickling as such, although some report that the child will show withdrawing movements; nor to itching powder as such—or, if at all, very slowly. As is generally true of all of his responses, the infant responds massively to strong stimuli; that is, he "reacts all over"—less strongly when replete or asleep, more strongly when hungry and awake, and always with a poor sense of direction. However, with repeated trials, he is usually able to locate a bothersome sensation or make an adaptive response, such as approaching and sucking the nipple.

The infant's reactions to skin conditions, binding clothes, and so on, all seem to be less acute than they will be later. He apparently recovers quickly (until he has learned to respond by fright or crying) from bumps, bruises, or pricks. In general, compared with older children and adults, he appears to require stronger stimuli in all sense modalities before he makes a response. However, he quickly learns the meaning of certain pressures and skin sensations, just as he learns refinements of reaction to stimuli in any other sense modality. His adaptation to the breast or bottle grows steadily more refined. At 6 months a slight push here or pull there will usually produce signs of cooperation in dressing. Certain pressures that were originally struggled against, such as hats and caps, are accepted or looked forward to at 6 months. Responses to tactile or touch sensations are reasonably refined, and the six-month-old baby often seems to enjoy contact for the sake of contact: stroking, patting, and other caressing stimuli to which no attention was paid in early infancy.

Touch (*Movement or Kinesthesis*)

Kinesthesis, the muscle sense, subtly pervades all of living. Through kinesthesis we "know where we are and where we are going." From about the fourth fetal month, stimulus receptors located in muscles, tendons, joints, and perhaps around blood vessels (see Zubek and Solberg, 1954) report constantly to the brain or spinal nerves sensations that later lead the human to know whether he is sitting, standing, or lying down; the degree of flexion or extension; and the amount, direction, and force of movement of his body and its parts. Even before anything like conscious awareness can be assumed to exist, these sensory reports lead to attempts to correct position, or to approach or withdraw or make other adaptive movements.

The effect of moving the child's body or some part of it through space has been studied less painstakingly than have his reactions to touch. Watson (1924, 1928), one of the earliest psychologists interested in babies, maintained that sudden "dropping" of an infant invariably produced signs of fear, and that such fear was inborn. Later studies and casual observations of infants indicate that this is not true of all babies. It may be that a child's response to such a situation is a function of his basic reactivity; some have held that it depends on the degree of security he feels. In other words, the meaning of responses to loss of support is not agreed on. Probably a majority of small babies show the Moro or startle response to loss of support, and for many this will be followed by crying and signs of agitation and excitement.

Watson also held that restraint or inhibition cf the child's ability to move was the basic cause of rage. Careful observation by others has failed to support his position, and many now believe that the infant's response to having his arms held is related to how he has learned to regard such restraint. If he senses hostility or rejection in the holding, he may show signs of rage; but if the restraint is loving or matter-of-course, no emotional response will appear. In many cultures swaddling is so complete that babies are virtually immobilized; but no satisfactory evidence exists that these babies are full of rage. Indeed, the Hopis, among whom confining cradle boards have been frequently used, are among the most peaceful of people.

Infants' spontaneous movements are varied but relatively uncontrolled. Babies seem almost to have a drive toward activity; and it is through random, massive activity that the muscle coordinations which result in sitting, creeping, and walking slowly evolve. When very young infants are held erect, stepping movements may occur, although these are different in pattern from those that later constitute walking. Such stepping movements usually disappear after the first few weeks of life.

By the time the child is 6 months of age he has learned much about being moved and moving himself. Infants, depending partially on how they have been handled, may take delight in "centrifugal" games—being danced with, whirled, and rotated by adults; in height—being lifted above the adult's head; in sensations of loss of support—imitations of dropping. Other babies show concern and purposeful although panicky grasping responses to such activities, often followed by crying. These differential responses are primarily a function of learning, although individual differences appear that, to ordinary observation, scarcely seem to be so attributable. Certainly infants at birth show pronounced differences in reactivity: for example, before learning can possibly have influenced behavior greatly, some children startle when support is lost while others show little or no reaction; some startle and cry in response to loud sounds while others are passive. Because of these differences in reactivity, similar learning experiences have very different effects on different babies

By 7 or 8 months of age many children sit alone and unsupported, and some can attain the sitting posture independently. A minority of babies are creeping or crawling; a few stand more or less alone. Reaching and grasping are rather well established; primitive efforts at self-feeding occur; an occasional child manages a cup precariously; and physical self-determination has progressed as dramatically as have reactions determined by the other sense modalities.

Throughout the first half year of life a majority of infants respond favorably to rocking and to relaxed cradling. Much modern psychological and pediatric advice favors the old-fashioned rocking chair or the cradle and encourages mothers to hold their children while they are being fed in order to simulate the breast-feeding situation as closely as possible. The tendency of many children to "rock" or "hobbyhorse" themselves to sleep is attributed by some to lack of sufficient contact and rocking on the part of parents in the very early days of infancy, although evidence on this point is far from final (Spitz, 1949). But the parent who takes such advice as an invitation to play constantly with the infant is likely to defeat the very purpose of the rocking, soothing movement. Such a child is kept in, or brought to, a state of fatigue and tension. Or, if the mother attempts to rock the child while she is very tense herself, she is likely to increase his tension.

Erikson, one of those who has thought deeply and creatively about the development of personality, believes that the sense of trust or security is developed during this first period of babyhood, and that frequent and relaxed bodily contact with the mother or mother-substitute is necessary for its development. Sullivan (in Mullahy, 1948), another creative thinker in the field, postulates a process of "empathy"—a "feeling with"—that goes on in the baby as he has contact with the mother. Although no words need be spoken (and indeed, they would not be understood by the infant), the infant senses the mother's love for, acceptance of, and relaxation with him; or conversely, her displeasure, tension, and rejection. To date, no one knows precisely how to define or observe empathy, but it is a common observation that relaxed and accepting mothers are likely to have relaxed and amiable babies. Lakin (1957), whose study is reviewed more extensively in Chapter 3, provides evidence supporting such a conclusion. Certainly, the infant's kinesthetic sensibilities are very important in his interactions with his mother, father, and other meaningful adults in his world.

Pain

During his first few weeks of life the infant seems to respond less directly and discriminatingly to pain than the older child. Some experimenters believe that the baby is relatively insensitive to painful stimuli immediately after birth. Some theorize that the process of being born exhausts the baby's sense receptors, leaving him slow or lacking in response to all sensation and particularly to painful stimuli. Some have held that the brain centers for localization of pain stimuli are inadequately developed in infancy. The evidence on this score is by no means final. However, there is apparently less immediate reaction to pain on the part of the newborn than on the part of the older child. A single stimulus of a painful nature frequently produces no response, although normal infants respond to repeated painful stimuli by attempting to withdraw the part of the body that has been stimulated and by the massive, total type of response, including crying, which is so characteristic of their response to any strong stimulus. The capacity to respond to single painful stimulations is acquired rapidly. The literature on the sense of pain has been capably reviewed by Pratt (1954) and Zubek and Solberg (1954).

By the time the baby is 6 months old, the type of reaction he makes to pain depends considerably on the type of handling he has received from his parents. This effect is even more striking with older children. The parent who is frightened and reacts strongly to any pain the child may experience probably induces the child to show exaggerated emotional responses even to mild pain stimuli. The relatively relaxed parent whc waits to see whether the child is genuinely hurt before he jumps is likely to have children who take alarm much less easily. Here again, basic differences in reactivity probably affect the results of learning. The hyper-reactive child, handled calmly, will still, emotionally speaking, be more easily wounded than the passive, inactive baby who is handled in equally relaxed fashion.

Because pain may be an antecedent of anxiety, one of the most chronic and painful of human emotional ills, more study of its role in the developmental process is badly needed.

Temperature

The infant definitely responds to thermal stimulation, although it is difficult to separate temperature from sensations of touch, pressure, and pain. About the only pure heat stimulation possible is by radiant heat, but because the heat strikes a large area of the body, this type of stimulus makes localization difficult.

It is obvious that, for purposes of survival, organisms must respond to gross temperature changes. The human infant, who is in general helpless and ill equipped from the point of view of instincts or efficient physical patterns of reaction, conforms sufficiently to the biological laws of survival to make responses where these are necessary to maintain life, as in all cases of extreme sensory stimulation and variation. His patterns of response are crude, primitive, and of little use in themselves, but, by arousing responses from responsible adults, they result in protection, food, comfort, and love enough so that the infant survives. Responses to temperature follow this general rule.

Pratt (1954) has provided an excellent summary of neonatal reactions to thermal stimuli. It is clear that there is a response to temperature from birth, and it is probable that the fetus is capable of responding to temperature variations. Presumably there is a physiological zero or neutral point for all the senses, and certainly there is for temperature. At this temperature point a minimum of stimulation and incentive to activity is provided. Although no really systematic investigations of all the zones of the body have been made, this physiological neutral point ranges from 91° to 97° Fahrenheit for those body areas that have been studied. Adaptation, or "getting used" to temperatures occurs rapidly for infants, as it does for adults. We are all familiar with the rather quick adjustment to the bath that initially feels much too hot, or to the initially too-cold water of the swimming pool.

Nurseries are usually kept at high temperatures, and high temperatures are recommended for the homes into which tiny infants are taken from the hospital. These recommended high temperatures make sense if one considers that the child has only recently come from the consistent temperature of his mother's body, about 100° Fahrenheit. Before birth, he has been accustomed neither to fluctuations in temperature nor to coolness, relative or absolute. When his postbirth surroundings approximate his body temperature, he reacts little, just as before birth. Where his environment differs sharply from his body temperature, he reacts strongly. To "cold" temperatures, the child shows withdrawing responses; he heightens his activity; he shudders, shivers, and "scratches," this last being apparently a primitive device for removing the stimulation. When the temperature goes moderately above physiological neutral, babies have been observed to show "seeking" movements, although they react less to moderate upward shifts than to downward ones. Sucking is most vigorous for liquids above 100° Fahrenheit.

Sensory Stimulation and General Development

Many studies (e.g., pages 101 ff.) show that babies are retarded in development when reared in institutions where there are many infants and few nurses. Development of reaching, grasping, so-called social behavior, smiling, and all types of coordinated sensory-muscular behavior lags behind that shown by babies reared either in their own or in foster homes. There is also evidence indicating that babies in an institutional setting cry far more than do babies living in a household (Aldrich *et al.,* 1945, 1946).

Some authors believe that nursery-reared babies languish because they do not receive consistent mothering. Spitz (1945), for example, presents a dramatic and appalling picture of high death rate, an almost vegetable-like and irreversible slowness in the rate of neuromuscular-intellectual growth, and emotional maladjustment as being characteristic of babies in nursery wards. Although his methods have been scathingly criticized (Pinneau, 1955), other evidence (see, for instance, Goldfarb, 1945) bears out the notion that mass rearing of infants slows their development in several respects, and suggests that the infant who is abnormally reared—who has not had some "tender loving care"—may suffer severe emotional impoverishment.

Hebb (1949, 1955) speaks less emotionally but equally convincingly of the need for rich perceptual stimulation in earliest infancy. Drawing on his own theories and research, as well as on the work of his students and colleagues, he concludes that the human infant is an exceedingly slow-learning organism compared with infants of other species. Hebb accepts the point taken for granted by many physiologists and neurologists: that the human brain is relatively undifferentiated and equipotential when compared with that of other species. To oversimplify, this means that there is little instinctual direction for babies: they behave as they learn to behave, not as their instincts or their genetically laid-down brain patterns direct them.

Hebb believes that in the first few months of the baby's life, learning is by trial and error: it is inefficient, slow, and passive in the sense that it depends for its occurrence entirely on the stimulation that is offered. Hence, if there is no stimulation, no learning takes place. Neurologically speaking, the first few months of the baby's life are spent in laying down "cell assemblies." These are the basic, relatively simple neural connections that result in the integration of the sense modalities and provide the basis for such responses as blinking, grasping, responding to a touch on the face by sucking, and for perceptions of form, color, and contrast.

If a rich foundation of such cell assemblies is not laid in the first few months of life, Hebb reasons, it may never be laid at all, and interference with, or slowed development of, higher perceptual-intellectual-emotional functions may result. His views receive support from experiments (e.g., by Thompson and Heron, 1954) in which animals deprived of sensory stimulation in infancy show deficient "intellectual" behavior in their adult life. Less clear-cut evidence (Melzack, 1954; Melzack and Scott, 1957; and Melzack and Thompson, 1956) indicates that immature social and "emotional" adjustment is also characteristic of these animals.

According to Hebb, once cell assemblies are established, higher-order "phase sequences" begin to operate, making possible the insightful, symbolic behavior that we consider typical of intellectual human functioning. By implication, the more bountiful the supply of cell assemblies, the higher the order of functioning of the higher processes mediated by the phase sequences. As Hebb himself states, his postulated neurophysiology is speculative, although it does not violate known laws. His thinking, which is congruent with research studies of infants reared in deprived circumstances as well as with the results of animal research, suggests that a rich supply of sensory stimulation is essential for the child in the first year or so of his life as well as later.

SUMMARY

This chapter has stressed the impact of culture, interacting with the child's sense organs and other physical attributes, on the development of the human organism.

Culture, although organized in a bewildering number of ways, is defined as *the major institutional and social patterns followed by a larger or smaller, but definable, group of persons.* Families, themselves subcultures, transmit to their children the broad patterns of the culture of which they form a part. Considerable cultural differences exist as a function of social class.

Culture may affect a mother's physical condition during pregnancy, and her condition, in turn, affects the development of the fetus she is carrying. For example, maternal stress may be related to physical and emotional adjustment in infancy; certain types of infection during pregnancy may damage the fetus, and so on.

In the United States the literature about infant care is enormous, reflecting popular needs arising from parental insecurity. The two principal reasons for this insecurity are lack of information about handling babies and the influence of the two major streams of child-development theory, behaviorist and psychoanalytic, both of which stress the crucial role of parent-child interactions in shaping personality.

Since the culture cannot influence a child unless it impinges on him through his sense organs, this chapter has presented a brief summary of sensory equipment and development. With respect to *vision,* sensitivity to light, as judged by pupillary reflexes, is present at birth, but the first really functional use of vision—focusing on a source of light—does not appear until about 4 weeks. From that time, visual efficiency develops rapidly.

Hearing may not be present for a few days after birth, probably because of the presence of amniotic fluid in the ear. However, auditory sensory equipment is structurally complete in the newborn. Ability to localize sound appears at about 20 weeks.

Little is known about the development of the sense of *smell,* but it does not appear to function at birth. The infant's *taste* receptors do function in early infancy, and in fact the acuity of taste seems to diminish through life.

The other sense modalities are *touch* (pressure or contact, and movement or kinesthesis); *pain;* and *temperature.*

In general, response to sensory stimulation progresses from crude and massive reactions to cumulative stimulation toward precise, adaptive reactions to discrete stimuli. By the time a normal child is 6 months old he shows much purposeful, adaptive behavior; is social within the limits of his powers; demonstrates complex learning; exhibits such idiosyncracies as taste preferences; and is ordinarily rather well attuned to his complicated environment.

Studies of infants reared in institutional settings strongly suggest that the intellectual and emotional development of such babies is seriously impaired. These findings have been explained in terms of inadequate and inconsistent mothering and, more recently, by a theory relating mature intellectual and perhaps emotional functioning to the richness and variety of sensory stimulation in infancy.

Methods and Problems in the Study of Child-Rearing Practices

IN the preceding chapter, stress was laid on the crucial influence of culture on children's development. During the formative preschool years this influence, which ultimately makes its impact on the child's sense organs and nervous system, is brought to bear primarily through the behavior of his parents. Of course, parental influence continues to play a major role in the lives of older children, but in more diluted form.

Central, then, to an understanding of development in the early years of childhood is a study of child-rearing practices: their types and their effects.

The point was made in Chapter 1 that a great volume of literature has been provided by professionals in child development in an attempt to meet the need posed by parental insecurity. However, the inconsistency of the advice given by the experts has caused many to reject *all* experts. Others, including some of the experts themselves, have concluded that little good evidence about the effects of child-rearing practices exists and, in consequence, have maintained that efforts to educate and guide parents are futile.

As with most human matters, the truth probably lies somewhere between the optimism of the early or more extreme child-development experts (or parent-family educators) and the pessimism of the more conservative or of those come more recently into the field. Admittedly, the record of the experts is not a happy one. At least two survey articles show that child-care recommendations have moved full circle between about 1890 and 1950 (Stendler, 1950; Vincent, 1951). In many respects, advice about infant care today adheres more closely to the practices of our grandmothers and great-grandmothers than to the lines of thought of the early behaviorists. But to the many, including the author of this volume, who assume that cultural and family factors are crucial in the development of personality and in social and intellectual functioning, the study of parent-child relations should nevertheless be one of the principal preoccupations of educators, pediatricians, psychiatrists, psychologists, social workers, and other professionals in human development and functioning.

Chapter 3 presents a detailed survey of the research literature on child-rearing practices. Regrettably few solid conclusions can be drawn from these studies. A major reason for this state of affairs is that many, perhaps most, of them are weak methodologically. This chapter is devoted largely to an exploration of weaknesses often found in such research. The motives for presenting such a critique are two: (1) Critically alert, the student of child development will be less gullible in his reading and listening; and (2) possessed of general information about methodological pitfalls, he may be more precise, objective, and orderly in his own observations and research.

DIMENSIONS OF RESEARCH IN CHILD DEVELOPMENT

Spiker has suggested that every research study in the area of child development may be described in terms of its position on four dimensions, each forming a continuum ranging between two extremes. Although some of these dimensions may tend to vary together, there is no logical necessity for them to do so. The four dimensions are: (1) normative–explanatory; (2) ahistorical–historical; (3) naturalistic–manipulative; (4) atheoretical–theoretical.

| NORMATIVE | EXPLANATORY |
| Descriptive, averages, types, frequencies | Causal relations, prediction |

| AHISTORICAL | HISTORICAL |
| Relations between two variables measured at same time; studies of phenomena at about same point in time; no exploration of their origins | Search in history of the organism for the origin and learning conditions of behavior |

| NATURALISTIC | MANIPULATIVE |
| Organism studied under real life, natural conditions | Conditions controlled and, if possible, placed in laboratory setting |

| ATHEORETICAL | THEORETICAL |
| Designed to answer immediate problems, or substantiate informal observations, or satisfy curiosity | Deduced or induced from body of logically interrelated concepts and postulates |

FIG. 2.1.   Four dimensions of studies in child development

Normative–Explanatory

A major (perhaps *the* major) goal of early workers in child development was to describe the behavior and characteristics of the developing human organism—hopefully, from conception on. The majority of the research findings discussed in the previous chapter are *normative* (e.g., the *average* baby localizes sound at about 20 weeks, whereas he fixates on a source of light at 4 weeks). Normative studies of child-rearing practices often seek to gather such information as average time of weaning, method of weaning, number of mothers who breast feed, time and method of initiating toilet training, and so on.

Collection of such norms can be helpful. A pediatrician becomes concerned if his small patient is not fixating light at, say, 8 weeks. A teacher, knowing that the average IQ of her class is 85, will pitch her instruction lower than if she knows it is 115, thus accommodating a majority of her class *but not each individual.* If the average mother begins toilet training at 11 months, one would suspect that mothers who differ greatly from the average (who start at 6 weeks or 3 years, for instance) may have special effects on their children.

In the *explanatory* approach to research, an attempt is made to go beyond the compiling of frequencies and averages. Such an approach concerns itself less with the average time of starting toilet training (for instance) and more with the effect on children's later development of differences in the time of beginning toilet training; or with the motives and intentions of the mother who differs greatly from the average (or adheres closely to it, for that matter).

Research at the explanatory rather than the normative end of this methodological continuum seems more likely to contribute to an understanding of human development, although the establishing of accurate norms may be an essential first step in explanation. Good norms help us "restrict the range of our best guesses." The teacher who knows that the average IQ of her class is low will be less likely to err in her teaching level than the teacher without such information. The author of a reading text finds it useful, even necessary, to know how extensive and difficult a vocabulary the average child in the second grade can master. He must know the frequency with which English words are used, so that the child can master early those that he most needs in order to comprehend what he reads.

But norms are *not* explanations. They do not enable us to predict the development of an individual child, nor do they help us, except in the sense of the preceding paragraph, to guide him. It is reassuring to the parent of a fourteen-month-old who is just beginning to walk to know that the average child walks at this age, but disturbing, and without implications for guidance, to the parent whose child is *not* walking four months later. Norms are, however, frequently taken for explanation, even by those who should know better. A parent, querying a child-development speaker, asks why her daughter, previously such a good child, has become naughty and now always says "No" rather than "Yes." The speaker asks the age of the child; the mother answers, "Twenty months," and the speaker says, "Oh, that is the time when negativism reaches its peak in girls." Both mother and speaker seem relieved, and each apparently believes that something has been explained. However, the *fact* is not the explanation. The explanation is an accounting of how or why the fact came to be.

Ahistorical–Historical

There are two types of *ahistorical* research. The first type poses a question that, illustratively, might be: Are children less resistant during dental work when their mothers remain in the waiting room than they are when their mothers accompany them to the dentist's chair? In a hypothetical study to answer this question, the investigator might form two groups of children: an experimental group, whose mothers remain in the waiting room; and a control group, whose mothers go with them into the dentist's office. The two groups should be about the same in age and number; they should include similar numbers of only, first, and second or later children; the mothers should be of about the same educational level (or social class); and so on. If there is less crying and resistance in the experimental than in the control group, the investigator concludes that, for children like those he studied, dental work will be done more efficiently if mothers remain in the waiting room. But, in the ahistorical approach, the research worker does not concern himself with factors in the history of mother-child relations that might account for the difference between the two groups; nor does he ask how the history of the child who cries and resists with his mother absent differs from that of the child who makes no resistance.

The second type of ahistorical research measures two variables at more or less the same time and relates them to each other. For example, an investigator wishes to find the relation between mothers' and children's intelligence. As close in time as possible, he administers intelligence tests to a number of mothers and children. He finds that there is a tendency for the brightest mothers to have the brightest children, and vice versa, and concludes that mothers' intelligence is *positively correlated* with their children's intelligence. But he does not seek to determine why some bright mothers have children who are not bright (did they, for example, read less to their children when they were little? has the home been a quarrelsome one? and so on).

The *historical* approach, as can be seen, has something in common with the explanatory approach, and holds that the experiences an individual has had in the past determine the kind of person he is at the moment, how he perceives his current environment, and therefore what he will do in the present situation.

A true historical approach to many of the pressing questions in parent-child relations involves longitudinal (long-time) study of large numbers of children and their parents. But such studies are so complex and difficult, as well as expensive, that almost no individuals and few research centers can undertake them. Not least among the difficulties is maintaining the co-operation of a representative or typical sample of families year after year.

Many investigators attempt to reconstruct the child's history by interviewing his mother, or mother and father. Inquiries are typically made about the circumstances of birth, feeding, weaning, discipline, and so on. This approach might be called the semihistorical approach, and is typified by the Sears, Maccoby, and Levin (1957) study mentioned in the preceding chapter.

Naturalistic–Manipulative

In the *naturalistic* approach, the subject is studied in his natural setting; *manipulative* research, essentially, is laboratory research, in which the experimenter exerts controls in order to study in as pure a form as possible the phenomenon in which he is interested. In this sense, astronomy is a naturalistic, physics predominantly a manipulative science. An observational study of the child in his own home, or in free play in a preschool setting, is naturalistic; a study of the difference in his performance on a test when his mother is present, compared with his performance when a female stranger is in the room, would be manipulative.

The bulk of research in child development has been and continues to be naturalistic, although the tendency toward experimental work with children is growing. The manipulative approach is much superior to the naturalistic in precision. However, some think it is limited in the contribution it can make to knowledge of human development because of the difficulty of reducing pressing human problems such as sibling rivalry, mother fixation, or dependency, to dimensions that can be studied in the laboratory.

Atheoretical–Theoretical

In the early days of child development, investigators tended to be atheoretical, even antitheoretical, in their approach to child behavior. Many considered theory sheer speculation, and wished simply to gather facts. But as the facts accumulated, the need for integration became obvious to more and more child psychologists, and theory itself became more objective and empirically grounded. Today few deny the usefulness of scientific theory. However, many practical problems not derived from or related in any close fashion to theory continue to demand and receive attention.

METHODOLOGICAL PROBLEMS

The remainder of this chapter treats two major types of problem that beset the scientific investigation of child-rearing practices. The first type is *methodological,* and pertains to the design and carrying out of empirical research. The second type of problem is *theoretical,* and pertains to the development of an adequate framework within which fruitful research can be carried out.

The following seven difficulties are among the most frequent in research on child-rearing practices, although they characterize other types of psychological, psychiatric, and sociological research as well: (1) contamination; (2) reconstruction through retrospection; (3) faulty logic; (4) poor definition of concepts; (5) direct influence of the investigator; (6) problems of sampling; (7) unsound generalization.

The research summaries and evaluations in Chapter 3 illustrate some of these faults in detail.

Contamination

The most frequent type of contamination occurs when the investigator knows the predicted nature of the relation between an *independent* and a *dependent* variable and has control over the measurement of both. The less objective and quantifiable the measurement of the variables (ratings or judgments based on interviews are notably subjective and difficult to quantify satisfactorily), the more likely contamination is to occur.

A typical piece of research, unless it seeks simply to describe children in terms of their height, weight, intelligence, or reading ability, is designed to test the relation between an *independent* (or, speaking loosely, *causal*) variable and a *dependent,* or *effect* variable. Depending on the kinds of questions being asked, the same factor may function as either an independent or a dependent variable. For example, in a study of the effect of lack of mothering on intellectual functioning, *intellectual functioning* is the *dependent* variable. In a study seeking to establish whether intelligence is related to superior school work, on the other hand, *intellectual functioning* serves as the *independent* variable.

As has been said, the possibility of contaminating research results always exists when the person collecting the data is aware of the predicted relation between the independent and the dependent variable. For example, one influential hypothesis about asthma, derived from psychoanalytic theory, holds that asthma occurs in children whose mothers have rejected yet overprotected them. It is maintained that such children are frustrated criers: they want to cry, but dare not for fear of losing their mothers' love. Hence they turn their crying in on themselves, producing the strangling, acute shortness of breath and difficulty in breathing that characterize asthmatic children.

In a test of this hypothesis, the dependent variable is the presence or absence of asthma. Since the criteria for asthma are fairly clear, asthmatic children can be readily distinguished from nonasthmatic children. But the question of whether or not a mother rejects her child is to a considerable degree a matter of the investigator's judgment. This judgment is most frequently based on interviews with or observation of the mother. If an investigator holds a strong theoretical bias (for purposes of this illustration, either toward or against psychoanalytic theory), and at the same time knows which mothers have asthmatic and which healthy children, his questions to the mothers of asthmatics may, quite unintentionally, be slanted either to pick up (for the pro-bias) or conceal (for the anti-bias) signs of rejection; and he may be differentially alert to signs of overprotection in mothers of asthmatics and healthy children. Similar possibilities for contamination exist when the subjects are aware of the relationship being studied.

The danger of contamination may also be present in studies not concerned with causal relationships, whenever the investigator holds certain expectations about results. For example, in studies of threshold measurement (the lowest intensity of a stimulus that can be perceived), it has been found that the experimenter's expectations concerning the location of the threshold can influence his methods and hence the point at which it is actually found.

Studies involving individual testing of intelligence may contain a similar type of bias. If a child is known to be or suspected to be of high intelligence, borderline performances on an item may be scored as passed; for a child judged to be of lower intelligence, they may be scored as failed. In experimental studies of learning, children are extremely sensitive to variations of expression on the experimenter's face, or to differential cues springing from the apparatus. When systematic variations are present, learning guided by *them*, rather than according to the goal of the experiment, may be responsible for the child's performance.

Reconstruction through Retrospection

The technique of reconstruction through retrospection is widely (and often necessarily) used in studies of the effects of child-rearing practices. For example, an investigator may conduct a study of the personalities of college students. He is interested in how some of the aspects of personality he has studied are related to the child-rearing practices used with his subjects. He constructs a questionnaire for mothers to fill out, or interviews the mothers about how the experimental subjects were fed as infants—whether or not feeding was scheduled, when and how the subjects were weaned, when and how they were toilet-trained, and so on. He relates these reported practices to the characteristics of the young people he has studied and concludes that such and such a practice has such and such an effect on personality, or that infant-training practices do not affect the personality of young adults.

A number of factors, of which forgetting is an important one, force us to regard such retrospective data with skepticism. For parents who have several children, memories about the development of one child blend with memories of the growth of others. Forgetting is also selective: parents are likely to remember the pleasant things about their children's development and forget the unpleasant ones. An experience of the author's illustrates this point: a friend with a new baby inquired rather desperately when the author's children had begun to sleep through the night. The confident answer, "At around 2 months," was given. Later, to assure accuracy, he checked the baby books kept for the three children in the family, and found that his statement had been glaringly false: none of the three had slept through the night consistently until he was about 14 weeks old.

Finally, a lack of frankness often accompanies reports of child-rearing practices. Most parents have had exposure to people who have told them how babies *should* be reared. On the other hand, no parent had done with his children precisely as he believes he should have. People try to put themselves in the most favorable light. Hence, parents' reports about how they reared their children are likely to be slanted to some degree in the direction they believe they *should* have done it, or in the direction they think the expert questioner believes they should have done it.

For reasons such as these, it is difficult to know how much reliance to place on research findings based on methods involving retrospection.

Faulty Logic

Another characteristic of research in this area, faulty logic, particularly fallacious causal inference, is regrettably frequent. Research illustrations provided in the section on contamination are, in this sense, instances of faulty logic. In a study of different toilet-training practices (Holway, 1949), some mothers were rated as strict, others as permissive, or tolerant. The children's fantasy play was then studied. That of children strictly toilet-trained was considered to indicate that they were more disturbed, less happy, than those permissively trained, and this difference was attributed to the training. The possibility was ignored that strict toilet training may be associated with other restrictive child-rearing practices, and that it may have been any one of the other practices, or all of them together, that produced the fantasy differences. Furthermore, it is possible that neither strict toilet training nor general restrictiveness was associated with disturbed fantasy play, but that the children with disturbed fantasy were harder to handle than other children, so that the mothers were driven into restrictiveness by the characteristics of their children.

Poor Definition of Concepts

The results of scientific study are dependable to the degree that an investigator has spelled out what he *means* and what he has *done*. Both the specification of the concept and its measurement determine the clarity of scientific definition.

Every scientific investigation must make use of concepts—abstractions from observed events. Some concepts are quite close to the phenomena they represent (for example, concepts such as *house* or *car*). Most of the concepts used in child-rearing studies, however, are abstractions at a higher level, much less easily related to events in the concrete world. Examples of such concepts are *maladjustment, dependency, aggression, overprotection.*

The concepts used by an investigator must be defined both in *abstract* terms, so that insofar as possible they mean the same thing to the reader or listener and to the originator; and in terms of the *operations* (measurements) defining them in the particular study. These operational or experimental definitions are adequate to the extent that they are satisfactory behavioral indicators of the concepts they are intended to represent. Without a clear *conceptual* definition, an adequate and useful *operational* definition is impossible.[1]

It should be obvious that concepts vary enormously in the degree to which they can be clearly defined and reliably measured. When a defini-

[1] Bergmann (1951) may be consulted for further discussion of this subject.

tion means the same thing to two people, when it includes a clear-cut method of measurement, and when measurements can be made repeatedly by the same person or by different people with the same results, *clarity of definition* exists.

Studies in the area of child-rearing frequently fail to satisfy these requirements. For example, Rank (1929) has advanced the hypothesis that maladjustments in children (and adults) may be due in part to "birth trauma," the pain and shock of the birth process. Ruja (1948) reasoned that this hypothesis could be tested by determining whether infants who had had difficult birth showed greater maladjustment than infants who had had relatively easy births. His criterion (behavioral indicator) for a *difficult birth* was the length of the mother's labor, as judged from her "in labor" admission to the hospital until the time of delivery. His criterion for *maladjustment of the infant* was the amount of time the child spent crying. The first criterion is open to criticism because, from the infant's point of view, it may be that precipitate, hurried labor is harder (more traumatic) than prolonged, gradual delivery. The second criterion is unsatisfactory because the most profoundly traumatized or damaged baby may be the one who lacks the energy to cry.

Ruja, not surprisingly, found no relationship between length of labor and amount of crying. However, because of his faulty translation of concepts into observable events, we cannot say that he has disproved or even offered convincing evidence against the hypothesis concerning birth trauma. Psychological literature abounds with evidence of equally poor definition.

Direct Influence of the Investigator upon His Research Results

Another problem frequently encountered in research on human relations, particularly if it involves child-rearing practices, is that *the investigator himself affects the results of the study he is conducting.* One of the potentially most profitable methods of studying children is to make repeated or continuing studies of the same child as he grows up. Such studies, known as *longitudinal* studies, have given us valuable information concerning the development of intelligence and the rate and pattern of physical growth. These are examples of topics on which the influence of the investigator is relatively small, and for which we have valid and reliable techniques of measurement. But longitudinal studies have thrown little light on the effects of child-rearing practices or on the question of how personality develops. There are two major reasons for this. First, it is difficult to ask meaningful (conceptually clear) questions about personality development. What, for example, is meant by *adjustment? dependency? maternal rejection?* Second, the investigator and the things he stands for and does influence the very child-rearing practices that are being studied.

The average person who does research with children has a real and special regard for them. If he sees them developing in a fashion that he knows is likely to lead to maladjustment, it is almost impossible for him to behave in a coldly dispassionate, purely scientific fashion. He must do something to help. But his behavior, though well-intentioned, distorts his results. The study becomes not a study of *parent-child* relations and their effects upon personality, but a study of *parent-child-expert* relations. Whenever the investigator, for extrascientific motives—no matter how "good" these are—directly affects the relations he is studying, the study he produces becomes different from what he originally intended.

The phenomenon of experimenter influence has been clearly demonstrated in the "Hawthorne studies" of the effects of different kinds of working conditions on the productivity of factory workers (see Homans, 1958). Regardless of the kinds of change introduced, and *regardless of whether these changes were in the direction of better or poorer physical working conditions*, the productivity of the experimental group continued to increase. The effect of physical working conditions was overshadowed by the effect of other changes: the workers' awareness of taking part in an experiment; their being set apart as a special small group; their altered relations with supervisory personnel. These social and attitudinal variables, directly related to the experiment itself, obscured the effect of the factors the experiment was initially designed to investigate. Something very similar seems likely to occur in longitudinal studies of personality, where, over the years, the investigator has continued an intimate interaction with the parents and children who form the core of the study.

Problems of Sampling

The problems of sampling range from the practical difficulties of obtaining human subjects to the question of making generalizations from the population studied to other populations, as is discussed in the next section.

Practical difficulties in obtaining subjects result, for example, in our knowing little about child-rearing practices in lower-class homes; such parents usually do not understand, and are uninterested in, research. On the other hand, because of the availability of students in college psychology classes and of white rats, much of psychological fact and theory is based on the study of such populations.

Central to the problem of making sound generalizations from a study is the nature of the population on which it was based. *Biased samples* limit generalization. The basic definition of a biased sample is this: *The measured sample fails to represent, and thus to predict, the sample it was originally supposed to predict.* Bias is essentially a matter of *systematic variation* of some type, as opposed to *random*, or chance, variation.

Since it is often impossible to work with a total *population*, or *universe*, a subsection of the population (a *sample*) must be selected for study. In a *random sample*, each member of the total population being considered has an equal chance of being selected as a member of the sample, or of being assigned to some particular method of study or experimental treatment in the total research program. The reason for randomizing selection is that if, and only if, a sample is random can the laws of mathematical probability be applied to findings based on that sample, and any sort of confident generalization applied to the population from which it was drawn.

The problem of the biased sample has been central, most markedly in the normative research approach. It is virtually impossible, from a practical point of view, to avoid a biased sample. For example, in studying the height and weight of six-year-olds, a typical procedure is to enlist the cooperation of the public schools of a city, or several cities, so that all, or a random, or a representative sample of six-year-olds can be measured during the shortest possible period of time. But such an apparently comprehensive sample will be biased because some six-year-olds will be absent from school during the time of the study, perhaps because they are ill. If a large enough group of six-year-olds is included in the study, the research worker will find a fairly good cross-section and number of illnesses. In general, the children who are ill at any given time include many who, because of chronic illness, miss more days of school than their healthier classmates, and who are also thinner and shorter than children of normal health. Hence, we obtain a group that averages somewhat taller and heavier than the universe (which would include *all* six-year-olds in the population).

In addition to the six-year-olds ordinarily in regular attendance at school, but absent on the day of weighing and measuring, there are other six-year-old children who never attend public school. Such children may have been born crippled or physically or mentally handicapped in some other way. They, like the chronically ill, will be found to weigh less and to be shorter than the group of six-year-olds regularly attending school. Their absence will further bias the sample in the direction of producing norms (i.e., averages and the range from the shortest or lightest to the tallest or heaviest child) that show six-year-olds to be taller and heavier than they would be if *all* six-year-olds were measured. Finally, some children will refuse to cooperate, or their parents will decline permission for them to be measured.

Results from such a study, then, do not pertain to "Kansas City, Missouri, six-year-olds," but to "cooperative Kansas City, Missouri, six-year-olds in attendance at public school at the time height and weight were determined."

Occasionally, another type of bias is introduced by an investigator. He formulates a hypothesis, designs a method to test it, secures the cooperation of subjects, and collects his data. The data fall in the direction of his prediction, but the results are not clear enough to reach statistical significance. He looks at his individual cases, and sees that most of them have behaved as he predicted they would; but a minority has not, thus reducing the overall effect he hoped to show. He checks with this minority and finds that each one had "seen through" the purpose of his experiment. He concludes that "seeing through" his plan has kept these subjects from behaving according to prediction, and discards their results, leaving the average behavior of the remaining subjects striking enough to support his hypothesis statistically. But he has not checked to see whether, among them, there are some who had also "seen through" the experiment. He has, in other words, systematically altered his final sample from that he originally studied. This investigator would not have erred if he had included in his original research plan a check for "seeing through," with the initial declared intention of discarding the results obtained from *all* subjects who "saw through" the experiment.

Still another type of bias results from substituting volunteers for persons originally scheduled to take part in a study or experiment. If a research worker plans to study the attitudes of working mothers toward disciplining their children, he might, for example, secure the cooperation of the management of a large plant. From the personnel records of women working in the plant he obtains information about the ages of the women employees, the number of children each has, their average education, and so on. Because of the large numbers involved, it is not feasible for him to study *all* the women, so he constructs a representative sample: a certain proportion of women with one child, or with two or more; so many with children under school age, so many with children in elementary school; so many over 40 years of age; so many widowed, and so on. He then selects from the files names of women that will satisfy these requirements of a representative sample, and approaches them to ask their cooperation. Most are willing to serve as subjects, but some are not. He then calls for volunteers, picking from them women who match the characteristics of those who have refused; or continues to go through the files, finding women with characteristics that match the refusers, until he has rounded out a sample fitting his original specifications.

In doing this, he has biased his sample. The "volunteers" differ from the refusers on the important dimension of cooperativeness. It may be that cooperators, compared with refusers, are more sympathetic toward psychological research, better informed about recommendations for "good" discipline, and hence different in their ways of disciplining their children. Such a bias consequently influences the soundness of the conclusions about the universe (here, the total population of mothers working in the plant).

Biased samples, then, are those that do not predict the sample they were originally intended to predict. This, most frequently, results from one of three processes: failure to measure all of the intended sample; elimination of subjects without previous specification of the conditions under which this will be done; and substitution of one type of subject for another.

Unsound Generalization

The three most common types of unsound generalization are:

1. Writing or speaking as though findings were more significant or clear-cut than they are.
2. Applying findings gathered in one situation to circumstances different in essential characteristics.

3. Applying findings from one population to another differing in basic dimensions.

Hypothetical examples of these are, for the *first:* using the well-established, moderately high correlation between the intelligence of mothers and their children as though it indicated that *every* child of a bright mother was himself bright, and vice versa.

An example of the *second* type of unsound generalization is the assumption that, because a child behaved inflexibly in an experimental situation (e.g., failed to change his approach as the type of arithmetic problem presented to him changed), he will act rigidly in a wide variety of real-life situations.

An illustration of the *third* type of unsound generalization is the assumption that the height and weight of the "cooperative Kansas City, Missouri, six-year-olds attending public school," mentioned previously, provide an adequate basis for judging normal height and weight of six-year-olds in Tahiti.

Generalization, then, should be made according to the scientific certainty of the original findings, to situations having as much as possible in common with the original research setting, and to populations as similar as possible to the research population from which the findings were obtained. The more closely these conditions are met, the sounder the generalization.

Increasing confidence can be placed in a finding if it has been replicated. If a relation between a certain type of reward and speed of learning has been demonstrated for white rats, monkeys, three-year-olds in Arizona and New York, eighth-graders in Minnesota, and college sophomores in California, one would be more confident in saying that it is a general truth or law than if this relation had been demonstrated for only one of these populations. However, one would still hesitate to say that it held for adult Australian aborigines.

Research workers in child development frequently *overgeneralize,* or generalize *imprecisely,* and advisers of parents and teachers err in this direction even more often than research workers themselves. For example, it is generally held that praise is better than punishment as a method of motivating children's learning. Yet, strictly speaking, this generalization is imprecise, because praise and punishment have seldom, if ever, been compared for their effect on *precisely the same behavior.* In teaching a child traffic safety, for example, one does not compare the results of *praising* him for standing on the curb and looking both ways before crossing the street with *punishing* him for the same behavior. A test in this situation would be to compare the speed with which he learned to use discretion in crossing streets under conditions (1) of being punished for darting into the street and (2) of being rewarded for staying on the curb until he had looked both ways. Still a third test, making for greater precision of generalization, would be (3) to train a group of children by praise for correct responses *and* punishment or criticism for mistakes. With such evidence, it could then be said that praise was preferable to punishment, or that a combination of both was better than either alone, in *achieving the training goal.*

Serious overgeneralization has also resulted from studies of children's eating. Davis (1939) found that children who were given their free choice of a variety of simple, nutritious foods tended, on the whole, to choose foods that were good for them. Although one day they might eat only one item, and on the next go on a binge of eating another, over a long period of time they quite voluntarily selected a well-balanced diet. As a result, a whole generation of parents has been advised to "leave your children alone. They will automatically choose diets that are good for them." Such advice overlooks the fact that the children in the study were offered alternatives only among foods that were simple and essentially good for them—such as eggs, bananas, and simple cereals—whereas the typical modern child includes among his alternatives foods such as chocolate candy, varieties of pie, and bleached-flour bread. Anyone who has watched children growing up cannot help wondering whether their own choices might not result in a diet composed almost entirely of white bread, candy, pop of various sorts, and chocolate milk.

STATISTICAL CONSIDERATIONS

A text of this nature is not the place to introduce an elaborate treatment of statistics. However, to understand subsequent reviews of research, as well as to appreciate some of the critical points developed in the preceding section (particularly *unsound generalization*), some knowledge of at least three statistical concepts is required. These are discussed (in perhaps misleadingly simple terms) in the following paragraphs.

Correlation

A correlation coefficient is an expression of *the relation between one thing and another*—the degree to which two things *vary together.* The correlation between height and weight in a sample of 50 young men can be illustrated as follows. First, array the men in order of their height, with the shortest man to the left, the tallest man to the right. Put a card over each man's head indicating his weight. Observation will show a tendency for the shorter men to be lighter, the taller men heavier. There will be a number of men who are heavier than those taller than they, and vice versa. *But, for the group as a whole,* greater height will go with greater weight. In other words, height and weight will covary.

Correlation coefficients, theoretically, can range from perfect positive (+1.00) to perfect negative (−1.00). The condition of a perfect positive correlation would be met if, in our illustration, the tallest man was the heaviest, the next tallest the next heavy, and so on down the line to the *shortest and the lightest* man. The more interchange in weight status between men of different height (e.g., the third from the shortest man is found to be the third from the heaviest), the lower the correlation. If there is *no covariance* between height and weight, but simply a chance relation, the correlation is zero. If the shortest man were the heaviest, the next shortest man the next heavy, and so on, until the *tallest* man was revealed to be the *lightest,* the condition for a perfect negative correlation would be fulfilled.

Prediction through Correlation

The principal purpose in calculating a correlation coefficient (r) is to predict one variable from another. Knowledge of a man's height is more useful if it also helps us to predict his weight than if it gives us no information about him other than how tall he is. Correlations are likely to lead to deceptive inferences about causality: if two things are correlated with each other, it is tempting to say that one "causes" the other. *Correctly, we should* assume only that they are related, but should also be encouraged to look for the *reasons* for the relation. In general, tall men are heavier than short men for the rather elementary reason that they have more bones to cover and coordinate with muscle and fat. *There is simply more to them.* But their height did not *cause* their weight.

A simple calculation is useful in appraising the predictive value of a correlation coefficient. It is easy (but incorrect) to assume that the rather high correlation of .70 between a test of reading achievement and intelligence for fourth-graders means that all the brighter children read better than those less bright. This correlation does indicate a strong relation between reading and intelligence. Hence, knowledge of the children's intelligence helps us predict their standing in reading ability among other children of their age. But the relation is by no means a perfect one. To determine how much of the *total variance of reading* (*all* the factors that influence, or determine, reading skill) is accounted for by intelligence, one multiplies the correlation between the two by itself: .70 $\times$ .70 is equal to .49. Translated, this means that 49 percent of the variance of reading in our sample of fourth-graders is accounted for by the children's intelligence. To put it in other words, the .70 correlation between intelligence and reading accounts for 49 percent of the *possible* range of factors that would enter into making a *perfect* prediction of where a child stood in his reading group. But 51 percent of the variance remains *unaccounted for* when we know only the intelligence-test scores of a group of children. Of this unaccounted-for 51 percent of the variance, the amount of practice children have had is responsible for some; some is due to parents' intelligence; some can be accounted for by the number of books in the home libraries, some by motivation, some by study efficiency, some by the acuity and coordination of vision, and so on.

The average correlation of about .50 that has been found between the intelligence of parents and children indicates that only 25 percent of the variance of children's intelligence can be accounted for by the brightness of their parents. A correlation of .20 between children's strength and their speed of response means that only 4 percent of the variance of speed of response is accounted for by strength, leaving 96 percent to be predicted from knowledge of other factors.

Much faulty generalization results from failure to calculate how much of the variance of one variable is due to another with which it is correlated. A correlation of .70 *looks* reassuringly high, but still leaves us with 51 percent of the variance unaccounted for.

Level of Statistical Confidence

The central task of science is to discover *lawfulness* in its subject matter. Child development seeks to determine lawfulness in human structure, growth, and function. Statistics are among the tools used to demonstrate lawfulness. Among other tasks we assign to statistics is that of providing us with an estimate of the confidence we can place in our findings. We are particularly interested in whether we can assume that they happened for reasons *other than chance.*

Ordinarily, we speak with "confidence" of results that are *statistically significant.* In this volume, statistical significance refers to any result at or below the .05 (or 5 percent) level of confidence. Such a figure (which may also be referred to as P—for probability—= .05) indicates that the results to which it refers are of such magnitude that they would occur by chance only five times in a hundred. The .01 (P = .01) level of confidence tells us that results like ours would be expected through chance once in one hundred times; the .001 level of confidence, once in a thousand times.

In our earlier example, a correlation of .70 was postulated between intelligence and reading achievement for 60 children in two fourth-grade classrooms. To establish the significance or level of confidence for this correlation, we can consult a table or go through certain computations. Either of these procedures shows it to be significant at less than the .001 level—that is, a correlation of this magnitude, based on a population of this size, would be expected to occur by chance fewer than once in a thousand times.

For another illustration, suppose that the investigator's purpose is to test the effectiveness of an accelerated reading program. By a process of random selection, half the children in four classes of fourth-graders are assigned to an experimental group. The remaining children constitute a control group. The purpose of the study is to see whether the experimental children can be significantly advanced in reading skill over children remaining in the regular reading program by supplying individual instructions and enriched reading materials. Some safeguard must be introduced, however, so that it can be said that any superiority they show is due to the reading program, and not to the "Hawthorne effect" (improvement in performance as a result of taking part in an experiment). This safeguard is introduced by giving the control children an amount of individual attention equal to that given the experimental youngsters, but social rather than instructional in nature; and supplying them with attractive materials that differ in *content* from those regularly used, but are at the same level of difficulty. Otherwise, the experiences of the two groups are the same.

The children are tested for reading achievement before and after the study. The experimental (accelerated) group does not differ from the control group at the beginning of the study, but has gained a full grade level at its end, while the control group has gained only a half year. Statistical computations relating to this differential gain result in a numerical expression of sufficient size to have happened by chance only once in a hundred times. In practice, we proceed from this indication of lawfulness to the conclusion that the accelerated reading program was responsible for the difference in experimental and control group gains.

Faulty generalization often results from overconfidence in expressions of statistical significance, such as placing too much faith in a single experiment or study that shows significance at the .05 or .10 level. Less often, insufficient, hence faulty, generalization is made because of skepticism about the level of confidence of a finding.

THE DEVELOPMENT OF A THEORETICAL FRAMEWORK

The discussion so far has emphasized the purely methodological problems encountered by studies of the effects of child-reading. But if they are to make their most effective contribution to knowledge in a given field, empirical studies must have a close and continuing relation with theory in that field. Theory—even if fragmentary—serves to guide research by pointing to areas in which meaningful relations are likely to be found, and enhances the meaning of specific findings by relating them to more general concepts and principles. Research, on the other hand, serves to test existing theories and to provide a basis for their modification or for the development of new theories.

At a minimum, the theoretical framework within which fruitful investigations of child-rearing practices can be carried out must specify two dimensions: (1) the *areas or stages of child development* upon which parental behavior has a significant impact; (2) the *types or characteristics of parental behavior* that significantly influence development. In this section we shall consider, first, certain approaches to the definition of developmental stages, and, second, some of the attempts to isolate significant characteristics of parental behavior.

Dimensions of Human Development

Almost all authors in the field of human development who have thought deeply about the matter have developed ideas about the most meaningful developmental dimensions. Many have arrived at a conception of *developmental stages.* To some, these stages are chronological divisions. Gesell (see, e.g., Gesell *et al.*, 1940), for example, appears to regard age as the most important developmental dimension, and refers to types of behavior that characterize the two-year-old or the twelve-year-old. He regards development as a wavelike phenomenon, in which a period of integration and social harmony is followed by a period of increasing disintegration until a relatively disintegrated, socially inharmonious trough is reached. This, in turn, is followed by periods of steadily increasing integration until another peak is reached. This wavelike process ends only with maturity.

Others have gone beyond the straightforward chronological conception of stages and, like Freud (e.g., 1933, 1938), take note of how, at different age levels, different organ systems and their satisfactions are predominant (for instance, during the first year of life, the mouth and eating). Freud believes that predominance of a given organ system, interacting with parental treatment of the child during its dominance (for example, style of feeding the child), plays a major role in forming personality.

Still others (e.g., Sullivan, 1947) talk, not so much of the genetically or biologically determined dominance of different organ systems, but of the child's maturing capacities—his ability to "understand" his environment. Others, perhaps because of the difficulty of measuring or evaluating developmental stages, resort to universal categories of socialization (e.g., feeding, toilet training, and so on), and, in effect, do not consider stages of development as such.

The next few pages describe some of these theoretical frames of reference in greater detail.

THE DEVELOPMENT STAGES OF FREUD

Freud was one of the first to consider in any dynamic way how the early life of the infant shaped his later personality. Well grounded in biology, Freud believed that the influences of learning in infancy upon the developing organism profoundly affected the well- or ill-being of the older child and adult. More than any other scholar, he is responsible for currently accepted ideas that all behavior is *caused,* none is random or meaningless; and that, to understand later behavior, we must understand development in infancy and early childhood.

The roots of personality, for Freud, were biological. Personality was shaped through the interaction between learning and the three vital organ systems of orality and eating, anality and elimination, and genitality and (eventual) procreation. These organ systems and processes he related to infantile sexuality.

The *oral system* is, of course, dominant during the first year of life. The child's first experiences with satisfaction and discomfort, and with kindly or unsatisfying human relations, come through his mouth and the feeding process. Deprived of food or otherwise harshly treated, the infant is overwhelmed by fear and anxiety. Throughout his life, he must devote an undue portion of his psychological energy to defending against such anxiety and

insecurity. In other words, he is "fixated" at the oral stage, and, unless for-
tuitous circumstances intervene, continues to be handicapped by the problems engendered during this early developmental period. The type of the
adult orally fixated, because of deprivation, is one who is miserly, arrogant,
aggressive and impatient, competitive, suspicious, depressed, and cynical.

Relaxed and generous, but not overindulgent, feeding is thought to
produce childhood and adult personalities characterized by cooperative,
peaceful, friendly, optimistic, and sharing-and-giving traits. When oral
overprotectiveness exists and there is a lack of parental encouragement to
move into later developmental or *psychosexual* stages, or when conditions
during later developmental stages are unduly harsh or unrewarding, the
child may become orally fixated in quite a different way. Feelings of unrealistic security and self-confidence are common; the individual is rashly
trusting of others, at the same time expecting them to "do everything for
him." By way of contrast, the orally deprived baby becomes prematurely dependent on himself ("self-sufficient"), but is at the same time insecure and
uncertain. Thus, he is later forced into unwilling and untrusting dependent
behavior. In this sense, similar personality traits (dependence) may have
sharply contrasting origins, just as very different-appearing behaviors may
have similar origins.

After, but overlapping with, the dominance of the oral-eating system
comes pre-eminence of the *anal-eliminative system.* Ordinarily, during this
period (from about a year or 18 months to around 4 years), the child is
asked to submit his will to that of his parents: to forego his own pleasure
and accede to the demands of society. During this stage, he learns the rudiments of control: to *withhold* (i.e., to be continent), and, voluntarily, to
give (i.e., to have his bowel movement, or to void, at the right time and in
the right place).

The *anal character* (fixation at the anal stage) may, according to Freud,
result from too early or too strict and harsh toilet training. Such a personality
is characterized by excessive orderliness, parsimoniousness, and obstinancy;
although, if the child never "knuckles down" to parental training, adult
traits of wastefulness, unpunctuality, extravagance, and vacillation may
presumably occur. The necessary adult trait of *dependence* (and all of us
must be able to handle dependency, since we are all dependent on others)
develops either naturally or abnormally during the oral stage. The equally
necessary trait of *autonomy* (loosely, self-determination) is thought to develop or be blunted during the anal developmental stage. Too strict toilet
training is thought by some to inhibit the natural exploratory interest of the
child; to cause him to be filled with shame, so that he is likely to "regress" to
the oral, dependent stage and fail to develop self-confidence and independent problem-solving behavior.

Hypothetically, anal fixation, like oral fixation, could occur either
through deprivation or through overgratification. A situation in which
much affection accompanied complete accession to the child's demands,

without imposition of limits, might constitute such overindulgence. If fixation due to indulgence occurred, one might speculate that the personality would include all-encompassing self-confidence, insensitivity to the needs of others, and extreme social dominance. However, at least two facts combine to produce fixation through *excessive limits* rather than through *overindulgence*. The first is that necessary limits on behavior have to be set for children of this age to protect them from bodily harm; second, even though their parents may be overindulgent, children early start bumping into limits set by their playmates and adults other than their parents.

During the *phallic stage* (between about 3½ and 5 or 5½ years of age) the child becomes entranced with his own power as well as his own body. Here again, according to Freudian theory, too harsh and restrictive treatment may impair self-confidence, curiosity, and ambition, and produce anxiety about the body and its natural functions, particularly in the area of sexual behavior.

Fixation at this stage through overgratification is unlikely in our culture, since discouragement of childhood sexuality is almost universal. Even the child handled indulgently by his parents will encounter taboos through his friends and their mothers, and through other adults in his world.

Of central importance in Freud's theory of personality development is his account of the *Oedipus complex* and its possible outcomes. If normal development is to occur, boys must renounce an intense relationship they have presumably had with their mothers, and girls do the same with their fathers. The resolution of the Oedipal conflict, which is assumed to occur between 5 and 6 or 7 years of age, ushers in the child's identification with the parent of the same sex. When the Oedipus complex is successfully resolved, the little boy presumably takes a natural, easy, proud attitude toward his maleness, the little girl toward her femaleness. When, for one reason or another (such as unduly harsh, rejecting, or overprotective parents of either sex), the Oedipus complex is not resolved, the child may identify with the parent of the opposite sex to the detriment of his own later development. Cases in point are those who are homosexual, sexually impotent, or frigid. Again, as with the oral stage, similar behavior may have very different origins; one girl may conceivably become homosexual because of a strong, tender mother, a weak father; another because her father was harsh and rejecting but to a lesser degree than her mother.

Following the resolution of the Oedipus complex, it is thought that the child represses his infantile sexuality and the primitive fantasies connected with the organ systems of orality and anality. This repression marks the beginning of the *latency* period, characterized by reality orientation and lack of sexuality. *Adolescence,* which begins with genital maturity, re-evokes many of the infantile fantasies and conflicts. But, if these have been handled relatively well by the parents and other meaningful adults, the child moves fairly easily into natural heterosexual maturity, when he is able to *give* as well as *receive* love.

Freud's conception of the stages of psychosexual development has been roundly criticized by many. It derives more from listening to adults talk about their own children than from consistent observation of children, although the correspondence of the stages to stages of physical growth is obvious.

The first three of Freud's stages—oral, anal, and phallic—lend themselves easily to a social-learning analysis of personality, since they involve organ systems subjected to training by *all* cultures. It is toward the Oedipus complex that heaviest professional criticism has been directed, pointed particularly at Freud's postulation of its universality. Although the Oedipus complex is understandable in the context of the European or United States home, particularly the middle-class home, it seems less concordant with family structure in other cultures, such as those in which multiple mothering is practiced.

Freud theorized that, at about 5 or 6 years, boys renounce incestuous thoughts of their mothers because of a combination of two circumstances: first, fear of the all-powerful father and the damage he may do to them (fear of castration); and, second, love for the father, which enables them to identify with him. But how does the first of these, a perception of the all-powerful, potentially dangerous father, develop in cultures where the father is a mild and tangential adjunct of the family and the mother or a maternal uncle is the undisputed head? Boys *do* grow up in such cultures, and there is no evidence to indicate that they are any more mother-fixated or less masculine than boys in a standard United States culture. If anything, they appear to have fewer sexual problems. If boys reared in these cultures *do* develop such perceptions of the father (and there is not solid evidence that they do), it almost becomes necessary for psychologists to subscribe to a biologically determined theory of personality, in which learning plays a relatively slight role.

Regardless of the criticism that has been leveled against Freud, no one else has come up with developmental dimensions that represent a substantial improvement over his ideas. His genetic theory of psychosexual development has made two profound contributions to our thinking about personality formation: first, that all behavior is *caused,* hence *lawful,* and that search for the causes is the central task of psychology; second, that the mind and emotions do not operate in a vacuum, but develop and function in the context of the individual's biological and physiological structure and function.

Freud has been criticized for mysticism and imprecision; but perhaps the two most pertinent criticisms are (1) what many believe to be an overemphasis on the influence of biological, organic needs on personality, even though great weight is given to the interaction of learning with these organic needs; and (2) the difficulty, *at present,* of making *independent* estimates or measures of the strength of organic drives in infants and young children, or of mapping the learning process as it goes on in infancy and early childhood. For example, we can infer the strength of the infantile oral drive and the way it was handled only from the behavior of older children and adults, coupled, at best (except in longitudinal studies), with retrospective maternal accounts of child-rearing practices. Drives and learning conditions that are measured in retrospect or by inference from the behavior they presumably help to explain are not scientifically very useful. To date, attempts to make the necessary independent measures of "constitutional strength" of the organic drives have been unsuccessful; hence their explanatory and predictive power is slight. As we shall see in Chapter 3, studies of child-rearing practices have not, so far, contributed definitive information.

A NEO-PSYCHOANALYTIC POINT OF VIEW

Sullivan (1947, 1953; see also Mullahy, 1948), whose theoretical orientation differs from Freud's in several decisive respects, approaches the problem of developmental stages in a different manner. Whereas Freud's stages are primarily determined by physical maturational processes, Sullivan's have a much more intimate relation to the interaction the child, as a developing self, has with other people in his environment. Freud's stress is on the demands the child's organ systems make on the world in which he lives, and on the results of interference with (or overgratification of) these demands. Sullivan emphasizes the child's way of perceiving the world and adapting to it, and concerns himself less than Freud with stages of growth (although these are not neglected).

The key concepts in Sullivan's theory of personality development are *euphoria, tension,* and *dependence.* Absolute euphoria may be equated with total equilibrium of the organism; absolute tension with the maximum possible deviation from euphoria. Sullivan further distinguishes between the tension of (organic) *needs,* which is reduced by their (specific) *satisfaction,* and the tension of *anxiety,* which, in contrast with that of needs, is nonspecific, is interpersonal, and is reduced by the feeling of *security.*

The earliest experience of the infant presumably consists of undifferentiated states of comfort (equilibrium, euphoria) and discomfort (disequilibrium, tension). That is, the infant is not aware of hunger, thirst, or cold as such; he has not yet learned to identify the specific satisfactions that will reduce his state of tension. Further, and of crucial importance to Sullivan's theory, the infant is *totally dependent* on the ministrations of another person to satisfy his needs.

Gradually, as a result of repeated alternations of tension and tension-reduction, certain kinds of learning take place. The infant learns that certain objects or activities will alleviate certain kinds of discomfort: he stops crying at the *sight* of the nipple or the bottle instead of waiting until the nipple reaches his mouth. At the same time, he is learning something even more important: that his discomfort is generally alleviated fairly quickly, or that it is not. Out of his early, relatively undifferentiated, preverbal experiences concerning his needs and their satisfaction, there develop certain generalized expectations—what, from the point of view of the adult, might be called attitudes of trust or distrust, security or insecurity.

It should be noted here that Sullivan attaches far less significance to the simple failure to satisfy the infant's needs (e.g., because the mother is temporarily absent) than he does to their unwitting frustration through *anxiety* in a situation where satisfaction would normally be expected to occur. Anxiety is initially induced in the infant by anxiety (which need not be related specifically to the mother-child interaction) in the mother, through a process Sullivan terms *empathy*. By this he means nothing outside the realm of sensory perception, but simply a feeling based on extremely subtle cues. Once the infant has experienced the highly unpleasant emotion of anxiety, however, this emotion becomes of central importance in his subsequent behavior.

Sullivan hypothesizes that the infant learns to make certain very important differentiations based on anxiety. There is, first the differentiation (personification) of the *good* (need-satisfying) *mother* from the *bad* (anxiety-evoking) *mother*. Later on comes the differentiation (personification) of *good-me* ("me" rewarded by the tenderness of the good mother), *bad-me* ("me" punished by the anxiety-evoking mother), and *not-me* ("me" overwhelmed by intense, sudden anxiety)—in other words, the rudiments of what will later be the self-concept, which, according to Sullivan, develops from the reflected appraisals of significant others in the child's life.

What is particularly important for Sullivan's theory is that these differentiations—the earliest associations of anxiety with certain behaviors and situations involving the self and other people—are made long before language can define with any accuracy or precision exactly *what* it is that is anxiety-provoking, what it is that is "bad," what it is that is to be avoided. The combination of utter dependence and relatively unclear and uninformed perception, in other words, produces a situation in which the possibilities for distortion are enormous. The creeping infant stopped by a sharp "No" from his mother has no notion that he is about to bump into a table; that atop the table is a lamp; that, if the table is bumped, the lamp will fall; that, if it falls, the lamp will break; or that, if it breaks, this will matter to anyone, and so on. These "reasonable," cause-and-effect learnings come much later, long after any number of "unreasonable" learnings may have occurred.

The significance of one of the developmental schemes used by Sullivan—his analysis of experience into three "modes"—becomes apparent in the light of this view of how learning proceeds. The *prototaxic* is the earliest mode of experiencing the world. The infant "knows" only momentary states; he distinguishes dimly, if at all, between his body and what lies outside; his experience is undifferentiated, without definite limits. The second mode of experence identified by Sullivan is the *parataxic*. The infant begins to differentiate among his experiences and to attach meanings to them. But these meanings are not logically related, and many of them are highly special and unique to him (*autistic*). When one's meanings are common or shared (when *chair* means *chair* to him consistently, just as it does to all those with whom he comes in contact), these meanings are said to be *consensually validated,* and experience is said to be occurring in the *syntaxic* mode. Syntaxic meanings follow reality and logic as we think of them.

It seems clear that the same child-rearing practices, and parental behavior in general, will have a very different impact on learning, including the learning involved in the development of personality, in each of these three modes. And although the age of the individual is to some extent related to his predominant mode of perception, the three modes are not mutually exclusive, nor are they ever altogether "outgrown."

In a further search for meaningful dimensions of personality development Sullivan, like many others, resorted to a *temporal* sequence, although to him the nature of the interpersonal relations of the child, and his capacity for different complexities and types of social relations at different levels, is of more concern than chronological age or neurophysical maturity. Sullivan says that *infancy* becomes *childhood* "as soon as the infant has picked up a vocal trick, saying perhaps 'ma' and getting tremendous response from the significant adult, without any idea of precisely what has happened but catching on the second time it happens" (1947, p. 8). In other words, infancy ends and childhood begins as soon as the rudiments of language are acquired.

Childhood continues up to the time when the child can get on fairly well with his peers; the *juvenile era* begins when playmates are badly needed and are, in most ways, preferred to adults. The "eruption, due to maturation, of a need for an intimate relation with another person of comparable status" marks the beginning of *pre-adolescence,* a relatively brief period which ends with puberty. *Adolescence* is marked by a shift of interest from a person of one's own sex to one of the opposite sex, and by the patterning of adult sexual activity. At *adulthood* one is able, for the first time, to establish a love relationship in which the other person is almost as important as oneself.

The significance of these developmental epochs lies in the fact that each begins with new (interpersonal) needs and new (interpersonal) relationships, and each therefore to some extent affords an opportunity for new and more appropriate learnings:

> It is in general true that, as one passes over one of these more-or-less determinable thresholds of a developmental era, everything that has gone before becomes reasonably open to influence; this is true even in the organization of the self-system, which, as I suppose I cannot stress too much, is remarkably inclined to maintain its direction. The changes which take place at the thresholds of the developmental eras . . . are far-reaching; they touch upon much of what has already been acquired as personality, often making it somewhat acutely inadequate . . . for the

sudden new expanding of the personal horizon. Thus the beginning phase of a developmental era may considerably affect those inappropriate aspects of personality which emerge from what the person has undergone up to then.[2]

The theory of personality development outlined by Sullivan is essentially one of social learning. This social-learning frame of reference is one to which we shall return again and again throughout the book, for it is the point of convergence of a variety of theoretical strands and empirical facts.

OTHER APPROACHES TO THE DEFINITION OF DEVELOPMENTAL STAGES

Chronological divisions have been adopted by a substantial proportion of United States child psychologists and educators, but few, if any, have attempted the psychological *plus* chronological division used by Sullivan. Child psychology texts typically include sections on *infancy*, which is variously defined as consisting of the first 6 months to the first 2 years; *early childhood*, a stage ordinarily extending from the runabout period (about 18 months) to school age; *the early school years* (kindergarten or first grade through third grade); *the intermediate school years* (fourth through sixth grades); *adolescence* (beginning at the age of puberty and extending, according to some authors, to the age of about 24); and *maturity*, which follows adolescence.

Some authors, for example Whiting and Child (1953) and Sears, Maccoby, and Levin (1957), in effect, do not try to formulate developmental stages at all but concentrate on *those organ-need and behavioral areas* in which every society, if it is to function, must guide (socialize) its young. The first three areas of socialization postulated by these writers correspond to the Freudian sequence of organ systems and needs: (1) *feeding and weaning;* (2) *elimination training;* and (3) *sex training.* Although the authors mentioned above have been much influenced by psychoanalytic thought, their emphasis is more on *learning as it affects functioning* than on *organ needs as they affect (or interact with) learning.* For their fourth and fifth universal training areas, they move from organ systems and functions to emotional expression: (4) *aggression training;* and (5) *dependency training.*[3]

The summaries of research presented in Chapter 3 follow this latter pattern. Taken up in turn are studies concerning feeding and weaning, toilet training, sex training, and training in the expression of aggressive and dependency feelings.

[2] Reprinted with permission from the William Alanson White Psychiatric Foundation and W. W. Norton and Company, from Sullivan, H. S.: *Interpersonal Theory of Psychiatry.* New York: W. W. Norton, 1953.
[3] For Freud, the type of training necessary in these two areas, and its outcome, is viewed almost as a by-product, or inevitable consequence, of training in the first three psychosexual stages.

Analyses of Parental Behavior

Up to this point, discussion has centered around the dimensions of *child development*. But meaningful categories for looking at and analyzing *parental behavior* as it impinges upon these dimensions must also be found.

THE SEARS, MACCOBY, AND LEVIN STUDY

Sears, Maccoby, and Levin performed a factor analysis of ratings and judgments based on a large number of interviews about child-rearing practices with mothers of five-year-old children. Their study resulted in the identification of eight factors that appeared to underlie a wide variety of discrete parental behaviors.

Factor analysis is a procedure for determining which of a large number of items (or, in this case, types of behavior) are statistically related to one another. In other words, it is a statistical procedure for *grouping* discrete items. The analyst then attempts to find a descriptive name for the factor that he believes the items of a particular group have in common. Of the 44 scales of maternal behavior devised by Sears, Maccoby, and Levin, 16 appeared to be related to each other in such a fashion as to form the first factor, the common element of which could plausibly be called *permissiveness-restrictiveness*. Stated so that they define the strict, or nonpermissive, end of the scale, these maternal behaviors (as judged from the mothers' *verbal description* and not from *actual observation*) are: high restrictions on play in the house and with furniture, and on making noise; high demands and standards for good table manners, being neat and orderly, and being obedient; strict toilet training and strict and rejective response to dependency; much emphasis on doing well in school; frequent use of physical punishment and severe punishment for aggression toward parents; low permissiveness for aggression toward parents, between siblings, or toward other children; low permissiveness for nudity, immodesty, masturbation, or sex play with other children.

The second factor identified by Sears, Maccoby, and Levin includes 10 types of items that the mothers reported about themselves, and was labeled *general family adjustment*. Stated so that they define the high, or "good," end of the scale, these items are: the mother reports high self-esteem, gives a high evaluation of the father, is very satisfied with her current life situation, is not anxious about her ability to rear children. She was delighted when she became pregnant with the child who was the subject of the study, as was the father. She reports no disagreements with the father about child-rearing, enjoyed an affectionate interaction with the child when he was a baby, as did the father, and says she has no difficulty following through on her disciplinary actions.

The third factor was called *warmth of mother-child relationship*. The 6 items constituting this factor, stated so that they define warm relationships, are: the mother has much affectionate interaction with the child, is warmly demonstrative to the child, finds ample time to play with him, accepts his dependency cheerfully, praises the child for good table manners, and leans heavily on reasoning as a method of training.

The fourth factor, *responsible child-training orientation*, includes some of the items from previous scales. Its 9 related items are: mother has high self-esteem; places high demands on the child for neatness and orderliness; enforces strict regulations on play in the house and with furniture; insists upon good table manners and strict obedience; uses much praise for good table manners and "playing nicely." To obtain obedience, she uses a combination of withdrawing privileges and offering many tangible rewards. Concerning a mother who scores high on this factor, the authors "get the impression that she keeps her attention rather continuously (and mainly pleasantly) directed toward the child, viewing him as a person who must be taught many things." (Sears, Maccoby, and Levin, 1957, p. 475)

The fifth factor identified in the study was *aggressiveness and punitiveness*. Mothers scoring high on the items related to this factor showed high demands for aggression toward other children and high permissiveness for such aggression. They themselves used much physical punishment and were severe in their punishment when the child was aggressive toward them. Needless to say, they were markedly nonpermissive about their child's aggression toward them.

The sixth factor was labeled by the authors *perception of husband*. Fathers who scored high were reported by their wives to be displeased when the wife became pregnant, to assume chief responsibility for child-rearing policies, and to be very permissive about the child's aggression toward other children.

The seventh and final purely statistical factor has been called *orientation toward child's physical well-being*. Health and safety practices predominate, and the mother who scored high tended to use scheduled feedings for the child as a baby; to demand good table manners, including eating everything on the plate; to be strict about bedtime; and to be firm about the child's wandering about the neighborhood. Such a mother was also likely to be anxious about her child-rearing ability.

Another pattern, less easily identified statistically but related to most of the seven statistical factors, also appeared from the mothers' interviews. This was the *pattern of control or discipline* used by the mother. Control techniques appeared to fall into two categories, one considered by the authors to be love-oriented, the other object-oriented. The love-oriented mother was likely to use praise as a method of reward, and to "withdraw" love as punishment. The object-oriented mother was more likely to use tangible rewards for good behavior on the part of her child (to bribe?) and to punish him either by physical discipline or by deprivation of privileges.

These seven statistical and one "clinical" factors in child-rearing represent the thinking and research of one team of highly skilled and experienced investigators. Like the author of this volume, they believe that social learning (primarily, learning from the parents in the early years of childhood) is paramount in the development of personality. This learning results from environmental experiences impinging upon the child as he passes through various developmental stages. To discover the "how" of this process is perhaps the single most important function of child psychology. This "how" can never be discovered until dimensions are formulated for child-rearing practices and for child development which are clear (i.e., which other people can understand and determine in the same fashion as the original investigators) and useful (i.e., related to significant aspects of the development of children). Eight child-rearing factors interacting with five developmental aspects (feeding and weaning, elimination, sex, dependency, and aggression) constitute Sears, Maccoby, and Levin's analysis of the major *parental-practice variables* as they are applied in the five most important *child-training areas*.

THE SEWELL, MUSSEN, AND HARRIS STUDY

Sewell, Mussen, and Harris (1955) have studied child-rearing practices using methods similar to those of Sears, Maccoby, and Levin. First they interviewed a large sample of mothers of five- and six-year-olds. From these interviews they made ratings and judgments about child-rearing practices and then performed a factor analysis of their results.

The children studied by Sewell, Mussen, and Harris were five- and six-year-old rural youngsters from Wisconsin, whereas those studied by Sears, Maccoby, and Levin were five-year-old suburban youngsters from the East Coast. Sewell, Mussen, and Harris probably used more direct interviewing techniques (phrased their questions more pointedly) than did the Sears group. They secured information about 38 aspects of child-rearing and also attempted to tap some parental attitudes and practices.

On the whole, Sewell, Mussen, and Harris found lower relationships among the different items of behavior subsumed under their factor headings than did Sears, Maccoby, and Levin. The seven factors they emerged with were: (1) practices generally considered to reflect permissiveness in early feeding situations; (2) permissive toilet-training practices (these two factors appear to be related to Sears, Maccoby, and Levin's first factor of "permissiveness-restrictiveness"); (3) practices involving much activity of the parent with the child (conceivably overlapping to some degree "warmth of mother-child relationship"); (4) nonpunitive treatment of behavior (possibly related to "permissiveness-restrictiveness" but not correlated with factors 1 and 2 in the Sewell study); (5) practices making for early independence; (6) practices reflecting casual attitudes of the parents in a number of situations: bowel training, napping, eating, mischievousness; (7) noninsistent reactions on the part of the parent.

The biggest overlap, then, between Sewell, Mussen, and Harris and Sears, Maccoby, and Levin is their agreement that at least one very important variable in child-rearing practices is the degree of permissiveness or strictness that a mother shows toward her children.

Sewell, Mussen, and Harris believe that they failed to find any true common denominator of different child-rearing practices, such as a general "acceptance or rejection of the child," or even consistency from one area of child-rearing to another. Some of their conclusions neatly illustrate this point. For example, parents who were permissive in feeding practices were quite active with their children and treated them casually, but punished for misbehavior. Parents who did *not* punish the child for misbehavior were not particularly likely to be permissive in early feeding or toilet training, nor did they participate in much activity with the child, but they also tended to treat their child casually. Again, parents who said they encouraged early independence of their child did not treat him casually and *did* engage in much activity with him. Common sense would say that the child most likely to become independent was the one who was treated casually and whose parents engaged in relatively little activity with him.

It should be mentioned again that these findings are based on what parents *report* they do with their children. It is not known whether they actually behave as they say they do, nor is it known whether the children are as their parents describe them (in the Sears, Maccoby, and Levin study; no descriptions of the children's behavior are provided by Sewell, Mussen, and Harris).

THE CRANDALL AND PRESTON STUDY

A third and final study to be reported here used statistical techniques other than factor analysis in a similar effort to get at meaningful dimensions of child-rearing practices. Crandall and Preston (1955), working with a smaller number of mothers whose children differed widely in age, but also using interview techniques, reported four major dimensions of maternal behavior. Their first major cluster they named *affection.* This cluster consists of rather highly interrelated maternal tendencies toward expressing affection, rapport (a close, friendly, mutually understanding relationship), approval of the child's behavior, and much contact between mother and child. It can be seen that this cluster of items has a similarity to the factor identified by Sears, Maccoby, and Levin as "warmth of mother-child relationship," and to the third factor isolated by Sewell, Mussen, and Harris, which relates to the amount of activity shared by parent and child.

Crandall and Preston's second cluster is labeled *protective.* The items included are babying, protectiveness, solicitousness, and child-centeredness. This cluster has no apparent relationship to any of the Sears clusters; it may be more or less opposite (hence logically related) to the factors of casualness and encouraging of independence identified by Sewell, Mussen, and Harris.

The third cluster of items found to be highly interrelated by Crandall and Preston they called *coactive control.* By this they mean, roughly, democratic control. Parents who scored high in this cluster justified their policies of handling their children to the children, endorsed and used democratic policies, were very ready with explanations, and were quite understanding of their children. No close resemblance to any of the Sears factors is obvious; there may be some resemblance to the Sewell factor of noninsistence, although the resemblance is not close. (The two most important items in the noninsistence factor are: father does not insist that child mind without question; mother does not insist that child mind without question.)

Crandall and Preston's fourth cluster they named *coercive control.* This cluster includes items indicating that the mother was very quick in enforcing either her demands or her suggestions, and was quite severe in her penalties. The similarity of this factor to several of the factors identified by the two studies discussed previously is obvious.

SUMMARY

The purpose of this chapter on methodology is to make students in the field critically more alert. It contains material designed to improve their observations and research concerning child development and child-rearing practices.

Research in the area of child-rearing practices and child development in general can be schematized as varying along four dimensions: (1) normative–explanatory; (2) ahistorical–historical; (3) naturalistic–manipulative; and (4) atheoretical–theoretical. Although these dimensions are logically independent, there is a tendency for some to vary together.

Seven major defects of research in the general area of child development, including child-rearing practices, are: contamination; reconstruction through retrospection; faulty logic; poor definition of concepts; direct influence of the investigator upon his results; sampling deficiencies; and unsound generalization.

Unsound generalization is often related to uninformed use of three statistical concepts. These basic concepts are *correlation* (a measure of relatedness); *prediction through correlation;* and *level of confidence.* Familiarity with these concepts is necessary to an understanding of research summaries given later in the text.

To be most useful, empirical studies should have theoretical relevance. A body of theory consists of *concepts* and a set of *propositions* stating the relations between them, these propositions being subject to empirical verification. The function of theoretical categories (concepts) is to direct attention to those areas of the field in which significant relationships are likely to be found. At a minimum, then, theory in the field of child development must specify (1) the important dimensions of child development and (2) the crucial elements of child-rearing practices.

Freud postulated a sequence of *organ needs* and *need-satisfactions,* rooted in biology, as most relevant to personality development. Different organ systems predominate at different times in the child's life, and their effect on later personality is determined by the way infants are handled during the predominance of each system. The three systems with which

Freud concerned himself are (1) *oral-feeding*, (2) *anal-elimination*, and (3) *genital-sexual*.

Sullivan, more than Freud, stressed infantile and childhood cognition and adaptation. He postulated three modes of experiencing the world: the *prototaxic*, the *parataxic*, and the *syntaxic;* and seven age epochs (important to him more because of the social phenomena that characterize them than because of the chronological age variable alone): *infancy, childhood,* the *juvenile era, pre-adolescence, early adolescence, late adolescence,* and of course, *maturity.*

Sullivan's concepts seem more susceptible of clear definition and translation into operational terms than Freud's, although Freud's psychoanalytic theories have elicited more attention and stimulated more research.

Other authors do not concern themselves with developmental stages as such but concentrate on areas of training common to all cultures. Most often agreed on are training in *feeding and weaning, elimination, sex, aggression,* and *dependency.* The next chapter is organized in accordance with this framework, which stresses the learning of the human organism rather than his biological needs.

There is no general agreement on the important elements of child-rearing practices, but the findings of three representative studies indicate that the following may be significant variables: *permissiveness-strictness; autocratic-democratic* practices; *punitive-nonpunitive* discipline; *warmth-coldness* of parental attitudes and practices; *casual-ignoring* behavior toward the child; and stress on *promoting independence* as opposed to *encouraging dependence* on the parents.

CHAPTER 3

Child-Rearing Practices

THE preceding chapters have introduced the concept of culture and mapped the sensory equipment through which culture impinges on the child. Many authors have analyzed the stages through which the child passes, postulating that the culture makes a different impact on the child during each stage. There is no close agreement about the characteristics, or even the dimensions, of these stages, although all agree that the beginning years of life are crucially important and that, during them, development is profoundly shaped by the treatment the baby and young child receives from his parents.

The material in this chapter is organized according to a social-learning analysis of child training, principally because independent definitions have not yet been formulated for the stages of development that such authors as Freud and Sullivan have set forth. Studies concerning feeding and weaning, toilet training, sex, aggression, and dependency are discussed in that order. The effects of deprivation and over-all parental attitudes, including general techniques of control and training, are also treated.

It is often impossible to draw solid conclusions about child-rearing practices in a given area, since the studies may be too few in number, poorly designed, contradictory in their results, or all three. But, when possible, conclusions and applications of research are presented.

The goals of this chapter are, first, to summarize the facts concerning child-rearing practices and the *effects* of these practices when such effects have been studied, and second, to give a rather detailed introduction to research, its evaluation, and the process of drawing from it conclusions and suggestions for practice.

FEEDING

Choice of and Success at Breast Feeding

One of the first decisions the mother must make about her baby is, Shall I breast-feed him or use some artificial method? A major study to which this chapter makes repeated reference has been done by Sears, Maccoby, and Levin (1957). Of the 379 mothers of five-year-olds whose interviews make up the data, 39 percent had breast-fed the child who was the subject of the study. In the majority of the cases, the child had been breast-fed for less than three months.

It seems logical that the decision to breast-feed may be linked with other decisions about "closeness" to or "intimacy" with the baby. It may be that women who desire both to breast-feed and to be in intimate contact with their new baby are more "motherly" than those who do not. In one interesting study (Klatskin, Lethin, and Jackson, 1950), it was predicted that a choice to breast-feed would be associated with a choice to "room in" with the baby. Under the rooming-in plan, the baby is placed in the mother's hospital room almost from birth, and she assumes all the care for him that she can. In the conventional nursery plan, new babies are kept in the hospital nursery and brought to their mothers for feeding at regular intervals. Nurses assume care for the babies other than feeding.

Klatskin, Lethin, and Jackson interviewed 1,251 mothers about their rooming-in and feeding preferences, *prior* to the birth of their babies. These mothers were all from low-income groups, although many of them were the wives of college students and medical internes and residents, so that their education was higher than would be predicted from knowing their husbands' incomes.

In the total group, 53 percent chose to breast-feed, 40 percent to bottle-feed, and the rest were undecided.

The difference of 14 percent between the Sears, Maccoby, and Levin data for breast feeding and the Klatskin, Lethin, and Jackson data may plausibly be attributed to the period of the child's life about which the mother was queried: in the Sears study, mothers *remembered* what they had *actually done;* in the second study, mothers predicted what they *intended* to do. In addition, the mothers in the Klatskin study had been officially encouraged by the hospital staff both to breast-feed and to room in.

Rooming-in was chosen by 54 percent of the mothers. Thirty-one percent preferred the hospital nursery, and 15 percent were undecided at the time of the interview. As predicted, choice of rooming-in was positively associated with choice of breast feeding. This association is shown in Table 3.1.

Of the mothers who preferred the rooming-in plan, with all its attendant intimacy with the baby, almost two thirds (64 percent) chose breast feeding, which also demands close and intimate contact with the infant. Of those who preferred the hospital nursery, only about a third chose breast feeding, while three fifths selected bottle feeding (35 percent and 60 percent, respectively). The "undecided" mothers were intermediate. About half of them selected breast, the other half bottle feeding (47 percent and 43 percent, respectively). This association of infant-care preference and feeding choice is highly significant, P being less than .001.

There are other interesting trends in the data: The group who chose rooming-in had the fewest babies and the biggest percentage of first-born babies. The members of the rooming-in group were also, on the average, the best-educated and were married to husbands at higher occupational levels. It is often popularly suggested that mothers of Southern European national origins and Negro mothers are more "motherly" than women from old United States families or than mothers whose national origins are British or Northwest European. In this study, there was a tendency (not statistically significant) in the opposite direction. More of the latter group preferred rooming-in; more mothers who were Negro or could trace their origins to Southern

TABLE 3.1: RELATIONSHIP BETWEEN PREFERRED PLAN FOR INFANT CARE FOLLOWING BIRTH AND MOTHERS' CHOICE OF METHOD OF FEEDING THE BABY.

	Baby-Care Plan					
Feeding method	*Rooming-in*		*Hospital nursery*		*Undecided*	
	N	%	N	%	N	%
Breast	438	64	138	35	83	47
Bottle	194	29	235	60	76	43
Undecided	49	7	21	5	17	10
Total	681	100	394	100	176	100

Adapted with permission of C. D. May, Editor, *Pediatrics,* and Ethelyn H. Klatskin, from Klatskin, Lethin, and Jackson (1950).

Europe preferred the nursery. However, this difference is probably due to educational differences that undoubtedly existed between the two groups. No differences in "motherliness" were found for different religious groups.

Another study (Newton and Newton, 1950) relates maternal attitudes toward breast feeding to actual success at breast feeding. In this study 91 mothers who had given natural birth to normal babies were interviewed about their feelings toward breast feeding. Trained judges sorted the expressed attitudes into three categories: positive, doubtful, and negative. The mothers were then observed to see how much milk they were giving the babies, and how much milk they actually had available. They were then classified as successful, unsuccessful, or abortive breast-feeders. The first group included mothers whose babies required no supplemental feeding after the fourth day of life; mothers were classified as unsuccessful if, after the fourth day of life, their babies required supplemental feedings; and as abortive feeders if they gave up breast feeding entirely before they left the hospital.

Of the 91 mothers, 51 were classified as showing positive attitudes toward breast feeding. Of these 51, 74 percent were successful in breast-feeding their babies. Only 2 percent (one mother) fell into the category of an abortive breast-feeder. Twenty-three mothers expressed negative attitudes toward breast feeding, and of them only 26 percent were successful breast-feeders. Thirty percent were included in the abortive bracket. The 17 mothers who had doubtful attitudes about breast feeding included 35 percent who succeeded at it; half of them (47 percent) were unsuccessful; a fifth (18 percent) were abortive feeders.

Mothers with positive attitudes gave their babies an average of 59 grams of milk at each fourth-day feeding; mothers with doubtful attitudes, 42 grams; and mothers with negative attitudes supplied only 35 grams of milk per fourth-day feeding. The authors of the study report that there were no real differences between the three attitude groups in the amount of milk actually available for the babies; and that such factors as experience with previous children and experience of actually putting the baby to the breast did not affect their results.

Adams (1959) administered a personality test and interviews to two groups of mothers, one group composed of 35 women who had chosen to breast-feed, the other of 23 who had chosen to bottle-feed. All were in the last trimester (three months) of pregnancy, and the groups were well-matched on a sizable number of factors.

A number of significant differences appeared between the groups. Mothers choosing to use the bottle were, as a group, more dependent, more rejecting of the child, and more dissatisfied with their own sex role. They also showed more signs of psychosexual disturbance. They seemed more maladjusted in areas concerned with eating, sucking, and elimination; manifested more sibling rivalry and guilt feelings; and were more preoccupied with themselves. More signs of penis envy—broadly speaking, jealousy of men—were shown by the group choosing to breast-feed.

These judgments were made on the basis of interviews and the analysis of responses to the Blacky test, a projective instrument revolving around a family of four dogs: the parents; Blacky, who is of indeterminate sex; and a younger brother (or sister) of Blacky. The person taking the test is asked to tell stories about pictures involving various members of the family.

Although there was considerable overlapping between the two groups of subjects, the tentative conclusion drawn from the study was that mothers choosing to breast-feed show a somewhat more secure and mature set of attitudes than those choosing to bottle-feed.

From these studies, all based in part on the interview method—and some of the dangers inherent in this method have been discussed—the following tentative conclusions emerge: Half or fewer of the mothers studied actually breast-feed their babies; positive attitudes toward breast feeding seem to be associated with success at it and with other types of intimate mother-baby relations. Mothers choosing breast feeding show certain personality characteristics judged to indicate greater maturity than mothers choosing to bottle-feed. However, this last conclusion is based on a rather small group of mothers—58 in all.

The Scheduling of Infant Feeding

Another choice that a mother must make early in the baby's life concerns his feeding schedule. Shall it be the traditional rigid schedule, with a feeding every three or four hours; or shall it be a self-demand schedule, in which the baby is fed whenever he appears to be hungry? Traditional pediatrics has favored the former practice; modern pediatrics leans more toward the self-demand schedule.

Perhaps the most convincing evidence favoring self-demand schedules is afforded by a study (Aldrich and Hewitt, 1947) of 668 demand-fed babies up to their first birthday. The babies eventually set up realistic-appearing programs for themselves, although early in infancy they ate more frequently than the conventional every four hours. About 70 percent of them had switched to an adult-type schedule of three meals per day by the time they were 10 months of age. At 1 year of age, they averaged 29.4 inches in height and weighed 21.8 pounds, figures that compare favorably with generally accepted standards. At this age, fewer than 1 percent of them were severe feeding problems, although an additional 7 percent were somewhat resistant to eating and required coaxing.

Other studies of individual children and of twins (e.g., Simsarian and McLendon, 1945; Trainham, Pilafian, and Kraft, 1945) also support the idea of self-demand schedules. A subfinding in a comprehensive study (Williams and Scott, 1953), which will be discussed in more detail later, indicates that children who have more rigid feeding schedules are less active in their first and second years than children fed more flexibly. But in this study, mothers who scheduled feedings strictly also engaged in a wide range of other restrictive practices, so that it is difficult to evaluate the influence of strict feeding schedules apart from the influence of other factors.

At a common-sense level, anyone who has watched new babies thoughtfully has reached the conclusion that they are highly variable and unstable creatures. Most moderately relaxed parents probably find it easier on their nervous systems to follow a self-demand feeding schedule, since ordinarily there will be less total crying under such a system than when careful schedules are enforced. However, if parents are oversolicitous and tense, self-demand feeding may be accompanied by overstimulation of the child to the point of interfering with his easy development. Currently, on the basis of the facts available, we can conclude only that self-demand feeding seems to do the baby no harm in terms of the characteristics that have been studied.

Cup Feeding

One other type of feeding, quite revolutionary, has been advocated and used: feeding the baby by cup from birth. Two types of study of this procedure have been conducted, only one of which (Fredeen, 1948) is relevant to this section. The reported weight gain for prematurely born babies fed by cup and by other methods is presented in Table 3.2.

Table 3.2 shows rather clearly the advantages of this type of feeding for premature babies, who are short on energy at birth. Other advantages claimed for this method of feeding are that the mother must of necessity have close, warm, personal contact with the baby as he is being fed: that is,

TABLE 3.2: AVERAGE WEIGHT GAIN, IN GRAMS PER DAY, OF PREMATURE
BABIES OF DIFFERENT BIRTH WEIGHTS, SOME OF WHOM WERE CUP-FED,
OTHERS CONVENTIONALLY FED.

Birth Weight of Premature Infants	Cup-Fed Babies		Other than Cup-Fed Babies	
	Number of infants	Average gain in weight per day	Number of infants	Average gain in weight per day
Less than 1.5 kg.	8	21.5 g.	4	19.7 g.
1.5 to 2.0	41	22.2	12	17.4
2.0 to 2.5	22	16.7	11	9.2

Adapted with permission of C. D. May, Editor, *Pediatrics*, and R. C. Fredeen, from
Fredeen (1948).

there is no way to feed by cup without holding the baby. Such bodily contact
is believed by most authorities to help babies' normal development. Bottles,
on the other hand, can be given by means of holders. Cup feeding is thought
also to be excellent for babies with disorders such as harelip and cleft palate.
Apparently cup-fed babies suffer less frequently from ear disorders (which
may be aggravated by the process of sucking).

Style of Feeding and Thumb-Sucking

The third major feeding decision that a mother must arrive at, after
making up her mind whether to feed by breast or artificially, and how or if
to schedule, concerns the total sucking time the baby shall have. Shall he be
fed rapidly or slowly? This decision, of course, can be made more easily by
the mother who chooses bottle feeding, where deliberate regulation of the
speed of securing food is possible.

Some psychoanalytic writers, most notably David Levy (1934) contend
that sucking is an instinct that *demands* gratification. If enough satisfaction
is not given by sucking for food, then gratification will be secured through
thumb-sucking, blanket-sucking, or some other type of nonnutritive sucking.
Levy observed calves, some of which had suckled from the cow, others fed
from the pail, and concluded that the latter did much more sucking than the
former at the ears of other calves. He then separated a litter of six puppies,
feeding three of them from slow-flowing, three from fast-flowing bottles.
The latter showed more nonnutritive sucking than the former. Much ado
has been made over these six dogs, who may well have influenced the handling of more babies than any other six dogs in history.

Kunst (1948) observed thumb- and finger-sucking in 143 orphanage
babies. She concluded that such sucking increases steadily as time passes
after the baby has been fed, regardless of whether he is asleep or awake.
Extranutritive sucking was most marked one and a half to two hours after
meals. The less rich the formula, the more sucking of the thumb. Evapo-
rated-milk formulas produced less nonnutritive sucking than other formulas.

Babies often begin to thumb- or finger-suck soon after birth, and the frequency of such behavior increases rapidly in the first 3 months, stays about the same until 6 months, then declines to 10 months. Teething babies are more likely to do it than babies who are not teething, and boys more likely to than girls.

Thumb-sucking[1] seems to be normal, at least in the sense that a very large proportion of children practice it. Klackenberg (1949) found half of a population of 259 babies sucking their thumbs at 1 year of age, and Brazelton (1956) reports that almost 90 percent of a group of 70 rather superior babies were thumb-suckers at some time during their first year, although by 1 year of age, only 4 of them continued to suck their hands except when they were under stress.

If sucking is a learned or partially learned response rather than an instinct or inborn drive, then babies with more practice at sucking should do more, and more vigorous, sucking, nutritive or nonnutritive, than babies with less sucking practice. Specifically, learning theory predicts that cup-fed babies will be least likely to do either strong extranutritive sucking; bottle- and breast-fed babies will do more; and breast-fed babies may well do the most.

Several studies have tested this differential prediction. The first (Davis *et al.,* 1948) divided 60 babies into three equal groups, one cup-, one bottle-, and one breast-fed during the first 10 days of life. Learning theory was supported to a moderate degree: breast-fed babies showed stronger sucking responses than the other two groups, although cup- and bottle-fed babies did not differ from each other. Sears and Wise (1950) studied 80 normal children from 2 years 3 months to 7 years 10 months of age to see how they had been fed, how long they had been sucking-fed, how severely they had been weaned, and what some of the differential effects had been. Some of these babies had been cup-fed from birth, more of them from about 2 weeks of age. They were classified as early-, middle-, and late-weaned according to the total amount of sucking feeding they had received. According to instinctual-psychoanalytic theory, it would be expected that the group weaned earliest would be most frustrated by weaning and would most frequently be thumb-suckers. In fact, the reverse was found. The tendency for the late-weaned to be rated most frustrated was statistically significant when they were compared with the other two groups. Although differences in frequency of thumb-sucking were not significant among the three groups, they were in the direction opposite to that predicted by instinct theory. The actual frequency of thumb-sucking was greatest, not in the

[1] The definition of a "thumb-sucker" is complex. Does it apply to a child who at any time sucks his thumb, even though this may be mild sucking for a few minutes before going to sleep or when tired? Or does it apply rather to the child who exerts strong thrusting pressure on lips, teeth, and palate for (for example) four hours a day? Lack of clear definition is partly responsible for our failure to have a clear answer to questions about the relation between thumb-sucking and adjustment, or thumb-sucking and dental malformation.

early-, but in the *late-weaned* group. Suddenness of weaning was related to the amount of frustrated behavior the child showed. Those more suddenly weaned were more frustrated by weaning.

Another careful experiment (Brodbeck, 1950) shows that intensity of sucking goes *down* during periods when very young babies (in their first 8 days of life) are cup-fed, *up* when they are required to exert strong sucking pressure to get their food. Those who obtained the most food for their efforts were also the strongest suckers.

A husband-wife team (Blau and Blau, 1955) used as their subject for study only one baby, who was alternated on nipples that required much and little effort to secure milk. On the free-flowing nipple, this baby required fewer feedings per day, took more food, went to sleep sooner after feeding, cried less, did less nonnutritive sucking, and was less active after and between feedings. He also did less regurgitating.

Yarrow (1954) followed 66 children, 28 boys and 38 girls, for a number of years. Almost two thirds of the children (64 percent) were reported to be thumb-suckers at some time or another during the period of study. Somewhat more girls (66 percent) than boys (54 percent) had been thumb-suckers, and half of the thumb-suckers were still sucking their thumbs at the age of 4 years. Almost all (90 percent) who had at any time sucked their thumbs started before 6 months of age, and almost two thirds of them (63 percent)had begun before the age of 3 months. Three fourths of the children had stopped thumb-sucking by 6 years of age (perhaps as a result of teasing on the part of schoolmates?), but some still persisted at 8 years of age. The duration and severity of the thumb-sucking had no relation to whether the child had been breast- or bottle-fed or to the age at which he had been weaned. However, there seemed to be a relation in babyhood (1 to 6 months of age) between thumb-sucking and length of time the child was allowed to suck at feedings. Those who were allowed to suck longer were less frequently thumb-suckers.

Three studies (Johnson, 1939; and Lewis, 1930 and 1931) relate to the effect of thumb-sucking on dental structure. The general conclusions are that thumb-sucking has a deleterious effect on bites that are already out of line, little or none on "good" bites. It is also suggested that although the structure of the baby teeth is altered by thumb-sucking, no effect is produced on the permanent teeth if the child stops sucking his thumb by the time the permanent teeth begin to come in (ordinarily during the seventh year).

From the time of Freud, thumb-sucking has been considered a neurotic symptom in children, a sign of fixation at the oral psychosexual stage, hence of immaturity and dependency. This has been more a matter of opinion than of fact. In the one study of the subject known to the author (Honzik, unpublished), an effort was made to study the personalities of thumb-suckers as opposed to those who had not sucked their thumbs. Thumb-sucking was more intense and more frequent among children from homes rated happier, and whose parents were better educated. Thumb-sucking little girls actually grew into young women who, according to the Rorschach Ink-Blot Test of Personality, were better adjusted in the sense that they more easily accepted their role as women. There was no difference in the young-adult adjustment of the groups of boys who had and who had not sucked their thumbs in childhood. This difference in frequency of thumb-sucking according to socioeconomic status and happiness of parents is probably due to the type of control techniques used. Better-educated and happier parents may discipline less harshly, hence be less likely to "break" their children of thumb-sucking.

In summary, then, there is no clear-cut evidence about the relation between thumb-sucking and style or length of feedings. Thumb-sucking is a frequent, even a normal, phase of development, which may provide real relaxation and peace to the baby or small child. Such evidence as exists indicates that it is not a neurotic symptom. There is no convincing evidence, either, that moderate thumb-sucking has any effect on permanent tooth structure or jaw alignment.

General Maternal Reactions, Feeding, and Colic

The general "emotional climate" of the feeding situation may be more important than whether the child is breast- or bottle-fed, weaned early or late, or allowed to suck for a long or a short period of time. Brody (1956) and Escalona (personal communication) have stated that the best over-all indicator of a mother-baby relationship is provided by watching how the mother feeds her baby. Escalona (1945) has also published informal observations of the feeding relationship between babies 10 days to 2 years of age, who were placed in the nursery of a women's penal institution, and their mothers and mother-substitutes. Among the tentative conclusions she reached was that the mothers and mother-substitutes were tense and used the babies as emotional outlets for themselves. She especially noted 10 babies under 1 month of age who refused the breast as a means of getting food. Of their 10 mothers, she described 9 as being very tense. When 6 of these mothers were given superficial psychotherapy, the child's eating improved. She also noted that as mother-figures were changed for 15 babies, the babies changed their preference from orange to tomato juice or vice versa according to the preference of the mother-figure. According to Escalona, the babies' eating behavior correlated with the institutional atmosphere. Even small disturbances were reflected in the babies' adjustment.

A study by Stewart *et al.* (1954), done more formally than the one just described, used as its data maternal interviews and observations of mothers interacting with their babies during two-hour clinic visits. A total of 10 boy and 8 girl babies and their mothers (and, to a lesser degree, their fathers) were used as subjects. Eight babies were characterized by the authors as excessive criers ("colicky"). *Excessive crying* was defined as "episodic crying in the first three months of life after 2 weeks of age, over a period of at least 2 weeks, occurring at least once a day, lasting not less than 90 minutes and not related to obvious physical discomfort." (p. 688) This is indeed a great deal of crying, as anyone who has lived around a small baby knows. The mothers of these babies were characterized as ambivalent about their woman-mother role, as quite dependent, and as feeling some rivalry with their children or their husbands. It was concluded that they either openly neglected the babies or overcompensated by fussing with them and giving them excessive attention. Fathers of excessively crying babies were described as passive individuals who gave little real support to their wives.

A contrasting group of 6 babies was defined as low criers, or "very good" babies. Mothers of such babies were described as welcoming children as a fulfillment of their femininity. They were relaxed and happy. For them, motherhood was a method of getting desirable attention and support; the babies' fathers were able to give this support and themselves accepted their paternity and masculinity with little conflict. Compared with the mothers of the excessive criers, the mothers of the low criers met their babies' needs for both stimulation and food much more realistically. Crying differences between the two groups of babies did not begin to show until after about 2 weeks of age. By the time they were 6 weeks old, the low criers ordinarily stopped crying when adults appeared (a matter of confidence and trust?), whereas excessive criers intensified their wails when adults appeared.

An ingenious study by Lakin (1957) sought to determine personality differences between mothers of colicky babies (corresponding to the excessive criers discussed immediately above) and noncolicky babies. Lakin secured the cooperation of two rather well-matched groups of 20 mothers each, one with "good" babies, the other with "colicky" babies. The groups of mothers differed in age, the mothers of the colicky being older, but were similar in education. All were relatively well educated; their husbands had high occupational status; and the ages and birth weights of the babies were similar for the two groups.

Lakin hypothesized that colic is due to a disturbance in the mother-child relationship. Specifically, he predicted that the mothers of colicky babies (1) would themselves have experienced poorer parent-child relationships, (2) would have had more conflict within themselves over their role acceptance (i.e., would have more difficulty accepting themselves as women, wives, and mothers), (3) would be more concerned and worried about whether they were adequate as females, (4) would be less happily adjusted to their marriages, and (5) would in general be less motherly than the mother of the low-crying babies. In the main, his data supported all hypotheses.

Lakin used a large number of techniques to test these hypotheses. He also carried out a long interview covering various aspects of child-rearing, marital adjustment, and so on. Among his interesting subsidiary findings were the following: The mothers of the colicky babies were more pessimistic than the other group—that is, they remembered fewer positive statements from a passage containing both positive and negative statements. They also more frequently drew pictures of mothers *with babies* in a figure-drawing test. Lakin points out that this fits in with the findings of other studies, in which professionally less secure people more frequently drew figures ?quipped with the "tools of their trade" (apparently, in an effort to reassure themselves by using props).

To an overwhelming degree, such routine factors as the babies' diets, birth weight, specific type of feeding, length of labor, allergy history, and so on, failed to differentiate between the two groups of mothers. Although probably no more interview-history items than would be expected to appear by chance were significant, those that did discriminate all appear logical. For example, compared with the control group, mothers of colicky babies stopped working earlier in their pregnancies, stopped sexual intercourse sooner, experienced more symptoms that are considered to involve emotional components both during and antecedent to their pregnancy, more frequently described themselves as habitually tense and nervous, and more frequently asked their mothers to come to help them out at the time the babies were born. There was a nonsignificant tendency for them to regard their husbands as being of little help with the baby. More of them had been depressed after the baby's birth, and (understandably, perhaps, in view of the colic) they felt more nervous and tense when the baby cried, had more trouble trying to interpret the crying, and believed that they were more tense and anxious in handling their babies. There was no difference between the groups in planned versus surprise babies, in their intention to breast- or bottle-feed, or in their desire to have more children.

The three studies described in this section—one an informal, clinical study, one an elaborate and formal investigation, and one falling somewhere between—suggest that, at the very least, babies' eating, as well as "how their food sits with them," is affected by tension on the part of the mother. This tension is probably communicated to them to an important degree during feeding.

Behavioral Consequences of Style of Feeding

The discussion so far has centered principally on the connection between different types of feeding and the child's concurrent adjustment. Psychoanalytic theory predicts that the consequences of different ways of handling children's oral needs persist indefinitely. Learning theory, although it would make a less certain prediction about the permanent effects of a specific method of feeding or weaning, would agree that there might well be long-lasting consequences.

As will be seen, widely different and flatly contradictory findings have come from the feeding-weaning studies. Those that have obtained results indicating major effects will be presented and evaluated first, followed by those indicating that there are few, if any, effects on personality.

STUDIES INDICATING MAJOR EFFECTS

In the first of the representative positive-effect studies (Holway, 1949), 8 boys and 9 girls, aged 3 years 3 months to 5 years 4 months were observed in a doll-play situation, and their play-fantasy behavior was recorded and analyzed. Their feeding and toilet-training histories were obtained from their mothers and rated. An unfavorable rating was given when the mother followed an exact feeding schedule; a favorable one when she allowed a complete self-demand schedule. A favorable rating was given for the longest breast-feeding time, an unfavorable one for the shortest; the mother's attitude or feeling tone toward the feeding schedule was also rated.

From the children's play, a measure of the amount of "reality" play (presumably "good") was obtained. Holway then separated the 17 children into two groups according to the type of feeding schedule used. Of their total observed play time, the 5 "self-regulating feeders" spent 97 minutes in what she called reality play, whereas the more rigidly scheduled children, 12 in number, spent only 37 minutes in such play. This difference between the two groups was highly significant. The first group spent an average of only 3.4 minutes in "unrealistic fantasy play" with the dolls, whereas schedule-fed children averaged 47.7 minutes in such play. This difference is again highly significant statistically. Inferentially, the tendency of the demand-fed children to indulge in realistic fantasy play testifies to their good mental health—their ability to face reality—and the trend toward unrealistic or "escapist" fantasy of the scheduled babies indicates their need to "escape reality."

One of the most extensive studies of the effects of type of feeding on later physical development was published by Hoefer and Hardy (1929). This study included 383 children from 7 to 13 years of age, classified in different groups according to whether or not they had been breast- or artificially fed, and according to the length of time they had been exclusively breast-fed. Hoefer and Hardy concluded that the artificially fed ranked in general physical development below all the breast-fed groups, and that the optimal period of breast feeding was from four to nine months. A greater number of artificially fed than breast-fed children were classed as undernourished, although the two groups did not differ in height. The artificially fed seemed also to have been more susceptible to childhood diseases, and were slightly but significantly lower in intelligence and educational attainment. On the average, they had begun to talk later.

Another study of this type was published ten years later, in 1939, and used as subjects British children who had come to a general clinic and whose fathers' occupations ranged "from the small shopkeeper, policeman and publican to the casual dock labourer and street pedler" and who were "in general, honest, straightforward, self-respecting." (Rogerson and Rogerson, 1939, p. 1,164) Interviews were conducted with those responsible for or intimately familiar with the life history of the child when the children were about 7 years old. All subjects had been seen at the clinic for at least six months and had started attending before they were 6 months old.

The children were classified into groups according to whether they had been entirely breast-fed by their mothers up until the time solid food was introduced (a group of 62 children called "the group without feeding difficulties"), or whether artificial feeding had been introduced (a group numbering 47 referred to as "those with feeding difficulties"). These two groups differed considerably in some important respects, although each included about the same number of boys and girls and the same number of children who had been delivered instrumentally. The mothers' ages were also similar, as was the age at which solid food had been introduced (about 31 weeks for both groups). But the so-called feeding-difficulty group included a higher percentage of premature and first-born children.

In infancy, the two groups did not differ from each other in restlessness, but a rough evaluation of general health showed 48 percent of the no-difficulty group in "good health," compared with only 30 percent of the feeding-difficulty group. Only 2 percent of the former group were described as in poor general health, whereas 15 percent of the latter group were so classified. This group also averaged more visits to the clinic for health questions.

At the age of about 7, the group that had been entirely breast-fed in infancy tended (not statistically significantly) to have poorer appetites, according to their mothers' statements. There was no difference between the groups in the percentage of children who had sleep disturbances. A tendency existed for the feeding-difficulty group to have been enuretic (day or night wetters), nervous, to have showed fears at school ages, and to have done less well in school. Where a younger brother or sister had been born into the family, more of the feeding-difficulty than of the completely breast-fed group had showed jealousy.

It must be borne in mind that this study was done on a non-United States population. In addition, all the mothers had been urged to breast-feed. Finally, the feeding-difficulty group included more premature babies (who are hard to get started in life and who frequently suffer from parental overprotectiveness) and more first babies (who may also be victims of parental anxiety and inexperience). In other words, the differences between the two groups may well have been due to factors other than style of feeding.

In another study (Maslow and Szilagyi-Kessler, 1946), college students were asked to take a test designed to measure their psychological security or insecurity. They then obtained from their mothers information about their breast-feeding history. Results showed that those who were breast-fed for less than three months, who were entirely bottle-fed, or who had been breast-fed for longer than nine months were more secure than those who had been breast-fed from three to nine months.

Many of the mothers of these students had come to the United States from national and cultural areas where prolonged breast feeding was the normal thing to do. The authors of this study reasoned that those mothers who could do so easily and comfortably tended to breast-feed for long periods, and that mothers who for some realistic reason could breast-feed for only a very short period of time or not at all felt guilty and made up for their "failure" by giving extra attention to their children. On the other hand, they suspected that mothers who breast-fed for a medium amount of time were self-consciously trying to fit in with the United States culture, in which long breast feeding was at that time unfashionable. Such mothers were therefore less relaxed and easy with their children. In other words, Maslow and Szilagyi-Kessler attribute their observed differences between groups less to style of feeding than to mothers' attitudes toward it.

The theoretical position of Whiting and Child (1953) is the increasingly popular one of attempting to translate psychoanalytic concepts into social-learning terms, with the intent of making the learning system more dynamic and the psychoanalytic system more precise.

Whiting and Child have worked with cultural anthropological material gathered from more than fifty different cultures and have attempted to determine how various child-rearing practices affected behavior of children growing up in different societies. The phases of child-rearing that they believe are *universal,* and hence both crucial and treatable by scientific method, are the oral, anal, sexual, dependence, and aggression areas. The variables of parental behavior with which they concern themselves are *initial indulgence* (the degree to which parents in a culture are generous and permissive) and its opposite, *initial anxiety* (the degree to which the child presumably experiences deprivation or hardship); *socialization anxiety* (the firmness, severity, or punitiveness, for example, that is typically connected with toilet training, dependence and aggression training, etc.; they hold that the less severe and intense the training, the less the socialization anxiety will be); and *age of socialization.* It can to some degree be assumed that late beginning of socialization is related to permissive socialization and thus to less socializaton anxiety. Such an assumption, however, does not hold for all societies or all people in a given society.

Whiting and Child find, as did Sewell, Mussen, and Harris (1955), that there is little relation between the way a society handles one of these phases of child-training and the way it handles another. A given society may be very indulgent in one area, very severe in another; may socialize firmly in one, mildly in another; may start training a child almost at birth in one area but indefinitely delay training in another.

One of the hypotheses advanced by Whiting and Child is that the amount of anxiety a culture induces in one of the child-rearing areas (e.g., the oral—feeding and weaning) will be reflected in the way it accounts for illness. For example, they predicted that a society which was rigid and depriving in its feeding practices would be more likely than an indulgent society to attribute illness to things that are eaten or drunk. This prediction was supported for the societies they studied: those societies with the strictest infant-feeding practices were also those most likely to attribute illness to eating or drinking some malign substance.

Again, Whiting and Child reasoned that if a society has given a child extensive and progressive satisfaction in one of the training areas, it is likely to believe that relief of illness will occur by means of treatment of that type. There is a tendency for those societies with the most initial oral indulgence (easy feeding-weaning practices) to believe that some sort of oral therapy (e.g., magical foods or liquids) will cure the disease.

Whiting and Child also looked for the presence of "guilt" in the cultures they studied. Guilt may be defined as feelings or emotions with which a person punishes himself, even though there is no likelihood that what he has done will be found out by anyone else. In other words, there must be the development of a conscience before there can be guilt. The operational definition of guilt used by Whiting and Child was the following: The people in a culture are capable of guilt, or have developed guilt as a method of self-control, in proportion to the degree to which people in the culture who are sick are blamed for their illness. A substantial correlation of —.42 was found between age of weaning and presence of guilt as defined by Whiting and Child. This means that the later the customary age of weaning children, the less likely they are to endorse the "guilty" belief that the sick are responsible for their conditions—or, to put it another way, early and harsh oral socialization practices are associated with strong feelings of guilt.

Psychoanalytic theory predicts that deprivation during the oral stage results in a distrust of other people. This prediction was supported by Whiting and Child's data: oral socialization anxiety was significantly correlated with ratings of fearfulness of human beings and with "over-all fear of others." The correlations were significant, but not high (.29 and .27, respectively). They support the notion that oral deprivation, including severe weaning practices, reduces trust in other people.

Whiting and Child, then, may be said to have provided support for the psychoanalytic ideas of the importance for later personality development of child-rearing practices during the first, or oral year. Severe treatment is associated with guilt and fearfulness, as they define it; permissive treatment with trust.

Goldman (1948, 1951) has attempted to relate weaning practices to personality type. The first step in her study consisted in defining an "oral optimistic personality" and an "oral pessimistic personality." The "oral optimists" had traits of general cheerfulness and hopefulness. They were positively interested in external events and people, had generous inclinations toward protecting the weak and needy, were sociable, unaggressive, moderately ambitious, and welcomed new things and experiences rather than clinging to the old. "Oral pessimists" were generally unhopeful and sour, and were passive-receptive in their attitudes toward life. They were socially aloof and withdrawn, and uninclined to be helpful or protective toward others. They appeared to be selfishly independent and self-sufficient.

From the group of 47 men and 68 women from whom these two personality descriptions had been derived, she selected the 20 who seemed most purely to be oral optimists and the 20 who could most clearly be described as oral pessimists, and obtained their feeding histories from their mothers. She decided that the age of 4 months was a critical time for weaning from the breast, and then compared the scores on her test of oral optimism and pessimism for those who had been weaned before and after this time. She found a highly significant difference in pessimism scores for the two groups—the early-weaned scored +.14 on oral pessimism, those weaned later, —.19. This difference is significant at less than the .01 level. When she compared the group weaned before 4 months of age with a group who had been "excessively breast-fed" (for longer than 9 months), the difference was from a +.14 to a —.35 score on pessimism.

Many traditional psychoanalytic writers have suggested that early-weaned babies will develop frustrated, impatient, and orally aggressive personalities. Goldman's findings suggest, rather, that the tendency is for early weaning to produce pessimism, passivity, aloofness, and self-centeredness.

STUDIES INDICATING FEW EFFECTS

One large study of feeding practices and behavior (Peterson and Spano, 1941) deals with 126 Ohio children and their mothers who had been followed for a number of years for research purposes. Fairly reliable data about infant-feeding practices were routinely gathered, and a great deal of information was available about the children included in the study. However, absolutely no significant results emerged; all relationships were low, almost all were statistically nonsignificant, and many were in a direction opposite to psychoanalytic predictions. To illustrate, there was a tendency for those children breast-fed longest to be *less* affectionate, cheerful, confident, and kind, and *more* resistant and socially apprehensive. But they were also less aggressive, cruel, jealous, and quarrelsome. Ratings of the mother's acceptance or rejection of the child were not related to her feeding practices. Indeed, the correlations with ratings of such factors as child-centeredness, solicitousness, restrictiveness, and severity of discipline were low and frequently opposite to what might have been expected.

Two studies (Sewell, 1952; Sewell and Mussen, 1952) have been published dealing with the population of 162 Wisconsin farm children of 5 to 6 years of age discussed in Chapter 2. No relationships were discovered between any type of infant-training practice and later personality or behavior of the children.

One study in which college students were given a security-insecurity test, the results of which were related to their breast-feeding histories, was summarized on pages 81–82. A similar study of college students at the University of Wisconsin (Thurston and Mussen, 1951) revealed absolutely no differences in the predicted direction between those permissively and those rigidly fed.

One of the most ambitious studies of child-rearing practices is the study by Sears, Maccoby, and Levin (1957) already referred to in Chapter 2. Three hundred seventy-nine mothers of five-year-old children were intensively interviewed concerning their child-rearing practices, and they were also asked to describe the behavior of these youngsters. The mothers who were interviewed are considered to be reasonably representative of an urban population. All lived in two large East Coast suburbs. They were for the most part members of the middle class and possibly the upper-lower class.

This volume contains the most extensive body of data concerning mothers' dealings with their children from birth to the age of 5. It should be remembered, however, that the children's behavior is reported *as described by the mothers, not as actually observed* by the authors of the book. Later publications by other co-workers on this large study will include reports of the children's observed behavior, but these are not available at the time of writing this text.

The children were all enrolled in a public-school kindergarten. No mothers of children in parochial schools were used as subjects, and selection of mothers was made so that there would be equal numbers of boys, girls, only, first, middle, and youngest children in the sample. All cases where either the wife or the husband was foreign-born, where husband and wife were not living together, where the child in question was not natural-born, was a twin, or was in some fashion handicapped, were also excluded

Feelings of pleasure or displeasure over the pregnancy, the degree of warmth in the mother-child relationship, and feelings of competence or inadequacy concerning child care were not related to mothers' decision about breast feeding. The only variable that was significantly related to a decision about breast feeding was "sex permissiveness" (i.e., the mother's tolerance about her child's sex behavior). Mothers who were not sex-permissive were less likely to breast-feed. It is likely, the authors point out, that such attitudes are related to the mother's personal modesty.

Breast feeding or its lack had no effect on such child behaviors (as described by the mothers) as aggression, conscience, dependence, feeding problems, bed-wetting, or disturbance over toilet training.

As far as the scheduling of feeding was concerned, nearly half of the mothers (48 percent) were relatively relaxed. They partially or completely followed the infant's rhythm and made no real effort to impose a schedule on him. But about a fifth (22 percent) followed fairly rigid or inflexible feeding schedules. Those mothers who appeared to be most anxious about child-rearing were the mothers who followed their pediatrician's advice most closely. Since, at the time of these babies' birth, scheduling was frequently or usually recommended, the scheduling mothers were also those most anxious about child care and rearing. According to the mothers' reports, type of scheduling and weaning did not affect the personalities of the children at 5 years.

About two thirds of the mothers began weaning before their child was 11 months old, and most of them finished the process within about four months. Babies whose weaning was started latest were most quickly weaned. Fifteen percent of the babies were not weaned by 2 years of age. There was some tendency for late, severely, *or* very permissively weaned children to show upset more frequently than early, gently, but decisively weaned babies. However, nearly as many babies weaned between 5 and 8 months showed upset as did babies weaned after they were 16 months old (30 percent and 35 percent respectively).

Fifty-five percent of the mothers reported that their children had only very mild or no feeding problems. More than a sixth (17 percent) reported considerable or severe feeding problems. The presence or absence of such problems was not related to whether a child had been breast-fed, scheduled or fed by self-demand, or to his age at weaning, but accompanied such behaviors or reactions of the mother as the following: severe toilet training, strong suppression of the child's aggression toward his parents, being negative toward or rejecting of the the child's dependency (resenting clinging or attention demands), using much physical punishment, and manifesting little warmth toward the child.

In other words, these mothers' reports of their children's behavior do not demonstrate effects on personality of infant feeding and weaning practices as such, but suggest instead that feeding problems, for example, may be associated with general restrictiveness on the part of the mother.

What, Then, of Feeding Practices?

How can this section on the effects of early feeding practices on later personality be summarized? What, if any, advice can be given to parents?

At least two authors have taken a thoughtful look at the type of advice that has been given to parents during approximately the last half century, up to about 1950 (Vincent, 1951; Wolfenstein, 1953). The record of the experts, whether they were medical or nonmedical in affiliation, is not a cheering one, or at least not a consistent one. For example, in 1920, 100 percent of the articles on the subject recommended *tight* feeding schedules; but in 1948, 100 percent of them recommended *self-demand* schedules. Other recommendations, though they did not make so full a cycle, were highly variable from one time to another. There is some evidence that this "expert" advice slowly affects child-care practices of the general population (Brim, 1959; Bronfenbrenner, 1959).

A review of the representative literature, such as that in the preceding sections, shows that the actual evidence for what is "good" and what is "bad" is not consistent or conclusive. The author is inclined to shrug his shoulders about recommendations for child-rearing practices in the feeding area. The best conclusion about the specifics of feeding seems to be that mothers who are well-meaning and who try relaxedly to do what they sincerely believe is best for their children—particularly when this is in harmony with the cultural ways of the community with which they are most closely associated—obtain the best results with their children. Such evidence as we have indicates that feeding disturbances, though less related to specific methods of feeding a baby, are tied in with many aspects of mothers' and fathers' adjustment, personality, attitudes, and tension or relaxation with their children.

TOILET TRAINING

Although toilet training has been a matter of consideration and necessity in all cultures since the dawn of civilization, and although reams of speculative and "clinical" material have been written on the subject, the number of careful studies of just what mothers and fathers do, how it works, and what, if anything, happens to the child as a result of it is small.

Sears, Maccoby, and Levin (1957) provide a good picture of how toilet training is actually carried on in twentieth-century United States. A summary of their data and of some of their tentative conclusions about the effects of toilet training is given below.

Modern child-development specialists ordinarily encourage mothers to postpone bowel training until some time in the second year, when the child has fairly complete postural control, can voluntarily control his sphincters, and can be expected to learn to make some signal about his needs. But the average age at which the mothers in the Sears, Maccoby, and Levin study began bowel training was 11 months. The average age of completing it was 18 months. Thus, the training procedure on the average required seven months, although some mothers managed it in a few weeks and others took as long as 18 months. Almost half (47 percent) of the mothers started toilet training before their children were 9 months old; fewer than 8 percent waited to begin until the second half of their child's second year. The children whose training was begun late learned most quickly.

As a group, mothers who were rated high in anxiety about sex started bowel training earlier than mothers more relaxed about sex, although the differences between the groups were not striking. The early-middle period of beginning bowel training (i.e., from 5 to 15 months) produced the least emotional upset (as described by the mothers) on the part of the children.

Sears, Maccoby, and Levin worked out a five-point rating of severity of toilet training. When ratings of 1 or 2 are considered mild ("child more or less trained himself . . . mild disapproval for some late accidents"), more than half (52 percent) of the mothers were characterized as mild in their training methods. When ratings of 4 and 5 are considered severe ("mother clearly shows disapproval; child may be left on toilet for fairly lengthy periods; . . . child punished severely for deviations; mother angry and emotional over them"), almost a fifth (18 percent) of the mothers were characterized as severe in their methods.

A number of other attitudes and practices were associated with severity of toilet training. Mothers who trained severely also put relatively great pressure on their children to use good table manners, be neat and orderly, be careful around the house and with furniture, keep quiet, and do well in school. They were more likely than lenient mothers to use physical punishment and deprivation of privileges, and reasoned less with their children. They strongly discouraged and punished aggression toward themselves and their husbands, and expected strict obedience. They laid heavy emphasis on modesty, and were more concerned about masturbation and social sex play than the lenient mothers. They were also anxious about their child-rearing capabilities and seemed, relatively, to lack warmth and esteem for themselves, their husbands, and their children.

In other words, Sears and his colleagues suggest, "toilet training" is not an isolated factor, but is accompanied by a whole set of other child-rearing practices affecting many phases of the child's social and sexual behavior. If this is true, it is impossible to single out toilet training as a determiner of personality. We must say that whatever is discovered concerning the relation between child behavior or personality and toilet training results from something more general—perhaps the Sears, Maccoby, and Levin factor of permissiveness-restrictiveness.

As their mothers described them, the severely toilet-trained children were more disturbed by training than those who were trained mildly. The very sizable correlation of .47 between severity of training and children's emotional upset was one of the highest correlations obtained in the study. However, the degree of warmth the mothers injected into the process was also an important variable, so that mothers who were warm in their attitudes but severe in their training produced fewer emotional upsets in conjunction with toilet training than did mothers who were relatively cold and severe (23 percent and 48 percent, respectively).

The problem of their child's learning to sleep dry at night is a major one for parents. The mothers included in this study most frequently trained their children by getting them up at night to go to the bathroom, and many of them attempted to limit the amount of late-afternoon and evening liquids. Many used more severe methods, such as making the children wash out their pajamas or bedclothes. Many mothers offered rewards for night-dryness. Almost half the mothers (44 percent) reported that their children were dry at night by the time they were 2. Four fifths of the children were night-dry by the time the study was conducted, leaving a fifth still having an occasional or frequent night accident at the age of 5 or 6. Children tended either to be bed-wetters or feeding problems, not both.

The age of beginning bladder training made no difference in the age at which the children gained full bladder control, but mothers who had high anxiety about sex *and* were relatively cold and undemonstrative toward the child *and* used severe toilet-training procedures were, as the authors say, "most efficient for producing prolonged bed-wetting." (p. 131) Warm, permissive mothers with anxiety about sex got their children dry at night earliest. This relation is an intriguing one. An area of behavior that is extremely important to the mother, but about which she is punitive and cold, may be one in which the child refuses to conform, thus expressing his rebellion and resentment. When the behavior is extremely important to the mother, *but* she is gentle and warm in her insistence on conformity, the child "compliments" or rewards her by taking note of her wishes, and doing as she wants him to.

Bed-wetting was not affected by severity of weaning, scheduled or self-demand feeding, or mothers' responsiveness to their children's crying. Such things as high demands for care with furniture and walls, strict requirements that the child stay in his own yard, demands for quick obedience, and pressure for good table manners and good performance in school also had no effect on bed-wetting.

Psychoanalytic theory maintains that bed-wetting is a child's way of getting back at, or punishing, his mother. The Sears, Maccoby, and Levin findings offer some support for this point of view, since there was some correlation between over-all severity of punishment and bed-wetting, particularly when the former was combined with a cold, rejecting manner toward the child.

Toilet-training practices in many different cultures were studied by Whiting and Child (1953). They found that anal indulgence and permissiveness were negatively but insignificantly related to a society's tendency to give anal-excremental explanations for illness. Anal socialization anxiety was not related to any of the factors they studied, but the progressive satisfaction given to the child in the toilet-training area (i.e., the degree to which he was "never given any trouble about it") was negatively related to a culture's use of excremental materials in warding off or curing illness. Whiting and Child found no relation between age of toilet training and the development of guilt, or between method of toilet training and fear and distrust of others.

The Whiting and Child findings about toilet training thus revealed less than their findings about feeding and weaning. Their principal result is tentative support of relatedness between permissive toilet training and lack of superstition about bodily wastes.

The Davis and Havighurst study (1946) reports the average age of obtaining bladder control at about 21 months; about 50 percent of the children they studied had achieved complete bladder control by 18 months. Sears and his colleagues report that a fifth of their mothers were quite severe in their training for bladder control. They state that 28 percent of the children in their study suffered emotional upset during bowel training, but give no similar figures for bladder training. However, about a third of the youngsters in the Sears study were still wetting their beds at 3 years of age or later.

Going as far afield as Australia, we find another study (Bostock, 1951) suggesting that breast feeding is unrelated to later enuresis, but that severity of toilet training is strongly related to it, as it is to acceptance of the child: unwanted children tend to receive more rigid training than accepted children. The congruence between these results and those of Sears, Maccoby, and Levin is immediately evident. McCandless and Heye (1951), using as subjects two different groups of children in a university nursery school, also found that maternal attitudes of acceptance, lateness of starting bladder training, and speed of achieving bladder control were linked to each other.

In the previously mentioned study by Williams and Scott (1953) of factors that are related to rapid as opposed to slow motor development, rigid toilet training (like rigid feeding scheduling) was associated with relatively slow motor development. A list of other factors that were associated with motor retardation reads very much like Sears, Maccoby, and Levin's list of factors associated with rigid toilet training. Children who were relatively retarded in motor development were weaned earlier, trained earlier, handled more punitively, and were more restricted in play space and experimentation; they had less bodily contact and time with others, and were less frequently breast-fed and for a shorter time.

Williams and Scott used as subjects Negro babies from two socioeconomic classes. The children more retarded in motor development were from the upper-class group of parents, who were also more generally restrictive in their child-rearing practices. Motor retardation or acceleration was judged from scores on an infant "intelligence" test—hence the somewhat surprising finding that those children who, according to confident prediction, will later score higher in IQ tests are, in infancy, less accelerated on a measure of development that stresses motor skills. In turn, slow development of motor skills is associated with relatively restrictive methods of child-rearing, which characterize parents from higher rather than lower socioeconomic classes and include relatively depriving or severe weaning and toilet-training practices.

Conclusions about toilet training are, for the most part, more clear-cut than those for feeding and weaning. This may be because children are older, hence better able to learn, when toilet training is begun.

Studies of toilet training do not in any consistent way support psychoanalytic theory, but they do suggest that psychoanalysts are correct in emphasizing the importance of toilet-training practices on later development. United States mothers, as we have seen, start toilet training earlier than the "experts" advise; and the earlier toilet training is started, the longer it takes to complete. The more severe the training, the more upset the child is by it. Rigid toilet training, in conjunction with a number of other practices that might be called restrictive, also seems to slow down motor development in infancy.

Mothers high in anxiety about sex start toilet training earlier than mothers who are more relaxed about sex. The most successful mothers in early training for night-dryness are high in sex anxiety but use mild training procedures and show much warmth to their children. The least successful mothers also have high sex anxiety, but combine with it severe training procedures and relatively cold attitudes and emotions toward their children. In a study of primitive cultures, little relation was found between anality and cultural folkways.

Finally, and probably most important, the rigidity with which toilet training is carried out is related to a number of other child-rearing practices, almost all of which may be thought of either as restrictive or as indicative of insecurity and low self-esteem on the part of the mother. For this reason, we cannot say definitely that toilet training alone is important in shaping a child's personality; but we can say that it is one of a number of indicators of the mother's relationship with her child, and that all of these taken together have important and probably durable effects on personality.

SEX TRAINING

Childhood Sexuality

Chapter 2 introduced the concept of infantile sexuality as proposed by Freud—a sexuality, or libidinous gratification, associated with the predominant oral, anal, and genital organ systems. Mishandled, the child may be condemned to a lifelong, neurotic attempt to make up for what has happened to him during these stages. Mishandling may occur either through deprivation and trauma or through overgratification.

Freud's views about infantile sexuality provoked strong emotional reactions and a storm of controversy. Unfortunately, his postulations have not been subjected to rigorous experimental test, and the great volume of material that has been written on the subject of sex in childhood is not often related to substantial or sound research. Most research in the area has been clinical. Purely anecdotal material also abounds. The conclusions of this section are therefore based more on clinical experience than on solid research.

Kinsey *et al.* (1948, 1953) tell us much about human sexual behavior, but, about children, almost all that we learn is that they are interested in sex, experience orgasms earlier than is commonly thought, and, from early childhood, show much more interest and participation in sexual behavior than the average adult guesses (or remembers).

In the United States, sexuality in children is currently much discussed in PTA groups and by "experts," but it still remains a matter of considerable discomfort to mothers and fathers. They appear to handle it by repressing or suppressing it, rather than by an intelligent use of learning principles.

Goals and Practices of Sex Training

The most comprehensive and the soundest survey of child-rearing practices in the area of sexual behavior is provided by Sears, Maccoby, and Levin (1957). These authors state that there are four goals of childhood sex training in the United States. The first (apparently universal in all modern cultures) is to inculcate the taboo against incest; the second, by no means universal although probably characteristic of all Western European cultures, is training against masturbation (training that almost universally breaks down at adolescence, particularly for boys); the third is to teach the child to avoid sex play with other children; the fourth is to control information: "Information control . . . is one of the methods by which adults attempt to induce the growing child to postpone sex gratification and limit sex activities in the early years." (p. 182)

Sears, Maccoby, and Levin point out that there are substitute gratifications for things the child gives up as he is weaned and toilet trained: solid foods are found to be tasteful and pleasant; parents reward one for cleaning one's plate; being dry and clean have their virtues. But for sex, there are no substitutes until the time of adolescence. This leaves mothers with no possibility of *guidance* through substitute rewards; they can only *inhibit* sexual behavior. To do this, they predominantly try to prevent stimulation (for example, supervise play carefully, dress children in loose, nonbinding clothing, observe stringent rules of modesty in the home); distract the child (for example, by changing activity if children seem to be getting "sexy"); "borrow sanctions" (such as telling the child addicted to nudity that he will catch cold, or telling him, as he manipulates his genitals, that he will hurt himself; avoid labels (for example, by using euphemisms for the genitals); and control information (most frequently by elaborate subterfuges such as "I found you under a rosebush").

Much control of sex is accomplished through training for modesty. Sears, Maccoby, and Levin queried their 379 mothers about how permissive they were about their children's going around indoors without clothes, and how severe was the pressure they exerted toward indoor modesty. Again using the two highest of five rating-scale points to define permissiveness (little or no restraint on nudity, for example), about one third (36 percent) of the mothers were permissive. Almost half (44 percent) fell at the other end of the scale, believing that the "child must be clothed at all times," or being only very slightly permissive. On the other hand, the mothers were not very severe in enforcing their scruples about modesty. If mild pressure is defined as their doing nothing more drastic than teasing or gently remonstrating about nudity, then three fifths (61 percent) of the mothers used mild pressure only. If severe pressure is defined as scolding, warning, punishing, and becoming angry and emotional, only 7 percent of the mothers used severe pressure.

Children "playing with themselves" elicited considerable emotional reaction from the mothers. Fewer than a fifth (18 percent) felt "that a certain amount is to be expected," or that "it's natural, just curiosity"; while one half (49 percent) considered it wrong or harmful or "might not do anything if it happened just once, but wouldn't like it " As with nudity, however, they did not back up their strong opinions with strong action, since 45 percent of them used mild or no pressure against masturbation, and only a twentieth were classified as using severe pressure against masturbation.

The picture concerning permissiveness about sex play among children is similar. Fewer than a sixth (16 percent) of the mothers believed in permissiveness, and almost three fifths (57 percent) of them expressed firm attitudes against it. But again, opinions were not backed up by stringent action. Almost half (46 percent) of the mothers said that so far as they knew, no incidents had occurred. When mothers mentioned that such incidents had occurred, 45 percent had been quite permissive in their actions, and only 13 percent had behaved severely and forbiddingly. Interestingly enough, more mothers who were rated high on their tendency to keep a close check on their children *did not know* of sex-play incidents.

Even though the mothers seemed to "talk loudly and carry a little stick" concerning children's sexual behavior, there was a high correlation between mothers' disapproval of a certain behavior and their taking definite steps to prevent it. The correlation between permissiveness and pressure was —.75 (i.e., mothers who were not permissive about a given type of behavior *did* punish when it occurred).

The mothers in this study who were not permissive about sex permitted relatively little aggression toward parents on the part of their children. They were more likely than permissive mothers to toilet-train their children severely, keep a close watch on their whereabouts, use physical punishment fairly often, and be strict about noise, table manners, and care of household property. They were also relatively cold emotionally toward their children, did not like it when the children clung to them or made attention demands, and put much emphasis on their daughters being feminine, their sons masculine. In other words, these mothers fell toward the restrictive extreme of Sears, Maccoby, and Levin's behavioral factor of permissiveness-restrictiveness.

Whiting and Child (1953), in their cross-cultural study of child-rearing practices, found no relationship between sex training and explanations of disease. However, in the small number of societies they studied which were very permissive toward childhood sexuality, there were also recommendations for sexual activity as a method of *getting over* illness. In cultures where sexual behavior was severely inhibited, there were moderate tendencies not to use and even to avoid or abjure sexual types of therapy for disease. A very high negative correlation (—.74) existed between the age at which training in sexual inhibition was begun and the development of guilt in the members of a society. Severe inhibition was also somewhat associated with fear of other human beings.

These two studies provide almost all the available data about sex training and its correlates. From them, we see that maternal permissiveness in the sexual area correlates with general permissiveness. United States mothers who have been studied seem to have generally negative attitudes toward children's sexual behavior, but they do not exercise very strong open pressure against it (perhaps because they themselves are guilty, uneasy, and uninformed in the area). When they punish, they punish the things they disapprove of. In a cross-cultural study, societies in which children's sexual behavior was indulged tended also to be those where sexual behaviors were considered therapeutic for disease. The same study demonstrated that early sex training was associated with the development of guilt (as defined), for which conscience is assumed to be a necessary foundation.

Clinical evidence and hypotheses about the effects of sex training abound, suggesting that both harsh and restrictive sex training and overly permissive training, including overexposure to sexual information and experiences, may leave the child sexually disturbed. Chapter 10 includes material, more of it theoretical than factual, on sexual development and the consequences for adult behavior of direct and indirect sex training.

The lack of solid data in this area is obvious and regrettable. There are, in the United States, strong sanctions against conducting research on sexual behavior at *any* age level, but particularly with children. However, any college counselor, any psychiatrist, can testify to the fact that a certain amount of sexual disturbance accompanies or underlies almost every psychological disability. The sex-based neuroses of our culture can be alleviated and prevented only when facts about the development of sexual behavior are more fully known and when the relations between different types of experience and training and later personality development and adjustment have been more fully explored.

DEPENDENCY TRAINING

There are reasonably adequate studies of childhood dependency, but the early training of dependency behavior (positive and encouraging, or negative and discouraging) has been little studied by people other than those mentioned in the two preceding sections: Sears, Maccoby, and Levin (1957) and Whiting and Child (1953). These authors, following Freud' leads, have also contributed much to theories of dependency and its relation to socialization; but the details of this treatment more properly belong in Chapter 10.

Sears, Maccoby, and Levin devote a 38-page chapter to the topic of dependency, using the material they gleaned from their interviews with 379 suburban mothers of five-year-olds. It must be repeated that judgments about the children's behavior were made from what the mothers *said* about the children, rather than from *observation* of what the children actually did. Such judgments are bound to be frail reeds. The mother who rejects dependency behavior may see the occasionally whining child as very dependent indeed; whereas the mother who craves a child "who is always a baby and needs me" might perceive the same child as almost rejectingly independent. However, the Sears, Maccoby, and Levin data are the best in the area and must be summarized here.

Almost equal proportions of the mothers perceived their children as, first, very slightly or almost not at all dependent (35 percent), and quite dependent or showing a great deal of dependent behavior (37 percent). More than half of the mothers reported that their five-year-olds did not cling to them, follow them, or seek to be near them; while about a tenth (8 percent) reported a great deal of this behavior. A fourth of the mothers reported that at one time or another their children had gone through a very dependent stage. Almost two thirds (62 percent) of the children at the time of the study put up no objection to their mothers' going out or leaving them with someone else (only 5 percent rather consistently raised a fuss about this). Only children were slightly but significantly more dependent than children with brothers or sisters. The latter seemed able to turn to their sibs for company.

Dependency behavior at 5 years of age had no relationship to the warmth the mother had given earlier, when the child was a baby, nor to breast or bottle feeding, nor to age of beginning or ending weaning. Neither did other infantile frustrations result in dependency at age 5, although they had frequently done so concurrently. The mothers ranged from being quite unresponsive to their babies' crying (16 percent) to quite responsive (usually or always picking up the baby immediately), with almost half falling in this response category. Such responsiveness had no relation with later dependency. Nor did early brief separation experiences seem to affect dependency at the age of 5.

The mothers ranged from low permissiveness toward dependency behavior (37 percent) to high permissiveness (30 percent). Two fifths (41 percent) of the mothers occasionally or never rewarded dependency; a fourth (23 percent) of them often or almost always did. A fourth were almost never irritated by dependency behavior, whereas more than one third (36 percent) were often irritable and punishing when the child hung and clung to them. As might be expected, these three tendencies—to be permissive, to reward, and not to be irritated—were positively interrelated one with the other.

When the mother had an accepting and tolerant attitude toward the child's dependent behavior, she was also likely to be affectionately warm toward him, gentle in toilet training, high in sex permissiveness, unlikely to use physical punishment for dependent behaviors, and tolerant when he was angry and aggressive toward his parents. She also manifested high esteem for herself and her husband. Irritable scolding and pulling away from dependent behaviors increased their frequency, according to the mothers' reports; and the most dependent children of all belonged to mothers who irritably rejected dependency demands for a time but eventually gave in to them, thus rewarding the child. This finding fits well with the results of experimental learning studies on partial reinforcement (see Chapter 4).

The cross-cultural material of Whiting and Child (1953) indicates that there is a relation within cultures between the tendency to be orally indulgent (permissive and generous suckling and late weaning) and to indulge dependency behavior. According to Whiting and Child, cultures that accorded high indulgence to children's dependency behaviors were not cultures in which illness was explained as being due to dependency. These authors also found that when an "avoidance therapy" is defined as isolating the patient or removing him from the home during his illness, there is a clear and positive relation between socialization anxiety for dependency and the tendency of a society to use avoidance therapy—that is, societies that discourage dependency also use illness therapy that involves isolating the patient or removing him from the home.

Whiting and Child found a moderate negative relation between the age at which independence training was begun and the degree to which the people of a society were judged to possess guilt. It will be remembered that these authors' definition of guilt for a society was the degree to which a patient was held responsible for his own illness.

To summarize this section, the majority of five-year-olds in the Sears, Maccoby, and Levin study were reported by their mothers to be sturdily independent youngsters. A mother's indulgence of dependency in her child was related, although not strongly, to a number of other permissive and warm behaviors on her part. Mothers who were irritated by dependency behavior yet eventually yielded to it believed they had the most dependent children. Only children were slightly more dependent than children with brothers and sisters. However, the mothers' descriptions of their children's dependency are particularly suspect, since they are liable to distortion by the mothers' attitudes toward dependency.

The cross-cultural findings of Whiting and Child show a relation between oral and dependency indulgence, whereas Sears, Maccoby, and Levin find almost no relation between dependency and other infant-rearing practices. According to Whiting and Child, cultures that indulge dependency do not use dependency explanations of illness; cultures in which high socialization anxiety exists for dependency use "avoidance therapies" for disease. The age at which training for independence was started was found to be negatively related to guilt in a culture.

AGGRESSION TRAINING

The Nature of Childhood Aggression

Sears, Maccoby, and Levin (1957) have an excellent chapter on aggression in childhood and the methods by which mothers cope with and attempt to socialize it in their children. Of the 379 mothers they studied, every mother at one time or another had been forced to cope with angry outbursts or quarreling on the part of her children, and almost all mothers (95 percent) reported instances of strong aggression directed by the child against his parents. Among United States mainland children in nursery school, one study (McCandless, Balsbaugh, and Bennett, 1958) reports that some sort of conflict, ranging from fairly mild to violent, occurs during free play about every 5 minutes for boys, about every 7 or 8 minutes for girls. Hawaiian nursery-school children show similar patterns, although they do not quarrel as frequently (about every 8 minutes for boys, every 10 minutes for girls).

Aggression in childhood, then, seems to be universal, or nearly so. As Sears, Maccoby, and Levin (as well as many others) point out, the aggressive child is the angry child, and an angry child is not a happy child. He is also likely to provoke retaliation on the part of those toward whom his anger is directed, and this in turn makes him even angrier and more aggressive. In recent years, there has been a tendency (particularly among well-educated middle-class parents) to believe that supressing a child is bad for him and that repressing aggression and feelings of hate will lead the child to build up still more anger and hate so that he either becomes neurotic or displaces his rage to other and innocent victims. They argue that it is all right for the child to express aggression toward his parents—that it is usually the parents who frustrate and hence anger the child, and that it is better, more direct, and "healthier" for the child to express anger directly against the source of his frustrations. Thus will his anger be drained off.

There are at least two reasons to question these assumptions. The first is that there is little place in civilized, cooperative living for the direct and primitive expression of aggression, when aggression is thought of as either physical or verbal attack. Certain "disguised" verbal aggressions, such as gossip or "frankness," are condoned to a greater degree than physical attack or direct verbal abuse, but even gossip and frankness that conceals hostility are more likely to produce complications in human relations than to oil the wheels of social interaction. Secondly, learning theory predicts that the expression of aggression and its consequent momentary tension-relief strengthens rather than weakens the tendency to behave aggressively. There is some evidence (Feshbach, 1956) to support this prediction. Nor does evidence (e.g., Mussen and Naylor, 1954; Purcell, 1956; Smith and Coleman, 1956) indicate that behaving aggressively reduces tendencies to be aggressive. If anything, these studies suggest that the opposite is true. Children and young adults with crude fantasies of aggression have been found to be more openly aggressive in their behavior than those whose aggressive fantasies are muted or contain elements indicating that the person is as concerned with the dangerous consequences of his aggression as he is with the aggression itself. In other words, aggressive fantasy *may suggest* or stimulate aggressive behavior, rather than drain off the motive to behave aggressively.

On the other hand, case histories gathered by psychiatrists, social workers, and psychologists, as well as social experiences that we all have had, indicate that bottled-up hate which cannot be recognized, or constructively drained off, is painful, even destructive, to the person. It may be that an honest recognition and acceptance of feelings is one of the most important facets of good adjustment. Normal people *do* become angry periodically, but the well-adjusted person is usually able to recognize and accept his anger. He has enough control over his impulses, and sufficient personal flexibility, to make constructive (or, at least, not destructive) use of his anger. Our society permits and rewards such possible disguises of aggression as competitiveness, ambition, standing up for one's rights, and being "righteously indignant" over needs for social reform. The literature about aggression, as well as ordinary social observation, clearly suggests that children's aggression cannot safely be so thoroughly squelched that they become milktoasts. On the other hand, blind acting out of aggression through physical violence and verbal tirades is socially destructive. Channeled in one way, aggression helps to build society; in another way, to destroy it. For such reasons as these, it is vital that we work to understand the means by which it can be constructively socialized.

Effects of Aggression Training

One of the earlier studies of aggressive behavior in nursery-school children (Appel, 1942) analyzes 641 different aggressive episodes involving 252 individuals. Property was involved more than any other factor, although there were many instances of unprovoked hostility. The older children were more persistent than the younger in their hostile behavior. Adult techniques varied widely in effectiveness. Most effective in stopping an aggressive episode was teacher diversion, which terminated hostility 93 percent of the time. Separating the children was slightly less effective, and arbitrary decisions on the part of the nursery-school teacher were quite ineffective. Interpreting the wishes and feelings of one child to another worked surprisingly well considering the age of the children, which ranged from about 2 to 4. Explaining property rights and suggesting solutions worked in about two thirds of the cases of conflict; very ineffective were such techniques as disapproving, moralizing, failing to understand, having children "talk it over," or being unsympathetic. When the adult was unsure of himself or his course of action, he was also unsuccessful in terminating conflicts.

Appel, after studying individual children, believes that their aggression may spring from either too much or too little discipline at home, from jealousy of their brothers or sisters, from excessive parental standards, or from home tensions.

Pauline Sears (1951) has studied some of the conditions that accompany fantasy aggression in children from about 3 to 5 years of age. As would be expected, she found that boys were more frequently and violently physically aggressive in their fantasy play than girls; but that the girls more frequently showed aggression through scolding and mischief, so that the hurt was mental rather than physical. Boys were much more hostile to a "father" doll than were girls. Children who were oldest in a family manifested less fantasy aggression than younger and only children, possibly because they had been subjected to more pressure from their parents against being rough with younger brothers and sisters. The pattern of fantasy aggression for boys whose fathers had been away from home for long periods of time was more like that of girls; they were markedly less aggressive than boys whose fathers had been home consistently No such effect was observed for girls whose fathers had been separated from the family.

The pattern of child-rearing that produces the most aggressive children, as revealed by the research of Sears, Maccoby, and Levin (1957), is one where the parents disapprove of aggression and, when it occurs, punish it with physical aggression of their own or threaten the child. This "counter-attack" on the part of the parent, though it may work for the moment, appears to generate still more hostility on the part of the child, which eventually breaks out. Sears, Maccoby, and Levin point out that the parent who uses physical punishment is providing for his child a model of aggressive, destructive behavior that the child is likely to copy, either then or later. But highly aggressive children are also produced by homes in which the mother is very permissive of the child's outbursts, whether or not they are directed against her. Where mothers were both permissive and physically punishing, they were most likely to produce highly aggressive children. Least-aggressive children apparently come from homes where aggression is disapproved of and is stopped, but where techniques other than physical punishment are used to stop it. The study reported above of techniques used successfully and unsuccessfully by nursery-school teachers fits well with these conclusions.

In their cross-cultural study, Whiting and Child (1953) report that the more aggression is indulged (i.e., the more the child is allowed to attain satisfaction through being aggressive), the less likely the society is to explain illness as some function of aggressive behavior; but the more severe the socialization anxiety about aggression (the more firmly a society stamps out aggression in its children), the more likely the society is to explain illness as a function of aggression. Finally, these authors demonstrate that the less the initial indulgence and the more the socialization anxiety for aggressive behavior, the more the people in the culture show an over-all fear of others.

Nakamura (1959) asked 78 undergraduate women to prepare auto-biographical workbooks while taking a course in the psychology of adjustment. He was interested in whether they considered their childhood discipline to have been positive or negative. Discipline was rated as *positive* if the subjects said they would use the same disciplinary techniques on their own children. Discipline was judged to be *negative* when the girls stressed physical punishment or the psychological hurtfulness of their parents' methods of discipline and rejected using the same sort of discipline for their own children. Nakamura hypothesized that overprotective parents would so impress their daughters with their power that the girls would be relatively unable to express hostility or criticism directly toward the parents, but would instead displace it to other people. He also predicted that positively disciplined girls would direct less criticism toward their parents than negatively disciplined girls. Both predictions were supported by his analysis of the autobiographies.

Studies of children's fantasy play have generally shown that a second session of fantasy play in the company of a permissive adult reveals more aggression than the first. This increase in aggression has generally been attributed to the child's increased feeling of freedom to do what he wished to do. Some investigators (e.g., Siegel and Kohn, 1959) believe that the determinants of children's aggression in any situation are a combination of the child's own need to be aggressive, his evaluation of and attitude toward aggression, the attitudes and values of other people in the situation, and his assessment of the likelihood of counteraggression on the part of others (particularly adults). These authors assume that our society consistently disapproves of open aggression. For this reason, they think, a child will construe an adult's *permissiveness* about aggression as actual *encouragement*.

As a partial test of their thinking, they took a number of pairs of boys and exposed half the pairs to two sessions of fantasy play in the presence of an unintrusive but friendly adult, the other half of the pairs to two sessions of fantasy play with no adult present. Every pair exposed to the adult-absent condition showed a drop in the amount of aggression from Session I to Session II, while two thirds of the pairs with the adult present showed more aggression in Session II. However, the over-all amount of aggression was approximately the same under the two conditions.

An alternative theory to account for these results is the following: Children are accustomed to having their parents assume considerable responsibility for their behavior, and this attitude toward their parents generalizes to other adults. The children with the permissive adult present felt "safe"—that is, they could increase their aggressive play, feeling that if things got out of hand, the adult would "take over." The children with the adult absent, on the other hand, had to be responsible for the consequences of their own behavior, hence had to move from Session I to Session II in the direction of increasing aggression control. From this study, it cannot be said with any confidence which is the more appropriate explanation of the findings.

It may be concluded that both parental permissiveness and parental punitiveness encourage or reinforce aggression in children, that aggression is so widespread as to be universal, that diversionary and reasoning-understanding techniques are most effective in terminating hostile behavior, and that, for the sake of good mental health and a smoothly functioning society, aggressive and hostile feelings should be handled constructively (i.e., transmuted into such socially acceptable forms as ambition, competition, and initiative). Aggressive impulses should be recognized and acknowledged, but their direct expression seems to create more problems than it solves.

EFFECTS OF INFANTILE AND EARLY-CHILDHOOD DEPRIVATION

Maternal Deprivation

Through the ages, mankind has been sentimental about the love of a mother for her child. The general public makes the tacit assumption that such a love is universal (despite much evidence to indicate that there are brutal and rejecting mothers, that *smother* in contrast to *mother* love exists, and that even the best of mothers can become mightily annoyed with her offspring). The assumption is also made by the general public that children cannot grow up normally without mother love. This assumption was made forcefully by Freud, and at present is more or less an article of faith on the part of all child-psychology and developmental personnel.

What effects does deprivation of mother love have upon a child? It is certainly not necessary for a child to grow up with his *natural* mother. But what of the child who, for one reason or another, is separated from his mother or his foster mother after he has come to know and love her? What of the child who grows up in a relatively impersonal institution? If separation from or absence of a mother-figure is damaging to normal personality development, is it so at some ages and not at others, or at all ages?

It is to such questions as these that the present section is addressed. The effects of institutional or intellectually very barren environments on the development of intelligence in both children and animals are discussed in Chapter 8. Here it suffices to say that the evidence from research with children suggests strongly that poor environments (including life in institutions) retard intellectual development; good environments capitalize on it, and may even facilitate it. For animals, where more extreme environmental alterations can be produced, the evidence is even more convincing: environments of isolation retard "intellectual" development, and this retardation is lasting.

But, while granting that intelligence is one aspect of personality, this chapter concerns itself with topics more conventionally related to emotional development and adjustment. One of the earliest papers concerning the effects on infants of living in institutions was published by Lowrey (1940). A psychiatrist, Lowrey became concerned about the psychological state of a group of children who were referred to him. These children, 28 in number, had been placed in a "model" institution when they were (with one exception) from 2 weeks to 11 months of age. Their psychiatric referrals occurred when they were between 2 years 11 months and 4 years of age. Their histories revealed that after leaving the institution, where model medical care had been provided, they had caught more diseases than would be expected of the general population. They also showed a high incidence of speech retardation, with poor vocabularies and more than the usual number of speech defects. They were frequently negativistic and had temper tantrums; they gravitated toward solitary activities and showed a fear of social contacts; they manifested uncontrolled demands for attention and material possessions and were very frequently hostile. Their IQ's were lower than would have been expected from their family backgrounds, only one having an IQ as high as 115 and one being as low as 52 (almost down to the upper limit of low-grade mental deficiency).

Lowrey concluded that infants should not be reared in institutions. If institutionalization is necessary, babies should be provided with intimate, continuing, consistent contact with at least one adult so that they can develop techniques of socialization and channel their emotions in such a way that they will be able to handle later family living.

One of the most assiduous of the workers who have attempted to answer the question, What are the effects of growing up without any consistent mother-figure (i.e., of living in an institution), is William Goldfarb. Alone or with co-workers, he has published a number of papers, of which the study summarized here is representative. In this study Goldfarb (1945) first summarizes some of his previous studies of children at ages 7, 8½, and 12. Each of these earlier studies had included rather well-matched (although small) groups of children. In each study one group of children had lived in an institution until they were about 3 years old and had then gone to foster homes. The other group, after a very brief period of time with their own families, had gone into and remained in foster homes. The over-all findings at all three ages were consistent with one another, although different methods were frequently used, and are in agreement that the institution-reared group showed "a profoundly deviate personality type characterized by (1) marked impoverishment, meagerness and lack of differentiation in all aspects of personality, and (2) marked passivity or apathy of personality." (p. 20)

Goldfarb states:

> Institution children were less secure, more isolated from other people, and less able to enter into meaningful relationships. They also showed more frequent speech retardation, school deficiency and mental

retardation . . . the institution children were more retarded mentally and were considerably more immature in perceptual reaction and in level of conceptual performance. They also more frequently showed problems such as restlessness, hyperactivity, inability to concentrate, lack of popularity with children, poor school achievement, fearfulness and excessive craving for affection. They were shown by experiment and case history to be deficient in drive and to be marked by an unusual degree of apathy or emptiness of emotional response. (p. 19)[2]

In the 1945 study, two groups of 15 children were studied. There were 9 boys and 6 girls in each group. The first group (institution children) were admitted at an average age of 4½ months to an infant institution, and stayed there for almost three years, being placed in foster homes, on the average, at a little past 3 years of age. They were tested a little while before being placed in foster homes and again seven months later. The other group of children (foster children) had always lived in their foster homes. They were equated with the institution children for age, sex, age at admission to care, and age at first and second testing. The true mothers of both groups were similar in national origin. The mothers of the institution children were of a higher occupational but not educational level, and the true fathers of the foster children were lower socioeconomically.

On the first and second tests the institution children averaged 68 and 76 IQ respectively. The foster children tested significantly higher—96 and 102 on the first and second tests respectively. Language development tests were also used, and the foster children scored higher than the institution group in intelligibility, language organization, total language score, and vocabulary. The groups did not differ from each other in motor development, nor, on the first test, on the Vineland test of social maturity. But on the second test (perhaps because of their difficulty in adjusting to foster homes) the institution children dropped in score from 100 to 89. whereas the foster children raised their social-maturity quotients from 103 to 109 from the first to the second test. A score of 100 on the Vineland is considered average for United States children. The difference between the two groups on the second test is statistically significant.

Goldfarb concludes from these studies that the foster children have better contact and relatedness with the external world; have more will to meet and reorganize experience with the external world; and are superior to the institution children in "the richness and maturational level of personality as expressed in imaginative and conceptual competence and even in the more primitive levels of perceptual reaction." (p. 30)

In another study, Goldfarb (1944) examined the records of 40 children with continuous foster-home experience and 40 who, from infancy, had lived in an infant institution for about three years. At the time of his

---

[2] Reprinted with permission of C. B. Farrar, Editor, *American J. Psychiat.*, and W. Goldfarb, from Goldfarb (1945).

study, the two groups were 7 years 7 months and 7 years 8 months respectively. They were matched for sex, age, age of admission to care, and years of dependency. Only 1 of the first group had had to move from a foster home at any time because of unacceptable behavior, whereas 12 (30 percent) of the second, or institutional, group had been forced to move from one to three times for such reasons. Goldfarb states that the institutional children showed aggressive, hyperactive syndromes, peculiar or bizarre syndromes, or emotionally unresponsive syndromes.

Spitz (e.g., 1945, 1946) has published a number of studies dealing with similar topics. He has found institution babies to be massively retarded in scores on a measure of infant adaptive reactions. Considering the fact that good medical care was provided in the institution he studied, there was an extremely high rate of death from all causes, including contagious diseases such as measles—which, although serious, do not frequently kill their victims. Spitz also reports that his institution babies were very retarded in motor development, even in such things as learning to sit alone, to walk, and so on (although Goldfarb's institution babies were reported to have normal motor development). Extreme lack of attention, Spitz believes, results in an infant disease called *marasmus,* which is literally a listless withering away into death. According to Spitz, babies separated in about the middle of their first year from their mothers suffer from depression and frequently go on to develop serious mental disease.

Spitz's studies have attracted wide attention. An initial phase of uncritical acceptance of the dramatic results he reported has been followed by increasingly critical reviews of his methods, data, and form of reporting, culminating in so devastating a series of critical articles and replies (Pinneau, 1955a, 1955b; Spitz, 1955) that there may currently be a danger of throwing out the baby with the bath. Spitz's is by no means the only evidence we have to indicate that barren environments of all sorts, including large and impersonal infant hospitals and traditional orphanages for young children, blunt the development not only of the human organism but of simpler nonverbal organisms such as rats, mice, dogs, and monkeys. There is some evidence to indicate that these effects are very long-lasting, the evidence for animals being more convincing than that for humans. Spitz maintains that such damage is irreversible. The findings of other authors (e.g., Pasamanick, 1946; Rheingold, 1956) seem to suggest that when the situation is altered, babies regain at least much of their lost ground. However, animal research indicates that prolonged and severe environmental deprivation early in the life of the organism produces lasting interferences with both "intellectual" and emotional responses (see Chapter 8).

What may be involved here is a phenomenon known as *imprinting,* which has been observed with some species of animals. If these animals do not have the opportunity to observe and practice behaviors typical of their species at an appropriate developmental phase (usually very early in their life), they seem never to acquire them but to behave, insofar as they are able, in a way similar to the species with which they had their earliest experiences. Beach and Jaynes (1954) have presented an interesting summary of research in this area. Gray (1957) has reviewed the literature concerning children reared in isolation, or in very deprived circumstances. He concludes that imprinting occurs with humans (a possibility that has intrigued many people), and that it is effective from about the sixth week to about the sixth month. The sixth week, he argues, is the time of first socialization. It is at about this time that babies begin to make elementary "social" responses, such as smiling, and can be conditioned (see Chapter 4) fairly stably. The sixth month is the approximate age when fear of strangers and animals begins. Such theories are interesting and should be followed up by research, but at the present time they remain speculative.

John Bowlby (1952), writing for the World Health Organization, made a survey of literature in the area of maternal deprivation and from it concluded that certainly before the age of 2, and probably before the age of 3, any severe deprivation of maternal care, whether this took the form of physical absence or psychological rejection, would damage the personality development of the child. Testing this prediction four years later (Bowlby *et al.,* 1956), he studied the adjustment of a group of 41 boys and 19 girls who had been separated from their families for periods ranging from a little less than five months to more than two years, at various ages up to 4 years, because of pulmonary tuberculosis. About half of them experienced separation from their families before the age of 2. Since there were from 40 to 60 children in residence at a time, the sanatorium had not provided them with substitute-mothering. These children were compared by Bowlby and his colleagues with a group of nonseparated controls who were in the same classes in school. At the time of the study the children were between 7 and 13 years of age.

There were few significant differences between the separated and the nonseparated children either in intelligence or in teachers' ratings of their adjustment, although on all scores the sanatorium children showed up less well than the nonseparated youngsters. For example, the average IQ of the sanatorium children was 107, that of the controls, 110. Those children who had been institutionalized before the age of 2 had an average IQ of 102, whereas those who had gone in after 2 averaged 110. This difference is significant statistically, but it is not of great practical importance.

A few of the teachers' ratings differentiated significantly between the two groups. The sanatorium children did more day-dreaming, showed less initiative, and got overexcited and rough in their play. Their attention was more likely to wander. They were also timid about competition, or seemed not to care how they compared with other children.

This study cannot be said to support Bowlby's earlier conclusions very strongly, although where differences between groups were found, they were in favor of children growing up consistently in one family.

In one study (Beres and Obers, 1950), 38 young people were studied psychiatrically sixteen to eighteen years after they had been discharged from an infant hospital. They had originally been placed there when they were from 2 weeks to 23 months of age, and had remained in the hospital until they were from 18 months to 4½ years old. Twenty of them were judged to have personal difficulties of an extreme sort, including mental retardation, psychosis, and neurosis, although 18 were apparently adequately adjusted. In view of the findings of Lowrey and Goldfarb, it is surprising to find almost half of the young people normal; on the other hand, considering the fact that the children were physically normal, the percentage of disturbance is very high, being tremendously above that in the general population.

A British report on 277 children separated from their families for any of a number of reasons, and received into a diagnostic and treatment center after some form of public care (Lewis, 1954), states that 51 percent were severely, 36 percent mildly disturbed emotionally. Of children received into the center from their own homes, 44 percent were severely disturbed, 30 percent moderately disturbed. The percentages of children manifesting *some* disturbance, then, were 87 and 74, a difference which is statistically significant. Lewis makes a number of analyses in an attempt to determine if, and at what age, separation from the mother produces emotional maladjustment, and concludes that lasting separation before 2 is the only type of separation that can be shown to be deleterious in and of itself. Early separation, according to Lewis, is not noticeably related to what such authors as Goldfarb have called emotional coldness and apathy; the most frequent type of emotional disturbance shown by these children was overaggressiveness.

All the studies reviewed so far in this subsection support, at varying levels of confidence, the proposition that institutional living in infancy is damaging to the personality and intellect of the child. If institutional living is thought of as "isolation," studies of animals reared in isolation (as reported in Chapter 8) lead to the same conclusion.

But research is a complex matter, and one study in the area stands out in flat disagreement with the others. In fairness to students, it must be summarized, although it cannot be explained. Orgel (1941) studied 16 children who apparently came from the same institution reported on by Lowrey, whose study was the first to be mentioned in this subsection. These youngsters had entered the institution soon after birth, and had gone to foster homes when they were between 3 and 4 years old. Orgel reports that 12 of them adjusted easily, with only minor difficulties. Two had trouble in their first placement, but adjusted easily in a second placement. Their adjustment problem, Orgel believes, was due to the foster parents' impatience. Two others had serious and long-enduring problems and "had to be treated through the environment of the foster home before they adjusted." (p. 372) Orgel concludes: "I could see no evidence of these children being unprepared for or unequal to the demands of a family setting. On the contrary, the great majority readily accepted and met the demands made upon them by the family settings, in spite of the almost constant interference of the majority of the natural parents." (pp. 372–373)

In a summary of this subsection, it must be noted that there is some conflicting evidence about what happens to babies as a result of separation from their mothers, if this separation results in their being placed in an institution of the traditional type. The bulk of the evidence supports the conclusion that such placement is emotionally and intellectually severely damaging to the child. Studies of animals reared in isolation, later to be reviewed, indicate that simpler organisms, too, suffer from lack of normal stimulation and interaction. Relatively prolonged ill effects are also suggested by most of the research on this topic. Whether such effects are due to separation from the mother as such is a moot point. They may result from lack of perceptual stimulation, and (at least for human babies) from lack of opportunity to learn dependency, to resolve it, and to channel emotions so as to live harmoniously with others.

When institutions *must* serve babies, pains should be taken to assure that environmental stimulation and close, intimate, and tender personal relations with adults are provided.

Existing evidence also suggests early adoption for infants who are to go to foster parents. Lynch and Mertz (1955) summarize data for 45 babies placed directly from nursing homes when they were between 7 and 20 days old. The results of such early placement were considered excellent. The mothers who were willing to release their babies early seemed to be more genuinely concerned about the welfare of their children than the mothers who opposed early release. The foster parents were delighted to obtain their babies early, and the babies themselves turned out well. The authors suggest that many so-called gray placements (i.e., other than through an established social agency) result because the natural mothers do not want their babies in intermediate foster homes (or, presumably, infant institutions).

Lack of Fathering

Little research has been done on the interaction of fathers and their children. One reason for this is theoretical: the assumption is frequently made, either implicitly or explicitly, that it is the mother who has the major effect on early personality development and that the father's role is relatively unimportant. At best, this assumption is a doubtful one. In many sections of modern United States society, fathers interact a great deal with their children from birth, and very often share with mothers all phases of child care.

The second reason for the dearth of information about the role of fathering is that it is more difficult to get research cooperation from fathers. Because they work during the day, the researcher must do his work on evenings and weekends. Fathers are justifiably reluctant to devote their leisure time to being guinea pigs. It may also be that fathers are less interested than mothers in the area of child development, hence less willing to serve as research subjects.

However, research done by Lois Meek Stolz and co-workers (1954) includes fathers, mothers, and children as subjects. This team of workers was interested in the effects of paternal absence during babyhood on the later adjustment of children. They secured the cooperation of 19 families in which the fathers had been away from home (in the armed services) at the time of the children's birth and for at least eleven months thereafter. The time away from the children following their birth ranged from eleven to thirty-three months. At the time the study was conducted, the "first-born children" on whom it concentrated were all at least of preschool age, and some were in the early years of elementary school (up to and including second grade). The attitudes, practices, and emotional adjustment of these fathers, mothers, and children were contrasted with fairly well-matched control groups of families in which the fathers had never been away for a substantial period of time after the children's birth.

According to this study, the war-separated fathers had looked forward with mixed feelings (including apprehension) to vocational rehabilitation after the war (all were college students at the time of the study), to earning a living and to being a husband, but few had planned their new relationships as fathers. Coming back into the home, they found themselves resenting the child who had "usurped" much of their wife's love and affection. The children themselves were frequently shy, distant, or resentful of the strange new man who had come into the home. The most frequent role played by the fathers was that of disciplinarian: their complaints were that the child was too dependent on the mother, not well-trained in routines, not "manly enough" (when the child was a boy). At the time the children were studied, the fathers were relating more naturally and easily to children who had been born into the family subsequent to their return than they were to their first-born children.

The children themselves showed some personality damage when compared with youngsters whose fathers had not been separated from them. An association with the fathers' absence rather than with other factors is suggested by the fact that there were no differences between the groups of children studied in such factors as conditions associated with pregnancy, labor, and childbirth; nor in child-rearing practices related to the children's organic needs. But the war-separated children had been harder to train in their routines, and were reported to have poorer relations with other children, than the nonseparated youngsters. This factor of reported poor social relations was substantiated by the investigators through actual observation of the children in their social groups. It was observed, among other things, that the war-separated children were more likely to be fringers and onlookers. They were also observed to have greater difficulty in acting naturally and easily with such adults as their teachers; and they seemed to be in conflict between being extremely obedient, on the one hand, and openly defiant, on the other. The war-separated youngsters were also believed to be more anxious, and to show more serious fears and more tension patterns. The boys seemed somewhat more distant emotionally from their fathers than the girls.

This study presents clearly a picture of difficulties occurring for both fathers and children as a result of the father's absence—difficulties that had not been resolved within the period of several years following the father's return to the home. The problems uncovered appeared to result from a complex family interaction that hinged upon the absence of the father; in other words, they were due more to complications in human relationships as a function of absence than to absence as such.

Lynn and Sawrey (1959) studied the effects of father absence in a population of Norwegian boys and girls. The fathers of half the group (21 boys, 19 girls) were sailors of officer rank who were away from home at least nine months of the year, often as much as two years at a time. These children, all in the second grade and between 8 years and 9 years 6 months of age, were matched with 20 boys and 20 girls whose fathers were consistently at home on such factors as whether they lived in town or in the country, mother's age, number of brothers and sisters, their own position in the family, teachers' ratings of intelligence, and father's status in the community. To be considered equal in prestige to a ship's officer, the fathers of the control group had to be at an occupational level involving supervision of others—for example, shop owners, high civil servants, or office managers.

Judgments about the children's adjustment to their peers, and the boys' *compensatory masculinity,* were made from interviews with the mother. A child was assumed to be compensating if, for example, a mother described her son as acting in an exaggeratedly masculine way, but also related instances of his behaving in a fashion more characteristic of girls than of boys.

The children were also given a Structured Doll Play test. In this test, dolls are placed in a series of typical family and age-mate situations. The child is told what the situation is, and is asked to resolve it through doll play. For instance, he is presented with a crib and a bed, and is told that the little boy has two places where he can sleep, and that either is all right. He is then asked to put the doll to sleep. After that, he is asked which of his parents will come in, and what will happen. On the basis of his resolution of a series of such situations, each child was given a score for maturity, frequency of father choice, reaction to separation (after separation, which parent was chosen to return to the doll figure—presumed to represent the child), and dependency.

In general, the authors' five predictions were supported, usually quite clearly. More father-absent than father-present boys showed immaturity. The father-absent boys, presumed to be insecure in their identification with their fathers, showed stronger strivings toward such identification. More father-absent boys were judged to show compensatory masculinity, and to be less well-adjusted in their peer relations. Father absence produced few differences between the father-absent and the father-present girls, except that the father-absent girls, perhaps because threatened by the absence of one parent, showed more dependence on their mothers than the father-present girls. This was not true of the boys.

Another study (Bach, 1946), conducted with children between the ages of 6 and 10, shows that boys whose fathers had been away from home from one to three years behaved, in a doll-play situation, more like girls than boys whose fathers had been in the home consistently. In other words, a possible problem of appropriate sex-typing appeared.

Bach also found, among his 20 subjects, 2 boys and 2 girls whose mothers, during long interviews, were consistently derogatory in the picture they painted of their absent husbands. The mothers of 2 other boys and 2 other girls were as enthusiastic about their husbands as the first group was negative. When the doll-play behavior of these two groups of children was compared, the children of the negative mothers showed many more fantasies in which the father in the doll-play situation was aggressive to the doll children, and in which he was *generally* aggressive. On the other hand, they showed the doll children more often yearning for affection from the father than the children whose mothers talked favorably about their husbands. Bach, plausibly enough, believes that the attitudes of the mother influence the way the child thinks of his absent father. However, it is possible that the mother *and* the child see the father as he really is. The study offers no information on this latter interpretation.

Research summarized earlier in this chapter in connection with the discussion of aggression (Pauline Sears, 1951) has demonstrated that preschool boys (three-, four-, and five-year-olds) whose fathers are absent from home show fantasy patterns that are different from those of boys whose fathers are with them: they are more girlish, less aggressive. It is of course possible—though none of the studies cited was designed to probe this relationship—that the effect of separation from the father varies according to the age at which the separation occurs.

Fathers' presence, then, seems to play an important role in the development of their children, particularly their sons. Children whose fathers had been away from home at the time of their birth and for about a year or more thereafter were less well adjusted on a number of scores than children whose fathers had been consistently at home. This maladjustment appears to have been related to complex interactions between father, mother, and child after the father's return—the child feels threatened by the stranger; the father, expecting immediate love from the child, finds that he must "win" the youngster, and so on. The fantasy play of boys whose fathers were absent for prolonged periods during preschool or early school years has been found to be less masculine than that of boys whose fathers were not absent.

A study of Norwegian children whose fathers were away from home a large percentage of the time provides results closely in accord with those obtained for United States childen: boys were affected more than girls; and, compared with boys whose fathers remained at home, were more immature and less secure in identification with their fathers. Some evidence suggests that "father-absent" children, particularly boys, suffer unusual difficulties in social relations with their peers.

THE PERSONALITY PATTERN OF THE FAMILY

Becker *et al.* (1959) have conducted one of the few studies that concern themselves with both fathers and mothers. They charted extensively the characteristics of the families of 25 children who were not in need of clinical services (for behavior problems) and of the families of 32 children who were in need of such services. The children were between 6 and 12 years of age at the time of the study. The parents were of Caucasian extraction, and were living together. The groups were quite well matched on variables other than the children's adjustment.

Factor analysis of the data indicated that the maladjusted children fell into two major groups. For purposes of convenience, the authors labeled the first of these the "conduct problem" group, made up of children who manifested uncontrollable or highly aggressive behavior. The second group was called the "personality problem" group. Its members showed such symptoms as shyness, undue sensitiveness, and feelings of inferiority. Both labels, of course, reflect personality problems, but they are applied in accordance with a widely used classification of children with behavior disturbances: those who act out their unhappiness (conduct problems); and those who "take it out on themselves" (the personality-problem group). They might also be called the "attackers" and the "withdrawers."

Becker and his colleagues found that the parents of the conduct-problem group, typically, were maladjusted and inclined to be arbitrary with their children, and were themselves likely to give vent violently and unpredictably to their emotions. The mother was likely to be active and tense, very free with suggestions, dictatorial, and thwarting. But the fathers, apparently rather withdrawn from the situation, tended not to enforce regulations. Such a situation, obviously, can easily become a vicious spiral: the mother, frustrated by the father, becomes shriller and shriller; the father, frustrated by the mother, withdraws more and more; and the hapless child is left in the middle, with an antagonistic parent on the one hand and a nonsupportive and withdrawn one on the other.

For the group of children with personality problems, the role of the father appeared to be significantly more important than that of the mother. None of her behaviors was particularly related to such symptoms; but the fathers were revealed to be maladjusted and thwarting of the child.

The authors conclude their study with the following italicized statement: "The many important associations between father and child behavior lead to the conclusion that future research, and perhaps therapeutic practice, should *give more consideration to the role of the father in child development."* (p. 117)

Peterson *et al.* (1959) report an apparent extension of this study and summarize their findings as follows:

> Personality problems seem largely independent of maternal attitude, but related to dictatorial attitudes and a lack of genuine concern among fathers. Conduct problems are related chiefly to maladjustment among mothers and to democratic attitudes and heightened feelings of parental concern among fathers. Both parents appear overly permissive, and characterization of the fathers of children who present conduct problems as generally weak and ineffectual may not be far wide of the mark. Democratic qualities are esteemed in our culture, but when they are combined with laxity, unwillingness to issue orders, exaggerated concern for children, and a tendency to shelter them in the fact of day-to-day problems the seeds of conduct disorders may be sown. (p. 126)[3]

In another study (Liverant, 1959), personality-test data from 49 sets of Caucasian parents of children referred for psychiatric help were compared with the test data of 49 carefully matched parents of normal children. Most of the families were lower middle-class people.

On the personality test (the Minnesota Multiphasic Inventory, usually referred to as the MMPI), the fathers of the disturbed children showed up as more concerned with body complaints and illness; they were gloomier in their outlook on life, yet at the same time appeared to be less mature and more impulsive; and they were more tense and anxious. The mothers, too, were more impulsive and less mature, and more depressed and anxious. They laid blame on other people for their problems, were less honest, and were inclined to act out ther aggressions and unconventional impulses.

Although these findings are based on a paper-and-pencil test, and do not directly represent real-life behavior, they fit well enough with the results obtained by Becker and Peterson and their colleagues.

All three studies, then, suggest that disturbed fathers and mothers have disturbed children. Children who might be described as "attackers" have mothers who are dominating and demanding, fathers who are unusually lax and withdrawn. The mothers of "withdrawers" do not differ as a group from the mothers of nonproblem children, but their fathers appear to be more dominating and restricting.

SUMMARY

This chapter has summarized the major studies of child-rearing practices in the United States, stressing their effects upon children when such

[3] Reprinted with permission of W. E. Martin, Editor, *Child Develpm.*, and D. R. Peterson, from Peterson *et al.* (1959).

effects have been studied. The chapter has focused on five areas of training common to all cultures: feeding and weaning, elimination training, sex training, dependency training, and aggression training. In addition, research on the effects of maternal deprivation in early childhood and on lack of fathering has been summarized. Finally, the results of three studies investigating the relation between children's personality disorders and the personality patterns of their parents have been briefly presented.

Concerning feeding and weaning, the conclusion suggested by the bulk of the evidence available is that style of feeding (breast, bottle, or cup) and time of weaning are of less importance in the concurrent and subsequent personality development of the child than maternal attitudes of affection, acceptance, and relaxation (or their opposites) which express themselves in the feeding situation. The evidence that exists, plus observation and common sense, indicates that a self-demand schedule is as satisfactory as scheduled feeding and may be easier on both the baby and his parents. Cup feeding starting in infancy does not appear to have ill effects, and may actually be preferable for low-energy children—for example, premature babies.

Perhaps because children are older when they are toilet-trained than when decisions about breast or bottle feeding are made, conclusions about the effects of toilet training are clearer than those about feeding and weaning. The findings do not consistently support psychoanalytic theory, but they *do* indicate that this theory is correct in emphasizing the importance of toilet training. United States mothers start toilet training earlier than the experts advise; and the earlier it is started, the longer it takes to establish. The more severe the training, the more upsetting it is to children. Rigid toilet training, in conjuncton with a number of other practices that might be called restrictive, also seems to slow down motor development in infancy.

Harsh toilet training seems to be related to many other child-rearing practices, almost all of which may be thought of as restrictive or as indicative of insecurity or low self-esteem on the part of the mother. It may well be that the conjunction of harsh toilet training with other types of restrictiveness, and the general mother-child relationship which this reflects, is responsible for the effects that harsh and rigid training appears to have on the development of personality.

United States mothers, in their sex training, seem to worry about and disapprove of sexual behavior in their children, but take few drastic measures to prevent or punish it. Modesty training is almost synonymous with sex training. Among primitive societies, internalization of control has been found to be associated with early sex training. Although it is common psychiatric knowledge that sexual problems usually accompany personal maladjustment, little sound information exists about the sexual training of children in the United States.

With respect to dependency training, Sears, Maccoby, and Levin (1957) found that most of the children in their study were reported to be quite independent by the age of 5. Mothers who are *generally* permissive seem also to be indulgent of dependency in their children. The most dependent children were reported to be those whose mothers expressed annoyance over dependency but eventually surrendered to the child's demands.

In primitive cultures, a relation has been found between indulging the child orally and being permissive about his dependency-seeking behaviors. Cultures that sharply discourage dependency in childhood also discourage it in adults. The earlier a culture trains for independence, the more likely its members are to show signs of strong internalized controls.

Aggressive behavior in children seems to result both from aggressive punishment by parents and from parental permissiveness concerning their children's aggression. All children are hostile and aggressive at times, and diversionary and reasoning-understanding techniques on the part of adults seem most effective in terminating episodes of hostility. The problem of socializing aggression is particularly acute since, on the one hand, overtly expressed aggression can seriously disrupt social functioning; and, on the other hand, strong repression can have equally serious consequences for the individual. A well-adjusted older child or adult should be able to recognize and accept the fact that he is angry and feels aggressive; yet be able to handle his feelings in a constructive (or, at least, nondestructive) fashion.

Most of the existing evidence indicates that when infants and very young children live in institutions, their intellectual and emotional development is impeded. In other words, "mothering"—the presence of a consistent, warm adult—seems to be very important for infant development. This conclusion is supported by research done with animals reared in isolation. Corollary to this is the advice that babies be placed for adoption as early as possible.

That the father, too, has his role is demonstrated by research on children living their infant and preschool years with their fathers absent from home. Boys, particularly, seem to suffer from such absence: they appear to have difficulty in developing "boyishness," work artificially hard at behaving in masculine ways, and possibly have difficulty in relating with their age-mates.

Although complete families (father, mother, child) have not often been studied, such studies being difficult to conduct, at least three studies indicate that disturbed families produce disturbed children. Constellations often found among families of disturbed children are: (1) both parents inconsistent, impulsively acting out their emotions, and arbitrary in their handling of the child; (2) a self-preoccupied, rather weak father and an aggressive, also self-preoccupied, but strong mother; and (3) "average" mothers (i.e., not different as a group from the mothers of nonproblem children) and arbitrary, demanding, and restrictive fathers.

Learning and Motivation

THE premise of this volume is that the processes fundamental for explaining human behavior are *learning* and *motivation*. The two cannot be separated from each other. Theories of learning are complex and, relative to other areas of psychology, well developed. The research literature is vast. For such reasons, this chapter is schematic; it is intended neither as a survey nor as a synthesis, but as a guide-line, laid out to clarify the earlier and later sections of the book.

A number of intriguing questions are raised in preceding and following chapters. Why, and through what mechanisms, does the sense of smell enter strongly into many emotionally charged behaviors, such as those labeled sexual? Literature on *classical conditioning* makes suggestions concerning this. What are the mechanisms through which deprivation in infancy slows intellectual development in human and animal babies? Ideas concerning *learning to learn* are relevant here. Why do studies on toilet training present clearer conclusions than those done with younger babies, concerning feeding and weaning practices? Research on *verbal mediation* suggests the reasons. Why do children in some sections of the United States decline in intelligence as they grow older, and why are children of some socioeconomic strata less intelligent than those from other strata? Research dealing with the *effect of reward on learning* contributes suggestive answers to these questions.

This chapter, then, contains a schematic outline of concepts that underlie the development of human personality and intellect. These principles should be applied retrospectively, to the literature on child-rearing practices and their effects, and should be kept in mind as research on intelligence, physical growth and socialization, sex typing and identification, and so on, is introduced. For each of these topics, the principles of learning provide useful ideas for organizing research findings, instituting new research, and in a practical way, guiding the development of children.

Any person who works with children should, ideally, have thorough training in learning theory and research. Lacking such training, he should do as much reading in the area as possible. Most good general psychology textbooks include a treatment of learning. As a supplement to this chapter, the beginning student might, for example, read the chapters on learning in Kimble (1956). Kimble's treatment is simple, but comprehensive.

MATURATION AND LEARNING

Definitions of Maturation and Learning

Although learning has been stressed throughout the discussion of material to this point, no attempt has been made to define it, nor have general principles been provided by which it may be understood. Growth (for example, changing in height and weight) does not involve learning but relates, rather, to the concept of *maturation*. By *"maturation" is meant development of the organism as a function of time, or age;* maturation refers to neuro-physiological-biochemical changes from conception to death. The fetus is more mature than the embryo; the eighteen-month-old is more mature than the newborn baby; the fourteen-year-old more mature than the six-year-old, and so on.

Increased height, weight, and strength, then, are in part the result of maturation (time and nutrition). But organizing these maturational phenomena so that performances previously impossible for the child can be accomplished involves *learning*. A baby sits alone in part because he has grown or matured. His head, in proportion to his torso and legs, is smaller; his back muscles, in consequence of both maturation and exercise, are stronger. As he has grown, he has practiced constantly. He has reared up from his stomach, using his arms as props; he has practiced balancing his head; he has used his legs. While lying on his back, he has tried to pull himself up by his hands and arms. Presently, he puts these separate learned skills together; and a new behavior, the effect partly of learning, partly of maturation, results: he sits up alone.

Learning, then, involves the acquisition of new skills, such as sitting up, talking, walking, or dropping one of two toys in order to pick up a third that is more interesting. It also includes acquiring new meanings. Nothing will long prevent the two-month-old from screaming when he is hungry, except the nipple in his mouth. But the six-month-old will quiet for a few moments at the sound of his mother's voice, or the sight of her preparing his bottle. As the bottle approaches him, he stops crying and reaches for it. The three-year-old will calm, when he is in the mood, for a considerable period of time because of his parents' statement that dinner will be ready in about ten minutes. These new meanings are themselves skills; they are methods of understanding and manipulating the environment and oneself. They lead not only to learning to do new things, but to learning *not* to do old things: not to behave in ways that lead to pain or disapproval. Tendencies to approach the stove, for instance, disappear early, although it is a rare child who does not get burned at least once before he learns to keep away.

Child and adult lives are full of such learning: to *do* things and *not* to do things; to *approach* or master, and to *avoid*. Learning, then, refers to the acquisition of new skills, meanings, and orientations, including avoidances and simple *"not doing"* what one has once done.[1]

[1] This kind of learning should be distinguished from fatigue, which may be thought of as not doing something, or doing it more slowly, because one is *tired*.

Perhaps as good a definition of learning as any other is the following: *Learning is a change in performance as a function of practice* (see McGeoch and Irion, 1952). It should be remembered that learning *not to do* can be just as positive a "performance" as learning to *do*. Behavior effects due to fatigue are not learning, although they may affect learning.

How does *learning* differ from *performance?* Learning can be considered as something that goes on, or exists, inside the skin of the human or animal. So defined, it is not available for measurement. Reduction in the amount of reward given for a task often results in reducing the efficiency of *performance* (reduces output). However, this need not eliminate *knowledge* of what is correct. In this volume, learning and performance are considered as closely related to each other, although it is granted that they are not identical.

Role of Maturation and Learning in Behavior

Much research has been done to determine the relative contribution of maturation and learning to human development. *Maturity* is the *physical* readiness to learn, including both neurological and muscular maturity. One does not, for example, try to teach a three-month-old how to walk, or an eighteen-month-old how to read. They are not mature enough; they are not ready for the developmental tasks of walking and reading.

Research on the relative importance of maturation and learning has provided few facts of value to psychology, whether psychology is considered as a *science* or as a *method of understanding children*. The effects of maturation and learning cannot be separated from each other, any more than one can break up H_2O and still have water, or demonstrate that hydrogen is more important to water than oxygen. However, maturation-learning research does have important implications for practice. If maturation is considered paramount (and traditional textbook treatment gives it such importance), the role of learning is minimized; if learning is considered paramount, the role of maturation tends to be neglected. Because of these practical implications, the traditional, logically rather pointless research dealing with maturation *versus* learning should be fully discussed.

Few, if any, three-month-old infants, regardless of the opportunity given them to practice, can sit alone, because they have not reached the necessary level of maturity. Their heads are disproportionately large and heavy compared with their torsos; their neck muscles are not yet strong enough to balance their heads; their back muscles are weak. But most normal eight-month-olds can sit alone, partly because of normal growth (maturity), partly because of practice, the rewarded result of which is *learning*. Spitz (1945) has shown that the eight-month-old, denied practice, does not sit by himself as a result of maturation in the partial absence of learning opportunity.

Dennis (1940) reports that Hopi Indian infants from the American Southwest who are confined to cradle boards learn to walk, when eventually given the opportunity, as early as other Hopi infants who have been reared without cradle boards. Since the latter, presumably, have had more opportunity for exercise and practice, Dennis concludes that maturation is more important than learning in motor development.

This research must be examined critically. Even the cradle-boarded Hopi infant has used *some* musculature (cradle boards include kicking room). He has been taken out of the cradle board at intervals for cleaning; and, because of the way he is carried, he has had much experience in balancing his head and using his arms and shoulders. He has seen other children walking and may have built up imitative tendencies, so that he is as ready to go, when he is released from the cradle board, as is the hypothetically more experienced unconfined baby. Indeed, the baby reared in the cradle board may have had more opportunity to observe the world around him than his ostensibly freer peer, since the cradle board makes it easy for his mother to take him with her wherever she goes. He has also had more experience with vertical posture. Because of his confinement, he may have more motivation to get out on his own than the baby whose activity drives have presumably been less blocked. Seldom or never having been separated from his mother, he may be psychologically more secure, hence more ready to strike out on his own. Even in this interesting piece of research, then, there has been no conclusive testing of the independent effects of maturation and learning on the development of a skill.

Several experiments (e.g., Gesell and Thompson, 1929; Hilgard, 1932) have sought to depict effects of maturation as distinguished from learning, using as subjects identical twin girls, T (for trained) and C (for control). This method of study is known as the *method of co-twin control*. It involves giving one of a pair of identical twins a certain type of experience, and delaying training for the other member of the pair. Since identical twins have identical hereditaries, differences in their eventual performance are assumed to be due to learning. If no differences in performance result, the assumption is made that identical heredities have resulted in identical maturational processes, which override the effects of differential learning.

On a number of different tasks, such as stair-climbing and fastening button strips to buttonhole strips, twin T was exposed early to the task, while twin C was given training later. After a time, during which twin C was also allowed to practice, the performance of the two girls on the task was measured. Few, if any, differences were found, despite the fact that twin C had had much less total practice. In general, it was concluded that maturation was more important in development than learning. That some learning *did* occur is indicated by the fact that, for at least a short period of time, T was superior to C.

The design of these studies has neglected the factor of motivation. By the time C started her practice, T may already have been bored with the task, while C was intensely interested. Rivalry may have entered the picture to some degree. Finally, no amount of practice on a task for which the child does not have the appropriate physical equipment and coordination will help him to master it.

Another well-known pair of twins, not identical, were Jimmy and Johnny. The psychologist who worked with them (McGraw, 1935) exposed one twin early to experiences such as tricycling; the other twin was given such opportunities much later. Then, as with twins T and C, differences in performance were measured. Again, after the control twin had had a relatively brief period of practice, negligible differences were found between the boys (although, obviously, the experimental twin had learned and had experienced temporary superiority over his sibling). McGraw also concluded that maturation was more important in development than learning.

Although the logical error of such studies has been pointed out, their conclusions have been interpreted as implying that one can minimize opportunities for children's learning, since maturation will take care of the developmental process. This interpretation ignores the fact that more subtle results of early and late teaching have been neglected in studies such as those cited. How, for example, were interpersonal relations between these two pairs of twins—T and C, and Jimmy and Johnny—affected? What may have been the effects of early exposure to routine tasks on twin T, whose sister, meanwhile, was going free? How did C react to having her sister *master* certain skills before she was allowed the opportunity even to *practice* them? McGraw's experimental twin was trained to master exciting aspects of his environment (e.g., tricycles) before the control twin. How did this affect Jimmy's and Johnny's self-concepts, and their relations with each other? The only bit of evidence we have about later personality differences is Gesell and Thompson's report (1941) on the personalities of twins T and C at adolescence: C seemed to be more creative and flexible; T more methodical, less imaginative, perhaps more practical.

CONDITIONED RESPONSES

The Classical Conditioned Response

It is widely accepted, and will be accepted here, that the simplest—perhaps the most primitive—form of learning is the *classical conditioned response*. The assumption is made that many of our automatic, persistent, emotion-laden responses, such as elation in spring and depression in February, develop through classical conditioning.

The first formal laboratory demonstration of the classical conditioned response was made by Pavlov, a Russian physiologist. He showed that, after a bell had been presented repeatedly in conjunction with food, dogs would respond to the bell presented alone in about the same manner as to food. Response to the bell alone was considered to be the *conditioned response* (CR), and the bell was called the *conditioned stimulus* (CS). Since, at the beginning of training, sight (and smell?) of the food produced a salivating response, food was called the *unconditioned stimulus* (US); and the response (in Pavlov's early work, the measure of response was the amount of saliva excreted) was designated as the *unconditioned response* (UR).

Figure 4.1 schematizes the presentation of the conditioned stimulus (CS), illustrates its temporal relation to the unconditioned stimulus (US), shows that the unconditioned response (UR) follows the US temporally and that, following training, the very similar conditioned response (CR) occurs (but earlier than the UR).

Time

Fig. 4.1.   A schematic representation of the classical conditioned-response experiment. Time is represented along the horizontal. Departures from the horizontal line represent the presentation of conditioned and unconditioned stimuli and the occurrence of conditioned and unconditioned responses

Research on classical conditioning with humans is less complete than with animals, but for both, circumstances favorable to developing conditioned responses seem to be the following, all of which are schematized in Figure 4.1: CS sets on before US is presented, and continues very briefly (a fraction of a second) after US ceases. At the beginning of conditioning, US is already associated with UR, and almost invariably produces it (food elicits salivation in dogs; electric shock is reacted to by withdrawal). US may be thought of as providing motivation: food appeals to the hungry animal; electric shock is painful, and the tendency is to withdraw from it. US is always presented whether or not UR (or CR—the distinction between them is difficult to make) results.

CR, once established, is likely to differ from UR, although it is designed to accomplish the same purpose (obtaining food, escaping shock). CR appears sooner after the onset of CS than does (or did) UR. Finally, CS loses its power to evoke CR unless it is occasionally coupled with *primary reinforcement* (in this illustration, food or shock). The "loss of power to evoke" is called *extinction,* and is probably related to forgetting.

The graphic pattern by which a conditioned response is usually considered to be acquired and extinguished is shown in Figure 4.2.

The ordinate of Figure 4.2 represents the percentage of trials on which CS elicits CR. Since one of the characteristics of CR is that it precedes UR in time (is an *anticipatory response*), the most common measure of conditioning is the counting of anticipatory responses, although some measures, such as salivation, do not lend themselves readily to this procedure. CS can also be presented without US to see whether it evokes CR; but in this case, each test is also an extinction trial, so that acquisition is slowed.

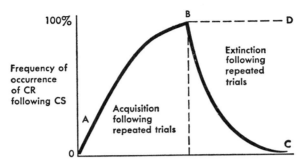

FIG. 4.2. Typical pattern of growth (acquisition) and extinction of a classical conditioned response

As can be seen from Figure 4.2, learning hypothetically begins at zero. That is, the bell alone does not originally result in salivation (or, in the case of shock, withdrawal). Gradually, CS acquires power to elicit CR, as shown by the section of the curve between points A and B. The horizontal line, or abscissa, of Figure 4.2 represents the amount of practice that has been given. At point B, learning levels off, or reaches its *asymptote*, usually at less than the 100 percent level of the power of CS to elicit CR. At point B in Figure 4.2, the experimenter stops presenting US with CS. Gradually the power of CS to elicit CR disappears (as a function of such extinction trials). Presumably, the experimental subject begins to stop regarding CS as a signal that food is in the offing. Finally, at point C in Figure 4.2, CS fails altogether to elicit CR, and *extinction* of the conditioned response is said to have occurred. The rising curve between points A and B represents the process of acquiring the conditioned response. The curve for extinction is an approximate inverted mirror image of the curve for acquisition.

It is not necessary, either for humans or for animals, to present CS without US to produce extinction. Presentation or adventitious occurrence of stimuli similar to CS, hence having much the same effect, may accomplish the same purpose. In children and adults, but not animals, verbal or other symbolic representations of CS may also result in extinction. The mental rehearsal of a painful experience may, for example, partially reduce its potency.[2]

Some evidence (Estes, 1944) indicates that an animal must have ex-

[2] When conditioning starts from zero, the shape of the acquisition and extinction curves is usually considered to be S-shaped. The question of shape is important in developing further theory, but does not concern us in this discussion.

periences with CS and its attendant CR *in the absence of US* (the primary reinforcer) for CS to lose its power. The same thing may hold for children *before they acquire symbols* (which they can use to rehearse, thus to extinguish conditioning). In the absence of practice, the persistence of conditioned responses in very young infants for as long as seven months has been noted. Thus, one might speculate that if a conditioned response is established and the experimental subject subsequently goes for a long period of time without again experiencing CS-CR, then CS may indefinitely preserve its power to elicit CR. This is illustrated by the dashes between B and D in Figure 4.2.

This interpretation has interesting implications for the practical handling of very young children (or older ones, for that matter), arguing as it does for the need to practice *unlearning* (extinguishing) maladaptive responses as well as *learning* adaptive ones. It is conceivable that stimuli associated with some trauma in infancy, if not re-experienced and adapted to, may years later evoke the same unfortunate emotional responses with which they were originally associated.

Such tentative theory gives a certain foundation to the advice that children be allowed to express reactions such as fear and hate, even when these are inappropriate, so that they may be extinguished. In a warm, relatively permissive, democratic atmosphere the child will feel free to exhibit a wide range of behaviors, "good" and "bad," helpful and harmful to him. His parent or teacher then has an opportunity to help him consolidate or acquire firmly the adequate or adaptive behaviors and to extinguish the inadequate or maladaptive ones. Without an active process of *unlearning,* it may be that the maladaptive behaviors and feeling will persist indefinitely. Such reasoning, at this stage of our knowledge, is admittedly speculative, but it is plausible and potentially useful educationally.

Classical conditioning appears to be an automatic process, and seems to depend neither on insight nor on more than the most elementary nervous system or intelligence. Indeed, there is some evidence (Munn, 1954) to indicate that it is difficult to produce classical conditioning in older children and adults, particularly when UR is subject to their voluntary control (as is true of responses involved in hand or finger withdrawal from an electric shock). Some have interpreted this resistance to classical conditioning on the part of older children and adults as distaste for being placed in a situation where they must learn against their will: they fight against learning. Perhaps, also, one must possess language if he is to resist classical conditioning. An older child has available cues that he can put into words immediately, saying, in effect, "The shock has stopped (or is intermittent). Why should I bother to respond to it?" Through such a mental set, or intent, he can inhibit *voluntary* responses, although classical conditioning of *involuntary responses,* such as the eye-blink, is easily accomplished with both adults and children.

Evidence is clear that conditioning occurs very early in life. Munn's summary (1954) indicates that sucking, blinking, limb withdrawal, respiration, crying, general activity, galvanic skin response (electrical conductivity of the skin), and fear reactions can, during infancy, be conditioned to tactile, visual, and auditory stimuli. However, a baby must be hungry (drive or motive must be present) before conditioning of the sucking reaction is possible. Newborn infants can be and have been conditioned, although their reactions often lack stability. Conditioned responses in older infants are usually more stable than those of the newborn. Such responses have been maintained over periods ranging up to seven months. Spontaneous recovery (temporary reappearance of CR) occurs following partial extinction training. The curve of extinction for conditioned responses (particularly feeding, which has been studied most) approximates a mirror image of the acquisition curve. Finally, continued presentation of CS and US together, after conditioning has been established, may result in a decrease in the frequency of CR.

This last point requires some elucidation. The decrease in frequency of CR following repeated presentations of the paired stimuli US and CS is represented in Figure 4.3. This figure is analogous to Figure 4.2 on page 123. The percentage of test trials on which CS produces CR is represented by the curve between points A and B. The decrease of which Munn speaks

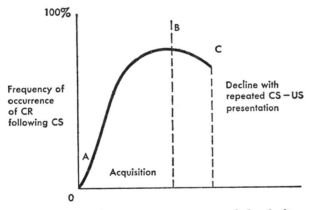

FIG. 4.3.   A schematic representation of the decline in power of CS to elicit CR when CS and US are paired together after learning has been established

is represented by the curve from points B to C. By the time point C has been reached, a considerable decrease in frequency of eliciting CR by CS has occurred despite the fact that CS has been followed in every case by US. Why should this drop occur? Why does CS lose its power even when it continues to be associated with reward?

At least two factors are necessary to explain this phenomenon. In some instances the reason may be reduction in drive. If a small amount of food (US) is given for each learning trial, the animal or infant becomes less hungry with each trial. We know that elicitation of CR depends on a state of drive or motivation, such as hunger. Hence, the lower the drive, the less likely the response is to occur. Even when the drive or motive is pain avoid ance, and US is electric shock, reduction of drive through repeated trials may occur because the individual in the experiment becomes adapted (or accustomed, or relatively insensitive) to shock of the intensity being used n the experiment.

A second factor that may help to reduce the power of CS to elicit CR is fatigue. The more times a subject practices a response, the more fatigue accumulates and detracts from the likelihood or probability of the occurrence of the response. This fatigue factor is probably largely responsible for Munn's conclusion above concerning spontaneous recovery (see Fig. 4.4).

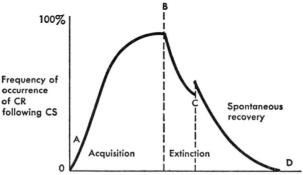

FIG. 4.4.   A schematic representation of spontaneous recovery during extinction training

Figure 4.4 is partially familiar. The curve between points A and B represents acquisition of the conditioned response, and the curve between B and C represents the beginning of extinction as we have seen it in Figure 4.2. However, extinction training has been interrupted by a rest period at point C. On the resumption of extinction training after rest, the frequency of CR in response to CS increases temporarily, although the continuation of extinction training reduces it to approximately zero power at point D. This increase in power at point C is probably due to the fact that fatigue has been dissipated, leaving CR with a greater probability of occurrence than immediately before rest. Many have had the experience of changing from a car with a standard gear shift to one with an automatic shift. At the beginning, driving the new car is accompanied by almost automatic manipulation with the left foot and leg to find the clutch that is not there. At the end of the first long practice session, the clutch-pushing reaction is almost extinguished. But after a night of rest it pops back again, although not as strongly as at first. This reappearance after partial extinction is known as *spontaneous recovery*. Old ways of doing things are always cropping up in our everyday life, with spontaneous recovery at least partly responsible. Many children's errors in schoolwork are probably due to this phenomenon.

Although studies of classical conditioning with human infants and chil
dren have been less extensive and less rigorously controlled than experiments with animals, they indicate that conditioning in infancy and early
childhood follows approximately the same patterns and laws as it does with
animals. Many of the responses of older children and adults also seem, at
least superficially, to belong to this family of the conditioned response, with
all its primitive, automatic, preverbal associations. Our disgust at the sight
or smell of vomit or feces is not an intellectual but a frequently violent, somatic, apparently automatic response. It seems plausible that the sight and
smell, for instance, of vomit (CS) have been associated in early childhood
with the stimuli of nausea (US) and the UR of vomiting, Our adult reactions of disgust, and even gagging or vomiting, are the persistent conditioned responses that have resulted.

More pleasing behaviors may be thought of in a similar way. For the
adult brought up in a temperate climate, the smell or sight of a flowering
apple orchard (CS) evokes responses of relaxation, pleasure, and well-being
(CRs). As a child, he may have associated the smell of apple blossoms with
warmth, space, and fresh air (complex sorts of US), and the unconditioned
responses of muscular freedom, comfort, and so on. Even in an urban flat in
February, the odor of apple blossoms may evoke some of the pleasant responses associated with spring. It may be hazarded that many of the responses associated with smells, tastes, half-caught vistas, faces of strangers,
and so on, belong logically, although in complex fashion, to the family of
the classical conditioned response. Much advertising is based on the evoca-
tion of such old CS-CR connections; and much social usage (for example,
the use of perfumes by women in polite society) depends on their existence.

Of course, in these illustrations, hundreds of separate conditioned
stimuli and responses exist, but the over-all process appears to belong in
the classical conditioned-response category.

Instrumental Conditioning

A second, and somewhat more complicated, type of conditioning is
called *instrumental conditioning*. In one of the simplest forms of instrumental conditioning, an animal—typically, a white rat—is confined in a
cage with a trip bar. Pushing this trip bar provides a pellet of food for the
animal.

In instrumental conditioning, or learning, an animal or a child does
one thing to accomplish *another*. In the case cited above, he pushes a bar
to receive a pellet of food. The pushing of the bar is the conditioned response (CR); the food he obtains is the unconditioned stimulus (US).
Eating the food (or salivating in its presence) is the unconditioned response
(UR). The bar itself, plus his own internal sensations, is the conditioned
stimulus (CS), and the animal's learning task is to utilize this stimulus as a
sign that, if CR is performed, US will present itself and UR can occur.
Figure 4.5 diagrams this process.

The learning, or establishing the conditioned response, seems to occur by trial and error. CR occurs first by chance during the time when, for example, the white rat is exploring the box into which he has been placed. However, it is common practice to attract his attention to the bar by smearing it with food. This is equivalent to giving a child instructions on how to proceed in a task, and is designed to shorten the learning process by orienting the subject properly to the work at hand.

FIG. 4.5.   Sequence of instrumental conditioning

A *gradient of reinforcement* appears to operate in learning, so that the behavior most relevant to securing the reward, or escaping the punishment, is most reinforced. In the first stages of learning, this applies to behavior made in closest proximity to delivery of US and making of UR. In the case of the rat, the responses most relevant to US-UR are to remain in the vicinity of the trip bar and to manipulate it (particularly the latter).

Reinforced less strongly, or not at all, is behavior that is far distant in time or space from the US-UR event, such as exploring the side of the cage opposite the bar. Probably the subportions of the larger response that originally tripped the bar are more strongly and precisely reinforced (in part because they require less effort) than the gross original response. For example, it might be that the rat originally tripped the bar by climbing on it, but eventually his behavior is streamlined so that he trips it, with minimal exertion, with his paws.

After the animal has learned the initial conditioned response—bar-pushing—he can be taught to acquire still other refinements of learning, such as to push on the bar only when a light is shining or a bell ringing. This is accomplished by rewarding him (giving him food) when he pushes the bar while the light shines or the bell rings, and not rewarding him for pushing the bar at any other time. This type of learning is one form of *discrimination learning* (see pp. 133–134).

Differences between classical and instrumental conditioning are immediately obvious. CS is present at all times in the example of instrumental conditioning given above, and the animal is free to approach or ignore it as he wishes. This gives him much more control over the situation than is afforded in classical conditioning, since he can determine the interval (amount of time) between CS and CR-US-UR. The frequency and number of responses or trials, and the time between them, are also up to him rather than the experimenter. US (food) results *only* when CR (bar-pushing) occurs; CR resembles UR little or not at all; and the CR-UR sequence is not forced as in classical conditioning.

With so many variables open to control by the subject, it is obvious that classical conditioning is somewhat more efficient as a highly controlled demonstration of learning; but that instrumental conditioning is a valuable technique for the study of motivation in addition to learning.

It is possible, at the risk of overgeneralizing, to move from the simple situation of the rat in the cage to the more complex behavior of human beings, from instrumental *conditioning* to the more complex case of instrumental *learning*, which has much in common with it.

Let us assume a small boy, Tommy, aged 3½ years. This small boy attends a nursery school, in the yard of which is a tree that includes a tempting fork 4 feet off the ground, in which Tommy wishes to sit. This tempting fork may be thought of as the unconditioned stimulus; sitting in it, as the unconditioned response. But there is no direct way to reach the fork: it is too high; the tree trunk is too thick for Tommy to climb. A conditioned response is called for to help him achieve US and obtain satisfaction from UR. He sees a ladder (CS) on the other side of the tree and climbs it (CR), reaches the tree fork, sits in it, and looks around him like a prince on high (UR).

Such behavior, though made up of multitudinous conditioned responses, both classical and instrumental, follows the pattern of the instrumental conditioned response. Because of its complexity, however, it is better referred to as *instrumental learning*. Most of our daily behaviors have arisen in this fashion: we use forks or chopsticks in order *to eat;* good manners and flattery in order *to secure warm responses* from others; and work in order to earn the salary *to pay our rent*. In other words, instrumental learning has a goal-oriented or purposive nature apparently lacking in classical conditioning, or behaviors that belong in the classical-conditioning category.

STIMULUS GENERALIZATION

Primary Stimulus Generalization

The simplest form of transfer of training consists of the application of a response or set of responses originally evoked by one stimulus to another stimulus or stimuli. If a person is trained to push a telegraph key upon the presentation of a medium-gray stimulus and a slightly lighter or darker gray stimulus is presented to him, he is likely to press the telegraph key upon the presentation of either. But if a white stimulus or a black one is presented, there is much less likelihood of his responding. Such *generalization* is due to the physical similarity of the stimuli and, in a sense, is a function of the subject's "confusion" (failure to discriminate) about what is and what is not the stimulus to which he has been trained.

Figure 4.6, which is a schematic representation of the *primary general-*

ization gradient, shows that response probability is greatest for stimuli much like the one used in training and decreases steadily with decreasing similarity of the test stimulus to the original.

The generalization model shown in Figure 4.6 is *negatively decelerating* in both directions from the stimulus for which training was given (i.e., the curve descends in a shallow concave shape from the peak response to the original stimulus). As is true of learning curves, there is disagreement about

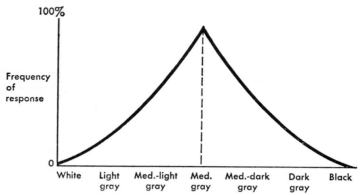

Fig. 4.6.   A schematic representation of primary stimulus generalization

the shape of the generalization curve, or gradient. Although this disagreement has implications for more complex psychological theory, it does not concern us here. The actual shape of the generalization curve probably varies according to the method used to test for generalization; the amount of training that has been given on the "correct" stimulus (apparently, the greater the training, the wider the generalization); the intensity of the stimulus (the more intense the stimulus, the wider the generalization); very possibly the type of stimulus (the shape of the curve from medium to bright stimuli may differ from that for medium to dim stimuli, for example; or the shape of the curve for colors may conceivably differ from that for sounds, lights, and so on).

There are some not entirely consistent data showing that younger children generalize more widely than older ones (Mednick and Lehtinen, 1957). This finding has an interesting, although frankly speculative, bearing on the notion that childhood experiences (learnings) have more widespread effects than similar experiences or learnings at a later age.

Generalization to Common Elements

If one has been trained to press a telegraph key to an outline of a square with three sides drawn in red and one in black, it might be predicted that the same response is more likely to occur with another square having two sides or one side drawn in red than with one all four of whose sides are black. In other words, the more elements complex stimuli have in common, the more likely it is that the same response will be made to them. Our hypothetical subject would probably also be more likely to respond to a circle drawn half in red, half in black, than to an all-black circle.

This type of generalization has not been studied much, but the gradient of generalization from an original stimulus to one having *many* elements in common with it, then to another with a *moderate* number of elements in common, and to another with *few* common elements, would probably resemble that in Figure 4.6.

Secondary Generalization

Secondary generalization refers to the process involved in making similar responses to stimuli that, objectively (in terms of primary stimulus characteristics), are different from each other. Such words as *gorgeous, pretty, beautiful, winsome, lissome, attractive,* all convey, at least to the masculine reader, the notion of a girl who has substantial "social stimulus value." But these words have little in common with each other in terms of primary stimulus generalization. Their similarity is *learned,* whereas, for all practical purposes, primary stimulus generalization can be considered innate.

Secondary generalization is a particularly useful concept in understanding human behavior. Independently, or in combination with primary generalization, it appears to underlie the ability to transfer learning in one situation to another that may, in terms of objective characteristics, be very different. The principle of secondary generalization is basic to our generalizations, principles, and classifications, providing guidelines for cognitive, planned behavior.

The secondary stimulus generalization gradient probably resembles that in Figure 4.6; but, instead of physical stimuli (such as a range of stimuli from white to black), *meanings* are the basis for generalization. *Mule,* for example, is more similar to *horse* than *chicken.*

Mediated Stimulus Generalization

At a colloquial level, *mediated generalization* might be defined as secondary generalization in action. When two concepts, or words, or any other stimuli have acquired, through training, the capacity to evoke a common response, and another response is then learned to the first of them, the second, although never directly trained or "attached" to the new response, will, upon test, tend to evoke it (see Fig. 4.7).

An anecdote that illustrates the real-life importance of mediated generalization concerns a small boy left with an elderly baby-sitter, who insisted that he call her "Grandma." She was a pleasant-appearing, bespectacled gray-haired woman, who proved to be a highly unsuccessful baby-sitter. By the time his parents came home, the child was bitterly unhappy.

A month or so later, the little boy's quite glamorous and youthful-looking grandmother, whom he had not seen for some years and had forgotten, came to visit and was introduced to him as "Grandma." His reactions were chilly. Indeed, it was days before he would make a friendly gesture toward her, or respond to one offered by her. The process responsible was, of course, verbally mediated generalization. To one lady, who had given him a bad time, he had learned to apply the term "Grandma." "Grandma," applied to another lady who came into his home, mediated to him the whole complex of unhappy associations he had had to the first grandma, and produced the same responses of dislike and avoidance.

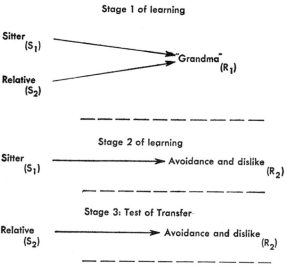

Stage 1 of learning

Sitter (S₁)

Relative (S₂)

"Grandma" (R₁)

Stage 2 of learning

Sitter (S₁) → Avoidance and dislike (R₂)

Stage 3: Test of Transfer

Relative (S₂) → Avoidance and dislike (R₂)

Fig. 4.7. A diagrammatic illustration of a case of verbally mediated generalization, illustrating an account in the adjacent text

In other words, although he had never had unpleasant experiences with his real grandmother, the experience with the baby-sitter who insisted on being called "Grandma" transferred, through learned meanings, to his real grandmother. The concept "Grandma" included two ladies; and the sentiments and reactions learned to the sitter (S₁) transferred, via words and their associations, to the real grandma (S₂) in the absence of his knowing anything directly, whether positive or negative, about her.

The child who has learned that a bad, punishing, rejecting parent is "boss", and who has also learned that teachers are "bosses," may transfer, via verbal mediation, the negative and frightened feelings he has toward his parents to the first teacher he encounters. Parents—particularly, it seems, punitive ones—often assist destructive verbal mediation by such preparation for school as this: "Just wait until you get to school! The teacher will whip you into shape!"

DISCRIMINATION LEARNING

Establishing Discriminations

In the preceding section it was noted that a child or adult trained to react to medium gray will respond, less often but still frequently, to medium-light or medium-dark gray. Such imprecise reactions (or generalizations) are likely to cause trouble in real life when the reaction is supposed to be to the correct thing *only,* not to something resembling it, however close the resemblance may be. Precise reaction calls for *discrimination* between what is correct and what is similar but incorrect.

In a simple case of discrimination learning, the subject is given a reward or reinforcement when he reacts to the correct stimulus—for purposes of illustration, medium gray. This reinforcement may consist of such things as money, a piece of candy, or praise. But when the closely similar stimulus of medium-light gray is responded to, no reinforcement, or punishment, or a delayed reinforcement (reinforcement distant in time from the response) is provided. Thus, approach-positive tendencies are built up to medium gray; and avoidance-negative tendencies to medium-light gray. The gradient of generalization, in other words, steepens: In Figure 4.6, for example, it would no longer extend from medium to medium-light gray, but only to medium grays so close together that they were beyond the limits of perceptual differentiation for the subject.

Such learning is easiest to establish when medium gray and medium-light gray are presented together (simultaneous discrimination); probably harder when they are presented one after the other; and still harder when, for example, an adult or child is asked to respond by pressing the left-hand telegraph key when the medium-gray member of the stimulus pair is presented on the right, but the right-hand key when medium-light gray is presented on the left. This last case is called *successive discrimination,* and is the sort that children are required to make constantly in the earlier stages of reading, when, for example, they are expected to respond one way to *s-a-w,* and another to *w-a-s;* one way to *l-a-d,* and another to *l-a-p,* and so on. Much practice is necessary in such cases before the complex stimulus, *l-a-d,* comes to be identified by the child as *"el-a-the one with the loop on the left and the line sticking up in the air,"* and is differentiated from the other complex stimulus, *l-a-p,* *"el-a-the one with the loop on the right and the line sticking down."* Only after such stimulus compoundings and differentiations have been patiently established, through endless teacher and parent reinforcements of "Yes, right," and "No, wrong," does the quick, effortless comprehension of *l-a-d* as *lad,* and *l-a-p* as *lap,* occur. It is fairly easy to learn to discriminate *d*'s presented simultaneously with *p*'s; *d*'s presented with *b*'s are less easily discriminated because of their greater similarity; and the appropriate function of these letters in successively presented words is discriminated least easily of all.

Acquired Distinctiveness of Cues

Secondary and mediated generalization involve the learning of similarities between, and common reactions to, two things that are not necessarily similar but "serve the same general purpose." *Acquired distinctiveness of cues* enables one to act *differentially* in situations that have considerable objective similarity to each other but call for differential behavior.

To the small child, a nickel and a dime are perceptually quite similar to each other, yet it is advantageous for the child offered a choice between them to choose the latter. Preteaching that *this* coin is a nickel and *this* one a dime, until the child has learned to attach the names appropriately, gives these objectively rather similar stimuli extra stimulus differentiation—makes them, cognitively, more unlike each other than they originally were because they have acquired added meanings or verbal stimulus properties. Thus, the appropriate discrimination or choice is facilitated in a later learning situation in which the child is expected to choose the more valuable, but smaller, coin. Children with such pretraining will learn faster than those without it.

Pretraining of this kind is one of the factors in reading readiness. The child who has been taught that d = "dee," while b = "bee," will be more ready to discriminate between *gab* and *gad* than the child who has not learned this. The child who has clearly learned that left is left, and right is right, and that in the United States one reads from left to right, will differentiate between *saw* and *was* more easily than the youngster who does not know his directions.

In other words, any addition of differentiating cues to objectively similar stimuli makes them more unlike, and hence, later, more easily discriminated from each other.

Transposition

The discrimination theory that has been discussed indicates that coming to choose, or prefer, one stimulus rather than another that originally had equal value results from having received rewards for choosing the first and no-reward, punishment, or a delayed reward for choosing the second. If *a* is correct, *b* incorrect, and if the child is confronted with both at the same time, he says, in effect, to himself, "Approach *a*, avoid *b*." If they are presented one at a time, he says "Approach" to *a*, "Avoid" to *b*. In the successive discrimination situation (such as learning the difference, in standard reading training, between a *b* and a *d*), he learns, "If *b*, then not *duh*, but *buh*; but if *d*, then *duh*, not *buh*." This is analogous to training the rat to approach left and avoid right for the white stimulus; and to go right and avoid left for the black.

But experimental psychology as well as real life frequently requires relative, or relational, rather than absolute choices. Let us suppose that a subject, *without specification of the principle,* is trained to choose the larger of two squares. Then he is presented with two different squares, the *larger* of them being the same size as the *smaller* of the two to which he has been trained. At least as often as not, and usually more often, a *relational choice* (according to the principle, "larger," rather than according to an absolute property of the stimulus—its size) is correct. Making such relational choices is called *transposition*.

Transposition can be predicted by learning theory, although the prediction is based on theories too complex to be presented here. This theory leads to the prediction that, if a very young child has been trained to choose the smaller of two squares, one of 100 and the other of 85 square inches, he will be more likely to transpose if his alternatives on a test trial are close in size to the original—for example, 75 and 60 square inches—than if they are very different from the original—for example, 30 and 15 square inches.

However, when children are old enough to have learned the concepts "smaller" and "larger," transposition or relational choice seems to occur regardless of the difference of the test-stimulus pair from the training pair. In this case, it may be said that verbal mediation has taken place. Examples of research demonstrating transposition have been provided by Kuenne (1946), and Spiker, Gerjuoy, and Shepard (1956).

Learning to Learn

For higher animals and children, problem-solving ability seems to increase with increasing practice, even though each new problem may be different from its predecessor (see, for instance, Harlow, 1949). This tendency is roughly analogous to mediated generalization, but what is transferred is a "problem-solving set" rather than a technique for solving a particular problem. This issue is discussed in more detail in Chapter 7. Such a "set" results in progressive efficiency in problem-solving, even when the problems have little in common. It is a general way of approaching life which is held to be desirable, and which is one of the aims of child-rearing and education.

DRIVE OR MOTIVATION

It has already been mentioned that organisms do not learn unless some *motive* or *drive* exists. A drive or motive performs one or more of three functions (Farber, 1955): it *energizes* or *sensitizes, selects,* and *directs.* Drives are frequently classified as *primary* and *secondary.* A *primary drive* is considered to be one related to the biological needs that must be satisfied if life and the species are to be preserved. Hunger, thirst, and sex are illustrations of such biological drives. *Secondary drives* have been learned, presumably in the course of satisfying primary drives. Dependency and a need for mastery are illustrations of secondary drives, and aggression and anxiety may also belong to this category.

Energizing and Sensitizing Functions of Drive[3]

When a drive *energizes,* it puts the organism into a state of heightened activity "designed" to encounter maximal stimulation in the "hope" of finding stimuli that will reduce the drive. When the drive acts as a *sensitizer,* stimuli pertinent to reducing the drive are more likely to be perceived than when the drive is not operating: their *perceptual threshold* is lowered.

In the beginning of an organism's life, the energizing function of drive is entirely, or at least partially, unlearned. This function may be illustrated by an example taken from the behavior of a two-week-old baby. If

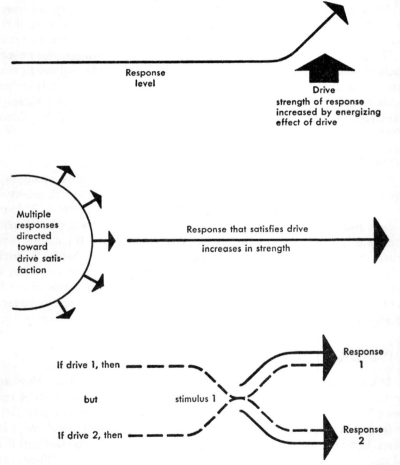

Fig. 4.8.   A schematic representation of the three major functions of drive or motive

---

[3] This discussion of the threefold function of drive is based on an analysis originally made by Melton (1950).

we first begin to observe him an hour after he has been fed and changed, we find him very relaxed, breathing evenly and deeply. His hands, arms, legs, neck, and head—indeed, his whole body—are still, almost limp. Observed at the second hour after feeding, he remains relaxed, but occasionally clenches and unclenches his hands. This motion is not an intense one. As we watch him during the third hour after feeding, we see his hands grow more active; he "flutters" with them. Presently, he makes motions with his arms; his head turns; his mouth purses; he moves his feet and legs. Then, as the third hour draws to a close, he is in motion "all over." He moves his head restlessly; arms and hands and legs move; his color heightens. Then his eyes open, and, after a moment of adaptation to the light, his body comes to even more vigorous motion. He vocalizes, whimpers, cries—first plaintively, then vociferously, with total body action and deeply flushed features accompanying the crying. Every parent recognizes the symptoms: the baby is hungry. The only thing that will stop this feverish activity for more than a few seconds is food. The intensity of the baby's hunger drive is directly proportional to his "time of deprivation" (the amount of time that has gone by since he was last fed).

Thus drive, in its energizing sense, has put the baby's whole body in motion so that he may make contact with a maximal range of stimulation in the "hope" that one of the stimuli encountered by his many responses will reduce his drive or satisfy him (in this case, supply him with the breast or bottle). The responses of sucking and head-turning to the bottle are the ones that eventually put him in touch with the nipple.

The sensitizing function of drive is similarly adaptive. When drive energizes, the organism is more active and presumably more likely to encounter drive-reducing stimuli. When drive sensitizes, the threshold for appropriate stimuli is lowered. Logically, it would seem that the sensitizing function of drive owes more to learning than the energizing function. All of the processes discussed earlier in the chapter may well have contributed to this sensitizing function: in some cases, it has been affected by classical conditioning, in others, by instrumental learning. Generalization operates, in that stimuli like those that earlier satisfied the drive are now perceived as worth exploring, while those that are clearly different from the original stimuli are ignored.

The added alertness that goes with the sensitizing function of drive puts the organism (child) in touch with the stimuli appropriate for satisfying whatever drive is operating.

At three o'clock in the afternoon, the three-year-old may run happily through the kitchen a dozen times, at no time attending to any of the stimuli it provides. But at 4:30 or 5:00, a trip through the kitchen is suddenly halted; he stops, cries, "I'm hungry," and begins to yank at the cupboard where he knows the cookies are, or the drawer where the bread and crackers are kept. He is suffering from "time of deprivation." His heightened hunger drive makes him more sensitive to stimuli that earlier had made no impression on him: the cupboards and drawers where cookies, bread, and crackers are kept.

Adults may work cheerfully all morning in a room close to a restaurant kitchen or bakery, at no time noticing the odors. But at 11:30, the smell stimuli suddenly impinge on them and they begin to feel ravenously hungry. This, too, is an example of the sensitizing function of drive.

Social or learned drives or motives may work in a similar manner. Preschool children who have been deprived of adult attention for a brief period of time will achieve more in an apparent attempt to gain attention (or satisfy their heightened dependency needs) than preschoolers not so deprived (see, e.g., Hartup, 1958). This result is analogous to the energizing function of drive. The young child in an institution reacts with exaggeration to the smallest attention of the visiting adult—perhaps an illustration of the sensitizing function of drive.

The Selective Function of Drive

The baby discussed above, who becomes progressively more restless with the passage of time since his last feeding, exhibits, in his most excited state, a number of different behaviors. He (1) cries; (2) thrashes with his arms and legs; (3) agitates his torso; (4) rolls his head; (5) intersperses crying with sucking movements; (6) agitates his legs. When the bottle is between his lips, all these movements except sucking diminish or disappear. As he grows a little older, the touch of the bottle or breast on his face will terminate all these responses except an adaptive head-turning in the direction of the nipple, seeking motions with his lips, and eventual sucking responses. Still later, the mere sight of the bottle will terminate the random behavior and cause him to get ready for the nipple. In other words, the reward (food) that reduces the drive helps the baby to *select* appropriate or facilitating responses: first sucking, then seeking, and, later, grasping.

The rat and the trip bar that provided the illustration of instrumental conditioning also illustrate the operation of the selective function of drive. The rat's original reactions to the CS (the trip bar) may have included nibbling at it, jumping over it, sniffing it, creeping under it, and, finally, tripping it quite by accident as he climbs on it. Having received a piece of food immediately after depressing the bar, he will soon tend to prefer the vicinity of the bar to other parts of the cage; an increase in the tendency to react to the bar by climbing on it, rather than sniffing it or going under it, will come later; and, finally, from the numerous responses involved in climbing, the more efficient response of pushing with one or both front paws will be selected as the method of responding to the bar.

All our learning involves *selecting* and *fixing,* through reinforcement, some responses and *eliminating* or *extinguishing* others. For our purposes, reinforcement may be said to strengthen the tendency for a given stimulus to evoke a given response; the most usual reinforcement occurs because the response that was made reduced the drive that was associated with or produced the stimulus in the first place. However, there appear to be instances of reinforcements provided by increased rather than reduced drive (as, for example, in sexual fantasy without orgasm). In any event, it is here assumed that reinforcement is provided, if not by drive *reduction,* at least by some type of drive *satisfaction.*

An adult, seeking a certain right-hand turnoff in a strange city, consults a city map before he begins his trip. He makes mental approximations of distances, and fixes certain landmarks in his mind. As he reaches the first of these landmarks, he begins to drive more slowly, and with more hesitation. He strains to read street signs well before he reaches them. He becomes mildly anxious. At last, he succeeds in making the appropriate right turn. On his second trip over the same route, many of his earlier behaviors have been eliminated. He is less anxious; he strains less to anticipate street signs; his hesitations are fewer. He moves later to the slow, right-hand lane of traffic. At the same time, some responses have become selected or strengthened: he recognizes the hospital that stands in the block before the necessary right turn. At sight of it, he smoothly and confidently moves into place for his turn.

This function of drive, then, is the one that helps to eliminate maladaptive or inefficient responses; and assists in establishing efficient, instrumental ways of behaving.

The Directive Function of Drive

The energizing function of drive is innate, serving the biological economy by increasing the probability of the organism's coming into contact with stimuli that will reduce the drive, thus enabling it to survive. More learning accompanies the sensitizing than the energizing function, but it too is directed toward survival. The selective function of drive is synonymous with learning, in the sense that it results in greater efficiency in satisfying drive. The directive function is learned—it is a *cue* function. For one drive plus a given stimulus, one type of behavior is appropriate; for another drive and the *same* stimulus, another behavior is chosen. This function of drive enables the individual to choose one of two or more behaviors already potentially available to him, each of which is equally appropriate to the stimulus (when "stimulus" is considered only as an objective event or thing). The drive *provides information* to the individual about how he should behave: it is, itself, an informative stimulus.

By way of illustration, let us consider three-year-old Sally. Sally has been up very late on Tuesday night, and awakens to go to nursery school on Wednesday somewhat the worse for wear. She arrives, passes the nurse's inspection, and enters the playroom. She sees a blue blanket in the doll corner (the stimulus) and approaches it. Her drive (avoidance of the unpleasant symptoms of fatigue), coupled with the blanket, suggests to her that she pick up the blanket, take it to a cot, and lie down with it to rest.

The drive, in other words, interacts with the objective stimulus and directs her behavior. But on Wednesday night Sally goes to bed early, and arrives at school rested and bursting with energy. Her drive is for exploration and play; this drive couples in an informational or cue fashion with the same blue blanket in the same doll corner. But this time, the information it gives leads to using the blanket as one prop in a lively game of housekeeping in which she plays the role of mother, and recruits several other children to play the parts of brothers, sisters, father, and baby.

In the same fashion, the lonely adult may welcome a large, formal social function; on the other hand, after a week filled with social activities, the notion of attending a similar function may be repugnant. Or, after moving to a strange city with accompanying mild or severe loneliness, the mental stimuli of friends or relatives prompt voluminous letter-writing; after six months, when many new friends have been made, the same mental stimuli may prompt only the grudging reaction: "Oh, I should write to Uncle Herbert, but I don't really want to!" The kitchen smells that were so hunger-arousing before lunch may be mildly unpleasant after a heavy meal. In each case, different drives coupled with the same objective stimuli have directed the individual to choose very different responses from among those available to him.

REWARD AND LEARNING

Although it is not accepted by all that a drive must be reduced if learning is to occur, it is granted that learning typically occurs when drive is reduced. The agent or thing that reduces the drive is commonly referred to as the *reward*. There may be cases where more stimulation or greater drive is sought (see, e.g., Hebb, 1955, and J. S. Brown, 1955). In such a situation, increased stimulation or drive may be thought of as the reward. In any event, reward, coupled with drive, is known to result in learning.

The aspects of reward considered to bear most directly on learning are its *amount, consistency,* and *immediacy*. A reward, of course, must be *relevant* to the drive associated with the activity that results in obtaining it before learning will occur. To the full but sleepy infant, more food is not a reward; nor are soda crackers to the extremely thirsty child. The delinquent is not interested in the approval of the community pastor; and to the shy, plain, but bright girl, another A will be less rewarding than being asked to go to the movies with a boy of her age.

It has often been stated (e.g., by Mussen and Conger, 1956), that learning is directly proportional to the amount, immediacy, and consistency of reward. According to this principle, the greater the reward, the sooner it follows the action designed to obtain it, and the more consistently it occurs, the higher the level of learning will be. There is some question about the complete accuracy of these conclusions.

At the present stage of research knowledge, it seems more accurate to say that *speedier* learning occurs with large, immediate, and consistent rewards; but that small, somewhat delayed, and inconsistent rewards eventually produce about the same *level* of learning.

There is evidence to indicate that behavior acquired through inconsistent reward (more commonly known as *partial reinforcement*) reaches its asymptote more slowly than under consistent-reward conditions. But such behavior is more resistant to extinction and will remain longer in the individual's behavior repertory. One tentative explanation for this fact is that the partially reinforced animal or child "continues to hope." He has had the experience of efforts sometimes being rewarded, sometimes not, so that extinction training is a less radical alteration for him than it is for the animal or child who has had consistent reinforcement (see, e.g., Crum, Brown, and Bitterman, 1951; Hake, Grant, and Hornseth, 1951; Jenkins and Stanley, 1950; and Lauer and Estes, 1955). Knowledge concerning the role of partial reinforcement, "hope" or expectancy, and extinction is incomplete at present. Although most of the research has been done with animals, the phenomena also seem to characterize children (see, e.g., Bijou, 1957; Rosenblum, 1956).

Human life is so complex, the relations between parents and children and teachers and children so varied, that it is fortunate that children seem to be able to learn, and learn well, from small, often delayed, and necessarily inconsistent rewards. Their *own symbolic behavior* often seems to constitute the only reward they get for many performances, yet they learn. On the face of it, complete consistency is impossible between parent and child, if for no other reason than that the parent is not always with the child. No teacher can give every one of the 25 or more children in her class a reward, even a word of approbation, every time he does something praiseworthy; nor can she administer punishment (reproof, correction, or criticism) every time he does something not praiseworthy. She has too many other children to deal with, and she cannot guide the child in every detail of his academic or personal learning during the school day.

SUMMARY

One of the most striking and exciting attributes of the normal child is that he *learns*. Learning is "a change in performance as a function of practice," although this definition ignores the difference between performance— that which is *manifested*—and learning, which may consist of "knowing better" or "knowing how," but not demonstrating it. Since learning, in the latter sense, is not subject to measurement, this volume does not make the distinction between performance and learning, although its plausibility is granted.

Maturation (roughly, growth and development) and learning cannot be separated in the development of a child, any more than we can separate H_2O and still have water. Nor can their relative importance be assessed, since both are essential, hence "all-important."

For babies, learning is likely to be slow, and to advance through a process of trial and error. Many aspects of it are almost automatic, as in classical conditioning, during which a new stimulus comes to evoke a response already present. Instrumental learning, more goal-directed, results in the child's being able to use tools to accomplish his ends. These tools may be words or behaviors.

Primary and secondary generalization play a major role in human learning. If a response is learned to one stimulus, the same response is likely to be evoked by other stimuli similar to it along dimensions of physical likeness (primary generalization) or meaning (secondary generalization). Transposition is akin to secondary generalization, and is the name applied to the ability of older children and adults to respond, in general, to the *relations between things* rather than to their absolute properties. Relational response is ordinarily more adaptive than absolute response, and underlies our ability to make generalizations.

Although it is important and useful to respond to life in terms of general laws, accurate discriminations are also necessary. Secondary generalization, transposition, and mediated generalization allow the older child and the adult to behave according to generalized abstractions; but acquired distinctiveness of cues enables them to make the fine distinctions that are equally necessary.

Drive and motivation can be separated from learning no more than learning can be separated from maturation. There are three major functions of drive: (1) the energizing and sensitizing function, which, by increasing the organism's activity, increases his chances of encountering the stimuli necessary to reduce his drive; he is also more alert to appropriate stimuli; (2) the selective function, which helps him to slough off behavior irrelevant to satisfying his motive, thus making him more efficient; and (3) the directive function, which, following considerable learning, enables him to act adaptively to the same stimuli under different drives, or different strengths of drive.

Reward, typically, results in strengthening (or establishing) the rewarded behavior. Although large, immediate, and consistent rewards may result in *speedier* learning, approximately the same *level* of learning appears to be reached with small, delayed, and inconsistent reward (or punishment).

Special Factors in Human Learning

THE preceding chapter contained an abbreviated discussion of some of the basic principles of learning. These principles mesh with the general point of view developed by the Yale-Iowa, or Hullian, theory of learning. This theory is by no means accepted by all psychologists, but it is relatively complete and has demonstrated its usefulness in predicting and understanding many aspects of human behavior. Its proponents believe most of its principles apply both to humans and animals, although much of the research on which it is based has used animals, not humans, as subjects.[1]

The most important psychological difference between the human being and other animals is that the human possesses a rich symbolic system, the most conspicuous aspect of which is speech. Speech makes possible an infinite variety of symbolization: using it, one can plan ahead, or practice a task unofficially by thinking about a previous practice session. Speech makes insight possible, and provides substitute or fantasy satisfactions for primary needs. All of these functions of symbols make the study of human learning much trickier than animal learning, and there are those who believe that the understanding of human learning will require a theoretical system entirely different from one developed for animals.

The following sections treat a number of tentative principles, some of which have been considered by learning theorists, others not. Many of the ideas presented are frankly speculative, since little, if any, research has been done concerning them.

EXPECTANCIES AND PROBABILITY

Consciously or unconsciously, we appear to behave as we do partly in terms of probability "estimates." No one with the slightest common sense darts across the street at an unlighted intersection if the chances are as low as 50-50 that he will reach the other side in one piece. Seldom do we make

[1] Animals are much used in psychological research because they are easier to work with than humans. The experimenter does not have to plead with them to cooperate. They can be studied without interrupting their schoolwork. One does not run the risk of "hurting their feelings." They do not confide to other potential subjects the purpose and procedure of the experiment. Their living circumstances can be controlled. They act naturally, and do not attempt to hide their feelings, or behave as they think you *want* them to behave, and so on.

a formal estimate of probability under such circumstances, but we do usually wait until it appears that the nearest moving vehicle is far enough away so that chances of a safe crossing stand at about 100 to 1. We vary our odds according to our needs, however. If we are about to be late for an extremely important appointment, we will take more chances in crossing the street than if we are heading back to the office or to class with a time leeway of ten minutes. We might predict that the urgency or importance of the goal we are seeking will affect the risk we accept concerning the route to that goal: we will take more chances for an urgent goal or a big reward than for a small reward or a goal to which we are relatively indifferent.

The urgency of his goals will push an insecure child into behavior with a low probability of success: he will take great chances with his physical safety to impress his peers. Showing-off and daredevil behavior are perhaps attempts to obtain such goals. The bully, who usually chooses "safe," or high-probability, behavior, as represented by "picking on" smaller and younger children, will, when cornered, actually fight with someone as big and skillful as he to avoid losing face. His prestige is very valuable to him, so that he will risk much to maintain it: when safe routes are shut off, he will make the risky choice of fighting someone who may win.

Other things being equal, however, if there are several different procedures an individual can use to achieve his goal, he will take the one he estimates to have the highest probability of success. Interesting treatments of the theoretical role of expectancy are provided by such authors as Brunswik (1951), Lewin (1935), Rotter (1954), and Tolman (1932), who present and treat in detail ideas relating to those above.

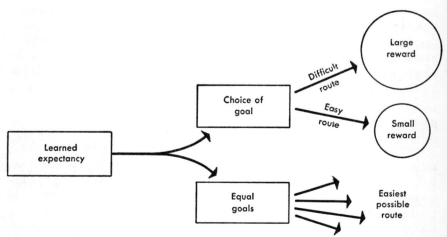

Fig. 5.1.   Expectancies determine the route of behavior

Motivation for one type of activity (goal) over another also depends to a substantial degree on the relative expectancy of success. The slow-learn ing child in a classroom full of normal and bright children estimates his chances of competing with his classmates at 0 to 100. Hence he does not try to accomplish even as much as he is able to, but chooses instead to be a trouble-maker. The nearsighted, scrawny junior-high student sees no chance of experiencing success at basketball in competition with his huskier classmates. He does not even report for basketball practice, but seeks his satisfaction in getting good grades, or in daydreaming.

A set of expectancies may be accurate with reference to the setting in which it has been learned, yet be both discouraging and maladjustive. If the slow-learning child of the previous illustration, who judges quite accurately that he cannot compete with his peers, generalizes this notion to the point where he does not compete even with himself, does not make *any* intellectual effort, then he seriously handicaps himself as far as his future success is concerned. When characteristics of children are compared with biased norms (standards), expectancies of limited accuracy may be developed that are seriously maladaptive. The girl who is as attractive as the average, but who grows up with three sisters who are raving beauties, may predict with a high level of personal certainty that she is homely and will never be able to catch a husband. She may generalize, or extend, this feeling to such a degree that she makes no effort to get along with boys. She may even snub them. Perhaps without knowing it, she is defending herself: "If I freeze them out first, they will have no chance to rebuff and hurt me." In such a case, obviously, she is causing her own expectancies to come true, thus reinforcing or proving them correct. But from an outsider's point of view, she could compete quite adequately in the "courtship market" were she able to relax and be self-confident in her behavior. The boy of average intelligence who grows up in a family of brilliant siblings may react similarly in the academic area, with a very similar result. He expects so definitely to fail that he *does* fail, and consequently proves to himself what he "knew" about himself all along. Such behavior might almost be called "self-fulfilling prophecies."

But unrealistic positive expectancies (which may also be based on biased samples) may lead to similar difficulties. The girl of somewhat above-average ability who goes to a school with low standards and is the brightest child in her class may develop a set of expectancies predicting success for herself as a lawyer or doctor or physicist. When she moves from high school to college, the falseness of her expectancies may be disastrously revealed. For the first time in her life she does badly. She has had no experience in dealing with academic failure or mediocrity, and accordingly she suffers deeply. The overprotected small child, going to public school for the first time and finding that he is not "king of the universe," may likewise experience great difficulty in his adjustment.

Expectancies such as those we have discussed are obviously learned. They are based partly on the information an individual has, or *thinks* he has, about an immediate situation. In the case of crossing the street, or entering a busy highway, he looks right and left, sees how many cars there are and what their distance from him is, and judges how rapidly they are moving. Depending on the information thus gathered and evaluated, he remains where he is or moves out. This, of course, is all done in terms of previous learning. One who has grown up crossing streets and driving in San Francisco or New York can assess his chances in heavy traffic accurately. One who has grown up on a ranch in Nevada may be confused and frightened by similar traffic.

Current expectancies, then, reflect previous learning. If a child has always been punished for being aggressive, and has thus been defeated, his expectancy of success in handling a new situation by being aggressive will be low (Rotter, 1954). If, on the other hand, he has repeatedly succeeded by acting in an aggressive fashion, his expectancy of success for aggressive behavior in a new situation will be high.

Rotter has also proposed that the effectiveness of a reward depends at least in part on the expectancy held for a given undertaking. If an individual has a low expectancy of success for behaving in a certain fashion, yet succeeds, the value or strength of reinforcement through success may be great. This may be related to partial reinforcement, as discussed in Chapter 4. After a chain of failures, a success is striking, hence particularly reinforcing. The shy girl who tries to flirt for the first time and finds that boys flock around her will have her flirting behavior strongly reinforced. The timid boy who suddenly finds that, by speaking up and being aggressive, he can get his way, will have such behavior much strengthened. Maturity, in many senses of the term, depends on such revelations: the adolescent who has always thought of herself or himself as gawky and unattractive overhears someone say, "What an attractive girl she has grown to be!" or "Isn't he getting to be a strapping young man?" Such a remark may alter expectancies radically. The saying, "Nothing succeeds like success," may be based on such an alteration of expectancies.

Failure may operate in a similar way. Criticism or failure may serve as an excellent motivating device for the bright and able child yet discourage and handicap the child who is already doing poorly; whereas reward does not do very much "extra" for the bright and successful but motivates the unsuccessful child highly. Rotter's notions fit well here: the bright child expects to succeed, hence success and praise do not surprise him or raise him to new levels of performance. He does not expect to fail or be criticized; hence, when such things happen to him, the effect is great. The punishment, as it were, is so severe that he redoubles his efforts to avoid encountering it again. The failing child expects failure and criticism, hence it has little effect on him except to confirm his beliefs and reduce his effort. But an experience of praise or reward is so striking and sweet that he works doubly hard to encounter such a state of affairs again.

An ingenious experiment (Spector, 1956) related to the propositions discussed above has been done with young men in a simulated military situation. Thirty-six teams of four men each were placed in a situation where their performance on a group task presumably had a direct effect on whether they would be promoted from corporal to sergeant. Half the groups were told that three out of the four men in the group would be promoted (high expectancy for promotion); half were told that only one of the four men would be promoted (low expectancy). These groups were then halved again, all the men in half the groups (regardless of previous information) being promoted, all the men in the other half of the groups failing to receive promotion.

After having completed two tasks and receiving or failing to receive promotion, the men were asked questions designed to tap their morale. These questions dealt with such factors as the attractiveness of the group for its members, satisfaction with the two tasks that had been assigned to the group, evaluation of the group's productivity, etc. A composite score of morale was made up from the answers to these questions.

From the highest to the lowest morale score, the results follow in orderly progression: men with low expectancy who received promotions reported the highest morale; men with high expectancy who were promoted came next; men with low expectancy who were not promoted were third; while men with high expectancy who were not promoted suffered the most damage to morale. The average morale scores for the different groups were in many cases not greatly different from each other, but their arrangement in the order obtained could happen by chance only once in 24 times. The actual fact of promotion or nonpromotion, however, had a greater over-all effect on morale than did high or low expectancy.[2]

The usefulness of an expectancy in guiding behavior depends upon the *completeness* and *accuracy* of the information possessed by the individual. The information which the urban three-year-old has about busy streets is perhaps as complete as that of the ten-year-old, but it is less accurate. Hence we leave the ten-year-old reasonably free to move around unsupervised, but keep a watchful eye on the three-year-old in all potentially dangerous situations. The girl of average good looks who has grown up in a family of beautiful sisters has neither complete nor accurate information about her own appearance, and may require much re-education before she revises her expectancies. We have seen how these expectancies govern her behavior, so that they are in effect confirmed. The friendly and gregarious eight-year-old who has had an overwhelming majority of experiences of being liked and accepted by strangers enters a new school with a broad grin and an open and friendly interest in his new classmates. They are flattered, relax, and soon accept him, thus confirming his expectancies. The occasional social

[2] This experiment must be criticized on one score: men whose internal expectancies did not conform with the instructions given them by the experimenter (men who were skeptical or who kept their own previous expectancies) were excluded from the analysis of results that reached statistical significance—an illustration of one of the research faults discussed in Chapter 2.

failure he may have causes him, in terms of this theory, to redouble his efforts to be accepted.

CURIOSITY

Many people who have worked with the higher mammals, such as monkeys and chimpanzees, or with children, have been struck by the tendency of such subjects to be "curious." Even when well-fed, not thirsty, and, as nearly as can be ascertained, generally comfortable or in "equilibrium," such subjects constantly explore their environment. Some investigators have postulated a "curiosity drive" to account for this behavior; others talk of an "activity drive." Hebb (1955) may have in mind a phenomenon such as this when he speaks of the organism's seeking an optimal stimuation level. It is difficult to see how the so-called primary drives (thirst, hunger, need for elimination, etc.) produce such common behavior as we see in the warm, dry, recently fed baby who kicks, chews, and bangs his rattle, waves his hands in a dance "just for fun," and is never still for a moment while he is awake.

Some studies present evidence suggesting that curiosity is a drive, possessing the properties of energizing and sensitizing, selecting, and directing behavior. In one of these (Montgomery and Segall, 1955), rats learned to discriminate between black and white when the reward for a correct choice was the opportunity to run for one minute in a situation new to them. In another (Montgomery, 1955), it was found that tame rats, who had been handled, preferred "risky" open elevated runaways; whereas wild rats, presumably more uneasy in the whole experimental situation, chose "safe" enclosed runways. Curiosity, operating as a drive, was thought to be responsible for both sets of results, and it was proposed that curiosity and fear are antagonistic drives, with fear inhibiting curiosity.

Glanzer (1958) has published an excellent theoretical review of the literature on curiosity and stimulus satiation, in which he suggests that an organism requires a certain amount of information—stimulation—per unit of time. If enough information is not present in the organism's environment, it will be actively sought. If too much stimulation is present, the organism tries to reduce the amount. In animals, this may take the form of freezing, avoidance, and even seizure. It has already been suggested (Chapter 1) that the human infant may seek to reduce stimulation by sleeping, although this avoidance or reduction phenomenon has not been studied as such in humans.

Glanzer sets up a postulate that, if correct, has profound implications for early child-rearing. He suggests that an organism's requirements for information are set by its past experience. If a high flow of information has been directed at it in the past, it will have high requirements later (be highly curious?). Coming from an impoverished informational environment, a low requirement or standard will be established. This postulate suggests differential effects of early and late experience—new information is predicted to have more effect on changing the organism's standard, and therefore its behavior, if given earlier rather than later in life. There is considerable direct and indirect evidence to support this prediction, with respect to both animal and human problem-solving behavior (intelligence). This material is presented in considerable detail in Chapters 7 and 8.

In explaining and predicting human behavior, a distinction is often made between *primary* and *secondary* drives. *Primary* drives refer to the "universal," and usually physiological, drives, such as hunger and thirst; whereas *secondary* drives are thought to be learned. Examples of drives usually considered to be secondary, or learned, are those for dependency, love and affection, and so on. The question has been raised whether certain drives, particularly curiosity, anxiety, and aggression, are primary or secondary drives (indeed, as will be pointed out a little later, the question has been raised whether they are drives at all). Such a classification is not of great *practical* significance, since in either case a drive operates in about the same way. Furthermore, our culture seems to provide opportunities for *all* its members to learn curiosity, aggression, and anxiety, thus satisfying the criterion of *universality* which a postulated drive should have if it is to be widely useful in explaining behavior.

There is a certain logical appeal, on the other hand, to considering curiosity as a well-established "habit of responding," or a well and probably universally learned set of expectancies. Very early in the life of any higher organism, its own activities have resulted in reward: by wriggling closer to the mother, mammals have found warmth; by sucking, they have found nourishment; by pawing and grasping, they have secured food more easily. A general learning might be postulated, functioning almost like a trait: "Something occurs following moving around and trying out things." This "something" may be good or it may be painful, but the probabilities are that, at least for children, curiosity results more often in reward than in punishment. It is to be hoped that the average parent rewards curiosity more often than he punishes it—questions are answered, new toys are purchased, and so on.

It might be postulated that secure children, who experience reward more frequently than punishment, will be more curious than children for whom the ratio is reversed. However, the principle of partial reinforcement may also apply to curiosity: even if curiosity is rewarded only occasionally, it will be reinforced as a response system (the needs it serves will be reduced, hence it will be consolidated), thus functioning in the practical sense much like a drive. Nor is it inconceivable for curiosity to develop when the learning history of the child includes a preponderance of punishments over rewards. In such a case, a portion of the motive or drive producing curious behavior would be anxiety: in effect, one had best be curious and learn about his environment in order to avoid the pain inherent in it. Curious behavior would then serve to reduce both anxiety and curiosity.

For humans, confirmation of expectancies, quite without other reward, may also be reinforcing. Things happen to the curious child. Even though they are apparently neutral in a reward sense, the mere confirmation of his expectancies is rewarding to him. There is no question that being able to say "I was right," without any other reward, is satisfying, hence rewarding, to older children and adults. Observation leads us to believe that younger children and even infants are also gratified by being "right." The game of peek-a-boo may have as part of its reward the constant confirmation of expectancies: "Mamma is still here, and I am still here." The endless glee resulting from opening, closing, and reopening a jack-in-the-box is perhaps another illustration of the rewarding nature of confirmation of expectancies. The morning ritual of checking for all the dolls, or looking to see whether the cat is in his accustomed place (without any apparent interest in playing with or petting the cat), may also illustrate this "expectancy-confirming" phenomenon. Confirmation of expectancies may thus be security-giving.

For our present purposes, curiosity is considered to be a drive or motive. Montgomery and his co-workers seem to have demonstrated that reducing curiosity results in learning in lower animals; observation indicates that curiosity exists in very young infants. Montgomery's research indicates that responses motivated by fear appear to inhibit or prevent curious responses, and the inhibition of *overt* curiosity about taboo subjects, such as sex, is a phenomenon familiar in our culture. Ordinarily, as children move into the elementary-school years, they ask other children, not their parents and teachers, about sex. Yet curiosity about sex persists.

Whether drive or habit, or a mixture of both, curiosity plays a basic role in human learning. It seems desirable to reinforce the behaviors that reduce or satisfy it, but *at the level at which it exists in the child.* An anecdote about the son of an astronomer is in order. The boy asked his mother about the planet Mars. "Why don't you ask your father?" she said. "He's the expert." The son's reply was: "Yes, but I don't want to know that much."

It is possible that mild frustration and partial reinforcement will result in stronger curiosity than consistent reward. Answers that come too easily are less rewarding than answers that require more effort. But consistent punishment of curious behavior, or indifference toward and failure to reward the responses designed to reduce curiosity, may either distort its expression and the means by which it is satisfied (as, in the sexual area, by "Peeping Tom" behavior), or result in apathy and resignation. The apathetic, bland acceptance of things as they are that has been reported as characteristic of institutionalized and extremely poor children may be due to the failure of their environment to reinforce curiosity behavior. One author (Hofstaetter, 1954) reports that most of our standard judgments of intelligence up to about 20 months of age are based on a factor he calls "sensorimotor alertness"—a term embracing behaviors that seem closely related to curiosity. The important idea that an information-rich environment in very early childhood results in the need for more stimulation (in more curiosity?) at later stages of development should not be neglected in research on child-rearing.

FIXATION

Not all human behavior is adaptive and rational. All of us have learned and persist in ways of behaving that range from being inappropriate and ineffective to being disruptive of our general well-being. The girl with such a fear of insects that even a fly fills her with acute discomfort and anxiety is not behaving rationally. Her behavior will not ruin her life, but it will be consistently inconvenient, embarrassing, and uncomfortable for her and, if her reactions are noticeable, for those around her. The adolescent whose sexual impulses are uncontrollably channeled into voyeurism, on the other hand, runs the risk of public disgrace and humiliation, and repeatedly places himself in a situation of serious personal danger. Yet he repeats his potentially ruinous behavior over and over again, even after he has been caught, beaten, and legally punished.

There are two common conceptions of fixation. The first, and more general one, refers to the forming of a very strong habit or association. The second, perhaps as widely used, is the Freudian, which refers specifically to either an arrest of libido at an immature stage of development (see Chapters 2 and 3) or its strong attachment to early and inappropriate love objects.

The present treatment of fixation regards it as a strong and persistent response which occurs regardless of whether it is appropriate or inappropriate, and even in the face of observable or predictable punishment. The assumption is, then, that this fixated response is somehow, in terms of tension reduction, rewarding. Such a conception of fixation seems to offer a model for Freudian theories of fixation; at least, it fits well with the Freudian defense mechanisms—postulated to reduce anxiety—which spring at least in part from fixation. The present conceptual treatment of fixation was, indeed, suggested quite directly by Freud, to account for the persistence of neurotic symptoms (and, presumably, those that serve more effectively as well). His treatment of fixation and the defense mechanisms has been further developed by such representatives of learning theory as Dollard and Miller (1950), R. R. Sears (1951), and Whiting and Child (1953).[3]

Because of its nature and frequency, it is important to try to understand fixation. Alcoholism, for example, can be thought of as a fixation. Estimates are that there are as many as 4,000,000 persons in the United States who are "problem drinkers." Men and women who persist in overeating despite their physician's well-based warning that they are "eating their way into the

[3] The conditioning paradigm for fixation has been developed in about this form by I. E. Farber (personal communication).

grave" may also be thought of as fixated on eating. The tendency to overeat is certainly one of the major health problems in the United States.

To develop a hypothesis of how a fixation is established, let us take the case of a small boy, Tommy, aged 16 months. Tommy is a toddler, not very steady on his feet. One day, before his parents can prevent it, the neighbor's bouncy terrier jumps at him, knocks him down, and stands over his face, breathing hotly at him and barking excitedly. Tommy screams convulsively, is very difficult to comfort, calms eventually, but goes into hysterics the next time he sees the dog. He also reacts with terror whenever he sees *any* dog. This terror generalizes to the tired old cat his parents own, and presently he shows acute fright reactions to all animals—even to the ducks at the zoo, to which he has previously enjoyed feeding stale bread. Such reactions go on for months; Tommy begins to have nightmares about animals, and no amount of reassurance, explanation, derision, or even punishment helps him. What has happened to Tommy?

The beginning of this behavior can be thought of as belonging to the family of the classical conditioned response, with the dog the conditioned stimulus, the sensations of being knocked down the unconditioned stimulus, the resulting pain and fear the unconditioned response, and the later fear, crying, and avoidance, the conditioned response.

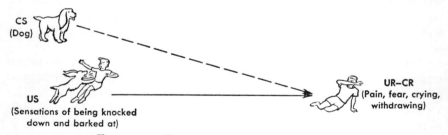

CS
(Dog)

US
(Sensations of being knocked down and barked at)

UR–CR
(Pain, fear, crying, withdrawing)

FIG. 5.2.   First stage in acquiring a fixation

Since this experience was an extremely *traumatic,* or frightening one, it is possible that conditioning, or more properly learning, could occur in one trial. Figure 5.2 demonstrates the observable, or overt, aspects of the first stage of the conditioning process. Figure 5.3 illustrates what may be happening "inside" Tommy.

The next stage of the fixation may be represented as it is in Figure 5.4. Here CS (the dog) arouses anxiety besides causing Tommy to be afraid, to cry, and to run away. *His being afraid, crying, and running away reduced his anxiety*—an anxiety rooted in his early, preverbal history. Hence punishment—such as scolding or derision, the meaning of which he has learned later, and which arouses either fear or shame—does not eliminate his hysterical behavior. Nor does comfort help greatly, since it (like scolding and derision) ordinarily occurs after the child has already reduced his anxiety in good part by crying and running away. For these reasons, the scolding, derision, and comfort do not become associated in a meaningful fashion with anxiety reduction. Since it is commonly assumed that anxiety is one of the most intolerable drives, anything that reduces it is heavily rewarded or reinforced, hence likely to be well-learned and extremely persistent.

Primary and secondary stimulus generalization also occurs in this situation, so that instead of reacting hysterically *only* to the dog that frightened him, Tommy reacts similarly to all dogs, cats, and to many or most other animals.

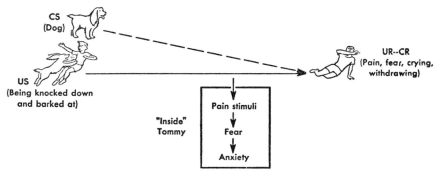

FIG. 5.3.   Internal aspects of the first stage of fixation

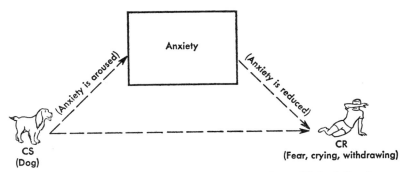

FIG. 5.4.   A diagrammatic representation of established fixation

The hypothetical case of the compulsive overeater is somewhat more complex than the illustration above. Let us create a fictitious adolescent, Mary, who, under her layers of fat, is a pretty girl, but whose fat causes boys as well as girls to shy away from her and poke fun at her. Physical examinations show nothing medically wrong with Mary; she could slim down if she would simply eat less. But, despite parental and medical urging and ostracism by her peers, she continues to eat "senselessly." Instead of slimming down, she grows even fatter. For Mary, going back to Figure 5.3, food may be thought of as the conditioned stimulus. Pain associated with hunger, perhaps as a result of rigid infant scheduling, is the unconditioned stimulus; and eating is the unconditioned-conditioned response that eliminates the hunger pains. If Mary's early hunger experiences have been painful enough, they may have evoked great anxiety, so that food (as the CS) evokes anxiety, and eating reduces it.

Through stimulus generalization, other anxiety-arousing stimuli may become conditioned stimuli for eating. Due to their similarity to the anxiety associated with eating, these new anxieties may in turn come to be reduced by eating. Since eating also satisfies the primary drive of hunger, it is a doubly reinforced response: Mary eats both to live and to keep herself from being anxious. In the face of such satisfactions, Mary foregoes popularity, parental approval, and good physical health.

Conditions under which fixation could conceivably be produced are listed and discussed below. In the present state of our research knowledge these are frankly speculative. But it seems reasonable that a response is likely to be fixated if one or several of the following conditions exist with reference to it:

1. A fixation depends on trauma or overlearning.

2. To be fixated, a response must satisfy a need (in the sense that this has been discussed).

3. Responses that require relatively little effort are more likely to be fixated than those that require great effort.

4. Responses that have been acquired and are maintained under conditions of partial reinforcement are most likely to be fixated.

5. It can be predicted, but less confidently, that the greater the reinforcement for a response, the more likely the response is to be fixated. Two reasons may be advanced for this prediction. First, let us think of the *likelihood that a response will occur* as a product of the amount of drive or need attached to it and the amount of previous learning that has occurred for it. Hence, if we have two competing responses of the same strength—one, for example, of avoiding a stimulus, the other of approaching it—the one with the greater drive or motive is more likely to occur and, under appropriate circumstances, to be reinforced.

For example, two-year-old Billy has been taught not to "raid the refrigerator." This habit (H) has a strength of 10, let us say. In combination with such a habit, Billy has a need or drive (D) of 10 to maintain the love and affection of his mother. The strength of his refrigerator-avoidance response, then, is D $\times$ H, or 100. Billy, however, has also learned to look to the refrigerator for food, and this habit has a strength of 10. If his hunger drive is low (5, for example), the two competing behaviors of raiding the refrigerator as opposed to "minding his mother" have respective excitatory potentials, or "likelihoods-of-occurring," that may be represented by the figures 50 and 100; Billy therefore avoids the refrigerator. The hungrier he gets, the stronger the drive that combines with the habit of refrigerator-raiding. When his hunger drive reaches a strength of 12, we see him moving in on the refrigerator. The "excitatory potential" for that response is now 12 × 10, or 120, and can compete successfully with his refrigerator-avoiding behavior, which has a strength of only 100. When both responses are at the same level (100 for both approach and avoidance), we may think of Billy as being in *conflict*. The greater the excitatory potential of the two matched responses, the greater the conflict may be (Brown and Farber, 1951). That is, if Billy is *very* attached to or afraid of his mother, and also very hungry, his conflict may be stronger than if he is only moderately attached to or afraid of his mother, and moderately hungry. It should be added that this account is oversimplified and ignores, for example, the fact that increased hunger drive may combine, not only with refrigerator-opening responses, but also with other responses.

Regardless of the level of his drive or habit, if Billy raids the refrigerator and gets away with it, his habit of doing so will be somewhat strengthened (reinforced). Habits accompanying the competing motive (regard for, or fear of, his mother) are not reinforced in this setting—hence lose in *relative* strength.

The second reason great reinforcement may be more likely to produce fixation than moderate reinforcement is that *the amount of reward has some bearing on the speed of learning.* Again using Billy and the refrigerator as an illustration, if Billy is *extremely* hungry, the *single* reinforcement of his refrigerator-raiding may have, for example, a value of 5 in increasing the habit, thus bringing its strength up to 15, comfortably (or uncomfortably for his mother) above his avoidance-habit strength of 10. But if he is more restless and bored than hungry, the increase in habit strength from a *single* refrigerator-opening response may be negligible, so that there is little or no resulting difference in the habit strength of refrigerator-raiding as opposed to mother-minding. In other words, a response made under high drive may increase in strength much more rapidly, each time it is made, than one made under low drive.

Related to the effect of amount of reinforcement on fixation is the effect of strong reinforcement in a strange situation, or when a child is under stress. It may be that strange situations arouse anxiety, and that anxiety adds to whatever motivation already exists. An event that reduces the anxiety *and other motives* may provide extra reinforcement for the response that brought about the event or is associated with it. A strong punishment in such a situation may, in similar fashion, reinforce whatever responses result in escape from punishment.

There is also some evidence to indicate that wider stimulus generalization occurs under circumstances of anxiety. One study (Levy and McCandless, 1952) indicates that subjects who were administered electric shock in a situation about which they had no information later expected more frequent shocks than those who had been shocked but had (or thought they had) information about the experimental circumstances. Evidence (Mednick and Lehtinen, 1957) also exists indicating that younger children show wider stimulus generalization than older ones, from which we can possibly infer that children generalize more widely than adults. If this is true, some basis is provided for arguing that the same experience may have more widespread effects on children than on adults.

APPROACH-AVOIDANCE, CONFLICT, AND DISPLACEMENT

Approach-Avoidance Gradients

The idea of approach-avoidance has already been introduced with reference to Billy and his refrigerator-opening behavior. Hunger combining with habit (previous learning) cause him to approach; but love for and need of his mother, in combination with habit, cause him to avoid. Lewin (1935) has discussed what he calls positive and negative valence (attraction-repulsion), and has hypothesized that negative valence lasts a shorter time and extends a shorter distance from the goal than does positive valence. Miller (e.g., 1951), working with similar concepts, postulated *approach-avoidance gradients*. Experimental work by Miller and his students (e.g., Murray and Berkun, 1955), as well as that of such workers as Judson Brown, has lent factual support to these ideas.

Taking a simple case, let us say that a white rat has been both shocked and fed in a goal box. In him will have been built up tendencies both to approach and to avoid the goal box. Figure 5.5A demonstrates the "spread" of the two gradients of approach-avoidance tendencies in terms of space from the goal box.

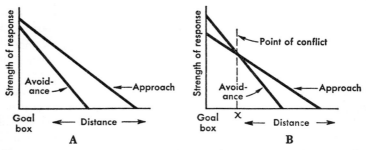

FIG. 5.5.   A schematic representation of approach-avoidance tendencies

It will be noted that in both A and B of Figure 5.5 the avoidance gradient is steeper (extends less far from the goal box) than the approach gradient. For Figure 5.5A, the avoidance gradient is not so high as the approach gradient, although at the goal box they are close together. It might be predicted that our white rat would move more slowly as the distance between the approach and avoidance gradients grew less, but that he would nonetheless proceed to the goal box and eat. This pattern might characterize Billy when his hunger reached the level at which he is ready to override his mother's prohibitions.

But in Figure 5.5B, the avoidance gradient at the goal box (or, in Billy's case, the refrigerator) is higher than the approach gradient. In the case of the white rat, this may be either because he is not very hungry or because he has been shocked more often or more intensely than he has been fed. In Billy's case, the same things might be postulated—that is, either he is not very hungry, or he has only recently been punished by his mother for refrigerator-raiding, or he is in a particularly dependent state so that he needs his mother very much.

Conflict

Since the avoidance gradient is steeper than the one for approach, Billy and the white rat are free to move to point X in Figure 5.5B, although again it might be predicted that they would move toward refrigerator or goal box more slowly as they approached it. At X, *conflict occurs and they are immobilized.* In other words, conflict can be defined as the place, or time, when *approach equals avoidance* in strength. This conflict may be resolved by time: as they hover at point X, they become hungrier. *Thoughts of food* (symbolic behavior) may serve almost instantaneously to increase Billy's hunger. For the nonthinking rat, only time, presumably, will accomplish this purpose. As their hunger drive increases, excitatory potential for approach is raised until the approach gradient is higher than the avoidance gradient and they move toward food. On the other hand, ideas of Billy's mother may enter his mind and raise his avoidance gradient to the point where conflict is removed by his leaving the entire situation. He "gets away from temptation."

The process of learning to read, or even of going to school at all, also illustrates approach-avoidance behavior. The good teacher is friendly and approachable; she "rules" with affection, kindness, and reward rather than with sarcasm and coldness. She attempts to understand each child in order to keep his anxieties and fears at a relatively low level and appropriate to the child's task rather than inappropriate. Some anxiety, when attached to appropriate, efficient responses, actually may result in their being more frequently made, hence reinforced. Thus, she strives to keep pupils' avoidance gradients low. By the same token, she tries to tie in her teaching with experiences from the children's own lives. She chooses textbooks that are suitably written, attractively put together, and interesting. In this fashion, she tries to raise pupils' motivation for learning, and this motivation in turn raises the approach gradient.

At the same time, teachers and parents are setting up different approach-avoidance gradients for activities that are detrimental to school learning. They praise (help to heighten approach gradients) when children do well in school. They typically criticize or punish when school success is low— that is, they set up avoidance gradients for pursuits that are incompatible with school success, such as dawdling, playing truant, daydreaming, and so on. There are social-class differences in the degree to which parents support the school (aid it in raising school-learning approach gradients; cooperate with it in discouraging behavior that may run counter to good school performance, such as regular school attendance, cooperation and courtesy in the classroom, etc.). Middle- and upper-class parents support the schools strongly; lower-class parents do so to a lesser degree. Observation and evidence (see Chapter 14) support such a point of view indirectly, and indicate that lower-class children do relatively less well in school than, for example, middle-class children. Many factors, of course, enter here, and this rather serious social problem is discussed in more detail in Chapter 14.

Displacement

Conflict has been defined as the state of an organism when affected by *equally strong approach and avoidance tendencies* toward a stimulus or goal. As has been pointed out, the organism may react with *immobility*. A child may *reason through* the conflict, thus *resolving* it, or may eventually approach because, as a function of delay, increase in drive occurs. The opposite may also happen: if avoidance tendencies increase sharply, the individual may simply *leave the situation* where conflict has occurred.

Ways of *avoiding* conflict, and of avoiding or diminishing the anxiety associated with it, also exist. Freud postulated a variety of defense mechanisms, such as repression, reaction formation and projection, and regression. One of the most important of these is *displacement*. Displacement seems most likely to occur when the original goal cannot be reached and when other goals, more or less similar to the original one, are available. Displacement is a *clinical* term, suggested by Freud. It is now thought that it is at least partially explainable by the *laboratory* term, generalization, which was discussed in Chapter 4. Miller (1948) and Dollard and Miller (1950) have given close attention to the concept of displacement, have related it to generalization and shown how it may be used as an important explanatory device for certain kinds of human behavior.

The girl angry with her teacher may *displace* her hostility so that she is saucy to her mother; or, if she fears her mother, or loves her so much that she cannot bring herself to be rude, she may abuse her younger brother. *Compensation* appears to be a special case of displacement: the boy who is shy, isolated, and inadequate in athletics may displace earlier efforts to excel physically onto his academic studies; or the boy inadequate academically may concentrate on becoming a star athlete or a school rowdy.

Miller (1948) discusses the assumptions that must be made before displacement can be used precisely in predicting human behavior. He states:

> Five assumptions are needed to deduce the tendency for displacement to occur in situations in which the direct response to the original stimulus is prevented by conflict. These are: (1) that the direct response to the original stimulus generalizes to other similar stimuli, with the amount of generalization becoming smaller the less similar

the stimuli; (2) that the response which conflicts with the occurrence of the direct response to the original stimulus also generalizes to other similar stimuli, becoming weaker the less similar the stimuli; (3) that the gradient of generalization of the conflicting response falls off more steeply with dissimilarity than does that of the original response which it inhibits; (4) that when two or more incompatible responses are simultaneously excited, the one with the greatest net strength will be the one which will occur; and (5) that the net strength of a response will be its strength minus that of any response incompatible with it which is excited at the same time. . . . In addition to these assumptions, two more will be useful in dealing with other aspects of the problem. One of these is (6) that an increase in the drive involved in either type of gradient will raise the overall height of that gradient. . . . The final assumption is (7) that gradients of generalization approximate the form of negative growth curves. (pp. 167–168)[4]

Granted these assumptions, most of which have been discussed earlier in this chapter, it is apparent that one stimulus can serve instead of another, one response take the place of another, substitute goals can be used, and, at least to some degree, gratification of some needs can be made to serve others.

An animal experiment by Murray and Berkun (1955) illustrates this process. Rats were placed in a three-alley maze, one alley black, one gray, and one white. Windows were cut in the walls between alleys to allow the animals to move from one to the other, as in Figure 5.6. The rats were first trained to seek food in the black (B) alley and goal box. After they had learned this, they were shocked in the black goal box until they had learned to avoid it. Previously they had explored all three alleys; but during training the alley windows had remained closed. On a test, the windows were opened. The dotted line in Figure 5.6 shows a typical rat's "path to the goal." At spot X in alley B, the rat comes into conflict (his approach gradient is crossed by his avoidance gradient). The rat retreats and passes through the window into the gray alley (G), similar to but different from the one in which he had been fed and shocked. At point X' he again reaches the conflict point and retreats to the white alley (W). Here, in this very different alley, his approach gradient is stronger. He goes all the way to the goal box and obtains food. He has "displaced" one goal with another.

One might call this process *substitution* when it is "conscious." For example, little children learn to argue rather than to hit with sticks or to kick; to ask for food from the refrigerator rather than to "snitch" it, etc. In displacement, presumably, the process occurs without the individual's being aware of the fact that he is displacing. Because of its clinical origin, many reserve the term *displacement* for socially and personally maladaptive behavior. The term *sublimation* can be applied to "truly happy" displacement

[4] Reprinted with permission of the American Psychological Association and N. E. Miller, from Miller (1948).

of libidinal drives—for instance, it might be said that the good nurse "sublimates" her own dependency needs; they become transformed into a desire to care for others. *Compensation,* as described above, is another case of displacement. Its social-personal utility (or mental-hygiene value) seems to fall between sublimation and displacement. The assumptions used to explain displacement in learning terms seem equally plausible for compensation and sublimation.

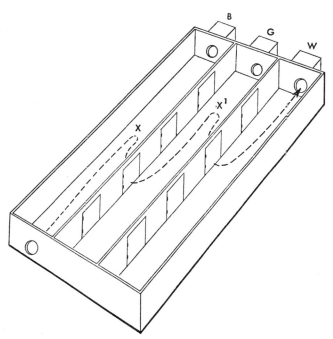

Fɪɢ. 5.6. A representation of the Murray-Berkun (1955) maze and a hypothetical goal path followed by a rat showing "displacement"

Figure 5.7 is a schematic three-dimensional representation of displacement. The horizontal axis from A to B represents goals that are moderately close to the original goal (located at point A). Instead of goals, stimuli, responses, or drives could be arranged along this axis in similar fashion.[5] For simplicity in writing, "goals" will be used in this section, although any of the other terms could be substituted.

The goals between A and B are unavailable to the human or animal because they lie in an area where the avoidance gradient is higher than the approach gradient. The approach and avoidance gradients intersect at the point indicated, since the slope of the avoidance gradient is steeper

---

[5] The interested student should consult Murray and Berkun (1955) for a detailed study of their animal experiment, suggested applications of their analysis to a psychotherapy case, and a schematic representation of their theory of displacement.

than that of the approach gradient. The goals between B and C on the horizontal axis can be approached along the "Displacement possible" arrow, since, from point B, the approach gradient is higher than the avoidance gradient. Presumably, the goal as close as possible to A will be the one selected for displacement. To the extent that the substitute goal is similar

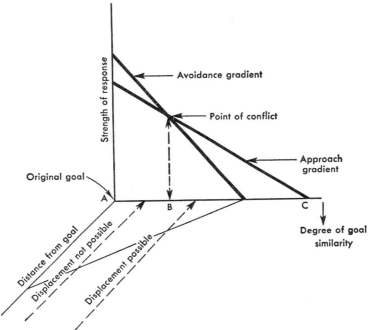

FIG. 5.7. A schematic representation of how displacement occurs as a function of conflict. (Adapted with permission of the American Psychological Association and E. J. Murray, from Murray and Berkun, 1955.)

to the original goal (satisfies the same or a related need), the displacement is successful—tension is reduced. When these conditions of similarity or "mutual" satisfaction do not exist, or are at a low level, the displacement is not successful. Thirst goals, for example, cannot be satisfied by hunger goals; or sex goals by dominance goals.

Treatment or Therapy

Displacement, particularly when it is persistent, can be thought of as a special case of fixation. What can be done about both fixations and displacements, particularly when they are very damaging to the individual?

Simple maturity, the learning that accompanies it, and resultant changes in self-confidence and self-concept often help. It is unlikely that runabout Tommy will continue all his life to fear dogs. Although anxiety and fear responses seem to be extinguished very slowly, they do eventually weaken. The world is full of friendly dogs; little boys are endlessly curious; eventually, it is likely that Tommy's approach tendency for dogs will become stronger than his avoidance tendency. If his new experiences with dogs are pleasant, approach tendencies will grow even stronger. As Tommy grows older, he also learns that it is "sissy" to show fear, so that he acquires "an avoidance tendency for his avoidance tendency" and, to show his bravery, goes up to dogs and pats them. Because he is unhurt, his approach tendency is further strengthened, his avoidance tendency further weakened.

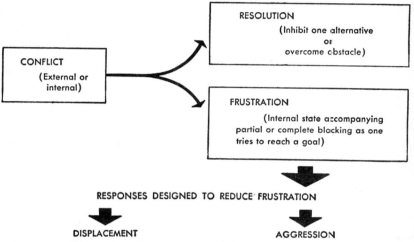

FIG. 5.8.   Various ways of handling frustration

Finally, as Tommy grows older, words mean more to him, and he understands better the connection between his fear and the event in his earlier childhood. Such understanding, or "insight," seems to reduce avoidance tendencies and to permit new learning to take place. The child's increased size, strength, speed, and coordination also combine to make dogs less threatening than when he was a runabout. Once his fear of one dog has been reduced, the generalization gradient works in reverse, so that unreasoning fear of *all* dogs is reduced.

This suggests a therapy for Tommy, and, by implication, for fixations in general. One recommendation is that parents acquire an old, tired dog, who is thoroughly accustomed to small children, and bring him into the home without any attempt to force Tommy into having traffic with him. Then, with comfort afforded to Tommy for whatever panic reaction he may have when he sees the dog, and repeated reassurances and explanations about dogs, "let nature take its course." The constant recurrence of anxiety will be wearing to Tommy and weaken his excitatory potential for anxious responses. His parents' reassurances may weaken them still further, and may also increase his approach tendencies (his interest) concerning the dog. Eventually he will reach the point where he can approach the dog. If the animal reacts in a friendly fashion or not at all, extinction begins to set in for the "avoidance-response-to-dogs," and the "approach-response-to-dogs" is reinforced. This extinction-of-fear behavior by the dog is the reason a "safe" animal should be acquired. If one is to work with the environment for therapeutic or training purposes, he needs to take precautions to see that the environment is going to fit the needs of the situation. In other words, don't, in such a situation, get a small, bouncy puppy with sharp teeth.

The principles of therapy for fixations of all sorts are very similar to those that have been described above. The alcoholic drinks himself into a stupor, fatiguing himself with drinking and building up, for a time, an avoidance tendency for alcohol. For a few days or weeks he stays "on the wagon." The compulsive eater gets gas pains, or is warned by the doctor, or is shocked by the scale reading; he goes on a diet for a few days, weeks, or months. But such "self-therapies" seldom work for long. The fatigue, the nausea, the gas pains wear off—the avoidance gradient is reduced; the old approach tendencies reappear; and the individual returns to his self-destructive behavior.

Some fixations can apparently be broken by understanding how the family of conditioned stimuli first came to be attached to the family of unconditioned stimuli. Such understanding can probably be gained only through words and a precise pin-pointing of the original experience. With experiences occurring in infancy, before the acquisition of language (as appears to be true of experiences associated with alcoholism and compulsive overeating), such pin-pointing and understanding may be difficult or impossible. The antecedents of such fixations are, in addition, undoubtedly both severe and complex. It may be for these reasons that conventional "insight" therapy for alcoholism and overeating is so difficult and so seldom successful.

For alcoholics, at this time, the most successful therapy resembles very closely that illustrated by the case of Tommy, in which understanding and pin-pointing play a minor role. A powerful avoidance gradient for liquor must have been established, perhaps by the almost complete ruin of the person through drinking. The support, warmth, and inspiration of such an organization as Alcoholics Anonymous may help to establish a strong approach tendency for abstinence, which counteracts the residual approach tendency for alcohol. Being able always to call on a brother Alcoholic Anonymous for support is undoubtedly important in setting up such a tendency.

One additional type of therapy can be mentioned here. This is Levy's *release therapy* (1939). It is apparently particularly successful with very young children (by whom, presumably, fixations have not been strongly overlearned) who have previously been well-adjusted, or reasonably so, but whose adjustment has deteriorated after some specific trying experience or experiences (a serious fright, an illness of the mother, a new baby whom they have not been able to accept, or a hospital experience such as a tonsillectomy). Release therapy consists of placing such children in a play situation that duplicates or resembles the situation that is thought to have caused the trouble in the first place (the principle of generalization operates here). The therapist is warm and reassuring. Ordinarily, children soon show strong emotions of the type they presumably showed in the original situation. But a typical extinction process apparently occurs. The conditioned stimuli of the hospital setting, for example, evoke the conditioned responses of panic and fear, but nothing happens: the unconditioned stimulus (pain and shock) no longer occurs following the conditioned stimulus (the hospital setting). Instead, the child is reassured; simple explanations are given to him; and presently he "recovers." Here, of course, the original circumstances of learning are relatively simple and accurately known Under such circumstances, therapy may be very effective.

One three-year-old girl, well known to the author, was compelled to undergo a tonsillectomy. The experience was very frightening, and the postoperative healing experience was also painful. A week or so after the operation she regressed in her sleeping habits and was wet at night frequently. Ordinarily a sound sleeper, she began to awaken because of bad dreams and fears. She sucked her thumb compulsively, showed shyness and fear around strangers, and in general behaved in a fashion unlike her usual rather well-adjusted self.

One evening she asked that her bedtime story be the recounting of her hospital experience. She demanded to have every unpleasant detail—from entering the hospital, through getting into the hospital bed and having the ether mask applied, to awakening in fear from the anaesthetic—recounted to her. She demanded the story not once but a half-dozen times on this first occasion. The next night she again demanded the story repeatedly. This went on night after night, but with fewer repetitions being requested as time went by. In a week or ten days, interest in the "story" had subsided, and during the same period her signs of maladjustment diminished and finally disappeared.

Although simple improvement in health probably accounted for a part of this recovery, much of it would seem to be explainable by the same principles of extinction and limited insight that we have applied to release therapy. For the child, the conditioned stimuli (the story of the operation) were constantly repeated without the occurrence of the unconditioned stimuli (the pain, fear sensations, nausea), so that the responses of anxiety, tension, and panic were extinguished. In addition, these conditioned stimuli were presented in a setting of security, with the child in her own bed, warm and safe. For such a child, with a fairly well-developed symbolic system, the scene of her original difficulties was, of course, evoked not literally but symbolically (see Chapter 4).

To conclude this chapter on special factors in learning, it must be admitted that, currently, no theory, whether derived from psychoanalytic or learning principles, is comprehensive or vital enough to encompass, explain, or guide the adult or child through states of despair, terror, tenderness, and dependence such as are constantly encountered. The child or adult whose defenses have broken down so that he is psychotic represents problems of adjustment and therapy that we only *begin* to understand, if indeed we even begin. But only by patient application and testing, confirming and rejecting of hypotheses formulated as explicitly as possible, can we ever hope to understand, guide, or cure.

SUMMARY

Possession of speech, together with a rich auxiliary system of symbols, makes the theory of human behavior both complex and fascinating. Some of the concepts needed to account for human behavior are treated in this chapter.

The first of these concepts is that of *expectancy and probability,* treated in a frankly speculative fashion in this chapter. Other things being equal, the human old enough to have developed a system of symbols (and possibly even the very young child) has learned to choose the response he believes to have the highest probability of success, even though extreme motivation may push him into behavior in which such probabilities are low. The choice of "life areas" into which a person puts his greatest effort also depends on his expectancies and his estimates of the likelihood of success.

Expectancies and probabilities are learned, according to the laws of learning discussed in Chapter 4. They may be accurate in terms of the individual's personal history, as in case of the moderately pretty girl who has grown up in a family of beautiful sisters, but inaccurate in the context of the larger society, and hence maladaptive (such a girl, with her expectancies "revised," could compete successfully with other women).

It may be that an unexpected consequence or reinforcement (success for one who expects to fail, failure for one who expects to succeed) is more effective in changing behavior than consequences that conform to expectancies and probability estimates.

Curiosity is probably a drive, although whether it should be considered a drive or a well-established habit is not completely clear at present. Children who are rewarded more often than they are punished for "curious" behavior are likely to be more curious than children for whom the reverse is true. However, even the child who is always punished for curiosity may manifest exploratory behavior, perhaps because he seeks to learn about his environment in order to avoid punishment.

A child's curiosity—his thirst for new information—may depend partly on how much information, or stimulation, has been given to him in infancy and early childhood. Given much information, he always desires much information; given little, he can tolerate—indeed, seeks—a life relatively devoid of information or stimulation. Mild frustration and partial reinforcement may intensify curiosity, which, regardless of whether we regard it as a drive or a habit, is fundamental to learning in our culture.

Much behavior that is irrational in appearance, and personally and socially maladaptive, persists indefinitely. *Fixation* is the term reserved for such behavior. Its apparently irrational, and maladaptive persistence is thought to be due to the fact that it serves, however inadequately, to reduce the anxiety associated with some specific and simple, or general and complex, earlier learning, usually painful in nature. Fixation seems to be related to classical conditioning, as discussed in Chapter 4. Overlearning, need satisfaction, ease, partial reinforcement, and high motivation seem to characterize fixated responses.

An individual possesses antagonistic *approach* and *avoidance* tendencies toward many stimuli, goals, responses, and so on, that he may potentially make, or may have to make. When his approach and avoidance tendencies (or gradients) toward a given goal, for example, are of equal strength, he is in *conflict.* This conflict may immobilize him; or he may reason it out (solve it symbolically, either strengthening his approach tendencies so that he achieves his goal, or his avoidance tendencies so that he "leaves temptation"). He may adopt one or another defense mechanism to reduce the anxiety associated with conflict.

One of the more frequent defense mechanisms for coping with conflict is *displacement*—the choice of another goal, stimulus, need-related behavior or response, as similar as possible (depending on the relevant approach-avoidance gradients) to the original. Avoidance gradients are steeper than approach gradients—generalize less widely—thus making displacement possible. The higher the avoidance gradient, the further or more different from the original goal the "displacement" goal must be.

Mechanisms of *sublimation* and *compensation* seem explicable by the same principles that apply to displacement. All can be closely related to principles of primary and secondary generalization and drive, as these concepts were developed in Chapter 4. The greater the drive in a conflict situation, the more intense the conflict. *Displacement,* as a term, is often reserved for "unfortunate" adjustments, and *sublimation* for socially approved ways of behaving. *Compensation,* in a mental-health sense, probably falls between these two. *Substitution* is *conscious* displacement, sublimation, or compensation.

Fixations, including displacements, which have occurred before language and other symbolic behavior has developed are particularly resistant to "insight" therapy. Examples of such fixations are alcoholism, food addiction, and certain types of homosexuality. When the events that resulted in the fixation (or displacement) are known, effective therapy for children often makes use of "massed extinction" (i.e., the repeated presentation of the original painful situation—actually or symbolically) to reduce the anxiety, coupled with reassurance designed to strengthen or raise the approach gradients to the feared stimulus. This process, together with (for older children) verbal explanation, seems to be fairly effective.

Current therapeutic theory, however, does not provide more than a beginning understanding of the many and complex ways in which human learning may go awry.

CHAPTER 6

The Self-Concept

As a child grows and develops, he learns, not only about the world about him—the type of learning that has been stressed so far in this volume—but about himself. Such learning is intensely personal, is in large part private, is heavily symbolic and often illogical, and is of vital importance to both private happiness and public behavior.

Each person lives with *himself,* and hence, to some degree, is always alone. No one can ever completely know the self of anyone else, although in the quest for understanding oneself and others there has developed much of human thought and philosophy, including psychology. Man has long held the hope of answering such questions as: Who am I? What am I? How did I come to be this way?—and their logical consequence, the search for purpose: *Why* am I?

The psychological construct, the *self-concept,* connotes this area of essentially private experience and self-evaluation—essentially private even though it is in part translated into action by most of the things we say and do, by the attitudes we hold, and by the beliefs we express.

The beginnings of the self-concept have been little studied. Sullivan, some of whose thought was summarized in Chapter 2, considers the self-concept or self-dynamism central to human personality, and he has devoted much thought to it. From the learning point of view, the self-concept is the apex—the culmination—of all the social and personal experiences the child has had. Conditioning and instrumental learning, primary and secondary generalization, reward and punishment, motives and drives, expectancies and probabilities, conflicts, fixations, and displacements—all these processes and experiences play a part, first in distinguishing *"others"* from *"me,"* later in an only partly articulate personal awareness and evaluation of "me," and finally in the mature "me," who may be cynical or trusting, happy or depressed, self-confidently male or female or the opposite, and so on.

All but very young children have formed some concept of themselves as people, and considerable study of the nature of the self-concept and its relation to behavior and adjustment has been made. A rather extensive review of this literature forms the bulk of this chapter. Although the self-concept is highly complex, most of the research done to date has concerned itself with a single dimension—the "good-bad" or positive-negative dimension. At the end of this chapter suggestions are made about some other characteristics of the self-concept that deserve attention but have been little studied, if at all.

The self-concept may be thought of as a *set of expectancies, plus evaluations of the areas or behaviors with reference to which these expectancies are held.* Confining ourselves, for the moment, to the good-bad dimension of the self-concept, we may say that the total self-concept of an individual may vary from extremely poor, or negative, to very good, or positive. The over-all self-concept may be visualized as an algebraic total: if, in considering the many areas making up the self, *more,* and *more important,* areas are regarded as good than as bad, then a positive self-concept can be inferred, and vice versa.

AN ILLUSTRATION OF
THE DEVELOPMENT OF THE SELF-CONCEPT

Let us examine a portion of the day of a rather bright and attractive four-and-a-half-year-old girl, whose self-concept is as yet vaguely formed. Dimly, she knows that she is well-loved and attractive. Upon awakening, she goes to her parents' room, is patted and kissed and sent on her way to get dressed for nursery school. She achieves this but neglects to brush her hair. She is sent back and, upon her return, although still not well-brushed, is told, "How pretty you look."

Her first period at school is an out-of-doors one. Her concept of her physical proficiency is poor, since she is small for her age and not particularly agile or graceful. She protests to her teacher that she does not want to go out, but is sent along. She finds almost all the children who are present running faster than she can run and climbing higher than she can climb. Someone runs into her and knocks her down; she sobs, then goes to the safety of the sandbox and plays quietly, perhaps alone, for the remainder of this period. The next period is an indoor activity period, where the choice of activity is free. The girl knows, in a poorly articulated fashion, that she is proficient at several things, among them the morning's offerings of woodwork, clay work, and painting. She chooses woodwork, and in half an hour has produced an object of several pieces and many nails that is accepted by her peers as a fine jet plane. She is admired for this by her teachers.

The next period is "the circle," when all children group around the teacher for general demonstrations, discussion, and "sharing." The girl is a little ill at ease in large groups and has a very soft voice. She sits in the circle, attempting, for security, to get as close to the teacher as she can. Her turn comes when the subject of jet planes arises; she eagerly extends her jet plane, but the big boy next to her, with the big voice, says, as he takes it from her, "See, she has the wheels too far back"; and the conversation and attention move on around the circle from her.

The rest of the morning is free; the weather is such that indoor equipment can be moved outside. She is verbal, imaginative, and proficient at dramatic play, so she takes several dolls, a carriage, and a baby bed outside and is soon the center and arbiter of a long and elaborate sequence of family play with three other girls and two boys. This lasts until she goes home.

A majority of this girl's expectancies, most of them rather soundly based on her credits and debits, have been confirmed on this particular morning: she has found parental love and admiration, has been defeated in large-muscle activity, has done well with finely coordinated small-muscle activity, has not excelled in the formal and competitive "circle," but has had a minor triumph in quiet dramatic play.

Projecting into the future, and oversimplifying, one might predict a generally positive self-concept for this girl. Her "failures" are not those that society regards as very serious for a girl; her successes are those that society holds to be desirable for females. We can almost see her as a young adult, looking prettily down her nose at gross motor activities—scorning tennis, for example; and, by this age, not being particularly affected if, when she is forced into a game of tennis, she does poorly. She may shun large, formal groups; speak up seldom in college classes, but do well on exams; and come vividly to life in individual creative enterprises and small informal groups. She may well be popular, a respected group member, but not a leader.

Slowly, it can be assumed, the things at which one is more successful (by means of which he solves his life problems) become more important to him, with either positive or negative results. If these strata of his success are socially useful, he becomes a valued member of society; if socially neutral, a nonentity; if socially destructive, possibly a criminal. When a certain type of proficiency is either important to survival and fulfillment (such as adequate attractiveness to the other sex), or is highly regarded by society (such as being brave), then a perceived deficiency present in the self-concept is very important and may contribute in a major fashion to the over-all self-image.

The self-concept, then, is a complex thing, and a function of the *importance* (or reward value) of its various facets and the *feeling*, positive or negative, about them.

For the girl in our example, by way of illustration:

Imaginative play, positive self-concept,
   high value .... +10
Large-muscle activity, negative self-
   concept, low value .... − 1
Formal group competition, negative self-
   concept, moderate value .... − 5
Individual creativity, positive self-
   concept, moderate value .... + 6
Personal attractiveness, positive self-
   concept, high value .... +10

Such a listing is, obviously, incomplete, and the assigning of numerical values an arbitrary device, but it permits us to represent schematically what is meant by "a generally positive self-concept."

Our illustration also suggests that the self-concept holds properties in common with drive (see Chapter 4), in that one *selects* some developmental, recreational, and avocational areas as a function of certain characteristics of the self-concept, and *rejects* others; or, because of its *directive function,* one person will behave one way (e.g., intellectually, through discussion), while another reacts to the same situation in quite another way (e.g., aggressively, through fighting). The girl in our illustration, given free choice, is likely to select individual or small-group informal activities where imagination can be exercised. One can see her, as she grows older, choosing drama before debate. One cannot see her going out for girls' intramural sports. She is not likely to be very disturbed by the prospect of a boy-girl party, where her attractiveness will stand her in good stead. However, as noted in Chapter 5, a real defeat in small groups or a genuine success in a formal activity, such as debate, may change her self-concept much more than a failure at tennis or a success in sewing class would.

Some authors (e.g., Sullivan, 1947) conceive of the self-concept as a unit, but one made up of many, many facets in dynamic equilibrium. This balance, whether it results in a positive or a negative self-concept, they believe to be essential in the adjustment of the child or adult because it represents the safest and most satisfactory solution to his life situation that he can manage at a given time. Since any disturbance of it represents a threat to the individual's well-being, however precarious this well-being may be, changes in or attempts to change the self-concept will be rejected. Those who hold such a point of view seek to account in this manner for the seeming irrationality of some of the behavior of most people: Why does the objectively successful man continue to regard himself as stupid? Why does the bright and talented girl consistently go to pieces when she competes for a part in the school play? It is argued that such behavior is designed to protect or maintain the status quo of the self-concept.

This reasoning is plausible, but such conceptions as *fixation* and accompanying anxiety reduction, as discussed in Chapter 5, fit better with the theoretical position adopted here. For our purposes, then, in recapitulation, we shall regard the self-concept as complex, made up of many facets, with each facet differing in importance—or reward value—from the others. Expectancies have been learned for each facet, so that the individual can predict success or failure in connection with behavior that pertains to a given facet. These expectancies have been acquired and can be changed according to the principles of learning previously discussed. The various aspects of the self-concept, in some senses, have properties similar to *drive:* to protect a good self-concept, we will strive hard (the energizing function) or will *select* those behaviors that preserve or enhance it (for example, if we are poor at sports we will drop sports; if good at talking, take up public speaking). We will also behave in ways that are congruent with our self-concept: the beautiful woman, coming into a new room, looks into the mirror; the homely one studies the pictures on the wall.

MEASUREMENT OF THE SELF-CONCEPT

We have discussed the idea of the self-concept in some detail. But, to be useful in science, an idea must have an objective referent: there must be a method of measuring it, and a number of methods have been devised to measure or estimate the self-concept. None of them captures the idea in its entirety, but most seem to catch enough of it to demonstrate that the self-concept is an important personality variable.

All measurements of the self-concept include the idea of *desirability* and *undesirability*. Desirability may be evaluated by one investigator according to an abstract social norm: to be good, or to be pretty, or to be intelligent, is ordinarily something that society at large values positively; to be bad, to be ugly, or to be stupid is something that society thinks of as a negative quality. Other investigators assess desirability and undesirability in terms of the evaluations of the subjects themselves: for one girl, to be vivacious may be "good"; another may be indifferent to vivacity; for still another girl, this quality may have negative connotations. One boy may think of "sophistication" as something he wants and values; another may think of it as a sissy quality of which he wishes no part.

Measurements of self-concept vary, then, along the dimension of how values are attached: some research workers use general social norms; others use the personal norms of the people they include in the study. In most measures of the self-concept, a number of terms, traits, values, or characteristics are presented to the subjects. Some research workers list adjectives such as *good, brave, beautiful, strong, honest* and ask the subjects of their study to estimate the degree to which each term applies to them. Ordinarily, a rating of 1 means "Very much like me" or "Very characteristic of me"; while a rating of 5 carries with it the idea of "I am almost never like this" or "This is not at all like me." The adjectives listed above are characterized by the *social* notion of desirability. Another list might read, *vivacious, ambitious, nonchalant, sophisticated, self-contained*. Here, the social value of the words is less clear-cut. Some will think of *vivacity* as meaning "alive, glancing, scintillating," whereas others will think of it as "jittery, artificial, birdlike." To some, *ambitious* means "hard-working, sober, wanting to advance." Others think of it as "pushiness, disregarding the rights of others." For such a list of adjectives, the subjects of any given study are ordinarily asked, as with the first list, to estimate the degree to which the adjective is characteristic of them; then, after they have gone through the list of adjectives, they are requested to estimate the desirability of the quality they have just rated. Again, a rating of 1 for desirability ordinarily means that they think the quality is a desirable one; a rating of 5 indicates that they dislike and devaluate it.

Regardless of which system is used, every choice of every subject is given a positive, a neutral, or a negative value. Ordinarily, these are added algebraically, and the resulting figure is thought of as an "index of the self-concept."

There are many other ways of getting at the self-concept. Some investigators use lists of traits more elaborate than simple adjectives. Examples are: "I go out of my way to look after people who are in trouble; . . . I am particularly fond of animals; . . . I think poorly of people who get ahead by questionable methods." Again, the subject makes a rating of how characteristic of him the statement is, and of how desirable the trait is. Other investigators use paired but opposite adjectives, such as *warm and outgoing* versus *cool and self-contained; constantly on the go* versus *relaxed and a little lazy.* Such investigators may ask their subjects to check where they think they stand on a line drawn between the two adjectives of a pair. After such a series of checks, estimates of the value of the quality to the person are made.

Still other research workers ask their subjects simply to answer the question, "Who Am I?" They use expert judges to help them classify the answers as indicating a positive or negative self-concept; or ask their subjects to go back over their answers and indicate with a plus all the answers they think are socially or personally desirable, with a 0 those they think are neutral, and with a minus those that are socially or personally undesirable.

Another common variation of the method is to have the subject do a "Q-sort." In this technique, a large number of statements or adjectives is given to the subject on separate slips of paper and he is asked to sort these slips on, for example, a seven-point scale. He is forced to distribute them according to a preordained quota system from those "least like him" to those "most like him." Of 100 such statements he is allowed to place only seven, for example, on the figure 1, meaning "most like me," and only seven on the figure 7, "least like me." In second and sixth positions, he may place twelve statements each; in third and fifth place, nineteen; and in the middle or fourth place, twenty-four statements. These statements may be judged positive or negative in terms of the abstract social norm by expert judges, or may be rated for desirability by each subject.

Another, less frequently used, method of measuring the self-concept consists of having the subjects respond to some projective technique, such as the Thematic Apperception Test. This test consists of a number of pictures. For each picture, the subject is asked to tell who the characters are, what has happened to them before, what is happening at the time the picture was taken, and what the outcome will be. Psychologically sophisticated judges then decide with whom the subject is most closely identified (who "stands for" the subject, or, according to psychological terminology, is the "hero"), and rate the attributes of this character in the story as positive, neutral, or negative. From these ratings, a judgment of the self-concept is made.

Some of these techniques, such as the Q-sort, are rather complicated to use with children, but variations of all of them have been used with children as well as adults. Compared with the number of adult studies, there are few studies of the self-concept in children. Those studies that have been done with children use, ordinarily, a simple technique of listing a series of adjectives or traits. They then ask the children to indicate whether these are "like them" or "unlike them." After this has been done, the request is made that the child indicate by a plus whether he thinks the quality is a "good" one; by a 0 whether he does not care one way or another; and by a minus if he does not like this aspect of himself. The "Who Am I" technique has also been used with children old enough to write. Self-concept studies of children younger than about fourth-grade age are rare, since each child would have to be examined individually (because of reading and writing difficulties); and an individual examination in an area such as this is likely to affect the results. The child, alone with the adult, is likely to respond, not in the way he feels or believes, but in the way he thinks the adult would like him to believe or feel.

One of the first questions that must be asked of any measuring technique, or of any behavioral indicator of a concept, is: Are its results repeatable; are they stable over time? If not, one is forced to question either the measure or the long-run scientific usefulness of the concept. In general, measures of the self-concept have demonstrated moderate stability over time. To support this statement, one representative piece of research can be introduced. Engel (1959) tested a group of sixth- and eighth-graders on a self-concept measure; then, after two years, repeated the same test (a Q-sort). After certain legitimate corrections of her statistical techniques, she arrived at a correlation of .78 between the first and the second test. The younger children showed as high a level of stability as the older, and boys were no different from girls in stability. In other words, even in the presumably unstable period of adolescence, a self-concept measure accounts for a little more than 60 percent of the variance of a second measure made two years later.

THE SELF-CONCEPT AND PERSONAL ADJUSTMENT

Introduction

Earlier in this chapter it was said that the self-concept, though essentially private, influences and is revealed by most of a person's behavior. If this is correct, then poor self-concepts should be reflected in other behavior that represents poor personal and social adjustment, and good self-concepts should be associated with good adjustment. The studies reviewed in this section indicate that the good-bad dimension of the self-concept is related to scores on anxiety tests as well as to more general measures of adjustment; to effectiveness in a group; and to self-honesty. All the relations are in the expected direction: persons with good self-concepts are less anxious, are judged to be generally better adjusted, are more effective in groups, and are more honest with themselves and less defensive.

People seem to assign positive evaluations to those of their traits that have been approved by their parents. Other research indicates that specific patterns of child-rearing are associated with certain maladaptive types of self-concept, and that the self-concept (presumably affected by patterns of child-rearing) is significantly related to achievement in school. The studies reviewed in this section follow the topical order of this introductory statement.

The Self-Concept and Anxiety

First, several studies of both children and college students indicate a relation between self-rejection, or negative self-concept, and measures of anxiety. In the first of these, Lipsitt (1958) asked a large number—300— of fourth-, fifth-, and sixth-grade boys and girls to indicate whether each of a series of adjectives was "very like them" or "very unlike them." They were then asked whether each of the traits was personally desirable or undesirable. This provided an over-all index of the good-bad dimension of their self-concepts. They also took an anxiety test. Children with poor self-concepts were more anxious, at a statistically significant level for both boys and girls, than children with good self-concepts.

The anxiety scale used (Castaneda, McCandless, and Palermo, 1956) appears to have a moderate degree of validity. Children who test high on it, when compared with children who test low, are less popular (McCandless, Castaneda, and Palermo, 1956); have more difficulty with conceptually complex learning tasks (Castaneda, Palermo, and McCandless, 1956; Palermo, Castaneda, and McCandless, 1956); and in at least some cases do less well with the more complicated school subjects (McCandless and Castaneda, 1956). Children referred for behavior problems test higher in anxiety than those not so referred (Rynerson, 1957); and Negro children in an area where racial role changes likely to produce tension are occurring test higher than their non-Negro peers (Palermo, 1959).

Another author, Coopersmith (1959), used this anxiety scale for a different sample of fifth- and sixth-grade children—102 in number—but used a *different* measure of self-concept. He found that children who had high self-esteem were significantly less anxious than those with low self-esteem. The youngsters with high self-esteem were also more popular (self-esteem and popularity correlated .37). The children were apparently rather accurate in their self-concepts, since teachers, in the main, judged the youngsters very much as they judged themselves.

Such relations between self-concept and anxiety are not limited to children. For example, Mitchell (1959) measured the self-concepts of

100 freshmen and sophomore women students, and correlated their anxiety scores with the adequacy of their self-concepts. The resulting correlation coefficient was —.41—the better the self-concept, the less the anxiety.

It will be recalled from Chapter 2 that one's confidence in a generalization increases in proportion to the frequency with which similar results are obtained from different populations and from different but related instruments. In this regard, then, rather convincing evidence exists relating poor self-concept to high anxiety, *as these are measured.*

Research done by Crandall and Bellugi (1954) will be discussed later in more detail, but should be mentioned in this context because it provides still further evidence (based, in this instance, on a presumably rather sophisticated sample of juniors and seniors in a highly rated private liberal arts college) that good self-concept is related to good adjustment. This research introduces still another experimental sample, and a different measure of adjustment—the Incomplete Sentences Technique, which provides an indirect index of adjustment. The subject's "creative" endings to sentence stems (such as "My mother . . ." or "When I . . .") are given adjustment ratings by expert raters. In other words, this study adds still more confidence to the generalization that good self-concept is related to good behavioral adjustment.

Effectiveness in Groups

The Mussen and Porter study (1959) bears on the question of the effectiveness in groups of people holding high or low esteem for themselves. This study used male volunteers from undergraduate psychology classes.

The young men highest in feelings of adequacy, and with favorable rather than negative self-concepts, were rated by other men who took part with them in "free-wheeling," or leaderless, discussion groups as being generally more effective than those who expressed feelings of inadequacy and negative self-concepts. The criteria that the group members—all of whom were initially unacquainted with each other—used in making their judgment of group effectiveness were, among others: contributing the best ideas to the group, degree of activity in the group, amount of intellectual stimulation provided to other members of the group, adequacy in explaining their ideas and clarifying the ideas of others, most influential in the group, and most appealing in that the rater desired to become better acquainted with him.

This study supports the suggestion made above, that self-concepts *are* translated into action, and contributes further support to the finding that good self-concepts are related to generally adequate social functioning, including popularity.

A related study (Dittes, 1959) supports the Mussen and Porter conclusion: the self-esteem ratings of 104 male college freshmen were positively correlated with ratings of adequacy made by fellow group members (Dittes does not give the correlation). Some of Dittes' subjects were led to believe that they were rejected by the group, while others were given the impression that they were accepted, or that acceptance was likely. Not surprisingly, he found that "Persons made to feel well accepted in a group found the group more attractive than did those made to feel poorly accepted." (p. 81) But an individual's rating of the *attractiveness of the accepting group* varied according to his self-concept, the group being rated significantly more attractive by those with low self-esteem. Dittes believes that low self-esteem should be considered indicative of a "strong need for acceptance." The implications of this study, in conjunction with others that have been summarized in this section, is that, while people with poor self-concepts are less popular than those who have high esteem for themselves, and while they are generally rated as less effective in groups, they have a stronger need for groups and, if anything, overreact to group acceptance. It would be helpful, from an educational and therapeutic standpoint, to investigate the effect of group acceptance on the self-concept and adjustment of isolated people with low self-esteem.

Accuracy of the Self-Concept

A rather subtle criticism can be applied to several of the studies reported in this section, particularly those that relate anxiety to self-concept. This criticism postulates that correlations are found between the two measures, not because there is *really* a relation between anxiety and poor self-concept, but because the method of measuring the two constructs ordinarily involves self-criticism (or its lack). To obtain a poor self-concept rating, an individual, when the usual techniques are employed, must say negative things about himself. Similarly, to get a high anxiety rating, he must admit to mildly derogatory or quite negative things about himself. Sample items from the Children's Manifest Anxiety Scale (Castaneda, McCandless, and Palermo, 1956) are: "It is hard for me to keep my mind on anything. . . . I feel I have to be best in everything. . . . I am secretly afraid of a lot of things. . . . Often I have trouble getting my breath. . . . My feelings get hurt easily when I am scolded." "Yes" answers to each of these statements are considered to indicate anxiety. Since this "admission phenomenon" (or willingness to be frank or self-critical) characterizes the self-concept test, the anxiety test, *and* the Incomplete Sentences Test, some have said that *it,* rather than a genuine relation between anxiety and self-concept, is responsible for the relations found.

This criticism would be less telling if it could be demonstrated that children judged as well-adjusted by some technique subject to the "admission phenomenon" are, on some other measure, more willing to admit derogatory things about themselves than children judged as maladjusted. That is, if the admission phenomenon results in their obtaining a favorable adjustment score on the personality test, it should operate to produce a low score on an instrument designed to elicit admissions of derogatory traits or feelings: if good personality scores result from the admission phenomenon, then its operation should assure that the "well-adjusted" will admit the fewest derogatory things about themselves.

Taylor and Combs (1952) provide the suggestion that such results as were summarized in this section are *not* due to the admission phenomenon. They used a sizable sample (202 in number) of rural sixth-grade boys and girls. Their hypothesis was the following: Well-adjusted children should be more accepting of unflattering things about themselves than poorly adjusted children. To test this hypothesis, a personality test, the well-standardized California Test of Personality, was given. Analyses of girls and boys were made separately. By sex, they were broken into two groups, the well-adjusted (those who scored above the median—that point above and below which exactly half the boys or girls fell), and the poorly adjusted (those who scored below the median). They were then asked to indicate whether such statements as the following did or did not characterize them: being lazy sometimes, talking back to mother sometimes, showing off in front of other children sometimes. Twenty such statements were included in this test. The well-adjusted boys admitted an average of 9.2 such items, the poorly adjusted ones only 5.1; the well-adjusted girls admitted 8.4, the poorly adjusted girls only 5.8. The differences for both boys and girls were highly significant statistically; and hence, by inference, willingness to admit derogatory things about oneself is positively, not negatively, related to adjustment. This finding suggests, then, that the relation between poor self-concept and high anxiety may be genuine, rather than due to an admission phenomenon common to the two tests. If better-adjusted children are *more* likely to admit derogatory things about themselves than maladjusted children, then their scores on an anxiety test, incomplete sentences tests, and self-concept tests should *maximize their poor adjustment* scores; and if maladjusted children are least likely to admit derogatory things, their poor adjustment should be *minimized* by their "No" answers to negative items and their "Yes" answers to positive items. In other words, the Taylor and Combs results suggest that relations obtained between anxiety and self-concept measures are, if anything, too low.

The Taylor and Combs study summarized immediately above suggests that honesty about oneself, which may also be thought of as accuracy, is an important aspect of the self-concept and may well be related to good adjustment. Chodorkoff (1954a) attempted to take account of accuracy of self-concept in an ingenious study using college men as subjects. The subjects did a Q-sort of themselves, and persons trained in clinical psychology used tests, items from their biographies, and other information to make the same Q-sort—that is, to state what characteristics were or were not applicable to them, and to what degree. If the subject's own Q-sort was very similar to that of the "experts," he was given a high rating on the factor of "accuracy of self-description." If the Q-sort of the subject was very different from that of the clinical psychologists, he got a low rating. The clinical psychologists also scored the subjects for general adjustment on the basis of various tests and information about their biographies. Another index of adjustment was taken from a standard personality test (the Rorschach Inkblot Test). In general, the more accurate the young men were in their self-descriptions, the better adjusted they were according to both indices.

One flaw of the study, of course, is that the clinical psychologists were using the same information to judge adjustment as that used to describe the young men in the first place. But still another test, *not* subject to this criticism, was utilized in the study—a test of defensiveness. It is commonly assumed in psychological literature that "defensiveness" represents poor adjustment. Defensiveness is frequently defined as the tendency to blot out of one's conscious mind, or deny, those things in his environment that are threatening or unpalatable. Chodorkoff first dictated to his subjects a series of 100 words, to each of which they were asked to make some verbal response. Of these words, 50 were "emotional," and 50 "neutral." For each subject 10 words judged to represent "personally relevant threatening stimuli" and 10 neutral words were selected, and these were then flashed before the subject repeatedly, starting with such short exposure times that the subject could not recognize them and increasing the exposure time until the word was recognized. A subject who recognized neutral words much more quickly than threatening words was considered to be defensive (was regarded as blocking out threatening stimuli), whereas a person whose reaction time for threatening and neutral words was approximately equal, or who recognized threatening words more quickly than neutral ones, was considered to be nondefensive.

The men who were more accurate in their self-descriptions (self-concepts) showed less defensiveness than the men who were inaccurate. Surprisingly, the *most* accurate men actually recognized the threatening words more quickly than the neutral ones. Chodorkoff suggests, quite plausibly, that one aspect of good adjustment is the ability quickly to recognize threat (and, presumably, to deal effectively with it).

Two studies, then, have used very different experimental populations (rural New York sixth-graders, and University of Wisconsin undergraduate men) and very different methods (paper-and-pencil tests, and experimental techniques) in an effort to relate self-honesty or lack of defensiveness to good personal adjustment. Both studies secured results supporting the hypothesis.

The Effect of Child-Rearing Practices

In line with the assumption that the self-concept is learned, it would be expected that one would develop a good self-concept, without attendant anxiety, about those of his traits that had been valued and rewarded by parents and other important persons during childhood, but would have a poor self-concept and marked anxiety about traits that had been punished, or had failed to receive reward. Child, Frank, and Storm (1956) attempted to check this hypothesis by asking male undergraduate students about how persons important in their childhood had reacted to such of their behaviors as competitiveness, aggression, mannerliness, and so on. The young men also indicated their own self-concepts and associated anxiety in these areas. The results of the study were not spectaculator, but *did* lend support to the hypothesis.

Ausubel *et al.* (1954) include, in a study of the effect of parental attitudes on children's self-concept, some findings supporting the hypothesis that children's self-concepts develop according to the pattern of parents' rewards and punishments, but that, when this pattern stresses objective success rather than the needs of the developing child, unfortunate personality characteristics may develop.

These authors developed a scale they call "Extrinsic Valuation." By this, they mean that the parents show excessive concern about the child's school accomplishment and, presumably, view it as a factor that enhances their own status. Children of such parents see their parents as overmotivating them, as planning for their careers in grandiose terms, and as displaying their school and other achievements publicly to an excessive degree. Children who reported their parents in such terms were themselves grandiose, according to their answers on a scale called "Could You Ever?" In this scale, the 40 ten-year-old boys and girls who were used as subjects of the study were asked 80 sex-appropriate questions dealing with their ability to achieve a number of goals which, in terms of probability of success, ranged from probable to highly improbable. Some of the questions concerned childhood achievements; others referred to what the child thought he could accomplish as an adult. "Grandiose" answers are those indicating that the child has an unrealistically ambitious or "cocky" notion of what he can do, both in the present and in the future.

Children who saw their parents as valuing them extrinsically were also more persistent (probably to an unrealistic degree) in believing they could do well "the next time" on a task at which they were consistently failing. The children were rated by an arts-crafts teacher, and by their classroom teachers, for emotional maturity. Those who saw their parents as valuing them extrinsically emerged with less favorable ratings for emotional maturity than those who perceived their parents as valuing them for themselves alone. The authors defined maturity as consisting of two traits: (1) *executive independence*—not asking for help on a task they were physically able to do; and (2) *ability to postpone hedonistic gratification*—putting off an immediate reward for some future, desirable goal. The relations reported here are those that achieved a satisfactory level of statistical significance.

Self-Concept and School Achievement

It might be predicted that poor self-concepts, implying, as they so often do. a lack of confidence in facing and mastering the environment, might accompany deficiency in one of the most vital of the child's areas of accomplishment—his performance in school.

The Coopersmith (1959) study of fifth- and sixth-grade children which has already been mentioned in this section supports this prediction. For the 102 children included in the study, a correlation of .36 was found between positive self-concept and school achievement.

Another research worker (Walsh, 1956) has interested herself in differences in self-concept between very bright boys (IQ above 120) who fell in the lowest quarter of their class in terms of academic achievement, and a group of carefully matched "adequate achievers"—those whose academic achievement was in the top half of their class. Twenty boys from the second through the fifth grade were included in each of these groups.

The Driscoll Playkit, consisting of a facsimile (floor plan) of a six-room house, toy furniture, and a doll family (father, mother, boy, girl, and baby), was used to elicit the boys' self-concepts. Nine incomplete stories were read to the boys, and they were asked to tell and play out the endings to the stories. They could make up a tenth story of their own in which anything they wanted could be made to happen. Judges inferred their self-concepts from their story-endings, making judgments about freedom of action; freedom and adequacy of emotional expression; feelings of belongingness (with their parents); response to environmental stimulation (whether the child used opportunities to gain direct satisfaction of his needs, conformed and obeyed without question, or saw his world as something he must defend himself against through such behaviors as rebellion, negativism, unreasoning opposition, etc.); and sex-typing (i.e., degree of normal "maleness").

There were extremely significant differences for three of these categories. The low achievers more markedly than the adequate achievers portrayed the boy doll or "hero" (from whose behavior their own self-concept was inferred) as being restricted, or not free to pursue his own interests and feelings, and as acting defensively. Results were statistically significant, but not as clear-cut, in the "belongingness" area. The low achievers more frequently depicted the boy doll as being isolated, criticized, or rejected.

This well-done study has obvious practical implications for education, suggesting as it does that children who have come to feel that their freedom is restricted, that they cannot pursue their own interests or express their feelings, that they cannot cope with their environment, that the world is "against them," and who do not feel close to their families, may express the conflicts so engendered by "rebellion" against the educational process— that is, by achieving far less than they are able to accomplish. For such children, active "emotional" education in addition to academic teaching may be necessary.

In sum, then, the self-concept *does* appear to be related to personal adjustment. Substantial evidence indicates that children and adults with poor self-concepts, when compared with those who have more positive self-concepts, are more anxious and less well-adjusted generally, are less popular, are less effective in groups (although they value groups that accept them more highly), and are less honest about themselves (or more defensive). The pattern of parental rewards and punishments seems to affect the self-concept, and, quite certainly, the self-concepts of bright but underachieving youngsters are less positive than those of children who are doing as well as can be expected in school.

DISCREPANCY BETWEEN THE PERCEIVED SELF AND THE IDEAL SELF

The studies reviewed in the previous section related self-concept—that is, how the person sees himself, or how he evaluates himself with respect to certain characteristics or attributes—to various other measures of adjustment and effective functioning. This section concerns itself with a quality that might be called self-satisfaction or self-discontent—What does it mean if a person sees himself as being very similar to the person whom he would, *ideally*, like to be, or, on the other hand, sees himself as much inferior to this idealized self?

The studies reviewed in this section are not in complete agreement. Generally, their results indicate that really sharp differences between one's perceived and ideal status are related to unhappiness; but they include suggestions that excessive self-satisfaction has its disadvantages, and that a certain amount of restless discontent may act as constructive motivation. They also indicate that dissatisfaction with oneself may be related to *general* dissatisfaction "with life."

Many studies, in addition to asking subjects for *self-perceptions,* obtain an additional measure: the subject, after indicating how he feels about himself, is asked to go through the same set of items again and indicate how he would like to be *ideally*. Since almost all of us would like to be "better" than we are, the *ideal self* is invariably judged to be at least as good as, and almost always better than, the perceived self. The difference between the scores for the perceived self and the ideal self is the *discrepancy* score: to obtain it, the score of the perceived self is subtracted from the score representing the ideal self. The larger this discrepancy score, the more dissatisfied with himself the person is presumed to be.

Most studies of this topic have used adults as subjects. However, the findings contain implications for children, and there are a few studies in this area that have actually used children as subjects. In the first of these (Hanlon, Hofstaetter, and O'Connor, 1954), the subjects were 78 boys who were juniors in a parochial school and who averaged 16.3 years of age. They were given the California Test of Personality, and asked to Q-sort 100 self-evaluating items both for their perceived self-concepts and for their ideal self-concepts. Their discrepancy score was then related to the over-all adjustment score on the California Test of Personality and to its subscales.

No particular relations were found between age or intelligence and self-ideal congruence, nor did the measures of adjustment show any particular relation to intelligence or age But the correlation between total adjustment and discrepancy was a highly significant .70. Similar figures for the subscales of the California Test of Personality, and P (probability that the relationship could have occurred by chance) are given in Table 6.1. The relations found in this study between self-ideal discrepancy and personality adjustment are, on the whole, higher than those found in any other study in the literature.

TABLE 6.1: CORRELATIONS BETWEEN SELF-IDEAL DISCREPANCY AND ADJUSTMENT AS MEASURED BY THE SUBSCALES OF THE CALIFORNIA TEST OF PERSONALITY.

California Test of Personality Subscale	Correlation with Self-Ideal Discrepancy	P
Self-adjustment	.70[a]	.001
Self-reliance	.48	.001
Sense of Personal Worth	.50	.001
Sense of Freedom	.40	.001
Feeling of Belonging	.55	.001
Freedom from Withdrawal Symptoms	.56	.001
Freedom from Nervous Symptoms	.39	.001
Social Adjustment	.59	.001
Social Standards	.08	NS (nonsignificant)
Social Skills	.52	.001
Freedom from Antisocial Tendencies	.22	.05
Family Relations	.30	.01
School Relations	.45	.001
Community Relations	.50	.001

[a] These positive correlations mean that the *less* the discrepancy, the *better* the adjustment.
Adapted with permission of the American Psychological Association and T. E. Hanlon, from Hanlon, Hofstaetter, and O'Connor (1954).

Bruce (1958), studied the self-ideal discrepancies of 184 sixth-grade children, drawn from 8 sixth-grade classes. Compared with the children who had low self-ideal discrepancy scores, the self-dissatisfied youngsters were significantly more anxious on the Children's Manifest Anxiety Scale, and were rated by observers as being significantly less secure.

Mitchell (1959) obtained results that are very similar to Bruce's results in his study of 100 college freshman and sophomore women. Among other data, Mitchell secured measures of self-ideal discrepancy and anxiety. His self-rejecting (high-discrepancy) women were more likely than the self-accepting (low-discrepancy) women to say about themselves such things as that they give up easily; are more sensitive than others; are less happy, less calm, and more restless; and that things pile up on them They believe they are more distractible and high-strung, that life is a strain, and that they cannot live up to their parents' expectations for them. Mitchell found an over-all correlation of .41 between self-ideal discrepancy and anxiety (the greater the discrepancy, the higher the anxiety score). However, as a group, the self-rejecting women did as well in school as those who were self-accepting, and did not differ from them in intelligence.

Two other studies relate directly to self-ideal discrepancy but are in disagreement with each other. Both use college students rather than children as subjects. The 56 men and women subjects in the first study, by Block and Thomas (1955), Q-sorted 80 adjectives for the typical measures of perceived self and ideal self. The self-ideal discrepancies, referred to as "self-satisfaction" (where little discrepancy means high satisfaction), were then correlated with the subscales of the Minnesota Multiphasic Inventory (MMPI).

Several interesting findings resulted from the study, most of them fitting well with the results of the studies summarized in the preceding section which dealt with the "goodness" or "badness" of the self-concept. For example, the students with high discrepancy scores also obtained high scores on MMPI subtests thought to indicate tendencies to project and feel that "others are against you," and demonstrated tendencies toward morbid self-preoccupation. But, on the other hand, highly self-satisfied subjects scored rather high on a test of defensiveness (unwillingness to admit to undesirable traits), and denied "characteristics and feelings of an adverse and personally disparaging nature." An interesting and apparently useful scale called "Social Maintenance" has been constructed from a number of MMPI items. People with mental illness who "do well" on the scale have, for instance, been found to be better prospects for rehabilitation into society than those who score low. Self-satisfaction showed a negative relation with Social Maintenance score: the highly self-satisfied did "less well" than those who were more self-critical, although the correlation was not high (−.34).

The authors went one step further in their analysis, checking to see what the differences in type of self-criticism were between those who were *extremely satisfied* with themselves, those who were *moderately content* (the "Middles") and those who obtained high scores for *self-dissatisfaction*. They conclude that the highly self-satisfied emphasize "social appropriateness over interpersonal intimacy," and wish to control "their expressiveness and spontaneity," but at the same time be accepted and popular. "Their uneasiness with the affective life is stressed by their preference to be ideally less sentimental, less dependent, and less jealous than the Middles." (p. 258)

The highly dissatisfied group was made up of students who were judged by the authors to be "confused, overly introspective, despairing and with unrealistic, contradictory aspirations," and who were seeking "a feeling of personal integrity," whereas the Middles appeared "to be reasonable and accepting in their self-appraisals. They would like more of what they value and less of what makes them uncomfortable. They accept the ambiguity of emotions and are comfortable in their relations with others. They have their problems, certainly, but they neither despair nor deny." (p. 258)

All of this suggests what statisticians refer to as a *curvilinear relation* between self-satisfaction and adjustment, in contrast to the linear relationships implied by the other studies we have talked about. Figure 6.1 demonstrates these contrasting relationships.

Fig. 6.1. Graphs representing, from left to right, a linear and a curvilinear relationship

The graph to the left in Figure 6.1 represents a linear relation. If we let the abscissa represent self-satisfaction, or congruence between perceived self and ideal self (0 meaning great, 4 meaning little discrepancy), and the ordinate represent adjustment from poor (0) to very good (4), then it follows from the graph that people with the least self-ideal congruence are least well adjusted, those with the greatest congruence best adjusted. The solid line in the curvilinear graph to the right, representing the Block and Thomas results, tells a quite different story. Both high congruence and low congruence are related to poor adjustment, although those with high congruence between perceived self and ideal self are better adjusted than those with low congruence. Degrees of congruence represented in the middle (entries of 1, 2, and 3) are the best adjusted of the group. This curvilinear type of relation is a common one in studies of human behavior (for example, policies of excessive strictness and excessive leniency both seem to have undesirable effects on the development of children).

In other words, the Block and Thomas study suggests a curvilinear relation between self-ideal discrepancy and adjustment; excessive self-satisfaction appears not to be the ideal human attribute, but too little self-satisfaction is also undesirable.

Another, somewhat similar study has been done by Chodorkoff (1954b), using as subjects 30 college men. Here too there is found a curvilinear relation between adjustment and self-ideal congruence. But Chodorkoff's findings are in opposition to the results obtained by Block and

Thomas. The curvilinear relation graphed by the dashed line at the right in Figure 6.1 represents Chodorkoff's findings. Both the high and the low self-satisfaction men received better adjustment ratings than those with moderate discrepancies.

There is no way to resolve these contradictory findings, and we can only say that they may have resulted from the different methods and the different populations used. Block and Thomas used men and women, Chodorkoff men only. Block and Thomas used a standardized, paper-and-pencil test to measure adjustment; Chodorkoff used primarily the Thematic Apperception Test and the Rorschach Inkblot Test of Personality as his basis for inferring adjustment. He and colleagues based a rating of adjustment for each subject on the results of the two tests.

We can only conclude that the relation between self-satisfaction and adjustment is not a simple one. When does self-dissatisfaction cease to be a "desire to improve oneself" and become a serious handicap? There is a very real difference between the person who sees himself as being not perfect, yet manages to live comfortably with himself as he is; and the person who tortures himself with inferiority feelings and self-doubts. But, using the methods of measurement we have available, these two types of people could obtain identical self-satisfaction scores. Block and Thomas' analysis of differences in the ways people are dissatisfied with themselves may represent a method of getting at the answers to some of these questions. Additional measures, not simply of the number and type of self-dissatisfactions, but of their intensity and "ego value" or "reward value" (see p. 175), also appear to be needed.

People who have used the Rorschach Inkblot Test in personality diagnosis have maintained that certain ways of responding to it indicate a tendency toward depression, and have developed methods of scoring the test responses for indicators of depression. One author (Bills, 1954) predicted that people with high self-ideal discrepancies would be more likely to be depressed than those with low discrepancies. He reasoned that "self perceptions of a lack of unity within the personality or of a discrepancy between the perceptions of self and the ideal self should be disorganizational experiences leading to feelings of depression." (p. 135). Bills obtained two comparison groups, one with high, one with low self-ideal discrepancy, and tested to see whether more of the former than of the latter would respond in a "depressed" fashion. Using men and women undergraduate students, he found this to be true for five of the six Rorschach indicators he used. Results for the sixth indicator closely approached significance in the predicted direction.

A socially brighter picture of high self-ideal discrepancy is presented by Martire (1956), who worked with college men. His findings indicate that high self-ideal discrepancies are associated with high achievement motivation (which may be somewhat loosely called ambition, or desire to do well)

This quality, of course, can have its drawbacks if it is too strongly present, or if it exists in an area in which a person for one reason or another simply cannot succeed.

One implication of several of these studies is that individuals are in conflict about those traits for which their self-ideal discrepancies are the greatest. Cowen, Heilizer, and Axelrod (1955) used college freshmen to test this implication. It was predicted that new learning would be slowed up if it involved the names of traits or qualities on which there was a large self-ideal discrepancy (conflict). From the self-concept test of each subject the authors of the study picked six neutral words and the six adjectives on which he had shown the greatest self-ideal discrepancy. They then tested to determine the differential speed with which one-syllable nonsense words could be associated (a memory bond formed) with the conflict and the neutral words. They found that, on the average, it took about five more trials to build up an association between a conflict word and a nonsense syllable than between a nonsense syllable and a neutral word.

Another ingenious study (Friedman, 1955) demonstrates that normal young men show a rather close relation between perceived self and ideal self; that neurotics have far greater discrepancies (are more dissatisfied with themselves); but that paranoid schizophrenics do not differ from normals in self-satisfaction. Judges then "constructed" the self-concepts of the heroes of Thematic Apperception Test stories told by the men, using the same procedure by which perceived-self and ideal-self measures had been obtained directly from the men themselves. These Q-sorts were called the "Projected Self." The normal men and the neurotics projected themselves rather accurately; but the paranoid men projected with little or no accuracy. In other words, the normals were rather *self-accepting*, and *projected* with moderate accuracy; the neurotics *did not like themselves*, but were *accurate in their projection;* whereas the paranoids were *self-accepting*, but *without accuracy of projection.*

Workers in the area of the self-concept have tended to confine themselves to the person as he *is* and as he *would like to be*, and to ignore the fact that a tendency to self-dissatisfaction or to self-satisfaction may perhaps spread out to all phases of life—may, in fact, be something akin to general pessimism or general optimism. Levy (1956) believed that this might be true. To test this hypothesis, he had college students, almost all of them men, do a Q-sort of 100 items to obtain a measure of perceived self. He developed another set of items referring to one's home town, and asked the same students to Q-sort them. Then the subjects did a *self*-ideal and a *home town*-ideal Q-sort. In general, the students who were dissatisfied with themselves were also dissatisfied with their home town, and vice versa. There was a highly significant correlation of .70 between the two sets of discrepancy scores. Levy wonders whether, rather than simply a self-ideal discrepancy related to personality adjustment, there may not be a maladaptive tendency for some people *generally* to perceive the *actual* as very different from the *ideal:* in other words, a pessimism factor may exist in personality. Luckey (1960) reports findings that support this point. In a study of happily and unhappily married couples, one of the most pervasive characteristics of the unhappily marrieds was that they perceived, not only themselves, but also their husbands or wives and mothers and fathers as rather cynical, depressed, begrudging people.

This topic of *discrepancy* between the perceived and the ideal self has been given separate treatment from the *self-concept* considered alone. There is some logical question about separating the two, since there are suggestions in the literature that the results obtained in self-ideal discrepancy studies would have been obtained as clearly and simply (or even more so) by employing a measure of perceived self only (e.g., Lipsitt, 1958). Ideal-self scores elicited from a population tend to bunch together at the favorable end of the scale, whereas perceived-self scores are normally distributed. This fact means that the *discrepancy* score is almost perfectly correlated with the *perceived-self* score, so that little additional information is gained from calculating it. The hypothetical set of scores below illustrates this point:

Subject A's perceived-self score is 20; his ideal-self score, 30; his discrepancy score, 10.

Similar scores for subject B are 15 and 31; his discrepancy score is 16.

For subject C, the perceived-self score is 10; the ideal-self score, 30; and the discrepancy score, 20.

In other words, we learn just as much about these people by the simple procedure of giving and scoring a perceived-self test as by adding the ideal-self test and computing the discrepancy score; almost all the difference among the three discrepancy scores above was contributed by the perceived-self score. However, even though such purely statistical considerations may have affected many self-ideal discrepancy studies, the study of self-acceptance and self-criticism continues to be important. More sophisticated ways of obtaining measures both of perceived self and of ideal self will contribute to such research.

In summary, most research evidence indicates that people who are highly self-critical—that is, who show a large discrepancy between the way they actually see themselves and the way they would ideally like to be—are less well adjusted than those who are at least moderately satisfied with themselves. Evidence indicates that highly self-critical children and adults are more anxious, more insecure, and possibly more cynical and depressed than self-accepting people. They *may* be more ambitious and driving, however. At least some evidence indicates that people experience conflict about the traits on which they have the greatest self-ideal discrepancy, and that this conflict is sharp enough to interfere with learning involving such areas. The evidence for a curvilinear relation between self-ideal discrepancy and adjustment is not clear, and there is some question whether the topic of self-ideal discrepancy is really different from the topic of positive and negative self-concepts.

SELF-CONCEPT AND THE "REAL" SELF

There is, of course, no way of knowing the "real" self. The closest approximation that can be made, in the current state of our knowledge, is to compare the statements of a person about himself with judgments of people who know him well. For understandable reasons, studies that compare the self-concept and the "real" self are infrequent: self-concept studies are easy to do on "captive" populations, such as a group of high-school students or college sophomores in an introductory psychology class. But to study the "real" self it is necesary to work with groups whose members know every other member well, and are willing to make the effort to cooperate with the research worker.

One of the few studies of "real" self and self-concept was done by Calvin and Holtzman (1953), using as subjects late adolescents (college men). These investigators elicited the cooperation of four fraternity groups, each member of which knew every other man well. In all, 79 men cooperated. All were given the Minnesota Multiphasic Inventory (MMPI) in groups. They were then seen individually so that background information for each could be obtained and each could rank his buddies (including himself in his rankings) on traits of leadership, tolerance, adjustment, drive, tactfulness, and social understanding. The pooled ranks of every other man for a particular man constituted his score for "inferred self." If a man ranked himself higher than his buddies rated him, he was said to be "self-enhancing"; if he ranked himself lower, he was "self-depreciative." The closer to his buddies' pooled ranking his own ranking was, the more "insightful" he was considered to be.

Men considered by their buddies to be relatively well adjusted had lower scores on the MMPI scales of depression, psychasthenia (morbid self-preoccupation) and schizophrenia; and also appeared to have traits that were more masculine than the men who were ranked as poorly adjusted. These correlations, while statistically significant, were not outstandingly high (in the high .20's and low .30's), but provide some evidence for the validity of some of the subscales of the MMPI. There were marked tendencies (correlations in the high .30's and low .40's) for men who were self-enhancing (who had better opinions of themselves than their buddies did) to score low on the depression, psychasthenia, and schizophrenia subscales of the MMPI, while self-depreciative men scored high, or in the poorly adjusted direction.

The authors of the study suggest that persons scoring high on these three scales "reflect a chronic state of marginal maladjustment including concern with one's self. Subjects who score high on the factor would tend to have difficulties in their social contacts, possibly by reason of their dissatisfactions, worry and disgruntlement, and their complaining and pessimistic attitude." (pp. 42–43) When the accuracy of the men's insight (the degree to which their rankings of themselves jibed with their buddies' rankings) was studied, it was found that men with more accurate insight had lower scores on the hysteria (attitudes of emotionality and immaturity) and psychopathic deviate (attitudes of social irresponsibility and delinquency) scales. They were also more masculine in their attitudes than men with less accurate insight. Such conclusions fit well with the conclusions reached by Friedman (1955) and Chodorkoff (1954a), who found that men who were more accurate in their self-descriptions tended to be less defensive.

In another study of young men in the Army (Howard, 1957), 51 men filled out a self-rating, and at least two of their buddies filled out the same rating for them. The discrepancy between their "real selves" (the buddy rating) and their own self-concept was then computed. It was found that the correlation between this discrepancy and their Army rating of delinquency was .56 (the greater the discrepancy, the greater the delinquency). When effects of intelligence were ruled out statistically, the correlation increased to .64. This again is evidence indicating that accuracy of self-perception is related to good adjustment, in the sense that well-adjusted people are less likely to be delinquent. This conclusion is interesting in the light of the Calvin and Holtzman findings that their inaccurately rating fraternity men had more emotional and less mature attitudes, and also scored higher on attitudes of social irresponsibility and delinquency than the men who rated themselves accurately.

Coopersmith's study (1959) of fifth- and sixth-grade children has already been mentioned in the section on self-concept and adjustment. In addition to his data about the self-concept, he secured teacher judgments about the children (their "real selves"). Some of his subjects rated themselves high, others low, in self-concept. Although the youngsters were in general accurate (in the sense that the teachers agreed with their self-estimates), disagreements between child and teacher judgments occurred. From the total population of self- and teacher-judgments, Coopersmith secured a group of *high* self-esteem children whose teachers thought *poorly* of them (the high-low, or HL group), and another group of children who thought *poorly of themselves,* but who were *highly regarded* by their teachers (the low-high, of LH group). When these groups were compared, the children who were objectively successful, but who regarded themselves poorly (the LH's) were found to be more popular, better academic achievers although more self-critical, and more ambitious. These youngsters appear to·"take it out on themselves," but are well-regarded by both teachers and peers, and are academically successful.

Coopersmith also selected two other groups for special study. In one of these, the good self-concept of the children agreed with the favorable "real self" teachers' rating. These youngsters comprised the high-high, or HH, group. Another group of children had poor self-concepts with which their teachers agreed (the low-low, or LL, group). The LL's were less popular, achieved less well, were more anxious, and held lower ideal concepts of themselves (yet, at the same time, were more self-critical) than the HH's.

In other words, humble yet successful children seemed to "do better" according to our United States criteria of success than less humble but equally favorably rated children, although at some personal price. Children who neither *thought* they were doing well, nor *were* doing well, were relatively unidealistic about themselves yet, in their own eyes, failed even to meet their relatively low standards.

Two studies, then, indicate rather clearly that accuracy of self-estimate is associated with a number of other indices of good adjustment, although another study suggests that this relation is affected by whether the self-concept is *high and accurate,* or *low and accurate,* the former condition being more likely to accompany good adjustment. In this study, self-depreciating children who were regarded by their teachers as successful were popular with their peers and academically successful, yet at the same time very self-critical.

SELF-ACCEPTANCE AND ACCEPTANCE OF OTHERS

The notion that people who are self-accepting are accepting of others has been frequently tested. This theory (Rogers, 1949) is of obvious practical importance, particularly to those who believe that personal maladjustment is socially learned. The maladjusted, self-rejecting person, if he also rejects others, is likely to be rejected by them in turn, with resulting exacerbation of his maladjustment. If, in counseling, the self-concept can be improved, and if this improvement results in increased acceptance of and by other people, then a spiraling effect of "cure" or personal improvement will result: a "newly friendly" world will help along the counselor and the client.

The majority of studies of this subject indicate a clear and significant relation between acceptance of self and aceptance of others for both men and women, although actual popularity does not seem to be associated with either self-acceptance or acceptance of others. At least seven studies support the prediction that self-acceptance accompanies tolerance of and liking for others, thus suggesting that the self-accepting person sees the world as a friendlier and more benign place than the self-rejecting individual. These studies are so congruent in their results that they need only to be listed here: Berger, 1951; Phillips, 1951; McIntyre, 1952; Crandall and Bellugi, 1954; Omwake, 1954; Fey, 1955; and Levanway, 1955. Of these studies, McIntyre and Fey also dealt with the relation between actual popularity and self-acceptance.

The one study (Zelen, 1955) in disagreement with these was done with sixth-grade children, but failed to separate the sexes in data analysis. Since, at this age, boys tend to reject girls socially, and girls boys, this failure to distinguish according to sex obscures the significance of the study's findings.

Fey (1955) has made a rather refined analysis of his data, and his conclusions throw some additional light on the more general finding. He secured measures of self-acceptance, acceptance of others, each subject's judgment of how well he was accepted by others, and an estimate of actual acceptability, or popularity. His subjects were a presumably quite sophisticated group of 58 third-year medical students, all or most of whom were probably men. His highly self-accepting (good self-concept) men were more accepting of others, and estimated their own popularity higher than did the less self-accepting men. But they were not *actually* any more popular. Men who were highly accepting of others estimated themselves as more popular than those who had little acceptance of others, but were not actually more popular (r between acceptance of others and actual acceptance by others was .20, which does not reach statistical significance). Interestingly enough, there was no accuracy at all on the part of the men in estimating their popularity, the r between estimated acceptability and actual acceptability being .00.

Fey then split his subjects into groups of men who markedly overestimated their popularity (had self-enhancing tendencies) and men who markedly underestimated it (were self-derogatory). He found the latter group to be significantly more popular than the former, with an average of 6 friendly mentions each to the self-enhancers' 1.5. Fey believes that individuals who are very self-accepting but who reject others are possessed of "defensively organized" attitudes of superiority, are unperceptive of their actual group status, tend to disparage others, and are consequently rejected because they are threatening to the security of other people. But men who have low acceptance of themselves, together with high acceptance of others, are seen as nonthreatening, hence rewarding; and are well liked. Fey believes that the "prototypic well-adjusted person" (the one with high self-acceptance of others as well as himself) "may not appear to 'need' friendship or to repay it . . . his very psychological robustness is resented, or perhaps it is perceived and rejected as a Pollyanna-like facade." (p. 275)

To summarize, self-acceptance (a lack of cynicism about the self?) seems to be associated with accepting other people. This appears to indicate that the self-accepting person views the world as a friendlier place than the self-rejector. However, perhaps because of the complexity of social interaction (our tendency to conceal hostility and to exercise techniques of good manners and warmth toward people whether we like them or not), acceptance of others has not been found to be associated with actual popularity. It has been suggested that self-disparaging people, particularly those who are objectively successful, are better accepted socially than the "prototypic well-adjusted person," perhaps because they present no threat to their friends. This conclusion is suggested both by the Fey study reviewed in this section, and by the Coopersmith study discussed on pages 195–196.

CHANGES IN SELF-CONCEPT

Change in self-concept is, of course, required by the process of maturing and is central to such activities as counseling, psychotherapy, and remedial teaching. Considering the importance of knowledge about development and change of the self-concept, it is surprising that little direct study has been made of these topics. Engel (1959), for example, has demonstrated that adolescents improve in self-concept over a two-year period, without therapy or other special attempts to change their self-image. Of the group she studied, those with initially negative self-concepts improved the most, although youngsters with good self-concepts maintained their original status. Rogers and his students (e.g., Rogers and Dymond, 1954) have shown that adult self-concepts tend to improve with psychotherapy; indeed, they regard improvement in self-concept as an indicator of successful therapy.

All of the present discussion of the self-concept has been based on the assumption that it is learned. It seems logical to think that the self-concept, based as it is on attitudes and values held about the *self*, has much in common with general social attitudes and personal beliefs and values. Any theory or research, then, that relates to changing attitudes *should* have relevance for changes in the self-concept.

Festinger (1957) has developed a provocative theory about attitudes and their change, from which have come interesting studies of children and college students. His theory is very briefly presented below, and the assumption (admittedly speculative) is made that it applies to self-concept as well as to more general and more objective (or thing-centered) attitude changes. Several ingenious experiments to test this theory have been carried out by Festinger and his students. Some of these are reviewed below. Following each review, and assuming underlying similarity of the principles governing self- and general-attitude changes, theoretical extensions for the self-concept are formulated on the basis of the research results.

Festinger maintains that when inconsistent perceptions are held by a person, either about himself or about his environment, he is placed in a state of tension, which Festinger calls psychological "dissonance." This is an uncomfortable state of affairs, which an individual attempts to alleviate or dissipate by bringing his cognitions closer together (reducing the ratio of inconsistent to consistent cognitions). It seems plausible to extend this theory to self-concept discrepancies. Indeed, considerable evidence has been reviewed which indicates that individuals with high self-ideal discrepancies are uncomfortable people, who may be struggling to get their self- and ideal self-concepts more in line with each other; and that improvement in self-concept is regarded at least by some as an indication of increased personal comfort and happiness. Certainly, much of counseling and psychotherapy has as a goal improvement in self-concept, reduction in self-ideal discrepancy, reduction of confusion and conflict in self-concept, and so on.

The first of the studies to be reviewed here was done by Festinger and Carlsmith (1959). They have published an engaging report of research supporting the following hypotheses: (1) If a person is induced to do or say something that is contrary to his private opinion, he will change his opinion so as to bring it in line with what he has said or done. (2) The greater the pressure used to elicit his dissonant behavior (above the *minimum* required to elicit it), the less likely he is to change his opinion. In other words, the greater the pressure, the more likely it is that he will be able to divorce his behavior from his personal conviction.

These authors induced undergraduate college men, through harmless and amusing deceits, to report favorably, to a putative next-in-line subject for the same experiment, about an excruciatingly dull experimental session to which they had been subjected immediately prior to the report. Relative rankings of this dull task were secured (1) from a control group that had not been induced to make such a report; (2) from an experimental group that had been offered $1.00 per man to make such a report (the minimal-reward group); and (3) from a second experimental group (the maximal-reward group), each member of which was offered $20.00 to make the report.

The task they were ranking consisted of the subjects spending a half hour putting 12 spools on a tray, emptying the tray, refilling it with spools, and so on, working at their own speed and using only one hand; then, for a second half hour, working with a board that contained 48 square pegs, the task being to turn these one at a time a quarter-turn clockwise, then another quarter-turn, and so on, again using one hand and working at their own speed. It is difficult to imagine a more anaesthetizing task.

In line with the hypotheses, the control group gave the task a mildly negative rating (one might say that it showed good manners); the minimal-reward group rated it as moderately enjoyable; and the maximal-reward group gave it a neutral rating. Subjects in the minimal-reward group also testified to their willingness to go through the procedure again, whereas the other two groups indicated reluctance.

This study suggests the following speculative prediction for self-concept change: If, through mild pressure or reward, an individual can be induced to do something contrary to his self-concept, he will alter his self-concept in the direction of his spoken opinion or overt action. If one who considered himself a poor speaker, for example, were in some low-pressure fashion induced to make a good speech, he might improve his conception of himself as a speaker. This prediction fits well with material in Chapter 5: Unexpected rewards may result in more alteration of expectancies than rewards that have been predicted.

In a second study, Cohen, Terry, and Jones (1959) gave one group of male college freshmen *an option* of listening or not listening to a propaganda session on a topic concerning which they held strongly opposing opinions. Another group was subjected to *strong pressure* to listen to the session. The low-pressure group moved almost four times as far as the high-pressure group in the direction of agreeing with the propaganda. The suggestion for self-concept change is obvious: One is more likely to induce an individual to make changes in his self-concept by non-directive, low-pressure methods than through high social pressure. This suggests that therapy voluntarily entered will be more successful than when entered involuntarily.

Brehm (1959) exposed adolescents to two sets of conditions, in one of which there were high social consequences (the young people's behavior was ostensibly to be reported to their parents); whereas in the other their behavior would remain secret. Brehm obtained like-dislike ratings from eighth-graders for 34 vegetables. Then an experimenter, posing as a nutrition researcher, asked the youngsters to take part in a food-testing program. The test, of course, was designed so that the vegetable each adolescent was asked to "test" was one he heartily disliked. He was told that he could eat it or not, as he wished. If he ate it, he would be given his choice of either two movie tickets or two records. For the *low-consequence* group, nothing more was said; but for the *high-consequence* group, the experimenter mentioned casually (when the youngsters had almost finished eating the dish of vegetables), "Oh I almost forgot to mention that one of the reports we plan to put out from this study will simply be a letter to the parents of each person who takes part, just indicating which vegetable that person ate." (p. 380) Mama, in other words, would know that he had consumed something which was "good" for him, but which he loathed.

After this tricky sequence, the subjects were asked to rate the 34 vegetables again. They were told, in a permissive fashion, that some people changed their opinions, while others did not. The high-consequences group changed significantly more in their ranking of the previously disliked vegetable than the low-consequences group, although this latter group also gave higher ratings to the test vegetables after having tested them.

Implications for self-concept change are obvious: If the behavior contrary to the self-concept is likely to be known by important other people (is going to become public), then the predicted self-concept change will be greater than if the consequences remain private.

Brehm and Cohen (1959), using sixth-graders as subjects, demonstrated that when a choice must be made between two highly *dissimilar* rewards (toys), the increase in preference rating for the chosen one, and the decrease in preference rating for the unchosen one, is greater than when the choice is made between two rather *similar* toys. The reasoning is that the subject sees himself as giving up more in the dissimilar than in the similar choice situation, so that more dissonance is produced, and more change of opinion results. These sixth-grade children also changed more in favor of the chosen and against the unchosen toy when they were required to choose among four rather than two alternative items. The assumption is that having to give up three things produces more dissonance than having to give up one. These results suggest the "sour grapes" phenomenon.

Speculative predictions for self-concept change are more difficult to make from this study than from the first three summarized in this section, but the following might be hazarded: Let us take, for example, a boy who has entered junior-high school, when for the first time clear choices of activity must be made, some being sacrificed so that others may be pursued. He has equally strong and equally valued conceptions of himself as an athlete and as a scholar, but must choose between two activities: debate and basketball. He chooses debate. It might be predicted that he will sharply devalue the importance of basketball, and possibly of all sports; but will sharply upgrade the importance of debate and other types of intellectual activity. The actual *direction* of his conception of himself as an athlete may not shift, but the *value* to him of this facet of his self-concept will change in a negative direction. Conversely, the value of intellectual activities will become greater, and the importance of the intellectual facet of his self-concept will increase. Less marked changes will occur if he has to choose between, say, swimming and basketball, or Science Club and debate. More marked changes will occur if he has to choose one of many activities than if he has to choose between only two.

In summary, one may predict from the Festinger dissonance theory that the self-concept will change in the direction of overt behavior relating to it. Change will be greater if the behavior is induced by low pressure, or accompanies a high degree of freedom of choice; and if the behavior is likely to have tangible consequences (i.e., is expected to become known by people important to the subject). Shifts in the importance or value of facets of the self-concept will occur when the individual is forced to choose behavior that relates to one facet but excludes another. These shifts will be to the advantage of the facet to which the chosen behavior is relevant.

OTHER QUALITIES OF THE SELF-CONCEPT

To this point, the discussion of the self-concept has followed the research literature rather closely. Research in this area has concerned itself almost exclusively with one aspect or quality of the self-concept: its positive or negative valence. Suggestions of other qualities of the self-concept that merit more consideration and research than have been given them are listed below.

1. *Complexity and breadth.* It can be assumed that normal adults have more complex and broader self-concepts than children; and that highly intelligent and cultured adults have more complex and broader self-concepts than, for example, adults of borderline intelligence, little education, and a narrow range of experiences. The person who lives only for his work would be expected to have a narrower self-concept than an individual with

a great variety of interests and activities. The married man and father will
have had to develop facets of his self-concept for which the bachelor has
experienced no need.

2. *Congruency and accuracy.* The self-concept should, it would seem,
conform rather closely to the actual life situation of the individual. Some
research on this topic has been reviewed. There are many occasions or
periods during the developmental process when the self-concept is out of
line with actuality. For example, the author has known many early-maturing children who, as far as their physiques were concerned, were full-
fledged adults, and who were reacted to by teachers and others as though
they were substantially older than they really were; yet who still carried
conceptions of themselves as children. On occasion serious, although usually temporary, maladjustments have resulted for some of these young
people.

Also common in our culture is the middle-aged individual who still
carries with him a self-concept of the dashing blade or winsome belle of 21.
One of the problems of old age is failure to change the self-concept to fit
failing health, diminished strength and endurance, and brittle bones.
Wheelchairs are full of old ladies who broke their hip because of the illusion that they could still scramble up a stepladder to change a light bulb.

As has been mentioned, many successful people still maintain the self-
concept of shy, inadequate adolescence. Less frequent, probably, is the
example of the essentially inadequate individual who sees himself as a
powerful and successful figure. Much of psychotherapy and counseling
has as its goal an increase in congruency of the self-concept.

3. *Clarity or articulateness.* Highly self-aware or inner-directed people
perhaps have clearer and more articulate, although not necessarily more
accurate or positive, self-concepts than those who are extroverted or outer-
directed. It is also possible that highly verbal individuals have clearer, or at
least more articulate, self-concepts than relatively nonverbal persons.

4. *Consistency.* Many maladjusted children and adults carry within
them contradictory and conflicting self-concepts. The self-concept of the
bully will usually be found to include incompatible facets of insecurity
and fright, on the one hand, and hostility, aggression, and combativeness,
on the other. It has been suggested that the Don Juan sees himself both as
a sexually inadequate individual and as one whom women find irresistible.

The stability of the self-concept is related to consistency. An extreme
example of instability of self-concept is provided by the manic-depressive
psychotic. In the manic phase, he may see himself as gregarious, charming,
powerful, successful, and leading "the good life." Depressed, he regards
himself as worthless, the world as bleak and gray, and things so hopeless
that often he attempts suicide.

Certainly, self-assurance varies to some degree with success and failure,
good times and hard times. But this veering, for a well-adjusted person,
should not be extreme.

5. *Flexibility.* The notion of flexibility is, of course, somewhat related to both congruency and accuracy, as well as consistency, but it includes something more: the ability to change roles and shift from one appropriate self-concept to another as occasion demands it. When he comes home from the office, a man should be flexible enough to drop the concept and role of a successful or driving manager of men and to assume, instead, the appropriate role of husband and father.

Flexibility is also somewhat related to the notion of complexity. By maturity, an individual should have varied self-concepts: in one situation, he may need to see himself as a leader and be able to adopt the appropriate role; whereas in another, the self-concept and behavior of follower may be required. Adults must usually change from a high degree of personal freedom and independence to breadwinning or housewifery and parenthood; from parents of preschoolers to parents of adolescents; from the family circle to the social circle and back again; from the security of the at-home routine to the excitement and unfamiliarity of the vacation; from an intimate circle of friends to occasions when they are the only strangers, and so on.

6. Still another dimension of the self-concept that appears to have been neglected in the literature, although considerable research is now accumulating, can be tentatively called *self-acceptance.* There are some who can regard themselves accurately, who can face the fact that they are not all they would like to be (that there is substantial discrepancy between their actual and ideal selves), yet who live happily and creatively with this awareness. There are others who are in constant turmoil because they are not what they think they should be. It may be that this latter type of uncomfortable adjustment acts as a drive or motive to spur such people on. Ambition may, in part, have such a base.

These, undoubtedly, are only *some* of the qualities of the self-concept that are worth investigating, but a chapter on the self-concept would not be complete without their introduction.

SUMMARY

The assumption this chapter makes is that the self-concept is learned, and can best be visualized as a set of expectancies, plus evaluations of the areas or behaviors concerning which these expectancies are held.

Most of the research that has been done on the self-concept has concerned its "good-bad," or positive-negative, dimension. Items (usually some form of questionnaire) designed to measure this dimension either are selected because they have consensual social value (positive *or* negative); or are rated personally by the individual being measured.

The considerable body of research on traits, attitudes, behaviors, and various qualities associated with the self-concept indicates rather clearly that good self-concepts are associated with such desirable characteristics as low anxiety and generally good adjustment, popularity, and effectiveness in group relations but relative independence from the group (i.e., an accepting group seems less important to people with positive self-concepts than to people with negative self-concepts). Those with good self-concepts seem more honest with themselves than individuals with poor self-concepts, and appear to be less defensive.

Parental attitudes shape the self-concept, and children whose parents value them "extrinsically" (i.e., for what they *do* rather than what they *are*) seem to be grandiose in their self-conceptions, less mature, and unrealistically persistent—even rigid—in certain attitudes pertaining to the self. Underachievers in school have poorer self-concepts than normal achievers, and reflect feelings of undue restriction on their freedom, of defensiveness, and of loneliness.

A related, but not necessarily independent, type of self-concept research concerns itself with the discrepancy between the actual and the ideal self. This area is labeled as "not necessarily independent" because of some indications in the literature that the amount of self-ideal discrepancy is a function more of the positive-negative variation of the self-concept than of variations in the ideal self. Generally speaking, the greater the self-ideal discrepancy, the less adequate the adjustment, according to a variety of criteria. The responses of those with high self-ideal *discrepancies* seem quite similar to those of subjects in other studies that have taken account only of the good-bad dimension of the self-concept.

In studies where the self-concept was compared with ratings of the individual made by others, those who were more "accurate" in their self-perceptions received scores on personality tests indicating good adjustment, and less often manifested delinquent tendencies. However, the effect of accuracy varies according to whether the self-concept is *good* and accurate, or *poor* and accurate, with good-accurate self-concepts more closely associated with good adjustment than poor-accurate ones. Children who are inaccurate in their self-concepts, in that they regard themselves poorly but are rated by their teachers as successful, are quite popular and academically successful, yet very self-critical.

Self-acceptance appears to be related to acceptance of others, although not to actual popularity. Those who are self-rejecting, but who *do* accept others, are rated as more popular than highly self-accepting men who are not highly *other*-accepting.

Although self-concept change has not been intensively investigated, the Festinger theory of dissonance (built around more objective attitudes than those that characterize the self) suggests a number of predictions about how such change takes place. This theory states that individuals holding inconsistent perceptions about themselves or their environment will attempt to eliminate the tension aroused by this inconsistency by bringing their conflicting perceptions closer together. The following speculative predictions were made from research suggested by this theory: The self-concept will change in the direction of overt behavior that relates to it; low social pressure for change will result in more change than high pressure; when the behavior is expected to have real-life consequences, more change will result that when no consequences are expected; shifts of value in facets of the self-concept will occur when an individual is forced to choose behavior that relates to and supports one facet, but excludes another.

Finally, several aspects of the self-concept other than the positive-negative dimension, which are important and in need of research, were discussed. These aspects are: complexity and breadth, congruency and accuracy, clarity, consistency, flexibility, and self-acceptance.

Intelligence: Measurement and Educational Practices

ONE of the major achievements of the science of psychology is the measurement of intelligence. Although much controversy surrounds the theory and assessment of intelligence, the research literature on this topic is perhaps as solid as any in the entire field.

Because much highly specialized research relating to intelligence has been done, two separate chapters are devoted to a review of pertinent findings. This method of treatment should not be taken as implying that intelligence is independent of other developmental phenomena. It is, of course, *interdependent,* influencing and influenced by almost all other aspects of development.

DEFINITIONS

Many volumes have been written on intelligence, and attempts to define it are legion. These attempts range from stating that "intelligence is what intelligence tests measure" to such definitions as "intelligence is the ability to do abstract thinking."

Some early (Thorndike *et al.,* 1926) as well as recent (Ferguson, 1954, 1956) workers in theory and measurement of intelligence have argued that there are many intelligences, or that intelligence is made up of a number of pure or "primary" factors, each relatively independent of the others. Thurstone and Thurstone (1950) have devised tests for children and adults that purport to measure a number of these primary factors, such as ability to deal with spatial concepts, number ability, word fluency, and vocabulary.

Spearman (1927), a pioneer in work with the concept of intelligence, held that there was a general, or g, factor that influenced all "intelligent" or sentient behavior; and that there were many special, or s, factors, some of which were heavily dependent on g (number ability, for example), whereas others were relatively independent (for example, music or motor ability). Still other authors speak of verbal ability and performance ability (e.g., Wechsler, 1944).

Recent Theoretical Developments

There has been relatively little recent theoretical concern with intelligence. Ferguson (1954), surveying the current scene, states:

> At present no systematic theory, capable of generating fruitful hypotheses about behavior, lies behind the study of human ability. Current approaches are largely empirical. . . . The concept of intelligence . . . is no longer a useful scientific concept except as subsuming some defined set of clearly distinguishable abilities. (p. 95)

After this somewhat negative pronouncement, Ferguson develops a theory of intelligence which is more a learning than a genetic theory, and which has perhaps been indirectly prompted by Hebb (1949). Ferguson believes that "ability" (or intelligence), as tested by our current intelligence tests, is made up of correlated types of overlearning. Overlearning, in interaction with an individual's biological heritage, has resulted in these separate abilities (which, when grouped, are called intelligence) reaching their asymptotes. That is, regardless of how much an individual tries, he will become no more proficient in performing such tasks; nor, regardless of how their practice is neglected, will efficiency in performing them decline much with time. Ferguson would say that a score on an intelligence test is highly useful in predicting success in school simply because the overlearned skills represented by an intelligence quotient have a substantial amount of transfer to the types of learning an individual must master in school.

Ferguson maintains that those abilities essential for satisfactory adjustment to a culture increase regularly as a child grows older, up to perhaps age 17; those abilities that are not necessary for adjustment to a culture fail to increase at the same rate, and indeed may not increase at all. By this reasoning he accounts for the differences in measured intelligence between people who live in different countries, or in rural rather than urban areas, or in institutions rather than homes, or in circumstances of cultural isolation rather than cultural intercommunication, or in one social class rather than another. Representative studies bearing on such cultural factors will be taken up in more detail in the next chapter. But further to illustrate Ferguson's provocative point of view, let us anticipate later material by saying that there is substantial evidence that children growing up in culturally isolated rural areas (for example, the mountains of eastern Tennessee) show a progressive *decrease* in intelligence as measured by standard intelligence tests: older brothers and sisters have a materially lower IQ than younger brothers and sisters. Ferguson would explain this by saying that the skills measured by a standard American test of intelligence are simply not very important in adapting to existence in the Tennessee mountains; hence, they decline with age.

One interesting study (Havighurst and Hilkevitch, 1944) indicates that a sample of 92 Hopi Indian children, relatively remote from the "standard" United States culture, scored substantially higher on a performance ("nonverbal") type of intelligence test than Indian children living closer to the standard culture. Indeed, with a mean IQ[1] of 115, they scored substantially higher than the group of white children on which the test had been standardized. They also tested much higher than a group of 29 Shiprock Navaho children, whose average score was 96, despite the fact that the Hopi youngsters were "much less acculturated." However, the 21 most isolated of the Hopi children—an "Old Oraibi" group—averaged 105 IQ, whereas the rest of the "more progressive . . . more subject to white influence . . . group averaged 117 IQ." (p. 430)

It might be conjectured, according to Ferguson's point of view, that the elaborate tribal organization and ritual, high artistic level, well-developed architectural abilities, and complete dependency on an environment so hostile that survival demands it be studied in exquisite and painstaking detail, all helped to develop high performance skills. The artistically and architecturally less proficient Navahos, who are, on the whole, herders rather than farmers, may have less opportunity to develop the skills measured by this intelligence test. The same thing may be true of the standardization group of Midwestern children, who lived in moderately comfortable, undemanding surroundings.

In this connection, Ferguson's statement applies: "Presumably children reared in different environments, which demand different types of learning at different ages, develop different patterns of ability." (1954, p. 99) Ferguson also hypothesizes that different abilities may be required at different stages of learning a task. "An individual might possess the ability to improve rapidly in the early stages of learning, but might lack the abilities necessary to attain high proficiency at the stage of high habituation or overlearning." (1954, p. 2) Most of us, that is, can learn the elements of playing the piano; few of us, regardless of how we practice, can become good enough to be concert pianists. Evidence exists to support this point of view. One study of young men (cited by Ferguson, 1956) indicates that in the early stages of learning a visual-motor task, the rate of learning depended most heavily on spatial and verbal abilities. Those who could best manipulate spatial concepts, those who were superior in verbal ability, picked up the beginning essentials of the task most rapidly. However, eventual mastery—a highly superior finished performance—depended more on speed of reaction time and the rate at which the individual moved. Another study (Ritchie, Aeschliman, and Pierce, 1950) used rats as subjects, and found that the first stages of learning depended heavily on the animal's visual discrimination ability, whereas perfecting the maze learning was a function of the animal's ability to utilize motor and kinesthetic cues. Bayley (1955), who has conducted longitudinal studies of the develop-

---

[1] The intelligence quotient is obtained from a measurement of the child's mental age. Mental age is then divided by chronological age, and the result multiplied by 100 to remove decimals. For example, a child tested on his tenth birthday and found to have a mental age of 10 will obtain an IQ of 100, which is considered to be average.

ment of intelligence in United States children, comes to a conclusion in part similar to Ferguson's. Bayley states:

> I see no reason why we should continue to think of intelligence as an integrated (or simple) entity or capacity which grows throughout childhood by steady accretions. . . . Intelligence appears to me, rather, to be a dyamic succession of developing functions, with the more advanced or complex functions in the hierarchy depending on the prior maturing of earlier simpler ones (given, of course, normal conditions of care). (p. 807)

Intelligence as Problem-Solving Ability

By and large, the concern of this book is with United States children who are normal, who live in relatively average situations, and who go to regular schools. For such a group, it is perhaps most practical to think of intelligence as *problem-solving ability*.

Such an ability is complex, not simple. Problem-solving involves concentration, speed, and depth or power, among other things. One type of problem may involve numbers, another spatial or geometric concepts, another only the use of words. One man may be an "intelligent" safe-cracker, yet unable to grasp algebra or foreign languages. A brilliant author may be "stupid" if he tries to become a farmer or woodsman or mechanic. There does, however, appear to be a moderate relationship between different types of problem-solving ability. The efficient safe-cracker, had he been socially oriented and more conventionally motivated, could probably have made an excellent mechanic. The author, were he as interested in farming or being a woodsman as he is in writing, would probably have done well at either pursuit.

APPROACHES TO MEASUREMENT

There are many different types of intelligence test, and many different versions of each type. The *Fifth Mental Measurements Yearbook* (Buros, 1960), for instance, includes reviews of 179 different intelligence tests, or instruments allied to intelligence tests. Such tests are most simply classified according to (1) the age group for which they are suitable and (2) their type. There are tests suitable for measuring intelligence (or something presumed to be akin to it) in infants, preschool-aged children, children of elementary-school age, adolescents, and adults (including certain extremely difficult instruments designed to measure the intelligence of the most superior adult). There are tests that must be given individually, whereas others are intended as group instruments. There are tests of so-called verbal intelligence (such as verbal reasoning analogies: "*Good* is to *bad* as *love* is to . . . . . .?"; and vocabulary tests); and there are performance tests. These latter do not involve the use of words in responding, although probably subjects guide their behavior by thoughts expressed to themselves in words. Examples of such tests are: solving paper mazes by drawing a trace through them with a pencil; fitting together individual pieces to make more complex forms; and replacing missing pieces into a picture from which they have been cut. There are tests, or individual items within tests, that tap speed (the faster the individual works, the higher his score); power (problems range from very simple to extremely difficult, but no speed limit is set); and breadth (for instance, range of vocabulary or information).

Binet, with whom intelligence-testing may be said to have begun, was trying to solve a very practical problem: How can we predict whether a child will succeed or fail in school? At present, intelligence tests accomplish this goal fairly satisfactorily: when a child is successful, as compared with other children of the same age and culture, at dealing with certain problems—such as defining words, repeating a list of numbers from memory after the examiner has said them aloud, figuring out the answers to such questions as, "What makes a windmill turn?," judging how a piece of paper that has been cut when it was folded will look when it is unfolded —he is classified as "bright." Other things being equal, when his IQ is high, he will do well in school. Doing poorly on such tasks in comparison with other children results in a low IQ, which usually means that a child will do poorly in school.[2]

Intelligence tests predict best for groups of children in elementary school, and predict less adequately the higher up the academic ladder we go. Almost all American children attend elementary school; they are exposed to a relatively homogeneous curriculum; and usually they have only one teacher, except for special subjects such as music, art, and recreation. In junior high school, prediction is made more difficult by the platoon system, in which different teachers teach different subjects. A math teacher, for example, may be very efficient in getting the best achievement from almost every child, whereas the social studies teacher may get the most from her favorites but have a discouraging effect on other, perhaps equally able, children. Such factors reduce the accuracy of prediction. High school presents further complexities: some children take part-time jobs; some take easy curriculums or electives, others more difficult ones. Some let their grades go, spending all their time in extracurricular activities or in pursuit of the opposite sex. A whole group—the slow learners—who could be diagnosed very accurately by intelligence tests, have dropped out of school entirely before high school or have been placed in special vocational schools.

In college, motivation and study efficiency affect success almost as much as intelligence. There is no one to enforce study hours; hence the student who finds it difficult to plan ahead will almost certainly have academic trouble, regardless of how bright he is. There is a wide range of electives—

---

[2] The school curriculum, of course, is itself a complex matter. A child who stands very high in reading ability may be relatively poor in arithmetic, although ordinarily he will still do better than the average of his class.

some easy, some difficult. Ordinarily, only the relatively bright go to college in the first place, so that again the "easy-to-predict" lower-intelligence group is no longer present. In college, then, intelligence-test scores predict actual achievement even less accurately than they do in high school.

Finally, few enter professional and graduate schools without possessing very high intellectual ability, so that the success or failure of graduate students is perhaps due even more to temperament, interest, efficient studying, and motivation than it is to intelligence as such. Testing experts continue to struggle with the creation of intelligence tests that will permit accurate predictions about success in law, medical, or engineering school as well as the other learned professions. They are also searching for measures of aptitudes ranging from mechanical skills to the qualities required for making good as a banker.

Predictions about how a student will do in professional training can be made with some success for high-school students. Accuracy of prediction is greater still for students of college age. But as yet there is no way to pick out the potentially successful engineer or nurse during the elementary-school years, although general intellectual ability can be measured rather accurately by the time a child is 2½ to 3 or 4 years of age. That is, a moderate degree of accuracy has been achieved in predicting how well a child will do in school, but forecasting his specific intellectual and performance strengths and weaknesses is still a psychological frontier.

INFANT INTELLIGENCE TESTS

The most widely used intelligence tests, or developmental schedules, for infants (children up to approximately 2 years of age) are the Catell (1940), Gesell (Gesell and Amatruda, 1941), Kuhlmann (1939), and Northwestern (Gilliland, 1949). To anyone who knows infants, it is obvious that finding test items that tap what we have called problem-solving ability is difficult, if not impossible. A *problem* involves a *goal* for the individual being tested, the *route* to which is not clear. The goals of the very young infant (younger than about 6 months) are quite primitive: he wants only to be full, dry, warm, and so on. But he has no direct methods of reaching these goals; he is dependent upon adults for his achievement. How, then, can we devise an intelligence scale for infants?

The builders of such scales have used as items sensori-motor responses to changes in the environment, behaviors that indicate social responsiveness, and relatively primitive problem-solving activities. Examples of these are, respectively: turning the head in the direction of a bell or light; smiling in response to the smile and/or verbalization of an adult; and dropping one of two cubes or toys to take a third different one.

All tests of infants are, of course, individual. In a careful analysis of tests given over the years to children who took part in a longitudinal study, Hofstaetter (1954) concludes that the major element tapped by the items that make up infant intelligence tests is "sensori-motor alertness." A child who is advanced in a sensori-motor way earns a high score on the tests; a child who is retarded earns a low score. But the nature neither of the test items nor of measurable intelligence in infancy (the two are related, and it is difficult to say which is which) changes with increasing age, so that this factor of sensori-motor alertness plays little part in intelligence-test items designed for children older than about 40 months.

The findings that have resulted from studies of infant intelligence tests are easily summarized:

1. Grossly mentally defective babies can be distinguished from normals.

2. Babies who live in institutions score lower than children in homes with true or foster parents.

3. Some authors (e.g., Spitz, 1945, 1946) maintain that institution-reared children never recover from their retardation; others (Pasamanick, 1946) indicate that when the environment becomes richer, or more nearly normal, infants recover the lost ground, at least to some degree. However, no studies clearly resolve this important issue. Studies done with animals throw some light on this point; they will be reviewed in the next chapter.

4. Scores on intelligence tests given to children younger than 18 months have at best a low relation to the scores they earn later on more conventional, problem-solving types of intelligence tests. Some controversy persists regarding this point. A representative study supporting the conclusion was done by Cavanaugh *et al.* (1957), in which the Catell was used for children through 24 months of age, the Stanford-Binet for older children. (This was a longitudinal study, the maximum number of children compared at any two ages being 191, the minimum 34.) But Knobloch and Pasamanick (1960) report studies obtaining correlations of .50 to .75 between tests given in infancy (apparently at about 40 weeks) and tests given at the age of 3 years.

5. When other factors are controlled, socioeconomic status and race have no influence on infant test scores (see, e.g., Pasamanick, 1946, and Knobloch and Pasamanick, 1960).

6. In the hands of a sensitive and well-trained tester, infant intelligence tests can reveal a baby's specific disabilities, such as deficiency in social responsiveness, vision, hearing, and so on. In other words, like a physical examination, they provide a moderately good picture of the child as he is.

7. Babies tested when they appear to be in a good mood test about the same on a later test, whereas those who were thought by the examiner to be disturbed or other than normal at the time of one testing score substantially higher when they are tested later (Gallagher, 1953).

8. Scores for the same baby on different tests agree poorly with each other, since there are consistently large differences in *average* quotients from one test to another. Individual scores also fail to show a high correlation

from one test to another (Harms, 1957). That is, a baby may stand toward the top of his comparison group on one infant intelligence test, but toward the bottom on another.

Probably the most important of these findings is that infant intelligence tests *can* and *do* reflect environmental deprivation. It will be recalled that Hebb (1949) would predict such an effect, and one can venture the guess that he would consider such retardation permanent. But for the broad normal range of babies, infant tests do *not* predict later intelligence in any really useful sense. The child who scores 180 on a Catell Infant Test may score 105 on a Stanford-Binet given when he is 6 years old; the child who scores 90 on a Kuhlmann may score 130 on a later Wechsler Intelligence Scale for Children. Socioeconomic class is related to intelligence at all later age levels; it shows no relation to intelligence as measured before about 18 months of age, nor does parental intelligence have any relation to babies' test scores. But certain regularities or irregularities of development *do* show up on the tests when they are skillfully used.

We are left with the conclusion that infant intelligence tests do not make the same highly useful predictions as intelligence tests given at a later age. On the other hand, no one expects a physical examination at 6 *months* to guarantee that a child will be healthy at 6 *years*. Why should an infant intelligence test necessarily be expected to predict that the "bright" baby will be a bright six-year-old? If the test tells us that the baby is progressing normally, it has accomplished a purpose. If it points out to us certain remediable lags in development, it has been valuable. It would, of course, be much more helpful, for all sorts of reasons, if later intelligence could be predicted more efficiently.

PRESCHOOL-AGE TESTS

Tests for children up to about 5 years of age are also given individually. They may be both verbal and performance tests. That is, some items require purely verbal responses; others, such as fitting together a jigsaw puzzle or form board, do not require the child to use words. Examples of verbal items at the preschool-age level are: asking the child to identify toy objects, such as miniature cars, dogs, and dishes; or pictured objects, such as birds or ships.[3] Performance items for young preschoolers (about 2 years of age) are building a low tower from one-inch cubes; fitting three simple geometrical forms cut from wood back into their recesses on a rectangular piece of wood. An item partly verbal yet also requiring performance is to identify different parts of the body by pointing to them upon request.

Such items approach the concept of problem-solving that we consider to be the core of intelligence, yet they are very simple and involve reasoning, testing, and rejecting different problem solutions, and so on, to only a limited

[3] Actual test items included in the more common standardized tests are not given here, but illustrations are derived from them.

degree. Hofstaetter's study (1954) of tests given repeatedly to the same children concludes that for youngsters from about 20 to 40 months of age, intelligence-test items are characterized by a factor that may be called *persistence*. This factor, he thinks, may be a "tendency to act in accordance with an established set rather than upon interfering stimulation." (p. 162)

From one point of view, persistence is the opposite of sensori-motor alertness (the tendency to react to whatever stimulation comes along). Persistence means that attention is given to one stimulus until an appropriate response can be made. This formulation makes good common sense: We cannot respond to the environment unless we can attend quickly and efficiently to many aspects of it; but we cannot begin to cope with any aspect until we can concentrate long enough on it to make a suitable response. Persistence, in other words, is defined more by the goal than by the stimulus.

Predictive Efficiency of Preschool Tests

As we have indicated earlier, one of the values of an intelligence test is the degree to which it predicts later intelligence-test scores of a child or group of children. Predictions of this kind are valuable for such problems as placing children in ability groups, deciding whether or not to let an underage child into kindergarten, or making diagnoses of mental retardation and special-class placement. Infant intelligence tests, we have seen, do *not* predict later intellectual status well, although they have certain values of their own. How successful in predicting later intelligence are tests of preschool-aged children?

As might be expected, the older the child is, the more accurate his intelligence-test score is and the better is the prediction that can be made of his young-adult intelligence level. In the Berkeley Growth Study (Bayley, 1949), "young adulthood" was thought of as 18 years of age. This ambitious study followed a group of children from birth to age 18. Intelligence tests given the children at 6 months of age actually had a slight, although statistically insignificant, *negative* relationship with intelligence as measured at 18 years. Tests given at 1 year of age showed about a .25 correlation with intelligence measured in young adulthood; by 2 and 3 years of age the correlation had moved to about .50 (thus accounting for 25 percent of the variance); for tests given at age 4, the correlation was in the high .60's, rising to the mid-.70's for tests given at age 5, 6, and 7. In other words, tests given in the early preschool years predict later intellectual development moderately well, although extreme variations in mental growth can and do occur from the preschool ages to maturity. The accuracy of prediction for tests given in the preschool years increases sharply as the age of the child increases, particularly up to about 5 years of age.

The correlations obtained in this same Berkeley study from another but less intensively studied group of children were lower than those given above. For this group, the correlation figure between tests given at 2 and again at 18 was about .30; for tests at 3 and 4 and again at 18, about .40; for tests at 5 and 18, .55; and for tests given at 6 and 18 years of age, about .60. The difference between these two groups is probably due to the fact that the examiners knew the children in the more intensively studied group better, and the children were more at ease in the testing situation; hence the test results were more accurate and the prediction better.

This divergence highlights the fact that a major reason for poor prediction from preschool tests may be the circumstances of testing. To possess scientific value, any measurement technique must have *high repeatability*. Repeatability is reduced when circumstances of error and random variation enter into test results. Examples of conditions that may produce random variation in scores are tenseness, fatigue, and illness on the part of children; and different degrees of relaxation, expertness, familiarity with the child, and warmth on the part of the examiner. It is not unlikely that the sex of the examiner also affects children differentially (Harms and Spiker, 1959). Young children are easily made insecure; their language is not necessarily clear; their attention span is short and they easily grow fatigued. One teacher of testing asks his students: "What would be your diagnosis if, while observing a test being given to a three-year-old by a rather experienced tester with whose techniques you could discover no major fault, you noted that the child squirmed, was easily distracted, glanced continually around the room, and seemed constantly to be retreating from the test?" He states that his typical student believes that the child is insecure and is attempting to avoid the issue of the test. His question then is: "Have you thought that maybe the child needs to go to the bathroom?"

Despite the relatively large correlations reported above between preschool and young-adult tests, the authors of one study (Honzik, Macfarlane, and Allen, 1948), involving 252 children who had repeatedly taken intelligence tests between the ages of 21 months and 18 years (further data from the Berkeley Growth Study), conclude that between the ages of 6 and 18 years almost 60 percent of the subjects changed 20 or more points. Some children moved rather consistently upward or downward as much as 50 points in score, and their changes tended to be in the direction of the intellectual level of their families. Special circumstances in their life history affected some but not other children.

Predictive Efficiency of Different Types of Items

For the most widely used test, the Stanford-Binet, items involving memory and the use of words are more effective in predicting later intelligence (correlate more highly with later IQ's) than items involving numbers, or not involving words (Bradway, 1945). However, the differences are not of great practical significance. But another careful study, done with a different preschool test (Goodenough and Maurer, 1942), reaches the opposite conclusion, so that the question of what type of item best predicts later intelligence remains open.

Some support is given to the first set of results by a study (Catalano and McCarthy, 1954) done with a rather small number (23) of institutionalized children between 6 and 18 months of age. The speech of these children was studied, and correlations were calculated between speech and Stanford-Binet intelligence tests administered when they were between 3 and 4½ years of age. All the correlations were positive, and some were quite high (for example, a .45 correlation was found between IQ and the number of different kinds of consonants the child had used during infancy). However, because of the small number and special type of children included, this study, though promising, can be thought of only as an exploratory one.

INTELLIGENCE TESTS FOR ELEMENTARY-SCHOOL CHILDREN, ADOLESCENTS, AND ADULTS

As soon as children reach an age when they can follow instructions, inhibit distractibility, and use a pencil, group intelligence tests can be used. The overwhelming majority of intelligence (or general aptitude) tests that are given are of the group type, although individual tests must be used with infants and preschoolers and are sometimes given to older children and adults as well.

Tests for school children and adults fall into the same categories as those for preschool children: *verbal* and *nonverbal*. On verbal tests, older children may be asked to define words, ranging from such simple ones as *letter* to such complex ones as *indefatigable;* or to unscramble sentences against a time limit—being allowed, for example, one minute to make sense out of the following: TOWN LITTLE FOLLOWED THE TO DOG ME. Adults and older adolescents, in a test of concentration and memory, may be asked to repeat as many as nine digits read monotonously by the examiner at the rate of one per second; or to give in reverse order as many as seven or eight digits read in the same fashion. Analogies of different levels of difficulty are a popular test item. A relatively simple example is: "*Sharp* is to *blunt* as *tall* is to . . . ?" Riddle-like situations are presented. The child is asked to read a passage against a time and an error limit, and to give back as many ideas as he can from the passage.

Performance items consist of such things as assembling elaborate form-board or jigsaw-puzzle tasks against a time limit; of running elaborate paper-and-pencil mazes; or of planning a route of search for an object lost in a field. These are commonly said to be nonverbal, or performance, tasks. Several authors (e.g., Sarason, 1953) have pointed out that this is probably not an accurate description, and have maintained that most Americans from early childhood on will give verbal tags to the tasks on which they are working, even though they do not say the words aloud. On a maze, for ex ample, they may say to themselves, "A left turn—no, there's a blind alley— better try a right turn." In other words, there is no clear distinction between verbal and performance intelligence-test items, although certainly factors of efficiency, speed, and spatial relationships enter into the latter that do not enter into the former. A survey of the literature indicates that there is a median correlation between verbal and performance intelligence-test quotients of about .65. In other words, there is a clear tendency for those who do well on one type of test to do well on the other; but, in prediction, one accounts for only a little more than 40 percent of the variance of the other.

There is scattered evidence in the literature that children of average or near-average verbal IQ, whose performance-test quotients are much higher, may have reading difficulties more often than would be suspected from their verbal IQ alone. Children from lower-class homes are likely to have verbal quotients equal to or lower than performance quotients, whereas the opposite is true for children from middle-class homes. There is also evidence to indicate that delinquents are likely to have performance quotients higher than their verbal quotients. Children or adults with brain damage apparently test lower on performance items than on verbal items. Although these findings hold for groups, they are of little practical importance in dealing with individuals.

According to Hofstaetter (1954), who has performed a factor analysis of longitudinal data from the Berkeley Growth Study, the common characteristic of intelligence-test items for older children is "what Freud has called 'provisional action' . . . or . . . the manipulation of symbols . . . the anticipation of future actions in the present." (p. 162) Again, this makes good common sense: First we attend to the multifarious stimuli in the environment ("sensori-motor alertness"); next we concentrate long enough on one stimulus to make an adaptive response ("persistence"); and, finally, we integrate both the past and the present, at a symbolic level, in order to thread our way through the complexities of a problem ("provisional action").

Other things being equal, group tests probably predict school success better than individual tests, since they have more elements in common with school learning tasks. Children ordinarily read and do arithmetic or spelling in groups. Hence a test taken in a group has more factors in common with the regular school situation than a test taken individually, where an alert examiner reassures the child and draws his very best from him. The anxious child will "go to pieces" in a group intelligence test, just as he will go to pieces in a group reading or arithmetic session—hence the test score predicts his performance accurately (what he will do, not what he could ideally do). The calm, efficient child who likes competition does his best in both types of situation; hence either group or individual test scores predict his school performance accurately.

A good school is, of course, interested in more than prediction of academic achievement. One common school aim is to help those with high potential but relatively low achievement. Here lies the value of the individual test: If a child scores 20 points higher on an individual than on a group test, yet his school performance is in line with his group-test score, the school psychologist or trained teacher infers that he has the capacity to do better than he is doing, and initiates action to make him a more efficient worker (attempts to bring his school performance in line with his score on the individual test). This effort may involve extra coaching, reassurance, counseling, working with the home, or a combination of such measures. A group test may predict quite adequately what the child with a severe reading difficulty is actually *doing* in school; but when his individual-test score is 30 points higher than his group-test score, the need for remedial reading is dramatically brought home.

SPECIAL CONSIDERATIONS
IN USING INTELLIGENCE TESTS

Many teachers and school administrators are skeptical of the uses of intelligence tests, which have indeed been widely misused. One teacher came to the author with the lament that she had, in her third-grade class, an engaging and well-liked child from a foreign-language home. "Mike" was doing well in school, according to her report, but she felt sorry for him because he was "feeble-minded." Further questioning elicited the fact that Mike had taken a group test in first grade, when he had had only the most elementary grasp of English. Inevitably, he had scored low, and had done poorly in school during his first year. As he learned English, his schoolwork improved, but the "feeble-minded" score remained on his record. At the suggestion of the author, he was retested on an individual test. His score was a very superior 130 IQ.

Another teacher had counseled with the parents of a first-grader, alerting them (to their utter dismay) to the fact that their child, Maria, would never do well in school and, indeed, might be considered retarded. The middle-class parents accepted this, albeit reluctantly. The consulting psychologist to the school, while leafing through the group-test booklets for the first grade, noted that one child had colored in the outlines of the test items rather than drawing lines from the criterion to the proper alternative. The type of test used was one where, for example, the child is asked to draw a line from the model in the left-hand margin of the page (perhaps the picture of a hen) to the one of several alternatives at the right that resembles the model (e.g., to the hen among a pig, a rooster, a duck, and a pigeon). This child proved to be Maria.

When the test was discussed with her, Maria tearfully confessed that her mother had taught her it was naughty to "mess up" a paper with random lines, and that she had therefore tried to "color" all the correct responses, but that this had taken her so long that she had become hopelessly lost. The teacher, routinely grading the tests, had failed to catch the nuances of

Maria's very neat coloring, and had assigned her an exceptionally low score. Maria, assured that it was indeed all right for her to draw lines on the test, scored comfortably high upon retest. The mother, too, learned a lesson about setting too severe standards for her child.

Even experienced test users frequently forget that the best of tests, given under ideal circumstances, can make only a partial prediction of how well a child will do in school. In our search for precision and exactness, we often fail to realize that IQs do not remain completely constant for any given child—that a child who tests high in first grade may be functioning at a very different level in the fifth grade. Such factors have led some to condemn tests entirely, thereby losing the substantal guidance they can contribute to education.

Opponents of intelligence tests are likely to say that "any teacher worth her salt knows how bright her children are without going through all that foolishness." Alexander (1953), among others, decided to test this statement. As his subjects he used 978 public-school pupils in grades three to eight, and their 35 teachers. Fifty percent of the teachers had completed 120 hours of college training, and their median teaching experience was 12 years. The study was done in about the middle of the second semester of the school year, so that each teacher had had ample opportunity to get to know the children.

Alexander asked each teacher to list the five pupils in her class who, in her opinion, were the most intelligent; and the five who were the least intelligent. They were then asked to list the five pupils who were working closest to capacity and the five who were performing furthest below their capacity in the major academic areas (e.g., reading, arithmetic). All the pupils were then given tests for intelligence (or academic aptitude), and for actual academic achievement.

Alexander found that the teachers were accurate in picking the highest and the lowest IQ's for only a few more than half the cases (57 and 58 percent respectively). They picked only about one fourth of the highest and lowest achievers (in relation to their capacity). The tendency of the teachers was to rank as "achieving up to capacity" those children who stood toward the top of their particular class, disregarding factors of age. They operated in about the same fashion in picking the low achievers. But even allowing for the fact that they tended to judge in relation to their own classes, they were accurate in judging the high achievers only about two fifths of the time, and the low achievers only about one third of the time. In view of the fact that marks indicating absolute success or failure are still very widely assigned by teachers and accepted as gospel by children and their parents, such a finding indicates that a majority of children are being graded according to some factor other than their actual academic achievement, and that they receive ratings of brightness or dullness that may be completely at variance with their actual ability. The very bright, high-achieving, but

young child would, under such circumstances, probably be graded lowe*ı*
than the older child who is working up to capacity, but who, because he i*ı*
older, is doing *relatively* less well.

"CULTURE-FREE" OR "CULTURE-FAIR" INTELLIGENCE TESTS

Those who say that teachers will "peg" their children according to their
IQ and discriminate against the low-scoring child while putting all their
efforts and attention into working with the high-IQ child perhaps have a
point. We have mentioned above that there is an almost universal tendency
to look for the exact and tangible. An IQ score has a deceiving appearance
of precision and unchangeability, and there is no doubt that many accept
the IQ altogether too uncritically.

One articulate and influential group of critics of conventional intelligence tests (Eells *et al.,* 1951) maintains that children of low socioeconomic class (children of "working families") are discriminated against by
our standard intelligence tests (as well as by our standard school curriculums, and for the same reasons). They say that intelligence tests abound in
abstractions and verbal conventions that form part of the culture of middle-
and upper-class children, but are foreign to lower-class children. For these
latter children, this group of critics believes, the world is one of harsh reality and down-to-earthness. The future is an uncertain thing, so they live in
the here-and-now. Abstractions will not buy bread nor win a fight in the
street; hence they have neither much use for, nor familiarity with, the abstract, preferring the concrete and tangible. Eells and his colleagues believe
that this factor of differential familiarity, rather than a "real" difference in
intelligence, is responsible for the intellectual differences found between
children from different socioeconomic classes. Like the present author, they
think of intelligence as being, in general, problem-solving ability.

In one elaborate study of this matter of "culture-free" intelligence tests,
by Haggard (1954), conventional, abstract items were rewritten in familiar, concrete terms. Examples of the standard items and Haggard's revisions
are given below:

Conventional Item	*"Culture-Free" Item*
Cub is to *bear* as *gosling* is to: fox, grouse, goose, rabbit, duck.	*Puppy* goes with *dog* like *kitten* goes with: fox, goose, cat, rabbit, duck.
A weighs less than B; B weighs less than C; therefore: B weighs more than C; A's weight is equal to B's and C's; A weighs less than C.	Jim can hit harder than Bill. Bill can hit harder than Ted; so: Ted can hit harder than Bill; Bill can hit as hard as Jim and Ted; Jim can hit harder than Ted.

Haggard points out that the second, syllogistic type of item proved to be the most difficult for his lower-class subjects.

Haggard studied 671 ten- to twelve-year-old children in his carefully done study of how they would perform on the two types of test under several different conditions. Among his numerous hypotheses were the following: The lower-class children would do much better on the culture-free form of the test than they did on the conventional form, but there would be little difference for the middle-class children; and practice and motivation would do the lower-class children more good, particularly on the culture-free test, than they would the middle-class children. He found that both the middle- and the lower-class children made much greater gains from one testing situation to another on the culture-free than on the standardized test, with some not clearly significant tendency for the lower-class youngsters to gain relatively more on the culture-free test than the middle-class children. Haggard was correct in hypothesizing that the lower-class boys and girls would do better on the culture-free than on the standard test; but the middle-class children also did better, so that class differences were just as marked on the culture-free as on the conventional test.

From the study emerged useful information that middle-class children enter testing situations better motivated than lower-class children. They also generalize training in test-taking better. Under optimal conditions, the differences in average test scores between social classes can be reduced, although they do not disappear. In other words, conditions of motivation and interest favoring the already relatively privileged middle-class children make the class differential in intelligence more pronounced than it "really is."

For years, studies of class differences in intelligence (see, e.g., H. E. Jones, 1954) have demonstrated that lower-class children score lower than middle- or upper-class children. Proponents of culture-free intelligence tests have predicted that much of this difference would disappear if their test, rather than a conventional test, were used. But studies with the new type of test (e.g., Angelina and Shedd, 1955; and Rosenblum *et al.*, 1955) fail to substantiate this claim. Knief and Stroud (1959), for example, found that social class correlates .31 with one of the more widely used culture-free tests, and .30 with a conventional intelligence test.

Findley and McGuire (1957), accepting the point that lower-class children are handicapped in taking conventional intelligence tests because they do less well on abstractions than middle-class youngsters, predicted that for types of problems that are not frequently encountered in any sector of the culture (for which there has been *no* differential in opportunity for practice between social classes), lower-class children would do *better* than their test score would predict; but that prediction from test scores would be accurate for middle-class children. Specifically, they predicted that between groups of middle- and lower-class pupils matched for IQ on a conventional test there would be a difference in problem-solving performance favoring the lower-class youngsters. That is, Findley and McGuire reasoned that lower-class children are actually brighter than indicated by their test scores, whereas the quotients are accurate indices for the middle-class children.

To test this hypothesis, they devised a rather elaborate block-sorting test of abstracting ability that did not involve language ability and was unfamiliar to all the children. This test was administered to 96 children from grades 3, 6, and 9, half of whom were lower- and half middle-class, and who were matched in IQ as measured by a standard group test. Contrary to the expectations of advocates of the culture-free intelligence test, the middle-class children did better on this "nonverbal" test than the lower-class children.

There are also rather clear indications that culture-free intelligence tests predict school success less well than the more conventional tests. This is to be expected, since the conventional tests presumably have more "operations" in common with school learning, as it is now structured, than do the culture-free or culture-fair tests. Altus (1956) and Love and Beach (1957) have demonstrated this point convincingly.

However, critics of any position, instrument, or idea must take care not to throw out the baby with the bath. Haggard has demonstrated that improvements in motivation and practice in test-taking can be helpful to lower-class youngsters, and that the measured intellectual difference between lower- and middle-class youngsters can to some degree be lessened by using nonconventional tests and modifying testing techniques.

From the intelligence-test differences between social classes, we would expect differences in school progress, middle- and upper-class children being expected to do better schoolwork than lower-class children. The actual differences in academic achievement between social classes are even more dramatic than the differences in intellectual level. On the whole, lower-class children achieve less well in school than their intelligence tests predict they will, whereas middle- and upper-class children approach their academic potential more closely. This state of affairs is one of the most serious of American school problems, and is undoubtedly due in part to middle-class bias by teachers and to curriculums and textbook materials that are foreign to the experiences of lower-class youngsters. In questioning the efficiency of the culture-free intelligence test, we do not intend to maintain that the schools, including their psychological personnel, are doing the best they can with lower-class children. This problem will be discussed more fully in a later chapter.

GROWTH AND DECLINE OF INTELLIGENCE

Hundreds of studies have been conducted purporting to reveal the rate of growth, the time of leveling off, and the onset and rate of decay of all sorts of human behavior that can be roughly classified as "intelligent." Findings vary widely, so that the conclusions set forth here (although they fall conservatively in the middle range of findings) can be disputed in terms of individual studies. Competent reviews of research in this area have been made fairly recently by, among others, H. E. Jones (1954), G. G. Thompson (1952), and Zubek and Solberg (1954).

Intelligence appears to grow less rapidly with increasing age. This pattern produces the negatively accelerating growth curve illustrated in Figure 7.1, which represents intellectual growth from about 10½ to 20½ years of age. This figure is adapted from H. E. Jones and Conrad (1944), who have drawn it to incorporate findings from three major studies of the growth of intelligence.

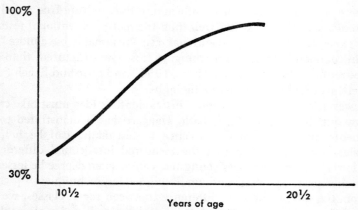

FIG. 7.1.   Intellectual growth from 10½ to 20½ years of age. (Adapted with permission of the National Society for the Study of Education and H. S. Conrad, from Jones and Conrad, 1944.)

Figure 7.1 reveals that somewhat more than 40 percent of mature intellectual status has been reached by 10½ years of age, and that growth from then on is progressively slower. No more "intellectual power" is added after about 19½ years of age, although of course individuals can add almost limitlessly to personal skills of all sorts. There is evidence to indicate that intellectual growth continues longer for the bright and superior and stops earlier for subjects of low intelligence (Gurvitz, 1951; H. E. Jones, 1954; Miles and Miles, 1932), although the most recent evidence that has come to the author's attention (Bayley, 1955; Owens, 1953) indicates that intellectual development continues well into maturity for relatively retarded as well as intellectually superior persons.

Figure 7.2 presents a curve of intellectual growth that, from birth to the late teens, is in the shape of a very shallow, steeply slanted S. This means that during infancy and the early preschool years there is a tendency toward positively accelerated growth (faster as the child gets older); at school age, growth has become negatively accelerated (slower year by year), as shown more clearly in Figure 7.1; and it is very gradual indeed (Figure 7.2) from the late teens on. Indeed, earlier studies, as reviewed by Zubek and Solberg (1954), for example, have rather consistently indicated that intellectual performance begins to drop at about the mid-twenties. This drop is minimal until a person reaches his forties. From this age, there is a steady decrease in efficiency for most mental functions. Tests that involve speed and, possibly, close attention or concentration seem to show decreas-

Fig. 7.2. A hypothetical composite age curve representing the growth of intelligence from birth to the middle years. (Adapted with permission of the American Psychological Association and Nancy Bayley, from Bayley, 1955.)

ing scores earliest in life (in the mid-twenties or even earlier); scores on power tests decline later; and scores on a type of test that Zubek and Solberg have called "breadth tests," such as tests of vocabulary and information, show a negligible decline, and in some studies an increase. Some of the information provided by Bayley (1955) on the development of intelligence during the years of middle age comes from tests that might be called power-breadth tests. In other words, intelligence seems very durable.

Owens (1953) re-administered the same test to 127 men after an interval of thirty or thirty-one years. These men had originally taken the tests as college freshmen, and, obviously, the second testing occurred when they were middle-aged and established.

The men whose cooperation Owens secured were not conspicuously different in general characteristics from those who refused to take part in the second test. He found that these mature men were significantly higher in total IQ than they had been as entering college freshmen. Their gains were most conspicuous in tests that presumably tap abilities called practical judgment, and on tests of synonym-antonyms, disarranged sentences, information, and analogies. Abilities to follow directions, handle arithmetic problems, and manage number series had stayed constant or decreased very slightly and not significantly. Men who were below 50 years of age in Owens' sample gained slightly more than those who were above 50, although both groups gained. Those who had completed the most college work gained more than those who had had less education; general science majors showed more upward movement than agriculture or engineering majors. Those who had moved from rural to urban settings during their life appeared to have gained more than those with other patterns of residence. Other characteristics, such as type of job held, income earned, physical exercise, marital status, number of children, and number of brothers and sisters showed no relationship to the amount of gain made by these men.

EDUCATIONAL PRACTICES AND INTELLECTUAL LEVEL

What are the responsibilities, and what special provisions exist, concerning the education of children at one or the other extreme of the intelligence distribution? A thoughtful observer is likely to conclude that American public schools do, on the whole, a fairly good job of "special education" —training children who are slow-learning, partially sighted or blind, partially hearing or deaf, cerebral-palsied, or with rheumatic hearts. It is true that these children are more adequately looked after in urban than in rural schools, and in states with large populations than in states with small populations. This thoughtful observer probably will not be highly dissatisfied with what the schools are doing for children in the middle ranges of intelligence—perhaps from 90 to 115 or 120 IQ. The schools are geared to the average child. But in our modern classrooms the prospect for the very superior child—from approximately 125 to 130 IQ and up—is less bright.

The Gifted

Intensive studies of the characteristics of bright and dull children have been made. As a group, the bright are taller, handsomer, stronger, healthier, show fewer behavior problems, are less likely to have cavities in their teeth, and do better work in school. Although a higher percentage of children from "good" families belong to the bright group than is true for families in the middle and lower classes, in terms of absolute numbers the majority of gifted children are middle-class, and vast numbers of children from lower-class families also classify as gifted. Children toward the lower end of the intellectual scale can be characterized in terms opposite to those we have used for the gifted: they are less popular, less healthy, do less well in school, and so on. But both the bright and the dull achieve below their capacity: the academic achievement of the bright in United States public schools is far lower than we would expect on the basis of their IQ.

Ketcham (1957) reports on a group of 40 gifted boys as they progressed from 6 to 12 years of age, and from the first to the seventh grade. At age 7, for example, their mental age averaged 9 years, 3 months, but their over-all educational age only 7 years, 2 months. The same figures for 42 gifted girls similarly followed were also 9 years, 3 months and 7 years, 2 months. At 12 years of age, the boys averaged 17 years, 11 months in mental age, and 15 years, 8 months in educational age; the girls, 17 years, 5 months in mental age, and 15 years in educational age. These youngsters were relatively accelerated in reading, lagged most markedly in arithmetic.

Paradoxically, this same tendency typifies public-school children at the opposite end of the intellectual spectrum.

It is probable that the phenomenon of underachievement, occurring in two such different groups, has very different causes. The bright are victims of underexpectation and understimulation; the slow learners are victims of frustration, defeat, and overexpectation.

Historically and currently, United States schools have used the following techniques with the gifted (although, by and large, no special provisions are made for them): they are accelerated, segregated, admitted early to school (a special form of acceleration), or given an enriched curriculum.

It has been widely held that *acceleration* is bad for a child. Pushed ahead a grade or two, he may be with children of similar mental age, but will lag behind his classmates in physical maturity and social development. To some degree and in extreme cases, this is undoubtedly true. But discreet acceleration of children whose physical size and social maturity is in line with their intellectual ability and reading achievement appears to do them good rather than harm. In the United States the most extensive work with the intellectually gifted has been done by Terman and his associates (e.g., Terman and Oden, 1947). Terman has found that the most successful gifted adults were those accelerated a year or more in school. No social-emotional disadvantages seemed to result from this acceleration.

Worcester (1959) should be quoted in this context: "It is interesting that, although acceleration has undoubtedly been used far more than any other method of providing for the rapid learner, and although there has been more research as to the outcomes of acceleration than there has been for any other method, and although almost all of the reasearch has shown results favorable to acceleration with hardly any study showing negative values, still a large proportion of teachers and administrators will have little or none of it." (p. 1) Worcester comments that acceleration is "a sort of daylight saving. We get the chores of the world done early in the day so that there may be more opportunity for the real joys of living a little later," (p. 3) and estimates that "if we got the top 3 percent of our gifted into their life work a year earlier, the country would have the advantage of some million years' additional use of its best brains, and it could probably find use for them. Only good effects, in general, have been found for up to two years of acceleration." (p. 4)

Segregation into special classes has often been tried for gifted children. Where research on the results has been carried out (e.g., Albers *et al.,* 1947; Ausubel, 1951; Bonsall, 1955; Carlson, 1947; and Havighurst, *et al.,* 1955) positive results have usually been reported. Both teachers and children enjoy the classes, and the children typically accomplish twice as much or more schoolwork then in their regular class. But for reasons that are logically not very clear, segregation has been condemned as undemocratic. Is it not better for the very bright child to encounter stiff competition from his intellectual peers than to coast along with his regular class, always getting the top A yet never really having to work for it? Does the "third from the top" child bitterly resent having the two gifted children in his class removed to a special class? Probably not; when they were in the regular class, he could *never* be first, no matter how hard he worked. With them gone, he may often be tops.

United States schools segregate in many ways. The best contact athletes are segregated into football or basketball teams; the best musicians are segregated into glee clubs and bands. No one argues that this is particularly undemocratic (although many are concerned about a school tendency to produce observers rather than participants in sports). Why then do we argue that segregation of the intellectually gifted group is undemocratic?

Such segregation, of course, presents school administrators with very real problems. Many parents whose children are *not* gifted secretly (or publicly) believe that they *are,* and often exert strong pressure on school authorities to place their youngsters in classrooms for the gifted. Such pressures, when they come from influential citizens, are hard to counter. It can be surmised that many a school superintendent has abandoned the practice of segregated classes for the gifted with a sigh of relief.

If superior children are to be placed in special, segregated classes, this placement should of course be made only after full consideration of *all* the child's needs. A simple measure of IQ does not provide enough information. We must know how efficiently the child is using his IQ, obtain an estimate of his social maturity, find out how placement in a special class will affect his relations with friends, parents, brothers and sisters. All these things should be known and taken into account before placement is made. If they are, one might predict outstanding success for special classes.

A common United States practice in education for the gifted is *enrichment.* Ideally, every class should be small enough to permit the teacher both to plan for and attend to the individual needs of each child in the group. Every teacher should be trained so that she can make such plans efficiently. Every classroom should have, among its books and equipment, materials simple yet interesting enough to appeal to its slowest-learning child and give him some feeling of mastery and success, yet complicated and difficult enough to challenge the brightest youngster. This represents a surprisingly wide range of material. It is not at all uncommon, for example, for a fourth-grade class in an ordinary middle-class neighborhood to include some children who do not read at all—who are *literally* functioning at a kindergarten or early first-grade level—and other children who are achieving at a college-freshman level as far as reading is concerned, and as high as eighth- or ninth-grade level in number skills.

The average classroom does not include such a range of teaching aids, and its class enrollment is so large that even the most dedicated and skilled teacher lacks the time to do careful individual planning for any but the "problem" children in her class. Far too few teachers are thoroughly trained to do individual planning, aside from having to spend a disproportionate amount of time on the "squeaking wheels" of the class—the children in the bottom fourth or fifth academically, and those with behavior problems. Since, in general, the very bright are relatively self-sufficient, manage at least to do all right with their schoolwork, and rather infrequently present serious behavior problems, they tend to be neglected.

Even well-trained teachers can pick out only about half the children in their classes with extremely high IQ's (see pp. 222–223). Reasons for this lie partly in the nature of teacher-training, and partly in the characteristics of United States children. For rather nebulous reasons, Americans distrust "eggheads." It is not particularly fashionable to be "the best student in the class." More emphasis is put on being popular or good at games than on intellectual achievement. This may be true of boys even more frequently than it is of girls. Consequently, very bright children may "hide their light under a bushel"—they simply don't try very hard. The present author has related elsewhere in a discussion of this topic (McCandless, 1957) an anecdote about an eleven-year-old friend of his who, during her first five grades of school, had consistently been the best in her class in work with numbers. During the sixth grade her arithmetic standing plummeted to about the class median. Asked how this had happened, she shrugged and said, matter-of-factly, "Girls are just not *supposed* to be that good in arithmetic."

These points illustrate some of the difficulties confronting teachers when they try enrichment. They cannot enrich the program of a gifted child if they do not know who he is; if they must spend too much time on children who, for one reason or another, are school problems; if gifted children, for cultural reasons, are dragging their heels; or if the classroom does not include appropriate types and ranges of material.

Another method that has been tried with the very bright child is *early admission* to school. This is a special form of acceleration, and many of the same reservations have been expressed concerning it. Few of these reservations are buttressed by facts. One of the most ambitious studies of the question has been done by Hobson (1956), concerning children in the Brookline, Massachusetts, public schools. For twenty-five years preceding his evaluation, these schools had been admitting to kindergarten children with mental ages of 5 or more years, but who were as young, chronologically, as 4 years on October 1 of the year they entered school. Criteria in addition to IQ were employed in admitting such children.

Hobson's sample is impressively large: his subjects include 550 under-age children and 3,891 regularly admitted children (to whom he refers as "others"), all of whom graduated from the Brookline schools between 1946 and 1955. Included in his "others" group were many underage children who had transferred to Brookline from other schools. These children in general did better than their older classmates, although they did less well than the carefully screened early-admitted children who had begun school in Brookline. Some of the representative findings are listed below.

"Graduation with honors" from Brookline high school demands a solid A and B average for all subjects taken in the last two years of school. Hobson's underage boys exceeded the "other" boys in better than a 2:1 ratio— 18.75 percent to 8.43 percent. Corresponding figures for the girls were 25.46 percent and 15.04 percent.

A second criterion of school success was broader than graduation with honors. Election to Alpha Pi in the Brookline schools depends on the student's accumulation of points, one third of which come from participating in extracurricular activities. Such items as election to class offices are included. Of the underage boys, about 13 percent received this honor; less than 6 percent of the "other" boys did. Corresponding figures for girls were 19 percent and 9 percent.

Hobson also studied two classes more intensively, obtaining about the same results as those given above. As a group, underage boys and girls averaged 18.8 extracurricular activities during their school years; the "other" group averaged only 12.1. The only category in which any possible disadvantage appeared for early admissions was boys' contact sports (such as football and basketball), where more of the "others" took part. But in other sports, such as tennis, the underage group was somewhat superior to the "others." Underage children were also more frequently accepted into "serious" universities (highly rated four-year colleges).

This careful study offers a strong argument against those who say that moderate acceleration handicaps children in the areas of social and motor skills.

In justice to United States public education, it should be added that attitudes toward training the gifted are currently becoming more flexible, that the major methods of furthering their progress are being re-evaluated, and that new adaptations of these major methods are being developed. For example, many school systems now have "enrichment" consultants; in many schools the first three or four years of school are ungraded, and children are allowed to progress through them as fast as they can master the work; and so on.

Other Exceptional Children

Segregation and highly specialized training are taken more or less for granted for other groups of exceptional children, such as the cerebral-palsied, deaf, and blind. There is some tendency, the full merits of which are not yet clear, to incorporate into regular classrooms all children who can possibly succeed. In one situation, blind children are provided with both intensive and extensive preschool experiences (to facilitate socialization); then, at an appropriate developmental age, are placed in the regular grades. Results are tentative, but encouraging, For the most part, however, such groups, including the low-grade mentally defective (below about 50 IQ), receive specialized and segregated training.

Controversy exists, however, about education for high-grade mentally defective and borderline children (with IQ's from about 50 to about 85), whose educational attainments by the middle of the elementary-school years are ordinarily below even the modest level that would be predicted from their IQ. *Deceleration* (failure to promote) and *segregation* have been the most frequent educational measures used by the public schools, at least in those systems where special procedures have been tried at all.

Convincing evidence exists (Goodlad, 1954; Sandin, 1944) that failure to promote a child is accompanied on his part by discouragement, progressive retardation, hostility (active or latent) toward the school in particular and schools in general, and symptoms of general maladjustment. But it is not clear whether this cluster of socially maladaptive behaviors and attitudes is the result of failure to promote or whether it accompanies the academic difficulties that lead to the child's not being promoted. In any event, the presence of large, physically mature, surly, older children (a majority of whom are usually boys from lower socioeconomic classes) in classes of younger boys and girls presents very real problems in the school situation. Probably a majority of United States schools now practice what is sometimes called "social promotion": regardless of the child's academic achievement, an effort is made to keep him with his age group. The results of this practice are particularly striking (and troublesome) when a child moves from elementary to junior high school. Typically, at this time, a child changes from a class that revolves almost entirely around one teacher to a platoon system, where different teachers teach different subjects; formal academic requirements ordinarily become more stringent. Where, in the first six grades, a child may have been limping along, in the seventh grade he becomes immobilized, with severe accompanying disturbances of all sorts.

There is no easy way out of this dilemma. Speaking very tentatively and without solid conviction, the author favors special or segregated classes, placement in which is made on a broader basis than an IQ test. Segregation of the slow-learning has been vociferously attacked as undemocratic and out of line with the philosophy of "developing the whole child." Anyone who has observed in the public schools knows that there is discrimination against pupils in "opportunity rooms." Common parlance for such classes by school children is "dummy rooms," and certainly some school systems make them little more than baby-sitting arrangements. However, clever and devoted teachers can produce remarkable results. One teacher (E. McCandless, 1943), working for two successive years with slow-learning children newly admitted to an institution for borderline mentally defective problem children, produced an average academic gain of nearly three grade levels per year. Prior to their commitment to the institution, these children, who averaged about 13 years of age at the time of commitment, had averaged a gain of only about .3 grade levels per year. Most of them had attended the generally very adequate schools of Detroit, Michigan.

Since academic achievement tests were administered independently of the teacher, there was no contamination of results in this study. The techniques used were those of individual diagnosis, strong personal interest in and attention to each child, and moderate firmness, although disciplinary techniques appeared to be milder and more democratic than those prevailing in other classrooms in the institution.

One interesting but tragic study (G. O. Johnson, 1950) charts the academic progress and social acceptance of mentally retarded children (average IQ, about 64) in regular public-school classes. The picture is a hopeless one. During each year of school attendance, the youngsters fell further and further behind academically. First-graders lagged 4.7 months behind their classmates academically (for a combination of arithmetic and reading); second-graders 9.5 months; third-graders 12.7 months; fourth-graders 17.6 months; and fifth-graders 27.8 months! This picture of progressive frustration and defeat holds true despite the fact that the mentally retarded children averaged almost two years older than their normal classmates.

Although these children comprised less than 6 percent of the total group of children studied, 40 percent of the most rejected children in the twenty-five classes included in the research came from the mentally defective group. Other children characterized them by such phrases as "rough, mean, teases, bullies, fights, misbehaves in school, poor sports, cheats, is dirty, smells." Not only were they actively rejected, but few children named them as friends. In these classes, social acceptance mounted steadily with intellectual level, the low (below 59 IQ) mental defectives being less acceptable than the highs, the borderline children more accepted than either group, the normal children still better accepted, and the superior youngsters (above 130 IQ) having the highest acceptance and the lowest rejection scores as determined by votes of their classmates.

Even though the number of mentally defective children in this study is relatively small, the picture the study presents is brutally clear. The life of the slow-learning child in the regular class is a miserable one of academic failure, increasing in severity year by year and compounded by social rejection. It seems that he *could not be worse off* in a special class, either academically or socially, even though other children in the school called it the "dummy class." In the special class he would at least be competing with other children of his own level, and could occasionally taste success. From a mental-hygiene point of view, it is perhaps better for him to have some victory and some acceptance from his peers, even though the majority of children derogate his class, than to be integrated but rejected.

In this section, we have reviewed the more common practices of United States public schools in educating special groups of children, particularly superior and slow-learning groups. Since relatively little definitive research has been done in this area, no definite conclusions about what practices are best can be drawn. The research that exists favors acceleration and segregation of the gifted, although such practices are not currently fashionable and considerable prejudice against them still exists. However, more flexibility and experimentation are being encouraged. The evidence is even less clear about deceleration (failing to promote) and segregation of slow-learning children. Both practices have drawbacks. The evidence we have surveyed indicates that mentally retarded children may be better off in special rooms than in regular classes, and that a number of socially maladaptive attitudes and behaviors characterize nonpromoted children. It is not clear whether these are the result of failure to promote or of general academic ineptitude and frustration.

SUMMARY

Psychological treatment of the concept of intelligence has been more successful in *practice* (i.e., in the well-developed area of intelligence-testing) than in *theory*. This chapter views *learning* as playing a heavy, perhaps a preponderant, role in the development and maintenence of intelligence in the physically normal human being. The basic definition of intelligence adopted here is that it is *problem-solving ability,* but that this ability is complex, involving among other things concentration, speed, depth and power, and probably breadth.

The types of intelligence test most frequently employed vary along the dimension of *age*: infancy, preschool, childhood, adolescence, and adulthood, although items on some individual intelligence tests range in difficulty from those designed for preschool children to those designed for highly intelligent adults. Some intelligence tests must be administered *individually;* others can be administered to *groups.* There are *verbal* and *nonverbal* (or performance) intelligence tests. Some intelligence tests emphasize *power* (no time limit); others, speed.

Test items used with children up to age 2 seem to have in common a factor of "sensori-motor alertness." The factor of "persistence," or goal-orientation, then enters; and after about 4 years of age, intelligence-test items seem to tap a factor of "provisional action," or symbolic, problem-solving ability. Infant intelligence tests do not predict intelligence as well as it is measured on tests given to older children and adults, but they have certain legitimate and valuable uses. Grossly defective functioning can be detected; sensory deficit can often be picked up by skilled testers; and a good "here-and-now" picture of the infant's status can be obtained. By the time a child is about 3, fairly good predictions of later intelligence can be obtained by skilled testers who know the children well.

The most common, and probably the most useful, employment of intelligence tests is to predict school achievement. Such prediction is most accurate for the elementary grades, becoming less accurate as the child progresses through junior and senior high school, college, and graduate school. There are several reasons for decreasing accuracy in prediction. First, those who are clearly going to fail drop out of school as early as they are allowed to. Second, the further the child progresses in school, the less standardized is his curriculum, and the more his individual study efficiency and motivation affect his academic performance.

"Culture-fair" or "culture-free" intelligence tests—those designed to minimize social class differences—predict academic performance less well than traditional tests, probably because they have less in common with the traditional curriculum. For the opposite reason, it may well be that group tests predict school success better than individual tests.

Intelligence seems to develop most rapidly during infancy and early childhood; probably about half of its potential is attained by about 10 years. Whereas it was formerly believed that growth in intelligence stopped at about 16 to 20 years of age, more recent studies indicate that intellectually superior populations are still gaining in intellectual power (as measured) in their 50's.

The gifted and the slow-learning present special educational problems, and the former, particularly, have been relatively neglected in American schools until quite recently. The most frequent educational procedures used with the gifted are acceleration, including early school admission; segregation; and enrichment. The last-named, although currently the most popular, is not often practical in the harried modern public school.

Although segregation of the slow-learning into special classes has many aspects that are distasteful to democratically-minded Americans, evidence suggests that it may be less damaging to the children than the steady and progressive frustration and defeat they experience in regular classes. Deceleration (failing to promote) does not appear to benefit children but, particularly from the time of junior high school, "social promotions" also present serious problems. More attention clearly needs to be paid to "special education" for both the gifted and the slow-learning, as well, of course, as for all other categories of exceptional children.

CHAPTER 8

Sources of Variation in Measured Intelligence

THE NATURE–NURTURE CONTROVERSY

A major, although only moderately profitable, psychological debate was carried on in the United States, during the thirties and forties of this century, concerning the question whether heredity or environment was more influential in determining the level of intelligence reached by a child. In the area of normal intellectual development, this controversy has for the most part been reduced to its common-sense merits. The debate is still being carried on, however, concerning the determinants of such disorders as simple mental deficiency (low intelligence without accompanying glandular or neurological disorder) and schizophrenia, the most serious and widespread of the mental diseases.

Anastasi and Foley (1948) have provided a sensible analysis of the dimensions of the heredity-environment problem. They maintain that the first approach should be to decide whether *structure* or *function* is being talked about; and then to ask further whether it is *hereditary* structure or function that is involved, or *environmental* structure and function.

Few argue with the fact that, under normal circumstances, the pattern of a child's physical growth and his eventual height, his tendency to be fat or thin, broad- or narrow-shouldered, brown- or blue-eyed, blond or brunette, is a matter of *structural* characteristics determined by *heredity*, although extreme nutritional deprivation or excess can greatly change the rating of body type (Shuttleworth, 1949) and may result in such alterations of structure as are produced by rickets. On the other hand, no one argues that heredity produced the change that occurs when an arm is crushed and must be amputated, or when a head injury or infantile case of whooping cough changes a previously normal child to one who is brain-damaged and mentally defective. These are obviously cases of *environmental* influence on *structure* which also results in changes in function.

Such diseases as Tay-Sachs disease (also called amaurotic idiocy) seem clearly to be *hereditary* interferences with *function* (with accompanying structural changes). In this disease, the previously normal child begins, most typically toward the middle of the first year of life, to show less muscular control, particularly of the head and neck; a cherry-red spot appears on the macula of the eye; muscular degeneration and blindness

239

progress rapidly; and death ensues. Phenylpyruvic idiocy (or amentia) is another example of a genetically determined functional disorder. The diagnostic sign of the disease is the presence of phenylpyruvic acid in the urine. It may well be that the metabolic disorder which accompanies this condition affects nervous tissue (or the phenylpryruvic acid does), with resulting low-grade mental deficiency. Except for intellectual deficit and a fine muscular tremor, individuals so affected appear quite normal. They achieve puberty, and grow to average height and strength.

Such functional-structural characteristics as near- or far-sightedness are probably partially determined by heredity. But no one (except possibly Tarzan) has learned to read without being taught. This is a case of *environmentally* determined *function*. Mongolism, one type of mental deficiency, seems to be caused by the uterine environment of the child, probably in the first three months of his intra-uterine development. Some types of microcephaly (a type of mental deficiency in which the head is very small and "pointed") seem to result from such environmental factors as the mother's having had German measles or heavy pelvic x-ray irradiation during her early pregnancy, although in other types of microcephaly there is apparently a hereditary component (Tredgold, 1947). These are cases of environment affecting function, although in the case of microcephaly, structure is also altered.

Concerning such conditions as those described above, there is little argument between hereditarians and environmentalists. For other types of ability and disability, however, it is more difficult to get agreement about whether the classification should be one of *hereditary function* or *environmental function*. Intelligence is one such trait.

Clear-cut facts about the inheritance or acquisition of such complex traits as intelligence and personal adjustment are hard to come by, for about the same reasons as those discussed in connection with the maturation-learning controversy (see Chapter 4). An argument about relative importance is meaningless on similar grounds. When each of two conditions or states is required for the existence of a phenomenon, neither can be more important than the other. Heredity *and* environment begin to exert their influence at the time a child is conceived. They cannot meaningfully be separated from each other. As one geneticist, Stern (1956), has ably put it, the environment comprises "all that is not genic. It means the intra-uterine surroundings of the embryo and fetus, the food and climate which impinge on the child and adult, and the psychological and cultural influences of home, school and society in their complex reactions upon the personality." (p. 48)

Ordinarily, there is an interaction between heredity and environment —an interaction overlooked in the classical studies of the Jukes and the Kallikaks. In the latter family (Goddard, 1912), young Martin Kallikak founded two clans, the first by begetting an illegitimate male baby with a presumably mentally defective barmaid during Revolutionary times. The lescendants of this child had remarkable records of criminality, mental leficiency, illegitimacy, and generally poor citizenship. But Kallikak's lescendants by a later union with a woman of his own social and intellec-ual status had equally conspicuous records of success and good citizenship. Overlooked in reports of these families was the fact that the environments of the two father-related clans differed to an even greater extent than their heredities, which, at least for the first generation following Martin, over-apped genetically by 50 percent. The children of intelligent, successful parents ordinarily grow up in security. They are well fed and well educated. The children of dull parents, who are typically rather unsuccessful in making their economic way through life, mature in a setting of deprivation, uncertainty, and depressed neighborhood conditions.

Human family histories are so fragmentary that accurate assessment of the attributes of ancestors is impossible, except in certain rare cases— for example, some royal families—and only partially so for them. (For example, intelligence tests have been in use only since the middle of the second decade of this century; and it is doubtful whether many royal children have been subjected to the Stanford-Binet.) Compared with most lower species of animals, the span between human generations is so great that any one scientific worker can ordinarily encompass no more than two generations in his professional life. Psychology and human genetics are new sciences, whose progress is so rapid that techniques useful for assessing one generation are outmoded by, and noncomparable with, techniques available for the second generation. As a matter of fact, techniques appli-cable in one *decade* are frequently outmoded by techniques developed in the second. This fact has added greatly to the difficulty of longitudinal research, particularly in the emotion-personality area.

An adequate study of heredity and environment necessitates control over mating as well as rather extreme manipulation of the environment.

In a Western European society such as ours, controlled mating is impossible. People marry whom they will. Manipulation to produce extreme environmental circumstances is, for good reasons, socially and legally impossible (for example, we cannot place the very superior two-year-old of very privileged parents in a situation where he would have no contact with humans). Yet to study environment and heredity in any conclusive fashion, extreme manipulations of heredity (mating of one mentally defective and one very superior person, for example) and of environment (as in the example given above) are necessary. It is for such reasons as these that some of our best information in this area comes from studies of animals, in which it is possible to manipulate both the genetic pool and the surround-ings. Some of these animal studies are reviewed later in the chapter.

Significance of the Nature-Nurture Question

Even though it is *logically* unclear and scientific answers are difficult, if not impossible, the nature–nurture question is discussed here at some length. This question merits full discussion for several reasons, of which the least important is that it has been historically and is currently a matter of preoccupation in the study of child development. More important is the fact that heredity is heavily weighted in placing babies for adoption, and any information that we can obtain about contributions to the variance of human intelligence is important information.

There exist very real reservations, possibly but not clearly justified by evidence, about placing for adoption babies whose parents are mentally defective or borderline in intelligence, or who are psychotic and even neurotic. Yet the evidence for the inheritance of these traits is not clear-cut. Rather impressive evidence exists (e.g., Skeels and Harms, 1948; Skodak and Skeels, 1949) to show that, given a good environment, many children who might have become simple mental defectives had they stayed in their true homes, turn out to be perfectly normal in all respects when placed in good adoptive homes. Little or no evidence exists about the effects of adoptive placement on children of psychotics or neurotics.

When an issue intimately affects the lives of many children and, in addition, has numerous other broad social implications, this issue, and the evidence with reference to it, should be examined. Because the data currently available are inconclusive, few scientists today are willing to take an extreme position. One widely accepted viewpoint has been advanced by Stern (1956):

> The genetic endowment in respect to any one trait has been compared to a rubber band and the trait itself to the length which the rubber band assumes when it is stretched by outside forces. Different people initially may have been given different lengths of unstretched endowment, but the natural forces of the environment may have stretched their expression to equal length, or led to differences in attained length sometimes corresponding to their innate differences and at other times in reverse of the relation. (p. 53)[1]

Relatively recent reviews of studies using human subjects and exploring the role of environment and heredity in intellectual development have been made by H. E. Jones (1954), McCandless (1952), and Pinneau and Jones (1955). No attempt to repeat these reviews will be made here. We will, however, try to summarize the findings concerning this issue under seven headings: (1) studies of adopted children; (2) studies using twins as subjects; (3) studies of the effects of institutional living and isolation on intellectual development; (4) investigations of the effects of preschool attendance; (5) research on the effects of socioeconomic class; (6) sub-

[1] Reprinted with permission of the Child Welfare League of America and C. Stern, from Stern, C.: *Hereditary factors affecting adoption. A study of adoption practices,* Volume II. New York: Child Welfare League of America, 1956.

cultural or simple mental deficiency; and (7) environmental influences on speech, including the relationship of intelligence and bilingualism.

STUDIES OF ADOPTED CHILDREN

The first conclusion that can be drawn from a study of the literature concerning the intelligence of adopted children is that they are above the national average in IQ. Skodak and Skeels's study (1949) of a group of 100 adopted children tested at an average age of 13.5 years showed them to have an average IQ of 117 whereas, for the nation, the figure is 100. This same group, containing a number of children who later dropped out of the study, had tested 117 on their first test at the age of 2 years, 2 months. There were 180 children in this initial group. For the 152 who took a second test, average IQ was 112 at 4 years, 3 months; and for the 139 who took a third test, the average was 115 at 7 years of age.

Another study (Skeels and Harms, 1948) reports on the average IQ's of three groups of adopted youngsters, all of whose true parents were inferior in social history (mothers were mentally defective, or fathers were in the lowest possible occupational brackets—semi- or unskilled labor—or both). Most of these children were tested at about kindergarten age. One group of 87 tested 105.5; another group of 111 tested at an average of 110.3; a third group of 35 tested at 104 IQ. These findings are representative of what has been found in other studies.

There are at least three reasons for the above-average IQ's of adopted youngsters. The *first* is that all obviously retarded children are screened out before adoption, so that there are few, if any, feeble-minded youngsters to pull down the average. The *second* is that adopted children, by definition, are badly wanted by their parents and consequently probably get more than an average amout of love, attention, and stimulation. *Finally,* since the majority of children are probably placed by social agencies, only the "better" homes are given babies for adoption.

Although intelligence scores of adopted children do not correlate highly, if at all, with the intelligence quotients or education of their foster parents, the average level of their intelligence is about the same as would be predicted for the true children of their foster parents.

The pioneering Skodak and Skeels study mentioned above found that the IQ's of adopted children averaged either 20 or 30 points higher than those of their true mothers. The difference in these figures is due to the fact that two different tests were used for the children. The authors took a sample of 180 children and followed them from the time they were placed in their adoptive homes, which in all cases was before the age of 6 months. Although not all the mothers had taken intelligence tests (63 had), there was a correlation of .44 between the IQ's of the true mothers and the IQ's of the children at the time the children were more than 13 years of age. Such a correlation, of course, accounts for less than one fifth of the variance in children's IQ (19 percent). One striking aspect of this study is the elevation of the children's IQ over that of their mothers. Whereas the mothers functioned, on the whole, at a borderline level, the children were significantly superior to the national average in intelligence.

This study has been severely criticized. It is maintained that the mothers were tested under disadvantageous conditions (i.e., fairly soon after they had had their babies, and ordinarily after they had decided to give them up). There is little doubt that these factors operated to lower the intelligence-test scores of the mothers;—emotional upset, unusual conditions, and so on, certainly contribute to errors in measuring intelligence. But the biographies of these 63 mothers indicate that they were marginal social persons, whereas the children, on the whole, were successful adolescents. Thirty-one percent of the children had IQ's higher than 99 percent of the true mothers. Seventy percent of the true mothers had IQ's below 95; only 16 percent of the children fell so low. Whereas 25 percent of the true mothers had IQ's below 75, only 4 percent of the children did. One evaluator of the study (Honzik, 1957) makes much of the correlation between the IQ's of the true mothers and the IQ's of the children, but partially ignores the fact that the children's intellectual functioning is a socially important level above that of the mothers.

The striking Skeels and Harms study (1948) concerns the intelligence of children whose true parents were socially disadvantaged. Skeels and Harms studied three groups of adopted children. The mothers of the 87 children in the first group all had intelligence-test scores of less than 75. The putative fathers of the 111 children in the second group were at the lowest occupational levels (semi- and unskilled laborers). A third group of 35 children was made up of children whose mothers tested below 75 IQ *and* whose fathers were at the bottom of the socioeconomic ladder in terms of their occupation. About 80 percent of the children in this study were illegitimate.

The IQ's of these three groups of children were 105.5, 110.3, and 104 respectively. In other words, all three groups tested above the national average, yet their true parents were, at the very best, marginal members of society in terms of intelligence and occupation. The correlations between the intelligence of the three groups of children and their true mothers were, respectively, .23 (significant at the .05 level); .22 (just missing significance at the 0.5 level); and .12, a statistically insignificant figure. For none of the groups does the intelligence of the true mothers account for more than about 5 percent of the variance in children's intelligence.

These two studies indicate that placement in an adequate adoptive home before 6 months is extremely effective in raising the general level of intelligence of large groups of children, even though for the one group a statistically significant relation exists between the intelligence of the children and that of their true mothers. Although there is some tendency for the less bright of the adopted children to be the offspring of the less bright of the true mothers, and for the brighter to be the offspring of the brighter, their general intellectual functioning has been moved from the feeble-minded or borderline level of their true mothers (and presumably their fathers) to one that is above the average. They approximate, not the intellectual level of their true mothers and fathers, but that of their foster parents, even though there is no correlation between their intellectual status and their foster parents' educational level.

A study by Leahy (1935) shows little effect of adoption on intellectual level of children. But the true mothers and fathers of the children who were the subjects of this study were far superior to the true mothers and fathers of the children in the two studies just reviewed.

STUDIES OF TWINS

The relation between the intelligence of nontwin siblings (brothers and sisters), fraternal twins (born at the same time, but from different eggs), and identical twins (born at the same time, and from the same maternal egg) have also been studied. It has been argued that since both heredity and environment differ to a considerable degree for nontwin sibs, their IQ's should show the lowest resemblance. For fraternal twins, according to this line of reasoning, heredity differs but environment is very similar; hence their IQ's should show a higher relation than those of sibs. Identical twins, it has been hypothesized, have identical heredities *and* environments; hence the relation between their IQ's should be the highest of any of the groups.

It has been argued that if this predicted pattern of relationships is found, the case for heredity is strengthened. Such a pattern has been found: in general, the modal correlation between the IQ's of nontwin brothers and brothers, brothers and sisters, and sisters and sisters is about .50; for fraternal twins, correlations in the .60's and .70's have been established; and for identical twins, IQ correlations are in the .80's and .90's.

These findings do not, however, necessarily support the heredity argument. The difference in the correlations between nontwin sibs and fraternal twins may well be due to increased environmental similarity for the latter; but the difference in correlation between fraternal and identical twins is not necessarily attributable to the identical heredities of the latter. Identical twins, by definition, are of the same sex and extremely similar in appearance; few people can tell them apart. The general culture has certain stereotyped ways of responding to pretty blonde or buck-toothed brunette females; to athletic and well-built or spindly and bespectacled males. Of an identical twin pair, "John" is almost as frequently labeled "Jim" as he is by his own name. In other words, for identical twins, not only is the heredity the same, but the environment is much more likely to be similar than it is for fraternal twins. When identical twins are reared together, therefore, there is no way of telling whether the increased IQ correlation typically found is due to common heredities or common environments.

Although the number of subjects is small, a major study (Newman, Freeman, and Holzinger, 1937) of identical twins who were reared separately strongly suggests that the more widely different the environments in which they grew up, the more divergent their IQ's were likely to be. In one of the 19 pairs studied, one girl had spent much time, during her early elementary years, in an isolated mountain setting where there were no schools, and had dropped out of school entirely when very young. Her twin sister had been adopted into a home where there was much emphasis on "getting ahead through education," and had been stimulated and even pushed, particularly by her foster mother. The Stanford-Binet of the first girl was 92; that of the second, 116—a difference of 24 points. The second girl was advanced in educational age over her sister by almost seven years. Of course, much of this difference was due to formal opportunity. The authors calculated a correlation between IQ differences and differences in judged educational opportunities for their subjects, and obtained a figure of .79 when Stanford-Binet IQ's were considered.

In other words, studies of twins suggest strongly that environment is of major importance in determining intelligence, but in no way discount the fact that heredity, too, plays an important part.

INSTITUTIONAL LIVING AND ISOLATION

Most studies of the effects of isolation and institutional living (e.g., Goldfarb, 1945) show that IQ's of children so brought up are quite low. A few studies of dubious scientific merit concern children reared by animals. These children are reported to behave not like human beings but like animals. However, folklore plays more part than science in relaying the data about these children (Dennis, 1951); for example, we do not know whether they may not have been abandoned in the first place because they were feeble-minded.

Another study (Spitz, 1945, 1946) of children reared in an institution found that during the first year of life their developmental quotient dropped from an initial level of 124 to 72, or from a classification of superior to one that could be considered defective. This study has been severely criticized (Pinneau, 1955) on the basis of its methods, and the criticisms are so severe and apparently well-founded that no more than limited confidence can be placed in its results. However, more careful studies by Goldfarb (1945) and Levy (1947) obtained similar results, as did a study of Chinese infants (Hsü, 1946), in which it was found that the longer the infants had been in a baby ward, the lower their developmental quotient was likely to be. Spitz maintains that the effects of such deprivation are irreversible, and the evidence of Goldfarb and Levy to some degree bears him out. Pasamanick (1946) found that baby-ward living had severely retarding effects, but implies that when the condition is remedied, the babies come back to normal. A study by Beres and Obers (1950) of 18-year-olds who had spent much of their early life in institutions indicates that a substantial number (about half) of them were normal emotionally (and presumably intellectually). Rheingold (1956) has demonstrated that one interested, around-the-clock "mother figure" can improve the social responsiveness of institutionalized infants.

Of course, there are institutions and institutions. Unpublished data (Harms, 1957) indicate that babies who are resident in a nutrition ward in which there are many nurses' aides and a warm, motherly chief nurse, who are fed in the laps of adults, and who have convalescent children running in and out of the ward, approach normal mental and emotional development even though many of their parents are of socially inferior stock.

Some of the studies mentioned above imply or state that the indisputable developmental retardation of infants brought up in baby wards where only routine attention is given by a large number of adults is due to the lack of a "significant and consistent mother figure." It might also be suggested that this retardation is due simply to lack of adequate sensori-motor stimulation. But the questions of the factors responsible and the degree of irreversibility remain open. Speaking from a social-welfare point of view, enough evidence has accumulated to indicate that group living for babies, in a baby ward where only routine care is given, is sufficiently damaging (whether temporarily or permanently) to justify recommendations against such arrangements.

Scott and his colleagues (1959) have performed an interesting study with Canadian men undergraduates, which supports the notion that sensory deprivation, even of short duration (three and four days) is rather profoundly disturbing to intellectual *function*. The inference drawn here is that it is equally and perhaps more disturbing to intellectual *development*. Scott *et al.* paid their subjects to lie for twenty-four hours a day in a comfortable bed in a lighted, semi-soundproofed cubicle. During the experiment they wore translucent goggles that admitted diffuse light but prevented pattern vision. Except when they were eating or toileting, they wore cotton gloves and cardboard cuffs extending from below their elbows to beyond their fingertips. A U-shaped foam rubber pillow and the monotonous hum of air-conditioning and other equipment limited their auditory perception. In general, the young men could put up with this situation for only about three or four days.

The experimental subjects (the total number was 29, but not all completed all the tests) were tested before the experiment, and at different times during it. Similar tests were given to control subjects who had not been isolated. In general, when compared with the controls, the experimental subjects, following as little as twelve hours of isolation, slowed down greatly in their performance of intelligence-test items, made many more errors, and (in a test of susceptibility to propaganda) changed their opinions more in the direction of a propaganda recording, manifested more interest in the propaganda, and gave a higher ranking of importance to its topic (psychic phenomena).

In other words, isolation and deprivation studies indicate that both intellectual development and (even after stable establishment) function may be disturbed by circumstances of inadequate stimulation.

EFFECTS OF NURSERY-SCHOOL ATTENDANCE

Considerable controversy has attended research on the effects of nursery-school experience on intelligence. Consistent intelligence gains (approximating an average of 5 1/2 IQ points for six months' attendance) have been reported for children attending the State University of Iowa Laboratory Preschools (e.g., Wellman, 1945). For 22 groups of children tested with one or another form of the Binet test before and after five to fourteen months of attendance at nursery-school, average IQ changes ranging from —0.6 to +10.1 points have been reported. Similar reports for 6 groups of children not attending nursery school indicate changes ranging from —4.5 to +0.8 IQ points on tests separated in time by five to ten months. The average IQ gain for all nursery-school children was +5.4; for the Iowa group, +5.5; for all children in the Iowa control groups, +0.7; for all children not attending nursery school, whether from Iowa or elsewhere, +1.1.

The Iowa studies show that these gains persist through time, and that the children's academic performance is rather consistently in line with the "new" rather than the "old" IQ's. The Iowa Preschools are heavily staffed (about one professionally trained teacher to every four or five children), and offer an emotionally supporting and intellectually stimulating program to the children enrolled. Children attend about three hours a day, five days a week. Although the children gain during the academic year, they do not gain over the summer holidays, when they are not in school, despite the fact that on the average they come from rather superior homes. The occupations of a plurality of the fathers are professional and semiprofessional or managerial.

Two studies (Starkweather and Roberts, 1940; Wooley, 1925), widely separated in time, report gains in IQ by children attending nursery school at the Merrill-Palmer School in Detroit. Another study (Barrett and Koch, 1930) shows that orphan children placed in a nursery-school program in an institution where, concurrently, the entire living schedule for the children was psychologically improved, gained an average of about 21 IQ points over a period of six to nine months. Their carefully matched controls (children not attending nursery school) gained only about 5 points. In another institution (Skeels *et al.*, 1938) where a nursery school was started without extensive accompanying institutional changes, children did not change in IQ as a result of nursery-school attendance; but their controls—children not attending nursery school—lost dramatically in IQ. The large average loss was, however, disproportionately due to the large IQ drops of certain of the children. This last study has been criticized on statistical grounds (McNemar, 1940), but re-analysis of its data by Wellman and Pegram (1944) has produced approximately the same results.

On the other hand, reports from nursery schools similar in type and presumed excellence, at such places as Western Reserve University (Anderson, 1940), Rhode Island College of Education (Bird, 1940), University of Minnesota (Goodenough and Maurer, 1940), University of California (H. E. Jones and Jorgensen, 1940), and Winnetka (Voas, 1940) do not show gains. A study (Frandsen and Barlow, 1940) of two groups of children, one of which attended nursery school at the Utah State Agricultural College and the second a WPA nursery school, showed borderline gains (3.34 IQ points in five and a half months of attendance). Children who entered the relatively privileged Moosehart children's institution from relatively underprivileged homes when they were less than 6 years of age gained about 6 1/2 IQ points during their first four years of residence. Most of this gain, 5+ points, was made during their first year of residence (Reymert and Hinton, 1940).

For schools reporting IQ gains following nursery-school attendance, the gains have been greater than could be accounted for by practice effects. However, practice effects, greater experience with a variety of adults in many types of situations (and possibly, in the case of the Iowa nursery schools, with the testers themselves), increasing maturity and poise on the part of the children, and a possible halo effect, all may plausibly account for some of the gain.[2] Arguments have been presented (Wellman, 1940) to demonstrate that none of these factors operated in the pioneering Iowa studies. Tests had been routinely administered to the nursery-school children for years before an analysis was made that demonstrated they were gaining in IQ; practice effects can be thought to be operating minimally when a child stays the same or loses in IQ from a spring to a fall test (the Iowa children averaged about a half-point loss over the summer months) yet gains from fall to spring; nursery-school children gained more than controls who had had the same number of tests, and so on.

A study in progress (Truax, 1961) provides some evidence that questions about examiner influence should not be given too much weight. Truax finds that children without siblings are the ones who gain in IQ in preschool. Those with brothers and sisters do not gain in IQ. Apparently, preschool provides children who have previously had little opportunity to

[2] A so-called halo effect may occur, for example, when the tester knows that a child is very bright and, almost unconsciously, rates borderline performance on an item as a pass. It also works in reverse: For a child who has previously tested low in IQ, borderline performance may be judged as a failure.

play with other youngsters with intellectual stimulation not otherwise available to them. There is no reason to think that examiner influence would differentiate between only children and those with siblings.

One interesting study (Worbois, 1942) used as its subjects elementary-school children and tested the differential effects of attending a rural consolidated or a rural one-room school. The different populations studied were rather closely matched for all factors but the type of school attended. The study was carried on for two years. The first group of children reported on experienced their first year of school while the study was in progress. Children attending a rural one-room school gained an average of one IQ point (from 105 to 106); rural consolidated-school children gained 5 points (106 to 111). The difference in these gains was significant. A second group, whose first two years of school coincided with the period of the study, showed a 16-point gain for consolidated children (from an average of 105 to 121); the one-room children moved from 104 to 108. This difference is highly significant. A third group of youngsters had their second and third years of school during the experimental period. The consolidated children changed from 112 to 116; the one-room children from 105 to 103. This was the smallest of the groups, and the difference in changes did not quite reach significance. Worbois believes that differences in the teachers' training, together with the richness of experiences provided, accounted for these differential intelligence gains.

To summarize, conclusions concerning the effects of nursery-school attendance on IQ are somewhat tentative. Evidence exists that children gain moderately in intelligence in many nursery schools, and that those who attend, on the whole, gain more than those who do not. But attendance at some nursery schools does not result in intellectual gains. Descriptions and personal observations of some of the nursery-school settings that we have discussed show no obvious differences between schools where gains occur and schools where they do not. Some aspects of the research work in this field probably operate to account artificially for part of the average gain.

Where information is available, it appears that the gains made in nursery school are permanent, and are positively correlated with academic performance.

EFFECTS OF SOCIAL CLASS AND OTHER SOCIAL FACTORS

The most comprehensive recent review of research on social class and intelligence is provided by H. E. Jones (1954, pp. 645–659). The evidence for social-class differences in intelligence is very clear-cut; the evidence is also clear that environmental opportunities substantially influence intellectual development. The social implications of this finding are readily apparent. No sensible person denies the important influence of heredity on all phases of human development, but the precise degree to which it affects so complex a phenomenon as intelligence is unknown. Likewise, no sensible person denies the influence of environment, although questions about the extent of its contribution to intellectual development are not yet answered. But we *can* do something about environment, little or nothing about heredity. Consequently, detailed studies of the range and type of environmental effects, and courses of action built upon the results of such studies, are of utmost social importance.

Dozens of studies (see, e.g., H. E. Jones, 1954) have been made of the resemblance in intelligence between parents and their offspring living in their own homes. Regardless of social class, level of parents' education, or parental intelligence, the correlation between measures of parental social status and children's intelligence is about .50.[3] It is ordinarily a little lower than this for social class as measured, for example, by occupation; often a little higher when parental intelligence or educational level is used as a criterion. Some studies show that fathers' intelligence is more closely related to children's IQ than mothers'; other studies show the reverse. The safest conclusion is that both parents contribute about equally. Kagan and Moss (1959), for example, found that the median correlation between the IQ's of boys (measured at ages between 3 and 10) and their fathers was .39, and between boys and their mothers, .41. Fathers' IQ correlated .51 with girl children's IQ; mothers' IQ, .48. Fathers' educational level had a median correlation of .24 with their boys' IQ, and .39 with that of their girls; mothers' educational level had a median correlation of .45 with sons' IQ; .57 with that of their girls. These findings suggest that mothers have more to do with the pattern of family stimulation, but that both parents (as would be expected) contribute equally to genetic endowment.

One of the more common ways of determining social class is by level of father's occupation. Class I is made up of professional men (lawyers, conventionally educated ministers, physicians, and so on); Class VII comprises unskilled laboring men. The 1937 revision of the Stanford-Binet test (Terman and Merrill, 1937) provided norms for 831 children be-

---

[3] The correlation between parental social status and children's intelligence is remarkably stable. For studies of our highly complex human nature and behavior, a correlation of .50 is high, but accounts for only 25 percent of the variance in intelligence. Yet this 25 percent represents the *combination* of parental genes and the environment provided by the parents. We must look elsewhere—no one knows precisely where—to account for the other 75 percent of this variance. Studies of the intelligence of grandparents, aunts, uncles, and great-grandparents may account for a larger share of the variance of children's intelligence than is usually considered likely. More sophisticated studies of motivation, personality, and *effective* environment should help still further in predicting children's intelligence. An *effective* environment is one the child actually experiences; an *objective* environment is the one the outside observer can see. The wealthy child, whose nursery is crammed with toys and books, may be said to have an intellectually stimulating *objective* environment; yet if his contacts with adults are confined to a nurse of borderline mentality, who is not literate enough to read him the books or interested enough to stimulate him in play with his toys, his *effective* environment is poor.

tween 2½ and 5 years of age, classified according to their social status. Class I children averaged 116 IQ; Class II children (whose fathers were semiprofessional and managerial) averaged 112; Class III (fathers clerical, skilled-trades, and retail workers) averaged 108; Class IV (rural owners) averaged 99; Class V (semiskilled, minor clerical, and small-business) averaged 104; Class VI (slightly skilled laborers) averaged 95; and Class VI (urban and rural day laborers) averaged 94. Similar results were obtained for other age levels up to the ages of 15 to 18.

This large study was somewhat unrepresentative of the national population, since rural and unskilled laboring groups were not fully represented. But here and in other studies, an average difference af about 20 IQ points was found between children of parents at the lowest and the highest social-class levels, regardless of the index used to measure social class.

Such a finding supports conclusively neither a hereditary nor an environmental point of view. It can be argued, probably legitimately but somewhat circularly, that people who "don't get ahead" are of inferior genetic stock, hence pass along a less adequate intellectual endowment to their children. That they provide less adequate intellectual stimulation is clear.

Our conclusion must be that the higher the socioeconomic class of the parents, the brighter, on the average, the children will be. One ambitious study has gathered together intelligence-test records of 45,000 children, fourth- through eighth-graders, from 455 schools in 310 communities in 36 of the 48 United States (McGehee and Lewis, 1942). The upper 10 percent of these children were classified as superior; the lower 10 percent as retarded. Fathers' occupations were scaled from I (professional) through V (unskilled, day labor). Class I produced 2.4 times as many superior children as would be expected, whereas Class V produced only .3; in the mentally retarded group, Class I parents produced only .14 times as many retarded children as would be expected, whereas Class V produced more than 1.5 times as many as expected statistically. Yet, in terms of sheer *numbers,* Classes II, III and IV (as the authors call them, the "great middle class") produced more than four fifths of the total (84 percent) of superior children and about two thirds of the "retarded" children. It should be noted that this study included as its subjects only those children actually enrolled in public school. Children of extremely low intelligence were thus excluded. Some evidence exists (Halperin, 1946) to indicate that the higher socioeconomic classes produce more than their share of such children, perhaps because they can afford better medical care so that a larger proportion of severely handicapped children born to them survive.

In general, urban children do better on intelligence tests than rural children, although much of this difference in test quotients results from performance on certain types of items: urban children do better than rural children on verbal items. Yet, since much of the manifest functioning of intelligence in our society is verbal, this is an important difference. Several studies exist (see H. E. Jones, 1954; McCandless, 1952) which demonstrate that children who mature in depressed rural areas, where schools are poor and there is a minimum of stimulation, decline progressively in intelligence as they grow older. Studies of Tennessee mountain children reported by Wheeler (1942) demonstrate the effect of a barren environment on children's intellectual development, yet contrast current tendencies with the more depressing picture that existed ten years before he gathered his data. In 1930, six-year-olds from this region tested an average 95 IQ. In 1940 they tested an average 103. Older children tested lower, both in 1930 and in 1940, than six-year-olds, so that in 1930 sixteen-year-olds averaged only 73.5 IQ; in 1940, 80. Some of the difference in scores between older and younger children is undoubtedly due to reading deficiency on the part of the older ones, since for them reading has a greater effect on test scores than it does for six-year-olds.

This study is representative of many which demonstrate that prolonged residence in a depressed socioeconomic-educational environment retards measured intelligence; and that, despite the warnings of geneticists, children tend to measure higher in intelligence from one decade to another. The tentative conclusion is that this increase in measured, functioning intelligence is the result of better schools for more people. Increased test sophistication, in an era where most children are exposed to tests from their early school years, may also have something to do with the results.

It has been demonstrated that Negro children from Louisiana measure higher in IQ the closer to New Orleans they dwell. Presumably, New Orleans has the best schools in the state, and the influence of the New Orleans school program diminishes with distance. Klineberg (1935), the author of this study, has also demonstrated that the longer Negro children from the South live in New York City and attend New York schools, the higher their IQ's will be. By the third emigree generation, they test about the same as their non-Negro peers, whereas genetically similar Negro children in the deep South test substantially lower than the national average. This difference shows up even for first-generation emigree children: those who have been in New York City for a short period of time test 81 IQ; those who have been there for two to three years test 84.5; and those who have lived there for longer than four years test 87 IQ. Klineberg offers some evidence to demonstrate that selective migration (i.e., the fact that the brighter Negroes move out of the South) is not responsible for this phenomenon. Certain of his more crucial findings have been independently verified for a population of Negro emigree children in Philadelphia, Pennsylvania (Lee, 1951).

Knobloch and Pasamanick (1960) found no differences in infant intelligence-test scores between white and nonwhite babies at 40 weeks of age, but found that (for example) their language intelligence scores differed by 16 points at the age of 3, in favor of the white youngsters. The major reason for this difference, they believe, is socioeconomic influence: the nonwhite youngsters have had fewer advantages and less stimulation.

Kent and Davis (1957), in a very different type of study, found that different types of parental discipline were associated with very different child IQ levels. They separated a sample of the parents of 213 children into the following four categories of family discipline:

1. *Demanding* parents—those who "set high standards . . . which take the child's weakness too little into account. . . . They provide good opportunities for the child to learn, and the home is a stimulating one, but they expect him to conform to a model of what they think he should be. This model is inflexible and they are intolerant of any departure from it." (pp. 27–28)

2. *Overanxious* parents, who "tend to be ambitious for their child, but in particular . . . are ceaselessly anxious lest he fall short of what they expect. . . . Their model is inconstant, although it may be emphatic. Also, they tend to be inconsistent in their use of reward and punishment; they are sometimes indulgent and sometimes intolerant, because they are apprehensive and uncertain. They sap the child's confidence. . . ." (p. 28)

3. *Normal* parents, who "are tolerant and patient, although firm. . . . They placidly enjoy each of their children and are affectionate toward them." (p. 28)

4. *Unconcerned* parents, who are content if their child keeps out of trouble and does not make demands on them. They are haphazard and inconsistent in their use of punishment.

The authors report no particular relation between fathers' occupation and discipline category, although there was a slight but nonsignificant tendency for fathers in the overanxious class to be in the lowest occupational category.

Kent and Davis administered the Binet test of intelligence (among other tests) to these children, and found that the IQ's of the children of demanding parents averaged 124; of overanxious parents, 107; of normal parents, 110; and of unconcerned parents, 97. Tests of statistical significance showed the demanding parents' children to be significantly brighter, the unconcerned parents' children significantly less bright, than the children of "normal" parents.

In other words (although undoubtedly at a severe emotional cost), effectively "driving" and highly stimulating parents "produce" bright youngsters.

To summarize, socioeconomic class is indisputably related to intellectual level. How much of this relation is due to heredity and how much to differential learning opportunities is by no means clear. Educational opportunities apparently affect measured IQ: where children have better educational opportunities, either as a result of migration from a disadvantaged area, or because of the passage of time, or because of parental demands on them, average IQ's rise or are found to be higher than those of children under less favorable circumstances. The longer the residence of a child in a disadvantaged area, the lower his IQ is, on the average, likely to be. In one such area, differences of more than 20 IQ points have been reported in favor of six-year-olds over sixteen-year-olds.

THE SUBCULTURAL OR SIMPLE MENTAL DEFECTIVE

We have already defined the group of simple mental defectives as neurologically and physically normal children testing below about 70 IQ on standard intelligence tests. Dressed in good clothes, and silent, they cannot be distinguished from normal children. Ordinarily, their IQ is not below 50, and the overwhelming majority come from the most disadvantaged of the social classes (Sarason, 1953). They comprise perhaps 2 percent of the American population—a relatively small percentage, but a tremendous number: more than 3,600,000 persons if we use as our base a United States census of 180,000,000 population. From their ranks comes a disproportionate number of relief, charity, delinquent, criminal, and promiscuous persons, although (see, e.g., Charles, 1953) even in this marginal group a majority seems to be self-supporting and law-abiding.

Intimate experience with, and deep interest in, this group has earlier led the present author (McCandless, 1952, pp. 684–685) to formulate two hypotheses concerning the way in which subcultural mental deficiency develops:

First, the environment from which the subcultural mentally defective person comes is one providing minimal opportunity for the learning of skills subsumed under the term *intelligence.*

Second, the environment from which the subcultural mentally defective person comes is one in which he has had maximal opportunity to learn "self-defeating" techniques—expectancies of failure, absolute as opposed to relative thinking, concrete as opposed to abstract thinking, belief in his essential worthlessness, and so on. Ferguson's thinking (1954, 1956) is also relevant in this connection.

Study after study (see McCandless, 1952; Sarason, 1953) reveals the hopelessness of the environment from which such children come: stark poverty, parental abandonment, social humiliation, rejection and defeat; parental drunkenness, feeble-mindedness, and psychosis; school failure and rejection by peers, progressively increasing with age; malnutrition; cultural barrenness of the home; parental indifference to the child's educational progress and community success; poor health, bad teeth, retarded growth.

It has been demonstrated that a relatively simple and circumscribed experience of failure can prevent children from taking advantage of practice that, under ordinary circumstances, would improve their score on intelligence-test items (Lantz, 1945). Such failure had the greatest influence on items that test "thinking process." It has also been demonstrated (Kendig and Richmond, 1940) that schizophrenics—the most seriously ill of the psychotics—do poorly on items involving motivation and concentration. Such people seem to have much in common with the "simple" mental defectives. If circumscribed experiences of failure and frustration can interfere so markedly with intellectual performance, it seems plausible that a lifetime of frustration will interfere far more. Such experiences characterize the lives of children and adults who belong to the group of subcultural mental defectives. In addition, of course, their lives are impoverished in terms of sheer cultural opportunities to learn.

Kephart (1940) has demonstrated that the longer simple defectives remained in their homes, the lower their IQ's were likely to be. Upon transfer to a relatively privileged institution, where there were about 2 employees to every 7 children, the pattern of IQ change reversed itself, particularly during the first year of residence. However, it should be stated that many of the children were tested under conditions of stress before being admitted to the institution. This fact would accentuate the picture of their steadily dropping IQ while in the community and in their own homes, and exaggerate the gain they made while in the institution, where tests were given by highly skilled examiners under standard and relaxed conditions after the children had begun to feel at ease.

The influence of the environment varies, however, according to the type of child. Kephart and Strauss (1940), in a study of children at the Wayne County Training School, separated children who were brain-damaged from those who were neurologically normal, and checked the rate of mental growth they had shown before and after admission to the institution. They concluded that neurologically normal mentally retarded children were more sensitive to environmental influence than children of about the same IQ who have suffered neurological damage.

Mundy (1957), in a study done in Britain, supplies evidence that the stimulation provided by community living results in more intellectual gain than residence in an institution for the mentally retarded. She matched 28 mentally retarded women between 18 and 50 years of age who had left the institution with 28 who remained, and found that, over about a two-year period, those residing in the community had gained about 11 points in IQ, whereas those who remained in the institution had gained only about 2 points.

How do subcultural mentally defective children function as adults? A number of studies, of which one by Charles (1953) is representative, indicate that although they do not do well, they do better than might be expected. Charles traced 127 children from an earlier study of opportunity-room children, all of whom had tested below 70 IQ (the average was about 60), and made as full an investigation as possible of them when they were between their mid-thirties and late forties. A disproportionate number— over 15 percent—of the group had died (twice as many as the national average; and of those dead, almost one third—mostly males—had died violently). More than one third had been entirely self-sufficient economically during their adult lives; fewer than half had had assistance from public relief funds. A smaller percentage than would be expected (on the basis of the national average) had married, although this was partly attributable to the fact that a number of the group were or had been institutionalized (about 18 percent either were in institutions for the mentally defective or psychotic, or had been institutionalized and then discharged). Those who had married averaged 2.03 children, a figure slightly lower than the national average. Those children of the original group who could be reached for testing (73 in number) ranged in IQ from 50 to 138, with an average of 95. Only 2 of these children were so retarded that they had to be institutionalized.

The divorce rate of the group was about the same as that for the nation; a greater percentage of the group than of the population as a whole lived in single-family houses; and over half of them owned or were buying their own homes (about the same as the national average). The men were, for the most part, laborers; the women housekeepers. Of the sample that could be reached, about 40 percent had been involved in some breach of the law. Twenty of the 127 were retested for IQ. When scores from the same test that had originally been used were averaged, the figure was 58 (about the same as the original score; but this particular test places adults at some disadvantage). A more modern and widely used test gave an average IQ of 81 for these 20 subjects. As is typical of subcultural mentally defective persons, an IQ based on verbal items was far inferior to one based on performance items (the respective IQ's were 72 and 88).

Probably more mothers belonging to the group of subcultural mental defectives have illegitimate babies than is true for the general population. It is also likely that more of their babies are placed for adoption than the babies of mothers who are intellectually and economically more advantaged. Are such babies in turn mentally defective? We have already reviewed some evidence that this is not the case (see p. 243). The average of the children who could be tested in Charles' study approached normal IQ, and ranged as high as 138 IQ (very bright, or superior). In another study involving 312 children separated from their mothers before they were 4 years of age (Snygg, 1938), the children of the 98 mothers whose IQ's were less than 70 averaged 91 IQ (low normal), even though their foster-home placements were not in any sense ideal. The over-all correlation between the IQ's of children and their true mothers was .13, accounting for less than 2 percent of the variance.

Speer (1940) studied a group of children whose mothers' average IQ was 49. The IQ's of children separated from their mothers before they were 2 years of age were normal. The average for this small group of 12 children was 100.5. The average IQ for a group of 16 children who stayed with their mothers until they were from 12 to 15 years of age was 53.

Another study (Stippich, 1940) reports the results from an investigation of children born to 48 mentally defective mothers with IQ averages between 60 and 63 (depending on which of three intelligence tests was used in computing IQ). All the mothers had been legally declared feeble-minded, and had been institutionalized. The children had been separated from their families before they were 1 year of age, and placed in boarding homes or institutions that offered less than ideal care for them. Even under such unfavorable circumstances, the children averaged 83 IQ at an average age of 5 years, or a minimum of 20 IQ points higher than their mothers. This study also included the similarly separated children of 29 mothers whose IQ's averaged 102. These youngsters averaged 97 IQ. Since it has not usually been found that environments other than rigorously depriving ones (such as impersonal institutional life) affect children before the age of about 18 months, this study provides support for a genetic point of view. In similar but deprived environments, children of brighter mothers are brighter at the age of 5 than the offspring of duller mothers. Even so, the children of the mentally defective mothers were a good 20 points higher in IQ than their mothers.

This section has offered evidence indicating that the longer children live in very depressed environments (including homes where the mother is mentally defective), the lower their average IQ is likely to be. There are indications that environmental reversal can change this developmental direction, although some of the evidence is weak. Several studies report normality or near-normality for children of feeble-minded parents placed early in foster homes, and report that there is no practically significant relation between the IQ of the mother and that of their true children when these are separated from the mother early. The most pessimistic of the studies still reveals an upward differential of a full 20 points between the IQ's of the feeble-minded mothers and their children, even though the children had been less than optimally placed.

LANGUAGE, INTELLIGENCE, AND THE CULTURE

Although our present tests of intelligence are very useful, they also have obvious defects, and their results are frequently misused. The definition of intelligence used in this book has been the rather traditional one of problem-solving ability. This ability, at least in conventional school programs, depends heavily on being able to handle abstractions; and these, in turn, are dealt with best by children who are high in verbal and number ability. Most of our current intelligence tests include many items involving these abilities. Of eight "primary abilities" separated by Thurstone, two have to do with words and word usage: the factor V, or verbal comprehension; and the factor W, or word fluency. Wechsler (1944), the author of probably the most widely used individual test of intelligence for adults and one of the more widely used tests for children, reports that scores from the vocabulary subtest of the total scale, composed (for the adult scale) of 42 words that the subject is asked to define, correlate .85 with the entire scale. Such a correlation accounts for almost three fourths of the variance of the full-scale IQ (72 percent). It has been pointed out that there is substantial evidence to indicate that performance (nonverbal) problems are solved better by those who give verbal labels to the tasks; it has been clearly demonstrated (e.g., Spiker, 1956) that children learn new tasks more efficiently when they have names for the elements of the process or for the pieces of equipment that must be manipulated successfully in order to demonstrate learning.

In other words, we are safe enough in saying that anything affecting the use of words probably has an effect on intelligence as we now measure it.

Vocabulary and general adequacy of speech vary by socioeconomic class. Speech is poorer in form and articulation, less in amount, and less precise for children at lower socioeconomic levels than for those at higher social levels (see, e.g., Irwin, 1948). The only glimmer of hope we have for predicting the later intelligence of children tested as infants lies, as has been pointed out, in measuring their speech sounds (Catalano and McCarthy, 1954). Children reared with scant adult attention, who are relatively isolated, or who live in institutions are retarded even more in their speech than in their general IQ level. This retardation has been shown to exist as early as 2 months of age. Children who, at elementary-school ages, test at the mentally retarded or borderline level started talking later than children who measure normal or bright. At least during the early years of their lives (presumably because they communicate primarily with each other, and depend to a lesser degree on adults), twins and triplets test lower in both speech and intelligence than singletons, although much of this ground is regained by school age. Their speech seems to be even more retarded than can be accounted for by their somewhat lower intelligence-test scores. Although the evidence is not entirely clear-cut, children who are bilingual during their preschool years—that is, typically, those whose homes use one language, while their schools use a different one—test lower than monoglots (speakers of one language). Although social class is involved, since children from such homes are rather more frequently from lower- than from upper-class homes, the effect seems greater than can be accounted for by social class alone.[4]

As we have seen, social class seems to be directly related to vocabulary level; yet children from some middle-class homes have been shown to have low vocabularies, while children from some lower-class homes have good vocabularies. One author (Milner, 1951) provides evidence indicating why there are such exceptions (at the same time presenting data to show that the child's language status and his socioeconomic status correlate somewhere between .78 and .86, depending on which of two statistical techniques is used).

The 21 high-scorers in Milner's study of 42 Negro first-graders came from homes ranging from upper-lower to lower-upper, this latter being the highest social class included in the study. The high-scorers were distin-

[4] For a comprehensive review of this area, see McCarthy (1954).

guished as a group from the 21 low-scorers by such factors as eating breakfast and dinner with their families, and engaging in conversation during these times. Their parents tended to use verbal methods of discipline, whereas physical punishment was more characteristic of the low-scoring children. High-scorers more frequently were expected to look after their own possessions and/or room, and received more praise and affection from their parents. More high- than low-scorers had been exposed to baby-sitters; and they went to bed later, frequently as late as 10 at night. Low-scorers were "bribed" with small gifts of money more frequently than high-scorers. The high-scorers, as might be expected, possessed more books, and indicated that their mothers and fathers more frequently read to them. More low-scorers said they could not recall ever feeling "real happy," and were more infrequently able to recall instances or situations in which they had felt happy. Low-scorers more frequently possessed as reading material only funny books or schoolbooks.

Such factors as those listed above are, of course, strongly related to social class; but where there are variations in language ability within a social class, it seems plausible that such variables as parental conversation, attention, praise, and so on, could account for the differences between low- and high-scorers.

The hypothesis just formulated is supported by an unpublished study of Irwin's (1961). Irwin secured the cooperation of a large group of mothers whose husbands were mostly skilled, semiskilled, and unskilled laborers. Ordinarily, such mothers do little reading to their children at any age, and almost certainly none in the first year or so of their babies' lives. Irwin persuaded 55 mothers to read aloud to their children for at least ten minutes a day from the time they were little more than babies (one year old). The participation in the study of another, control group of mothers was elicited by offers to check on the development of their babies. Otherwise no change was made in the interaction between them and their children.

Irwin measured the youngsters' speech development regularly and found great differences in all phases of speech by the time the children were 20 months of age. These differences appear to be highly significant statistically, although analysis of data has not been completed. The study is especially provocative when we consider the relations that have been found between speech and intelligence. Irwin reports the experimental mothers' amazement and chagrined amusement: "You asked us to read ten minutes a day," many exclaimed, "but I can't get away from that kid. He wants me to read to him all the time."

Once established during the preschool years, can a child's language level be changed? Since language is so closely related both to intelligence and to school achievement, the answer to this question is important. Dawe (1942) attempted to answer the query in a study that involved 11 pairs of children resident in an orphanage. When she began her study, the children ranged in age from 3 years, 7 months to 6 years, 10 months. Her experimental, or trained, children were very carefully matched with the control children for school group attended, sex, chronological and mental age, IQ, and vocabulary. All the children were going either to the orphanage nursery school or to kindergarten, and Dawe did her speech and language training on weekends for a total of 92 hours over a period of about seven and a half months.

At the beginning of her study, the experimental group averaged low-normal—IQ 80.6—as did her control group—81.5. The training consisted of help in understanding words and concepts, looking at and discussing pictures, and listening to poems and stories. Occasionally she took them on short excursions, although this proved to be difficult within the framework of the orphanage.

Dawe's experimental group of children gained an average of more than 14 points in IQ during the training period, whereas the controls dropped an average of 2 points. At the beginning of training, average IQ's of the two groups were almost identical. At the end of the study they differed enormously, not only on the test originally given to them but on another form of the test. Even on a performance test there was an average difference of 5.5 points in favor of the experimental children, although language presumably does not greatly affect success on such a test (an assumption which, as we have pointed out, is rather dubious). This latter difference, however, was not a significant one. Dawe's training did not include test-coaching, although her method of teaching may have helped the experimental children to approach more efficiently problems with elements similar to those included in intelligence tests.

Both groups of children gained in vocabulary, the experimentals 17½ score points (words), the controls 10 score points. The experimentals gained significantly more than the controls. Information-test scores also increased significantly more for the experimental than for the control children. In addition, Dawe obtained measures of such factors as attentiveness and intellectual interest. Dramatic improvements in almost all aspects of these important traits occurred for the experimental group, but such measures were not available for the controls.

ANIMAL RESEARCH

It has been pointed out that for practical reasons studies using humans as subjects cannot throw definitive light on the relative influence of environment (social learning) and heredity on the development of human intelligence, nor on any other complex psychological trait. The research worker cannot subject his human subjects to extreme environmental or hereditary variations; nor, indeed, can he exercise any very rigorous control over his subjects' environment or heredity. These considerations apply to a far lesser degree to research work done with animals.

It is unusual to include animal studies in a volume devoted to child

development. We have done it here, however, because of the practical social importance of knowing to what degree the environment can modify
the organism. We can make *no direct translation* or *application* to human
beings of research results or theories based on animals; but *suggestions* about
human development may, and frequently do, arise from such results.
Further, if we make the reasonably tenable assumption that animals are
simpler organisms and are more "genetically and instinctually bound" than
man, then we can argue with some force that if environment affects an animal to some degree, it is not unlikely to affect the more complicated, self-
determining, adaptable child or man to an even greater degree.

This section is not designed to include a comprehensive review of all
environmental studies of animals, but selected studies will be reviewed
and general conclusions drawn concerning the effects of early experiences
on later development—emotional, social, and physical as well as intellectual. Most of these research studies have been suggested by the work of
Hebb (1949, 1955), whose theories have already been discussed.

Isolation and Problem-Solving

One of the most elaborate experiments, although not the earliest in the
series, was done by Thompson and Heron (1954). These authors used as
subjects 26 Scottish terriers, all of them descendants of one litter, hence
genetically quite similar to one another. Thirteen of the animals were
reared as pets, in private homes or in the laboratories, from weaning time
(at about 4 weeks of age) until they were about 8 months of age, when they
were put in ordinary dog cages. During this period the dogs were exercised
outdoors every day when the weather permitted, were fed well, and had a
moderate amount of experience with humans.

Thirteen of their brothers, sisters, and cousins were reared very differently after weaning. Three conditions of isolation were imposed on them:
Two dogs experienced *severe isolation,* spending all their time up to between 7 and 10 months of age in one of two types of rather small cages
(30 × 40 × 60 inches). Every day they changed cages through a sliding
door. One cage was kept in darkness, whereas light was allowed to enter
the other; the dogs therefore spent every other day in the dark. Eight pups
experienced *moderate restriction,* two to three of them per group living for
8 to 10 months in ordinary dog cages whose walls were cardboard-covered,
so that they could not see out. Light came in from the top of the cage. They
had contact with humans about ten minutes a day while the cages were
cleaned. Three pups were *slightly restricted,* and lived for about 7 months
in cages similar to those of the moderately restricted group, except that the
cardboard was removed from the front and top of their cages. They thus
had considerable perceptual experience, but only of the environment immediately outside their cage.

At the end of this "experimental treatment" period, the restricted animals were handled precisely as were the normally reared ones. The experi-

mental animals were reported to be quite hyperactive after their release, and for the first few weeks to months demonstrated considerable sensori-motor disturbance: they bumped into things, had trouble with stairs and steps, and so on. After this time, however, they seemed normal enough. The experimental and control groups lived under similar conditions for somewhat more than a year after the end of the period of isolation. At this time, "intelligence" testing of the animals was begun.

Although very simple from an adult human point of view, these tests fit well enough with our definition of intelligence as problem-solving behavior. Six tests were given the animals, an orientation test I and II, a barrier test I and II, an attention test, and a maze test consisting of eighteen different arrangements of wire panels within a seventeen-foot square maze. These arrangements ranged from very simple to rather complex.

Fig. 8.1. A diagram of the testing situation for Thompson and Heron's orientation tests I and II

For the first orientation test the animal was placed in corner D of an eight-foot square, as shown in Figure 8.1. He was given 10 trials on which he ran to food at corner A. All of the animals that were given this test—8 normals, 3 slightly restricted, 5 moderately restricted, and 2 severely restricted—easily acquired this habit in 10 trials. After the habit had been learned and while the animal was watching, the food pan was switched 90° to corner C (to the left rather than to the right of the dog). Attention was further brought to the food by banging the pan on the floor and holding the food out so that the dog could see it. Five trials were then run for all animals. The pan was then changed to corner B, and another 5 runs were made by the animals; after this, another trial from D to C was given; then 2 trials from D to A; and a final trial using corner B as a starting point, requiring the animal to move to corner A to get his food. An error was scored when a dog did not go directly from his starting corner to the food.

The average number of correct trials out of 14 tests was 13.7 for the normally reared (control) animals, but only 5.9 for the restricted (experimental) dogs. The poorest of the control animals did better than the best of the experimental group. The difference was highly significant, P being less than .001. All the experimental animals continued to go to corner A first before proceeding to the new position, although they were eventually able to locate the food.

Orientation test II was slightly more complicated. A starting box, open on one side, was placed in the middle of the square so that its opening faced wall AB, as shown in Figure 8.1. The animal went to food located in corner A for 10 trials; the box was then rotated to face in turn walls BC, AD, and CD. One trial was given in each position. The starting box was then rotated back to its first position for 3 trials. After that the food was moved to corner B for one trial, and the dog, before being placed in the starting box, was taken to it and allowed to sniff it. For these 7 test trials the control dogs averaged 5.1 correct runs (i.e., ran directly to the corner where the food had been placed rather than to an incorrect corner); but the experimental animals averaged only 2.7 correct trials (P for this difference was again less than .001). Only one of the experimental animals did better than the poorest control, doing as well as 3 other controls. The least efficient control dog had experienced the shortest period of time living as a pet.

Fig. 8.2.   A diagram of the approximate arrangement for Thompson and Heron's barrier tests I and II

In barrier test I, a chicken-wire barrier was extended at right angles from wall BC about two feet from corner B, as shown by the solid line in Figure 8.2. The food was placed behind it as the dog watched, and after he had had 5 trials of going from corner C to get the food before the barrier was put in place. A correct trial consisted of the dog's avoiding an error zone— that is, the dog was correct if he angled from corner C out past the end of the barrier and then went directly in to get the food. Control animals averaged 6.75 correct runs out of 10 trials; experimental animals 2.4. This difference was significant at less than the .001 level. The experimental animals again manifested behavioral rigidity, frequently moving straight forward from corner C to the barrier, then circling it.

For barrier test II an addition was made to the barrier, as represented by the dotted line in Figure 8.2. The animals were placed, one at a time, in this partial enclosure after having been allowed first to sniff the food outside the barrier. Time for reaching the food was measured for each trial. To get at the food, of course, the animals had to turn their backs on it, run through the opening, and around. The average time for the control animals was 29.4 seconds. The experimentals on the average required 72.1 seconds. This difference is significant at less than the .05 level, and there was only one case of overlap between the groups.

Another test was designed to measure the dogs' attention span. After they had learned to go immediately to the one of two doors behind which they had watched the experimenter place a pan of food, they were tested to determine how long they could "keep this in mind." That is to say, they were required to wait behind a door for periods of time ranging from 5 to 300 seconds before being allowed to run to the easily opened door behind which they had watched the placement of the food. Even without delay, 6 of the 7 experimental dogs were never able to handle this problem, and the one successful dog solved the problem for a delay of only 25 seconds. The *least* apt of the 5 control animals tested handled a 50-second delay. These differences are obviously highly significant.

The final test given was the maze test. All dogs were given 5 easy trials to get them accustomed to the maze, then were given progressively more difficult problems. There were no group differences for the easy problems, and the average score for the control dogs was lowered by one pregnant female, who tired easily and gave up. Even when her scores were included, the controls averaged a total of 237 errors, whereas the experimentals made an average of 344 mistakes. This difference is significant at less than the .01 level. All dogs learned in a similar fashion: that is, both groups steadily improved in performance, and the learning curve showing the effects of practice was the same in shape for the two groups. At all points on the curve, however, the experimentals did less well than the controls.

This striking study has been reviewed in detail because it has so many implications concerning the influence of early stimulus or environmental deprivation on later problem-solving behavior. Dogs reared in isolation as puppies, even when given a long period (more than a year) of living in a relatively normal environment, clearly do less well than dogs reared as pets on a series of tasks that seem to involve a factor we could call intelligence.

It has been pointed out that we cannot apply animal research directly to humans. On the other hand, the implications of this study (done with higher mammals) are too striking to be completely ignored or dismissed. The authors describe the deficit of the dogs as "a lack of ability to discriminate relevant from irrelevant aspects of the environment, or to adapt to changes made in the experimental situation. There also seems to be some disturbance in the attention processes of the restricted animals." (p. 29) It will be remembered that Hofstaetter (1954), in an analysis of common factors in intelligence-test items for infants and preschoolers, found that the items thought to measure intelligent behavior before the age of speech are characterized by a factor he calls "sensori-motor alertness." This factor is of great importance up to 20 months of age. The major factor in intelligence-test items appropriate for children from about 20 to 40 months of age seems to be "persistence," or "a tendency to act in accordance with an established set rather than upon interfering stimulation." (p. 162) Certainly, the deficiencies of the restricted dogs in the Thompson and Heron study could be described by Hofstaetter's words. In fact, the two descriptions are almost interchangeable.

Results similar to those obtained by Thompson and Heron have also been obtained (see, e.g., Bingham and Griffiths, 1952; Thompson, 1955) using rats as subjects and employing similar research techniques.

Special Stimulation in Infancy

Other investigators have secured results congruent with those reported above. In one study (Gibson and Walk, 1956) rats were reared in identical surroundings and with identical treatment, except that on the walls of the experimental animals' cages hung pieces of black metal cut into the shapes of equilateral triangles and circles. The cages of the control animals had blank walls. For most of the white rats used in this study, hereditary influences were controlled by splitting litters, putting half of one litter in an experimental and half in a control group. At 90 days of age and without any "meaning" ever having been attached to circles or triangles, the animals were set to learn a discrimination problem involving these two geometric shapes. The rats exposed to the two stimuli proved far superior to the control group in learning the problem, the difference between groups being significant at much less than the .01 level.

Forgus (1956) has done several studies along the same general lines. One of these exposed groups of 11 baby rats to cutout forms—a circle, a triangle, a cross, and a square. The cages of the animals were blanked in, so that the forms were the conspicuous elements in the environment. These forms were placed on the walls of their cages as soon as their eyes had opened (at 16 days of age), and moved around from time to time to avoid any direct association ("meaning") between them and obtain food and water. The forms were kept in cages until the rats were 41 days of age.

Another group of rats was similarly reared, except that the forms were not put into their cages until they were 41 days old, and were left there until the animals were 66 days of age. Appropriate groups of control animals (in most cases, members of the same litter as the experimental animals) were reared identically, except that they were not exposed to the forms.

The rats that had been exposed to the forms from infancy were placed in a discrimination situation similar to that in the Gibson and Walk (1956) study when they were 41 days of age. The animals used as controls for this group also started to learn the discrimination (between a triangle and a cross) at this age. Animals who had been exposed to the forms only from the time they were 41 days old, and their controls, began the discrimination problem when they were 66 days old. After the problem had been learned, the forms were rotated 90° to see how well the rats could generalize. Table 8.1 shows the results for the four different groups.

TABLE 8.1: NUMBER OF TRIALS REQUIRED TO LEARN A DISCRIMINATION PROBLEM BY RATS EXPOSED TO FORMS EARLY AND LATER IN LIFE, AND THEIR CONTROLS.

	Number of Trials Required for Learning	Number of Errors Made on Generalization Test
Forms in infancy	33.8	4.7
Forms at 41 days	39.4	11.1
Early controls	48.2	19.7
Late controls	46.5	19.6

Printed with permission of J. Blackburn, *Canadian J. Psychol.*, from Forgus (1956), with appreciation to the University of Toronto Press.

The figures of statistical significance for this table indicate clearly that an advantage accrues both in learning and in generalizing to the rats exposed early in life to the forms. They did better in learning and generalizing than rats who were exposed later in life, and the late-exposed rats in turn did better than rats never exposed to the forms before discrimination-testing. The early and late controls showed no difference in their discrimination learning, although the animals tested later moved through each discrimination problem faster than those tested earlier; they seemed more confident or less fearful.

In another interesting study, Forgus (1954) reared rats in three different types of environment. Group I lived in a good-sized black-painted cage, in which a number of white objects, such as blocks, alleys, tunnels, elevated platforms, and inclined planes, were placed around the walls so that the animals had free access to them. Group II rats lived in a similar cage, but a clear plastic frame was placed so that they could see but not reach the playthings. Group III lived in small, black, unfurnished boxes.

On various tests, Forgus found that group I and II animals moved around faster than group III animals, were less emotional and frightened, and showed much more varied behavior. They were also much more efficient at a problem that involved insight. But where visual discrimination was necessary to solve a problem, group II (the group that had looked but not manipulated) usually did somewhat better than group I. Forgus reasoned that this was because group II animals had spent their lives being able to do nothing *but look.* Consequently, when problem-solving depended on using their eyes, they would do better than animals reared like group I, whereas group I animals would do better than animals who grew up under conditions similar to those of group II at problems demanding manipulation, and in situations involving no visual cues.

Forgus tested this reasoning in an experiment (1955b) in which his group I and group II animals were reared in the fashion just described. They then started discrimination learning in a maze that provided visual cues. These were removed before learning was complete; and the experiment was continued to see which group learned faster and made fewer errors. Group I, the "visuo-motor" group, learned in an average of 19.5 trials, and made an average of 60.5 errors during the learning. But group II ("visual only") required an average of 26.6 trials, and made 83.1 errors on the average. These differences are statistically significant.

Forgus, with Luchins (Luchins and Forgus, 1955) has performed another experiment of the same general type. In this study the experimental animals were brought up in cages equipped with blocks, alleys, and elevated platforms, and were played with by humans for about an hour a day. The controls lived in a barren cage without much contact with people. Experimental tests showed that in a new situation the experimentals were much more confident: they moved around far more. They explored their environment more (a greater number of alternate routes to a goal was used by them than by the controls). They showed more insightful and efficient behavior in solving problems than the controls; and they showed that they could more rapidly drop an old method of problem-solving that had become inefficient.

Handling and Gentling

Another investigator (Levine, 1956) studied the effects of handling rats (1) very early in their lives (from the day after birth through 20 days of age); (2) later in their lives (from 50 through 70 days); and (3) not at all. When all the animals were 71 days of age, they were subjected to training designed to teach them to avoid an electric shock. The early-handled differed consistently from the nonhandled group in the speed with which they learned to do this (they were faster, and made fewer errors); and in the indications of emotional disturbance they showed—that is, they defecated less, and fewer of them "froze." (Freezing is a frequent maladaptive reaction of rats to stress.) On the whole, the later-handled group fell in efficiency between the early- and the nonhandled groups. On most measures it was not significantly different from either.

Weininger, whose work is based on Hebb's thinking, has published three papers, one of them with co-workers, on the effects of gentling white rats in infancy (Weininger, 1953, 1956; Weininger *et al.*, 1954). His technique of gentling, typically, is to take a rat from about the time of weaning (approximately 21 days) for ten minutes per day in his left hand, holding the rat gently against his chest and stroking it with the thumb of his right hand from the head to the base of the tail at the rate of about 50 times per minute. Weininger has found consistently that the gentled animals gain weight faster and to a higher eventual level than do nongentled rats. This is a symmetrical weight gain; that is, the gentled rats are not only heavier but longer and bigger. They do not, however, actually eat more than the controls, but presumably utilize their food better.

Weininger's gentled rats showed less fear of open spaces: they ventured further and more frequently into the middle of a six-foot metal enclosure, where the light was brightest (rats fear open spaces and light). They hugged the walls of this open cylindrical space much less than the nongentled rats. When placed under severe stress (immobilized by bandages without food or water for 48 hours), more of the nongentled showed heart damage on autopsy, and suffered more extensive duodenal and stomach bleeding. The nongentled rats seemed to have enlarged adrenal glands *after* this experience of stress; another group failed to show this differential enlargement *before* stress. Still another group, exposed to even more severe (120-hour) stress composed of immobilization, food and water deprivation, and marked, though accidental, heat deprivation, showed the same symptoms on autopsy. More of the nongentled rats than of the gentled rats died under such circumstances. Levine and Otis (1958) also found that the earlier their albino-rat subjects were handled, the more resistant they were to stress.

At least three other studies (L. Bernstein, 1952; McClelland, 1956; Morgenson *et al.*, 1957) using rats as subjects support the findings reported above, including one which demonstrates that consistently handled animals learn faster than nonhandled ones, and that early handling is superior to later handling. The author of this last study (L. Bernstein, 1952) emphasizes that his results may be due, not just to an enriched objective environment, but also to the building of a positive "emotional" relationship between the investigator and the animal.

Gentling, then, as done in the studies reported above, seems to produce important differences in animal behavior. However, one apparently carefully done study (Scott, 1955), using the same gentling techniques as those used by Weininger, found no behavioral or weight differences between gentled and nongentled rats. There is no obvious explanation for this difference in results, and we must at present rest content with the conclusion that the bulk of the evidence favors positive results from gentling, but that some important research exists to discount its importance.

Isolation and Emotionality

The influences of restriction (as described in the 1954 Thompson and Heron study) on the emotional responses of dogs have also been studied by Canadian investigators. Melzack (1954) studied 17 Scottish terriers, 8 of them reared from puppyhood to maturity in homes, 9 reared for a similar period in the restriction cages described earlier. They were tested about one month after release from the cages, during which time they lived relatively normal lives; and again about one year after this. During the year, all had been normally handled.

Melzack exposed the dogs to a mannequin head, a bear and a chimpanzee skull, a toy car, a balloon, an umbrella, and a live rabbit. After an animal had been in the experimental room for one minute, one of these objects was moved toward him in zigzag fashion for one minute. The umbrella was opened to a 36-inch spread, and the balloon blown to a 10-inch diameter over a 30-second period before being moved toward the dog. Recording for behavior concerning the rabbit was not made until it had made its first move.

Table 8.2 shows the frequency of different kinds of behavior between the two groups. The third and last columns show the significance of differences between groups.

TABLE 8.2: DIFFERENCES IN EMOTIONAL BEHAVIOR SHOWN BY MELZACK'S SCOTTISH TERRIERS, RAISED UNDER NORMAL AND RESTRICTED CONDITIONS, TESTED SOON AFTER RELEASE FROM RESTRICTION AND ABOUT ONE YEAR LATER.

Behavior	Test at 3–5 Weeks			Test 10–12 Months Later		
	Restricted	Free	P	Restricted	Free	P
Excitement	3.9	0.5	.001	1.6	0.2	.045
Avoidance	1.9	5.5	.001	4.0	3.5	NS
Aggression	>0<	0.2	NS	>0<	2.2	.03
No emotional response	1.3	0.8	NS	1.3	1.2	NS

Printed with permission of the American Psychological Association and R. Melzack, from Melzack (1954).

These differences are rather striking. The normally reared dogs showed relatively more adaptive behavior (attacking or getting out of the way), whereas the restricted dogs behaved in an "immature," excited, nonadaptive fashion. As can be seen from Table 8.2, these differences decreased with time, but were still in evidence nearly a year later. The same dogs had also been tested for intelligence in about the same fashion as Thompson and Heron's dogs. Like them, they had been found less apt at problem-solving behavior.

It may be that "intellectual" differences account for some of Melzack's findings, although the emotional tests given to the animals seem to involve few elements of problem-solving. The study is not contaminated—that is, the experimenter did not know which dogs had been reared free, and which under restricted circumstances. Melzack states, in conclusion:

> When the restricted dogs were first released, their level of excitement was higher than any yet observed in the normal controls and was maintained for longer periods of time. . . . (The study) adds further support to the view that diffuse emotional excitement is a primitive disturbed response out of which avoidance and other forms of emotional

behavior develop. It demonstrates, however, that this behavior is primi tive only in so far as it appears prior to integrated forms of emotional behavior. It may appear at any stage of the animal's life when the situation differs greatly from any that the animal has already encountered (p. 197)[5]

In another study Melzack (1952) reports that the restricted dogs showed remarkably maladaptive reactions to pain; that is, they were much slower in learning to avoid an electric shock. Two of his 7 restricted subjects never learned to do so during the experiment. In this situation (the experimenter was directing a mobile toy car that administered a shock to the dog), the control dogs were smooth and coordinated in their avoidance responses, the experimental dogs wild and haphazard. A retest two years later showed that the experimental dogs were still much less adroit at this avoidance than the control dogs had been at about 9 months of age. The experimental dogs also used very little "sense" in avoiding lighted matches or pinpricks, or in moving from the "hot", or electrically charged, side of an apparatus to the safe side. They actually spent much more time around the experimenter *after* he had burned or pricked them than they had done before, whereas the control dogs shied away from him. Some of the experimental dogs came snuffling back up to the fire immediately after having been burned by it.

Melzack and Thompson (1956) tested dogs reared under the same circumstances as those described above for the adequacy of their social behavior. When the restricted animals were put into competition for a plate of food with normally reared animals of the same age, they consistently lost. The normal dogs scored 57 wins (i.e., drove the other dog away); the experimentals only 7 wins. This difference is significant at the .001 level. Even when the normals were substantially younger, the experimental animals lost. Their social curiosity, when exposed to a strange dog on the other side of a chicken-wire fence, was less adaptive: whereas the normal dogs soon tired of sniffing and exploring the other dog through the fence, the experimental dogs showed the opposite tendency. The experimental animals also showed less adaptive reactions to a human experimenter playing the part of a friendly, a timid, and a bold man.

Early Experience and Aggression and Sexual Behavior

Aggression is often thought to be an inborn trait for all species. We know that, in man, learning influences its expression strongly, but it might be considered relatively unmodifiable in lower species. However, one study (Kahn, 1951) demonstrates that mice, subjected while young to a severe beating by other mice, grow up to be relatively timid and unaggressive. Evidence also exists that mice reared in groups are more aggressive as adults than mice reared alone (King and Gurney, 1954). Rats reared in litters

[5] Reprinted with permission of the American Psychological Association and R. Melzack, from Melzack (1954).

of 6 (Spitz, 1954) when contrasted with those reared in litters of 12, seem emotionally more secure, are less fearful, eat more, but compete less effectively both for food and for sex objects. The future of any species depends upon its adequate sexual behavior. Such behavior should presumably be the least modifiable by environment, particularly in the lower species. Yet several representative studies illustrate how profoundly this presumably instinctual behavior may be modified by social learning.

In one study (Kagan and Beach, 1953) rats were separated from their kind just before puberty. At the time of their separation, their behavior with the opposite sex had been primarily playful. Males so separated and replaced at adulthood in cages with females in heat behaved inefficiently, consistently interrupting their adaptive sex behavior with the play behavior that had been appropriate during their "preadolescence."

In another study (Hayward, 1957) it was found that as adults, male rats that before pubescence had been consistently shocked in the presence of adult female rats in heat, but not shocked in the presence of adult males, avoided the in-heat female much more than a control group that had not been shocked in preadolescence. The experimental rats behaved inefficiently when they came into the presence of the female, and spent far more time with the available adult male rat than did the controls, although they did not show homosexual behavior. Actual ejaculation did not, however, occur for either the control or the experimental rats in this study. The author entertains the thought that the electric shock may have disorganized both groups.

Male guinea pigs with previous sexual experience (Riss and Goy, 1957) have been found to show much more sex behavior with an in-heat female following periods of living socially than they do after periods of living in isolation. When males were separated from other animals very early in life, the disturbance of sexual function was more profound than when separation occurred later (Valenstein, Riss, and Young, 1955).

To summarize this section on animals, research that has been done to test the effects of early experiences on the later behavior of a wide variety of animals—dogs, rats, guinea pigs, mice—demonstrates that such experiences exert a profound influence on problem-solving behavior ("intelligence"); social behavior, including aggression; responses to pain; sex behavior; and even such presumably genetically determined phenomena as weight and size.

SUMMARY

It is difficult to assign differential responsibility to "heredity" and "environment" (or nature and nurture) for intellectual development. Since no organism can function without both a heredity and an environment, and since environment begins to exert its influence at least as early as conception, it is scientifically impractical to say that such and such a percentage of the variance in intelligence is accounted for by genes, and the remainder by environment. However, since the nature-nurture question arises urgently in practical matters (such as early adoption of children, or placement for adoption of children from inferior social stock), it is important to review what evidence we have concerning the respective contributions made to intellectual development by environment and heredity. Some relatively recent animal research gives more definitive information on the matter than does research with humans. Both nature and nurture can be more effectively controlled for animals than for humans, and the generation span for most animals is much shorter than that for humans. Selective breeding, impossible in scientific studies of humans, is acceptable for animals; and severe environmental manipulations that cannot be performed with humans are possible with animal populations.

This chapter has reviewed research literature on eight major topics:

1. Research on adopted children indicates that they are on the whole brighter as a group than own or true children, probably for at least two reasons: severely retarded children are seldom placed for adoption; and adopted children are ordinarily sent to relatively superior homes, where they are very much wanted.

Children of socially inferior parents (i.e., whose mothers are feeble-minded or of border-line intelligence and/or whose fathers occupy a low socioeconomic status), when placed in average and superior homes, are more intelligent than their true parents. Indeed, they approach the intellectual level of their foster parents, particularly when they are placed in adoptive homes very early. However, a positive correlation between the intelligence of foster children and that of their *true* parents has been found, although this correlation accounts for little of the variance in children's intelligence. Studies on this topic show that, when adoption occurs early, true parents' intelligence (or education) accounts for between 0 and 10 percent of the variance in the intelligence of their children. It is doubtful, however, whether the adopted children of very inferior parents will average as high in intelligence as adopted children whose parents are normal or superior in intelligence. The evidence on this point is not clear.

2. Studies of twins indicate that the correlation of intelligence for *identical* twins reared together is very high—in the .80's and .90's; for *fraternal* twins reared in the same home correlations are lower (usually in the .70's); and for *nontwin siblings* reared together, the correlations cluster around .50. The correlation between intelligence for identical twins reared *separately* is lower; and the more disparate the environments in which they have been reared, the less similar they are in intelligence. Some of the correlation in intelligence between identical twins may be due to the similarity of social stimuli they evoke.

3. Evidence concerning the effects of residence in conventional institutions on the development of very young children is quite clear: standard institutional living exerts (at least temporarily, and probably lastingly) retarding and disturbing influences on intellectual and emotional growth.

Children growing up in culturally isolated areas ordinarily test low on standard intelligence tests. When families migrate from such areas to urban centers, the longer the family's residence in the urban center, the higher the children's intelligence scores.

4. Nursery-school attendance has frequently been found to be associated with gains in tested intelligence, although some careful studies have failed to show such gains. Where nursery schools have been set up in institutions for orphaned or deprived children, attendance at nursery school appears to have arrested the drop in intelligence that is typical for children who reside in institutions. When the institutional regime has been concurrently improved, nursery-school attendance has been accompanied by significant gains in tested intelligence.

5. Socioeconomic class is definitely related to intellectual level: the lower the social class, the lower the intelligence according to conventional measures. Lower social class is also ordinarily accompanied by inferior opportunities for education and by less encouragement from parents for conventional intellectual achievement.

6. Subcultural mentally retarded children are those who are neurologically normal, but who usually test between about 50 and 70 IQ. Most such youngsters are born and mature in families from the very lowest socioeconomic group: their childhood is harsh; they receive little intellectual stimulation at home; they do poorly in school. On two counts, therefore, they might be expected to be low in intelligence. First, they have had little opportunity to learn the skills that make for adequate performance on intelligence tests; and second, they learn many self-defeating attitudes through their repeated experiences of defeat and failure. Even so, more of them succeed as adults than might be predicted from their childhood histories.

7. Language development during infancy has been shown to be more highly related to later tests of intelligence than any other measure of infant "intelligence." With adult attention, the language development of infants can be accelerated: for example, the more reading infants have been exposed to, the more advanced their language development is likely to be. Love-oriented techniques of child-rearing, and a home atmosphere characterized by relatively high intellectual stimulation, are typical of families whose children are accelerated in language, regardless of the social class from which they come.

8. Research using animals as subjects indicates that they are retarded in problem-solving ability as a result of having spent their early months in isolation, and that isolation also appears to distort their "emotional" and "social" development. Introducing specific perceptual cues into animals' infantile environment helps them use these cues in later learning and problem-solving. Such animals perform better than animals that have not previously encountered the stimuli, even though their histories have included no *specific* learning related to the cues. Gentling early in development apparently helps animals to withstand later stress; and experiences while young have been shown to alter animals' sexual, competitive, and aggressive behavior profoundly.

Physical Growth and Motor Development

EVERY facet of social and personal development is affected by the body. The first, although by no means the most profound or important, impression a person makes on others in ordinary social living is likely to be based on his physiognomy and on his body and the way he handles it. Typically, one's first comments in attempting to describe a stranger concern his physical characteristics and his age: the dimensions most commonly used in such descriptions are height, weight, general body build, coloring, and attractiveness. Unusual and striking attributes of grace or awkwardness, thinness or obesity, apparent strength or weakness, and voice pitch are also likely to be mentioned.

An individual's conception of his body appears to be closely related to his self-concept. If he thinks well of himself, he is likely to be tolerant and accepting of his body; if he is self-rejecting, he rejects his body image (Laverne C. Johnson, 1956; Secord and Jourard, 1953). Self-rejection has been found to be associated with perceived parental rejection. This perceived rejection includes notions of being regarded as unattractive, or weak, or sickly by one's parents.

The nature of one's body and its functioning probably has much significance in the development of a pattern of interests, and possibly in selecting a vocation, although there is no conclusive evidence about this relationship. It is obvious that the weak and awkward boy will not, for example, become a professional athlete. His sturdy and graceful age-mate has before him a wider range of available interests, hobbies, and occupations. Bodies and faces that are markedly unattractive by cultural standards handicap their possessor in his social and heterosexual life, and create additional problems to be solved in an existence that, for most people, is already sufficiently complex.

For many years there has persisted in the United States the stereotyped notion that one type of growth or development occurs at the expense of other types. Commonplace are the cliches: "all brawn and no brain"; "beautiful but dumb"; "the mad genius"; and their like.

Much research has been done on the relation of physical growth to other variables. The conclusions are not particularly helpful for guiding a particular child, although the generalization that "all good things cluster together" has been generally borne out. A large group of children selected because they are far above average in intelligence, and compared with another large group of the same age and sex distribution selected because they are far below average in intelligence, will be found to be heavier, handsomer, healthier, stronger, and better coordinated. However, many of these relations are the result, not of intelligence, but of social status. The bright children come from wealthier homes, which provide them with better nutrition, better schooling, and more chances for constructive physical exercise. Although height and weight may correlate better than .60 with intelligence, intelligence and motor coordination are unlikely to show a correlation higher than the low .20's.

DEVELOPMENTAL NORMS

The first step in any field of scientific endeavor is to make such descriptions and quantifications of its data and to establish *norms* based on them. Norms, of course, do not explain either growth or behavior, but they are useful in locating extremes and in charting the progress of both the normal and the atypical child.

The word *normal,* when used to describe a child, refers to one or more of his characteristics that, quantitatively, fall close to the middle of the distribution of such characteristics for a sizable and presumably representative sample of children of his age and ethnic group. *Normal,* then, means "average." It does not imply optimal or ideal, although the word often has this latter connotation. That this connotation can lead to fallacy is well illustrated by research concerning pubescence. The *average* boy reaches sexual maturity, as judged by the appearance of coarse, kinky pubic hair, between 13 and 14 years of age. But studies by Ames (1957), Mary Cover Jones (1957), and Mussen and Jones (1957), for example, indicate rather clearly that the *early*-maturing boy has social and psychological advantages over the late-maturer (and probably over the average-maturer). The evidence is less clear for girls. These studies will be discussed in more detail later in this chapter.

To a degree, norms restrict the range of best guesses which we must make constantly in our practical dealings with children. Since complete data about any phase of the development of children do not exist, such "best guesses" are necessary; children must be reared, taught, and counseled. Take, for example, the professional worker in a children's psychological clinic. One of his first and most important tasks is to locate the factors that have contributed to a child's problems. If the child comes from a typical middle-class family and neighborhood and his IQ measures 108, then the chances are slight that intelligence as such contributes significantly to his problem. But if his IQ is 85, the suspicion immediately arises that intelligence is an important factor. The same considerations may be applied to physical growth and motor development. Extreme deviations may be influential in producing poor adjustment or, as in the case of unusual beauty and symmetry for girls or great strength and coordination for boys, may aid greatly in social and personal development.

Many workers in physical growth use the term *norm* not in the sense of a statistical average but as defining the range of acceptable variation. The reader should be alert to discover the sense in which the word is being used.

PRINCIPLES OF PHYSICAL GROWTH AND MOTOR DEVELOPMENT

Certain general principles (each of which has significant exceptions) have emerged from research on physical growth and motor development. Two of these generalizations concern developmental direction.

The first, or *cephalocaudal,* principle refers to the fact that growth and motor development proceed, in general, from the head to the tail end of the human organism. At birth, the part of the body that most closely approximates adult size is the head; the legs least closely approximate adult size. The first effective motor control is exerted over the major muscles that lift the head from a surface when the baby is in a prone position. Later, arm, shoulder, and abdominal muscles are used so that the baby lifts his torso. Only later still are leg and thigh muscles employed so that the pelvis can be lifted clear of the surface on which the baby lies.

An adult built along the lines of a baby would be a top-heavy monstrosity. The baby's crown-rump height is approximately 60 percent of his total height; the adult's height equals only about 50 percent of his standing height.

There are exceptions to the cephalocaudal principle. For example, during the fifth and sixth weeks following conception, the fetus grows an external tail. This decreases in length during the seventh and eighth weeks, and by the time of birth has become the coccyx (end of the spine). It is also true that the baby is only somewhat less adroit in reaching and holding with his feet than with his hands. Many six-month-olds hold the bottle efficiently between their feet as they feed themselves, but manipulation with the feet rapidly becomes less effective after the child begins to use them in the "heavy duty" of walking.

The second, or *proximodistal,* principle refers to the fact that growth and motor development proceed from the axis of the body outward to the periphery. This principle can be vividly demonstrated. The baby's early reaching is accomplished by gross movements from the shoulder. The arm and hand are used, not flexibly, but as a unit. Only well along in his first year does the baby make independent finger movements, or oppose his thumb and his fingers.

The third principle is that of progression from *general to specific action* patterns, and from *general gross to specific refined control.* There has been considerable argument, some of it heated, about whether development proceeds from the general to the specific, from the specific to the general, or whether it occurs in both directions. The best conclusion that can be drawn is that the most obvious or conspicuous development is from the general to the specific, but that development in the opposite direction also occurs, and that the processes complement each other.

The infant, pricked with a pin, reacts all over his body: he cries, kicks, and thrashes with his arms. But at 6 months, he reacts much more specifically and adaptively: he may cry, but he also withdraws efficiently if withdrawal is possible. Early grasping attempts have their fulcrum at the shoulder, are crude, and involve much heaving, puffing, and grunting. By a year of age or earlier, the baby manipulates cubes and pellets with well-coordinated movements of the wrist, and with the thumb in opposition to the fingers, which operate individually or work in unison. There is minimal involvement of other bodily parts, except for the coordination of his head and eyes with what he is doing with his hands.

However, it is obvious that many discrete neural connections and specific areas of muscle growth have occurred before even the grossest motor activity is possible. In other words, the argument about the direction of motor development has little practical value; although, from the observer's point of view, the most obvious development proceeds from general to specific.

Increasingly effective *motor chaining* also occurs. This development parallels the other types of learning that have been discussed. By *motor chaining* is meant simply that the child becomes more efficient in any motor activity he practices. Inappropriate muscle sequences drop out, and those that remain become smoother and more effective in accomplishing their purposes.

A striking illustration of the chaining process is the difference in walking between the average eighteen-month-old and the average two-year-old. The former "walks all over," and he walks for the sake of walking; for the latter walking is relatively efficient and automatic and, rather than being perceived as a goal in itself, serves simply as a means of getting the child to the place where he wants to go.

In the development of highly complex motor skills, all the processes of learning and development that have been discussed occur, and in many different sequences. An accomplished Spanish dancer, for example, has moved in his or her performance from relatively crude, gross movements to refined and at first partially independent movements with the feet, legs, arms, and hands. Chaining of responses has occurred. But eventually, the separate skills, movements, and postures must be integrated—changed from the specific back to the general (but a very different "general"). Only then is the performance "convincing," or "good." Such a process is necessary for all complex motor skills, including superior athletic performance as seen in boxing, swimming, or tennis.

PATTERNS OF PHYSICAL GROWTH

At least three broad postnatal growth curves have been identified. The first may be called the *neural curve*. This curve, which includes growth trends of the head, the brain, the spinal cord, and the eye, is illustrated in Figure 9.1. Neural growth is rapid during infancy, changing rather abruptly to a much slower rate during early childhood.

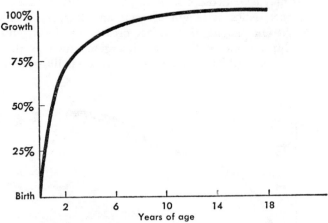

FIG. 9.1.   Neural growth pattern

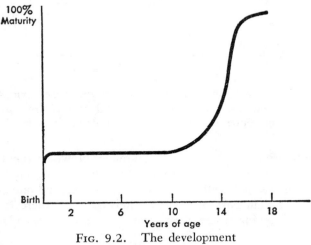

FIG. 9.2.   The development
of primary sex characteristics

The second pattern of growth might be called the sexual or *reproductive*. Figure 9.2 illustrates the development of the primary sex characteristics—genitals, ovaries, and testes. The secondary sex characteristics—

breasts, body and facial hair—follow a similar pattern of development. There is a slight increment in early infancy, but almost no change between late infancy and late childhood. A striking increase in rate of growth occurs before and around puberty, followed by a slower gain that tapers off in and during adolescence, although testes continue to grow until the middle twenties.

The third growth pattern is the one most obvious to the casual observer of the child. It may be called the *somatic* pattern, and includes such easily observable characteristics as length of arms and legs, girth of chest and abdomen, weight and height, the surface area of the body, and width of shoulders and hips. Some of the internal organs, such as the liver and kidneys, also grow according to this pattern, which is illustrated in Figure 9.3.

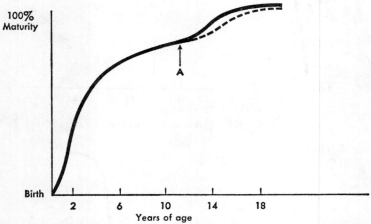

FIG. 9.3.   The general growth curve for the more obvious body dimensions and some of the major internal organs. From point *A*, the solid line represents girls' growth; the dotted line, boys'.

As can be seen from Figure 9.3, the rate of growth is rapid (following a brief initial decline, probably in weight only) during infancy. During childhood, the rate of growth is moderately slow. Around pubescence (and earlier for girls than boys by approximately a year), there is moderately rapid gain, followed by a slow year-by-year increase in later adolescence.

FACTORS THAT MODIFY PHYSICAL GROWTH

Preoccupation with modifiers of physical growth is characteristic of parents. How can I make my child gain (or lose) weight? Is there anything I can do so that he will be taller (or shorter)? Is he gaining at about the right rate? These are questions the pediatrician and nutritionist face constantly, and they concern matters in which not only parents but scientists have a legitimate interest.

Answers to such questions are by no means complete. Today, United States infants gain in weight and height much more rapidly than a generation ago. This may be the result of vitamin-enriched diets, or to the earlier addition of solid food or, as far as anyone knows, to mutation or increased atmospheric radiation. Young people achieve their maximal height as much as two years earlier than they did two or three generations ago (although the average height of old American stock at full maturity is not greatly different—perhaps a half inch—from what it was in 1900). This maximal height is reached now by the age of 16 (girls) or 18 (boys), whereas formerly girls kept growing until they were about 18 or 19, boys until they were about 21.

Research on the factors that modify physical growth is incomplete and results are inconclusive. A certain adequate level of vitamins in the diet is necessary for normal growth, but there is little agreement whether a child partaking of an average United States diet is getting enough vitamins or too many. There is no question that a variety of foods—calciums and other minerals, starches, proteins, and fats—is essential, but there is not full consensus about the proper proportion of these food types. Some advise starting the infant early on solids, others suggest keeping him on milk until the second half of his first year.

Few generalizations about growth modifiers can be made. It is agreed that children need sunlight, sufficient sleep, fresh air, exercise, and varied diets made up of milk, fruits, vegetables, and meats. Beyond these recommendations, little can be said.

ANATOMICAL CHANGES

Meredith (1957) lists various categories of physical change that are of interest to the student of physical growth. His clear and useful classification is the one that is presented here.

Changes in Kind

Life starts with change in *kind*. The union between sperm and ovum produces a new entity, the zygote. This simple structure is modified during prenatal life to include blood cells and bone cells, muscle tissue and adipose tissue, nervous system and skeletal system, and limb segments. In the second month of prenatal life an external tail begins to grow. A few weeks later it disappears. Most of the cartilaginous portions of the skeleton of the baby and the preschool child change to the bone of the older child and adult. The bones of the aged are more brittle than those of the young. All of these changes are examples of changes in kind.

Changes in Number

During adolescence, the number of bone masses drops from around 350 to fewer than 220, principally because of epiphyseal union. The five-year-old has in his head from 48 to 52 teeth in one or another stage of development, but by the time he is 15 he has ordinarily lost 20 deciduous (temporary) teeth. With increasing age, more teeth are likely to be lost, the wisdom teeth typically going first either because of decay or because the jaws cannot accommodate them.

HAIR CHANGES

There are striking developmental and sex differences in hairiness. For the male, hair around the genitals begins to proliferate, darken, and change in texture around adolescence (on the average, at 13 to 14 years), until by the time of the middle or late teens, the adult type of relatively thick, coarse, and curly pubic hair surrounds the genitals and covers a large portion of the groin region. Most frequently, distribution is roughly triangular with the apex of the triangle extending toward the navel. The appearance of axillary hair (coarse and curly hair in the armpits) follows the appearance of pubic hair. Next comes thickening and coarsening of facial hair, and the adolescent boy begins to shave. The growth is first noticeable on the upper lip. It extends outward and upward and downward with time until, in his middle twenties, the average male is bearded over his lower and lateral face and the upper throat region. Last in the maturational sequence is mature hair type and distribution on the extremities. Thicker, longer, and coarser hair begins to show on the lower legs, extending upward with time toward the crotch and buttocks and on the lower arm, developing progressively toward the elbow in one direction and the back of the hand and finger joints in the other. For a substantial portion of the male population, similar coarse hair begins to develop around the nipples, extending in area until, by the middle twenties, the entire chest is hairy, and there is extensive coverage of the upper back and shoulders. Many males, however, develop little or no chest hair. Body hairiness appears to be genetically determined.

At about the time pubic, axillary, and facial hair has reached its maximal density and distribution for the male, the inverse process begins at the top of his head. By the time they are 30, many men have conspicuously receding hairlines, and some are partially bald. This loss of hair is a continuous process which seems to be genetically determined, and (to the chagrin of many) is apparently irreversible.

There are conspicuous ethnic differences among males in the distribution and quantity of bodily and facial hair. If ethnic groups are divided (such a grouping is, of course, very rough) into the White, the Negroid, and the Mongoloid, bodily hairiness decreases in the same order, with Whites the hairiest and Mongoloids the least hairy. As adult males, the last group, typically, will have thin beards, relatively narrowly circumscribed pubic hair, comparatively little hair on lower arms and legs, and essentially hairless chests.

There is no known relationship between sexual function and hair distribution, despite the popular stereotype of the virile and hairy-chested male. But there is, among white United States males, a certain amount of positive value attached to the possession of abundant bodily and facial hair. Slow or negligible development of bodily hair may pose a certain adjustment problem for boys, analogous to but probably milder than the problems created by delayed pubescence.

Ethnic differences among females are less marked than among males, although the differences that exist are similar in direction to those for the various male populations mentioned. There are conspicuous sex differences in the values attached to bodily hair in many cultures, certainly in that of the United States. The manufacture and distribution of depilatories— agents for removing hair from the arms, underarms, legs, and face—is, in the United States, a huge business, whose purchasing public is overwhelmingly feminine.

The pattern of hair change for girls around and following pubescence is similar to that for boys, although less striking. First, as with boys, longer and coarser hair that later becomes curly begins to appear around the genitals. This hair extends laterally and upward, and eventually assumes the distribution of an inverted triangle, but one whose area is confined to the genital region rather than, as with the male, extending upward toward the navel. Soon after the appearance of the first pubic hair, as with boys, axillary hair develops. Some girls also develop marked facial hairiness, which follows the same, although a less striking, pattern as that for boys. The hair of the lower legs and arms becomes thicker, longer, and coarser, although only rarely to any degree approximating that of the typical male. The development of face, arm, and leg hair, which is viewed joyfully by the average boy, may be a matter of shame, embarrassment, and anxiety for girls, particularly if its development is sufficient to be conspicuous. Ordinarily, the female develops very little or no chest-breast hair.

Women's hair also thins with age, although not as conspicuously as that of men. However, in old age, many women are quite thin on top. Following menopause, women are likely to be troubled by increased growth of facial hair similar in type to, but not as striking as, the adolescent growth of facial hair in boys.

Changes in Size

Most lay people, when they consider physical growth, think primarily of changes in size, particularly in height and weight. Such changes are perhaps the most conspicuous and dramatic instances of growth, but constitute only one of its aspects.

There are periods of positive growth (or gain), of negative growth (decrease), and of little or no change in either direction. For example, the ligaments from the testes to the floor of the scrotum increase in length from 3 to 6 months of prenatal life; in the seventh prenatal month, these ligaments shorten by 50 percent; and by the time of birth they have shortened another 25 percent.

For the first few days after conception there is no change in the size of the zygote. Following birth, almost all babies lose some of their birth weight. From around 20 to 30 years, there is a minuscule change in standing or sitting height, but height decreases steadily, although not rapidly, during the mature years and old age. Height actually decreases between a quarter and a half inch from the time of getting out of bed in the morning to the time of retiring again at night, but this loss in height is recovered again by morning.

The thymus gland (presumably a regulator of growth) increases in weight almost to puberty, then declines strikingly in size. For both sexes, the genitals remain at approximately their infantile size until shortly before pubescence (11 or 12 for girls, 13 to 14 for boys). At this time and through middle adolescence begins a dramatic growth process—one that is often embarrassing, particularly for boys, who fear that their larger penis will show through their clothing (although they are, in actuality, usually very proud of this indication of their manhood). The typical sex-driven adolescent boy is frequently tormented by fear of betraying that he has an erection, which at this stage of development is frequently precipitated, often unpredictably, by casual environmental stimuli or fantasy. Penis length ordinarily reaches its maximum at about 17 or 18 years, although the testes increase in volume until in the middle twenties. Girls begin to bud around adolescence, and their breasts increase rapidly in size until, usually at 17 or 18, they reach a stage of development that may be considered mature. However, with increasing age, breasts change in shape, becoming more pendulous. Pregnancy and nursing also produce marked changes in the size and shape of the breasts.

When her breasts first begin to grow, the girl is likely to be as embarrassed by her new bosom as the boy is by his larger penis. Later, however, deficiency in this area will cause her as much agony as is caused the boy by undersized or underdeveloped genitals. The commercial supply of devices designed to increase the apparent size of the breasts is a big business.

It has earlier been pointed out, and illustrated in Figure 9.3, that the curve for height and weight gain shows a rapid increase in infancy, a much slower gain in childhood, another rapid increase a year or two before pubescence, and, in later adolescence, a slow year-by-year gain. Maximal height for boys is reached as much as two years earlier than it was fifty or sixty years ago—ordinarily, by the time the boy is 18 or 19.

The same trend is followed by girls, who today usually reach their mature height by about 17 years of age, whereas their grandmothers were probably still growing at 18 or 19. However, we do not have as much information about the growth of females fifty and sixty years ago as we do for males, since much of the information about the latter group was obtained from men entering military service.

A popular conception exists that each generation in the United States is taller than the preceding one. What actual gain there is in mature size is slight. Meredith estimates (personal communication) that in the United States it has not been more than a half inch, if that, since the latter part of the nineteenth century. But there are striking differences in the rate of growth in height and the age at which mature height is reached. All during childhood, children are taller today than formerly, but maximal height is also attained earlier.

The average mature white man in the United States is about 5 feet 8 inches tall; the average mature white woman about 5 feet 3 inches. Height, given adequate nutrition and normal health, is partially or completely determined by heredity, and shows marked ethnic differences. In the United States there is little, if any, difference in the height norms for Negroes and whites, although probably more members of the Negro population have faulty or insufficient nutrition. The Mexican-American population is, on the whole, slighter and shorter than the "Anglo" population in the same area, although again a portion of this difference is probably due to nutritional factors. Those of Oriental origin, although substantially taller—probably by an inch or two—than their progenitors, are as a group shorter and slighter than the white population (Greulich, 1957). The subsections of the population whose parents and grandparents came from Europe will usually be found to be taller and heavier, on the average, than their parents and grandparents; but, for all practical purposes, they merge into general population. Those of North European and British Isles national origin are, on the average, taller than those from South Europe (Meredith, 1939).

The growth curve for weight is about the same shape as that for height. The fat-rumped, relatively narrow-shouldered boy of 11 to 13 may take some comfort from the fact that for boys, shoulder width increases somewhat more rapidly than hip width, so that his adult proportions will be somewhat closer to the ideal adult figure than his present ones.

The weight curve, unlike the height curve, does not reach an asymptote in the late teens. Typically, weight increase continues into and frequently beyond the "sagging forties." As one passes middle age, this trend is usually reversed; the old are relatively thin. Overweight is a major problem in many societies in which the food supply is more than sufficient to provide for bodily needs. In the United States it is probably one of the most serious health problems. Chronic obesity based on overeating seems to have deep roots in emotional maladjustment; clinical reports indicate that it is almost as hard to "cure" as alcoholism, and indeed, "Fatties Anonymous" clubs have been organized. Many children seek security in eating, and food-based obesity is considered the symptom of a serious emotional problem when found in children.

Weight, like height, is principally determined by heredity under constant environmental conditions; but, more than height, it is subject to environmental manipulation. A regime of proper nutrition and appropriate exercise will keep most children and adults relatively trim. However, equivalent amounts of food affect different individuals differently. One may burst at the seams with weight gain; another, on the same rations, maintains a constant weight.

Changes in Shape

We have already referred to the changes in proportion from infancy to and following adolescence. Prenatal changes in shape are even more dramatic than they will be at any time after birth. Avey (1954), for example, shows that at the end of week 2 following fertilization, the embryo is shield-like in shape, but a month later is cylindroid and strongly bent.

The preschool child, whether boy or girl, is potbellied. During the first few years after pubescence, the typical boy has a concave abdomen. In his early twenties, this concavity begins to fill out, and from 30 on he is likely to be fighting the battle of the bulge, or else passively surrendering to it. His feminine counterpart will have been more curvilinear than he since puberty, and she too will have problems of sagging and bulging where she does not want to. Childbearing to some degree makes her problems more serious than those of the male.

Around adolescence, sex differences in proportion become more marked. For both boys and girls, the winged shoulder blades of childhood pull in so that backs are flatter transversely. As has been mentioned, pot-bellies recede. Boys' shoulder width increases somewhat more rapidly than their hip width, giving them an approximation of the narrow inverted triangle that is the ideal, although rarely attained, masculine figure. The opposite is true for girls, whose bodies are assuming the proportions that will fit them for easiest childbearing.

With the advent of teeth and the loss of baby fat, the shape of the face has more and more approximated a long oval, and the jaw has become more pronounced. When the teeth are lost, the face again becomes more compressed.

Changes in Position

Changes in position are not as immediately striking after birth as some of the other changes that have been described, although they are dramatic indeed during fetal development. The most obvious position changes in postnatal life involve the teeth. It has been mentioned that at 5 the child has between 48 and 52 teeth at one or another stage of development. In the process of acquiring his permanent teeth, two sets of teeth—the deciduous and the permanent—have moved upward or downward, depending on which jaw they are in, and have otherwise extensively changed their position.

At birth, the big toe is more widely spaced from the others than it will later be; and has been even more widely separated earlier. For most boys, the testes have descended from the abdomen to the scrotum before birth, although for some this process, either naturally or through surgery, follows birth. In the course of its development, the stomach moves from a vertical to a transverse position.

Changes in Pigmentation

The hair of many babies who will later be platinum blond is relatively dark; but is replaced by blond hair which, during later childhood and maturity (to the despair of many women) darkens, and then, in middle or old age, changes to gray. Like the hair, the skin progressively darkens, but the iris of the eye is likely to become lighter because of the resorption of pigment granules.

Changes in Texture

Changes in texture are striking and easily observable. The older preschool child has lost his baby fat and no longer has the "sponge-rubber" feel of the six-month-old infant, whose fatty tissue is easily compressible. The postadolescent girl "feels" different from the preadolescent, having, as she does, a greater percentage of fatty tissue than formerly. The postadolescent boy, on the other hand, has more muscle and less fat in his tissues than before adolescence. His muscles are harder. The bones of the aged are more brittle than those of the young adult. From the time of early maturity, the skin progressively loses its elasticity, so that crow's-feet and wrinkles develop. The pubic and axillary hair of adolescence and maturity is very different in texture from the down it replaced.

CHANGES IN FUNCTION

To this point, we have been discussing anatomical changes. But changes in physical and physiological function are of equal importance. Such changes seem to have influenced Freud in setting up the psychosexual stages that constitute so important a part of his theory of personality.

The Mouth

The little baby (up to 7 or 8 months) is essentially a passive receiver as far as the mouth and feeding are concerned. He has no teeth. His most effective motor function is sucking. But between 6 and 8 months, for most babies, teeth begin to erupt and the mouth can be used for something else than sucking. Indeed, as teeth irritate the gums, the baby begins to mouth and chew; and when teeth actually appear, nipping and biting are added to his behavior repertory. Among the Sioux, according to Erikson (1945), the addition of biting behavior results in a sharp change in the baby's relationship with his mother: where, previously, he had been enveloped in love and permissiveness, now, when he bites while feeding, he is thumped resoundingly on the head. This is his first experience of outside interference with his pleasure, and Erikson wonders whether this frustration, coming as it does so sharply after a history of great indulgence, may not be the root of the capacity for fury that characterized the Sioux as a warrior.

The Sphincters

A second change in function results from an interaction between maturation and the learning-teaching environment in which the child lives. The sphincters that control the elimination of urine and feces operate involuntarily during the first year of life. Voluntary, predictable control over them is difficult to establish before about 18 months at the earliest, with control often not being accomplished by 2 years. Even in adulthood, under conditions of stress or extreme visceral tension, sphincter control may be lost; and the loss of this control is a frequent accompaniment of severe emotional disturbance and the diseases of old age.

Posture and Locomotion

Between 7 and 8 months, the neck, trunk, abdominal, back, and leg muscles become sufficiently strong to permit the body to function in a sitting position. This landmark is important to the child. He can voluntarily make his world assume an entirely new perspective; things that he could not see before except when someone lifted or carried him are now visible at will.

A little later, still new coordinations and strengths are achieved, and he can crawl and later creep to a desired object from the spot where he espied it. By 10 or 11 months the baby, with constant practice, has reached the stage where he can pull himself to an upright position by using the side of his playpen, a chair, or the coffee table. Many babies learn to pull themselves erect before they know how to get down again, and the inexperienced parent is frequently concerned by his baby's tendency to pull himself erect, stand for a time, scream inexplicably, then calm when replaced in a sitting position. In a little while, the baby goes through the same sequence. This pattern disappears when the child learns to lower himself. Soon after standing, the child edges around his support, and some time between about 12 and 15 months sets off alone, walking independently.

Again, one can appreciate the importance of these landmarks in motor development only if he attempts to put himself in the position of the baby. Just as the world does not look the same from a lying-down and a sitting-up position, so it looks different from a sitting and a standing position. The object across the room has an entirely different meaning if it can be crawled or crept to, even though this is an effortful undertaking. It has a different meaning still if it can be walked or run toward.

The upright position is one of mankind's greatest developmental advantages, almost rivaling the ability to use symbolic behavior. It frees the hands, which in turn are uniquely structured to allow man to oppose his thumb and fingers for refined manipulation and exploration. In the phylogenetic sense, it may be speculated that the upright position made finger-thumb opposition possible; and that this in turn enabled man to gain a refined control over his environment impossible for any other species: with hands freed, and thumb and fingers working pincer-wise, it became possible to manufacture implements and weapons, to build fire, and to make shelter. It is conceivable that as he mastered more and more of his environment, man began to experience the need for labeling its complexities, so that, slowly, gestures, symbols, and words developed.

Laterality

During the first year, many babies are ambidextrous. But by the second year, a majority of them have developed a preference for one hand over the other; and by the end of the preschool period, about 9 out of 10 United States children have established a clear preference for the right hand. This preference does not, however, necessarily extend to all functions. A person may eat with his left hand, write with his right, yet shovel snow left-handedly. The left-hander may bat a ball right-handed, or vice versa. Nor does right-handedness imply the dominance of the right eye, the right foot, and so on.

There is no well-established theory about laterality. The cerebral-dominance theory, once widely accepted, is now considered at best speculative and at worst wrong. This theory said that if the left side of the brain were dominant, the individual would, for example, be right-handed; whereas if the right hemisphere of the brain were dominant, he would be left-handed. Implicit in this theory was the idea that damage would be done to the child if his preferred handedness were changed. Many authors have attributed stuttering and reading and writing difficulties (particularly reversals, mirror images, etc.) to forced change in handedness.

If indeed such problems accompany a handedness change, it now appears more likely that they are a function of the way the child was taught to change rather than of the change itself. Our society is a dextral, or right-handed, rather than a sinistral, or left-handed one, and has gone through periods when left-handedness has attributed to it "sinister" implications. The very derivation of *sinister,* coming from the Latin *sinister* (meaning "left"), testifies to this association. An adult can get some notion of what it means to a child to have his handedness arbitrarily and peremptorily changed if he forces himself to spend a half hour writing with his unpreferred hand and, at the same time, imagines some authority figure standing over him supervising, enforcing, and criticizing.

It is likely that heredity has something to do with handedness, although the evidence is scanty. Social learning, including direct imitation, probably plays at least as great a part. Some have maintained that adopting a left-handed preference is a sign of negativism.

The advice that might be given to parents concerning handedness is this: In a mild way, encourage children to be right-handed, since there are advantages to this in terms of using classroom chairs, tools, sporting goods, and so on. Encourage right-handedness by handing the young child the things he wants in his right hand. If he persists strongly in left-handedness, let him alone. However, make sure that he learns the correct orientation skills for left-handed people. Such tutelage will avoid, for example, the crabbed and roundabout way of writing that many left-handers develop.

Reproductive Organs and Sexual Behavior

Intricate developmental patterns bring the human organism to maturity. Sexual maturity is delayed until most physical and muscular growth has occurred. Then physical growth slows and stops, while the primary and secondary sex characteristics develop rapidly to their mature status.

Although the male baby and the little boy have experienced penis erections, only after pubescence can the true reproductive function be performed: erection and ejaculation of mature semen containing sperm. However, even from infancy, both boy and girl babies appear to be capable of experiencing either orgasm or orgasm-like states.

For the girl, entry into pubescence is marked by the onset of menstruation: the sloughing off of the nutritive tissue that accompanies ovulation, which occurs approximately monthly during the years of her reproductive potential. For some time following the first period, her menstrual cycles are likely to be irregular. For most girls a period of sterility, lasting for a year or two, apparently follows the first menstruation, although this period is highly variable from individual to individual (Montagu, 1946). It might be speculated that this state of affairs serves a useful purpose in helping to ensure full bodily growth before assumption of the tasks of pregnancy and motherhood.

It is not definitely known whether such a period of sterility follows pubescence for boys. In general, it is more difficult to establish criteria of sexual maturation for the boy than for the girl, since the "crossing over" is much less dramatic. According to Kinsey, Pomeroy, and Martin (1948), the middle and late teens—a time when, in our culture, free sexual activity is not generally permitted—mark the period of greatest sexual drive and potency for boys.

The overwhelming majority of boys—probably almost 100 percent in our culture—explore sex actively, to the degree of achieving orgasm, before marriage. Kinsey estimates that 95 percent of boys have experienced orgasm by age 15. Cultural sanctions are more relaxed for the male than for the female. Kinsey *et al.* (1948, 1953) report that the male sex drive is more urgent and, compared with that of the female, can be more easily aroused by fantasy, pictures, and other symbols. The male sex organ is also more visible and easily available for manipulation. Even without manipulation, seminal pressures produce tumescence (erection) in sleep, so that following pubescence most boys experience occasional or frequent orgasms during the night. These are known popularly as "wet dreams."

Girls less frequently experience orgasm before marriage although, according to Kinsey and his associates, almost two thirds of them have done so. Spontaneous orgasms are less likely to occur for girls than for boys: between the ages of 16 and 20, 91 percent of boys report such experiences, whereas only 7 percent of women do. Masturbation to orgasm (or climax) is less frequent for girls than for boys, the respective percentages being about 25 and 99. However, the *proportion* of orgasms due to masturbation is about the same for the two sexes.

Premarital intercourse is likewise less frequent for girls and women than for men, with about 50 percent of girls entering marriage as virgins. For boys, depending on their educational level, between 2 percent (for the lowest educational level) and 33 percent (for the best educated) enter marriage without having experienced intercourse. Premarital sex activity varies sharply according to social class. Middle-class males are considerably more inhibited than those of the lower class. The nature of sex activity also varies according to social class: premarital sexual activity for middle-class boys and girls is more likely to be solitary and to consist of masturbation, whereas lower-class youngsters are more likely to experiment socially and with a partner of the opposite sex. Extramarital sex seems, on the other hand, to continue later in life for the middle- than for the lower-class person, particularly the male. Early-maturing males tend to be more active sexually (in all types of sex activity) than late-maturers, but the same trend does not hold for women. At the time of Kinsey's survey (the 1940's, for the most part), the sex activity of younger women seemed to be substantially greater than that reported by older women, whereas very little change since the 1900's was manifested by men.

In line with other sexual activities, the male of the species is more likely to explore homosexuality actively. Kinsey *et al.* (1953, pp. 474–475) report that an accumulative incidence of homosexual responses had ultimately reached 28 percent for the female population he studied, with 13 percent having had overt homosexual contacts to the point of orgasm. The same figures for men were 50 percent and 37 percent. The women had also engaged in homosexual contact for shorter periods of time, and more frequently than men had had only one or two partners.

Some of the figures reported by Kinsey and his colleagues (1948, 1953) indicate that more lower- than middle-class males have had homosexual experiences, although the trends are not clear. The opposite is true for women, for obvious social reasons: the middle-class female is more likely to be a career woman and/or to remain a spinster, and to be sexually inhibited. Heterosexual courting starts earlier and is more vigorous in the lower-class group. Supervision of heterosexual contacts is closer for the middle-class girl, and the boy who courts her is likely to be less aggressive than the boy who courts the lower-class girl. All of these factors result in relatively greater oportunity for, and pressure toward, sex activity with other women than is true for the lower-class girl. The class difference in homosexual incidence for males (if it *does* exist) may, of course, be due simply to the greater freedom of social-sexual expression of all types that seems to characterize the lower class, and not to any difference in degree of heterosexual orientation.

The curve of sexual desire for the male changes steadily, declining from its peak in the middle and late teens to a fairly low but long-persisting level in the mid-fifties. A highly variable "male menopause" in the fifties or sixties has been postulated by many, but is not well documented by research; and there are many evidences of full-fledged sexual and reproductive activity on the part of males in advanced old age. The notion of the dangerous forties, particularly for middle-class males, appears to have some validity: the male, his virility flagging and his wife fading, seeks one last fling. This phenomenon is of course psychological and social, and may characterize only societies such as ours, which, besides being youth-centered, are organized on principles of monogamy and sexual restraint.

The course of development of female sexuality (Kinsey *et al.*, 1953) is quite different from that for men. The young girl rather typically is "not awakened," and, indeed, many girls feel no conscious sex desire until after their first complete heterosexual experiences. For many women, sex desire is highest preceding and following menstruation (Landis and Landis, 1957). The average woman experiences a rise in her sexual appetite, following its typically low level in the teens, which often continues into and beyond the middle forties. These trends produce complications in the relations between the sexes: the enthusiastic young bridegroom or suitor encounters a relatively cool partner; the tired middle-aged husband may prove singularly frustrating to his eager spouse. Although the capacity for reproduction ceases following female menopause, a substantial amount of interest in sex remains, often into old age.

Although Kinsey, who has been quoted frequently in this section, has gathered more data concerning human sexual behavior than any other investigator, it is possible that his data may overstate the case. All of his subjects were volunteers, who differ in many systematic ways from a randomly selected population. At least one study (Maslow and Sakoda, 1952) indicates that women volunteers are likely to have unorthodox attitudes toward sexual behavior, and may either indulge or profess to indulge in more sexual activities than nonvolunteers.

PHYSICAL FACTORS AND PERSONALITY

It has already been mentioned that between the ages of 11 and 13 girls are, on the average, taller and heavier than boys. Also, most girls reach physical maturity, although not necessarily "official" pubescence, earlier than most boys by about two years. The problems associated with this differential rate of maturity are obvious to anyone who visits a sixth-, seventh-, eighth-, or ninth-grade classroom, or who knows children in this age range. Whereas many of the girls are interested in dating and dancing, their male peers are frequently a head shorter than they, physically immature, and markedly uninterested in things heterosexual. The girl is thus reduced to going out with boys who chronologically are considerably older than she; or the boy is forced into the company of someone larger and more mature than he. This maturational difference has occasioned some to propose that girls should start school earlier than boys. Although there is merit to this suggestion, it is impractical for obvious reasons.

The Effect of Early Physical Maturity on Boys

Research workers at the University of California (e.g., Mary Cover Jones and Bayley, 1950; Mussen and Jones, 1957; and Mary Cover Jones, 1957) have investigated the consequences of early and late physical maturing for boys, and H. E. Jones (1949) and Mary Cover Jones and Mussen (1958) have reported results for early- and late-maturing girls. These workers report on data from a longitudinal study of California children, some of whom are still participating in their middle thirties.

The Jones and Bayley study (1950) uses skeletal age, as judged from x rays of the long bones of the hand and the knee, as its criterion of physical maturity. From a group of 90 boys who were studied for an average of about four and a half years, the 16 most consistently accelerated and the 16 most consistently retarded were studied intensively by means of observations and ratings both by professional adults and by the boys' buddies.

At the age of 14, ratings of physical maturity made from nude photographs showed almost no overlap between the two groups. The physically accelerated boys were taller, heavier, showed more advanced pubic hair, and had larger genitals. From 13 to 15 years of age the physically retarded boys tended to be long-legged, of slender build, and relatively weak during the period when they lagged most markedly behind in size. The retarded boys were rated by adults as lower in physical attractiveness, less masculine, less well groomed, and more animated and eager ("childish"). They sought attention more, were more affected and less matter-of-fact, and were tenser. However, they did not differ from the more advanced group in ratings of popularity, leadership, prestige, poise, assurance, cheerfulness, or social effect on the group. They were considered to be less mature in a heterosexual social situation.

FIG. 9.4.   Differential growth of an early maturing and a late maturing boy.
Drawings represent the boys' statuses at yearly intervals from 11½ to 16½ years
of age. (Adapted from Shuttleworth, 1949.)

When rated by their buddies, the physically retarded boys showed up about the same as when rated by adults, but the differences between them and the physically advanced group were less marked. Buddies estimated the physically retarded to be more restless, talkative, and bossy. They believed that they were more attention-seeking and less inclined to have assurance in class. Their buddies regarded them as less popular, and as less likely to be leaders. They were also rated as less likely to have older friends, as being shorter on a sense of humor about themselves, and as having a less attractive general appearance.

The Mussen and Jones study (1957) uses data taken from the Thematic Apperception Test, given to 17 late-maturers and 16 early-maturers when they were 17 years of age. In this test, the subject is shown a series of pictures and is asked to tell a story about each one: who the characters are, what has happened, and how it comes out. From the story he tells, a number of judgments (sometimes of dubious validity) can be made. As has been mentioned in Chapter 6, psychologists assume that the story-teller—the subject—projects his own needs and ideas onto the central character of the story he tells (the hero). This hero's actions, then, are assumed to be those that the story-teller sees as reasonable or desirable for himself. The hero's motives and needs are assumed to be those of the subject of the investigation. The TAT is one of the most useful measures of personality—Lindzey and co-workers (1952, 1955, 1956, and 1958), for example, have contributed evidence to show that it is, within broad limits, valid—although care should be taken not to overgeneralize from it.

In the Mussen and Jones study, it was found that more of the late- than of the early-maturers used TAT themes such as the following: the hero (with whom the boy presumably identified) was described in negative terms (for instance, as being an imbecile, a weakling, or a fanatic); the hero is rejected, scorned, or disapproved of by parents or by the authorities; the hero leaves home and/or defies his parents; the hero falls in love, or has a romance; the hero is helped, encouraged, or given something by someone other than his parents. One other theme came close to distinguishing significantly between the two groups: More of the late-maturers described the hero as feeling helpless and seeking aid or sympathy.

These patterns cluster sensibly together, and allow us to make tentative inferences about certain tendencies of this group of physically retarded boys. They are more likely than physically advanced boys to possess negative or derogatory self-concepts; they seem to blame their parents for their status, although perhaps not consciously; and they feel relatively weak, alone, and helpless. Hence, they seek assistance and affiliation.

The physically advanced group more frequently than the retarded group told stories in which the hero was aggressive in a physical and asocial fashion. They also tended somewhat more frequently to say that the picture elicited in them no thoughts or feelings. Here, perhaps, is an indication of self-confidence—an assurance that they can get away with aggressive behavior if they feel that way; and a tendency to be rather matter-of-fact, or unimaginative, as was observed by the raters in the Jones and Bayley study discussed above.

There were no differences between the two groups of boys in the number who told stories in which the hero is prevented by his parents from doing something he wants to; in which he establishes good relations with his parents; attempts to gain a high goal or do something creditable; or seeks fame and/or high prestige status. In other words, we can infer, very tentatively, that although the physically retarded boys bear somewhat more hostility toward their parents, they have, when compared with the physically advanced boys, an equal amount of positive feeling; and that the two groups subscribe equally to the cultural notion of the successful, occupationally climbing, bold man.

Mary Cover Jones (1957) has reported on two groups of 20 males (although at one point in her article she talks of 43 subjects), one early-, the other a late-maturing group. Average physical differences between the groups at age 14 were enormous: for example, the average height of the early-maturers was 5 feet 8 inches; that of the late-maturers only 5 feet even. Their respective average weights were approximately 127 pounds and 93 pounds. Ratings of body build showed the early-maturers to be more "mesomorphic"—i.e., with rugged bone and muscular structure.

However, at the time of Jones's follow-up, when the boys had become men averaging 33 years of age, physical differences had partially disappeared. The early-maturers averaged 5 feet 10 inches in height and 172 pounds in weight. The average figures for the late-maturers were 5 feet 9½ inches and 165 pounds. Although the early-maturers still appeared to conform more closely to the cultural notion of a "good build," differences between the groups were slight.

A number of questionnaires and tests were administered to these men, and significant differences were found on several measures (more than would be predicted by chance). These differences are quite harmonious with those obtained from an analysis of the TAT stories used by Jones and Mussen. The men who were early-maturing as boys scored higher than those who were late-maturing on measures of "good impression" and dominance; the late-maturers averaged higher scores on a test where high scores are said to refer to rebelliousness, touchiness, impulsivity, self-indulgence, assertiveness, and insightful self-preoccupation. Late-maturers scored significantly higher on a test of "succorance"—the tendency to look for help and support from others. There was a significant tendency for early-maturers to be less impulsive and more responsible.

Ames (1957) also studied this same group of 40 men from the California Growth Study, concentrating on different aspects of their behavior. Ames' findings are dramatic. An index of skeletal age, which he used as his criterion of maturity, predicted social behavior at the age of 33 better than *any* social measure obtained for the subjects during the time they were being studied (when they were from about 11 to about 18 years old). Some of Ames' correlations are worth listing and discussing here. His information about the men's adult status came from interviews with them. As has been pointed out before, the interview method has real weaknesses, but frequently (as in this case) it is the only method of study available.

Ames judged the men's occupational status, and found a correlation between skeletal maturation rate and status of .47, a highly significant figure, which means that the early-maturers were more successful occupationally than the late-maturers. Hypothetically, the boys did not differ originally in social class. When the degree of the men's informal social participation (their tendency to go out to have a good time) was rated, it was found to correlate .48 with skeletal maturation rate. Formal social participation (lodges, clubs, church affairs, and the like) correlated .44 with maturation rate. The relation of skeletal maturation rate to occupational social participation (business socialization) was a lower but still significant .35.

Fifteen of these 40 young men held positions in which they supervised or directed the work of subordinates. Of this group, only 3 were late-maturers. Eight of the men held some type of office in a club, lodge, or civic group. Of this number, none was a late-maturer.

The best single prediction of adult social behavior resulting from *social behavior data gathered when these men were boys* was obtained from a measure of clubhouse popularity, based on watching the boys in a number of social situations during which they were interacting with both boys and girls. This measure correlated .39 with adult informal social participation and was the only significant correlation found between adolescent social measures and adult status and social behavior, although even it reached significance at only the .05 level.

Kinsey, Pomeroy, and Martin (1949) used as their criterion of physical maturity the age at which their subjects reported first ejaculation. Boys and men reporting early sexual maturity are considered by Kinsey and his colleagues as "the more alert, energetic, vivacious, spontaneous, physically active, socially extrovert, and/or aggressive individuals in the population." (p. 325) Late-maturers were more frequently described as "slow, quiet, mild in manner, without force, reserved, timid, taciturn, introvert, and/or socially inept." (pp. 325–326) Early sexual maturity is associated with the almost immediate adoption of a pattern of regular consummatory sexual activity. Late-maturers delay adopting such a pattern. Early-maturers report consistently higher levels of sexual activity from adolescence on .until their fifties, although the differences between them and late-maturers become less extreme with age. But, over the years, early-maturers average about one fifth more sexual outlets than late maturers.

Implications of Physical Maturation and Personality Studies

Such data as those reported in the preceding section are impressive. It seems as though one of the most important things that could happen to a boy to assure his future good adjustment and success would be to mature early physically.

However, these findings, although dramatic and important, need to be considered thoughtfully. First, it should be noted that although some of the correlations (particularly from the Ames study) are high, even for the highest (between informal social participation and skeletal rate of maturation, .48), less than 25 percent of the variance of one variable is accounted for by the other. In other words, knowing a boy's skeletal maturation rate improves the accuracy of prediction about his social life in his thirties, but still leaves 75 percent of the variables that make him a "social drip" or "the life of the party" unknown.

Second, the samples used by Ames and Mary Cover Jones were small and highly selected. Also, as in any longitudinal study, two factors operate to make the sample of adults very different from the sample that was originally obtained. First, there are many dropouts. These may leave the study for a number of reasons: lack of interest in research, lack of time to cooperate as subjects, departure from the area, and so on. Lower-class subjects are more likely to drop out than middle-class subjects. Other subjects may not get along with the investigator. We do not know what the characteristics are of those who drop out, but there are many questions that should be asked, both about those who remain and those who leave a longitudinal study. Second, the long-time study of parents and their children may actually change the family relations, as has been pointed out in Chapter 2.

We know from the Mary Cover Jones and Bayley study (1950) that the adult raters regarded the physically precocious youngsters as the more attractive. Might this fact have resulted in friendship bonds between the research workers and the more stable and mature of the early-maturers, so that in their thirties they were willing, for friendship's sake, to cooperate in the study, whereas the less stable and emotionally mature members of the advanced group dropped out? It is also apparent that the late-maturers were more in need of help and support, and perhaps more dependent on adults. Is it possible that an active sympathy in the research worker was aroused by these relatively immature and dependent youngsters, so that considerable warmth and security was given them? As adults, then, when asked to return to the study, may not the most immature and dependent of the late-maturers have agreed to cooperate, perhaps hoping in some way to re-establish the pleasant bonds that had existed in their teens? We do not know the answers to these questions, but the factors implied by them may have affected the results reported by Jones and Ames, and should at least be considered in evaluating these studies.

In any longitudinal study, the investigators have an unknown influence on the populations studied. Could these influences have been positive for early-maturing, independent youngsters and negative for late-maturing and dependent boys? The California Growth Study was well enough designed, and its staff members sufficiently skilled, to make such an interaction unlikely, but at the same time its possibility must be considered.

Whatever questions we may ask about design and sample in these studies, we cannot overlook the implications of their findings. It is probable that the differences in adjustment and social behavior noted between groups of early- and late-maturing boys are socially mediated—that is, are a function of the way society reacts to the mature and the immature fourteen-year-old, rather than of the physiological or biochemical factors making for maturity or immaturity.

Body Build and Personality in Boys and Men

For thousands of years, philosophers and physicians and, more recently, anthropologists and other scientists have speculated (and done research) on relations between body build, function, constitution, and temperament. Efforts to classify body type apparently date back at least to Hippocrates (460?–377? B.C.). Tucker and Lessa (1940) state: "It is a curious and perhaps significant fact that 2500 years ago Hippocrates said that there are two roots of human beings, the long thins and the short thicks. Almost all simple classifications of type since that time have nearly the same basis, despite variety of nomenclature and detail of description." (p. 419) Kretschmer (1925) used a somewhat similar classification of body type in his controversial but influential hypotheses about the relations of body build to temperament and mental illness (for example, that long lean people, if they succumb to mental disease, will become schizophrenics; short blocky people manic-depressives).

In their scholarly review, Tucker and Lessa include a bibliography of 334 items, a large number of which refer to body build or constitution and temperament.

Sheldon has received much attention for his work in the area of body build and temperament. He and his colleagues (1940, 1942) have interested themselves in methods of characterizing body build and relating it to personality. One of his works (1949) takes an extreme position, and is endorsed by few; and the statistical assumptions of his whole technique of classifying or describing body build have been strongly and tellingly criticized (e.g., Hammond, 1957; Humphreys, 1957; Meredith, 1940). However, his work has had so much impact that this text would not be complete without a brief description of it.

Sheldon has worked mostly with college-age students—that is, people in late adolescence. His data are ordinarily nude front, side, and back photographs, and he has worked more with male than with female subjects. Each photograph is rated from 1 (having very little of) to 7 (having very much of) on three dimensions: endomorphy, mesomorphy, and ectomorphy. The barrel-chested, big-bellied individual would receive a high *endomorph* rating; the muscular, broad-shouldered, narrow-hipped, rather big-boned individual would be rated high on *mesomorphy;* the lean and skinny individual, whose external body surface is large in relation to his weight, would obtain a high rating on *ectomorphy.* Figure 9.5 consists of line drawings illustrating these patterns at 11½ years and Figure 9.6 shows the same boys three and a half years later.

FIG. 9.5.   Front and rear views, reading from the left, of an endomorph, a mesomorph, and an ectomorph boy, aged about 11½ years. (Adapted from Shuttleworth, 1949.)

FIG. 9.6.   The three boys shown in Fig. 9.5, in the same order from left to right, at 15 years of age. (Adapted from Shuttleworth, 1949.)

Each photograph is given three ratings: a 7-1-1 would describe an almost impossibly pure case of endomorphy; a 1-1-7 an equally improbable example of ectomorphy. Sheldon also rates on *dysplasia* (bodily disharmony), *gynandromorphy* (bisexuality), *texture,* and *hirsutism* (hairiness).

However, these are subsidiary values and of relatively little interest to us here. Attempts to somatotype children have been only moderately successful, and the somatotype has been found to vary sharply with nutritional condition (see, for example, Figure 9.7 and Shuttleworth, 1949).

Sheldon postulates personality patterns that go with these different body builds. He maintains that the individual high in endomorphy will have a personality type that he names "viscerotonia"; the personality type accompanying high mesomorphy is "somatotonia"' and ectomorphs are "cerebrotonic." The viscerotonic is generally relaxed, sociable, loves food

FIG. 9.7. A demonstration of the changes occurring as a result of near starvation on the body build of a pronounced mesomorph. The somatotype rating changes sharply in the direction of ectomorphy.

and comfort, and has an affectionate attitude toward people. The somatotonic is muscularly active, bodily assertive, and has great personal vigor. The cerebrotonic is restrained, inhibited, and shrinks from social obligations.

Should Sheldon be proved correct in his belief that there is an immutable, biological link between body build and temperament, the hope of improving society through education and social welfare would be sharply curtailed. The evidence in support of Sheldon's theory is very weak, although not entirely negative (see, for example, Child, 1950; and Janoff *et al.,* 1950). However, even if linkages between body build and personality (or between time of physical maturity and personality) should be found, it is not necessary to go to genetics to account for them. If a certain type of body build or quality arouses characteristic and consistent negative or positive social reactions, then, according to social-learning theory, predictable and differential types of personality development will occur.

One ingenious study (Brodsky, 1954) suggests that there *are* differential social reactions to characteristic body builds. Brodsky prepared five 15-inch silhouettes of males, representing: (1) extreme endomorph; (2) endomesomorph; (3) mesomorph; (4) ectomesomorph; and (5) ectomorph. He also constructed a questionnaire containing such items as the following: Which one of this group of five men is most aggressive? Which one of this group of five men is least aggressive?

To secure divergent research populations, Brodsky recruited 75 male medical and dental college students from Howard University, all or almost all of whom would be expected to be Negro; and 50 male college students from George Washington University, all presumably white. The questionnaire was given to the men in groups numbering no more than 5. There were no important differences in the way the two samples of respondents answered, so Brodsky pooled his groups. This homogeneity in opinion of superficially quite different groups of men lends weight to the notion of a "cultural stereotype," or characteristic way of regarding body build.

The various traits were usually assigned by the respondents to the "pure" silhouettes—the endomorph, mesomorph, and ectomorph. Those assigned to the given silhouette by a third or more of the respondents are listed below:

More than one third of the respondents labeled the *endomorph* silhouette as representing the man who eats the most, eats the most often, will make the worst soldier, will make the poorest athlete, will be the poorest professor of philosophy, can endure pain the least well, will make the least successful military leader, will be least likely to be chosen leader, will make the poorest university president, will be the least aggressive, will drink the most, will be least preferred as a personal friend (but, ironically, would have many friends), will make the poorest doctor, and will put his own interests before those of others.

This picture is an almost consistently negative one. If there is any truth to the notion that a person behaves as he is expected to behave, a dismal picture of the direction of personality growth of the endomorph is presented by this study.

The *mesomorph* fares as favorably as the endomorph does unfavorably: the respondents said that he would make the best athlete, the most successful military leader, and the best soldier. They chose him as the man who would assume leadership, as well as the man who would be elected as leader. He was judged not to smoke at all, and to be self-sufficient, in the sense of needing friends the least. However, he was most preferred as a friend, and was judged to have many friends. Respondents also said that he would be the most aggressive, would endure pain the best, would never have a nervous breakdown, and would drink the least.

The stereotype of the *ectomorph* is far less socially desirable than that of the mesomorph, but in general more favorable than that of the endomorph. The ectomorph was judged to be the most likely to have a nervous breakdown before the age of 30, to eat the least, and the least often, to smoke three packs of cigarettes a day, to be least self-sufficient, in the sense of needing friends the most (but, unfortunately, was judged to have the fewest friends), to hold his liquor the worst, to make a poor father, and, as a military leader, to be likely to sacrifice his men with the greatest emotional distress.

This study illustrates that there may be certain characteristic ways of reacting to different types of male physique, and that the pattern of reaction is such as to favor the mesomorph. In this context, it should be mentioned that Jones's early-maturers, best adjusted according to her criteria, were more mesomorphic in average body build than her late-maturers.

These relationships remain only suggestions until more research has been done, but *provocative* suggestions they are.

The Advantages to the Male
of Early Physical Maturation and Strong Body Build

It has already been noted (Mary Cover Jones and Bayley, 1950) that adult raters give more favorable ratings to early- than to late-maturing boys, and that their peers esteem early-maturers somewhat more highly (although other research does not give strong support to this conclusion). It is not unlikely that positions of leadership are allocated earlier by adults to such boys. Hence, if expectations in any way govern development, the boys will develop into more responsible and mature people, more socially self-confident than late-maturers.

Certainly, there is a period of years during junior high school when the early-maturers excel at athletics because of their superior height, weight, and strength. Athletic prowess, for boys, is a matter of tremendous prestige. At maturity they do not, as a group, lose their status as far as height, weight, and musculature are concerned, and may as individuals remain burlier than average- and late-maturers (although within the group their adult height is distributed much like that of the male population as a whole).

It must be remembered that the vital capacity of these boys—the amount of oxygen per unit of time that the body can utilize—lags behind their more obvious physical capacity. In other words, although they may appear very grown-up, they have not reached adult stamina, nor will they do so for two or three years after they have achieved maximal height and adult weight. Stolz and Stolz (1951), in this connection, cite the case history of Ben, a boy tall and rugged for his years, who was placed early in competitive athletics but was not able to perform, and consequently lost much prestige. This failure appeared to be due to his lag in vital capacity— he simply could not gulp in and utilize the large amounts of air needed for persistence in hard physical activity.

Early-maturing boys possess a clear heterosexual advantage for a period of several years, maturing as they do at about the same time as the girls in their classes. Consequently, their drives and interests are relatively well matched with those of their feminine age-mates, and they are able to take out their girls without the embarrassment of being the shorter and slighter member of the pair.

Late-maturing boys, on the other hand, although for the most part they catch up in height and weight with their early-maturing peers, undergo a long period of social disadvantage during an important formative period of their lives. During this time, they are likely to be perceived and treated as relatively immature and irresponsible, are at a disadvantage in athletics, and are biologically unready for, and hopelessly outclassed in, courtship competition. As Kinsey has pointed out, early-maturing boys not only precede late-maturers as far as initial sexual experience is concerned, but they establish a regular pattern for sexual satisfaction much earlier and, for many years, retain a higher rate of sexual output than late-maturers. This pattern may produce considerable conflict for early-maturers during adolescence (before sexual activity is condoned), but its net effects should be positive, including as they do an important and enduring source of satisfaction and a contribution to a self-concept of sexual adequacy and virility. Such a self-concept should also favor satisfactory and appropriate sex-role identification (see discussions of this topic in the following chapter).

Physical Maturation, Body Build, and Adjustment in Girls and Women

Fewer data exist for girls than for boys concerning the relationship between body build and temperament, and between time of sexual maturity and later personality. H. E. Jones (1949) has made many provocative suggestions concerning these relationships. He has suggested, for example, that for girls in our society, early development is disadvantageous, late physical maturing advantageous—a pattern opposite to that for boys, but resulting from similar general social principles. There is some tendency for early-maturing girls to be stockier, later in their development, than their late-maturing sisters. In our culture, the stocky figure is not the fashionable one. The social gap between the early-maturing girl and the boys in her class is of course striking—a span of important years goes by before there is any boy of her age who is tall enough so that she can appear in public with him without feeling conspicuous. Sexual maturity attained while psychologically immature may engender confusion, conflict, and uncertainty. The early-maturing girl may be driven beyond her depth in courtship, dating boys substantially older and more sophisticated than she, with attendant social-sexual complications. H. E. Jones (1949) has reported that late-maturing girls were judged by adult observers to have attained higher prestige, and to show more leadership, than early-maturers. They were also rated as having greater social-stimulus value. In summarizing a study in press at the time of this writing, Mary Cover Jones and Mussen (1958) state that, over a three-year period of time, late-maturing girls were more frequently mentioned in the high-school paper, and were elected to more offices in extracurricular activities. However, an analysis of TAT stories told by these

FIG. 9.8. Differential growth of an early and a late maturing girl. The first four pairings are drawn at yearly birthdays from 8 through 11 years. Other pairings are at half-year intervals from 11½ years through 14½ years of age. (Adapted from Shuttleworth, 1949.)

girls at the age of 17 revealed few differences between early- and late-maturers (only 2 out of 20 differences were statistically significant). If anything, on this measure of "fantasy," the early-maturers showed more characteristics believed to be favorable than the late-maturing group.

Trait Status and Personal Concern

Earlier in this chapter mention was made of the intimate relation between self-concept and attitude toward one's own body. It was also pointed out that a healthy, well-proportioned, strong, and graceful body undoubtedly aids, although it does not necessarily accompany, good emotional development and adjustment, whereas graceless and unattractive bodies often make personal adjustment more difficult.

The advantages, particularly to boys, of early physical maturity have been discussed. It has been pointed out that, by men at least, mesomorphic body build is more favorably regarded than endo- or ectomorphic structure.

It is probable that most children, particularly before and during adolescence, worry considerably about the development of their primary and secondary sex characteristics. Schonfeld (1950), for example, believes that inadequate masculine physique (including delay of puberty, small sex organs, or deficiency in secondary sex characteristics) can be a matter of considerable concern to boys and result in serious personality conflicts or psychosomatic complaints (physical ailments often considered to be psychological in their origin). His report is based on a population of 256 boys seen by him, who had expressed concern over their physical development, or whose parents had been worried about it. Most of these boys, he found, were normal in the sense that their development fell within the limits of normal variability.

Schonfeld has reported very good success in treating these boys. Thirty-five percent of them were adequately taken care of simply by reassurance, and the majority of the rest profited from re-education, psychotherapy, and, in some cases, hormonal treatment.

Angelino and Mech (1955) report that girls, too, worry about their physical development. Most of their worries center on the possibility that deviant height and weight development will interfere with, or complicate, their social and emotional life.

There is no question that children should receive more information than most of them are now given about the ways their bodies grow and are likely to grow. Few youngsters (or, for that matter, their parents) understand the wide variability in physical growth and the onset of pubescence. One boy, known to the author, began at 14 to have nightmares and to lose weight. He became moody and depressed, was insolent to his parents whereas previously he had been a model boy, withdrew from his former circle of school friends, and showed deterioration of a previously highly superior academic performance. This boy was a somewhat late-maturing youngster who was, in addition, one year advanced academically, so that at 14 he was in a grade where he was the youngest by almost a year, and where some boys were almost 17 years of age.

On the basis of professional advice, his parents decided to leave, where he could find it, a little volume prepared by Shuttleworth (1949), which, by means of pictures and easily understandable text, portrays the great variability in reaching pubescence. The boy's natural curiosity led him into the volume, and, almost as if by magic, his symptoms of conflict disappeared. A few months later he talked with his parents about his earlier conflicts and worries, and told them how obtaining factual information on the basis of which he could peg his own physical development, compare it with that of his older friends, and predict its course, had alleviated his concerns. Not all adolescent worries, of course, can be so easily dissipated.

Many adolescent worries are quite unrealistic, as, to some degree, were this boy's. Although objectively inadequate physical development can lead to conflict and disturbance, conflict and disturbance can also be tied, in symptomatic fashion, to perfectly adequate and normal physical development. A well-developed but insecure girl can (and many have been known to) blame her lack of social success on the fact that she is "too fat" or "too busty," when in reality she has excellent proportions. A normally sturdy, muscular boy can, in an almost neurotic fashion, think of himself as skinny, or an attractive but stocky boy believe that he is fat.

SUMMARY

The human body, the way it is handled, and general physical appearance are fundamentally linked to social living, self-concepts, and very possibly choice of vocation. Charting how the body grows and develops is an important task assumed by scholars in child development and physical anthropology. One major goal of such scholars is to describe and establish the norms, or general characteristics, of physical growth and body build and function. These norms do not *explain*, but they assist in establishing a range of acceptable variation, which is useful both psychologically and physically.

A second task assumed by research workers in the field of physical growth is to uncover general principles of development. To date, the cephalocaudal (head to tail) and proximodistal (center axis to periphery) principles of development hold up well for both physical growth and motor development. The third principle is that of development from general to specific action patterns, This principle has aroused considerable argument; the best conclusion that can be drawn is that, whereas the most conspicuous development is from the general to the specific, development in the other direction also occurs: the processes are complementary.

Different parts of the body grow according to different patterns. The *neural* pattern is one of rapid increase during infancy and slow gains during later childhood and adolescence; the *sexual* pattern is one of little change (long latency) up to somewhat before the time of adolescence (12 or 13 years for boys, 11 or 12 for girls). At this time the primary and secondary sex characteristics "mushroom," usually reaching mature development in five or six years. The *somatic pattern* (including changes in height and weight) is one of rapid growth in infancy, moderately rapid growth in childhood, a spurt preceding pubescence, and a tapering off from the middle to the late teens.

Other scientific goals in the study of physical growth include determining the factors that modify physical growth, and their relation to growth, health, stamina, and so on at all age levels. For example, how does growth vary from season to season, or from one climate to another? Does excessively rapid growth in infancy exert a positive or deleterious effect on the health of adolescents and adults—and so on. Another goal is to determine the relation between physical growth and other aspects of development: How are patterns of growth related to strength and speed, or to intelligence?

Physical growth, by definition, involves change. The seven varieties of anatomical change that have been most studied are the following:

1. Changes in kind (the zygote is very different in kind from the sperm and egg that make it up; pubic hair is very different from childhood down).

2. Changes in number (at 5, the child has 48 to 52 teeth in one stage of development or another; by adolescence, 20 deciduous—baby—teeth have been lost; by late adolescence one or more third molars—the wisdom teeth—have often been lost; and by old age it is common to have lost all of one's teeth).

3. Changes in size (the child steadily increases in height, for example, to 18 years or so, but in middle and old age height actually decreases; the primary sex characteristics develop very slowly during childhood, but increase dramatically in size before, during, and for a time after puberty).

4. Changes in shape (the proportions of the adolescent are very different from those of the baby; the chest becomes broader and flatter during childhood, more circular again after middle age).

5. Changes in position (elbows and knees at first project outward from the sides of the body—later the knees rotate toward the front, the elbows toward the back; feet move from paralleling the axis of the lower leg toward the perpendicular).

6. Changes in pigmentation (hair usually grows darker during childhood and ordinarily grays in middle and old age; skin darkens in middle age).

7. Changes in texture (muscles harden, particularly for males during and after adolescence; in middle and old age, bones become brittle and skin loses its elasticity).

Changes in function also occur. The mouth becomes less an instrument of sucking, more an instrument of biting, chewing, and vocalizing; the sphincters come under voluntary control; legs are used for walking. the penis acquires the function of ejaculation.

Babies seem to be divided about evenly as far as "natural" hand preference is concerned, but by about their second year, 90 percent or more of them have chosen or been trained to right-handedness. When it is possible to develop a right-handed preference without undue pressure on the infant, this should be done; our culture is *dextral,* and it is obviously more convenient to be right-handed.

Sexual behavior varies greatly according to social class, and men seem to indulge more in sex, including its fantasy aspects, than women. Overt sexual behavior seems to be more "social" among those with less education (i.e., they tend more to *mutual* sex behavior, less to such solitary sex behavior as masturbation). Almost all boys and men have masturbated to orgasm, and most have experienced intercourse, before marriage; whereas about 50 percent of women enter marriage as virgins, and only about one fourth of them have masturbated. Women's sex desires reach their maximum later than those of men, and these trends may produce complications in the relations between the sexes.

Attainment of physical maturity is an important landmark in our culture. It comes at a time when the child is changing in many ways— indeed, social change for young people in their early teens is as dramatic as physical change, and the two are closely linked in their dynamics and their results.

For boys, almost all the consequences of early physical maturity— immediately and for fifteen or more years thereafter—appear to be fortunate. Early exposure to opportunities for leadership, the prestige they enjoy in athletics during this important and formative period, the closing of the social gap between them and girls of their own age—all seem to give them a "start" that is better than that enjoyed by the late-maturing boy.

For girls, the evidence concerning the effects of differential physical maturity is unclear. Temporarily, early maturity may be to their advantage, but long-lasting positive correlates of early maturity have not been revealed.

There is no convincing evidence that body build is associated with personality, although one interesting study indicates that if there are correlations between personality and body build, social mediation could account for them. In United States culture, the mesomorphic (muscular) body build is regarded far more favorably than the ectomorphic (long and lean), which in turn meets with more approval than the endomorphic (stocky). If social expectancies have an influence on personality, the positive expectancies held for the mesmorph should influence him favorably, whereas the negative expectancies for the mesmorph may have deleterious effects.

Socialization, Sex-Typing and Identification

THE TERM *socialization,* as the psychologist uses it, refers to a wide range of behaviors and processes. We say that a child has begun to be socialized when he first responds to other people (usually, his parents) by some recognizable, consistent, and predictable sign that they are meaningful stimuli for him. Some say that the first real sign of socialization is the smile (Gray, 1957), which typically appears as a response to the father or mother around the age of 6 to 8 weeks. The following are other early signs of socialization: The child stops crying when he sees his mother; laughs at the sight of his parents; plays peek-a-boo; waves "bye-bye"; pulls at his mother to indicate his need for help when he cannot reach something he wants; gestures, pulls, or attempts to climb the adult to show that he wants to be held; cries when his parent leaves him; acts differently with strangers than with his parents or intimates.

These are all *social responses.* Socialization, however, implies not only social responsiveness but also *social* (and, ultimately, personal) *controls:* the child stops doing something when his mother says, "No, no," or does something he doesn't want to do when he is asked by her to do it. As he grows older, he can often be heard saying "No, no" to himself as he reaches for the forbidden ashtray or figurine, even when his parent is absent. The time comes when he signifies that he has to go to the toilet, and later he inhibits urination or defecation for considerable periods until he can be helped or can go independently to the toilet. As he grows still older, he will eat only his share of the brownies his mother has baked, saving their share for older brothers and sisters away at school. He may bring home to parents and siblings a portion of the birthday cake he has been offered at a party. Eventually, he postpones some of his own immediate gratification to do things that may be rewarding only in the far-distant future: he relinquishes basketball after school to do his homework or practice the piano; he saves money from baby-sitting or a paper route to apply it to a family vacation or a later college education.

First, then, comes social *response;* later come social and impulse *control.*[1]

---

[1] In sociology, the term *socialization* is ordinarily restricted to the second meaning, "adopting society's rules of behavior."

THE AGENTS OF SOCIALIZATION AND THEIR GOALS

Socialization implies not only an object—the child—but an agent, at first (ordinarily) the parents. It is thought that socialization (in the sense of control) will not occur at all until and unless the parents, *in and of themselves,* become reinforcers or rewarders to the child. If this parental role is lacking, social response will also be severely retarded. Typical parents acquire reward value (or reinforcement properties) by giving the child routine but tender physical care: the baby is fed, washed, dressed, bathed, put to bed—not coldly and mechanically, but with cooes, pats, kisses, and lullabies. It has been demonstrated (e.g., Rheingold, 1956) that early infant routines accompanied by social stimulation, including bodily contact, produce more socially responsive babies than routines carried out coolly and efficiently, but impersonally and quickly. Babies handled in the latter fashion speed up in their rate of social development when the type of treatment is changed to one of tender, loving care, and quickly learn social responsiveness. Rheingold, Gewirtz, and Ross (1959) have also demonstrated that a baby can quickly be conditioned to make social responses and to increase them in frequency when an adult responds socially to the baby's vocal responses.

Once the child is responding socially, it becomes necessary to train or channel his responses so that they are acceptable to his parents, brothers and sisters, and society at large. "Bye-bye" and "peek-a-boo" are well-regarded in one-year-olds, but inappropriate in this form for kindergartners. Wet diapers are all right at age one, but frowned on at age four. Crying for food is appropriate behavior in the nine-month-old but not in the fifth-grader. More and more control and direction of behavior are demanded of the child from the time he first begins to make social responses until he becomes a civilized, law-abiding, relatively unselfish adult.

The process of social control and adaptability starts with the child's interactions with his parents and family, and continues with his playmates, relatives, and teachers. These socializing agents must provide a pattern of reward, acceptance, permissiveness, and punishment that enables the child to gain law- and amenity-abiding adulthood yet remain or become relatively secure, calm, happy, appropriately masculine or feminine, and vocationally self-sustaining.

According to Erikson (1956), the socialization process consists of eight phases—the "eight stages of man." Erikson has been deeply influenced by Freud, but he also adopts a strong social point of view in his account of personality development. His "eight stages of man" were formulated, not through experimental work, but through wide-ranging experience in psychotherapy, including extensive experience with children and adolescents from low as well as upper and middle social classes. These stages are linked less than Freud's to organ systems, and more to the types of learning that go on at different age levels. Each stage is regarded by

Erikson as a "psychosocial crisis," which arises and demands resolution before the next stage can be satisfactorily negotiated. These stages are conceived in an almost architectural sense: satisfactory learning and resolution of each crisis is necessary if the child is to manage the next and subsequent ones satisfactorily, just as the foundation of a house is essential to the first floor, which in turn must be structurally sound to support the second story, and so on.

For Erikson, the eight stages of development are the following:

1. *Learning trust versus mistrust.* Chronologically, this is the period of infancy—the first one or two years. The child, well-handled, nurtured, and loved, develops trust and security—a basic optimism (see Chapter 3). Badly handled, he becomes insecure and mistrustful.[2] Freud, it will be recalled, refers to this as the oral phase, and Sullivan believes that, during it, learning is empathic.

2. *Learning autonomy versus shame.* The second psychosocial crisis, Erikson believes, occurs during early childhood, probably between about 18 months or 2 years and 3½ to four years of age. It coincides generally with Freud's anal stages and, in our culture, is the period when one of the most obvious "learnings of control"—toilet training—is being acquired. The "well-parented" child emerges from this stage sure of himself, elated with his newfound control, and proud rather than ashamed. Autonomy is not, however, entirely synonymous with assured self-possession, initiative, and independence, but—at least for children in the early part of this psychosocial crisis—includes stormy self-will, tantrums, stubbornness, and negativism. For example, one sees many two-year-olds resolutely folding their arms to prevent their mothers from holding their hands as they cross the street. Also, "The sound of *NO* rings through the house" (or the grocery).

3. *Learning initiative versus guilt.* Erikson believes that this third psychosocial crisis occurs during what he calls the "play age," or the later preschool years (from about 3½ to, in the United States culture, entry into formal school). During it, the healthily developing child learns to imagine, to broaden his skills through active play of all sorts, including fantasy; to cooperate with others; to lead as well as to follow. Immobolized by guilt, he is fearful; hangs on the fringes of groups; continues to depend unduly on adults; and is restricted both in the development of play skills and in imagination. This stage seems to combine Freud's phallic and Oedipal stages.

4. *Industry versus inferiority.* Erikson believes that the fourth pyschosocial crisis is handled, for better or worse, during what he calls the "school age"—presumably up to and possibly including some of junior high school. Here the child learns to master the more formal skills of life: relating with peers according to rules; progressing from free play to play

[2] In this connection, it may be profitable to return to the discussion of Sullivan's theories in Chapter 2, pages 56 and following.

that may be elaborately structured by rules and may demand formal team-work, such as baseball; mastering social studies, reading, arithmetic. Homework is a necessity, and the need for self-discipline increases yearly. The child who, because of his successive and successful resolutions of earlier psychosocial crises, is trusting, autonomous, and full of initiative will learn easily enough to be industrious; but the mistrusting child will doubt the future; the shame- and guilt-filled child will experience defeat and inferiority. This stage corresponds to Freud's latency period.

5. *Learning identity versus identity diffusion.* During the fifth psycho-social crisis (adolescence—from about 13 or 14 to about 20) the child (now the adolescent) learns how to answer satisfactorily and happily the question of "Who am I?" But even the best-adjusted of adolescents experiences some identity diffusion: most boys and probably most girls experiment with minor delinquency; rebellion flourishes; self-doubts flood the young-ster, and so on.

Erikson believes that during successful early adolescence, mature time perspective is developed; the young person acquires self-certainty as opposed to self-consciousness and self-doubt. He comes to experiment with different—usually constructive—roles rather than adopting a "negative identity" (such as delinquency). He actually anticipates achievement, and *achieves,* rather than being "paralyzed" by feelings of inferiority or by an inadequate time perspective. In later adolescence, clear sexual identity— "manhood" or "womanhood"—is established. The adolescent seeks leader-ship (someone to inspire him), and gradually develops a set of ideals (socially congruent and desirable, in the case of the successful adolescent). Erikson believes that, in our culture, adolescence affords a "psychosocial moratorium," particularly for middle- and upper-class American children. They do not yet have to "play for keeps," but can experiment, trying various roles, and thus hopefully find the one most suitable for them.

6. *Learning intimacy versus isolation.* The successful young adult, for the first time, can experience true intimacy—the sort of intimacy that makes possible a good marriage or a genuine and enduring friendship.

7. *Learning generativity versus self-absorption.* In adulthood, the psychosocial crisis demands generativity, both in the sense of marriage and parenthood, and in the sense of working productively and creatively.

8. *Integrity versus despair.* If the other seven psychosocial crises have been successfully resolved, the mature adult develops the peak of adjust-ment: integrity. He trusts, he is independent and dares to essay the new. He works hard, has found a well-defined role in life, and has developed a self-concept with which he is happy. He can be intimate without strain, guilt, regret, or lack of realism; and he is proud of what he creates—his chil-dren, his work, or his hobbies. If one or more of the earlier psychosocial crises have not been resolved, he may view himself and his life with disgust and despair.

These "eight stages of man"—the psychosocial crises—are plausible and insightful descriptions of how personality develops. But at present they are descriptions only. We possess at best rudimentary and tentative knowledge of just what sort of environment will result, for example, in traits of trust versus distrust, or clear personal identity versus diffusion. Helping the child through the various stages and the positive learnings that should accompany them is a complex and difficult task, as any worried parent or teacher knows. Search for the best way of accomplishing this task accounts for much of the research in the field of child development, particularly research such as that summarized and discussed in Chapters 3 and 6.

Socialization, then, is a learning-teaching process that, when successful, results in the human organism's moving from its infant state of helpless but total egocentricity to its ideal adult state of sensible conformity coupled with independent creativity.

Types and Urgency of the Socialization Problem

Adequate socialization is perhaps the human being's most important single accomplishment. An occasional total social misfit achieves, albeit unhappily, the status of genius; but the vast majority of socially maladjusted people lead lives that are miserable for them and produce misery for their fellow men. Wars reflect the ultimate failure of socialization of groups; psychosis, delinquency, narcotic or alcohol addiction, psychopathy and crime, homosexuality, possibly certain types of mental deficiency, and neurosis are extreme examples of failure in socialization by individuals. Tragically, in a nation with perhaps the most advanced natural science and technology in the world, we have at present only the most rudimentary science of socialization. In United States society the frequency of such failures of individual socialization as those listed above is as high as, or higher than, that of other Western European, Eastern, or "primitive" cultures. We lead, for example, in our rates of delinquency, crime, and divorce; and are well toward the front in our incidence of drug and alcohol addiction, psychosis and neurosis, and sexual aberration (perhaps only because we have the best statistical and census facilities).

The terrible social urgency of these various problems, plus the likelihood that failures of socialization originate in early childhood, is the reason this book gives such diligent attention to the admittedly very incomplete data about socialization. Some have said that all psychology is social psychology, and perhaps this should be the case.

The discussion of socialization follows logically from the content of the last several chapters. A basic assumption accepted here is that socialization occurs as a result of the learning process, as this has been described in Chapters 4 and 5. Neither the innate evil nor the innate good of man is assumed; only his almost infinite malleability through learning. Much social learning is clearly conscious: children learn not to walk on the tulip bed because their parents have said frequently, consistently, and emphatically that this is not to be done, and because they themselves can see the damage to the flowers which they, as well as their parents, enjoy. More subtle and complex learnings occur through a combination of tutelage, maturity, and personal intellectual effort.

A five-year-old friend of the author's announced one day that she had begun to enjoy her kindergarten rest time, except when Ellen, a "fighting friend" of hers, got to sit on the teacher's lap. "This," she stated with annoyance, "is just not fair!" Her mother asked, "What *would* be fair?" With little hesitation she said, "It would be fair if I got to sit on her lap first." After a minute of thought, she added, "But David (her good friend) ought to have a turn, too. Then me again." A long pause followed, then the beginning of insight: "But maybe all the other kids feel like I do—maybe they all want to sit on Miss Rickard's lap. Maybe they don't think it's fair when *I* get to."

Still more subtly, perhaps unconsciously, other social learnings occur. Learning to dislike the odor and sight of urine or feces is probably not conscious learning, but is picked up from subtle parental cues. Indeed, as has been pointed out, it is likely that many of the learnings that belong to the family of the classical conditioned response are unconscious, yet we know that they are strikingly effective.

There is little reasonable question that large individual differences exist in the ease with which children are socialized, although there is not much acceptable *scientific* evidence about individual differences in socializability. Today the "bad seed" idea of genetic transmission of psychopathic and criminal personality is not accepted; nor is it by any means clear that there is an important relation between genetics and most mental illness or even the majority of cases of mental deficiency. But there are strong suggestions of subtle interactions between constitution and environment that make it harder for some children than for others to grow into reasonable, controlled adults. Research by Sontag (1941), for example, suggests that children born following certain types of difficult pregnancy are more active, impulsive, and irritable than children whose mothers have had uneventful pregnancies. Observations and individual case histories accumulated during some of the longitudinal studies of development (e.g., Ames, 1957; Mary Cover Jones, 1957; Mussen and Jones, 1957) suggest that interactions between the social and physical environment and physique, time of reaching physical maturity, and activity level may produce very different effects on personality.

The life of a placid girl baby born as an only child to tired, middle-aged parents will, for example, be very different from that of a hyperactive, impulsive little boy born to the same parents. But if the phlegmatic little girl were born to a youthful couple whose way of life included strenuous activity from early morning until late at night, the consequences for her personality would almost certainly be very different. Late physical maturity can be much more traumatic for a boy with an early-maturing brother only a year younger than he than for a boy with *no* younger brothers or brothers *much* younger than he or brothers who are also late-maturers. And so it goes.

All the considerations and circumstances described in the previous chapters apply to socialization. Socialization depends, first of all, on sensori-motor stimulation. Intelligence certainly plays a major role. The child of low intelligence is by definition less sensitive to the complex environmental cues that can guide his socialization. The extremely bright child may be so much more perceptive than his age-mates that his very acuity puts him out of touch with them, thus complicating his process of socialization.

The child whose parents differ markedly from their community may also have special socialization problems. The permissively reared child in a strict, conforming neighborhood may constantly run afoul of neighborhood parents other than his own, and be rejected by his community playmates because of his freedom of action. Members of minority groups, whether ethnic or religious, experience peculiar complexities in socialization, as do children whose parents belong to a socioeconomic level diverging sharply from that of the rest of their neighborhood.

THE SOCIALIZATION PROCESS

Pressures toward Socialization

Every society has developed sanctions concerning the behavior of its members. The most nearly universal one is directed toward control of sexual behavior: all known contemporary societies include rigid incest taboos. Every organized society must have prohibitions concerning aggression. Such prohibitions range from forbidding physical combat among preschoolers to prohibiting murder. Rules, formal and informal, exist in all societies for the protection of property. Certain minimal standards of parental conduct toward children are ordinarily prescribed. Some nations have state religions; others, such as the United States, have informal sanctions that encourage but do not require the individual to profess and practice religious belief.

In other words, through implicit and explicit codes, most of which have a moral, or right-wrong overtone, societies set up standards of behavior for their members. Great latitude may be granted the individual in some societies, relatively little in others; and a specific society may vary widely in permissiveness from one time to another. Freedom of political thought and action in a democracy is, for example, usually curtailed during a time of war and the period of readjustment following war. The penalties for deviation from acceptable conduct vary widely: the death sentence for murder is common in Western European civilizations; but the middle-class mother who breast-feeds her baby beyond 18 months is only gossiped about. Random heterosexual activity by young males, although against formal canons of law and Judeo-Chrisian religious teaching, is winked at and even envied; the same sexual activity on the part of a girl may result in her being firmly, albeit informally, ostracized.

In short, the political-religious organization of any organized society blends with, influences, and is influenced by the informal sanctions of that society in defining correct conduct for its members and in setting up the methods by which parents and the community guide and direct children's conformity to social norms. For example, our society has quite clear expectations about dependency, sex, and aggressive behavior on the part of children and adults of different ages and sexes. It also says that parents should not use brutal punishment on their children, nor neglect them in obvious ways. It is assumed that parents should love and protect their children, and set good examples for them. Yet our culture is in many ways contradictory: the obedient, conforming, sexless *ideal* nine-year-old boy is expected to become the independent, enterprising, adequately masculine *ideal* twenty-one-year-old who welcomes his chance to serve in the armed forces. Many things that are taught children must be unlearned by them before they become successful adults.

Socialization Theories

The development of any individual depends upon how he sees and reacts to the socializing forces of the culture of which he is a member. How does the whole process look to the child? Society prescribes the sort of a man or woman he is to grow into, and lays down certain rules to guide his parents and teachers. But what are the forces and perceptions *within him,* as an individual, that cause him to respond in one way or another to these forces *on the outside?*

There are two broad theoretical orientations to the socialization process. The first is represented by both psychoanalytic and social-learning theory. Each of these subscribes to the idea that the adult end-product is a direct function of the teaching forces of the family and the environment as the child perceives them and as they affect him. If these forces are benign, the resulting human product is a happy one; if malign, the net result is unfortunate. The organism is thought of as shaped by its experiences. It becomes good or bad as these experiences are good or bad. Psychoanalytic or Freudian theory places more emphasis than social-learning theory on certain critical developmental stages, during which certain prescribed types of experience have a maximum of effect, and somewhat discounts the influence on emotional or personality development of learning experiences after the ages of 5 to 7. Social-learning theory tends more to regard the human being as modifiable at any age. However, the influence attributed by each theory to *learning* is enormous.

The second broad strand of socialization theory holds that the forces of growth and development within the organism are essentially creative. If the child is *accepted,* if his developmental needs are not blocked by society, he will grow into a happy, creative, socialized individual. Such a theory does not discount the effect of learning, particularly when it is imposed in a negative, restrictive, and frustrating fashion. It simply argues that, given moderately constructive circumstances, the organism is self-directing, and that its self-direction is intrinsically constructive. Active teaching is assigned a lesser role in such theory than in Freudian or social-learning theory. The essential condition in the child's environment is acceptance. If that condition is met, everything will work out well. This theory was perhaps first enunciated in modern times by Jean Jacques Rousseau in *Emile*. Such contemporary theorists as Rogers (1951), Maslow (1954), and Gesell (e.g., 1954) hold this viewpoint in common, although they differ in many of their derivations from it and their reasons for adopting it.

The difference between these two broad theories can perhaps be made clearer by an analogy from horticulture. The first theory would heartily endorse the principle, "As the twig is bent, so shall the tree grow." A good environment of proper soil, light, water, and fertilizer would be recommended. But active pruning, shaping, grafting, and cross-fertilizing would also be practiced. The second theory would also argue for an environment of proper soil, light, water, and perhaps fertilizer. But it would take the position that nature knows best how the tree is to grow. Pruning, shaping, grafting, and cross-fertilizing are to be left to the natural course of events plus the innate nature of the organism. There is a difference between the two theories (they are brutally simplified here) along the activity-passivity dimension, with *more* and *less* teaching activity, respectively, being regarded as "desirable" by the first and the second theory.

According to the first theory, the child will become social, altruistic, self-confident, or what have you, to the degree that he learns he must adapt himself to others in order to have his own needs gratified. The ease of this process, and the cost of it to the individual, will depend on the skill of the teacher and the appropriateness and effectiveness of the teaching process. According to the second theory, the germs of adequate adaptation or socialization are present in all people, and will come to soundest maturity in a benign and accepting but rather passive environment. It is probable that of the three theorists mentioned in connection with the second position, Gesell places more emphasis on inborn constitution and heredity than Rogers; that is, Gesell would not say that, given a suitable environment, everyone will turn out all right.

It is not known which of these two theories about socialization and development is correct—or whether, indeed, either of them is. Each places a heavy burden on those responsible for the environmental aspect of socialization—the first, or "learning," theory perhaps more than the second, or "developmental," theory. Both, with the possible exception of Freud as a representative of the first and of Gesell as a representative of the second, are optimistic. There are cross-overs between representatives of the two theories: Freudian theory seems almost to assume the "innate asociality of man," in the sense that the selfish, hedonistic, libidinous infant must be transformed into the altruistic and pleasure-postponing adult. Social-learning theory makes no assumptions about this issue, but postulates that altruism and pleasure-postponement are learned rather than innate. Freud, like Gesell, places heavy emphasis on universal, developmental-maturational sequences in growth, but does not put Gesell's emphasis on heredity as a determinant of individual differences.

Learning that Other People Are Necessary

Freud has spoken of the socialization process as a change from the *pleasure principle* of immediate need-gratification (characteristic of the very young child and infant) to the *reality principle,* which presumably governs the much older child and adult. This change seems to begin when the child realizes that his own gratification depends on the cooperation of other, older, stronger, and more proficient people, usually his parents. If he offends them by his own impulsiveness and "selfishness," then they in turn can keep gratification from him. At first it is likely that he conforms to their desires only to ensure that his own are met. Only later—often not until well into adolescence—does he begin genuinely to consider the needs of others because of an altruistic, "highly socialized" pleasure that he takes in seeing them happy.

The foundation of socialization is simply this: A socialized individual attaches importance and pays attention to people and the rules that have been developed to mold them into and keep them functioning as a society. If he is successfully socialized, he also rather *likes* people and has a generally positive attitude toward the majority of the rules of his society. Both introverts and extroverts can be thought of as being successfully socialized, since there is more than one method of successful socialization. The scientist or artist working alone in his laboratory or studio, and the insurance salesman, politician, or reporter who deals with dozens of people every day, are both socialized, although in different ways, to the degree that they direct or inhibit personal behavior in deference to people and social rules.

How is this regard for people and social rules developed? In discussing this question, the author has drawn most heavily on the work of Dollard and Miller (1950), Whiting and Child (1953), and Sears and his co-workers (Sears, Maccoby, and Levin, 1957). They in turn have been influenced by such theorists as Freud (e.g., 1938) and Hull (e.g., 1952), and have themselves been prolific in their research.

If a child is to learn to attach importance to people and rules, he must first attach *meaning* to them: to find out that they are useful, powerful, and associated with both rewards and punishments. The infant is helpless in satisfying his own needs. Without adults, he would die. Adults feed and warm and soothe and cleanse him. Soon, as a result of these ministrations, adults themselves come to have positive meaning for the baby; in the terminology of social-learning theory, they are perceived as "secondary rewards" or "reinforcements." The infant seeks them out not only to satisfy his *primary* needs, but also for themselves, to satisfy his newly developing *social* needs. As we have said, the smile that appears from 6 to 8 weeks of age is one of the first signs of socialization.

Evidence such as that presented in Chapters 3 and 7 indicates that babies who have had little opportunity to interact with adults are seriously retarded and perhaps permanently blunted in socialization. We might also speculate on the consequences for socialization of *complete and consistent reward* in infancy. It is reasonable to suppose that those who have never been cold fail to appreciate warmth, and that those who have never been insecure or afraid attach relatively little importance to security and freedom from fear. The child, in other words, to become socialized, must first have experienced many warm and loving relations with adults; but he must also have learned the importance and value of these relations by having experienced at least their temporary loss.

In real life, this question is largely academic. There is no way to rear a baby so that he does not experience temporary and rather frequent loss of attention and love. Not the most diligent of mothers can always feed her baby the instant he becomes hungry. In even the most child-centered family, there are times during the child's early life when his parents are not there at the moment he needs them. The child probably sees such experiences as "abandonment" or "deprivation of love." They presumably result in enhancing his appreciation of love and attention, and increase the reward value that adults have for him.

In addition to the deprivations that must of practical necessity occur for all children, parents impose deliberate deprivations or other penalties on their children in order to produce the behavior the parent considers desirable, or to eliminate undesirable behavior. These deprivations range from "love-oriented" manipulations ("Mommy thinks it would be nice if you went to the potty," or "It makes mommy feel bad when you are a naughty boy") to object- or thing-oriented techniques. These in turn range widely, from depriving or threatening to deprive the child of some of his television time, or outdoor play, or allowance, through depriving him of physical comfort by spanking or slapping him. Corporal discipline and "punitiveness" are commonly placed under this heading of "thing-oriented" discipline.

Love-oriented techniques, although they may be vicious in their extreme form (the mother who, when only slightly thwarted, retreats to her room in tears to place a damp cloth over her eyes), seem to result in more dependable social control through the exercise of the child's own conscience than thing-oriented techniques (see, for example, Sears, Maccoby, and Levin, 1957; and Miller and Swanson, 1960). But research in this important area is very incomplete.

To become socialized, in short, a child must have learned that his parents and (through generalization) other people are important, and that he is dependent on them. Dependency, as a *theoretical construct,* should be distinguished from dependent *behavior*. In the first sense, it refers to the *reward characteristics of the parents and others*, which have presumably been developed through a combination of good mothering and fathering, coupled with anxiety about the loss of this parental nurturance. In the second and more common sense, it refers to the clinging, lap-sitting, affection- and assistance-seeking behavior usually referred to as dependent.

Those parents who have helped their child to acquire dependency (in the theoretical sense of the word) have provided a powerful tool for his later, more complicated socialization. If his parents, that is, are important and generally rewarding to him, then, through the process of generalization, other adults, children, and their rules also become important.

Basic Drives and Personality

As Freud and his followers, particularly Sullivan and Erikson, have recognized, the basic drives around which a child's dependency (and probably important aspects of his later personality) is organized are those that involve much interaction with adults. These are the drives he cannot satisfy himself, or whose expression he must alter to conform to adult standards.

The child can *breathe* on his own; no one tells him *how* to breathe; no one teaches him *to* breathe. Thus it is not likely that air hunger and breathing are extensively involved in personality development. On the other hand, the baby interacts constantly with adults in such matters as eating and cleanliness, and, as he grows older, he must *change* his ways of eating and eliminating to conform to adult expectations. In our culture, he must also learn to inhibit or hide sex behavior or interest. These changes, suppressions, and concealments are all based on interaction, some of it usually unpleasant, with adults, and the expression of dependency and aggressive needs must themselves be altered with increasing age.

It is plausible, then, that the drives most significantly related to early personality development and socialization are the hunger and eliminative drives. Because these drives require the mediation of adults for their satisfaction, the child learns dependency; through deliberate or spontaneous manipulation of his dependency need he is taught elimination, sex, and aggression control, and his expression of the dependency need itself is changed.

Alterations in Dependency

Although early learning of dependency, in the theoretical sense, logically appears to be the foundation of socialization, dependent *behavior* must be sharply modified during the developmental process. The sort of dependency typically shown by the child between 1 and 2 years of age is inappropriate in the later preschool years. It is typical for the child of 2 to cling to his mother, to be shy with strangers, and openly to seek affection; but the child of 4 is expected to have modified this "babyish" behavior.

It has been found that, by the preschool years, children who are most dependent on adults are least popular with their age-mates (Marshall and

McCandless, 1957; McCandless, Bilous, and Balsbaugh, 1960; and Marshall, 1960[3]). Interestingly enough, being dependent interferes more with girls' than with boys' popularity (McCandless and Marshall, 1957), probably because of differences in the type of dependency shown by boys and girls (Heathers, 1955; McCandless, Balsbaugh, and Bennett, 1958). The latter seem more frequently to employ what might be called *emotional* dependency; they cling to adults, apparently seeking reassurance and affection, or openly ask for affection. Boys do not differ greatly from girls in amount of over-all dependency, but the type they show is different. They are more likely to be *instrumentally* dependent: that is, to seek help in accomplishing the aims of their work and play. "Help me put the wheel on the truck . . . Where is the big plane we had yesterday? . . . Will you move this ladder for me?" These are dependency requests of the type made more frequently by boys than by girls, and they seem not to interfere with popularity.

Boys also appear to be more task-oriented than girls (McCandless, Balsbaugh, and Bennett, 1958). They will more often go to almost any length of compromise or combat to continue their activity, whereas preschool-age girls, when blocked or engaged in conflict over an activity, more often drop it; or, rather than handling the conflict themselves, ask the adult in the situation to settle it for them.

There is some indication that these different modes of dependency and different ways of making use of adults in conflict situations result from learning: mothers of daughters more frequently than mothers of sons intervene in their conflicts and help them work out solutions.

For reasons probably similar to those implied above (society condones and perhaps even approves dependency in girls, but condemns it in boys), dependent behavior has been found to be more consistent from childhood to adulthood for girls than for boys. Kagan and Moss (1960) have found rather substantial relations between dependent behavior in girls, as rated from their case histories at the age of about 7 and as rated independently by a second investigator from interviews when they were in their early twenties. There was no indication in the behavior of young adult men whether they had been highly independent or dependent in their seventh year. The authors attribute this difference to the effect of the culture. It is all right for girls to be dependent; hence they do not "disguise" their dependency as they move through later childhood and adolescence. The dependent boy, on the other hand, is "punished"; hence, whether he "feels" dependent or not, he assumes the cloak of independence.

Jakubczak and Walters (1959) have found that dependent nine-year-old boys are more suggestible than nondependent youngsters of the same age, and that they are swayed more by the opinions of adults than by the opinions of their peers. This finding suggests that the dependent youngsters were oriented more to adults than to their peers, and provides a possible

[3] Personal communication.

clue about why dependent youngsters are less popular than nondependent ones.

Generally, in the preschool years, dependency and "seeking to do well at tasks," or achievement orientation, have been found to be negatively correlated. One study (Crandall, Preston, and Rabson, 1960) has found that the mothers of achievement-oriented four- and five-year-olds—presumably, nondependent children—reward their children when they seek *approval* and when they try to accomplish difficult tasks. The mothers' general affection, and their pattern of reward when children sought emotional support or help, were unrelated to the children's achievement efforts, although it appears from the data in this study that those mothers who not only were affectionate but also rewarded their children's requests for help, emotional support, and approval may have been the mothers of children with the highest achievement orientation.

To some degree, a negative relation between dependent behavior and achievement orientation may be "built in." Achievement is usually defined as *independent* task-orientation, perseverance, and so on; hence, measures of dependency should be negatively correlated with it. But task-orientation which the child uses as a means of obtaining social reinforcers (approval, praise, affection) may well be positively related to dependency (e.g., Endsley, 1960[4]).

We have said that the behavorial manifestations of dependency must change with the age of the child—it is generally inappropriate for eight-year-olds to sit in the laps of their mothers in public. How does this change in behavior come about while the parent at the same time satisfies the child's "inner" need for dependency? There are five possible ways in which the change from immature dependent behavior to more mature independent behavior can occur. (1) The reward value of the parent is in some fashion reduced as the child grows older; or (2) the threat of the loss of love, which presumably intensifies theoretical (and behavioral) dependency, is reduced; or (3) the parents gradually transfer their rewards from dependent to independent behavior, yet continue to satisfy the drive for dependency; or (4) the reward value of peers increases; or (5) the child's increasing size, strength, and skill afford him increasingly frequent and wide-ranging opportunities to master his environment, thus reinforcing his independent and autonomous behaviors. Successful autonomous or independent behavior is probably strongly reinforcing, and is probably generalized widely, since it indicates to the child that he can now gain a given goal quite directly and *by himself*—in other words, he need no longer depend on a mediating agent whose behavior he cannot always predict. If independence succeeds in one area, the child will probably try to extend it to other areas.

It is most likely that (2), (3), (4), and (5) are the conditions that operate. With increasing ability to symbolize, to incorporate past experience by thinking about it, and to envision future experience, the child of con-

4 Manuscript in preparation.

sistent and loving parents comes to see that his parents have loved him in the past, love him *now*, and will presumably continue to love him in the *future*. Thus the fear of loss of love is reduced: the eight-year-old realizes, as the three-year-old does not, that a baby-sitter for an evening does not signify parental desertion. Parents (as indicated by the Crandall, Preston, and Rabson study) may combine affection with reward for achievement, yet continue to accept and even reward immature requests for help and emotional support,[5] thus helping their children make the transition from the more immature dependent to the more mature achievement-oriented or independent behavior with a minimum of sudden change and insecurity. It seems certain (from the research summarized above, and from observation) that peers become increasingly important to children, and that peers reinforce independent behavior, particularly that which does not obviously seek to elicit adult affection and support. Finally, with increasing age, strength, vocabulary, and so on, the child becomes more and more able to master his environment.

This section, then, indicates that a necessary condition for socialization —in the sense of both social response and social control—is learning that other people are necessary, and that one should therefore modify his behavior in accordance with their needs and wishes as well as his own. The fact that people are "important" can be thought of as theoretical dependency, and it is the lever society uses to mold the self-centered child into the considerate adult. Good mothering and fathering, plus anxiety about losing such a state of affairs, appear to be responsible for the development of dependency, so defined.

In the young child dependency is expressed in dependent *behavior;* but in our society the seeking of help, affection, and nurturance from adults must be transformed into independent, achievement-oriented behavior. This change is apparently accomplished by an increase in the importance of approval from peers; by a shift in parental approval from dependent to independent behavior, while at the same time the child is assured that he continues to be loved; and by the child's own ability to remember the past, understand the present, and predict the future. The obvious fact that increasing size, strength, and adaptability help the normal child to master more and more aspects of his environment also aids in acquiring independent behavior.

SEX-TYPING

Sex-typing can probably be most plausibly distinguished from *identification* by saying that it is *imitative,* or *modeling,* behavior. The little boy,

[5] This conclusion from the Crandall, Preston, and Rabson study was reached from an inspection of their pattern of correlation coefficients, but not from a formal analysis of their data; nor is it among the conclusions presented by the authors.

with or without thinking much about it, practices ways of behaving that he has learned are characteristic of men; the little girl does things that she has learned typify women. Sex-typing is synonymous with sex-role differentiation, a term which covers all of the processes by which men become different from women (and women from men). We say that *sex-role identification* has occurred when masculine or feminine behavior is no longer deliberate or imitative, but automatic and generalized to all areas of the self, from the style of walking and thinking to the style of sexual behavior. The term *internalization*—a difficult one to define—is used by many to describe what happens when identification has been accomplished. To take an analogy from walking, for the eighteen-month-old the process is deliberate, self-conscious, painstaking, and poorly coordinated (i.e., imitative); but for the twelve-year-old or the adult it is natural, smooth, and unself-conscious (i.e., identification has occurred).

Lynn (1959) considers three phases of the identification process: sex-role preference, sex-role adoption, and sex-role identification. A little boy, deep in his heart, may prefer to be a little girl; but social pressures cause him to adopt the behaviors of a little boy. Unless he changes his sex-role preference, of course, it is unlikely that he will ever make a genuinely natural and sincere masculine identification, although he may be able to live his life as a socially acceptable male. As will be seen later in this chapter, more little girls apparently prefer to be little boys than vice versa, although most of them seem to be able to live out their lives very satisfactorily as girls and women.

The fortunate child, of course, is the one who has so adequate a father (male model) and mother (female model) that he comes early to prefer the sex role dictated by his physiology, moves naturally into its rehearsal, and eventually identifies easily with it.

Another author (Colley, 1959) points out that there are three areas in which an individual may be said to assume masculinity or femininity. The first he calls the *biomode,* or physiological area. The boy with somewhat feminine characteristics will have a harder time here than the child who is ruggedly masculine in physique. The converse will be true for girls. The second is the *sociomode,* or the preferred way of behaving, which is, of course, similar to Lynn's (and D. G. Brown's, 1958) sex-role preference. The third is full identification, which Colley calls the *psychomode,* or internalized identity.

Time of Appearance and Nature of Sex-Typing

By the time the child reaches the runabout age (from perhaps 18 months on), adults begin to expect sex differences in behavior. Many subtle as well as obvious pressures are placed on children to produce such differences. Sex-typing precedes and is a part of identification, and results from a pattern of rewards and punishments administered by parents, teachers, older brothers and sisters, and playmates. It is probably based on imitation.

Other things being equal, it is likely that the adult figures who will be imitated are the ones whom the child sees as appropriate, rewarding, and capable models.

By the early preschool years, many signs of sex-typing have appeared, even for children who spend a part of their time in permissive preschool settings where there is no obvious pressure on little boys to "act like little boys" or on little girls to "be ladylike." The preference of boys for wheeled toys, gun play, rough block-building, running and tussling, rope play, and the like is striking in groups of children long before they reach the age of 3. Girls in the same age groups play more quietly, utilize dolls rather than guns in their play, and prefer dramatization and playing house over rugged construction and cowboy play. But during the preschool period there is much crossing-over in type of activity. Girls frequently desert the sandbox or doll corner for the jungle-gym. Boys with equal frequency take part in quiet dramatic play with girls.

Parents' Role in Sex-Typing

Compared with that of girls, the fantasy play of little boys contains significantly more aggressive themes, particularly of the physical type. To what extent this is the result of imitation of their fathers and their perception of the father's masculine role is not clear, although imitation probably plays a part. There may also be a factor of frustration: fathers ordinarily assume the ultimate disciplinary role in the family, and probably discipline their sons more severely than they do their daughters. Fathers also very possibly monopolize some of the mother's time that the boy would like to have. If little boys, at these ages, are especially close to their mothers, this would prove frustrating to them—more so than to girls. Then if, as seems likely, frustration instigates aggressison, boys growing up with their fathers around will be more aggressive (directly or in fantasy) than boys whose fathers are away; and girls less than boys will be affected by the father's presence or absence.

It has been demonstrated (e.g., by Pauline Sears, 1951) that little boys whose fathers are not living at home show less aggressive fantasy play than those whose fathers are living with them—that is, they are more like girls. This result may be due either to lack of opportunity to imitate the father or to less frustration at his hands.

Another study by Pauline Sears (1953) suggests that warm, permissive, easygoing—in other words, *rewarding* fathers—have sons who are most likely to sex-type appropriately. Using 202 boy and 177 girl kindergartners as subjects, Sears obtained reactions to a standard set of family dolls and a doll house. Family conditions were judged from interviews carried out with the mothers. Hence, all information about what the father did was channeled through the mother and does not represent actual observation of interactions between him and his son.

It was found that boys who chose the father role (were appropriately sex-typed) were more often reported to have fathers who were warm, permissive, and fairly easygoing with their sons. Boys who took the mother role in play came from homes in which the mother, but not the father, was high in warmth. Mothers of such boys were quite permissive with respect to the child's sex behavior, restricted him in his mobility outside the home (thus constituting themselves the major source of authority and influence?), and were critical in their evaluation of their husbands (mediated unfavorable impressions of the father to the children?).

Another study (Levin and Sears, 1956), although not directly relevant to sex-typing, suggests that when children have incorporated their parents' standards, they are likely to model their behavior on that of their appropriate-sexed parent. Aggression in a doll-play situation was studied with almost 250 five-year-old boys and girls as subjects. These youngsters were said to be "highly identified" with their parents if they gave indications of having achieved a measure of internalized control over their behavior. Signs of guilt, for example, were considered as evidence of identification. For the subgroup of highly identified boys who were usually punished by their fathers, doll-play aggression was most frequent and intense. Identification in girls was associated with a high degree of aggression only when the girls' mothers were severe punishers and usually did the punishing.

Parents begin selective reinforcement of sex-appropriate behavior very early. The father, in his playtime, is likely to be rougher and to play more boys' games with his son than with his daughter; the mother will do more playing and take part in more mutual activity with her daughter than with her son, and their play will be gentler. Toys bought for boys and girls differ almost from babyhood. Boys are given toy tractors, footballs, and bats; girls receive dolls, dishes, and doll furniture. Differential pressure is put on the two sexes for conformity, lack of aggression, quietness, neatness, and good manners, girls being subjected to more pressure than boys. Boys also appear to be more active and to have more energy than girls. Work by Garn and Clark (1953) indicates that boys actually may have higher basal metabolic rates than girls. This does not mean that boys have more energy available, but suggests that, as far as their bodies are concerned, they "live faster"— that is, even in conditions of rest, they burn up more energy. All these factors result in the early appearance of sex differences in behavior.

SEX-TYPING AND SOCIAL CLASS

Sex-typing may also be related to social class. In one study (Rabban, 1950), children were divided by sex into middle- and lower-class groups. Lower-class boys were the first clearly to identify themselves with masculine interests, whereas middle-class girls were the last to take on a pattern of feminine interests. Lower-class girls and middle-class boys were intermediate between these two extremes. The average lower-class little boy manifested sex-typed behavior quite clearly, according to reasonable criteria (choice of masculine rather than feminine toys), by the time he was about

4 to 5; not until some three or four years later did the average middle-class girl manifest similarly appropriate sex-typed behavior.

Speculations about the reasons for this discrepancy are various. It seems likely that masculine and feminine roles are more clear-cut among the lower- or working-class population than they are in the middle class, and that the masculine role is more attractive than the feminine. Working-class men do heavy work on their jobs and assume little care for their children or the house. Working-class women, when employed, usually take such traditionally feminine jobs as housekeeping, cooking, or laundering. But among the middle-class group, both father and mother may be teachers, or lawyers, or work in the family business. Wives frequently handle the family finances. Mother drives the automobile with equal or greater frequency, particularly when father commutes. Father helps with the dishes and may do the shopping as he comes home from the office. Hence, models for the child's behavior are less distinctive. It is also likely that lower-class parents have less tolerance for individual differences on the part of their children than do middle-class parents: not only are working-class boys encouraged to act like boys, for example, but they are punished or ridiculed for *not* acting like boys. Middle-class women may also be more restless, more in competition with their husbands, and less satisfied with their roles as housewives and mothers than lower-class women, although this is speculation. However, if such speculation should prove true, then middle-class mothers may be assumed to present a somewhat unenthusiastic and blurred feminine model for their daughters.

Indirect support for this hypothesis is provided by an ambitious study (D. G. Brown, 1957) done with 303 boys and 310 girls, aged 5½ to 11½ years, who were enrolled in public schools from the kindergarten through the fifth grade. The children were all from middle-class homes.

The technique Brown used in his study is called the "It" test. "It" is a modified stick figure, vaguely resembling some illustrators' conceptions of "The Gingerbread Boy," but executed as a line drawing without features. The assumption behind the test is that the child will consider or "identify" himself as "It," and that the sex role and activities he chooses for "It" are actually those that he would choose for himself. In other words, the test is a projective technique, although an unusually straightforward one.

The actual testing procedure consists of having "It" indicate a preference for being a boy or a girl; choose between a number of pairs of toys, one of which is clearly masculine, the other clearly feminine; indicate a preference for one of several differently drawn figures, which range from boyish boys through girlish girls, and so one. Masculine choices are given higher scores, feminine choices lower ones, so that the higher the score, the more masculine the sex-role preference is presumed to be. Following Brown (1958) and Lynn (1959), we might say that this is a test of sex-role preference rather than of sex-role adoption or identification.

At every grade level up to the fifth, a majority of girls indicated a preference for boys' toys, and a majority of them said that they would rather be the father in the family than the mother. Boys made appropriate sex-typed choices much earlier. Even among kindergartners, 75 percent of the boys preferred boys' toys, and 77 percent preferred the father role to that of the mother. Among boys the percentages for both these choices reached the 90's by the second grade and remained consistent from then on. But even at the fifth-grade level, 37 percent of the girls preferred masculine toys and 21 percent of them stated that they would rather be a father than a mother.

Hartup and Zook (1960) have done an interesting study using three- and four-year-old nursery-school children, and find, as did Brown, that boys of these ages have more appropriate sex preferences than girls. Unlike Rabban, they did not find lower-class children to be more firmly sex-typed than middle-class youngsters. This finding may have reflected the youth of the subjects or perhaps the effect of nursery-school attendance. Since nursery schools are ordinarily quite permissive, lower-class children may have been under less pressure for sex-typing; or middle-class children, under such circumstances, may have more opportunities to learn appropriate sex-typing than they would have had in the absence of a group experience; or both of these factors may have been operative. Since 61 percent of the fathers of the lower-class children were absent from the home, the number of subjects from "normal" lower-class homes was small, hence subject to sampling error (see Chapter 2). Finally, the lower-class subjects in this study came mostly from the upper lower class, which has much in common with the middle class. In other words, the conditions in the Hartup and Zook study were so different from those in the Rabban study that they cannot be directly compared.

SEX-TYPING AND CULTURAL STEREOTYPES

Another of Hartup and Zook's findings raises some questions about the "It" technique, *if* "It" is presented to girls with its sex unspecified. Girls more often than not may see "It" as a boy: hence their rather high masculinity scores may be earned simply because they assign to "It" the masculine interests and preferences that they consider appropriate for boys. The fact that there was a highly significant shift in the direction of femininity for girls when the experimenter identified "It" as a girl supports this contention. Regardless of this, however, four-year-old girls scored as more feminine than three-year-old girls, and four-year-old boys as more masculine than three-year-old boys.

One interesting finding from the Hartup and Zook study was that the four-year-old girls were more feminine than Brown's ten-year-old girls. A possible explanation advanced for this is that for four-year-olds, the feminine model is almost entirely limited to mothers (and possibly pre-school teachers), who are doing very feminine things such as cooking, washing, baking, tending children, and so on. But in school years, through television, reading, and observation, girls see women doing a much wider variety of things, including some high-prestige activities that may be thought of as masculine. In other words, with increasing age (up to fourth or fifth grade) the masculine role becomes more attractive, and girls change from their moderate preference for the female role at the preschool years to their relative rejection of it in elementary school.

THE EFFECT OF SIBLINGS

So far we have considered the influence on sex-typing of parents, social class, and cultural stereotype. It has also been demonstrated that the presence of older brothers or sisters affects sex-typing. In one study (Fouls and Smith, 1956), 38 children between the ages of 4 years, 9 months and 5 years, 9 months, were selected as subjects. There were 10 only sons and 10 only daughters in the group; 10 of the boys had an older brother less than 10 years of age; 8 girls had an older sister less than 10. None of the children had an older sib of the opposite sex. The children were asked to make their choices of paired pictures, one of each pair depicting feminine, the other masculine play.

As might be expected, the boys significantly more often than the girls chose masculine play, and children with an older sib of the same sex seemed to have their sex-typing speeded up, in that they, more often than the only children, chose activities appropriate to their sex. One may speculate that the presence of two models—father and older brother for boys, mother and older sister for girls—facilitated sex-typing.

Approach-Avoidance Tendencies and Sex-Typing

It is possible to relate the concept of sex-typing to the ideas of approach-avoidance gradients that have been discussed earlier. We might speculate, on the basis of evidence concerning child-rearing practices in different socio-economic classes (e.g., Maas, 1951), that lower-class fathers provide less attractive and loving models for their sons than middle-class fathers, but that the latter offer less clear masculine models. Open aggression, a masculine trait, is, for example, frowned upon in middle-class society, but condoned by the lower class. Under such circumstances, the approach tendency toward masculine behavior will be stronger for middle-class than for lower-class boys, but it will be less clear to them precisely what it is they are to approach. On the other hand, girlish or sissy behavior on the part of the lower-class boy will be clearly and firmly disapproved of by both parents and peers; whereas in middle-class boys such behavior is more likely to be tolerated. The avoidance tendency for feminine behavior will therefore be very strong for lower-class boys, and substantially weaker for middle-class boys. It is probable that the masculine model provided by peers is not only clearer but also more compelling for the lower-class boy, since he is more likely to be dependent on his peers than his middle-class counterpart.

For lower-class boys, then, early, appropriate, and rigid sex-typing should occur, based as much on "avoidance of femininity" as on "approach to masculinity," or "attractiveness of the role." Middle-class boys would be expected to sex-type later, but more flexibly and with more genuine satisfaction.

The process of sex-typing for girls is less clear than it is for boys. Some of the reasons for this have already been touched on. Lynn (1959), for example, reasons that, although girls start out by identifying with their mothers (as do boys), the process of adequate sex-typing and identification is "corroded" for them by a number of social pressures. Males are accorded more prestige and privileges than females in our culture; boys are punished for adopting aspects of the feminine role, but the adoption of part-masculine roles is not strongly discouraged for girls. Lynn makes four predictions about differential identification: With increasing age, boys will become more firmly identified with the masculine, girls less firmly identified with the feminine role; more girls than boys will adopt aspects of the role of the opposite sex; and, whereas boys will tend to identify with a cultural stereotype of masculinity, girls will identify with aspects of their own mother's role rather than with a general cultural stereotype. It should be noted that Hartup and Zook's data, gathered independently of Lynn's predictions, support them quite directly, particularly when considered in conjunction with Brown's study. So do the data of Payne and Mussen (1956), although less directly. These are summarized later in this chapter.

The lower-class girl, like the lower-class boy, has a clearer (but again, on the whole, probably less warm, attractive, and successful) model for feminine identification than the middle-class girl. Probably she, like her brother, is punished more often than the middle-class girl for showing aspects of the role behavior of the opposite sex, although this has not been clearly substantiated. On the whole, the feminine role is relatively less desirable in the lower than in the middle class, so that her over-all push toward appropriate role behavior is weaker than her brother's; but the model, even though less attractive, is clearer than that for the middle-class girl. The lower-class girl, like the lower-class boy, may be more strongly pushed toward appropriate role identification by her peers, as well as by her early assumption of such feminine tasks as housework, baby-sitting, and so on.

Sex-Typing in Other Cultures

There is evidence for near-universality of sex differences in behavior. One study (Barry, Bacon, and Child, 1957) uses as data cultural anthropologists' records for a total of 110 cultures. For the five different traits studied, enough information was recorded to make possible judgments about sex differences in from 31 cultures (for achievement) to 84 cultures (for responsibility).

In the majority of cultures, girls were trained to be *nurturant* (to look after others) and *responsible* to a greater degree than boys. For boys, *achievement* and *self-reliance* were more heavily stressed. A majority of the 69 cultures for which information was available did not put differential emphasis on *obedience;* but 35 percent of the cultures stressed obedience more for girls, whereas only 3 percent stressed obedience more for boys. These data also suggest considerable variability among cultures.

In the cultures studied, stress on sex differences was greatest where the pattern of life included hunting or herding of large animals, following a nomadic rather than a settled residence pattern, and growing grain rather than root crops as the staple of diet. Sex differences also tended to be more clear-cut in cultures sanctioning multiple rather than single wives. The reasons are obvious: In hunting or herding of large animals, men, with their superior strength and speed, play a role sharply different from that of women. The nomadic way of life, because of its general hardships, sharpens sex distinctions. Grain crops require more land and muscle than root crops. When there are several wives, there is little likelihood that the man will have to take over the homemaking role at any time; with just one wife, he may be compelled to take on feminine tasks when, for example, his wife is ill, is having a new baby, and so on.

Sex-typing may be defined as imitative or modeling behavior. It should be thought of as sex-role *adoption,* rather than an indicator of sex-role *preference* or sex-role *identification.*

In our culture, starting at the runabout age—probably as early as 18 months—adults and older children begin to respond differentially to little boys and little girls. They reward masculine behavior in the former, feminine behavior in the latter. By the age of 2 or 2½ years, clear differences in play preferences have appeared: boys prefer more rugged activities (play with wheel-toys, climbing, and so on); girls engage more in quiet activities (play with dolls, dramatic play). The play of boys contains more physically aggressive themes than that of girls.

Little boys whose fathers are living at home show more aggressive themes in their fantasy play than boys whose fathers are away from home, but fathers' absence seems to have little effect on girls' fantasy play. Boys manifesting appropriate sex-typing have been shown to have warm, permissive, and fairly easygoing fathers.

Lower-class children seem to achieve appropriate sex-typing earlier than middle-class children; and in both social classes boys sex-type earlier than girls. It is probable that the appropriate roles are clearer for lower-class children than for middle-class children: their fathers engage in rough work, and are more clearly the heads of their households; mothers do not engage in masculine activities, and are placed in an inferior role. Children in the lower class may also be punished for failure to sex-type appropriately. In our culture the feminine model, whether lower or middle class, is probably less attractive than the masculine model.

Children with older siblings of the same sex appear to sex-type earlier than children who do not have older brothers or sisters, and almost all cultures seem to put pressure on children for appropriate sex-typing. Training for girls emphasizes nurturance, obedience, and responsibility; for boys, achievement and self-reliance are stressed.

IDENTIFICATION

Definition

The problem of arriving at a definition of identification is a knotty one. Sanford (1955) agrees with others who have written on the subject before him that identification has probably been used in more ways—with more different meanings—than any other psychoanalytic term. From his own thinking and the writing of others, Sanford points out that the following meanings of the term have been employed: copying or modeling; adhering to a group of which an individual feels a part; acceptance of a cause; empathy and vicarious living; sympathy; love; closeness; and loyalty. In addition, workers with projective tests such as the Thematic Apperception Test say that the subject *identifies* with the central character or hero of the story he tells.

The definition used here stresses *sex-role identification,* and is essentially a learning definition. The boy who has made a male identification is the boy who has happily and thoroughly adopted maleness as his way of life; he thinks of himself as a male; he accepts and likes this state of affairs, its advantages and its disadvantages; and he assumes the responsibilities that being male demands. His fantasy behavior is male, just as his sexual behavior, pattern of interests, and style of walking, talking, and gesturing, are male. It is assumed that the boy has learned to be male for various social-personal reasons, and that ordinarily (and ideally) his best model for this role is his father. In other words, it is likely that a boy must be *identified with* (i.e., love, respect, and, in many ways, imitate) his father in order to arrive at a consistently and genuinely *male identification.*

With respect to the girl, identification can be defined exactly as it is in the paragraph above, substituting *girl* for *boy, mother* for *father,* and feminine for masculine pronouns.

According to Freudian theory, full identification with the parent of the same sex takes place when the Oedipus conflict has been resolved. Incestuous wishes toward the parent of the opposite sex are repressed, and the child incorporates or introjects the image of the parent of the same sex. The boy then becomes genuinely male, the girl genuinely female. Psychoanalytic theory takes little note of what we have called sex-typing. Here again, we wish to distinguish between sex-role preference, sex-role adoption (based on imitation or modeling, and used synonymously with sex-typing), and identification, as defined above. Theoretically, it seems that appropriate sex-role preference certainly, and appropriate sex-role adoption almost equally certainly, must precede and accompany appropriate *identification*. Learning theory does not assume any literal *incorporation* of the image of the like-sexed parent in identification, but only a general modeling or patterning. Sex-role identification is possible, for reasons that will be discussed later, even when there is little warmth toward the parent of the same sex, but it is logical to assume that acquisition of an appropriate identification will be easier and probably less ambivalent when accompanied by good parent-child relations, just as imitation and sex-typing will be.

The term *identification* is usually employed to include sex-role identification and *other* important aspects of personality, although the present author has chosen to emphasize sex-role identification as being the clearest of the various meanings. Even those who have not made an appropriate sex-role identification, however, have assumed many of the attitudes, values, and beliefs of their parents and other significant figures in their lives. It is commonly held that such human attributes as conscience and self-determined morality, guilt, the motive to achieve, and so on, arise only through identification, which may be with either or both parents. As will be pointed out on page 344ff., "cross-identification"—that is, assumption of some of the values and standards of the parent of the opposite sex—is advantageous in our culture.

Identification for Boys

FREUDIAN THEORY

In Freudian theory, the little boy first identifies with—incorporates in part—the mother. At around 5 or 6 years of age incestuous wishes toward the mother become very strong, but are counterbalanced by the child's fear of his father's strength and the possibility of punishment, particularly castration. Since this fear is great and the loss of his genitals unthinkable, and since the small boy cannot hope to vanquish his father and win his mother, he copes with his father's strength by "becoming one with him"—by introjecting him—thus avoiding threat as well as, presumably, enjoying the mother vicariously. This process is sometimes called "identification with the aggressor," and might be summed up by the popular phrase, "If you can't lick them, join them."

SOCIAL-LEARNING THEORY

The learning position on identification takes little account of the Oedipus conflict, although it would not deny that this conflict may be frequent in some cultures. It also grants that the young child, boy or girl, probably (although not necessarily) loves his mother more than he does his father. It may well be possible for boys to make an adequate male identification and at the same time continue loving their mother more than their father. Identification is probably easier and better consolidated if the boy has had a loving and a strong father than if he has not; and the mother who loves her husband *and* her son, and wishes her son to be like her husband, probably facilitates the identification process.

The boy in a normal family, during his early childhood, probably loves his mother best. But he also has affection for his father, and, under fortunate circumstances, this affection grows stronger with age. As a result of it, and of general cultural influences, the boy, early in his preschool years, begins to imitate his father (to sex-type), and eventually makes his masculine identification.

In other words, learning theory holds that a father with whom a boy identifies, in the sense of loving and respecting him, facilitates appropriate sex-role identification in his son, and that this factor, rather than fear, is a major one in successful identification. A study done by Payne and Mussen (1956) bears on this topic. Junior- and senior-high boys were asked to complete a set of stories in which they were likely to reveal whether they regarded their fathers, their mothers, and the total family structure as rewarding or unrewarding. These boys, their fathers, and their mothers were given a series of tests, among which was a personality inventory and a test of masculinity-femininity. Boys whose scores on the personality inventory were much more like their fathers' than their mothers' were assumed to have modeled closely after their fathers: in the authors' words, to have identified with them. It was found that the most highly father-identified boys (those most similar to their fathers) also appeared to have the best male identification, since their scores for masculinity were substantially higher than those of boys showing little similarity to their fathers. They also saw their fathers as rewarders, not punishers; and as relatively more rewarding than their mothers; for them, the total family pattern was a happier, more rewarding one.

A distinction is often made between infantile and ego identification (for example, Bronson, 1959). In *infantile* identification, the child wishes to *be* the security-giving object in his environment—the mother or the father—in order to avoid frustrating reality. Under the stress of anxiety, he imitates (introjects?) adult behaviors, believing that these, in a magical way, will make him identical with the model he is imitating. In *ego* identification, on the other hand, the realistic differences between model and child are perceived, the model is admired and loved, and hence the child wishes *to be like* the security-giving object *in the future*.

Bronson predicted that sons from families where there were stressful father-son relations would be more likely than sons who had nonstressful relations with their fathers to show signs of infantile identification, but not of ego identification. She obtained ratings of father-son relations for 42 boys between 9 and 13 years of age, and measured the sons' covert and overt masculinity. The former was inferred from the boys' TAT stories, the latter from their tendency to choose masculine as contrasted with feminine toys.

Bronson also predicted that boys who had stressful relations with their fathers either would show extreme masculinity (i.e., would attempt directly to copy their image of their fathers) or would reject the father-image and show feminine patterns of behavior, whereas boys with nonstressful relations would fall intermediate on the overt-masculinity test (i.e., could take from the father-image what was useful to them, but without need either to copy the father defensively or to reject him and what he stood for). Scores from the toy-preference test supported this prediction. Bronson also reasoned that boys with less rewarding fathers (with whom they had stressful relations) would not make a satisfactory covert male identification— that is, at the fantasy (or unconscious?) level, they would reject masculinity—whereas boys with rewarding fathers would make satisfactory covert masculine identifications. The TAT data supported her prediction.

That the boys from stressful families actually rejected more often than they imitated their fathers' patterns is indicated by the fact that there was a $-.74$ correlation between their masculinity scores on the toy-preference test and ratings of the fathers' masculinity. This correlation for the boys from nonstressful homes was $+.37$.

The Payne and Mussen and the Bronson studies both support the notion that boys highly identified with their fathers do not necessarily pattern directly after them to any strong degree. Payne and Mussen found no relation between the masculinity scores of fathers and sons for highly identified boys, and the .37 correlation found by Bronson is not high. It might be said that the son who is securely identified as a male does not need to imitate his father slavishly, but can look to his environment for behavior models that may serve his purposes better than his father's. In other words, a ruggedly masculine but highly adequate father can rear a son with somewhat effeminate behavior, but with appropriate sex-role identification; or a rather effeminate but good father can rear a son who is ruggedly masculine in behavior as well as appropriately sex-identified.

THE "POWER" THEORY

A third theory of identification exists (Parsons, 1955), which is a logical extension of Freudian and learning theories. It argues that identification occurs, not solely because the father is a threat and not only because he is a benign model, but because he is *both* an effective rewarder and an effective punisher. In other words, a son identifies with him and models after him because he is *powerful.*

Mussen and Distler (1959) conducted an interesting test of these three hypotheses about identification (the "loving" parent; fear of the parent; and "power" of the parent), using a group of kindergarten boys as subjects. According to psychoanalytic theory, boys at this age should be intensely involved in the Oedipus conflict, hence should make ideal subjects. Mussen and Distler used scores on the "It" test (described on page 333) as their criterion for identification, which, like the present author, they consider to mean adoption of the appropriate sex role. It has been pointed out that the "It" test may measure sex preference rather than identification, although it certainly seems a promising measure for the latter as well.

The authors secured experimental (highly masculine) and control (relatively feminine) groups of boys, 10 in each group. The groups were matched on socioeconomic status. A structured doll-play situation, involving a mother, father, and boy doll and simple furniture, was used, and the boy was asked to play out a number of stories, of which the following is illustrative:

This boy lives on a very busy street. His mother and father have told him never to cross the street alone. He is playing in the front yard, and his mother and father are not there. His good friend on the other side of the street is playing with his new bike, and the boy wants to cross the street very much. What happens?

Mussen and Distler extracted a number of scores from the stories the boys told: *nurturance* (tenderness and care) from the mother and the father; *punishment* from the mother and the father; *nurturance* from *both* parents (when the child specified that it was not the mother or father singly, but the parents together who gave help and tenderness); *punishment* from both parents; and a total *power* score for both mother and father. The power score was the sum of the nurturance plus the punishment scores for the mothers and for the fathers.

The clearest finding was that the highly masculine boys reported their fathers as significantly more nurturant than the less masculine youngsters did. There was also a tendency, although it did not quite reach statistical significance, for the highly masculine boys to report their fathers as more punishing. When the two scores—nurturance and punishment—were added to constitute a "power" score, the fathers of the highly masculine boys were scored as much more powerful than the feminine boys' fathers (the probability was .007, a very high level of significance). The fathers' nurturance scores for the masculine boys were higher than the punishment scores (3.7 and 2.8 respectively), whereas they were almost identical for the feminine boys (2.2 and 2.1). None of the results for the mothers distinguished between the two groups.

Although the number of subjects is small, this study suggests rather clearly that boys identify with strength, that parental strength is a combination of reward and punishment (a sensible enough conclusion), and that, possibly, an excess of reward over punishment is conducive to appropriate identification (this last conclusion is the author's, not that of Mussen and Distler).

A CROSS-CULTURAL STUDY OF IDENTIFICATION

Following a theory of identification similar to that of Mussen and

Distler, Whiting (1959) reports an interesting cross-cultural study. He reasons that "a person will identify with, hence accept the moral values of, any person who is a successful rival with respect to resources which he covets, but cannot control." (p. 188) In other words, when the father's relation with the mother is envied by the son—when she nurtures the father, and the son must at times do without—then the boy will identify with his father. Whiting reasoned that cultures high in guilt—in internalized control—will be cultures in which the son is most likely to be envious of the father.

He classified a large number of cultures according to the likelihood that within them the father is likely to be nurtured by the mother, with resulting denial of nurturance to the son, thus arousing the son's envy. This situation, Whiting believed, would be most likely to occur in nuclear households (where father, one wife, and children live together under one roof). It would be next most probable in extended households (where grandparents, grown children, and their families all live together and may provide nurturance for the child when he needs it). Third in order of predicted envy on the part of the son is the polygymous family living under the same roof, where two or more wives can nurture the father as well as the sons. Least envy was predicted for polygymous families where wives live with their children in separate houses, and the father only visits. Whiting's predictions were confirmed at a high level of statistical significance.

IDENTIFICATION AND OTHER PERSONALITY FACTORS

Sutton-Smith and Rosenberg (1959) argue that boys who are "indecisive, dependent, affectionate, and more prepared to admit to anxiety or weakness"—in other words, boys scoring high on the Castaneda, Palermo, and McCandless Children's Manifest Anxiety Scale (1956)—will show more signs of feminine identification than boys who score low on the test.

The authors selected the 42 most anxious and the 42 least anxious boys from a large original group of fourth-, fifth-, and sixth-graders, and gave them a game-preference test. This test includes a list of games, preference for which differentiates boys from girls. Girls, for example, clearly prefer Fox and Geese and Crack the Whip; more boys than girls prefer darts.

The results of the study indicate that boys scoring high in anxiety are clearly more feminine in their game preferences than boys scoring low in anxiety.

Miller and Swanson (1960) studied a group of University of Michigan male undergraduates. They used a projective drawing test to measure "unconscious" masculinity (i.e., what the man was in his "inner core"), and a conventional masculinity-feminity test to measure "conscious" masculinity. One might conjecture that these measures refer, respectively, to sex-role preference and sex-role adoption, as discussed by Lynn, and that, when a man scores "masculine" on both indices, he has made a genuinely masculine identification.

Miller and Swanson distinguished between men who were feminine at both the "unconscious" and the "conscious" levels (FF); feminine on the "unconscious" but not the "conscious" level (FM); and men who were masculine at both levels (MM). They reasoned that there would be no men who were "unconsciously" masculine but consciously feminine, and found only 3 men scoring thus out of their tested population of 522. This result provides some support for the validity of their techniques.

In the various tests taken by their subjects, no differences appeared between the FF and the FM groups. This finding suggests that the important variable in general adjustment is the "unconscious" or "core" identification. But the MM group differed from the other two in several important respects. Fewer of them came from families in which, it was assumed, severe demands had been placed on the child very early in life (i.e., more of the MM's came from presumably relatively permissive homes). The MM's also handled conflict and guilt in a more mature fashion than either the FF or the FM group.

CROSS-IDENTIFICATION

Implicit in learning theory, and probably in psychoanalytic theory as well, is the idea that "cross-identification" is desirable—that is, that the boy should model *preponderantly* after his father as far as his attitudes,

FIG. 10.1. Contrasting motives for identification, according to Freudian (fear), social-learning (love), and power (love plus respect—possibly tinged with fear) theories, as applied to boys.

SOCIAL LEARNING

Boy

Love for father as a positive reinforcer

Sex-typing (modeling on positive image)

Identification with father

Sex-role identification

Conscience, guilt (internalized control)

POWER

Boy

Father as rewarder <u>and</u> effective punisher

Sex-typing (modeling on loved <u>and</u> powerful figure)

Identification with father

Sex-role identification

Conscience, guilt (internalized control)

FIG. 10.1. *Continued*

interests, and behavior are concerned (and entirely, as far as his "maleness" goes); but that some (sympathetic) modeling after the mother should also occur. In our complicated society, where masculine and feminine roles are often not clearly defined, a certain amount of cross-modeling seems to be desirable for boys. Some traits commonly labeled feminine make society run more smoothly: sweetness, tact, the willingness to compromise, intuitiveness, sympathy, interest in people as well as things, appreciation of the arts—all of these are as useful for the male in a Western European culture as they are for the female. It also seems likely that if a boy has genuinely liked his mother and respected—even incorporated—some of her traits, he will, as an adult, make a more sympathetic and understanding husband and father to daughters without necessarily losing any of his prowess as a male.

In summary, there are three theories that attempt to account for identification in boys. Classical Freudian theory holds that the boy identifies in self-protection and because of fear: the father is so powerful and so threatening that, to defend himself and to gain such power, the boy incorporates the father-image. Learning theory argues that boys identify with their fathers because they have been rewarded by them, love them, and wish to be like them. A sociological theory combines Freudian and learning theories, holding that children (boys and girls) identify with *powerful* parents— that is, parents who can both reward and punish. Whereas Freudian theory lays stress on the Oedipal conflict (the son's incestuous love for his mother, coupled with fear of his father's possible punishment directed against this love), neither the learning nor the sociological theory attends particularly to the Oedipal hypothesis.

Existing evidence supports the prediction that boys identify more completely with loving fathers and with powerful fathers, particularly when this power is preponderantly benevolent, than they do with rejecting and punishing fathers. It may be that envy is a motive toward identification: when mothers "look after" fathers, sometimes to the neglect of sons, boys may become envious of their fathers—see them as being powerful and as having desirable prerogatives—and hence be motivated to identify with them.

Some maternal identification appears to be desirable for boys—that is, society probably benefits when its males are interested in people, have positive regard for the arts and social welfare, and so on. It also seems likely that a man with some positive (or cross-) identification with his mother, even though thoroughly masculine in his own adjustment, would make a better husband and father of daughters than a man who rejected the mother-image and incorporated none of it in his own behavior.

Identification for Girls

Psychoanalytic theory holds that the identification process for girls is more complex than for boys. It involves, first, a close association with or love for the mother; then renunciation; then love, modeling, and identification again. According to Freudian theory, the little girl, at the age of about 2, discovers that she has no penis, and for this she blames her mother and turns away from her toward the father. Preference for him remains dominant until about 6, when she again turns toward the mother because, like the son in the family, she realizes that she cannot genuinely replace her mother and that, if she tried, she would lose the mother's love. So she too relinquishes her incestuous wishes and incorporates strength: her mother's image. Fear is less important for girls than for boys in this process.

Such a theory strains credulity and has no direct support. However, evidence exists that little girls of about this age *do* become extremely negative, and in many ways turn their affection from their mothers to their fathers. Some studies of parental preference find girls at around 5 actually stating that they like their fathers better than their mothers, although the usual pattern for both boys and girls is to state a preference for the mother (e.g., Ammons and Ammons, 1949; and Simpson, 1935).

It may be that for girls, at about the age of 2, mothers begin to enforce the social expectations of good manners, obedience, and neatness to a greater degree than they do for boys. This change from a stage of permissiveness-without-substantial-demands that has existed between mother and daughter earlier is sufficiently frustrating to the girl to cause her to turn to her father. He is pleased: he loves the mother *and* her daughter, and responds warmly, thus increasing the strength of affiliation with him. But at the kindergarten—first-grade level, the little girl is faced with the inevitability of her femininity. If her mother is a successful person, she provides the best available model for the appropriate sex role. Then identification takes place.

As for boys, it seems desirable that considerable modeling after, or cross-identification with, the parent of the opposite sex should continue to exist. The sex roles in our culture are *not* extremely clear-cut. Girls *do* compete. There is a place in their lives for striving, for doing well, for achieving, for being aggressive. Hence modified incorporation of these "masculine" traits is useful. Girls' marriages, and their mothering of their sons, should be helped if they have a sympathetic understanding of and liking for the male traits they will encounter in their husbands (and have grown to like first in their fathers)—traits which, in a muted degree, they understand and respect as part of themselves.

One study (Lazowick, 1955) bears directly on this matter of identification of boys and girls, and is the only research study known to the author that deals with the matter of cross-identification. Although its subjects were college-age young men and women and their parents, and the number of subjects is not large (15 young men, 15 young women, and their 60 parents), it is important because it bears on the end-result and reveals some of the dynamics of identification.

Essentially, the study deals with similarities between parents and their

children; and with the children's associations of pleasantness and unpleas-
antness (like and dislike) with certain masculine or feminine terms
(*father, man, mother, woman,* and the like). A measure of anxiety (used,
in this study, as an index of poor personal adjustment) was obtained for
the college men and women, and the low-anxiety ("well-adjusted") were
compared with the high-anxiety ("poorly adjusted") subjects.

Among the more significant findings were the following:

The lower the anxiety in boys, the more similar (the more adequate
the identification?) they were to their fathers. Boys resembled their fathers
more than girls resembled them (but not at a highly significant level).
The low-anxiety ("well-adjusted") boys also resembled their mothers more
than did the high-anxiety boys (support for the idea of cross-identification). Actually, low-anxiety boys were more like their mothers than low-
anxiety girls were. The fathers and mothers of low-anxiety subjects were
more like each other (had a more harmonious marriage?) than the parents
of high-anxiety subjects.

When the male subjects were asked to talk about the similarity of the
words *father* and *myself,* and women about *mother* and *myself,* the low-
anxiety subjects gave more harmonious descriptions than the high-anxiety
subjects. The terms *father, mother,* and *family* had more overlap, as far as
their associations with the word *unpleasant* were concerned, for high-
than for low-anxiety subjects. The low-anxiety subjects seemed, more than
the high-anxiety subjects, to identify with both parents.

It should be noted that the association between good adjustment (as
defined) and the degree of identification with *both* fathers and mothers is
higher for boys than for girls.

A number of other studies fall rather well in line with Lazowick's,
indicating that clear identification with the father is more important for
the boy's adjustment than is clear identification with the mother for the
girl. The reasons for this remain cloudy, unless, as has been mentioned,
they have to do with masculine prestige in Western European cultures.
Representative of these studies is that of Susan Gray (1959), who worked
with fifth- through eighth-graders in an upper-middle-class school, and who
found that boys with stronger identifications were judged as better adjusted
on almost all of her tests than boys with weaker identifications (although
they were not judged as more masculine). There were no real differences
in adjustment for girls with low and high mother identifications.

Helper (1955), using a similar, very special population of adolescents,
obtained very similar results. He worked with 50 freshmen and subfresh-
men in a small high school. His findings indicate that for boys, patterning
after the father in self-concept was at least in part a function of the praise
or reinforcement the boy received for being like his father. The degree of
"likeness" or "identification with" the father was also found to be related
to popularity for boys. That the same findings did not hold for girls with
respect to their mothers may be related to the fact that this high school

was an intellectual and career-oriented one, in which standard feminine traits of homemaking and motherhood may have been less highly valued than traits of competitiveness and intellectual achievement.

In summary, the process of identification appears to be more complex for girls than for boys. Girls who are strongly identified with their mothers do not seem to be superior in adjustment to girls who are less strongly identified, although this relationship does hold for boys. As for boys, however, some cross-identification with the parent of the opposite sex appears to be desirable: girls may have to support themselves; the girl who, while thoroughly feminine, has a certain amount of identification with her father should appreciate her husband more and be a better mother to her sons, and so on.

The lack of clear information about identification for girls may be due to the fact that, in our culture, the feminine role is less highly regarded than the masculine—hence, mothers may reject this role and provide unclear models for their daughters.

Social and Personal Forces in Identification

What happens to boys and girls with "defective" fathers or mothers, or both? With poor marriages and faulty child-rearing practices as common as they are in our culture, how do so many children nevertheless achieve adequate sex-typing and identification and became normally functioning, reasonably happy men and women?

There are at least four factors that may promote identification in the absence of adequate parental figures. The first is the transmission, through mediating processes, of favorable attitudes toward an absent or deceased spouse. There is some indirect evidence to indicate that mothers who pass on favorable opinions of their absent husbands rear children whose ideal father relationship, hence presumably their opportunity for adequate identification, is better than that of children whose mothers pass on unfavorable attitudes about the absent father (Bach, 1946).

Second, there are parent-surrogates in every culture and, in our culture, particularly for girls. A good kindergarten, elementary, or junior-high teacher can go a long way toward providing a favorable female model for the girl whose mother is weak, vicious, or absent. The average boy, on the other hand, does not encounter a male teacher until he is in junior high school, and often not then. But uncles, aunts, and neighborhood friends all can, and do, help provide models for the child of either sex who has no parental model on which to build. As has been mentioned, studies indicate that boys can make a satisfactory identification with fathers who themselves are not particularly masculine in their patterns of interest and activity. The reason for this may be that the boys can accept themselves easily as males if they see their fathers as warm, understanding, and rewarding. Then once this basic psychological identification has been made, the boys go ahead to copy from other males in their environment behaviors that are most suitable for them.

The popularity of Scouting with small boys may in part result from their need for a male model for identification. The hero worship that is given the good athletic coach may also originate in this need. Girls have some advantages over boys in our culture; their mothers are more available to them. Fathers go to work early; they come home late and, frequently, tired. Weekends are often so filled with activity that the father has little time for his son. The mother, in the ordinary course of the day, has more opportunity for informal interaction with her children. But, of course, if the mother is unsatisfactory, the girl is doubly threatened by this increased exposure.

A third factor pushing the child toward an appropriate sex-role identification is a general force in the culture. Boys are rewarded for acting like boys, punished for acting like girls. The same process holds true for girls. Teachers, the peer group, the community, all exert pressure for masculinity or femininity. These pressures, although not necessarily completely effective, are powerful.

Finally, there is suggestive although not definitive evidence that people have selective memories—that they remember the good, forget the bad. A child, even when his parent has preponderantly neglected, rejected, and punished him, forgets the bad times and remembers the good ones. He thus creates for himself a model for identification, however flawed the original may have been. Such a child may, of course, unconsciously follow the inadequate pattern set by his parent.

Identification is one of the most important of the socialization processes. Failure of identification seems to produce a variety of results, ranging from schizophrenia through homosexuality, impotence, and frigidity to unhappy marriages and the repetition by parents of the inadequate parental performance they themselves knew as children.

Even in personality breakdowns, however, there remain evidences of the struggle toward identification, in the sense that the patterns of behavior of mentally ill young men resemble those of their fathers. Singer and Opler (1956) made intensive studies of the patterns of life of Irish-American and Italian-American families, and from these constructed family models for the two groups. They then predicted the consequences for sons. In Irish families, it was hypothesized, the mother is strong and chaste, the father weak, relatively inadequate sexually (it will be remembered that native Irish marry perhaps latest of any group in the world), withdrawn, and uninterested in wife and family. In Italian families, on the other nand, sex is an approved way of expressing affection; the father is dominant, the mother relatively passive and warm, and very feminine. Even in complete breakdown into schizophrenia, the authors predicted, sons would show patterns indicating both that they had attempted to identify, and the nature of their attempt. An investigation of the behavior of adult male

Irish- and Italian-American schizophrenic males provided evidence supporting the predictions. The Irish-Americans showed more effort to control internally. They inhibited impulses more and manifested more fantasy. The Italian-Americans were assaultive, violent, and generally impulsive, and were rated as less cooperative on the wards. Each group, in other words, had struggled toward and modeled after the paternal model.

Social Class and Identification

Socioeconomic effects on sex-typing have already been discussed. Evidence exists that, at least for men, identification is characterized by less warmth and affection in lower-class subjects than it is in middle-class subjects. In a study by Singer (1954) the Thematic Apperception Test was administered to normal and schizophrenic adult males who came from lower and middle socioeconomic classes. References to parental figures in their stories were scored for the presence and amount of warmth. In general, middle-class normal men made more warm and affectionate references to parental figures than lower-class normals. Normal men, regardless of social class, showed more warmth toward parental figures than schizophrenics; but even among the schizophrenics, the middle-class subjects showed more warmth than the lower-class subjects. These results are presumably due to the fact that children receive more over-all warmth in middle- than in lower-class homes; and that homes producing normal sons, when compared with those producing schizophrenic sons, are warmer and happier, whether middle- or lower-class.

Two interesting studies, reviewed in more detail in the following chapter, indicate that middle-class mothers are more aware of the interests and activities of their adolescent sons and daughters than lower-class mothers; and that this awareness is significantly correlated with their children's identification with them (patterning after them). Cass (1952*a*, 1952*b*) found identification (similarity) less highly correlated with awareness for the lower-class mothers of nondelinquent children; the correlations were lowest when the children were delinquent. This suggests that the awareness of the lower-class mothers may well have taken the form of supervision or control rather than of a genuine, friendly interest. In line with this interpretation are Cass's findings that children of mothers who were highly aware of them, but exerted relatively loose control, were more strongly identified with the mothers than children of high-control, low-awareness mothers. The delinquent group of children, when compared with the matched normal group, reported more conflict with their mothers; their mothers showed less awareness of them, and were (as reported by the children) more strictly controlling. Of course, it may have been that such children required strict control, or that they resented even moderate control, or both.

This discussion of identification and social class has considerable relevance for those who work with children. Lower-class children, as a group, are likely to have less positive attitudes toward adult authority figures than middle-class children. But apparent coldness and indifference on their part may be based on previous experiences of rejection, and may well cloak a yearning for a warm relationship with an adult. On the average, lower-class children are less bright and less academically motivated than middle-class children. They may also be more aggressive and overtly sexual, as well as unkempt and ill-dressed. If, to these factors, is added an apparent indifference or even hostility to the teacher, the temptation to "give up on them" or even actively to reject them can become very strong. The teacher who is aware of some of the possible forces lying behind this façade will be less likely to yield to the temptation.

SUMMARY

Socialization may be defined as learning to respond to social stimuli, a process that possibly begins with the social smile. It also implies learning to attach importance to other people and to societal rules. Socialization involves active "teaching" by parents, other adults, older children, and peers.

Socialization may proceed by stages. Erikson, one of the abler writers in the field, talks of "the eight stages of man," or the eight psychosocial crises through which an individual must pass to reach a healthy, mature adjustment. These stages are: learning trust versus mistrust; autonomy versus shame; initiative versus guilt; industry versus inferiority; identity versus diffusion; intimacy versus isolation; generativity versus self-absorption; and integrity versus despair.

Two broad strands of socialization theory exist. Freudian and learning theory belong to the first, which holds that the human organism is shaped by its experiences—that it is a direct function of the teaching forces of the family and environment as perceived by the child and affecting him. The second argues that the forces of growth and development within the human organism are creative: if a child is accepted and if his developmental needs are met, he will grow into a happy, creative, socialized individual.

All societies are organized to reward successful socialization and provide powerful incentives for it, and to punish lack of successful socialization. Love-oriented techniques seem to be more effective in producing socialization than "thing-oriented" techniques (including physical punishment), although the evidence is not definitive.

The foundation of successful socialization is dependency, learned by the child at the hands of attentive (need-satisfying) parents when he is very small. Dependency also implies anxiety over "loss of love."

Dependency refers to the child's attaching importance to other people; dependent *behavior* refers to the seeking of help, affection, and nurturance. It is dependency in the latter sense which must be transmuted from infantile and childish to more mature forms. This process probably occurs as a result of the following: (1) the approval of peers assumes increasing importance; (2) parents shift their approval from dependent to independent behavior, yet continue to assure the child that he is loved; (3) the child is increasingly able to remember the past, understand the present, and predict the future; (4) the child grows in size, strength, and adaptability.

Sex-typing makes its appearance very early, seems to be universal, is probably based on rewards and on imitative learning, and is the forerunner of identification. It should be thought of as sex-role adoption, rather than sex-role preference or identification. Early in children's lives— probably as early as 18 months—adults and older children begin to reinforce differential behavior in boys and girls. Boys whose fathers live at home show more masculine behavior, particularly in their fantasy play, than do boys whose fathers are away from home; and the sons of warm, permissive, fairly easy going fathers appear to be most likely to sex-type appropriately. Fathers' absence makes little difference in the fantasy play of little girls.

Lower-class children, probably because their parental models are clearer, sex-type earlier than middle-class children. Regardless of class, boys sex-type earlier than girls, perhaps because in our culture the feminine model is less attractive—has less prestige—than the masculine model. Boys with older brothers and girls with older sisters sex-type earlier than only children.

Almost all cultures apply pressure for appropriate sex-typing. Typically, girls are trained to be nurturant, to obey, and to live up to their responsibilities, whereas boys are trained for achievement and self-reliance.

The process of identification appears to be more complex for girls than for boys. Although boys who identify with their fathers are better adjusted than boys who have apparently failed to make this identification, the same cannot be said for girls in relation to their mothers. Both boys and girls would seem to profit from some "cross-identification" with the parent of the opposite sex.

Authoritarianism and Prejudice

SOCIAL attitudes affect our behavior profoundly. Such attitudes can be divided into many categories. Some people are generous and open toward others; some are cautious, reserved, and withdrawn. Some hold liberal, others conservative social attitudes which affect the way they vote, the policy of social action they advocate, and even the church to which they belong. Some believe in strictness as a way of dealing with delinquents and criminals; others believe that affection, understanding, and tolerance should characterize all approaches to such social problems.

Social attitudes in large part determine the way parents rear their children, and these child-rearing attitudes and practices, we believe, in turn shape the personalities of the children. As we have seen, one of the clearest dimensions of child-rearing practices is that of authoritarian-nonauthoritarian control. It pervades the family; it varies from culture to culture; and, in a rough way, it divides governments into two camps. Authoritarianism was one of the issues in World War II. Debate continues hotly about whether, for example, the United States should have friendly dealings with dictatorships, or should renounce them.

This pervasive characteristic of social organization—the nonauthoritarian or equalitarian as opposed to the authoritarian—has been thought by many both to derive from and to influence the personalities of the individuals who make up a society. Many aspects of personality and social attitudes could be chosen for discussion in chapters such as this and the next, but the one on which most research has been done concerns authoritarian as contrasted with equalitarian personalities: how each develops, and how equalitarianism and authoritarianism relate to other types of social and personal behavior. Concepts of authoritarianism and equalitarianism are so important that this and the next chapter are devoted to an examination of relevant psychological research. Since it is impossible to review all of the research that has been done on personality variables and social attitudes, it seems appropriate to select a given *illustrative* and *socially important* area and develop it more fully and critically than would be possible if a policy of wider coverage were adopted. In other words, research on equalitarianism-authoritarianism is presented here as representative of research on personality and social attitudes in general.

THEORIES OF AUTHORITARIANISM AND ETHNOCENTRISM

The concept of the "authoritarian personality" has been most influentially developed by Adorno *et al.* During World War II, a group of investigators centered at the University of California attacked the problem of race prejudice, believing that any answers that might be provided about its origins and social development would be helpful in understanding some of the roots of anti-Semitism and Nazism. Their investigations of race prejudice, most particularly prejudice against Jews and Negroes, led them to theories about personality—particularly the authoritarian personality—that were much broader than the ideas of prejudice with which they began.

Every general term must be defined by behavior. It is widely held that the authoritarian personality is rigid, or inflexible; that it is concrete in its thinking and does not handle abstractions easily; that it is conforming, being conventional, for example, in its morality and its politics; that it does not willingly or accurately examine its own thoughts and its own adjustment; that it manifests an exaggerated respect for authority, including "overprotestations" of love for parents. These protestations, however, are combined with underlying hostility toward parental or other authority figures. The authoritarian personality places extreme emphasis on masculinity or femininity, and is hostile (prejudiced) toward groups other than the one to which its owner belongs. It prefers absolutes: black is black and white is white; there are no grays—in other words it is intolerant of ambiguity. It suspects evil in others.

Measures of race prejudice correlate fairly highly (usually in the .50's and .60's) with measures of authoritarian personality. In a number of places in this and the succeeding chapter, it is necessary to assume that groups of people who are high in race prejudice are also high in authoritarianism. It will be made clear when measures of prejudice (a narrower, more specific concept) are substituted for measures of authoritarianism (a more general psychological construct).

Turning now to *prejudice,* there seem to be two types, equally troublesome in their effects but different in their origin. The first is "pathological" prejudice. Here the individual displaces his own frustrations, self-contempt, and self-destructive dispositions onto convenient scapegoats: he seizes upon a social situation, or a group in society, that enables him to project his own difficulties in hostile action or attitudes, thus (albeit in an unhealthy way) reducing his hostilities and anxieties about his own problems. All societies provide scapegoats, and in a great many societies minority groups are conspicuously available and safe candidates for scapegoat roles —prejudice is manifested against them.

The other type of prejudice is "normal." A reasonably well-adjusted and happy person may grow up in a culture that holds derogatory attitudes toward some peoples. Just as he assimilates or learns the positive attitudes of this culture, so such a person learns the negative ones and becomes "normally" prejudiced.

Many psychologists, psychiatrists, sociologists, and so on, believe that autocratic families (or nations) produce authoritarian personalities; and that one of a number of typical traits of the authoritarian is race prejudice. There are at least two major theoretical explanations for the relation between authoritarianism and prejudice. The first, and currently the most widespread, arises from Freudian psychology and concerns itself most with attempts to explain *pathological* prejudice; it has paid little attention to "normal" prejudice. The second has been advanced by sociologists and psychologists interested in learning theory. It attempts to account for both varieties of prejudice, and has drawn heavily from (yet been critical of) the neo-psychoanalytic thinking of such people as Adorno, Frenkel-Bruns-wik, Levinson, and Sanford (1950).

The Psychoanalytic Point of View

The neo-psychoanalytic theory of Adorno *et al.* holds—and, as we shall see, the evidence is by no means clear, nor is the reasoning totally sound—that the authoritarian personality is the result of child-rearing practices (most specifically, those connected with toilet training). When toilet training is too severe or too early, it is believed that the child who has not yet acquired language learns, not only to be continent, but also to dread any situation that is unclear or ambiguous. Because he has been richly rewarded for being dry (when he did not know why he was being rewarded) and resoundingly punished for being wet or dirty (without recognizing why he was being punished), he expects unknown and very possibly unpleasant things to happen to him whenever he is in an unclear situation: he is intolerant of ambiguity. He attempts to reduce the anxiety engendered by ambiguity by forcing things into rigid molds and clear classifications.

The process described here also engenders in the child hostility against his parents. But because of their power, and the love (in addition to hostility) that he holds for them, he cannot express this hostility directly toward them. It is, therefore, displaced. The combination of these two tendencies—intolerance of ambiguity and the need to displace hostility—leads him to classify people as either in-group or out-group, fellow citizens or foreigners, whites or Negroes, Aryans or Jews. Toward the out-group, he expresses exaggerated rejection and dislike; toward the in-group, exaggerated fealty.

As we shall see in the course of this chapter, such a theory of prejudice is certainly oversimplified, and perhaps wrong, but the social importance of prejudice is such that any theory about it should be examined carefully. In many ways, prejudice resembles fixation (see Chapter 5).

Masling (1954), a sympathetic but critical viewer of the psycho-analytic theory of authoritarianism, has selected certain quotations from

Adorno *et al*,[1] interspersing the quotations with comments of his own. In all, he provides a rather full presentation of the Freudian definition of authoritarianism. To quote Masling, authoritarians . . .

> "worry about egocentric and material things. They think in terms of blame and they appear to express aggression against the weak." . . . authoritarians are conventional, submit uncritically in the face of authority, are anti-intraceptive, superstitious, and stereotypic in their thinking, are preoccupied with the "dominance-submission, strong-weak, leader-follower dimension," overemphasize the conventionalized attributes of the ego, have exaggerated assertions of strength and toughness, are cynical and destructive, tend to believe that "wild and dangerous things go on in the world," and have "exaggerated concern with sexual 'goings on'." In addition, authoritarian men are overly masculine and women overly feminine. . . . The authoritarian is characterized as achieving "social adjustment only by taking pleasure in obedience and subordination. This brings into play the sadomasochistic impulse structure both as a condition and as a result of social adjustment. . . . In the psychodynamics of the 'authoritarian character,' part of the preceding aggressiveness is absorbed and turned into masochism, while another part is left over as sadism. . . . Ambivalence is all-pervasive, being evidenced mainly by the simultaneity of blind belief in authority and readiness to attack those who are deemed weak and who are socially acceptable as 'victims.' . . . He develops deep 'compulsive' character traits, partly by retrogression to the anal-sadistic phase of development. . . . [His religious belief is compulsive and punitive; he has overt rigidity of conscience with] strong traces of ambivalence. . . . The over-rigid superego is not really integrated, but remains external." (P. 316)

This is strong prose indeed, and Masling finds little evidence that the traits listed cluster together in the populations he studied. He states:

> . . . the characterization of the authoritarian has been overdrawn. All things evil have been posited in one end of the distribution; all things healthy and democratic have been attributed to the other. It has been natural to slip from a rigorous, scientific, "show-me" frame of reference, to one which has been heavily influenced by the researcher's concern about world conditions. The concept of the authoritarian personality may be a valuable, heuristic tool, but only if it can be divorced as much as possible from value judgments. There seems to have been a tendency to use the term "authoritarian" as a mild profanity which one could use to describe other people (never oneself). It is suggested that the

---

[1] This volume, the "Bible" for psychoanalytically oriented thinkers and researchers in the authoritarianism area. will be referred to repeatedly.

concept be re-examined in the light of the data, purified of value judgments, and put to use again as a research instrument. (P. 318)[2]

Frenkel-Brunswik (1954), who is one of the co-authors of the important Adorno volume, has replied to Masling's critique, arguing that the authors of *The Authoritarian Personality* had no intention of linking this concept with "mental health" as it is conventionally thought of. She states:

> We had even come to the conclusion that the use of projection mechanisms as manifested in prejudice helps rather than hampers the authoritarian in preserving his mental balance, especially in view of the fact that in this case defense mechanisms act through channels which are partially socialized. (P. 466)

Later, she adds:

> In fact, as we have concluded on the basis of our interviews, the authoritarian may, and frequently does, function extremely well in most routine contexts of life; he probably even betters the equalitarian under certain narrowly circumscribed conditions, such as when the culture provides socialization for the mechanisms involved. (P. 468)

Frenkel-Brunswik also defends the empirical base of the value terms used:

> Such terms as "aggression against the weak"—to which Masling objects as evaluative—acquire a different flavor as soon as we remember that "aggression" designates a certain way of functioning in a descriptive manner or as a dispositional term, and thus is a legitimate part of the behavioral vocabulary, and that "weak" is defined by a certain objective locus in the social hierarchy. Similarly, "superstitious" designates nothing but the presence of a belief in supernatural explanations of natural phenomena. The sting that is bound to remain in any reference to such attitudes is given by the fact that they are in general ill suited for coping adequately with the complexities of social and cognitive problems. They tend to lead to consequences that are detrimental to society, to others, and often to their holder himself; but this tendency is empirically verifiable like any other factual trend. (P. 468)[3]

Both Masling and Frenkel-Brunswik make sound points. Social scientists have overextended the theory of the authoritarian personality; they have often committed each of the research and interpretive errors

[2] Reprinted with permission of the American Psychological Association and J. M. Masling, from Masling (1954).

[3] Reprinted with permission of the American Psychological Association, from Frenkel-Brunswik (1954).

discussed in Chapter 2. At the time Masling wrote, a "cold shower" was clearly indicated. On the other hand, the practical and theoretical problems presented by authoritarian personalities, and by prejudice, are so pressing and potentially fruitful that they merit major attention.

The Learning-Sociological Point of View

Accounting for "normal" prejudice is not only important but probably simpler than trying to explain *pathological* prejudice, since the former seems to depend in a relatively straightforward fashion on the principles of *substantive* (nonemotional) learning; whereas for the latter, emotional learnings, drives such as anxiety and aggression, factors of personal security, fixation, displacement, and so on, must be taken into account. The argument about "normal" prejudice is that, if a person has been brought up in a culture which, for example, dislikes Negroes, he learns the attitudes, opinions, and stereotypes of the culture so that he, too, dislikes Negroes. But if he moves to a culture where such attitudes do not exist, his dislike of Negroes will be reduced or his frame of reference will be altered in such a way that he becomes less prejudiced.

Christie and Garcia (1951) have been interested in the implications of this point of view about the development of both authoritarianism and prejudice. They believe that lack of education produces authoritarianism: the less one has been taught about relativism (as opposed to absolutism), the less he knows about history, and the less information he has about cultural diversity, the more likely he is to be authoritarian—to subscribe to absolutes and immediacies. According to such a view, authoritarianism does not necessarily have its roots in psychodynamics. It is, rather, culturally determined. Authoritarian and/or prejudiced persons, given a different culture (anthropologically speaking), or *more* culture (educationally speaking), would become more equalitarian and less prejudiced. They are neither maladjusted nor evil, simply ignorant.

The social-learning theorist finds it difficult to embrace the version of psychoanalytic theory which holds that the authoritarian personality springs full-blown from the anal psychosexual stage, and is a direct function of fixation due to the trauma of early and severe toilet training. However, within social-learning theory, it is reasonable to entertain sympathetically the notion that the mother who is severe in her toilet training also engages in a number of other child-rearing practices that might well make a child an authoritarian.

According to Sears, Maccoby, and Levin (1957), the following child-rearing factors were associated, at least to a modest degree, with severe toilet-training practices: tendencies to put relatively great pressure on children to use good table manners, to be neat and orderly, to be careful around the house and with furniture, to keep quiet, and to do well in school. Mothers who were severe in their toilet training were also likely to use physical punishment and deprivation of privileges (these are thing-oriented control techniques), and to reason little with their children. They strongly discouraged as well as punished aggression from their children toward themselves and their husbands, and expected strict obedience. They stressed modesty and were more concerned about masturbation and social sex play than the mothers who followed more lenient toilet-training practices. They suffered from marked anxiety about their child-rearing capabilities and (relatively) lacked warmth and esteem for themselves, their husbands, and their children.

They sound, in other words, as though they might be rearing children for a police state, where conscience or inner controls are not particularly necessary because external controlling forces are always present. Children so reared may well learn rather directly to fear insecurity and unclarity; to be hostile yet unable to express their hostility directly toward authority figures; to fear, distrust, and dislike minority groups; and to be rigid.

MEASURING AUTHORITARIANISM

The F-Scale

The most frequently used test for authoritarianism is the F- (for "fascism") scale (Adorno *et al.*, 1950). This scale was designed for adults, but it has been modified many times and some forms have been simplified so that they are suitable for children. An enormous quantity of research has been conducted using this test and its modifications.

Different versions of the F-scale include different numbers of items. Most of these items are so worded that a *yes* answer contributes to the score for authoritarianism and a *no* answer is considered to indicate equalitarianism. The following are examples of the items used:

Obedience and respect for authority are the most important virtues children should learn.

Human nature being what it is, there will always be war and conflict.

An insult to our honor should always be punished.

Most of our social problems would be solved if we could somehow get rid of the immoral, crooked, and feeble-minded people.

The person taking the test is asked to rank an item $+3$ if he is strongly in agreement with it; -3 if he is in strong opposition to it. The mid-point, or zero (0) marking, is not ordinarily used.

Evaluation of the F-Scale

Research findings for the F-scale range from strongly supportive to strongly rejecting. Included in publications about the scale has been a spate of criticisms, directed mainly at its mechanics—specifically, the way items are worded (affirmative answers are generally keyed to indicate authoritarianism). The assumptions that underlie the scale have attracted less critical attention. For example, is authoritarianism a unitary trait, or is it a mixture of conformity, aggression, tendencies toward displacement. and so on, each of which is more or less independent of every other, and all of which, together, do not in any logical fashion define the broader trait or characteristic of authoritarianism?

It has been maintained that the F-scale measures nothing like pure authoritarianism. Since for most items a *yes* answer adds to the authoritarianism, or F-, score, it has been argued that what is really being measured is "conformity" or "obligingness" or "acquiescence"—the tendency to be good-humored, to get along with the expert, to say "yes." Examples of some of these critical papers are those by Bass (1955), Chapman and Campbell (1957), Gage, Leavitt, and Stone (1957), Jackson and Messick (1957, 1958), and Jackson, Messick, and Solley (1957).

These criticisms have merit although some of the research techniques devised to support them have been awkward (cf. Christie, Havel, and Seidenberg, 1958, for a fuller discussion of this point). The entire debate centers on the *content* as contrasted with the *style* of the F-scale (cf. Jackson and Messick, 1958). Certainly it can be seen, at a common-sense level, that if one reads such items as those used above for illustration, and answers them honestly, then the positive answers logically contribute to an authoritarianism score. But if one is paying little attention to the content, and is inclined to agree with strongly worded statements presented to him by an expert (a teacher or a research worker), then *yes* answers contribute not to a score reflecting authoritarianism, but instead to one representing something that might be called "acquiescence."

Further, *agreement with what is said by the items* (their content) may or may not coincide with the *habit of agreeing with items* (response set), whatever their content. Hence, a person may score high on the F-scale because he is authoritarian *or* acquiescent, or both; or score low (be rated as equalitarian) because he is equalitarian *or* negativistic, or both. But the scale cannot identify persons who are authoritarian *and* negativistic, or equalitarian *and* acquiescent.

Zuckerman, Norton, and Sprague (1958), using as subjects student nurses, conclude that the factor of acquiescence contributes about half the variance to the authoritarianism score. In other words, acquiescence is an important part of the test score, but so is authoritarianism. These authors suspect that those who are both acquiescent and authoritarian may be authoritarian *followers,* whereas those whose high F-score is due entirely to their agreement with the content of the items may be authoritarian *leaders.*

These authors also used a form of the F-scale in which some items were reversed, and employed as a measure of acquiescence the number of item pairs on which the subject agreed with both items (thus contradicting herself logically, but being consistent in her style of responding). This acquiescence, or response set, score correlated .47 with the score on the conventional F-scale.

Brown and Datta (1959) conclude, on the basis of their study, that response set (or acquiescence) plays a relatively minor part in determining the score for the F-scale, and believe that response set may serve different purposes for people of different educational levels. For the well-educated person, acquiescence may represent a "basic disposition to structure ambiguity in a creative process which permits agreement rather than rejection by the S," (subject of the study), whereas "in less well-educated groups . . . response set may merely be a way of defending against lack of comprehension." (p. 133)

Christie, Havel, and Seidenberg (1958) have made a thorough evaluation of the F-scale. Several studies which obtained results indicating that the F-scale measures conformity more than it does authoritarianism have used the technique of reversing the meaning of items so that response set or acquiescence would result in a high *equalitarian* score. If the correlation between the original, affirmatively worded scale and the reversed scale were positive and high, the conclusion would be that respondents were answering according to content: *authoritarianism* was being measured. If the correlation were low or negative, the conclusion would be that response set was an important determining factor. Use of this technique has resulted in low and even negative correlations between the original and the reversed scales, thus supporting the assumption that conformity or response set operates in an important fashion to produce high F-scores.

Christie and his colleagues point out that such item reversals have frequently been awkward, since *logical* opposition does not necessarily involve *psychological* opposition; and that, in some of the reversal studies, items have been mechanically reversed without attention to psychological reversal. A second criticism of the item-reversal studies is that they employ extremely worded statements in the reversed items. One characteristic of authoritarians has been thought to be a tendency to espouse absolutes: *everyone, no one, any sane person,* and so on, form reasonable categories for the authoritarian. The statement, "No sane person could think of setting fire to a barn," might therefore appeal to the authoritarian personality. This item, *logically* reversed, might read, "Any sane person can think of setting fire to a barn." The equalitarian may endorse the notion that normal people can have very odd thoughts, and for that reason tend to agree with the statement, but the extreme wording may repel him—whereas it may appeal to the authoritarian. A more appropriate form of the statement, designed for endorsement by an equalitarian and rejection by an authoritarian, might therefore be: "Some, under the grip of a temporary need, could think of setting fire to a barn."

Finally, Christie, Havel, and Seidenberg believe that early undergraduates (who have been the subjects of these studies) are among the most suggestible of populations, hence will show more yielding and response set than many other populations. Christie and his co-workers conducted a number of different studies which demonstrated their points, and concluded quite reasonably that "the data do not support the identification of acquiescence with authoritarianism."

Considerations such as those outlined above probably account for the contradictory results that have been obtained from research on the F-scale. The main difficulty may be summarized as follows: One can be quite certain that conformers ("acquiescers") and authoritarians differ from each other to some degree, and that those who are negativistic differ in important ways from those who are equalitarian. Hence, into the relations between the F-scale and the various traits and behaviors with which it has been correlated have entered two different, although apparently correlated, bipolar dimensions: authoritarianism-equalitarianism, and acquiescence-negativism. This fact has undoubtedly reduced the correlation of the F-scale with some variables, and increased its correlation with others.

In other words, the F-scale, mainly because of its structure, seems to be measuring two things that, although correlated, are different from each other. This confuses the results that have been obtained from it. Ideally, we should have a test of conformity or acquiescence (if there *is* such a unitary trait), and of authoritarianism (again, if there is such a single trait). What we have in the F-scale appears to be a mixture of the two. Perhaps we should content ourselves with saying only that scores for the F-scale represent the degree to which the individual who has earned the score possesses "F-ness."

It may well be that authoritarianism can be measured with more sophistication and greater effectiveness by an instrument resembling that used by Stern and Cope (1956). These authors have devised a number of items to which *yes* answers are authoritarian in nature, but have also included a number on which, to score as authoritarian, the respondent must answer *no*. In this way, they control for the factor of acquiescence. They emerge with four possible scores: authoritarian; anti-authoritarian (equalitarian); irrational (where the answer pattern is illogical because of inconsistent answers, of which all no's or all yes's may be examples); and rational answers (refusing to espouse any extreme point of view). Most investigators working with the F-scale have ignored such subtleties, and have proceeded on the assumption that those scoring high on the scale were authoritarian; those scoring low, equalitarian.

Another factor complicating inferences from the F-scale is that many of the items have positive or negative social value—that is, they reflect sentiments, or facts, or conclusions of which society either approves or disapproves. Social approval is differently assessed by different populations: the uneducated may evaluate an item one way; the educationally sophisticated, another. The item may have one set of values for men, another for women; or it may differ in value according to the age of the respondent. These varying social assessments, and their influence on responses, have not received the attention they should have in F-scale research.

Regardless of its faults, the F-scale has been so widely employed as a research instrument, and the number of socially important relationships into which it has entered is so great, that it and its related measures of ethnocentrism must be carefully explored. The scale may be thought of as a loose measure of what is commonly called authoritarianism.

A discussion of measures of prejudice involves considerations similar to those introduced in this treatment of authoritarianism. These difficulties will be discussed as they arise.

Personality Characteristics of Conformers

The preceding pages have raised the question whether the F-scale is a measure of conformity or authoritarianism. Perhaps, however, this question does not reflect on the validity of either the F-scale or the construct of authoritarianism. It was suggested on page 358 that conformity itself is an aspect of authoritarianism, and this suggestion is sufficiently important to have stimulated considerable research.

Three studies suggest that persons scoring high on the F-scale are more conforming than persons who score low, and two studies have been devoted to exploring the other personality characteristics of people who are highly conforming. Crutchfield (1955) used as his subjects 50 men who averaged 34 years of age, all of whom were engaged in a profession where leadership qualities were important. In order to see how many of them would yield to group pressure, he arranged for each man to work in a private cubicle, but "in communication" with other "judges." False majority judgments that disagreed with his own were reported to the subject. The more a man changed his judgments in the direction of the false group judgment, the higher he was scored for conformity, or yielding. The correlation between F-scale score and conformity was .39.

Nadler (1959) has performed a somewhat similar study, using as his subjects 70 day- and evening-school college students. He secured a measure of yielding similar to that just mentioned, and correlated it with the scores on a modified F-scale. The correlation between yielding and the F-score was even higher than that obtained by Crutchfield—a highly significant .48. This, again, is an illustration of the concept of "confidence" in a finding: with two very different populations—one of mature men, the other of college students—similar statistical relations are revealed. The more frequently a finding is repeated, and the more diverse the populations from which it is obtained, the more confidence can be placed in it.

Wells, Weinert, and Rubel (1956) worked with 124 college students assigned to two matched groups. Half of the students were asked to judge from a drawing of an automobile collision which of the drivers of two cars had been responsible for the accident. From the picture, it was obvious that car A had run through a red light and crashed broadside into car B. For students with no conformity pressure, 60 of 62 made such a judgment. Four "confederates" or "stooges" reported aloud before each of the other 62 students made their judgments, registering unanimous "agreement," and giving reasons, that the driver of car B had been at fault. Twenty-one of this "pressured" group of 62 students conformed, or agreed with the deliberately incorrect group judgment. All students were then given the F-scale. The average score for the conformers was 119 (the higher the score, the more authoritarian); the average score for the nonconformers was 92. This difference is significant at less than the .001 level.

The studies that have been cited in the preceding paragraphs indicate that high F-scores accompany high tendencies to conform. The next question to be asked is, What does this mean? Relations between the F-scale and conformity scores may be due to the fact that there is a relation between authoritarianism and conformity; or between acquiescence, as tapped by the F-scale, and conformity; or the two effects may combine to produce the relation. This last possibility appears to be the most probable.

Tuddenham and McBride (1959) give us some evidence on the characteristics of conformers. In an amusingly written but alarming article, they show that college students and moderately successful adults in their mid-thirties can be moved by group opinion in the direction of endorsing (agreeing with) truly preposterous statements. In other words, urges toward conformity can result in presumably intelligent adults assuming positions that, from any intelligent point of view, are ridiculous.

Statements presented to the experimental subjects in the Tuddenham and McBride study include the following:

> Sixty to 70 percent of the population of the United States is over 65 years of age.
>
> Male babies have a life expectancy of only 25 years in the United States.
>
> The average American man is between eight and nine inches taller than the average American woman.
>
> On the average, Americans eat six meals per day.

The Tuddenham and McBride study indicates that conformity, although it may be intellectually ludicrous, is at least comfortable. Those who were not swayed by the "rigged" group opinions that, on the average, induced the experimental subjects to agree with such opinions, were less comfortable people. The nonyielders in this study expressed more anxiety, had more unresolved questions about their performance, and were more likely than the yielders to *blame themselves* for the discrepancy from the rigged group norm. It is possible, of course, that the psychological discomfort expressed by the nonyielders results directly from their perception of themselves as deviants from the group, and was, thus, derived directly from the experimental situation.

Tuddenham (1959) has carried out another study of personality factors associated with yielding and nonyielding. The yielders were more conventional in their behavior and values and seemed, on the whole, to be "good guys": well-socialized, conscientious people who were generally conforming, good-natured, affiliative, and nurturant. They were, on the other hand, less intelligent, lower in community status, less perceptive and psychologically sophisticated, and less accepting of themselves and other people. Yielding, according to Tuddenham, seems to be more a feminine, and nonyielding a masculine, behavior, although nonyielders are more likely to admit having personal problems than yielders (are more willing to be introspective).

Tuddenham found that the picture presented above was clearer and more consistent for men than for women, perhaps because "the yielding-independence variable is less closely related in women to attitudes toward the self and the sex role, and is hence somewhat less predictable from other variables." (p. 284)

PREJUDICE AND PERSONALITY

Studies of "Normal" and "Pathogenic" Prejudice

Authoritarianism as such has been little studied in children. But the assumption implicit in the preceding pages of this chapter, that authoritarianism and ethnocentrism (or race prejudice) are closely related to each other, has been widely accepted, and there have been a number of studies of ethnocentrism using children as subjects. Several of these studies have been selected for more intensive review here. It should be noted that most of them concentrate on pathogenic prejudice, and have been inspired by Adorno and his colleagues (see p. 358).

Mussen (1950) was interested in several aspects of prejudice: (1) Will prejudice decrease simply as a result of learning about members of a minority group—for example, by living with them for a time? Theories about "normal" prejudice (see pp. 361–362) would predict such a result. (2) What are the personality dynamics of those who increase, decrease, or do not change in prejudice as a result of greater familiarity with the minority group?

The subjects in Mussen's study were 106 white boys from 8 to 14 years of age, who had been placed for four weeks in an interracial camp. Early during their stay they had taken a test of anti-Negro prejudice, the Horowitz Faces Test. The test was re-administered when the boys left the camp. The Horowitz test is a picture test showing full-face views of eight Negro and four white boys. The higher a young subject ranks the Negro boys in a twelve-rank hierarchy of preferred friends, and the more frequently he chooses Negro boys as possible companions or associates in various activities or situations, the less prejudiced he is judged to be. Levitt (1956) has severely criticized this test. However, Mussen (1950) has shown that the prejudice scores derived from it for his sample of boys correlate moderately well (.52) with youngsters actual choices of cabin-mates during their stay in the camp.

Of particular interest to Mussen (1950) were various subgroups: those who, as a result of their camp experience, lowered their prejudice score; those who increased it; and those who stayed the same, whether originally high or originally low in prejudice. Although many individual children changed scores, *for the group as a whole* there was no significant change in the level of prejudice as a result of the interracial camping experience.

In addition to the test of anti-Negro prejudice, Mussen administered the

Thematic Apperception Test to his group of subjects. Correlating the data obtained from the two instruments, he found that the boys who were initially high in prejudice, when compared with those who were low, appeared to be more hostile and to have a need to dominate others. In their TAT stories, they appeared to show more hostility toward their parents and to believe more frequently that "the world was against them."

Characteristic of the boys who *increased* in race prejudice as a result of their camp experiences were strong needs to defy authority and strong hostile feelings. These youngsters also seemed to feel that open expression of aggression was likely to lead to punishment, retaliation, restraint, and prohibition. They appeared to regard themselves as victims of aggression.

The boys who *decreased* in prejudice told TAT stories in which the heroes showed relatively few aggressive needs, and in which aggression was not necessarily followed by retaliation and punishment. Their TAT stories revealed rather favorable attitudes toward their parents and their general social environment. Interviews obtained as they were leaving camp indicated, tentatively, that they had enjoyed their camp experience more than the boys who had increased in prejudice.

Mussen's study offers evidence to support the thesis that prejudice serves personal needs; does not bear out the prediction that, for *groups,* "getting to know them" automatically reduces prejudice; but indicates that when prejudice is *not* related to personality needs, acquaintance with a minority group may reduce prejudice.

Pettigrew (1959), like Mussen, was interested both in normal and in pathological prejudice. If prejudice is considered to be normal—that is, a product of straightforward learning—then, in the United States, anti-Negro prejudice should be higher in the South than in the North; but in the South the correlation between prejudice and authoritarianism should be lower than in the North, where there is at least token disapproval of prejudice. It also follows logically that there should be a higher correlation between anti-Negro and anti-Jewish prejudice in the North than in the South. Both should be more closely related to personality needs in the North than in the South, where there are more opportunities to learn anti-Negro than anti-Semitic prejudice.

Pettigrew interviewed a random sample of 180 Northerners and 186 Southerners from four small northern and four small southern towns. On the whole, his southern sample was slightly younger, less well educated, and included a larger proportion of native-born than the northern sample. During his interviews (which were presented as attempting to determine the influence of mass information media), he asked a number of questions from the F-scale and from a Negro and Jewish prejudice scale. The set of questions about Negroes included two types: stereotyped beliefs (they are a happy-go-lucky people), and exclusion-discrimination (they should never mingle with whites).

As he predicted, Pettigrew found his southern sample to be much more prejudiced against Negroes than the northern sample, the difference being more marked for the exclusion-discrimination than for the stereotyped-belief items. This finding illustrates the influence of direct learning; but his results also indicate the presence of pathological prejudice equally in North and South. For example, in the North, the F-scale correlated, not highly but significantly (.27), with anti-Negro prejudice; the correlation for southern subjects was .34. Correlations between anti-Negro and anti-Semitic prejudice also supported the prediction that prejudice is related to personality. This correlation was very similar in the North (.55) and the South (.58). For both the northern and southern samples, the better-educated were less prejudiced and less authoritarian, but education affected these relations more strongly in the South than in the North (for example, in the North, the correlation between education and anti-Negro prejudice was —.30; in the South it was —.47).

Pettigrew's study illustrates clearly that both theories—prejudice as *directly learned,* and prejudice as related to *personality dynamics*—must be considered in any accounting for ethnocentric attitudes. The better-educated Southerner *and* Northerner have reduced their prejudice, but education has affected the former more than the latter because, usually, he has further to go. However, the authoritarian, whether Northerner or Southerner, has seized upon *general* prejudice (i.e., against both Negroes and Jews) as a method of satisfying personal needs.

Personality Characteristics Associated with Prejudice

A study by Gough *et al.* (1950) sheds some light on personality characteristics associated with prejudice in children. Gough and his colleagues devised a test with each item of which the subjects—242 fourth-, fifth-, and sixth-grade pupils in two schools in a large midwestern city—were asked to indicate agreement or disagreement. Sample items, all of which concerned Negroes, are the following:

> They work hard.
> I would like to go on a picnic with them.
> They often hurt other people's feelings.
> I would like to see one of them get elected President of the United States.
> They are pretty dumb.

Other tests given to the children in this study concerned anti-Semitic prejudice and general intolerance. The characteristics of the most intolerant children were then compared with those of the most tolerant. There were approximately 40 children, both boys and girls, in each of these groups.

On the basis of their findings, the authors conclude that children's race prejudice is related to general intolerance, thus supporting the frequently made assumption of a relationship between authoritarianism and ethnocentrism. There were indications that the more intolerant children were also more constricted (less free and more apprehensive about creative self-expression), more cynical, more suspicious, more fearful, and less confident and secure than the tolerant children.

It must, of course, be borne in mind that these conclusions were based, not on the children's real-life behavior, but on their answers to questionnaire items. There is not necessarily a one-to-one relationship between the two.

Although reactions to frustration and failure are discussed in more detail in Chapter 13, it is necessary to anticipate this discussion briefly. Rosenzweig (1944) has classified reactions to frustration into *intropunitive* (turned in upon oneself), *extrapunitive* (turned outward toward others), and *impunitive* (repressed). It has been suspected that persons who are prejudiced are more likely to be extrapunitive than those who are not. Rosenzweig has developed the Picture Frustration Test (e.g., 1950) to measure the direction of expressions of hostility. This test is in the form of cartoons, in which, for example, someone has spilled soup on another person. The "balloon" above the soup-spiller is filled in with some statement, such as "Oops, I'm sorry"; and alternative possibilities are provided for filling in the balloon above the victim. These possibilities range from impunitive (for example, "Oh, that's all right. This suit had to be cleaned anyway") to extrapunitive ("You clumsy ox. Just who do you think you are? I ought to poke you in the nose!") to intropunitive ("It's my fault—I have my chair too far out in the aisle"). The respondent's "punitiveness" direction is judged from the type of response with which he fills in the balloons.

Using this technique, Lesser (1958) investigated the relationship between anti-Semitism and extrapunitiveness. His subjects were fifth- and sixth-grade Jewish boys (20 in number, from 10 to 13 years of age) and non-Jewish white boys (24 in number, aged from a little more than 10 to a little more than 13). Lesser's definition of anti-Semitism was sociometric: the number of Jewish boys chosen as being one of a boy's three best friends was subtracted from the number of Jewish boys among the three the boy most rejected. Scores ranged from +3 (very anti-Semitic) to —3 (very pro-Semitic). Scores for the non-Jewish boys average 0—they liked as many Jewish boys as they rejected. For the Jewish boys, the average was —.44. These average scores are not significantly different from each other.

Lesser then correlated anti-Semitism scores with extrapunitiveness scores for the two groups of boys separately. The correlation for the non-Jewish youngsters was .60, and for the Jewish boys .48. These correlations are high, and they are not significantly different from each other. Lesser thus provides support for the notion that youngsters holding anti-Semitic prejudices are also extrapunitive. They take out their wrath on the world, not on themselves. That this is not a healthy trait is suggested by Albee (1950), who found the prognosis (prediction of recovery) more favorable for adult schizophrenics and other psychotics who were intropunitive than for those who were extrapunitive. Albee, however, was dealing with actual behavior rather than test-inferred direction of punitiveness.

Berkowitz (1959) has used a research population of 48 women college students to demonstrate a similar point. His anti-Semitic college girls measured higher on a test of inclination toward hostility than girls low in anti-Semitism; and, when frustrated by a prestigeful outsider (the experimenter), vented (displaced) their aggression on their innocent working partners. Girls low in anti-Semitism actually said that they liked their partner *better* following than preceding frustration.

Research done by Cowen, Landes, and Schaet (1959) indicates that aggression displaced because of frustration is particularly likely to be directed toward Negroes. Using college students as subjects, Cowen and his colleagues administered an F scale, an anti-Negro scale, a general antiminority scale, and a patriotism scale. They then frustrated their subjects with two unsolvable puzzles, and retested them. Anti-Negro scores increased sharply and significantly, particularly for the men in the study, although there was no significant change in scores for the other tests.

Gough (1951 *a, b, c,* and *d*) has published four studies in which he attempts to measure attitudes and traits that are associated with prejudice in high-school boys and girls. He used a number of different samples of subjects and several research procedures, most of them involving pencil-and-paper techniques. It is not necessary for our present purposes to analyze these in great detail, although Gough's findings (as represented in his first two studies) are relevant here.

High race prejudice accompanied lower intellectual, social, and educational levels, poorer grades, and less sociability and participation in school activities. Those highly prejudiced testified more to uneasiness and discomfort in social situations, and complained more than the low-prejudice subjects of personal dissatisfactions, problems, and annoyances. Their prejudice was not confined to one out-group but was spread to many. Politically, they were nationalistic and conservative, and stated feelings of being victimized and exploited (Gough, 1951 *a*). These findings fit well with the Lesser study: the more prejudiced saw themselves as more frustrated, and indicated that they took out their frustration on others.

In his second study Gough (1951 *b*) standardized a prejudice test. Five clusters of items characterized those who were high in prejudice: (1) anti-intellectualism; (2) a pervading sense of pessimism and lack of hope and confidence in the future (cynicism, distrust, doubt, and suspicion); (3) a hostile and bitter outlook, including admissions of temptations to injure the self or someone else; (4) grumbling and discontented evaluation of current status; and (5) a rigid, somewhat dogmatic style of thinking. The highly prejudiced high-school students also showed signs of lack of poise and self-assurance; an underlying perplexity and an ominous fearfulness; and feelings of estrangement and isolation that mystify and frighten them (this is reminiscent of Erikson's adolescent "role diffusion," discussed on p. 318).

From this study Gough concludes that "all of the tendencies mentioned are socially isolating in varying degrees and would be expected to interfere with and impair the efficiency of social interaction and response." (p. 253)

Prejudice and Authoritarianism

Gough's studies, taken as a group, strengthen the assumption that prejudice is a special aspect of the authoritarian personality, since his highly prejudiced adolescents tend, as a group, to show characteristics that are usually combined in a definition of authoritarianism (see pp. 358 and 363).

The assumption of a moderate-to-strong relation between authoritarianism and prejudice is further strengthened by Jensen's study (1957) of college students. Jensen used Gough's prejudice (Pr) scale to measure prejudice in 712 freshman students at San Diego State College. These young people were tested almost immediately upon entering college, as were the 312 of them who returned a year later. A number of college seniors and students at a nearby junior college were also tested. The California F-scale was also given to several of these subgroups. Some of Jensen's more striking results are summarized below.

Students who dropped out of college during their first year obtained higher Pr-scores than those who remained. Pr-scores were much lower for sophomores than for freshmen, 69 percent of the students who remained showing lowered scores. Of the 11 percent whose Pr-scores stayed the same, most had obtained exceedingly low scores in the first place.

The correlation of Pr with F (i.e., of prejudice with authoritarianism, as measured by these two scales) varied considerably from one subgroup to another. For education majors at San Diego State College, this correlation was only .27, but for the junior-college students, it was .65.

Students with high Pr-scores also showed a number of scores on the Minnesota Multiphasic Inventory of the type considered to indicate maladjustment. Jensen says of their personalities, as judged by the MMPI:

> . . . the emphasis is on the obsessive-compulsive syndrome . . . , and there is comparatively little hysterical and repressive tendency. . . . The impression is that prejudiced, authoritarian persons have less well-developed ego defenses and are thus more exposed and vulnerable to psychological stress, in the face of which they develop tendencies toward pessimism, cynicism, low morale . . . and psychological isolation . . . , along with the more primitive defenses of a compulsive, ritualistic, and schizoid nature. (p. 310)

Jensen has also provided one of the few real-life tests of the relation of personality to prejudice. Members of the faculty of the college were asked to submit the names of students they knew personally and considered either well or poorly adjusted, in the sense of being likely or unlikely candidates for psychological counseling. None of the faculty had any idea of the reason for this request, nor was the faculty aware that a study of prejudice was being conducted. A list of 30 poorly adjusted and 59 well-adjusted students was submitted. The mean Pr-score of the former was 9.9; of the latter only 5.6. This difference is significant at less than the .001 level.

No differences in Pr-scores were found between men and women.

Prejudice and Intellectual Functioning

Kutner (1958) has made an elaborate study of the way prejudiced and nonprejudiced children attack intellectual problems. He accepts the assumptions that (1) rigidity and concrete-mindedness accompany and may even underlie prejudice; and (2) the person who is prejudiced is also authoritarian. His study is reviewed in some detail, since he has studied these phenomena with very young children.

Kutner used 60 seven-year-old public-school children as his subjects, and measured their prejudice by interviewing them. During the interview they were asked such questions as the following: "Some people are Jewish and some people are Catholics. Some Jewish people say that the Catholic people are not very nice. They say that Jewish is a better religion than Catholic. They don't like to make friends with Catholic people. What about that? How do you feel about Catholic people?" (p. 48) The interviewer knew the children well, and obtained free and full answers to his questions.

On the basis of these interviews, children were classified as prejudiced or nonprejudiced. In the prejudiced group were 18 children, 10 boys and 8 girls. The nonprejudiced group included 42 children, 27 girls and 15 boys. The two groups were not significantly different from each other in IQ (although scores were not available for all), sex distribution, father's occupation, age, or religion.

Kutner defined "very unprejudiced" children as, for example, denying unwarranted assertions of virtues of their own group; or denying or enhancing denial of negative traits ascribed in the interview question to an ethnic group. "Prejudiced" children, on the other hand, spontaneously express hostility against ethnic groups quite aside from the interview statement; or they make enhanced spontaneous additions to attributed negative traits, with rationalizations, and so on.

Of the most defensibly usable of the children's responses to the interview items, Kutner found that an encouraging 58 percent were clearly nonprejudiced, and only 12 percent clearly prejudiced.

Besides the interview, Kutner administered three tests of mental functioning to his group of subjects. The first of these was a concept-formation test. Each child was presented with four large objects: a red square, a green circle, a white triangle, and a red triangle; and four small objects: a blue triangle, a red square, a white circle, and a blue square. These were cut out of desk blotters. The children were told that they must put the things together in groups so that each group included the same number of things, and only things that belonged together. The possible solutions were either two groups, one of large and one of small objects; or four groups, consisting of two large and two small subgroups (i.e.—although this is not clear from Kutner—two large triangles and a large circle and square in the large groups; and two small squares and a circle and triangle in the small groups). The children were scored as obtaining a spontaneous correct solution, including verbalization of the correct principle; or a guided solution, in which the child did not verbalize the principle correctly or in which the experimenter had to guide him all the way to the solution through standard hints; or failure. Table 12.1 summarizes the results for the two groups of children.

TABLE 12.1: PERCENTAGE OF NONPREJUDICED AND PREJUDICED CHILDREN SECURING VARIOUS DEGREES OF SUCCESS ON A CONCEPT-FORMATION TEST.

| | Percentage of Group | |
	Nonprejudiced	Prejudiced
Spontaneous solution	46.3	29.4
Guided solution	34.1	11.8
No solution	19.6	58.8

Adapted with permission of the American Psychological Association and B. Kutner, from Kutner (1958).

As can be seen from Table 12.1, the nonprejudiced children performed significantly better on this test than the prejudiced youngsters. This difference seems not to be a function of intelligence, since Kutner's analysis shows that passing or failing the test is unrelated to general aptitude.

Kutner concludes: "In situations requiring the formation of general concepts . . . more prejudiced children tend to be deficient in forming adequate concepts, less prejudiced children tend to develop adequate concepts.' (p. 24) In other words, for these children, low prejudice is associated with better inductive reasoning.

Kutner next administered to his seven-year-olds a deductive reasoning test made up of nine problems. Of these, the first was an introductory item ("Electric lights never twinkle. This light is twinkling. Is it an electric light?"). Four others were problems of "formal logic," in which the reasoning was straightforward and there was only one correct answer. Examples of this type of item are: "Jane is taller than Jill. Mary is shorter than Jill. Who is the tallest of all?" and "The green bug runs faster than the red bug; the red bug runs faster than the blue bug. Which bug is slowest of all?"

The second type of item was considered to be ambiguous, since it could be answered correctly in any of a number of ways. Illustrations of this type of problem are: "It runs but it has no feet; it roars but it has no voice. What is it? Why?" and "You're going to the store. On the right-hand side is a farm; straight ahead is a lake. Which way is it to the store? Why?"

The prejudiced group of children was not inferior to the nonprejudiced on the problems of formal logic, but did significantly less well on the ambiguous items. Kutner believes this difference results from rigidity, which, he thinks, underlies prejudice. He concludes: "It appears that the accuracy of deduction is dependent upon the nature of the problem to be solved: the more prejudiced children having much more difficulty in arriving at valid conclusions on problems involving some ambiguity than do less prejudiced children. Both groups, on the other hand, have equal success (or difficulty) on problems of formal logic." (p. 27) Furthermore, the nonprejudiced children, when baffled, seemed willing to give up by saying, "I don't know," and averaged 1.3 such responses for the whole test. The prejudiced children averaged only .56 such responses. Kutner says: "It would appear, then, that prejudiced children are not only less capable of producing valid conclusions but the invalid ones they *do* produce are *dogmatically held*. Another way of interpreting this result is that prejudiced children tend not to admit what, to E(xperimenter), might be seen as an admission of weakness." (pp. 31–32)

O'Connor (1952) reports findings that support Kutner, even though she used Harvard college students as research subjects. O'Connor administered a test of abstract thinking and one of prejudice, and found that the two were significantly and negatively correlated (in the high .30's).

Using still another population (30 senior medical students), Neel (1959) found that the higher the F-scale score of these young men (the more authoritarian they were), the less well they dealt with ambiguous psychiatrically related material (such as advising a young woman who complained about frigidity, and whose physical examination was negative, about "a good book on sex"). They also received lower test grades on course material related to "humanitarian philosophy," although they equaled the less authoritarian men in mastery of formal course content.

Neel's study had an interesting inspiration. For years, several senior medical students in each class had complained bitterly about a required course in psychiatry. All efforts to mitigate these complaints through improving instructional methods and materials had failed. The author finally conjectured that it was the human-relations material itself against which the students were rebelling. The study was based on the assumption that authoritarian personalities reject human-relations and adjustment content per se, and will do poorly with it (because of their own personality adjustment), regardless of how well it is presented. Neel's study offers moderate support for her assumptions.

Studies Reporting Negative Findings

The studies reviewed in the three preceding subsections, using different experimental populations and various measures of prejudice, authoritarianism, and personal adjustment, suggest strongly that prejudice is related to authoritarianism and general adjustment, and that it is associated with certain types of learning disability.

However, Masling (1954) has reported findings from studies of his own and others that (at least for adults) do not demonstrate a relation between authoritarianism (or prejudice) and adjustment. For 34 men and 48 women who were psychiatric patients, no relation was found between ethnocentrism and scores on the Minnesota Multiphasic Inventory; for 963 representative citizens of Philadelphia, scores on an authoritarianism-equalitarianism scale were not correlated with scores on a scale designed to measure personal security; for 64 summer-school students who took the F-scale and an incomplete-sentences test, there was no relation between authoritarianism and personal adjustment. Finally, 49 Navy recruits hospitalized for personal-adjustment problems did not differ in their authoritarianism score from 1,000 not so hospitalized.

Davids and Eriksen (1957) have reported similar results for a group of 48 naval men of college age (although few had attended college). In this study, authoritarianism was significantly but slightly related (—.24) to intelligence, but no relation was found with three measures of personal adjustment. The authors argue that authoritarian college students, placed in the relatively democratic atmosphere that characterizes most colleges, become neurotic; whereas the same thing is not true for the Navy men.

McCandless and Holloway (1955) used the Horowitz Faces Test as a measure of anti-Negro prejudice for 154 fourth- and fifth-grade children in a midwestern public school. There were 77 boys and 77 girls in the group. The authors then tested the relations between race prejudice and various behaviors that, they reasoned, would characterize children who were intolerant of ambiguity. The general hypothesis was that prejudiced children would be more intolerant of ambiguity than unprejudiced children. An illustrative specific prediction was that there would be differences between the two groups in deciding which of two equal weights was the heavier. It was predicted that children intolerant of ambiguity would find a period of indecision unpleasant, and hence would "stampede" into a choice. For the 30 girls and 25 boys who took the test (this aspect of the study was dropped before all subjects had been tested, because there were obviously no differences), there were no decision-time differences between those high and low in prejudice. None of the other five hypotheses advanced by the authors (e.g., prejudiced children will choose as friends other prejudiced children, whereas nonprejudiced children will not discriminate) was supported.

On the whole, it can be concluded that impressive relations exist between authoritarianism, prejudice, and personal adjustment, although in some populations no relation has been found between authoritarianism and maladjustment or intolerance of ambiguity, as measured.

Prejudice as Seen by the Minority Group

The research that has been summarized to this point in the chapter concerns the personality and social characteristics of those of a majority or core group who are prejudiced. What of those who receive the prejudice?

Goff (1949) interviewed 150 ten- to twelve-year-old Negro children, and a number of their parents, about the types of prejudiced treatment they had received, their reactions to it, and the type of advice parents had given their children about what to do when they encountered prejudice. These children were drawn from upper- and lower-income groups in New York City (where overt sanctions against the free movement of minority groups are relatively slight), and from St. Louis (where more restrictive practices are in effect with reference to Negroes).

Of the 150 children, 95 percent reported experiences that they interpreted as problems in Negro-white relations. The most frequent problem, mentioned by 77 percent of the children, was ridicule. More than half of them complained of radio and movie stereotypes, and almost half (41 percent) had actually experienced aggression from white children. A tenth (11 percent) reported physical ill-treatment from white adults.

Five percent of the children reported no difficulties. Goff believes that this figure of five percent is too high, since some children had been carefully protected by the community or their parents, or both; but that poor rapport in the interview, or difficulties in expression, may have been responsible for "no reported difficulties" on the part of some of the youngsters. In other words, she believes the percentage of children reporting problems should have been even higher.

The sex of the children was not related to the presence or absence of reported difficulty, but subtle manifestations of prejudice were more likely to be noticed (or reported) by girls. Lower-income children, who are more likely to be completely segregated from whites, seemed to be more sensitive to implied prejudice than upper-income children. There was some indication that heavily segregated communities bred cultural isolates.

The children reported that their most frequent feeling was resentment in situations where they encountered ridicule, physical ill-treatment, aggression, and indirect disparagement. Inferiority feelings most often were aroused by rude treatment and discrimination. Fear was not often admitted (probably because the children were ashamed to admit it), and occurred most frequently in response to aggression. Girls admitted fear more frequently than boys, as would be expected. Indirect disparagement was the derogatory treatment most likely to be accepted as "true" by the children (i.e., such treatment caused them to question their own adequacy!).

Interestingly enough, upper-income girls were more likely to fight in response to ill-treatment than lower-income girls, who were more likely to display inertia. Boys were more likely to fight than girls.

The counsel given by parents to the children stressed withdrawal and avoidance when confronted by discrimination. In only 42 percent of the cases where parental guidance had been given did the children report it as being helpful.

To sum up, from the victim's point of view, race prejudice is an ugly, hurtful thing, in the face of which he feels angry, inferior, and helpless. He is placed in a situation where there is "frustration and failure without solution."

Stevenson and Stewart (1958) have conducted an interesting study of the development of racial awareness in young children. They used as subjects 225 Negro and white children, boys and girls, aged 3 to 7 years, who lived in Austin, Texas. As one measure of racial preference, they gave each child his choice of playing with colored (Negro) or white boy-girl pairs of dolls. At the ages of 3, 4, 5, 6, and 7 respectively, the following percentages of white children chose the white dolls: 52, 60, 64, 82, and 82. For the majority, in other words, a clear preference had been set up by the time they were 4, and by age 6 more than four fifths showed such a preference. Comparable percentages for the Negro children were 50, 39, 35, 33, and 65. At the ages of 4, 5, and 6, Negro children appeared to be rejecting dolls that represented their ethnic group. Only at age 7 did a modest majority pick the Negro doll.

It should be noted that Stevenson and Stewart did not equate the dolls' "intrinsic" attractiveness, although the colored dolls were identical in dress and physiognomy with the white dolls, the only difference being "skin tone." Furthermore, it is almost certain that both Negro and white children have had more experience in playing with white than with colored dolls (indeed, the authors report that they had been unable locally to purchase Negro dolls to use in their study). An additional, although unavoidable, defect in this study is that the socioeconomic status of the Negro children was lower than that of the white youngsters. The Negro children therefore probably tested lower in intelligence, although this may have little or no effect on racial awareness or preference as such.

In another phase of the Stevenson and Stewart study, the authors showed the children a series of pictures, of which the following is typical: two Negro and two white boys are shown playing in the background, and a child whose ethnic group cannot be determined is lying in the foreground. The experimenters then said to each child: "This little boy was playing in the yard. Another little boy was very mean to him and pushed him down. Which one of these little boys do you think pushed him down? Which little boy is going to come over and see if he is all right?"

A higher proportion of the white children than of the Negroes chose a child of their own ethnic group as the "hero" or "good guy"; the Negro children were more likely to choose a Negro child as the "bad guy" than were the white children to choose a white child.

At the ages of 3, 4, 5, 6, and 7 respectively, the following percentages of white children chose a white child as the villain in the picture described above: 32, 32, 40, 20, and 32. But, in the same order, a Negro child was chosen as the villain by the following percentages of Negro children: 65, 56, 45, 71, and 85.

For this picture, the differential trend in choosing a hero was not as clearly marked or statistically significant as the choice of a villain, but at five of the six ages, more white children chose whites as heroes than Negroes chose Negroes. The percentages for whites for the five age levels in order were 52, 76, 56, 56, and 60; and for Negroes, 48, 39, 41, 47, and 75. In other words, at each age level, a majority of the white youngsters believed that a white child would be the "good guy" in the story; but at each age level except age 7, the majority of the Negro children chose as the hero one of the two pictured white youngsters rather than one of the two pictured Negro children.

The implications of this study, although tentative, lead to the hypothesis that racial awareness, including differential preference, is developed very early in life; and that society is so organized as to lead the Negro child to devalue and perhaps even to reject his own ethnic group. The consequences of such a rejection for the self-concept of Negro children are serious, and should be investigated further.

SUMMARY

Attitudes of authoritarianism and prejudice have been selected as representative of the range of social beliefs and predispositions that children develop—beliefs that influence their behavior and have much to do with the conduct of society. A specific but representative attitude area was selected to permit more extensive review of appropriate theory and research than would have been possible with a wider range of attitudes and values.

The authoritarian personality is thought to be characterized by (among other things) rigidity, concreteness of thought, conformity, intolerance of ambiguity, disinclination toward introspection, exaggerated loyalty and affection toward parents and members of the in-group (yet with underlying hostility toward them), and hostility toward the out-group.

Psychoanalytic theory views prejudice as pathological, and believes it to be closely related to authoritarianism. A person is hostile toward alien ethnic or religious groups in order to satisfy certain unconscious or unadmitted personality needs of his own. His hate is *displaced*. Another theory regards prejudice as normal. If one lives in a prejudiced society, he learns prejudice directly and, given a different environment, will reduce his prejudice. Such a theory can be extended to include pathological prejudice on the assumption that certain types of restrictive child-rearing practices so circumscribe and frustrate the child, at the same time tying him to his parents, that he becomes basically resentful yet overconforming, and must find scapegoats on whom to vent his hostility.

The most widely used measure of authoritarianism is the California F- (for fascism) scale. This scale has been criticized because only affirmative answers contribute to the authoritarianism score. Critics maintain that the scale does not necessarily measure authoritarianism, but may instead, or in part, measure a tendency to be agreeable—to acquiesce, or conform. Research indicates that there is merit in the criticism, but that as a group subjects *do* respond to the content of F-scale items, not just to their style; and that F-scale scores are related to many other behaviors that have been subsumed under the more general construct of authoritarianism.

A number of studies of authoritarianism and prejudice, using populations ranging from second-graders to senior medical students and noncollege adults from the South as well as the North, support the hypothesis that prejudice is both "normal" *and* "pathological." For example, it has been found that whites living in the South are much more prejudiced against Negroes than those living in the North; yet at the same time a high level of education serves to reduce their prejudice more than it does that of Northerners. A study of boys in an interracial summer camp indicates that simply living with those of another race does not reduce prejudice, and may even increase it—particularly for boys who are initially rather prejudiced and who seem to believe that "the world is against them."

Although most studies indicate that authoritarianism and prejudice accompany maladjustive personality traits, such findings have not always been obtained. For example, "authoritarian" young men, not well educated, who were living in a military setting, showed no signs of maladjustment. Under such circumstances, the authors of the study conclude, authoritarianism is an "approved way of life"; hence does not bring the highly authoritarian person into conflict.

Studies including as their subjects second-grade children, college students, and senior medical students reveal that measures of authoritarianism and prejudice are associated with difficulty in solving abstract problems, difficulty in learning material related to a humanitarian philosophy, difficulty in handling ambiguous academic psychiatric material, and poor personal adjustment. They are also associated with a tendency to project hostility and blame, with general cynicism, and with underlying personal insecurity.

A study of the development of prejudice shows that for white children in Austin, Texas, racial awareness begins at least as early as 4 years of age; and that Negro children apparently learn to discriminate against those of their own ethnic group. Interviews with those against whom prejudice is directed (the minority group) suggest that serious personality difficulties may develop as a result of being "prejudiced against."

CHAPTER 12

The Development of Authoritarian Personalities

THIS chapter is concerned less with the personality characteristics of the authoritarian and the prejudiced than with the question of how authoritarian personalities and prejudiced attitudes develop among families with different child-rearing practices and in different social classes. Before proceeding to this question, however, it is necessary to mention again that in investigations of child-rearing practices and social class, our concepts and methods have frequently left something to be desired. For child-rearing studies, these difficulties have been discussed in some detail in Chapters 2 and 3. With respect to social class, although there are many disagreements about its measurement, almost everyone will agree that, at the very least, there is a blue-collar class and a white-collar class. Furthermore, regardless of how social class is defined and measured, quantitative expressions of it as it exists in our society exhibit solid relations with (that is, help to predict) human attributes ranging from IQ level to capacity for delaying impulse gratification.

We have, therefore, concepts—somewhat cloudy but useful—that we may call "social class," "patterns of child-rearing," and "authoritarian personality." The concern of this chapter is with the relations among these three.

CHILD-REARING PRACTICES, PREJUDICE, AND THE AUTHORITARIAN PERSONALITY

None of the theories of authoritarianism and prejudice discussed in the preceding chapter holds that these attitudes come into being *spontaneously* or *automatically*. Both psychoanalytic and social-psychological theories accept the assumption that prejudice or an authoritarian personality is something that is *developed*. The theories posit different mechanisms for this development, but each assigns responsibility to *some* experiential, social factor; none, for example, endorses instinct or heredity as a causal dynamism.

Among the most prominent to suggest that child-rearing practices were dynamically related to later race prejudice and authoritarianism were Adorno and his colleagues (1950). As was mentioned in Chapter 11, the research of this group began with efforts to investigate race prejudice.

Studies of prejudice against various minority groups led them to the conclusion that prejudice was not usually confined to a specific minority group, but was general: for example, those prejudiced against Negroes tended to be prejudiced against Jews and Orientals as well. A broader term than prejudice—*ethnocentrism*—seems to describe this phenomenon accurately. Ethnocentrism is defined as an emotional attitude that one's own race or nation is superior to all others; and, in addition, it implies a rejection of other races, nations, or groups other than one's own.

Further studies in this general area led Adorno and his co-workers to the still broader conception of the authoritarian personality, as defined and discussed at length in the preceding chapter. The most general personality-attitude construct employed in this chapter is, then, the *authoritarian personality*. One of its most frequent manifestations—in fact, one of its *usual* manifestations—is *ethnocentrism;* ethnocentrism, in turn, is ordinarily accompanied by specific *prejudices* against minority and other outgroups. The most common measure of the authoritarian personality is the F-scale, but a very large number of specific prejudice scales exists. Some of the studies reviewed in this chapter relate to authoritarianism, but they employ only specific prejudice scales as their measure. Such studies, it should be kept in mind, relate directly to authoritarianism *only to the degree that the prejudice measure used correlates with a more general measure of authoritarianism.* In this chapter, authoritarianism is often inferred from the use in a study of a specific measure or measures of prejudice because of the often-demonstrated correlation between them; but such a study provides less convincing support for a relation between the independent variable (e.g., child-rearing practices) and authoritarianism than if a direct measure of authoritarianism had been used.

Studies of Parental Practices and Attitudes

TYPE OF DISCIPLINE

Adorno and his colleagues (1950) made inferences about the childhood and the parent-child relations of their authoritarian and nonauthoritarian, prejudiced and non prejudiced adult subjects from interview and TAT data. Frenkel-Brunswik (1948, 1951, 1953, 1954a) worked directly with children and their parents, and concluded that parents of very authoritarian and ethnocentric children used harsher and more rigid forms of discipline than parents of children scoring low in authoritarianism or ethnocentrism. She states (1954a) that ethnocentric adolescents describe "the perfect father" as disciplining, strict, punitive, and a good provider, whereas nonprejudiced children see him as companionable and relaxed. Frenkel-Brunswik found that ethnocentric children see the discipline that has been meted out to them as threatening, traumatic, overwhelming, and bewildering. She believes that these perceptions accurately reflect the type of home in which such children have been reared. Parents of ethnocentric children, she believes, do not use an individualized approach with their children, but concern themselves principally with transmitting a set of fixed rules and customs. This interferes with the children's development of a clear-cut personal identity and integration.

An interesting study by Block (1955), one of the few research workers who has used fathers as subjects, presents a picture of *actual* authoritarian parents that is very like the one Frenkel-Brunswik constructed from her interviews with authoritarian children. Block made a rather detailed personality study of the 20 high (restrictives) and 20 low (permissives) scorers on a test of child-rearing attitudes given to a group of 100 Army officers. He describes the restrictives as follows:

> The picture which emerges of the fathers expressing restrictive attitudes toward child-rearing is almost a prototype of what has been variously labelled "the authoritarian personality" or "the over-controlled." These fathers are constricted, repressing, essentially dependent individuals with great feelings of personal inadequacy. Besides over-controlling their inner needs and tensions, they find it psychologically necessary to over-control the situations within their environment for which they hold responsibility. Their approach to child-rearing, while of particular importance for the forming of personality in the child, should be understood as but one of many manifestations of their basic personality structure. (pp. 45-46)

The restrictives, according to Block:

> . . . still lack in themselves a perception of self-integrity and a differentiation of the social environment which can enable them to treat their own children differently from the way they had been treated by their own threatening fathers. In effect, the restrictive father, acting upon the residues of his own childhood anxieties, is revenging himself upon the wrong generation. This cycle of personality transmission is thus self-perpetuating but *self-defeating*.[1]

Block's implication is clearly, "like father, like son." Frenkel-Brunswik and Havel (1953) present evidence to support this implication, at least for ethnocentrism. They report correlations between ratings of parental prejudice and children's prejudice ranging from .20 to .60.

Harris, Gough, and Martin (1950) found that certain maternal attitudes toward child-rearing were related to prejudice in their child subjects. Although the results are not entirely clear-cut, they present evidence that mothers of prejudiced children were more authoritarian, fussier, tended to want quiet children, and were in general less effective with their children than mothers of nonprejudiced children.

Evidence that harsh parental treatment may result in personal attri-

[1] Reprinted with permission of W. E. Martin, Editor, *Child Develpm.*, and J. Block, from Block (1955).

butes reflecting authoritarianism has also been provided by Mussen and Kagan (1958). They measured tendencies to yield, or to conform, by a technique similar to that discussed in Chapter 11 (see p. 367). They also gave the 20 male college students who took part in their study the TAT, evaluating the stories told according to how severely the heroes were punished by story characters judged to represent their parents or other authorities. The subjects whose TAT scores indicated that they had received high punishment from their parents (or, at least, believed they had) were significantly more often yielders than "independents"; those whose scores indicated mild punishment were more often independent in their judgments.

Harsh parents, Mussen and Kagan conclude, may have more conflicts with their children: their children, then, have more experiences with their parents in which yielding, or conforming, reduces anxiety. Consequently, through generalization, these children adopt yielding as a way of life. Mussen and Kagan also state that conformists have been shown to manifest marked distrust toward other people, which, they speculate, "may also be generalized responses stemming from original fear and distrust of the parents." (p. 60)

Further evidence supporting the fact that types of parental punishment affect the child's notion of appropriate punishment, as well as his need to direct hostility and punishment toward others, has been provided by Radke (1946) and Lyle and Levitt (1955). Radke's study indicates that children prescribe for others the same sorts of punishment they receive from their parents; and Lyle and Levitt have demonstrated, for a fifth-grade population, that there is a correlation between children's authoritarianism and their tendency to see their parents as punitive. Authoritarianism and punitiveness on the part of the children were also found to be related. These correlations, although not high, were statistically significant.

Such studies as those by Mussen and Kagan, and Lyle and Levitt, raise the extremely important question of whether children's *perception* of their parents' behavior accurately reflects the parents' *actual* behavior. Few studies have been done that bear on this important question, but what evidence is available indicates that children both perceive and report their parents' behavior more or less accurately, and that boys are as accurate as girls. Bronson, Katten, and Livson (1959), for example, found that children's ratings of parents' behavior in the areas of authority, affection, and involvement were in all instances highly and significantly related to psychologists' ratings of the parents. One hundred families who had been studied for eighteen years were involved in the study, making it quite convincing.

Still other studies suggest relations between authoritarian attitudes and methods of rearing children. For example, Hart (1957) administered the Traditional Family Ideology scale, which presumably measures authoritarian trends in child-rearing practices and family organization, to 126 mothers of children aged 2½ to 5½. She also conducted interviews with the mothers about their practices concerning feeding and oral activities, cleanliness training, sexual behavior, aggression, and dependent and independent behavior of their children. On the basis of the interview material, Hart classified the mothers' responses into two categories: love-oriented and nonlove-oriented techniques of control. She found that the higher a mother's authoritarianism score, the more she tended to use non-love-oriented techniques. Correlations in the area of complex human behavior usually run rather low—in the .20's, .30's, sometimes in the .40's and .50's—but Hart found the correlation between mothers' authoritarianism and the number of situations in which nonlove-oriented techniques were used to be a highly significant .63. Such factors as the age of mother and child, sex and birth order of the child, and number of children in the family bore no relation to mothers' authoritarianism.

The scale used in Hart's study—the Traditional Family Ideology—correlates .73 with a version of the F-scale (as reported by Titus and Hollander, 1957, in a review of literature dealing with the F-scale).

CHILD-REARING ATTITUDES

Zuckerman and his colleagues (1958) indicate that harsh child-rearing attitudes accompany high authoritarianism as measured by the F-scale. Their correlation between harshness, as measured by the child-rearing attitudes scale, and the F-scale was almost identical with that found by Hart: .61, despite the fact that they did not use mothers, but 88 student nurses, as subjects. Zuckerman and his co-workers took elaborate steps to eliminate the "yielding" or "response-set" influence on the F-scale (discussed in detail in Chapter 11); even with this influence controlled, the correlation between their measures remained in the .40's.

Kates and Diab (1955) used both men and women college students as subjects in a study to determine the relation between authoritarianism and child-rearing attitudes. They found correlations for their women subjects to be in the .30's (for the most part) between presumably "pathogenic" (poor) child-rearing attitudes and authoritarianism; but uncovered *no* relation between child-rearing attitudes and authoritarianism for the men.

This last study, taken in conjunction with others reviewed in this section, suggests that, among college students, child-rearing practices may be of more concern to women than to men, perhaps because of the emphasis of our culture. It is appropriate, even necessary, for girls and young women to interest themselves in children, their care, and their development; but such an interest is not expected to be manifested by men, particularly unmarried men. In addition, college women, more than their male classmates, may have had experience in caring for younger sibs, baby-sitting, and so on.

Since psychology is a young science, its students, teachers, and practitioners must be tolerant of ambiguity, uncertain results, and the lack of flatly demonstrated generalizations. From the studies that exist for a given area, they must determine the most likely trend and hope for further definitive research—or, even better, do such research themselves. But they must not overlook negative evidence. Gallagher (1957), for example, has done a study with college students somewhat similar to those summarized above, but found no relation between authoritarianism and attitudes that were judged to represent harshness toward children. However, he did not perform separate analyses for the 44 college women and the 15 college men who took part in his study, and it may be that results for the college men reduced his correlations. In addition, the scale of attitudes toward children used by Gallagher was not a *direct* measure of child-rearing attitudes. It included, for example, items related to information about child development; and there is no particular reason to expect a relation between authoritarianism and factual knowledge about how children develop. In other words, Gallagher's results introduce a note of caution into our conclusions for this subsection; but, because his methods differed from those of investigators who obtained positive results, his study is not directly comparable and its results cannot be clearly considered contradictory.

Taken together, the studies reviewed in this section suggest that authoritarian and prejudiced children are more likely to have parents who are overcontrolling and who use predominantly nonlove-oriented child-rearing techniques. Fathers holding harsh child-rearing attitudes seem to have patterned themselves on their own fathers, to be rather unaware of the individual needs of their children, and to feel personally inadequate.

The evidence indicates that children adopt their parents' attitudes: prejudiced children tend to come from prejudiced homes, and children who have been reared punitively seem themselves to be punitive. At least one study indicates that parents who are perceived by their children as punitive may produce conforming or yielding children.

An important question about this area of research is: Do children's perceptions of their parents represent what the parents are *actually* like? At least one study, using a sizable sample of 100 families, indicates that the children's perceptions of their parents agree by and large with the judgments of professional psychologists who have studied the parents.

Other research indicates that relations between personality characteristics and attitudes toward child-rearing may be a function of direct personal involvement with children. At college age, such relations have been found for women (who, according to the dictates of our culture, should be interested in children, even though not yet mothers), but not for men. But correlations between child-rearing attitudes and personality characteristics have been found for older men who *are* fathers.

The emphasis in this section on the desirability of love-oriented techniques of child-rearing should not lead one to the belief that spontaneous expressions of feeling, even to the point of a spanking, are irreparably damaging to children. The important factor may be, not *absolute consistency* of love-oriented techniques, but their *predominance*.

Some Other Correlates of Authoritarianism and Prejudice

In Chapter 11 the distinction was made between normal and pathological prejudice. Christie and Garcia (1951) were interested at least as much in the determinants of normal prejudice as in the antecedents of pathological prejudice (which has been the focus of the preceding subsection). They selected 57 pairs of college students, one of each pair from California, the other from "Southwest City." They characterize Southwest City as a town that might have come directly from Sinclair Lewis' *Babbitt*. Their pairs were well-matched: for example, on sex, age, fathers' median income, political preference, and so on. The distributions of F- and E (thnocentrism)-scores for the two samples (as well as the larger samples from which the matched pairs were drawn) were very similar in type, but the *average* scores were much higher for the Southwest City subjects. F- and E-scores were highly correlated: .63 for Southwest City, .56 for California subjects. Christie and Garcia conclude:

> Less psychoanalytically oriented theorists than Adorno and his colleagues might speculate that lifelong immersion in an implicitly authoritarian subculture establishes the frame of reference underlying one's perception of the world and the value judgments made about human nature, and that this factor would account for the increased evidences of authoritarianism in Southwest City. (p. 469)

Young, Benson, and Holtzman (1960) have also published a study related to environmental influences on anti-Negro prejudice (although they did not concern themselves with the broader concepts of authoritarianism). They report that the prejudiced attitudes of University of Texas undergraduate students are remarkably resistant to change. The three years of ferment over desegregation between 1955 and 1958 had produced no *average* changes in prejudice score—that is, the average prejudice score of a sample of University of Texas undergraduates measured in 1955 was almost identical with the average score of a comparable group measured in 1958. However, there were *sex differences* in change: men students, as a group, had become *more* prejudiced; women less prejudiced. Since, according to theory, women (mothers and future mothers) transmit the culture, there is some encouragement about tolerance in their finding.

Young, Benson, and Holtzman divided their large sample of students (508 in number) into a number of subgroups in order to study various factors that might relate to prejudice. Eight personal and demographic factors were found to be associated with anti-Negro prejudice at a statistically significant level:

1. *Area of residence.* Students who came from east Texas were most prejudiced; those from west Texas were intermediate in prejudice; and those from the Rio Grande Valley were least prejudiced.

2. *Religious affiliation.* Of the major religious groupings studied, Baptists showed the highest prejudice; Catholic students were intermediate; and Jewish students were least prejudiced.

3. *Church attendance.* Those who attended church *very* regularly and those who did not attend church *at all* were less prejudiced than those who claimed that they attended church once or twice a month.

4. *Scholastic standing.* Students earning good grades (B average or above) had lower prejudice scores than those earning poor grades (C average or below).

5. *Type of curriculum.* Social science majors were the least prejudiced group; pharmacy and business majors showed the highest prejudice.

6. *Urban-rural residence.* Students who had come from urban areas (cities of more than 50,000 population) were less prejudiced than students residing in small-town and rural settings.

7. *Fraternity-sorority membership.* Members of sororities and fraternities were more prejudiced than nonmembers.

8. *Fathers' reported income.* Students who claimed that their fathers earned more than $20,000 per year were significantly more prejudiced than those who reported paternal income as $5,000 per year or less.

Another interesting study investigated the relations between religious devoutness and anti-Semitic and anti-Negro attitudes (no direct measure of authoritarianism was used). O'Reilly and O'Reilly (1954) devised a scale of devoutness—the "extent to which the subjects (Ss) agreed with the Catholic Church on certain social, moral, and religious questions." (p. 378) This scale was administered, along with anti-Semitism and anti-Negro prejudice scales, to 92 men and 120 women attending Roman Catholic universities and seminaries. Almost all the subjects reported that religion had had a very marked influence on their upbringing.

For women, the devoutness scale correlated .39 with the anti-Semitism scale; for men the correlation was .31. The anti-Negro and anti-Semitism scales were rather highly correlated (.69 for women and .68 for men). Students scoring high on the devoutness scale also favored parish segregation for Negroes. Of those who favored segregation, 76.5 percent scored in the upper half of the devoutness scale, whereas 74.5 percent of those scoring low on the devoutness scale opposed parish segregation. As far as the present author knows, data do not exist concerning parental practices and children's devoutness, but it is reasonable to predict that there are significant relations of some type.

It has been argued, more often from clinical than from formal research evidence, that minority groups, or "inferiors," adopt—even *over*-adopt—the attitudes of the majority group, or their "superiors"—perhaps as a matter of self-protection. The butler may be more snobbish than his employer, the headwaiter haughtier than the prosperous clientele he serves, the "poor white" more prejudiced toward Negroes than members of his ethnic group who are above him in social class. Two studies are interesting in this connection. Authoritarian ideology in Negro college students has been studied by Steckler (1957), who concluded that Negro students were very conservative and that, in general, there was evidence that they had "identified with the aggressor"—that is, adopted the values and attitudes of the majority group. C. U. Smith and Prothro (1957) actually found that southern white freshman students scored lower on the F-scale than Negro college freshmen from the same state.

In other words, the conditions of one's rearing and his own status are likely to be related to attitudes of authoritarianism or equalitarianism. Those growing up in authoritarian surroundings acquire authoritarian patterns of reaction; and those who experience prejudice may become even more authoritarian than those who exercise prejudice.

AUTHORITARIANISM AND SOCIAL CLASS

Less is known about the relation between socioeconomic status and authoritarianism than about child-rearing practices and authoritarianism. Before the topic can be usefully approached, an attempt must be made to arrive at general but differential descriptions of lower- and middle-class child-rearing practices. This is a difficult task.

For present purposes, two papers have been selected that attempt to define the relation between lower- and middle-class parents and their children. The author grants his possible bias in selecting these particular studies, although his own general and professional clinical experience is congruent with their conclusions. This whole question is discussed more fully in Chapter 14.

Maas (1951), using interview techniques with a small sample of ten- to fifteen-year-olds, some from the lower-lower class, the others from the "core culture" (an amalgam of lower-middle and upper-lower classes), contrasted child-rearing practices of the two groups as he inferred them from the interview. There was greater social freedom and tolerance of physical aggression in the lives of the lower-class children; but, at the same time, they had experienced a psychologically closed, hierarchical, and quite rigid parental relationship. The core-culture children, on the other hand, reported a more open, relatively equalitarian and flexible relationship. Lower-class parents were seen as relatively closed and inaccessible to the child's communications, and the child was relatively mute with them because of the threat of explosive anger. Core-culture children did not seem fearful of expressing either positive or negative attitudes toward their parents, nor did they either fear or identify with the potentially threatening power of adults; lower-class children often experienced intense fear of parents and expressed feelings of rejection or unworthiness because of disobedience. Such children, under duress, may explode in a manner similar to their parents, or redirect their hostile aggression (as well as tender feelings) toward siblings or other contemporaries.

Maccoby and her colleagues (1954) found that, in general, lower-

Authoritarian Personalities

class mothers espoused more rigid child-rearing practices, used more physical punishment, and allowed less aggression toward parents than did middle-class parents.

Viewed in this framework, the following results fit together moderately well:

Singer (1954), using TAT protocols obtained from a normal and a schizophrenic population of men, found some evidence for warmer family and father-son relationships among middle- than among lower-class subjects.

Cass (1950, 1952*a*, 1952*b*) investigated the relation between mothers' awareness of their daughters and the identification of the daughters with the mothers. To measure identification, she asked four different groups of mothers (two middle-, two lower-class) to fill in a check list of favorite interests and activities. When the pattern of a daughter's check list was quite similar to her mother's, Cass considered her highly identified, and vice versa. The mothers were also asked to predict how their daughters would fill in the check list. The more accurate the mother was about her daughter, the more "aware" of her daughter she was considered to be.

A rather high relation was found between mothers' awareness and daughters' identification for the two groups of middle-class mothers of nondelinquent daughters ($r = .59$ and $.48$). For the two groups of lower-class mothers and daughters there was a low relationship between these variables. For lower-class mothers and nondelinquent daughters, the correlation was $.32$; for lower-class mothers and delinquent daughters, the correlation was only $.11$.

Cass also found that average scores for awareness and identification were higher for middle- than for lower-class mothers and daughters.[2] The average awareness scores for the middle-class mothers were between 13 and 14 (these figures represent the number of items checked by the daughter that were accurately predicted by the mother); the lower-class mothers of nondelinquents scored 12 items correct; the lower-class mothers of delinquents, 8. Identification scores for middle-class daughters averaged about 9; for lower-class daughters about 7.4.

Cohn and Carsch (1954) found significant F-scale differences between a group of 117 German factory workers who had attended only *Volkschule,* or *Volkschule* and *Mittelschule* (less well educated), and a better-educated group of 23 subjects who had attended *Hochschule.* The mean F-scale scores were 5.40 and 4.57 respectively, this difference being significant at less than the .01 level. (The higher the score, the more authoritarian the person is considered to be.)

Finally, Adorno and his colleagues report, among other relations, the

[2] These figures come from personal communication with Dr. Cass, and, although they are in the expected direction, the differences have not been tested for statistical significance.

following mean F-scale scores for combined University of Oregon and University of California groups: 3.39 for men and 3.82 for women; for middle-class men and women, 3.62 and 3.69, respectively; and for working-class women and men, 3.86 and 4.19, respectively. A preponderantly upper-lower-class group of Maritime Service men scored an average of 4.06; and a group of San Quentin prisoners, mostly lower-class, scored 4.73. A group of professional women scored 3.43.

The evidence of a relation between lower-class socioeconomic status and authoritarianism is tenuous, but a connection is suggested. If verified, it seems logical to suggest that this relation is due to an interaction between child-rearing practices, general educational-cultural factors, and social threat, with lower-class parents as a group using stricter and less love-oriented ways of bringing up children, having a less adequate education, and being more vulnerable to threat from authoritarian figures in general (such as the police and the boss). In addition, they are more directly in contact and competition with minority groups; hence are more likely to be threatened by them.

THE DEVELOPMENT OF AUTHORITARIANISM

A tentative theory of why authoritarian children differ from equalitarian children is advanced in this section of the chapter. It will be noted that in the present treatment, learning theory has been enriched by psychoanalytic theory, which, in turn, has been sharpened by learning theory. The latter, influenced by sociological theory, takes more account of "normal" prejudice than psychoanalytic theory does. It should be noted that a number of the predictions made from social-learning theory are similar to those that would be made within a Freudian framework, particularly as developed by Frenkel-Brunswik (e.g., 1948, 1954a).

Theory can often be most economically developed by dealing with the extremes of the population distribution: hence, this section is concerned with children who are extremely authoritarian, considered as a group; and with children who are extremely equalitarian, considered as a group. The assumption is made that child-rearing practices for the two groups will differ sharply, with a minimum of overlap between the attitudes and methods of parents of authoritarians and parents of equalitarians. These extreme groups, of course, form a very small part of the total population, so that most parents fall somewhere between consistent and extreme authoritarianism and consistent and extreme equalitarianism. Similarly, few or no children or adults can be expected to be "all" authoritarian or "all" equalitarian in personality characteristics. The concept of the authoritarian personality is complex, so that a person may show high prejudice, for example, but at the same time be moderately flexible in behavior and attitudes. Nor, human nature being what it is, is it likely that the most extremely authoritarian parent is authoritarian in *all* his practices with his children *all* the time. But he will differ from the equalitarian parent in being *more* authoritarian *more* of the time.

Child-Rearing Practices and Intolerance of Ambiguity

The first major hypothesis about authoritarian parents is that they are personally intolerant of ambiguity. They like things clear-cut; ambiguous and tentative situations or problem-solutions make them uncomfortable; and they prefer the absolute to the relative. Hence, in contrast to equalitarian parents, they tend to use an either-or approach to child-rearing: depending on the situation and the child's behavior, they are either all-punishing or all-rewarding. Discipline and punishment are not diluted with tenderness, acceptance, and reasoning. Conversely, love and approval, when given, are unmixed with reservations or qualifications. This all-or-none attitude is perhaps due to the fact that authoritarian parents do not question the correctness of their behavior with their children, and at any given time they may actually perceive the child as "all bad" or "all good."

This either-or method of treatment will have very different effects upon the child, depending on his chronological age. Up to about 2 or 2½ years of age, before he is able to use or understand complex verbal symbols, he will see this parental treatment as highly inconsistent and arbitrary. That is, from *his* point of view, the child is doing nothing more than behaving naturally. He does not discern his behavior as good or bad, right or wrong. His parents receive some of it with punishment and rejection, some with affection and reward; but he is unable to make the proper or appropriate reference of the parents' treatment *back to his behavior.* Such a state of affairs bears a resemblance to the concept of partial (or at least inconsistent) reinforcement, and may produce at least two major effects. The first of these concerns the child's emerging self-concept and his relationship with his parents. Since the parents' treatment is perceived as arbitrary, the child's self-concept may become (at least temporarily) quite confused and his attitudes toward himself ambivalent. Similarly, his attitudes toward the parent-child relation will be confused and ambivalent—Erikson's mistrust and premature bipolarity (p. 317)?

However, the child will come eventually, but with difficulty and through trial and error, to associate a preponderance of reward with, for example, behavior A (keeping himself clean); and of punishment with behavior B (wetting his pants). Hence he will consolidate behavior A and extinguish B, even though the *earlier* history of both behaviors *as seen by him* has been one of partial or inconsistent reinforcement (it is perhaps not entirely justifiable to consider partial and inconsistent reinforcement as equivalent, although in principle they have much in common). However, even after the child has learned what his parents expect of him, the ambivalent attitudes engendered during this learning process are likely to be retained, although perhaps not at a conscious level.

After effective verbal mediation—true speech—sets in, the child will see his parents' reinforcements as they intend and practice them: that is, as highly consistent.

Equalitarian parents, on the other hand, may tend more than authoritarians simply to accept their children until they are old enough to make appropriate references of differential parental reinforcements to their behavior. Hence, during early childhood, the child of nonauthoritarian parents experiences relatively consistent and positive reinforcement: his behavior, undifferentiated by him, is met with equally undifferentiated acceptance and love on the part of his parents.

From this first hypothesis, that parents of authoritarian children are themselves authoritarian and intolerant of ambiguity, four predictions follow logically:

1. The things that the authoritarian child eventually learns through his parents' teaching are relatively difficult to extinguish, since, from the child's point of view, they have been not only excessively but partially or inconsistently reinforced. It may be that partial reinforcement for humans produces responses that are more difficult to extinguish than responses that have been established through consistent reinforcement. There is some evidence that this holds true for animals as well as children. It may also be that extreme reinforcements (either rewards or punishments) produce more rapid (and possibly better) learning than mild reinforcements, although evidence on this point is not clear.

2. The responses of the child of authoritarian parents will be more intense than those of the child of nonauthoritarian parents, since frustration has added to his ordinary drive level.

3. The child of authoritarian parents will develop clear, persistent, and widely generalized expectancies of punishment in new or unclear situations. With these expectancies will be associated subjective discomfort and anxiety, producing a condition resembling "intolerance of ambiguity."

This prediction (as well as the first) is based on evidence that some of the responses associated with secondary drives, such as anxiety, are extremely difficult to extinguish. Hence such intolerance of unclarity may be exceedingly persistent. Also, some evidence exists that punishment or reward administered in unstructured situations is generalized more widely than in situations that are clearly structured (Levy and McCandless, 1952). There is evidence that younger children (7 through 9 years of age) generalize more frequently and widely than children 10 through 12 years of age (Mednick and Lehtinen, 1957). Finally, it may be that anxiety and stress situations result in increased generalization. Hence, the child will be persistently anxious in a wide-ranging series of unclear or ambiguous situations, not *just* those similar to situations in which he has been punished; and his anxious responses will be extinguished with difficulty.

4. With age and increasing ability to mediate verbally, the child learns to refer the social rewards and punishments he receives to the appropriate

behavior. Then, like his parents, the authoritarian child comes to react dichotomously (in an either-or fashion), and to make sharp distinctions between, for example, "right" and "wrong." Such distinctions are unusually intense and persistent because they help the child to ward off or allay anxiety; they are facilitated because he has become able, through acquiring language and increased time perspective, to realize the consistency of his parents' reinforcements, which are now seen as relevant to his behavior. It is possible that authoritarian parents are *objectively* more consistent than nonauthoritarian parents in their child-rearing behavior, although in his runabout years, their child may not have perceived this consistency.

Child-Rearing Practices and Child Conformity

The second major hypothesis about the families of authoritarian children is that the parents, themselves highly conforming to approved adult standards of behavior, will give strong positive reinforcement to their children for acting in socially sanctioned ("adult") ways, such as being quiet, orderly, and successful in competition. Deviant or "childish" behavior will be punished with equal strength. From the point of view of the parent and the *older child* (although not from that of the *very young child*), such reward and punishment are consistent as well as strong. This hypothesis leads to two predictions:

1. The child of authoritarian parents will develop clear, easily available, and consistent methods of responding to familiar situations, and will suffer from little apparent indecision, self-doubt, or conflict in such situations, although anxiety may underlie his seemingly assured behavior.

2. It will be more than usually difficult for the child of authoritarian parents to learn to make different or new responses to familiar situations and stimuli: he has a standard way of responding, and it is difficult for him to change.

Quality of Reward

The third major hypothesis argues that for the authoritarian as well as the equalitarian parent, rewards to the child will usually exceed punishments in frequency, since parents ordinarily prefer the positive to the negative approach, love their children, and want to do the best they know for them. But the rewards of authoritarian parents (see also the first hypothesis in this section, p. 396) will be less diluted, or more intense. Two predictions follow from this consideration:

1. The child of authoritarian parents will perceive his parents as need-gratifiers to a greater degree than the child of equalitarians, since authoritarian parents present themselves as "always right," whereas equalitarians are often frankly uncertain.

This situation may change sharply at adolescence, when the child seeks independence from his parents, begins to question the values by which he has been brought up, looks more searchingly at society and the value systems of families other than his own, and often becomes rebellious. At this time, the child of the authoritarian parent, particularly if his upbringing has been short on love, may reject the parental image sharply; whereas, in the equalitarian home that has been rich in love, the child may see that his parents are really "not so bad after all," and make a final, adult, and lasting identification with them and their values.

2. The authoritarian child will pattern his attitudes and behavior after his parents, perhaps to a greater degree than the child of the non-authoritarian family, since, by the nature of his training, he will strive more to please, and not to offend, his parents. They, having no conscious question of their own rightness, will reward him strongly and consistently for patterning after them. The equalitarian parent, more thoughtful and, at the superficial level at least, less sure of his own admirability, may view such imitative patterning with mixed feelings.

If equalitarian parents have given their child much love, and have used predominantly love-oriented techniques of control, we would expect the child to be sensitive to his parents' feelings and considerate of them— that is, to strive to please them, just like the child of authoritarian parents. He will not see a straight-line pattern of "modeling after them" as the *only* way to please them, nor will they themselves. But he *will* strive for behavior models that satisfy not only himself but his parents.

The behavior modeling of the authoritarian child may go in either of two ways: *copying,* which will involve close modeling on the parents' attitudes and values; or *rebellion,* in which the child seeks to make himself as different from his parents as possible in all of his values, beliefs, and behaviors. How many beatniks have come from authoritarian homes?

Source of Reward

The fourth hypothesis about the development of authoritarianism is that authoritarian parents are more likely than equalitarian parents to teach their children that *all* rewards and punishments come from them. This hypothesis leads to two predictions:

1. For children of authoritarian parents, persons (including other "authority figures") who are easily differentiated (distinctly different) from their parents afford them little positive *or* negative reinforcement. They do not regard the rewards that such people can offer them as worth while (or they mistrust these rewards); and they are not afraid of the punishment such people can administer. Hence their disregard and perhaps contempt for weak (including minority-group) persons, or permissive teachers, or kindly neighbors.

2. The child of authoritarian parents, who has been taught that his parents are all-powerful, will expect that all of his behavior, conforming or deviant, will come to light (will be judged). Hence, he will be more con-forming than the nonauthoritarian youngster, will have a high expectation and fear of retaliation for misdeeds, and will be more accepting of and

influenced by external techniques of control. He will not wish to be conspicuous, except possibly in such socially approved areas as academic competition. He may be uncomfortable even then, particularly if he is "too good." However, he will misbehave if he is quite certain that he will not be caught, or if he has no fear of (or respect for) the person who might possibly catch him.

Concern with Status and Power

The fifth hypothesis suggests that very authoritarian parents are more concerned with status and power than with love and affection. Their child may thus be viewed by them as an enhancer of their own status and power rather than as an individual in his own right. This hypothesis also leads to two predictions:

1. The children of authoritarians will learn to gratify their own love and affection needs by developing techniques for satisfying status and power needs, will frequently be unrealistic in their ideas of the socially valued goals they can reach, and will value external success (status and power) disproportionately. Ausubel and his colleagues (1954) have found that children who believe their parents to hold a primarily "extrinsic" valuation of them—like them for what they can do, rather than for what they are— *do* have unrealistically optimistic ideas of their ability to be successful, often have unrealistic levels of aspiration, and hold to these aspiration levels with a tenacity outside the limits of common sense or adaptive behavior.

2. The child of authoritarian parents will be relatively task-oriented and matter-of-fact, and will manifest relatively little overt affection-seeking behavior (not, at least, as an older child—as a preschooler, he may be more dependent than average, seeking to make up for what he does not get at home). He will seek to gain *approval* through independent, task-oriented behavior, but will do little direct seeking of *love*. This type of *task-* rather than *person*-orientation may have been forced on him early in his life through the control techniques mentioned in the discussion of hypothesis 1 (p. 396)—that is, the methods of control applied to him as a very young child have resulted in his perception of human relations as anxiety-provoking rather than security-giving. He has also learned to devalue himself as a person, and has come to realize that he cannot be loved for himself but only *approved* or *disapproved* of on the basis of his *objective* performance.

This last consideration, coupled with the others that have been introduced, suggests why authoritarians have been said to be anti-intraceptive (i.e., to dislike thinking about and looking into themselves). They dislike intraception because, if they look too closely at themselves, they see the ambivalences, uncertainties, and insecurities for which they are compensating. It is more comfortable to keep thought and attention fixed securely on the objective world and on measurable achievement.

Trust and Hostility in Authoritarians

The five hypotheses that have been developed on the preceding pages, when considered together, lead us to two further general predictions. The *first* of these is that the child of authoritarian parents will lack trust, and probably be less optimistic than the child of nonauthoritarian parents.

Second, the child of authoritarian parents will have built up more of a reservoir of hostility than the child of equalitarian parents (e.g., Siegel, 1956). Because of the nature of his relations with his parents, he cannot reduce this hostility by directing it at them or their surrogates. It seems permissible to conjecture that he relieves the pressure of this reservoir of hostility by displacement either to "safe" objects and persons, or to equally safe fantasy, or perhaps to both.

The term "reservoir" is not a satisfactory one. Nor do we have any plausible theory about how a "reservoir of hostility" might be built up and maintained, although we see that there are chronically hostile people around us. However, such a concept may not be necessary in this context. Because they are frustrating and threatening, an authoritarian has reason to be hostile to others who are not rule-bound, who present him with ambiguous situations, who (from his point of view) are immoral, who were or are disliked by his parents, or who are socially prescribed objects of hostility.

Three additional considerations may be advanced to account for authoritarianism in the lower class. First, lower-class children are not as well educated as middle-class children. Other things being equal, the lower the educational level, the higher the authoritarianism and prejudice. Second, lower-class children lead more difficult lives in all respects, from their experience of parental discipline on through personal insecurity, than middle-class children. Such frustrating circumstances produce aggression; this cannot, as has been mentioned, be safely expressed toward parents and peers. Hence it is displaced to, among others, those belonging to minority groups. Third, lower-class people have to live shoulder-to-shoulder with minority-group persons, who also compete with them for jobs, housing, and so on; hence, minorities are directly frustrating in a sense that they are not for the middle class.

SUMMARY

This chapter has concerned itself with the question of how authoritarian personalities and prejudiced attitudes develop among families with different child-rearing practices and in different social classes. The three major concepts involved are *child-rearing practices, social class,* and *the authoritarian personality.* In some of the studies cited in the chapter, a measure of *prejudice* has been used to infer authoritarianism; although high correlations have usually been found between the two, such an inference supplies less convincing evidence for the conclusions reached than do studies using a more direct measure of authoritarianism.

With some exceptions, research on parental attitudes and authoritarianism indicates that overcontrolling parents who employ predominantly nonlove-oriented control and socialization techniques are most likely to bring up children who are authoritarian, and that authoritarianism in parents is related to espousal of harsh child-rearing practices. Such a relationship between authoritarianism and severe child-rearing attitudes has usually been obtained in studies using women as subjects, whether the women were mothers or not; for men, the relationship has been found only when the subjects were *actually* fathers. This finding suggests that personality-attitude relationships may occur principally in areas that are of *personal* importance.

Studies of both fathers and mothers suggest that those holding harsh child-rearing attitudes are likely to be unaware of the needs of their children and to feel personally inadequate. Evidence also suggests that children emulate their parents' attitudes, including authoritarianism and prejudice, although correlations between the attitudes of children and their parents have not been uniformly high.

Many studies of parental attitudes and practices utilize a technique of asking the child to evaluate his parents, rather than observing the parents directly. In evaluating these studies, one must ask: How accurately does the child's perception or judgment of his parent reflect the behavior of the parent? At least one study indicates that the level of accuracy is rather high.

Several studies indicate that both authoritarianism and prejudice vary markedly depending (apparently regardless of child-rearing practices) on whether one has been exposed to a culture in which authoritarianism and prejudice are tolerated or approved. In communities where prejudice is accepted, children and young people manifest more prejudiced attitudes than where it is not accepted. Some evidence exists to indicate that members of minority groups may actually adopt the authoritarian and prejudiced attitudes they have experienced at the hands of the majority group.

There is moderately supportive evidence for a relation between authoritarianism and prejudice, on the one hand, and membership in the lower socioeconomic class on the other, probably because of a combination of factors: lower-class parents seem to employ harsher child-rearing methods than middle-class parents; lower-class children are more directly exposed to threat and receive less reward from authority figures in general; and lower-class children are more likely to live in a highly frustrating situation (characterized by overcrowding, poverty, and so on) where they are forced into competition with minority-group children—first in play and school and, later, for employment.

In the concluding section of the chapter five major hypotheses relating to the development of authoritarianism were formulated: (1) Authoritarian parents are intolerant of ambiguity; (2) authoritarian parents, much more than equalitarian parents, reward their children for social conformity and punish them for individualism or social deviation; (3) like equalitarian parents, authoritarian parents ordinarily give more rewards than punishments to their children, but their rewards are greater and less qualified; (4) more than equalitarian parents, authoritarian mothers and fathers set themselves up as exclusive need-gratifiers; and (5) authoritarian parents are relatively more concerned with status and power than with love and affection, whereas the reverse is true for equalitarian parents.

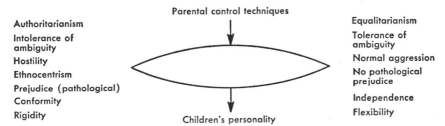

Parental control techniques

Authoritarianism	Equalitarianism
Intolerance of ambiguity	Tolerance of ambiguity
Hostility	Normal aggression
Ethnocentrism	No pathological prejudice
Prejudice (pathological)	
Conformity	Independence
Rigidity	Flexibility

Children's personality

Fig. 12.1. One theoretical view of the relation between authoritarian-equalitarian and other personality dimensions. The necessary clustering of traits as diagrammed has been questioned by some research workers, as has the concept of authoritarianism as a unitary trait.

From these five hypotheses, a number of predictions were made. For example: It will be more difficult to change the behavior of an authoritarian than of an equalitarian child; authoritarian children, like their parents, will be intolerant of ambiguity, authoritarian children will have more latent hostility than equalitarian children, and will be less trusting; the authoritarian child, in familiar, well-charted situations, will behave at least as efficiently as, and perhaps more efficiently than, the equalitarian child.

Chapters 12 and 13 should be regarded as interlocking with each other and, together, as representing the vitally important area of attitude formation and the translation of attitudes into behavior. It is to be hoped that the following generalizations have been made explicit in these two chapters:

1. Authoritarianism, ethnocentrism, and prejudice are related but not identical concepts and, like almost every other major social attitude, may be either "normal" or "pathological," or both. This is another way of saying that they may be directly learned and, like any other direct, cognitive learning, fairly easily changed as a person acquires new information; or they may be expressions of deeeply ingrained, even fixated, personality needs, in which case change will be much more difficult.

2. Regardless of whether an attitude is normal or pathological, parental attitudes and child-rearing practices have played a substantial role in its development; but the general culture has also affected it.

3. Authoritarianism is a very *general* concept, defined in many ways. Its various operational definitions are sometimes, in some groups and in

some people, highly related to the general concept; but in other groups and in other people, the relations may be much lower. For *groups,* prejudice and authoritarianism usually show a high correlation; but for a given group (for example, in a stable, well-adjusted group of young people growing up in the Deep South), the correlation may be low. It should not be forgotten, either, that generalizations of only a moderate level of confidence (for example, based on a correleation of .50) cannot in any definitive way be applied to an individual. A correlation of .50 accounts for only 25 percent of the variance of the variable one is attempting to predict. In other words, an individual may be very rigid in some or many of his attitudes and behaviors, *but* at the same time be unprejudiced and equalitarian, hold little or no latent hostility toward his parents, and be thoroughly extroverted.

4. Concerning authoritarianism, as for almost all other important social attitudes, more questions remain to *be* answered than have *been* answered. Because of the necessity of integrating the large amount of complex material in Chapters 12 and 13, the author has been forced to look for trends and general laws, to formulate conclusions, and to make summaries. He has had to assume that studies using very different methods, but coming out with about the same results, *really* bear on the question to which he has related them. He has had to accept as suggestive results that, although significant statistically, are not powerful in predicting either groups or individuals (e.g., correlations in the .20's and .30's). One cannot, in other words, regard the conclusions reached from the literature on social attitudes as being as firm as conclusions reached from the literature on intelligence or physical growth. Attitudes are less tangible; research tools are more ambiguous and usually both less reliable and less valid; and theory is both looser and more complex.

Nevertheless, important suggestions have come and are coming from research on personal-social attitudes; and the task of the researcher or writer in the area, while immensely difficult, is also immensely important both to the science of psychology and to society.

Child Development and Childhood Education

A SOCIETY stands or falls according to its values. If these meet the needs of the majority of its citizens, and if it resists destruction from without, then a society stands. If its values do not provide for its citizens' welfare, or if they are intolerably threatening to other societies, or if the organization of the society cannot withstand outside pressure, then (at least this has been true in the past) the society falls. One of the most important—perhaps the most important of the factors in the continuity of a society is the transmission of knowledge and values to the society's young.

Earlier chapters (particularly 3 and 10) have discussed relations between parents and children and have explored the effect of the culture on the child's daily living. But little has been said about another profound influence on United States children—the public and private schools as they affect the academic, personal, social, intellectual, and physical development of their charges.

For understandable reasons, the areas of academic growth and change have been most carefully investigated. Measuring instruments have been devised for all sorts of academic skills. But only surface knowledge exists concerning the influence of schools on children's personal, social, motor, and intellectual development. The reasons for this dearth of knowledge are several. The community's first expectation is that the school should transmit the substantive (or factual) culture to its pupils. Dispute rages about its responsibility for other areas of development. Partly for this reason, research in such areas as personality has been neglected. Also, it is relatively easier to conduct research about academic growth: the questions to be asked are quite clear; no one quarrels about the legitimacy of the research; and techniques of measuring academic achievement are comparatively clear-cut and easy to develop.

But no phase of development proceeds independently, and all phases need to be studied. There is urgent need for more research dealing with such topics as teaching methods of all sorts, special educational procedures, and the effect of recreational programs on social skills and motor development. An example of a relatively simple (but as yet unanswered) question is: Do United States toys and recreational programs neglect the development of the child's torso, arms, and shoulders? We know that our children tricycle, bicycle, and run, thereby developing their breathing capacity and leg muscles. But do they pull and climb and lift sufficiently for the optimal development of their arms, shoulders, and backs? The incidence of creaking backs among the middle-aged (and not-so-middle-aged) suggests, but does not prove, that this type of development has been neglected.

There are more questions than answers about the impact of the public schools on the development of United States children. These questions can be answered only through research, and research in the public, private, and parochial schools demands conviction on the part of teachers and school administrators, flexibility and tolerance on the part of research workers, understanding by the public, and more research workers (either functioning as part of the public-school staff, or cooperating with the staff).

A detailed discussion of research concerning such things as teaching reading or arithmetic is best reserved for education textbooks. However, some of the points of view and theories that have been developed by child psychologists and developmentalists can profitably be brought to bear on selected phases of the child-training and educational process. That is the goal of this chapter.

GENERAL ASSUMPTIONS ABOUT CURRICULUM

The elementary, secondary, and liberal-arts curriculum is primarily a learning experience. Its goal is to have students assimilate in increasing breadth and depth the most significant aspects of human knowledge. Every society selectively emphasizes that knowledge characteristic of and unique to it: for example, United States children learn more about United States than about British culture, and more about the traditions and ways of the Western world than of the Eastern. The "rightness" of this, of course, is open to question, although the factual correctness of it is not.

A second assumption (more often questioned than the first) is that to be effective, any curriculum, at any level of sophistication, must be geared realistically to the child's needs and level of development; and that each student should have available to him competent and realistic guidance.

The educational process has received considerable philosophical attention. Two major theories—the "classical" and the "progressive"—have been advanced, defended, and denounced, but all too little investigated. The classical theory regards the child as a learning machine, and accounts for his acquisition of reading or number skills in much the same way that sociologists and psychologists account for "normal" prejudice (as discussed in Chapters 11 and 12). If the child has a sufficient number of exposures to an idea (or a skill), and if he is rewarded for improvement and punished for failure, he will eventually master it. This educational philosophy is adequate enough as far as it goes, but, historically, it has tended to ignore differences among children, has been associated with authoritarian classroom practices, and has been naive in failing to allow for the subtle effects of motivation, including frustration, level of aspiration, achievement motive, and achievement anxiety. These concepts are discussed in some detail in this chapter.

The classical philosophy of education places much stress on high academic standards, traditional subject-matter content, drill, and conventional discipline, but frequently fails to attend to some of the side-effects of these practices. An illustration of some of these side-effects is furnished by the following anecdote, concerning a young couple who acquired an irresponsible puppy. Among this puppy's other undesirable habits was that of chewing the drapes. The first time he did this, they decided to rub his nose against the rough wallpaper and throw him out of the ground-floor window. They repeated this process the second, third, fourth, and fifth times he chewed the drapes. On the sixth occasion, he chewed the drapes, rubbed his *own* nose against the wallpaper, and voluntarily jumped out of the window.

Many adult attitudes and behaviors reflect this type of teaching: learning occurred, but it was not what the parent or teacher intended. How many people in the United States regard art with near-distaste because their art-appreciation courses consisted of memorizing the titles and painters of 200 great works, or are utterly indifferent to poetry as a result of analyzing hundreds of lines for the type of meter and the number of beats to a line?

In contrast to the classical philosophy, progressive educational philosophy is strongly pupil-centered. Its extreme proponents hold that the child needs simply to be *exposed* to the opportunity to learn in order to become educated. This school of thought resembles the self-realization theory of social development as this was discussed in Chapter 10: accept the child, and he will "flower." In its extreme form, progressive educational philosophy neglects the contributions of learning research and theory, perhaps underemphasizes the value of classical knowledge, overemphasizes some of the superficial aspects of "adjusting to the society," and takes an oversimplified view of "discipline" and behavior control. However, the movement has been beneficial in forcing educators to consider individual differences among children. It has laid heavy stress on motivational factors in learning, and has made it possible to consider the effect of such crucial social and emotional factors as social-class differences, anxiety, and unresolvable frustrations. These factors have usually been neglected in the classical approach to education.

As this volume is written, education in the United States appears to be in a healthy ferment. The best of both of the extreme educational philosophies outlined above is being considered and incorporated into practice: Respect for traditional, substantive learning, application of the laws of learning (including practice), and so on, are being joined with regard for individual differences among pupils, concern for personal adjustment, increasingly sophisticated use of motivational principles, and other factors, in a fashion that should help improve the efficiency and happiness of students of all types.

LEARNING, LEVEL OF ASPIRATION, AND ACHIEVEMENT MOTIVATION

An effective curriculum must meet the children who take part in it at their ability level, must allow for their motive systems and their interests, and must move them forward as rapidly as possible toward its objectives. Foremost among these objectives are knowledge of the culture, development of a respect for knowledge, and acquisition and maintenance of self-respect.

Children's adjustment to a curriculum will be shaped to a substantial degree according to the principles of *level of aspiration* and *achievement motive*. This section reviews research and theory relating to both of these concepts.

Definition of Level of Aspiration

"Level of aspiration" refers to how well an individual wishes to perform in the future, compared with how well he has done in the past. As a concept, it is closely related to expectancy and the self-concept, as these were discussed in Chapters 5 and 6. Level of aspiration (a basic reference is Lewin *et al.*, 1944) is related to goal-seeking behavior: How difficult are the goals an individual seeks? If they are higher than those he has reached previously in performing the same task (that is, if he wishes to achieve more next time than he did last time), he is said to have a high level of aspiration. If his aim is low—as low as or lower than goals he attained before—he is said to have a low level of aspiration.

In other words, "level of aspiration" carries a personal connotation: it refers to a person's ambitions about his own performance. But level of aspiration can also be viewed in an absolute context. A great but aging scientist sets his goals so that he expects himself to do less in 1970 than in 1969. In terms of the *personal* frame of reference, his level of aspiration is low; but *absolutely* (compared with what the average man in the United States aspires to) his level of aspiration is high. A vigorous young day-laborer may aspire to do better in 1970 than he did in 1969. Defined in personal terms, his level of aspiration is high; but the scientist's absolute aspiration is far higher than the young laborer's. In research, however, the term *level of aspiration* most often refers to the personal and relative, rather than the absolute, and is defined by what the individual aspires to in comparison with what he has done previously.

Like all abstract concepts, "level of aspiration" must be translated into observable behavior before it can be scientifically or practically useful. Many translations (behavioral measures) have been devised. Two studies, summarized below, have been selected to illustrate the methods by which level of aspiration may be measured. The conclusions of the first study illustrate the effect that parental aspirations may have on the aspiration level of their children. The second study illustrates the effect of social climate on level of aspiration.

Representative Level of Aspiration Studies

Little and Cohen (1951), on the basis of their observations of asthmatic children referred for treatment to a university hospital, were led to suspect that mothers of asthmatics pushed their children harder than typical mothers do. They devised a simple but practical level of aspiration task: shooting darts at a bull's-eye target. Each child was given 21 trials at this task. Actually achieving the bull's-eye earned the highest possible score; attaining the concentric ring next to the bull's-eye gave him the next highest score; and hitting each ring concentrically outward resulted in progressively lower scores.

After his first trial with a dart fired at the target the child was asked how well he believed he would do the next time, but was warned that he would be penalized if his "bet" or prediction was too wide of what he actually did on the next shot. The difference between his prediction and his previous performance was called his discrepancy (or D) score. If his bet was for the third ring away from the bull's-eye, for example, but his immediately preceding performance had been for the fourth ring from the bull's-eye, he would be assigned a D-score of +1—his aspiration was one circle better than his previous performance. But, had he predicted the fifth ring from the bull's-eye, his D-score for that trial would have been —1. The study allowed for 20 such predictions, and D-scores were averaged for each child.

Thirty asthmatic children and their mothers were included in the experiment. They were compared with 30 nonasthmatic children, either their brothers or sisters who were not asthmatic, or children who were in the hospital for ailments other than asthma. The subjects ranged from 4 to 12 years of age. Before each child made a prediction, his mother (who was watching) predicted privately how well he would do next time.

The authors' technique worked well; even the four-year-olds were able to get the idea and perform the task. Their results supported the predictions Little and Cohen had made before they started the study: mothers of asthmatic children appeared to expect more of their children than mothers of nonasthmatics did. The average D-score for the mothers of asthmatics was +1.6, whereas that of the mothers of nonasthmatics was only +0.1 (this difference was highly significant statistically). In other words, the mothers of asthmatics expected their children (on the average) to better their performance by almost two bull's-eye rings, whereas the mothers of nonasthmatic children predicted that their youngsters would do about the same next time as they had done last time.

The children's aspiration patterns followed their mothers', which perhaps indicates that their levels of aspiration were modeled after what they thought their mothers expected of them. The average D-scores (ambitions) of asthmatic children were twice as high as those of nonasthmatic children(+1.85 and +.93 respectively).

The second illustrative study (Pauline Sears and Levin, 1957) indicates that children in relaxed and permissive circumstances change their level of aspiration in the direction of assuring themselves maximal success. The authors used 19 four- and five-year-old children as subjects, and devised interesting and ingenious techniques for measuring level of aspiration. Each child was given a pegboard, with different sections painted green (to indicate the easiest task), yellow (for next easy), brown (for intermediate), blue (for rather difficult), and red (for most difficult of all). The child inserted a peg into the colored section to indicate the level of difficulty of the performance he planned to undertake. The tasks, also identified by color (green easiest, red most difficult) were: jumping for balls at different heights over the children's head; copying designs with blocks, the designs ranging from very easy to quite complex; pulling weights on a pulley, the weights ranging from light to heavy; matching designs to a model; and broad-jumping. The children were given six trials for each task; for a first experimental session, the order of tasks was predetermined by the experimenters. All children had a second session a few days later in which *they* chose the order of their tasks.

After a success, the children tended to become more "ambitious"—that is, they went on to a more difficult task. They showed no consistent pattern after failure. But during the second session with the very permissive experimenters, the children's choices were for lower levels of difficulty than during the first session. In other words, under circumstances of general relaxation and friendliness, the children "aimed" lower than when they were new to the situation.

Outline of Level of Aspiration Findings

A person's level of aspiration is undoubtedly affected by many things. His previous history has taught him to be generally optimistic or pessimistic about how well he can do at a given type of endeavor (he has formed expectancies about his performance—see Chapter 5). His level of aspiration will vary according to the importance of the goal he is seeking—he may be more cautious about important goals than about goals that hold no great value for him, although the literature is not conclusive about this. He tends to be either markedly more daring or the opposite—markedly more cautious —if he states his level of aspiration in public. His level of aspiration will vary more if his principal motive is to avoid failure than if it is to achieve success (this conclusion is treated more extensively a little later, in the discussion of achievement motivation). If he is competing against a group that he considers about equal to him in ability—that is, if he has been informed about how well such a group has done on a similar task—his level of aspiration may be higher than if he thinks he is "competing" against the standards of a group much superior to him.

Experimental evidence has not yet been gathered to illuminate all these influences on level of aspiration, but a brief, oversimplified, and general review of results in the area of level of aspiration studies can be attempted, and tentative inferences can be drawn for child development and training. Following success, level of aspiration is raised; it is lowered after failure. Following either success or failure, maladjusted children and adults react either more extremely, more variably, or both, than do normals. Following failure, the level of aspiration of maladjusted subjects may shoot far up, unrealistically; or some may go up very high, others down very low. Their reactions following success are more predictable than those following failure, but remain more erratic than those of normal subjects. For a normal middle-class population of children, the level of aspiration is moderately positive, but not unrealistically so. The principles implied by level of aspiration research appear already to be well established by the ages of 4 and 5. Under permissive, nondemanding circumstances, individuals appear to relax their level of aspiration to assure themselves the greatest chance of success, although they remain "optimistic."

Most studies report only modest correlations between level of aspiration from one situation to another. Because of the differential learning histories of complex human organisms, such a finding might be predicted. On the other hand, there is probably a moderate relation between levels of aspiration for different tasks in similar areas (e.g., for arithmetic and reading in the area of academics; or for basketball and volleyball in the area of athletics).

Implications for Child-Training

In the present context, the findings summarized above are all interesting, but perhaps the most pertinent one concerns the hopeful or optimistic nature of aspiration level. Apparently most normal children seem both to expect and to hope that they will do somewhat better "next time" than they did the time before. Both the Little and Cohen and the Sears and Levin studies illustrate this trend. On the basis of their research (and the general body of research in this area), the general, practical prediction can be made that children actually like to "stand on their toes." Reaching for concepts and skills which are perhaps a little too difficult for them at the moment, but which can—hopefully—be attained, is both natural and challenging for children. In other words, the following practical recommendation might be made: Keep each child reaching, but see to it that he has some hope of grasping what he reaches for.

Experimental work on level of aspiration demonstrates that experiences of success result in a person's raising his level of aspiration, while, on the average, experiences of failure result in its lowering. It is reasonable to suggest that if patterns of success or failure persist over long periods of time, the level of aspiration may be affected relatively permanently. Long-time experiences of success may result in increasing confidence and optimism, and in redoubled effort, whereas persistently repeated failure may result in resignation, pessimism, and, possibly, reduction of effort. G. O. Johnson's findings (1950) concerning mentally retarded youngsters in regular classrooms fit well with these predictions. His retarded children fell academically further and further behind the standing of their class in each advancing year of elementary school during which they were studied.

Level of Aspiration and Social Class

In Chapter 12 it was pointed out that, regardless of how social class is defined, there is little argument about the fact that the United States can be divided into at least two classes: the white-collar and the blue-collar class. Evidence was introduced in Chapter 12 suggesting that child-rearing practices differ according to social class, and that these practices influence the development of authoritarianism and prejudice in middle- and lower-class children. It seems equally likely that social class affects the aspiration level of children.

One of the most ambitious studies of the relations between level of aspiration, social class, and various personal traits was conducted by Douvan and Adelson (1958). This study merits detailed discussion.

The most usual treatment of social class considers three strata: the upper class (relatively aristocratic); the middle class (professional and white-collar); and the working, or "lower," or blue-collar class. It is generally held that upper-class boys aspire merely to hold their own—they have little hope of doing better than their fathers, and are content if they do as well; middle-class boys are thought to be quite ambitious, wishing to exceed their fathers' status; and lower-class boys are believed to possess little hope of bettering their fathers' position, although such a prospect does not cheer them.

Douvan and Adelson have done some interesting thinking about upward mobility (doing better than father), which they classify into three types. The first type, according to them, is that of the "desperately scrambling Philistine," who is exhausted in his pursuit of status. He defines his own identity and personal worth exclusively according to whether or not he is successful. His family teaches him to be competitive: don't be happy, make MONEY. He measures his success not by his actual achievement, but by how he compares with others. He is a "keeper-up-with-the-Joneses." But, as Douvan and Adelson point out, there are always some who have done better, and who have more money and social prestige than he has. He always runs the risk of being pushed off the social or occupational ladder by a competitor.

The second upwardly mobile pattern they describe is one that might be produced by the "authoritarian personality" family described in Chapters 11 and 12. Such an upwardly mobile person is ambivalent toward success (has mingled feelings of attraction and repulsion, approach and avoidance). Douvan and Adelson believe that the response of such upwardly mobile people is to the dominance and prestige of the more privileged stratum through a defensive identification with it (i.e., this stratum is strong, dangerous, and threatening, so one had best join it, not fight it). In the process, one denies and decries his own background and status. The origins of such feelings lie in the child's early encounters with authority and status in his own family. He is likely to have had harsh and forbidding parents who allowed him no expression of hostility. He has *accommodated* to parental strength through identifying with it. Arising from this process are manifestations of the authoritarian personality: a conscious overidealization of the parent and authority, together with unconscious rebellion and hostility, rigidity, conformity, and resistance to examination of one's own motives and thoughts. The motive to move upward socially and occupationally arises from the need to emulate the parents, yet this mobility arouses conflict because it implies a struggle with powerful authority figures.

Douvan and Adelson's third type of upwardly mobile child and adult is considerably happier. Young people falling into the third category have a "hope of success" pattern. Their interest in success is directed by a rational ego; consequently, they can mobilize their energies effectively. Their aspirations are realistic, not grandiose. When they aspire to very substantial improvement of status, this aspiration is based on a realistic judgment of their own capabilities, and in general their aspirations for improvement are relatively modest. They are likely to come from families that encourage autonomy (self-determination and independence). Such a family is not obsessed by status, yet accepts and transmits to its children in a straightforward fashion a culturally central value of solid achievement. The shifts in identity necessary for the child—from child to adolescent to young man or woman to successful independent adult—do not involve the child in conflict, because he has been taught that such shifts are not only inevitable but desirable. Douvan and Adelson believe that this third, happy type of upward mobility is most frequent in our culture. They therefore predicted that upwardly mobile children, as a group, would show more desirable personal and social characteristics than downwardly mobile youngsters.

Douvan and Adelson studied 1,000 boys 14 to 15 years of age, all of whom came from urban nonfarm families. The fathers of the group on which they reported in greatest detail were small business owners, self-employed artisans, or men who worked at white-collar jobs, including sales and clerical positions; or who were skilled and semiskilled manual workers. The boys were classified as upwardly mobile if they aspired to an occupation higher than their fathers'; downwardly mobile if their vocational aim was lower than their fathers'; and stable if they wished only to equal their fathers.

Table 13.1 shows the percentages of upwardly mobile, stable, and downwardly mobile boys of fathers in different occupational groups. In class one—professional—it is impossible (because of Douvan and Adelson's methods) for a boy to be upwardly mobile; or for the boys of unskilled workers to be classified as downwardly mobile.

Before continuing with a discussion of Douvan and Adelson's results, it should be pointed out that Table 13.1 gives scant support to the notion of occupational resignation on the part of lower-class boys; or of driving am-

TABLE 13.1: PERCENTAGE OF BOYS FROM DIFFERENT PATERNAL OCCUPA-
TIONAL LEVELS WHO ASPIRED TO DO BETTER OCCUPATIONALLY (UPWARDLY
MOBILE), THE SAME (STABLE), OR LESS WELL (DOWNWARDLY MOBILE)
THAN THEIR FATHERS.

Father's Occupation	Number	Percentage of Boys who Were		
		Upwardly mobile	Stable	Downwardly mobile
Professional	136	—	67	33
White collar	183	46	29	25
Manual skilled	335	58	34	8
Manual unskilled	70	84	16	—

Adapted with permission of the American Psychological Association and
Elizabeth M. Douvan, from Douvan and Adelson (1958).

bition, relatively speaking, on the part of middle-class boys. A substantially
higher percentage of the former (84 percent) than of the latter (46 percent) wish to surpass their fathers.

Douvan and Adelson's results do not provide a direct test of their ideas
about three types of upward mobility, but they *do* suggest that upwardly
mobile boys are happier and more effective than downwardly mobile
youngsters. When compared with downwardly mobile boys, the upwardly
mobile excelled in the following characteristics: they took part in more
group-membership and leisure-time activities; did somewhat more dating
(although no more of them held jobs); did more, and more intellectual,
reading; and expressed more enjoyment in their activities. They also had
more plans for future activities. More of them said that they had chosen an
occupation because it was interesting and would give them status, but fewer
of them had selected it because it was easy. They preferred success to security. They were more likely than downwardly mobile boys to save money
and to plan for the future. They were more interested in getting satisfaction
from assuming adult roles, less interested in simply being popular with their
group. More of them said that they kept promises because they were trusted
by their parents or other adults; fewer of them kept their word because they
were afraid of punishment. More of them said they would be honest with
their parents, but more of them also said they would not worry unduly about
breaking a promise either because of an emergency, or because they felt
personally mature ("I am sensible enough to judge what is right"). Fewer
would break promises because of feelings of rebellion, or on impulse, or because their parents were not around to police them. Fewer of the upwardly
mobile boys thought that there was such a thing as an unbreakable rule.
More of them believed that friends can be just as close to one as family.
More of them considered adult leaders as helpers rather than decision-
makers; fewer of them relied on authority; and fewer of them regarded one
of their family members as their ideal. They were more humorous, less self-

rejecting, yearned less for impossible changes. More of them believed that change of status was within their own power.

In general, they reported that they had received less physical punishment than downwardly mobile boys; their punishment had been more psychological—for example, "withdrawal of love." Fewer of them portrayed their parents as punishing and harsh, although they said that they had had more disagreements with their parents. The parents voiced more disapproval of how they spent their money. They were more likely to share leisure-time activities with their parents.

In general, there was no relation between mobility aspiration and degree of certainty about what would happen to them, nor were there relations between mobility aspiration and age, family economic status, or fathers' education. However, the upwardly mobile boys possessed significantly more verbal ability than those who were downwardly mobile. It may be conjectured that this is partly the result of the greater amount of time they have spent with their parents, and is also related to other child-rearing practices (e.g., pp. 254, 259–61). In general, the "stables" fell between the upwardly and downwardly mobile boys in the characteristics that have been summarized.

Rosen (1956) worked with male students in two New Haven high schools. His upper-class subjects, according to test, showed higher need for achievement on a TAT-like test, and seemed to be more future-oriented and individualistic. Their achievement-need score was positively related to their school grades; and their values included an ambition to attend college. Brim and Forer (1956) report similar results, adding that being Jewish and male is associated with the tendency to plan one's life ahead. They believe that the tendency to plan one's life is a function of having learned that planning is good, while at the same time possessing a social status that makes the future sufficiently predictable to permit planning with some degree of positive expectation.

Empey (1956) reports that lower-class high-school students aspire to lower occupational levels than upper- and middle-class youngsters, but that (as with Douvan and Adelson's sample) they *do* aspire to an occupational status higher than that of their fathers.

Hieronymus (1951), working with 910 ninth-grade boys and girls from a moderate-sized midwestern town, found that socioeconomic status was more highly related to socioeconomic expectation (how well the children expected to do) than was intelligence. For girls the correlation between socioeconomic level and socioeconomic expectation was .61, for boys .63. Similar correlations for intelligence were only .36 and .41. Socioeconomic status was also correlated (in the neighborhood of .30) with positive attitudes toward education, and seemed to be an important factor in determining a positive attitude toward education ($r =$ approximately .50). High socioeconomic status, favorable attitudes toward education, and high socioeconomic expectations all combine to assist the student in doing well at school. Hieronymus concludes that he has provided evidence to support the hypothesis that socialized anxiety (and by this he means simply the desire to do well—ambition) is a factor in the selective process of American education.

Campbell (1955), working with New Zealand (presumably) secondary-school children 12 to 14 years of age, finds that those who are progressing at a greater rate than expected are not particularly different in intelligence from those making normal progress, but that they have significantly higher sociocultural scores. He suggests that of two types of secondary school (one more, one less academically oriented), placement for border-zone children (in terms of their academic achievement) should be made according to social class: the border-zone middle- or upper-class child should go to the academic, the border-zone lower-class child of the same achievement level to the nonacademic school.

In other words, a generally positive level of aspiration—the desire and intent to do better than one's father has done—seems to be associated with a complex of positive factors: greater optimism, greater orientation toward "doing the job well," greater self-determination, and more effective performance. There is no suggestion in existing research that more lower-class than upper- or middle-class boys are resigned to their status. At the same time, the relative level of aspiration (how high one aspires to climb) appears to depend on the place in the social ladder from which one begins.

Achievement Motivation and Achievement Anxiety

A discussion of the literature devoted to level of aspiration leads to the conclusion that (at least in United States culture) a *positive* level of aspiration is associated with many other desirable traits. A consideration of the concept of level of aspiration leads logically to the idea of an *achievement motive*—a widely generalized "wish to master" or "desire to do well." The achievement motive has much in common with such concepts as autonomy, independence, and generativity. These concepts have already been discussed, particularly in Chapter 10. Inevitably, in a culture like ours, any motivation as important as the wish to achieve is highly esteemed and is likely to be associated with *anxiety* about achievement, just as problems in any other important developmental area may result in anxiety.[1]

Anxiety is currently one of the most frequently—perhaps one of the most loosely—used motivational concepts. It is a central concept in both psychoanalytic and learning theories of personality. Scales to measure it have been developed for use with both children and adults (for example, Castaneda, McCandless, and Palermo, 1957; Sarason, 1957, and Taylor, 1955).

---

[1] The relation between delayed or inadequate physical development and anxiety was discussed in Chapter 9; the relations between the self-concept and anxiety were suggested in Chapter 6; and the association of anxiety and fixation was discussed in Chapter 5.

The simplest—deceptively simple—definition of anxiety regards it as a highly noxious drive state or stimulus condition. A child (or adult) will go to considerable lengths to avoid or reduce it.

To amplify this definition of anxiety, one might say that it probably originates with physical or psychic pain. However, the original connection between the pain stimulus and its response has been forgotten. This "forgetting" or "repression" provides a distinction between anxiety and fear: in fear, the connection between stimulus and response is remembered. Another distinction relates to the multiplicity of connections or associations with anxiety and fear: anxiety stimuli are widely, fear stimuli narrowly, generalized.

The time of greatest incubation or growth potential for anxiety is probably the first preverbal year or years. In our culture the opportunities for acquisition of anxiety are so widespread as to be, for all practical purposes, universal. Hence, it is not necessary to argue about whether it is a primary ("unlearned") or secondary ("learned") drive. Anxiety may be either situation-specific (attached, for example, to test-taking situations, or high places) or chronic (as in the hypertense person), just as, in varying circumstances, anxious behavior may meet with positive or negative social reactions.

Anxiety as a *response* must be considered in contrast to our earlier treatment of it as a drive. Anxiety responses are ordinarily thought of as nonconstructive. We think of the anxious person as one who goes to pieces under stress, is tense and jerky, "gets tied up in knots." Such responses do not usually elicit positive social response; they make other people tense. But many anxious responses, even though they are accompanied by discomfort in the person who makes them, can be socially constructive: compulsive neatness is useful to a scientist or a certified public accountant; promptness is socially esteemed, although seldom practiced in our society; and we give approval to children who strive desperately for high grades.

In any event, responses motivated by and associated with anxiety are remarkably resistant to change (see Chapters 5 and 12). Anxiety is likely to be most intense in areas of human endeavor that are most highly valued by society, or with which society most concerns itself, such as sexual behavior, school learning, vocational achievement, popularity, adequacy of sex-typing, and the like. Chronic anxiety is likely to be associated with behaviors that pervade the most central areas of living (e.g., eating, eliminating, social relations).

Therapy for anxiety assumes many guises. Some therapies, such as tranquilizers, do nothing for the anxiety itself, but may merely reduce the intensity of its *symptoms*. Elimination of symptoms may also reduce the feedback from the symptoms to the organism: if a person finds that he is betraying his anxiety, or is behaving and feeling in ways that he labels anxious, his behavior or feelings may further increase the intensity of his anxiety state (as, for example, odors from a bakery may intensify hunger).

Insight therapy dwells lightly on anxiety symptoms, but seeks to help an individual to discover (or recover) the *origin* of his anxiety. The assumption is that, once he understands how a given set of stimuli has come to arouse anxiety in him, these stimuli will lose their power to evoke both the anxiety drive and the socially maladjusted responses designed to reduce it. Whether such behavior changes are automatic is doubtful. It seems more logical to think that, when anxiety drive is reduced, an individual can be more easily retrained along socially acceptable lines. Anxiety-motivated but socially constructive behaviors would not need to be retrained; they could simply be *preserved*. Following successful therapy, however, they would no longer be associated with personal discomfort.

One might predict that chronic anxiety will be higher for those who in their early childhood have been "badly reared" than for those who have been "well reared," although, as we have repeatedly said, it is difficult, in any clear scientific sense, to say what is meant by these terms.

The relation between chronic and situational anxiety is not entirely clear. The two should be positively correlated, in the sense that the stimuli belonging to a pervasive and general drive become associated with all the situations that are relevant to the drive. The chronically anxious person may be compared with the individual in a famine-ridden country: for him every act is designed to reduce hunger, and even far-fetched stimuli (grubs, for example) are used as food; but for the comfortably situated resident of a district with a full larder, stimuli associated with hunger operate selectively—three or four hours after a meal, and in particular surroundings, such as restaurants and dining rooms, in which one eats. In other words, under conditions of *chronic* hunger or anxiety, a disproportionate share of behavior results from the energizing and sensitizing functions of the drive (see Chapter 4) and is directed toward its satisfaction (in this case, reduction). With *situational* hunger or anxiety, the larger proportion of behavior is related to motives other than hunger or anxiety; only in selected and appropriate circumstances, biologically or socially determined, does an individual direct his behavior to reduce hunger or anxiety. These two designations of anxiety, then, are not inconsistent with each other. Their apparent difference relates principally to threshold and to facilities or opportunities for satisfaction. For these drives, satisfaction is almost always synonymous with reduction.

It is important to distinguish *achievement motivation* from *achievement anxiety*. For the person who is motivated toward achievement, achieving something (succeeding, solving a problem) has reinforcing properties. It is rewarding, and constitutes a goal.

The definition of *achievement anxiety* is more difficult. Such anxiety is probably situational (i.e., it arises only when stimuli associated with the achievement motive are present). It can be further assumed that pain or punishment, as well as reward, has been associated with achievement or achievement-directed behavior; and that the reward-punishment ratio has been about 50-50, or has even been tipped in the direction of punishment.

Anxiety about achievement could presumably develop in the absence of any very strong achievement motive, as a consequence of punishment for poor achievement imposed on the child by (for example) the school system. For such a child, however, simple avoidance learning would be a more likely result than anxiety. It is probable that a fairly strong drive must be present in order for a drive-related anxiety to develop.

Achievement anxiety, then, should be stronger the stronger the achievement motive. Hence, maximal anxiety about school achievement should occur for the child who is maximally motivated to do well, but whose achievement history has been characterized by a ratio of punishment (*of a given type*) to reward ranging from approximately 50-50 to 100-0.

Although punishment was undoubtedly at first imposed *externally* on the child, he is likely to internalize it eventually, since the presence of a strong achievement motive or motives implies internalization of control (see Chapter 10 on identification). This, in turn, implies adoption of self-punishing and self-rewarding behavior. Thus, even a straight-A student can experience a majority of self-administered punishments or failures because he is, despite his A's, more often second than first in his class; while a straight-C student who considers himself lucky to avoid D's may give himself consistent positive rewards.

Our society is so organized that the second type of individual is rarer than the first, at least in the middle class. However, the second may be more frequent than the first in lower and possibly upper socioeconomic classes.

Relating achievement motivation and anxiety to social class requires one to examine the relation between achievement need, or motive, and conscience. It can be assumed that the need for school achievement is only one manifestation of conscience, which involves the incorporation of a set of standards valued by adult society (again, see the identification section in Chapter 10).

Conscience, as we have postulated, develops or fails to develop as a function of the type of control techniques that have been used with children from the time they are about 1 to 5 or 6 years of age. Love-oriented techniques of control perhaps operate as follows: "If I behave in such and such a way, I please significant others—my parents; if in another way, I displease them." Once this concept is learned, it generalizes to people other than the parents. The child eventually includes *himself* as a *person*—an important and socialized person. Thus he becomes his *own* rewarder or punisher. He has developed a conscience, and its probable concomitants of guilt and anxiety.

Nonlove-oriented child-rearing techniques, particularly when the proportion of punishment sharply exceeds that of reward, fail to achieve the same end. From the child's point of view, parents punish; hence he must modify his behavior according to their desires. Significant others, through generalization, are seen as possessing the same punitive properties as the parents. The child asks: "Why label myself as a socialized person if the only reward is permission to punish myself?" In such circumstances there are theoretically few reasons to develop a conscience, and internalization of parental standards does not occur. Hence, there results a personality low in anxiety, high in fear and shame, and high in direct self-gratification (including a low need for school achievement).

From what has been said here and in Chapter 12, we see that achievement motive should be highest in the middle class, lowest in the lower-lower class, and perhaps about equal for the upper-lower and the upper classes. Achievement anxiety should be highest for middle-class children, because of the interaction between their motives, the love-oriented control techniques their parents have used, and their self-punishment for failure to do well. Upper-lower and upper-class children should be aligned somewhere between middle and lower-lower class youngsters.

In accounting for a specific value, such as need for achievement, it may not be necessary to refer to the total concept of conscience. It may simply be that scholastic achievement is not valued very highly among lower-class parents; hence they do not transmit this value to their children. Since the need for achievement is low, anxiety associated with failure to achieve is also low.

Middle-class children probably have differentially more added to their achievement motivation (and anxiety?) than children from other social classes because their teachers are also middle-class, and thus provide them with models to be imitated. Middle-class parents also provide academic achievement models that are not furnished by lower-class and perhaps not by upper-class parents.

Whatever sex differences exist in school achievement anxiety probably vary with the age of the child. It is possible that, in elementary school, boys do not experience the same subjective pressure to achieve that girls do; but, by junior high and secondary school, the prospect of independence and responsibilities intensifies the pressure on boys. During college, it may be predicted that boys will have more achievement motivation and achievement anxiety than girls.

Achievement Motivation versus Fear of Failure

The preceding section suggests that the achievement motive may be a rather pervasive and stable trait and that, as far as academic achievement is concerned, it may be heavily concentrated in middle-class children. This section also suggests that "fear of failure" is closely related to the concept of achievement anxiety.

An interesting body of literature has accumulated concerning achievement motivation (or need for achievement) and fear of failure (see, for example, McClelland, 1958, and Atkinson, 1958). This literature relates closely to the notions of expectancy and self-concept (see chs. 5 and 6), and to level of aspiration, school achievement, and general "ambition," or desire "to get ahead." The theory and research chosen to develop this topic here have been provided by Atkinson and his co-workers (Atkinson, 1958; Atkinson *et al.*, 1960; and Atkinson and Litwin, 1960).

Atkinson reasons that any competitive situation—and for the average child, both his family and his school situation are likely to be competitive— arouses one of two major motives: either to achieve success (the achievement motive) or to avoid failure. Some children and adults work hard for success, without seriously considering the threat of failure. Others think less of succeeding than of avoiding failure (the illustration given on p. 421 is relevant here: some work to get A's, others to avoid D's). Yet both motives operate in the same person: for the striver-for-A's, the drive toward success is stronger than the fear of failure, yet he undoubtedly also fears failure; for the avoider-of-D's, the threat of failure is paramount, but he would also like success, as represented by a B or an A.

Atkinson and his colleagues have made some interesting and generally accurate predictions about these two types of person—the strivers-for-success (those who are achievement motivated) and the avoiders-of-failure. The first type, Atkinson reasons, is likely to be a middle-of-the-roader in his aspirations or ambitions; whereas the second type, the failure-avoider, will be either excessively cautious or extravagantly reckless in the things he tries.

Atkinson has developed a behavior theory about motivation, arguing that motivation is equal to the strength of the relevant motive, multiplied by the expectation of success for behavior related to the motive, which is multiplied again by the incentive (or value) of the goal. In other words, motivation $= f$ (motive $\times$ expectancy $\times$ incentive). In the context of this chapter (as for Atkinson), the important motives to which this equation is to be applied are the achievement motive and the failure-avoidance motive.

The three terms in Atkinson's equation may be thought of as follows: *Motive* may be innate, or it may be learned. It is analogous to *drive,* as this concept has been discussed in Chapter 4. *Expectancy* (as discussed in Chapter 5) is a function of the individual's learning. On the basis of his experience he expects, at some level of confidence, either to succeed or to fail at any given undertaking. If he is an excellent basketball player, he will expect to make 3 out of 4 of his free-throws; if a novice or unskilled, he expects to make one out of 10, or fewer. Atkinson reasons that *incentive* is an inverse function of the expectancy of success (this conception has been discussed in Chapter 5). Incentive (reward value) will be greatest for undertakings attended by little hope of success, least for undertakings accompanied by a high expectancy of success. In other words, Atkinson's definition of incentive is equal to 100 percent probability minus the expected probability of success: for the proficient basketball player, a successful free-throw will have an incentive value of 1.00 —.75, or .25; whereas for our novice, it will have an incentive value of 1.00 —.10, or .90.

This formula leads directly to the prediction that, for those with a high need for achievement, middle-of-the-road ventures, bets, and aspirations will be preferred to extreme gambits; whereas for those whose dominant motive is to avoid failure, middle-of-the-road courses of action will be avoided and extreme alternatives—very conservative, or very reckless—will be chosen. If such theoretical predictions can be verified, our understanding of children's attitudes toward competitive athletics, games in general, and academic aspirations will be much increased.

Let us consider first the implications of Atkinson's formulations for the child who is motivated more by the desire to achieve than he is by fear of failure. If motivation $= f$ (motive $\times$ expectancy $\times$ incentive) and incentive $= 1.00$ minus expectancy of success, and if an arbitrary weight of 10 is assigned to motive and three levels of expectancy of success are considered (90 percent success, 50 percent success, and 10 percent success), we can solve the Atkinson formula as follows:

First instance: Motivation $= 10 \times .90 \times .10 = .9$
Second instance: Motivation $= 10 \times .50 \times .50 = 2.5$
Third instance: Motivation $= 10 \times .10 \times .90 = .9$

This solution demonstrates that, with positive, approach motives (the principle of approach and avoidance gradients or motives was introduced in Chapter 5), subjective expectancies hovering around the 50-50 level result in maximal motivation. An achievement-oriented child (and it has been demonstrated that teachers can select such children—McClelland, 1958) will put forth greatest effort if he figures his chances of reaching the goal as about even.

The Atkinson formula applies to failure-avoidance as well as achievement. If the motive in the equations above is thought of as *avoidance-of-failure* rather than approach-to-success, it can be seen that the second instance results in the strongest avoidance tendency. Because failure is painful, the child will choose either extreme—caution or recklessness—but will avoid the middle instance, the 50-50 probability.

This explanation may help account for the general finding cited earlier (p. 413) in connection with level of aspiration studies—that, following failure, people manifest more variable levels of aspiration than they do following success. If the experience of failure has raised their motivation to avoid failure and made it stronger than their motivation to achieve success, then they will have been driven to extremes of caution or recklessness; consequently, considered as a group, they will be much more variable (or erratic) in their level of aspiration bids. The Atkinson formula is also instructive when we consider neurotics—a group which probably lives more to avoid failure than to achieve success—and contrast them with normals, who (as a group) probably strive more to obtain success than to avoid failure. The summary statement about level of aspiration (p. 413) indicated that deviant groups were more variable (less predictable) in their level of aspiration bids following success than were normals, but that the difference in variability following success was less than the deviant-normal difference in variability following failure. If deviants are shaky in their self-confidence, whereas normals are fairly stable, an experience of failure will be more likely to move the deviants from an *achievement* orientation to a *failure-avoidance* orientation than it will be to alter the goals of normals. Hence, deviant groups should be more variable than normal groups after failure than after success.

Atkinson and his colleagues, and McClelland, have provided experimental evidence that gives modest support to the predictions they have made. They have used a variety of populations as subjects, ranging from kindergarten and second-grade children through college sophomores and juniors, and have employed experimental tasks ranging from playing shuffleboard to obtaining superior college grades.

In sum, it seems possible to separate children and adults into groups according to whether their dominant motive is to attain success or to avoid failure. When they are success-oriented, they are likely to choose middle-of-the-road ways of behaving; but when their predominant motive is to avoid failure, they are likely to go to extremes, selecting either excessively cautious or excessively reckless behavior alternatives. The research that has been done (Atkinson *et al.,* 1960) indicates that they are more likely to be reckless than conservative. However, in the Atkinson study, the experimental subjects were always confronted with an audience, and this circumstance may have driven them in the direction of bravado. In private, they might have behaved differently.

FRUSTRATION AND FAILURE

Definition of Frustration and Failure

In the literature of child development, *frustration* typically has a "bad" connotation. It is not good to frustrate your child; failure is psychologically damaging.

A closer analysis of the two terms, *frustration* and *failure,* leads us to interesting and provocative conclusions that differ from the stereotypes. *Frustration* can be defined in either of two ways. First, it can be thought of as an internal state resulting from or accompanying partial or complete blocking as one tries to get to a goal (or away from some stimulus he is avoiding). Second, it can be considered as the *act* of blocking. The "internal state" idea (see J. S. Brown and Farber, 1951) includes the hypothesis that frustration adds to total drive or motivation level (i.e., frustration "stirs the person up," thereby adding a certain amount of drive to that which he already has). Frustration is an "irrelevant" drive, in that it is not related to the motivation initiating the sequence of behavior. A hungry child, blocked from getting food, is frustrated; but his "frustration drive" is irrelevant to the hunger drive that prompted his behavior in the first place. However, frustration adds to his total drive level, thus intensifying the responses he makes to obtain food. Frustration may lead him to attack whoever or whatever is blocking him.

Failure, very simply, means not getting what one is trying to get. It is a descriptive term that refers to "successful blocking," or the *mechanics* of frustration; hence, it is related to the second definition of frustration given above. Failure, of course, is likely to produce frustration (considered as an inner drive).

The most perfunctory examination of the day of the average adult or child forces one to the conclusion that blocking and its accompanying frustration are not necessarily either "good" or "bad." They simply exist. One is frustrated when the alarm clock goes off in the morning. One is frustrated if the meaning of a paragraph does not come clear during the first reading. One is frustrated if someone else gets a higher grade than he does on a test. One is frustrated if the pavements are icy. One is frustrated by having to set the table rather than read the comics.

If frustration is bad, and if each failure is psychologically damaging, then each of us is lucky to get through any given day without coming apart at the seams.

What earlier writers probably meant by "frustration is *bad*" is that *hopeless* frustration (particularly in areas of great personal or social importance), and failure with *no* alternatives, are bad—prolonged partial or complete blocking, which has no possible happy solution and which occurs in important need areas, may be severely damaging to personal development and adjustment.

Theories of Frustration

A widely accepted theoretical treatment of frustration has been presented by Dollard and his colleagues (1939). These authors postulate that aggression is always instigated by frustration, although, depending on the learning history of the individual, many reactions other than aggression may occur in response to frustration. Like Brown and Farber, Dollard and his co-authors regard frustration as a drive with highly unpleasant qualities, so that a person is strongly motivated to reduce his frustration. Hence, any behavior that provides escape from frustration—reduces frustration drive—is reinforced.

Research has revealed a number of ways in which individuals of different ages react to various types and degrees of frustration. They may, for example, become passive, or withdraw, or regress (revert to more immature ways of behaving). They may persevere, and work harder; or they may become dependent and ask for help. They may persist blindly in maladaptive behavior (demonstrate rigidity). They may displace their aggression, or reject the task, or "go all to pieces."

Dollard and his co-workers believe that, according to his learning history, an individual may respond in any of these ways, and any behavior which succeeds in reducing frustration will be more likely to appear when he is next frustrated. When a response does not succeed in reducing the frustration, it is weakened so that eventually the next-strongest potential response appears.

For example, let us assume that a child has three potential responses to frustration, diagrammed in Figure 13.1. Response A (the strongest) is to be polite and considerate; response B is to ask help of the adult (i.e., to be dependent); and response C (the weakest) is to become angry and abusive. The prediction is that in the course of repeated frustration, the first few

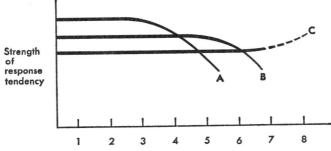

Strength of response tendency

1 2 3 4 5 6 7 8

FIG. 13.1.   A schematic representation of the appearance, disappearance, and strengthening of three types of reaction to repeated frustration. *A* refers to politeness, *B,* to dependency, *C* to aggression. The abscissa represents frustration episodes.

responses will be polite and considerate. If these responses do not successfully resolve frustration, this pattern of behaving will be weakened and the child will show dependent behavior. If, in turn, this fails to reduce the frustration, response C (aggression) will occur, and, if successful, will be strengthened.

Otis and McCandless (1955) have demonstrated this phenomenon experimentally. Preschool children were placed in a mild frustration situation, in which two nursery-school building blocks were placed end to end as a "road." For each of eight trials, the child started with his car or doll from one end of the road and the experimenter (who adopted a very impersonal role) started from the other end. Upon meeting the child's car in the middle, the experimenter would say, "My car is blocking yours," and would leave it at that. She did not respond to the children's "good manners," nor to their requests for help. Three different groups of children dropped from their behavior repertories the mannerly or dependent attempts to remove the road block and substituted for them, in the manner schematized in Figure 13.1, aggressive attempts at solving the problem. In other words, this study offers support for the idea that behavior (in this case, nonaggressive behavior) which does not reduce frustration will be weakened, or partly extinguished; and suggests that frustration is an instigator of aggression, which will appear overtly when the strength of the tendency toward other types of behavior is weakened.

As has been mentioned (pp. 425–426), Brown and Farber (1951) have worked with the conception of frustration as a drive. Their formulation of the theory fits well with (and extends) the formulation of Dollard and his colleagues; and the Otis and McCandless results are in accord with it.

Rosenzweig's theories of frustration (e.g., 1938, 1941, 1944) were discussed briefly in Chapter 11 (p. 372), but will be reviewed more fully in the present context. Rosenzweig believes that there are at least three characteristic patterns of reaction to frustration: the *extrapunitive*, the *impunitive*, and the *intrapunitive*. The first type of reactor lashes out immediately at figures or people in the outside world; the second type attempts to remove emotion from the situation (perhaps denying the frustration, or simply persisting calmly in trying to solve the problem constructively); and the third type blames himself. Rosenzweig also classifies reactions to frustration as *need-persistive* (the need remains, and the individual keeps on trying to gratify it) or *ego-defensive* (the person is threatened and takes steps to save face, although he may do this constructively). Rosenzweig further distinguishes *primary* frustration—a situation of privation in which the goal-object of an active need is unavailable (e.g., the absence of food when one is hungry); and *secondary* frustration, in which an obstacle prevents access to the goal-object. These obstacles are of several types: *passive* (such as a locked door, or a state of dissatisfaction); *active* (such as the burglar who bars the way and threatens); *external* (to the person); and *internal* (such as a state of conflict).

Nothing in Rosenzweig's treatment is contradictory to the theories of Dollard or of Brown and Farber. However, Maier (e.g., 1956), who has done most of his work with rats, introduces a different account of the effects of frustration. To him, the frustrated person's behavior is without a goal. When he is frustrated severely and for a prolonged time, task-orientation disappears and the person's behavior becomes goalless.

Maier's formulation is not unlike that of Child and Waterhouse (1952), who believe that because of previous learning, frustration stimuli arouse tendencies to respond in a manner that interferes with efficient, goal-directed behavior. The assumption that Child and Waterhouse make is that learning experiences during frustration are usually unfortunate. The things done when one is frustrated are maladaptive, and become attached to the internal stimuli of being frustrated—perhaps because they have removed the unpleasant sensations of frustration. When frustration stimuli occur again, these interfering tendencies reappear. However, there is nothing in the formulation by Child and Waterhouse to say that constructive responses to frustration cannot be established.

Maier (1956) also speaks of fixation (blind adherence to a response that is usually or always wrong) which may occur as a result of frustration, particularly when blocking is prolonged and severe. Maier lists seven conclusions, based on research with rats and young adults, which are of interest at this point in our discussion; although it cannot be said with assurance that they are relevant to children's behavior, they may be useful in suggesting new hypotheses and developing new knowledge.

From a number of studies done by him, his students, and his colleagues, Maier concludes the following:

1. Animals placed for 16 days in an unsolvable problem situation are more likely to fixate than when placed in a similar problem situation for 8 days. The inference that may be drawn from this is that prolonged frustration is more damaging than shorter periods of frustration.

2. The rate of punishment accompanying an unsolvable problem seems to affect fixation. Mild electric shock given to human subjects on 75 percent of 50 trials produced more fixations than the same absolute number of shocks distributed over 150 trials. The implications for children seem clear: The higher the ratio of punishment to total behavior, the more likely it is that behavior will be disrupted.

3. Feeding animals after electric shock results in fewer fixations than does shock alone. To draw inferences from this result, one must speculate rather freely. After a child has been punished, or has failed severely, comfort and explanation will minimize the ill effects of the experience.

4. For rats, guidance during the early stages of learning prevents fixations later, when the rats are placed in an unsolvable problem situation. By implication, children who are familiar with or who understand a situation in which they experience punishment or severe failure will be less adversely affected than children for whom the situation is strange. In addition, if one has a "plan of attack" or a "cognitive map," punishment and frustration will damage him less than if he is proceeding aimlessly.

5. Difficult learning problems result in more fixations than easy ones. It is simple to draw implications for children from this conclusion, which seems to be closely related to conclusion (1) above: Severe frustrations or failures are more likely to disrupt behavior than mild ones.

6. For humans, the use of the word "wrong" instead of electric shock to indicate an error produces fixations about as frequently as the shock. Again, the implications for children's behavior are clear. The implications of verbally mediated generalization were developed quite fully in Chapters 4 and 5, and Maier's conclusion provides evidence for the effectiveness of this mediation. Human beings, after they have acquired language, can be punished just as effectively by the use of symbols—words, in this case—as by physical punishment. The jingle, "Sticks and stones can break my bones, but words can never hurt me," is not necessarily true.

7. Finally, Maier finds that failure to confirm expectancies seems to be an important influence in the formation of fixations in a discrimination learning problem for rats (when, for example, the rat must learn that the black card behind which he has learned to find food is no longer correct, but

that the food is now concealed behind the white card). This finding argues for consistency in handling children—or for giving advance notice if the rules of the game are to be changed.

Frustration and Child-Training

Since frustration and failure are unavoidable, parents and teachers should seek ways to help children resolve their frustrations and arrive at accurate and constructive substitutes or explanations for their failures. Good child-training, including academic training, is aimed at such goals.

AVOIDING IRRELEVANT FRUSTRATIONS

Good parents, good teachers, and good schools seek to avoid *irrelevant* frustrations. Learning to read or to do long division are, by their very nature, frustrating. But we wish to confine the frustrations that necessarily accompany learning to those that are *task-relevant;* hence, learning should take place in esthetically and socially congenial surroundings. It is for this reason that teachers today more frequently than before use sociometric groupings, permitting children to work with and sit beside friends of their own choosing. It is partly for this reason that new schools are characterized by open, light, cheery, and attractively furnished rooms. It is for this reason that color and lighting schemes have been devised which will produce the least distraction or glare, and the old type of fixed desk has been abandoned wherever possible.

School psychology and counseling have come into being so that the academically irrelevant frustrations of social maladjustment or an unhappy home life can be reduced. Textbooks have been age-graded. Teachers increasingly study the development of normal children in order to understand the crises and frustrations (as well as the special satisfactions) of the different developmental stages and, whenever possible, reduce the academically irrelevant frustrations that may accompany them.

Most school systems now practice so-called social promotions, by which academically slow children are kept with their age-mates even though they may not be able to compete academically with them. The theory behind this practice is that the social frustration of being left back is greater than the increasing frustration of inability to compete. Grade-skipping for the superior student has been largely abandoned for similar reasons: fear that the social and personal frustrations encountered by the child in an advanced grade would more than offset the academic advantages. Both these points are debatable, and should receive more study than they have received so far. In the Brookline public schools (Hobson, 1956), for example, carefully screened children admitted early to kindergarten did better on all scores, including academic achievement, than children admitted at the normal age. By the time of enrolling in junior high school, the problems presented by socially promoted children who cannot cope with the advanced curriculum perhaps more than offset the intended advantages of social promotion. On the other hand, a gangling adolescent still in the fourth grade poses serious problems for other children in his class, for his teacher, and for himself. The accelerated child *may* be socially out of step for a time, particularly if he is male and especially at adolescence. However, he may be inordinately bored if kept in a homogeneously taught classroom where the average child is far below him in ability. Age-graded reading texts may be less frustrating *mechanically* to children, but many of them, with their endless repetitions and plot simplicities (even banalities), are thoroughly boring as well.

There are no simple answers to such probelms. But, in principle, the steps taken to reduce irrelevant classroom frustrations are sound, and, as *experiments* (not dogma), they are worth trying.

BUILDING FRUSTRATION TOLERANCE

A first principle, then, for dealing with frustration in child-training is to reduce irrelevant frustrations to a minimum. But, inevitably, frustrations remain. A practical recommendation for reducing their impact, and building up tolerance for frustration, is to start the child with mild frustrations and move him toward more severe ones. By such training, we try to help the child look for constructive ways of coping with frustration and failure. We do this by exposing him first to very clear-cut, black-and-white types of problems (or discriminations), providing guidance and emotional support as he works at them. As the child grows more and more capable of solving these problems, we narrow the discriminations and make the problems more complex and less clear-cut.

Excessive motivation is likely to impair performance in complex situations where a *correct* response or set of responses has not been established. The higher the drive state when such behavior choices must be made, the more likely it is that an already established "wrong" response will be made. Many inappropriate response tendencies that are ordinarily below threshold —that is, not likely to appear in behavior—will be strengthened under conditions of excessive motivation, and thus may interfere with performance. Since frustration is presumed to add to general drive level, and excessive frustration (or excessive anxiety) to add to it excessively, the recommendation follows that frustration should be kept within moderate limits. If it is not, it may cause an individual to perpetuate errors (behave in a rigid fashion) or be slow to select the single correct response or set of responses from competing but erroneous responses.

PROVIDING FOR INDIVIDUAL DIFFERENCES

Although the tremendous variation among children in a classroom subjects children to a wide variety of human-relations learnings, and adds interest to the teacher's task, this variation is also a major source of frustration for children. To confine this frustration to a minimum is a major and extremely difficult task for the teacher.

Almost everything that has been said earlier in this chapter relates to the topic of individual differences, and extensive literature on child development and education is devoted to this topic. By way of illustrating the problem, a hypothetical but not atypical fifth-grade class in a small town has been selected for description.

The teacher of such a group may have 36 or more children in her class, of whom about half are boys, half girls. Some of the girls in the class have already reached puberty, and most of them are in their prepubescent growth spurt. Two of the boys are pubescent. They are the oldest members of the class, and both of them have previously been "held back."

In terms of social status, this teacher's charges range from two children of itinerant farm workers, who come (shabby and ill-washed) into her classroom after an hour's ride on the school bus, carrying inadequate lunches in bags, to the daughter of the community's leading doctor, who walks the two blocks to school from her large and handsome home and goes home for a hot lunch.

The lowest IQ in the group is 77, the highest 145. One child in the room reads at the second-grade level, whereas another tests as high as the median for high-school seniors. The range in number proficiency is narrower, extending from second to ninth grade. The families of some of the children have never taken a daily newspaper, but one family subscribes to both a morning and an evening paper, and takes the Sunday New York *Times* as well. Some of the children have traveled no farther than a few miles outside the town limits, but the doctor's daughter has toured Europe, and one of the itinerant farm worker's children has attended schools in thirteen states.

One child in the room is Negro, and one Mexican-American (his parents do not speak English). Religious affiliations of the children's families include orthodox Judaism, agnosticism, Roman Catholicism, and Protestant groups ranging from the so-called fundamentalist to the progressive or liberal. The age range is from 10 to 14 years. One child has spent a year in a school for delinquent and predelinquent boys.

This picture seems extreme. But, for the elementary-school teacher in the small-town or consolidated school, and for junior-high teachers in all except the largest cities, it is not unrepresentative. In more populous urban centers, of course, the informal (and formal) residential segregation that exists restricts this variability in background. The school population becomes more homogeneous in high school because the less able students drop out, but even in high school variability remains very great.

With a population like that of our hypothetical fifth-grade classroom, individual differences in needs cannot be met in a fully satisfactory way. Most teachers are compelled to pitch their teaching at, or somewhat below, the median of the class, to spend a disproportionate amount of their time working with slow-learning or trouble-making children, and, to a regrettable degree, to allow the upper two fifths of the class to teach themselves. The result is severe frustration for the slowest-learning children in the room, and almost equally extreme frustration, due to boredom and too easily achieved success, for the two or three fastest-learning children.

One result of this procedure is that far too many intellectually gifted United States children do not learn to work by the time they reach college. Almost a third of Terman's "geniuses," for example, actually failed out of college for one or another reason (see Terman and Oden, 1947), although each possessed the potential to obtain advanced academic degrees. Accumulated hostility toward education may also have developed by the time a child becomes an adult and a taxpayer.

In the face of such difficulties, the American dream of universal education has nevertheless been achieved to a remarkable extent. The literacy rate is high, there is no hopeless schism between "aristocrat" and "peasant," and most children derive considerable satisfaction from their schooling. Individual needs are met, as best they can be, through the interested and dedicated teacher's knowledge of socioeconomic conditions, and through her efforts to understand the different problems of the children in her class. One of the most desirable characteristics in a teacher is the ability to put herself (or himself) to some degree in the child's place: to feel the lost-ness, the insecurity, even the hopelessness of the itinerant farm worker's child; to understand and sympathize with the doctor's daughter, who has always had everything (whereas teachers have often been forced, at least, in part, to work their way through school).

The most important tools for accommodating to individual differences are, then, compassionate knowledge of children's backgrounds and flexibility in dealing with them. Second, the schools must supply work materials of sufficient range so that no child needs to go unchallenged, yet no child needs to experience complete failure. Third, teaching should be done in subgroups formed according to modern principles of teaching and social grouping. As has been mentioned above, these groups should be as compatible as possible, and should be academically more homogeneous than the class as a whole. Modern testing techniques are sufficiently sophisticated to accomplish both of these goals. Sociometric tests (the determination, in strict professional confidence, of who are the good friends of each child in the class) are easy and quick to administer; and effective achievement tests exist for all areas of academics. Given social and educational data such as these, even our unwieldy class of 36 or more fifth-graders can be divided into "committees" for the benefit of all. It is probable that even such matters as classroom discipline can be improved by taking such steps.

Psychological literature now includes suggestions, based on experimental research, for dealing more effectively with special types of children in the classroom. For example, an experiment by Douvan (1956) suggests that concrete rewards are more effective in motivating lower-class children than are appeals to "intellectual excellence," which is the ordinary "coin of the realm" in the classroom. Douvan classified high-school seniors into three groups—middle class, working class, and "marginals" (children whose fathers held working-class jobs, yet who regarded themselves as middle-class). All these young people were failed on an experimental task, but half the members of each social-class group were told that they were expected to do as well as other comparable children (the "internal intellectual standards" group), while the members of the other half of each of the groups were told that if they did well, each would receive a $10.00 reward.

After the failure experience, a measure of achievement motivation was made for each socioeconomic group. The average number of achievement motives recorded for middle-class children for the "intrinsic intellectual appeal" condition ("Do the best you can") was 7.6, whereas working-class children scored only 4.9 achievement motives. The difference was significant statistically, and the marginals did not differ from the middle-class children. But, when the reward was tangible—hard cash—there were no differences between lower- and middle-class children: the average number of achievement-motive themes for the former was 8.1; for the latter, 8.3. The marginals obtained an average of 7.9, not significantly different from either of the other groups.

The implication of Douvan's study is that educational motivation—and perhaps motivation in general—should be made more concrete or tangible for lower- than for middle-class children. "Their academic consciences are not so well built-in."

THE SCHOOLS, HUMAN RELATIONS, AND PSYCHOLOGY

Among people concerned with education, controversy rages about the merits of "classical" versus "developmental" curricula. Although discussion of the merits of the controversy is outside the scope of this book, the following position is taken: Matters concerning human relations and social responsibility are not taught fully or adequately in United States elementary and secondary schools (and probably not in colleges). Covering them adequately does not preclude a "tough" substantive curriculum. Most people, upon serious thought, would admit that the world's and the nation's problems are less those of guided missiles and nuclear warfare than they are those of faulty human relations. The physical sciences are generations ahead of the social sciences.

What, basically, is homemaking: How to cook, or sew a set of drapes—or how to get along with a husband, children, and the neighbors? What is traffic safety: A matter of steering a car or a matter of using good manners and common sense? A local newspaper account tells of a driver passing on blind curves at a high rate of speed, with a load of strangers in his own car, who crashed head-on into a family-packed automobile, killing himself, most of his own passengers, and all of the family in the other car. This driver, only a few miles back on the road, had been stopped and warned by the highway patrol. Obviously, his driving skills were adequate, or he would not have got so far along the mountain road; but he had not learned that an automobile is a poor vehicle for expressing personal needs for power and aggression.

Studies of "Change in Human Nature"

Objections to teaching human relations in schools are frequently expressed by some version of the cliché, "The idea is fine, but you can't change human nature." Research literature now includes enough studies (sociological and psychological, survey and experimental) to enable us to dismiss this generalization with confidence.

Two studies have been conducted to determine the effectiveness of the program of the Wayne County Training School, a residential center for high-grade mentally defective delinquent or predelinquent children. In a sense, it is a luxury institution: at the time these studies were run (during the depression years of the '30's), there was a ratio of about 2 employees to every 5 children. The institution's grounds and buildings were attractive; the children were relatively well-dressed; counseling, therapy, and special education (both academic and vocational) were available for all children. Almost all the children, boys and girls, came from broken and disorganized families who lived in deteriorated urban slums. Children remained in the institution for an average of about three years.

In the first of these studies of children paroled from the institution into the community, Kephart and Ainsworth (1938) found that nearly three fourths of the boys had become law-abiding, self-supporting citizens, and had remained so for a period of from five to ten years after their return to the community. This was true despite the fact that the era of the study was also that of the social confusion and despair of the great Depression, and despite the fact that a population of this type is one of the least promising of the various problem subgroups of our society. Girls (Bijou, Ainsworth, and Stockey, 1943), who are more vulnerable than boys to accidental environment forces, were rehabilitated almost as successfully as boys—70 percent of them did well in the community during the study period of five to ten years following parole.

A study of the Hawthorne-Cedar Knolls School (Curran, 1955) provides similar but even more encouraging results: almost 85 percent of its resident population of disturbed and delinquent boys were successful after being returned to the community. For children treated in the "standard" state reform or training school, the estimate of recidivism (continued delinquency) is between 70 and 80 percent—hence, only 20 to 30 percent are successfully rehabilitated.

Experimental studies of "change in human nature" include one demonstrating that it is possible to teach children constructive reactions to frustration and failure (Keister, 1937); two that demonstrate success in making shy children more self-assertive or ascendant in experimentally devised social situations (Jack, 1934; and Page, 1936); one showing that highly ag-

gressive and competitive preschoolers can be trained to make more cooperative and socially approved responses (Chittenden, 1942); and one indicating that children's fears can be reduced through experience, reassurance,
and explanation (Jersild and Holmes, 1935).

A summary of the first of these studies illustrates the methods (and the
positive results) of the others. From a group of 82 preschoolers, Keister selected the 12 who showed the most maladaptive reaction to failure on a test
she devised: fitting back into a flat box a number of gaily painted wooden
figurines. The task is difficult for adults, almost impossible for children. The
children's constructive and nonconstructive behavior while working on the
problem was recorded. Examples of constructive behavior are: "Attempts to
solve alone; shows interest." Nonconstructive reactions consisted of such
behavior as, "No overt attempt to solve; asks another to solve; sulks; cries;
whines."

After this test, the experimenter (a young woman trained in preschool
teaching methods) worked with the children over a period of about six
weeks, with sessions for the different children ranging from 8 to 33 minutes
in duration. She taught them constructive approaches to a series of tasks
ranging from quite easy to quite difficult, employing techniques of reassurance, praise, and sometimes direct suggestions, and putting the children
through the training series in such a fashion that a child did not go on to a
more difficult task until he had succeeded on an easier one. She provides a
number of comments made by the children, of which the following is illustrative: "I'm sure havin' a hard time. But look! This is steadier now [his
block construction]. I'm makin' him better. I think it will stay this time.
Now it's gonna stay, I s'pose. See! It's gonna stay." (Keister, 1937, p. 70).

After these training situations the children were retested on a puzzle box
similar to but different from the original. Table 13.2, modified from Keister,
illustrates the dramatic nature of the differences in response to frustration
before and after training.

Keister used as a control group 12 children from the same nursery
school who had showed moderately poor reactions to the initial frustration,
and retested them when she retested her experimental group. Although the
controls had experienced the general benefits of the preschool program, they
did not show any significant improvements in reaction to the second
frustration task.

Social climates may also affect behavior powerfully. Behavioral changes
produced by variations in social climate have been demonstrated to be remarkably permanent by such "real-life" studies as the Wayne County Training School and the Hawthorne-Cedar Knolls studies discussed earlier (p.
435). However, a more specific picture of these changes is provided
by experimental studies.

The classical study in this area is that by Lewin, Lippitt, and White
(1939). Four groups, each made up of 5 ten-year-old boys, were placed

TABLE 13.2: DIFFERENCES IN RESPONSE TO FRUSTRATION AS A RESULT OF TRAINING TO PRODUCE FRUSTRATION TOLERANCE.

Behavior	Before Training;[1] Mean Minutes (N = 15)	After Training;[2] Mean Minutes (N = 12)[3]	Difference[4]
No overt attempt	6.0	2.1	3.9
Attempts to solve alone	8.5	11.2	2.7*
Asks another to solve	3.6	0.5	3.1
Asks help	2.5	2.4	0.1
Destructive behavior	0.6	—	0.6
Rationalizes	2.8	—	2.8
Shows interest	6.0	11.0	5.0*
No emotional manifestation	2.5	1.3	1.2
Indifference	1.0	—	1.0
Smiles	0.3	—	0.3
Laughs	—	0.1	0.1
Sulks	0.8	—	0.8*
Cries	1.7	—	1.7*
Whines	2.6	1.0	1.6
Yells	0.3	—	0.3
Motor manifestations of anger	0.2	—	0.2

Adapted from Keister (1937).

[1] Mean length of the experimental period was 14.5 minutes.
[2] Mean length of the experimental period was 13.3 minutes.
[3] Keister lost 3 subjects, either because of withdrawal from school or because of irregular attendance.
[4] Differences marked * are significant below the .05 level.

under the guidance of leaders who were, by turns and with different groups, authoritarian, democratic, or *laissez-faire* (indifferent and passive).

The boys in one of the authoritarian groups were rebellious and, in the other, passive; they displayed little "we" feeling, "went to pieces" when the leader left the room, and showed much hostility toward each other. The *laissez-faire* boys disliked their groups, were bored, quarrelsome, inefficient in group projects, and disorganized. The boys in the democratic groups showed least hostility toward each other, were "we-minded," held together best when the adult leader was absent, and worked constructively and happily. Later interviews with the boys showed that all but one had liked their democratic leaders better than their autocratic leaders.

This study has had profound educational effects, and its results are pleasing to all of us who espouse the democratic way of life. But it must be pointed out that the study has certain defects. Perhaps the most serious one is that the design of the study included no "benevolent authoritarian" group climate. The author, because of his own experience, is convinced that such an atmosphere is probably the most effective and efficient one in which an adult can begin his relations with, for example, delinquent groups. Once accepted, respected, and liked by them, the leader can begin to help the children become self-disciplined instead of having to be controlled by others.

Fresh from his experience as one of the four group leaders in the Lewin, Lippitt, and White study (and ardent in his convictions concerning democracy, warmth, and child-centeredness), the author went into a situation where he was partially responsible for the conduct of two cottages (residential centers for 30 to 40 boys each) of adolescent, mentally retarded, delinquent and predelinquent boys. Under the new regime of sweetness, light, trust in their better nature, and permissiveness, these youngsters went completely to pieces, making life miserable for their cottage personnel, themselves, and the writer. After some months of this nightmare, and after a particularly atrocious betrayal of trust, the author finally took one of the "gang" leaders over his lap and spanked him thoroughly—an embarrassing and temporarily painful experience for the gangling adolescent boy.

Following this incident, the atmosphere of the two cottages changed overnight; these slum youngsters had been talked to in their own language. Only then was it possible to put into action an effective democratic organization of the cottages. The effectiveness of this organization was attested by the fact that, after about two years, one of the cottages—during the acute manpower shortage early in World War II—operated well for some months with no adult living in it. During this time, an adult came in at meal- and bedtimes; but during the rest of the day, the residential group of 13- to 15-year-old low-IQ delinquent slum boys managed their own lives. There was no mayhem and there were no runaways, although on the average (under closely supervised conditions) one boy in 30 ran away weekly.

It is doubtful, however, whether democratic organization would have been equally effective had not the boys learned before the spanking episode that the adults responsible for them, though gullible, had real affection for them and were fair.

Another, but less obvious, flaw in the Lewin, Lippitt, and White study is related to the role-playing done by the four leaders in their three leadership roles. The four leaders were graduate students or postdoctoral fellows in child and clinical psychology. All were convinced and liberal equalitarians, living at a time when Hitler, the arch-authoritarian, was consolidating his power and preparing for world conquest. Each preferred and put his heart into his *democratic* leadership role, becoming perhaps the *warmest* and most dedicated democratic leader in recent history. But, when his turn came to play the authoritarian, he tended to become *cold* and *hard*—a veritable Captain Bligh. In the *laissez-faire* role, detachment of a profound sort became the order of the day. In other words, the crucial variable involved *may* have been warmth.

Despite its flaws, this study was a pioneering one that should be replicated.

In another study illustrating the changes that can result from shifts in group climate, McCandless (1942) checked the social structure of one of the Wayne County Training School cottages mentioned above, but before democratic organization was introduced. This checking consisted in part of asking the 13- to 15-year-old boys to list their three best friends in order from first to third. The "stars" (the most popular boys) were those whom the cottage supervisors, who made their ratings without knowing popularity status, agreed were "muscle men"—physically domineering boys. Boys rated by the supervisors as "mature and interested in conforming to adult standards" were low in popularity.

Some months after the cottage had been reorganized along democratic lines, these measurements were repeated, and the social structure of the group was found to have shifted dramatically. The relatively mature boys had become the stars, whereas the muscle men had dropped sharply in popularity and no longer held positions of group leadership. One of these boys had become quite disturbed by what was happening to him and, during the period of the study, had run away from the cottage repeatedly.

Several experiments in public-school mental health are now under way in the United States and Canada. These programs and studies place their emphasis on *preventive* and *creative* mental health, in contrast to more traditional research emphases on *remediation and cure*.[5]

One of the most extensive of these programs is the Preventive Psychiatry Project directed by Ojemann at the Iowa Child Welfare Research Station. Ojemann's approach to preventive psychiatry involves the concepts of a *surface* and a *causal* approach to human relations. He and his co-workers have made analyses (e.g., Stiles, 1950) of traditional curricular material (such as children's stories, and courses in civics), concluding from these that the United States approach to education is principally *surface,* fails partially to take account of human motivations, and neglects attempts at understanding the motivations of others.

Ojemann and his colleagues have prepared curricular materials which, although they do not ignore the traditional content of civics, for example, stress the motivations of members of society as these have been translated into social organization and law, and also consider how social organization and law in turn affect the individual. They have also prepared a number of causally oriented stories, which emphasize "psychological problem solving" and attempt to teach the child to look for the causes of behavior. The preventive-psychiatry program emphasizes the complexity of human nature and the multiplicity of causes that may underlie the "simplest" piece of behavior. The idea of "probabilistic thinking" is also stressed. For example, a child's fear may be caused by some specific unfortunate experience or set of experiences; but if this hypothesis does not work out, a secondary hypothesis may be that the child has a poor relation with his father; if this hypothesis is

[5] The Group for the Advancement of Psychiatry (GAP, 1951) has summarized these programs.

rejected, then we must look still further in our attempt to understand the child—operate, perhaps, on the assumption that his fear is symbolic of some apparently unrelated disturbance.

In the Ojemann project, it is assumed that the teacher's daily behavior (in addition to the more formal curriculum) is a vital causal (or surface) force operating on the child.

Ojemann and his co-workers are conducting research in a number of different school systems. Their undertakings include workshops in which teachers are trained in the causal approach; and the effects on school classes of being taught by such teachers are being examined. These studies provide for control classes composed of children similar to the experimental children, but taught by teachers without causal training. Although conclusions remain tentative—such research is enormously complicated—preliminary results are encouraging. It cannot yet be said, however, whether the signs of improved mental health in the experimental children are due to the causal approach as such or to the lift in their teachers' morale. Whatever the cause, the teachers, after their training, appear to be more understanding of children, more interested in the general process of normal development, and more enthusiastic about their work.

The implication of the research reviewed in this section is that human nature *can* be changed. It is possible, by firm and intensive treatment, to turn delinquent children into self-supporting, law-abiding citizens. Children's methods of reacting to frustration and failure, their ways of handling fear, and their aggressive behavior can be modified radically and constructively. Children seem to "do better" in an atmosphere of democracy, although (particularly for delinquent and lower-class groups) an initial group climate of benevolent authoritarianism may be necessary. Several studies now under way, which emphasize preventive mental health rather than treatment, have yielded encouraging though tentative results.

Evaluating a Child's Mastery of the Curriculum

A hotly debated issue in United States education concerns evaluation or "marking." Procedures for evaluating the progress of elementary-school children range all the way from interviews with parents, in which many phases of the child's development are discussed, to the traditional report card, on which everything from conduct to reading is graded by letter: A for excellent, F for "flunk," with no explanations given either parent or child. In junior and senior high school, such unqualified marks constitute the most typical form of evaluation.

Parent, child, teacher, and school counselor or psychologist (where there is one) must know at least three characteristics of the child's academic progress in order to guide him soundly: the child's personal potential, his ranking in his local group, and his standing on national norms. This is not to say that they do not need to know many things about his personal and social development as well.

THE CHILD'S PERSONAL POTENTIAL

The first and probably most important piece of information about the child's progress is how well he is doing in relation to his ability. In our society, much is made of competition (successful or unsuccessful) with others, but very little is said about "competition with oneself."

There has been much talk about the evils of competition, by modern educators who have deplored its existence in the classroom. It has been pointed out that society requires cooperation more than it does competition, and that education should stress the former.

Research studies on competition and cooperation indicate that children do more work while competing than while working alone (just as hens eat more corn when another fowl is present and eating than when they are alone); that "natural" teams (e.g., boys against girls) accomplish more when competing against each other than do "artificial" teams (randomly or arbitrarily assigned); and that children working toward a group goal, with no competing team, do the most work of all. For a fuller discussion of this subject, see Hurlock (1959), Jersild (1954), or Thompson (1952).

In the broad sense, ours is certainly as much a cooperative society as a competitive one, and perhaps more so: the flow of traffic (erratic as it often is) depends upon driver cooperation and conformity. In our daily living, we depend upon (cooperate with) the milkman, the postman, the grocer. To exist, labor and management cooperate more than they compete.

There is little question that a substantial share of our personal and social crises—our breakdowns in human relations—occur because of a failure to cooperate: because of our insensitivity to the needs of our fellow man, or his insensitivity to ours. While driving, we indignantly refuse to allow the pushing, honking, glaring motorist to pull in ahead of us from a side street; but should he smile hopefully and raise his eyebrows questioningly, we would gladly accommodate him, and gain from this a pleasant sense of having done good.

For such reasons, one tends to agree with the liberal educator that cooperation is insufficiently stressed in our schools. The corollary that is often drawn, however—that competition is bad and should be eliminated from the classroom—must be argued. Competition is here to stay, just as frustration is. Like frustration, competition is neither good nor bad; it is simply inevitable.

Hopi and Zuni Indian societies have been presented to us (e.g., Benedict, 1953) as free from competition. It is said that in these societies, each man lives as much for his neighbor and his group as for himself. However, Dennis (1955) obtained the *anonymous* wishes of Hopi adolescents about outcomes of competition, and found that in these circumstances the proportion who wanted to win was about the same as that of a population of non-Hopi Virginia adolescents. This competitive spirit may have been taught the Hopi youth in their "American style" schools, of course, although it seems unlikely that what has been said to be the spirit of the culture could be so easily contravened; more probably, the secret wish to win persists despite the well-documented public Hopi living pattern.

In our society, children and youth need to know how to compete effectively, realistically, and gracefully. Everyone wins *and* loses; each person must adjust to both circumstances, and it is perhaps as difficult to learn to handle a win gracefully as it is to lose in good style.

It might be very profitable for parents, teachers, and others who deal with children and youth to shift their emphasis from competition with others to "competition with the self"—that is, to living up to the potential one has. Certainly, the schools should provide information about a child's *actual* progress in relation to what he can do *potentially*. If children were assigned grades on such a basis, the pattern of many "report cards" would be greatly changed. For example, as a group, the intellectually superior perform much less well than would be expected (see pp. 228–232), even allowing for the statistical concept of "regression to the mean."[6] If grading were done according to potential performance, using conventional letter markings, many superior children might receive C's or F's, even though their *absolute* performance is better than that of other children in a class. Using this "self-reference" system, the slowest child in the class, working up to his capacity, might receive an A.

THE CHILD'S RANK IN HIS LOCAL GROUP

The standing of a child within his classroom group typically determines the teacher's evaluation of his performance. This comparative evaluation is probably the most important single criterion by which a child forms his self-concept about his academic prowess.

Evaluation based solely on how children in a given class compare with one another can lead children to very inaccurate perceptions of their academic ability. A relatively bright child in a blighted neighborhood may develop grandiose notions of his ability; a bright child in a highly superior class may develop an unjustifiably poor notion of his ability. Isolated or rural communities frequently develop "delusions of grandeur" in at least the top students in a class.

Girls, who are more conforming, probably work somewhat harder, and are socially more mature than boys, typically get higher grades than boys, although their actual standing on standardized and objective tests of aca-

[6] Exceptional status (extremely high or extremely low) with respect to one trait does not imply equally exceptional status with respect to other traits (unless the traits selected have a very high correlation). Mentally retarded youngsters, for example, will be closer to the national average in height than they are in IQ; intellectually superior children will be closer to the national average in study efficiency and motivation than in intellectual status.

demic achievement is not higher (particularly after elementary school) than boys'. Teachers' grades correlate well with girls' achievement on objective and standardized achievement tests, but show much lower correlations with boys' ratings on the same instruments. The exceptionally bright child who is young for his group may be graded no higher (or may be graded lower) than older children in the group who, intellectually, are less able (see pp. 222–223). Grades often seem to be based on conformity and good manners almost as much as on performance.

Other deficiencies of the marking system, and a discussion of the difficulty teachers experience in selecting the bright children in their classes, have been discussed in Chapter 7.

Despite the weaknesses of a grading system based on relative standing in a classroom, knowledge of this standing is important in guiding children. Parents need to know, and their child *does* know, where he stands in relation to his classroom group. Teachers should, of course, mark with scrupulous fairness. It is probable that boys are somewhat penalized by the average teacher's marking, and, since breadwinners in the United States are preponderantly male, this is a serious defect in the grading system. If relative academic failure discourages a substantial proportion of boys from going on to exploit their potentialities, educators should explore the problem thoroughly.

THE CHILD'S STANDING ON NATIONAL NORMS

The third major type of academic evaluation involves a comparison of the child's performance with national norms. In Iowa, for example, the top-ranking student in some high-school graduating classes stands lower on objective and standardized tests of academic achievement than the lowest-ranking student in other high schools. In some areas of the United States, as many as *two thirds* of high-school graduates fall below the *median* (midpoint) of high-school graduates from other sections of the country (e.g., Bloom, 1956).

Such discrepancies can (and *do*) lead to serious complications when, for example, the valedictorian of an inferior high school goes to college and begins competing with students who have been better trained than he. An equally serious problem, although perhaps not as traumatizing to the individual, is the lowering of self-concept that may occur for children in the middle or toward the bottom of the class distribution in highly efficient and rigorous school systems. Such youngsters may be quite capable of mastering advanced training, but be discouraged from trying to attend college by their relatively mediocre elementary- and secondary-school performance.

For reasons such as these, the child and those responsible for his guidance should know how he stands on norms extending beyond his classroom and school. Such norms exist, and tests standardized on a large and representative population should be administered routinely to children in all schools. Only through the repeated use of such tests can all the important goals of evaluation be achieved: (1) comparing the child's year-by-year growth with his ability; (2) comparing his performance with the achievements of his classmates (thus giving the teacher a valuable check on her own objectivity); and (3) comparing the child (and the school) against broader norms. Certain disadvantages of such full reporting are inevitable— some children are moderately shocked, others made cocky, some parents push their children excessively, and so on—but the advantages of full and factual guidance seem to outweigh the disadvantages.

A fifth-grade friend of the author's attends a school where these three types of evaluation are routinely carried out. He is a bright but underachieving child, and such a picture of him appeared clearly on his progress report. At a conservative estimate, he could, at the end of his fifth-grade year, have been achieving about as well as the average United States child beginning the eighth grade; he was actually doing about as well as the average child at the beginning of the seventh grade. He stood at or near the top of his class in intellectual potential; but his actual achievement (whether measured by standardized tests or by teachers' marks) ranked at or slightly below the median of his class. According to the national norms for the test he was given, he scored better than 90 percent of United States children on all subtests but one.

From a study of his test profile (his scores on various subtests, such as reading comprehension, number performance, number comprehension, spelling, map reading, and so on), this boy provided his own educational guidance. The test profile showed that his two lowest scores were in reading comprehension and reading speed. This deficiency in reading, he was able to see, handicapped his performance in everything else, and the remedy was more free reading. As a result, he moved toward a goal that his parents and teachers had for some years been trying to achieve: he began to read extensively on his own, and subsequently improved in academic standing both within his class and according to broader norms.

BREADTH OF EVALUATION

To this point, discussion of evaluation has been limited to description and measurement of academic progress. However, evaluation should be creative as well as descriptive. It should be designed to discover and record a range of talents broader than intellectual and academic proficiency. Parents, teachers, and schools in general should be on the lookout for such gifts as exceptional artistic and athletic ability. Floyd Patterson, as a case in point, attained championship status as a prize fighter; but he might have been an even greater champion, and some or many of his academic and personal troubles might have been prevented or alleviated, if his gifts of speed, power, and coordination had been discovered through creative evaluation when he was, for example, in the third grade. His talents must certainly have been present, at least in nascent form, as early as his elementary-school years.

Skill in such activities as music, art, tennis, and swimming are correlated only very modestly with measured intelligence and academic standing, and may easily be overlooked in a school system that is oriented exclusively toward academics (of course, this is not to deny that the basic function of schools is their academic function). Discovery and development of nonacademic talents may be a key to the adjustment problems of many children—the path by which they escape from the academic mediocrity that has given them a sense of failure. Thus, creative evaluation may not only make a positive contribution to society, but be of therapeutic value to many individuals as well. Currently, however, such evaluation is given a minor role—usually, lip service only—in most United States school systems.

Failure to stress creative evaluation may have later unfortunate effects on the schools' public relations. For example, it has been suggested that successful men in the business community often obtained poor or mediocre academic records as children. May not some of their later suspicion of—or, at best, lack of enthusiastic support for—the schools be an outgrowth of their school experiences? To become successful, they must have possessed attributes of drive, clear thinking, and initiative that could have been, but were not, recognized and rewarded during their school years. The next chapter portrays the adjustment of lower-class children to schools; usually, this adjustment is frustrated and unhappy—certainly not of the type to cause the lower-class child, as an adult, to show much sympathy for the school system at whose hands he has suffered.

ACCEPTANCE OF EVALUATION

If evaluations are to be accepted by children and their parents, they must be accurate, fair, and comprehensive. They must also be adequately interpreted. To achieve both of these objectives, teachers, school administrators, and counselors should acquire sound knowledge of evaluation procedures, including testing methods and sophisticated interpretation of test results. Weaknesses as well as strengths of tests should be recognized. Subjective influences on class grades should be recognized and allowed for. Aspects of evaluation other than the academic should be developed.

School people should have some training in counseling and should work to develop attitudes that accompany successful counseling—for example, tolerance of individual differences; acceptance, without condemnation and rejection, of parents and children *as they are;* recognition of the worth and integrity of the human personality; awareness that almost all parents, no matter how misguided they may seem, genuinely wish to do the best they can for their children.

Some teachers seem almost to want the children in their classes for their own. Regarding themselves almost as substitute parents, they manifest a certain amount of resentment toward the children's real mothers and fathers. Although it is understandable and desirable that teachers should enter their profession because they like people, and *particularly* children, this liking should be realistically based and nonpossessive. Teachers should be on guard against rejecting parents because their own lives are empty, or because their own maternal or paternal needs are not fully satisfied.

SUMMARY

This chapter has discussed emotional factors affecting all areas of the child's (and adult's) life. Topics have ranged from level of aspiration to evaluation of performance in and out of school.

Central to understanding both school and life performance is the concept of *level of aspiration*. This term ordinarily has a personal frame of reference: an individual has a positive level of aspiration if, for "next time," he predicts that he will do better on a task than he did the last time he tried it. However, the term can also be applied in an absolute sense: one man aspires to write great literature or to achieve fame through science, while another wants only to be personally secure.

Most children and adults believe and hope that their future achievement will be superior to their past performance. The implications of this finding are that children should be kept reaching, but that their reaching should be so structured as to afford reasonable hope for a successful outcome. The level of aspiration is usually raised after success and lowered after experiences of failure. Maladjusted groups of children and adults are more variable in their predictions about performance, following both success and failure, than are normal groups.

Suggestive evidence exists that persistent success or failure may have long-lasting effects on an individual's level of aspiration (his "ambition"). Success will buoy him up; failure will depress him. In the academic sphere, middle-class children seem to possess more positive levels of aspiration and stronger achievement motives than lower-class children.

The achievement motive may be thought of as a widely generalized *positive* level of aspiration. A person with high achievement motive regards problems, obstacles, and competition as a challenge to be met: he works for success. Others seem to be motivated more by fear of failure than by desire for success. An adjustment that is predominantly achievement-oriented appears to result in middle-of-the-road aspirations: the individual is neither overly cautious, nor is he reckless. But predominant motivation to avoid failure seems to result either in undue caution or, more frequently, in reckless attempts to achieve.

Achievement, of course, is heavily stressed in our culture. Both those who are generally motivated to achieve and those whose generalized motive is to avoid failure have acquired or learned such adjustments, usually in their family setting. Anxiety about achievement often accompanies both learning to value achievement and learning to fear failure. Achievement anxiety may be "situation-specific" (i.e., it may arise only in situations where achievement is expected, and where competition exists), or it may simply be one of many manifestations of chronic anxiety. Achievement anxiety probably leads to inefficiency in performance more often than it does to efficiency, although if an individual possesses all the "right" or correct responses for dealing with a situation or solving a problem or taking a test, anxiety may increase his efficiency rather than interfere with it. Anxiety about achievement may have much in common with fixation, and may be very difficult to extinguish.

The author takes the rather widely accepted position that frustration can be defined in two ways: first, as failure to achieve a goal, or blockage (of a more temporary sort) of a person's efforts to reach a goal; and second, as a drive induced by such failure or blocking. Frustration in the first sense cannot be considered either "good" or "bad," but must be thought of as inevitable and ubiquitous. The important child-training consideration, then, is not how to avoid frustration, but how to handle it and resolve it constructively.

When frustration is considered in this light, the following recommendations emerge for parents and teachers: (1) Attempt to avoid *irrelevant* frustrations in training and teaching children; (2) help children acquire a general "frustration tolerance" by starting them with easy learning tasks, discriminations, and problems; guiding their solutions; and moving them, after success, to more difficult problems; and (3) keep frustration (in the sense of a *drive*) moderate, insofar as this is possible, since severe frustration seems to interfere with performance more often than to facilitate it, particularly in complex learning situations for which there exist many competing responses, of which the majority are inappropriate (wrong).

A major source of frustration is the enormous variability among children in a family or classroom. In a typical classroom, the superior child is likely to be frustrated by lack of challenge to his abilities, while the inferior child is consistently frustrated by his inability to keep pace with the rest of the class. Meeting this problem of individual differences in ability, personality, physical characteristics, and so on, is one of the most difficult problems faced by the schools. Failure to challenge bright youngsters may result in their learning inefficient study methods, acquiring only low motivation, and failing to develop tolerance for future failures; while failure to meet the needs of slow-learning children may induce self-defeating attitudes of discouragement and pessimism. Similar, although perhaps less extreme, problems may arise in any family where there is more than one child.

Evaluation of children's performance is necessary, both in the family and in the school setting, although it assumes a more formal guise in school. Whether evaluation is done formally or informally, in the family or in the school, it should be guided by three principles. First, the child should be evaluated in terms of his own capacity: has he done as well as he is potentially able to do? Second, he should be evaluated in terms of his reference group, if for no other reason than that he compares himself with this group. Since his own comparison may be distorted (this problem was discussed in

Chapter 6 in relation to the self-concept), it is essential that he be given an accurate evaluation. The immediate reference group may consist of either the child's brothers or sisters or his classmates at school. Third, the child's performance should be evaluated according to broad norms based, for example, on a state-wide or nationally selected population or even, conceivably, on a representative international population. Thus, the relatively able child who competes rather unsuccessfully with a superior set of classmates can be made to realize that he is quite competent according to broader standards; or, if he has been consistently compared with below-average children (as many bright lower-class or rural children are), he will know that the future may hold more competitive difficulties for him than he has met in the past.

United States public schools have tended to neglect teaching "human relations." A substantial body of research literature indicates that important aspects of "human nature" *can* be changed through education—for example, delinquents can be reformed; and children who are low in frustration tolerance be taught to meet failure constructively.

The Middle-Class Teacher and the "Every-Class" Child

AMERICANS do not like to think of their society as being characterized by social class. With the term is associated an idea of snobbery that sits uneasily on the consciences of those who are proud to be citizens of a democracy and who, in their heart of hearts, believe that "every boy can become president."

On the other hand, everyone realizes that social class exists. It is probably here to stay. There is no town so small that it does not have a "wrong side of the tracks" and a "right part of town." In small towns, these differences are less striking than in big ones, but they exist nonetheless. In rural areas, some farmsteads are "nice," others are "slummy"; although residential distinctions are less clearly marked in rural than in urban areas.

Children from the lowest social classes in large cities may come later than rural and small-town children to recognize their low social status, living, as they are likely to, in segregated slum areas where everyone else is like them. The lower-class rural or small-town child is exposed very early to the fact that his house is shabbier, his clothing less good, than that of the child who lives two blocks away, or on the next farm.

People clique together socially: professors are more comfortable with doctors than they are with businessmen. When businessmen gather socially, they are not likely to be found in company with members in good standing of the plasterer's union. The banker's daughter is more likely to marry the lawyer's son than the telephone lineman's boy.

There are social-class differences in tastes. An Associated Press article (February 22, 1959, Des Moines, Iowa, *Register*) tells of a beer that is popular with the working but not with the middle or upper social classes. According to this report, the company that makes the beer is trying discreetly to give it more snob appeal without at the same time losing the blue-collar clientele. Children of some social classes are more likely to go to college (even though they may not be any brighter) than children of other social classes. Although this difference is partly economic, it is not entirely so, as we have seen in earlier chapters.

Not only do social classes differ in preferences for beverages, food, clothing, and manner of speaking, they also differ in values, religion, intellectual interest, and social beliefs. These differences are exceedingly likely to lead to breakdowns in interclass communication: members of one class almost literally do not understand what members of another class are talking about, what they are striving for, or why their goals are important to them. When there is so gross a deficiency in communication, there is little understanding; and when there is little understanding, suspicion and even hostility are likely to develop. Adding to this likelihood of suspicion and hostility between social classes is the fact that there are frequently very important conflicts of interest between them. The middle- or upper-class landlord resents the cost of improving rental properties occupied by members of the lower class, and his tenants are justifiably bitter about the condition of their dwelling places. The aristocrat resents higher taxes on his inherited fortune; the lower-class widow desperately needs an increase in her "Aid to Dependent Children" funds. The successful medical practitioner resists any move toward "socialized medicine," while the poor neglect their health because they cannot afford doctor and drug bills.

This problem of breakdowns in communication and conflict of interest is particularly acute in public- and parochial-school education, where teachers, who are almost without exception middle-class people, must try to communicate clearly and effectively with children of all social classes. Although the content of this chapter refers primarily to the child's life in school and to his relations with his teachers, it is equally relevant for other professional and lay people who work with children and families: nursing and public-health personnel; speech therapists; recreation, probation, and social workers; public-health oriented doctors and dentists; and members of youth-oriented service clubs. Members of all these groups are, in overwhelming majority, middle-class; yet their clientele comes from all social classes, particularly the working or lower class.

The lack of communication between social classes can, and often does, have extremely unfortunate consequences in such areas as labor-management relations. A substantial portion of our difficulties with delinquents is the result of such failure of understanding and communication: the delinquent's difficulties often start as a result of the discrepancy between his lower-class standards and interests and the middle-class values of his teacher. When communication with the school has completely broken down, social work and legal agencies take over—but they too are staffed by the middle class, so that the situation may be little or not at all improved.

Problems of communication also exist between different ethnic and national groups. Education for vast numbers of Negro and Puerto Rican children, for example, is complicated both by their social-class position, which is lower, on the average, than that of the so-called core culture, and by their membership in a minority group. To the Puerto Rican child's difficulties usually is added the handicap of speaking a foreign language.

DEFINITIONS OF SOCIAL CLASS

One of the most widely used definitions of social class is that provided by Warner, Meeker, and Eells (1949). Their "Index of Status Characteristics" is made up by assigning points to four of five social characteristics. The most heavily weighted variable is occupation (of the father, for children; of the self for mature and established adults). A rating of 1 is given to doctors, dentists, judges, professors, and so on, or to persons with large capital investments or high status in business, management, or government. A rating of 7 is given to unskilled laborers, domestic servants, or migrant workers. Each social characteristic is given such a rating, from 1 (high) to 7 (low).

Next most heavily weighted is the source of family or personal income. A rating of 1 is given when at least half the income comes from inherited savings and investments; income from salary or commission, including pension, earns a rating of 4; and a value of 7 is assigned to income from public relief or "nonrespectable" income.

Housing is third in importance in calculating this index. An individual receives a rating of 1 if he lives in a large house of nine rooms or more, in good condition and set in adequate grounds; he is given a 7 if he resides in a house or apartment in bad condition, or in a dwelling not originally intended as a home (such as one that has a store front).

The fourth characteristic from which the index is computed is either the area lived in or the educational level of the father (or the self, for adults). Areas of residence rated as 1 are select residential areas in "the best part of town"; slum areas and neighborhoods in bad repute earn a rating of 7. Since it is difficult to rate "area" in small towns and rural sections, "education of father" may be substituted for the area rating. A 1 is assigned if he has completed as much as one or more years of graduate work at a college or university. For older people, a rating of 7 is assigned for education below third grade; for younger people, a rating of 7 is given for education stopping below eighth grade.

Social class has been defined in a number of other ways, although most of the definitions involve either paternal (or maternal) occupation or education, or both. Centers (1950, 1951) has developed a "psychological" measure of social class: in effect, he has determined differential attitudes and beliefs that characterize different segments of the population. People are assigned by him to one social class or another depending on the pattern of their answers to his attitude and belief questions. However, Centers also often uses the more conventional variables (such as education or occupation), either independently or in conjunction with the psychological method of classification.

There are obvious deficiencies in these definitions of social class. In one city, the Presbyterian minister, a man trained to the doctoral level, lives in a "poor" part of town: his parsonage is in the same block with a filling station, a bar, and a beer storage warehouse. This man would receive an occupational rating of 1 according to Warner and his colleagues; on his source of income, he would be rated 4, since he is paid a salary; his house would merit a 3, since it is a medium-sized house in fair condition; if he were rated on the area in which he lived, he would receive a 5 at best, and probably a 6; but if the permissible alternative of rating his education were chosen, he would obtain a 1. If, of these last two ratings, area of residence were used, he would be classified as lower middle class; however, if the basis of ranking were education, his social classification would be upper middle. Actually, in the city in which he lives, he belongs to the highest social level. Usually, however, the numerical ratings are less variable from one "rating zone" to another than in the example chosen.

Although differential social-class ratings have been worked out for farm populations (e.g., Belcher, 1951; Kaufman, 1944, 1946; and Sewell, 1940, 1943) they are not widely used. In one classification system all farmers are listed together as being in class 4 of a hierarchy in which 1 is high and 7 low. But the social differences between the "gentleman farmer," who has inherited large blocks of land, the struggling tenant farmer, who pays rent either in cash or in kind, and the farm laborer are as great as those between a medical doctor or a lawyer and an unskilled laborer.

Despite varying definitions, however, almost all studies of social class have demonstrated differences between classes for variables ranging from intelligence through rate of delinquency to child-rearing practices.

Social-Class Characteristics of Teachers

For a number of years, the writer has been a "teacher of teachers." Repeatedly, after using the Warner Index of Status Characteristics as an illustration of how social class is measured, he has asked the students in his classes (who probably represent the more "ambitious" educators) to indicate (anonymously) their social class. Without exception (indeed, almost by definition), these teachers are middle-class, and the overwhelming majority of them have improved their class status (i.e., they have advanced further educationally and, usually, economically than their parents). In other words, they are upwardly mobile, are proud of their status (although they deplore some of its disadvantages, such as poor salaries, community snooping into their personal affairs, etc.). They also want their own children to continue upwardly mobile—that is, to do still better than they themselves have done.

The Value System of the Middle Class

What are the values of the middle class? No one can say with certainty, nor can a complete list be constructed; nor, if one were constructed, would all members of the middle class agree with the inclusions in the list. However, the following set of values and beliefs appears to be subscribed to by a majority of the middle class, and perhaps particularly by those members of it who compose the professions and lay groups that work with children. Since, of all such groups, teachers ordinarily have the most extensive and immediate impact on children, this list and the discussion accompanying it are linked to teachers, although the broad reference is to the middle class in general.

The list represents the author's experience and general reading. It has not been drawn directly from research, although many specific pieces of research are synthesized in it.

The majority of the United States middle-class population, and perhaps especially teachers, appear to support the following values:

1. Most members of the middle class believe in God, and act on this belief to the extent of attending church. Usually they do more about church than merely attend. The majority of public-school teachers in the United States are Protestant.

2. Belief in personal cleanliness—clean clothing, clean bodies, clean teeth, clean hair, and clean fingernails—characterizes the middle class in general, and teachers in particular.

3. Teachers, like the middle class as a whole, believe in thrift. Teachers as a group do not have much money to save or invest, but by and large they believe firmly in the American adage that "a penny saved is a penny earned." Through their organizations, they have worked genteelly but with moderate effectiveness toward retirement plans, teacher annuity and group insurance associations, discount buying, and so on. Luxuries, including vacations, are planned for; it is disgraceful to be long overdue on debts. Payments on large debts or installment obligations may be small, but they are punctual. Falling behind in money matters causes real anxiety. For the middle class, possessions are both a sign of status and an indication of security. Ownership of a house, a lot, some real estate, some good stocks is important not only in and of itself, but because of what it represents.

4. Intellect should be used before emotion and should be the controlling factor in managing one's affairs, whether these are personal or concern the larger community. Teachers and the middle class in general are as emotional as anyone else, but they are somewhat ashamed of their emotions and believe that life should be handled according to the dictates of common sense and reason.

5. For such reasons as those expressed in (4), teachers and other members of the middle class try to avoid expressing strong emotion and are guilty and ashamed when they do. Of the various emotions, those that are openly aggressive or sexual in nature are particularly to be avoided. People should live peacefully and chastely together.

6. If aggression *must* be expressed, the avenues for expressing it should be socially acceptable. Teachers and other members of the middle class do not like to get into loud abusive arguments, physical combat, or barroom brawls. Their hostilities are likely to be expressed verbally, in the form of

gossip (or, at the worst, sarcasm), rather than in more direct and violent ways. Physical aggression is seldom employed, except possibly behind the wheel of a car—honkings, inconsiderateness, glarings, and the like. Although poor driving manners are frowned upon, their use is a not uncommon way for the middle class to vent its spleen—as can be seen easily any weekday at the morning, noon, and late-afternoon traffic peaks.

7. The middle class prides itself on sexual restraint. The stereotype of the teacher, probably as inaccurate as other stereotypes, is a prim and spinsterish woman and a repressed, dour, and somewhat effeminate (or at least not conspicuously virile) man. Coaches escape this stereotype, but they too are expected to lead lives that, sexually, do not go beyond the respectable joys of conventional wedded bliss.

8. Clean and correct language is a matter of middle-class pride. It is permissible for the middle-class male to swear, even sulphurously, if he bangs his thumb in a do-it-yourself project, but only if he is alone or, possibly, in the company of other men like himself. Most particularly, swearing should never be indulged in, no matter what the provocation, when children are within earshot. Shady stories are all right when men are together, but not when women are present. Verbal exchanges between the sexes should be well-laundered. This particular canon has been considerably relaxed in recent years, although the freedom and frankness of verbal exchange between the sexes almost never reaches the point that is typical of the lower class, particularly of the lower-lower class group. The standards of the upper-lower class are not far from those of the middle class, just as the standards of the upper-middle class are not far from those of the upper class.

9. Since the middle class believes in restraint of impulses, particularly those of sex and aggression, and endorses moderation in all things, it follows logically that temperance in the consumption of alcoholic beverages is also advocated. The strictures in this regard are firmer for women than for men, but definitely apply to both sexes. Alcohol releases inhibitions, and alcohol is expensive. Hence it is to be used sparingly if at all. Although the absolute prohibition of teachers' drinking that formerly existed in many parts of the United States has been considerably relaxed, it still holds in many places in the South and the Midwest, where the teacher is expected to set a model of abstemiousness and virtue—all along the line and without exception—for the youth with whose education he is charged.

10. The middle class believes in, although it does not always practice, scrupulous honesty in speech and action (including financial dealings). Although in practice there is much "white-collar crime," in principle middle-class people do not condone lying and stealing (although the managers of hotels, as they tally their towels and ashtrays, have some reason to doubt the extent to which these values are binding). Teachers, being public servants whose salaries are a matter of community knowledge, are more constrained to financial honesty than many other occupational groups within

the middle class. Not for them is the padding of the expense account or the partial evasion of the income tax. Their financial affairs are matters of public knowledge. The leading newspaper of one midwestern state, for example, periodically publishes the salaries of all employees of state-supported institutions of higher education. The teacher, if he has larcenous inclinations, must content himself with a few pencils or an occasional package of writing or typing paper. If he falls too far behind with his creditors, his job is likely to be forfeited—indeed, his creditors are not unlikely to be the members of his school board.

11. The middle class remains firmly convinced, although again does not necessarily act on its conviction, that hard work and self-discipline will bring success. That is to say, if one is not impulsive, if one does not gratify his immediate needs for pleasure but postpones them for the sake of later satisfactions, he will in the long run be happier, have more money in the bank, and be more esteemed, both by the community and by himself. This middle-class ethic is as old as the fable of the grasshopper and the ant. In such a society as ours, the principle is sound enough although many regard it as dull—but it works better for middle than for lower-class people, who, usually, do not make it regardless of how hard they work.

Paradoxically, the middle class also holds such beliefs and values as these: "The breaks are a help. . . . You have to get to know the right people. . . . Influence will get you a long way," etc.

12. Along with sentiments endorsing hard work and self-discipline goes a belief that one should acknowledge and live up to the expectations of others and should do his duty, unrewarding as this may often appear to be. Actually, the middle class believes that doing one's duty is virtuous in and of itself.

Examples of the esteem in which doing one's duty and working hard are held are such statements as these: "You can't let other people down. . . . If you have an obligation, live up to it. . . . I have always tried to do what my mother taught me at her knee was right. . . . If a job is worth doing at all, it is worth doing well. . . . All that I ask of any employee is an honest eight hours' work in a day. . . . Genius is 90 percent perspiration and 10 percent inspiration. . . . A man is just as good as his word. . . . I must maintain my position, and live up to the obligations it entails. . . . The devil finds work for idle hands to do."

13. Finally (and these thirteen points are meant rather as illustrations of middle-class beliefs and values than as a complete list), the middle class believes firmly in learning for learning's sake. Learning and schooling (which are by no means completely synonymous) are seen as vehicles for getting ahead, for bettering oneself. A college education is also viewed as a virtue in and of itself, regardless of the practical use to which it is put. A middle-class family feels disgraced if one of its children fails to finish high school. Girls should have a college education, whether they use it or not, because it "broadens" them. The reading of a biography has higher merit

than the reading of a piece of fiction, and heavy or historical fiction is viewed with more favor than light or humorous fiction. However, appreciation of culture purely for its own sake is more an upper- than a middle-class virtue. Paradoxically, *too much* learning is viewed with suspicion. The United States seems most to esteem the well-educated but practical man. It is uneasy about the scholar—unless he puts his great fund of information to work at some pursuit such as writing encyclopedias (which are held in high esteem because they are practical repositories of knowledge) or (in years not so far gone by) winning television quiz shows that emphasized breadth of information rather than depth of thinking or knowledge.

Such, then, is a crude, incomplete, and subjective map of the beliefs and values that characterize the middle class, one rather typical section of which is made up of teachers. Society not only entrusts these teachers with the imparting of skills, facts, and knowledge to its young, but (since school policy is set by middle-class people) explicitly expects them to pass these values on to their pupils by precept and example.

MIDDLE-CLASS VALUES AND LOWER-CLASS CHILDREN

Population by Social Class

What is the distribution of United States school children by social class? This question is difficult to answer, but an approximation of the distribution of persons over 14 years of age by social class has been made from the 1950 federal census. The census gives the occupational listings of people over 14. From these figures, the author has estimated that 39.4 percent of the population is middle- or upper-class; 55.3 percent belongs to the working class; and 5.2 percent are farmers. As has been pointed out, it is difficult, although not impossible, to classify farm population according to social class. Because of this difficulty, the farm-operating population will be omitted from the present discussion, although the 5.9 percent of the population engaged in farm labor and foremanship will be included. This group, for the most part, falls into the lower-lower socioeconomic bracket.

The 55.3 percent of the population belonging to the working class is made up in a ratio of about 3 to 2 of skilled craftsmen (who are usually classified in the group that Warner, Meeker, and Eells call upper-lower class) and unskilled workers (who, according to the same criterion, are considered lower-lower class). In other words, about one fourth of the adults in the United States are lower-lower class; almost one third, upper-lower class; and fewer than two fifths, middle and upper class. Since there is a tendency for lower-class families to have more children than middle- or upper-class families, one can estimate roughly that of pupils attending United States public elementary schools, nearly two thirds come from lower-class homes. At least one fourth, and probably more, of United States children come from lower-lower class homes.

The reader should keep in mind that these figures are approximations only (although Hollingshead in 1949 reported roughly these proportions in the midwestern "Elmtown" he studied), and that they are based on a strictly occupational classification. It may also be that distinctions between the middle and the lower classes have become increasingly blurred during the long period of prosperity dating from the early 1940's.

Regardless of the accuracy of the figures suggested above, the large number of lower-class children who must be educated remains beyond dispute. Their teachers, however, are overwhelmingly middle class, either having been born into the middle class or having worked themselves up to it. The implications of differences in social class between teachers and their pupils are set forth in the remaining sections of this chapter.

Concentration of Research by Social Class

Most psychological and sociological research concerning social class has been based on research populations ranging from the upper-lower to the lower-upper class. Little research has been conducted with lower-lower individuals or groups, except insofar as children from this class have served as research subjects while attending public school or have been present in one or another type of residential treatment center. Their parents usually do not understand the purposes of research and hence do not cooperate with it. Neither have upper-upper subjects often served in psychological or sociological research. Their children are frequently "sequestered" in private schools, and they are themselves relatively unapproachable. It would, for example, take a psychologist or a sociologist with considerable temerity to request a research interview with, let us say, a senior Vanderbilt about her methods of child-rearing. It is not unlikely that, approached by an intensely devoted research worker, upper-upper class parents would take part in research; but their social position is sufficiently threatening to the conforming and usually somewhat deferential middle-class investigator that they are seldom asked.

This factor of subjective threat may also be partly responsible for the fact that lower-lower class parents have seldom been recruited as research subjects. A tough-minded, intensely motivated research worker could probably secure information about, for example, their child-rearing practices. But in the process he might be sworn at and even punched in the nose. He would have to go into residential areas that are objectionable to him, besides posing the threat of possible physical danger. He would have to translate his questions into simple and highly practical terms. Most research workers do not have these personal attributes of toughness, dedication, and flexibility. Hence, research subjects are rather generally drawn from the middle class, who talk the same language as the research worker, who hold standards similar to his, and who believe in "knowledge for knowledge's sake," just as he does. With such people, he is comfortable.

This focus on the middle class is more pronounced in studies of families (where the parents are involved) than it is in studies of the children themselves, although, as has been mentioned, upper-class children are not often available as research subjects in either public schools or institutions. Some work has been done with them at the college level (e.g., MacArthur, 1955*a*, *b*), since they attend such institutions of higher learning as Yale, Harvard, Princeton, Vassar, and Sarah Lawrence.

In other words, what is said here about the middle-class teacher and the social class of the children with whom she works is based on limited scientific information—information that does not include upper-class children and parents, and information that underrepresents, if indeed it represents at all, the values and beliefs of parents at the bottom of the social heap—the lower-lower class parents.

A substantial portion of the following sections is based on the author's experience with children from urban lower-lower classes, whose behavior had been sufficiently deviant to require their being sent to a residential treatment center for children of below-normal intelligence. In the course of working with them, it was both necessary and easy to get to know their brighter brothers and sisters (although these children and young people often had problems not much less severe than their institutionalized sibs), and their parents (who had their problems as well).

Some of the material is based on the author's close association with lower-lower class farm laborers and their families, both migrant and relatively stable.

The focus of this chapter is on the 25–30 percent of lower-lower class children in the public schools. It is they, more than upper-lower class children, who are referred to by the often-used designation, "lower class."

Values of the Lower-Lower Class

How do the beliefs and values of the lower-class child, particularly the child from the lowest socioeconomic stratum, jibe with the beliefs and values of his middle-class teacher?

1. First, how does the lower-class child regard God and religion? Lower-class parents are less likely than middle-class parents to belong to or attend church. When they do, their church is more likely to be one of the fundamentalist Protestant sects or the Roman Catholic Church than the Episcopalian, Methodist, Presbyterian, Baptist, or Jewish churches of their teachers. Hence, to begin with, there is often a religious gap between teachers and such children. This gap does not exist, of course, in parochial schools, where teacher and child are of the same faith. However, even in such schools, the teachers are principally middle-class people, while many of the children are from the lower class.

2. The second principle of middle-class belief, that of cleanliness, is again one that is not shared by lower-class children. These youngsters come typically from large families. If they live in town, their residence is not unlikely to be a cold-water flat; if they come from rural areas, their homes are not likely to include running water. The competition for the bathtub,

if there is one, is high; and water costs money on the meter, or effort if it has to be carried from an outdoor pump. The mother has many things to do besides scrubbing the children and their clothes. Baths, if taken, must often be taken semipublicly, and, according to Kinsey (1948), there is a tendency toward taboo of nudity among the lower classes.[1]

Hence, for practical if for no other reasons, cleanliness is a luxury that lower-lower class parents and children find it hard to afford. Since they must live without it, it may well be that they relegate it to a low place in their hierarchy of values.

3. As far as thrift (the third of our postulated middle-class values), is concerned, the lower-class group has nothing to be thrifty with. One must *have* money to save money. A certain faith in the dependability of the future is essential if one is to plan for it. For the typical lower-class child, faith in the future has received little support—he has learned instead that he had better grab while the grabbing is good, because if he doesn't, one of his brothers and sisters, or his parents, or his peers, will grab instead; and the supply is limited. The lower-class child does not understand what the teacher means when she talks about or exemplifies thrift. As far as he is concerned, she probably "has extra holes in her head." He simply does not comprehend the principle of saving.

4. He is equally uncomprehending when he is asked to put reason before emotion. Reason has never won a street fight, nor enabled him to get the biggest share of the can of beans, nor served to keep his father from beating his mother when he got drunk. The virtues of reason and the desirability of suppressing emotion are values that the lower-lower class child has had no chance to learn. He sees only that reasoning breeds delay of action and serves to reduce the intensity of behavior. Without immediate action and intense drive, the child may not survive in the tooth-and-claw existence that for him is almost routine. Hence, he not only does not share his middle-class teacher's value but holds one opposite to it, and for reasons that in his experience have intense validity.

5. For such reasons, lower-class children fail to appreciate the fifth article of middle-class faith: that strong emotion, particularly sexual and aggressive emotion, should not be manifested. When one is battling for survival—for his fair share of the limited supply of food in the window cooler or ice box, for his turn with the local girl who will let the boys go as far as they want—intense emotion facilitates and spurs action. Standing back, thinking, and suppressing result in failure to reach the goal. Striking out, yelling, and pushing cause others to stand back so that you can go ahead.

It is true that the results of many studies of social class and personal adjustment have been influenced by the "admission phenomenon" (willingness to respond accurately to an interview or questionnaire). Middle-class children, for example, have been taught that aggression is "wrong." Queried,

[1] Kinsey reports that although sexuality is freer among the lower classes, body exposure is permitted more often among middle- and upper-class populations.

or given a questionnaire about aggression, they deny many of their aggressive acts and feelings. Lower-class children, on the other hand, have learned different values about aggression, and may be freer (more honest) in admitting overt and covert aggression. The admission phenomenon thus may increase the differences in expressed aggression between the social classes: the middle-class child denies some of his aggression; the lower-class youngster admits it all, or possibly even adds to it (since, for him, it may seem desirable to be aggressive).

McKee and Leader (1955), however, studied competitiveness and aggression as expressed in the *behavior* of middle- and lower-class three- and four-year-olds. The children were placed in pairs in a block-building situation. Table 14.1 shows the number of pairings of lower- and middle-class children in which neither child (0), one child (1), or both children (2) demonstrated aggression during the experimental situation.

TABLE 14.1: NUMBER OF CHILDREN IN LOWER- AND MIDDLE-CLASS GROUPS WHO SHOWED AGGRESSION IN AN EXPERIMENTAL BLOCK-BUILDING SITUATION.

Social Class	Number of Children per Pair Showing Aggression		
	0	1	2
Lower	5	5	18
Middle	12	8	8

Chi-square for this table is significant, with P between 0.5 and .02.

Adapted with permission of W. E. Martin, Editor, *Child Develpm.*, and J. P. McKee, from McKee and Leader (1955).

This study, which supports the notion that lower-class children display aggression more openly than middle-class children, even as early as the pre-school years, clearly was not affected by the admission phenomenon.

Griffiths (1952), in a study of 3,387 parents, 900 of their children aged 6 to 14, and 760 teachers of these children, found that middle-class children showed greater conformity to middle-class values than lower- (or upper-) class youngsters, were less aggressive in their behavior, and were more likely to be submissive and withdrawing. In general, the children, regardless of social class, became more conforming as they grew older.

It might be inferred that for lower-class children, open aggression would be related to status among their peers (i.e., that the more aggressive child would be the more popular one). Lesser (1959) became interested in checking this possibility, and asked upper-lower class children in two sixth-grade classes to name the boys (not the girls) who showed most of the following types of aggression: (1) provoked physical aggression (i.e., *fought back vigorously when pushed around*); (2) outburst aggression, of the temper-tantrum sort; (3) unprovoked physical aggression; (4) *unprovoked verbal* aggression; and (5) indirect aggression, such as tattling or damaging other children's popularity.

Such estimates of aggression were obtained for 74 boys aged 10 to 13½, and an estimate of their popularity as well as the degree to which they were rejected was also obtained. The index of popularity was the number of rejection votes the child received subtracted from the number of acceptance votes.

The results indicate that only the first type of aggression—fighting back when picked on—was positively related to popularity ($r = .31$). All other forms were negatively related to popularity, with indirect aggression (which in turn was negatively related to provoked physical aggression) correlating —.69 with popularity among one's schoolmates.

Apparently, at least for this population, only "legitimate" (provoked) aggression was positively associated with friendship status in the group, and even this not to a high degree.

One cannot assume, then, that aggression contributes to popularity among lower-class children, even though, as a group, they may be more aggressive than middle-class children. Most of the types of aggression studied by Lesser showed *negative* relations to popularity, and the one positive correlation he found was low and for "justifiable" aggression.

The lower-class child has more chance to acquire combative and aggressive sexual behavior through imitative learning than the middle-class child does. His world is full of fights, of sexual aggression, of the police. His mother may have "called the cops on" his father; his father may have made direct, open, and even brutal sexual advances toward his mother in his presence. The discipline that has been imposed on him is more likely to have been physical than verbal. One writer (LeShan, 1952) describes the discipline in a lower-lower class family as consisting, in the majority of instances, of threatening (and probably administering) immediate punishment (or reward)—for example: "You go back to bed or I'll beat you with this leather strap." Of 101 observed instances of discipline in this study, 57 were of this type.

The lower-class child's inclination to use his reason, and to try to predict logically, is further discouraged by the inconsistent nature of parental discipline. LeShan reports that of the 101 observed instances of discipline, 28 were unpredictable both from the point of view of the child and from that of the observer. He gives the following illustration: "The father had brought a three-year-old daughter some candy cigarettes. The child pretended to smoke them, flicking off the ashes, etc. When she did this, the father took them away from her and spanked her for 'putting on the dog'." (p. 590) He also tells of a mother who described the weaning of one of her children thus: "Yeah, one day she threw the bottle out of her crib and I gave it back to her and she didn't want it so I never gave it to her again." (p. 591)

LeShan also states that "the lower-lower class child plays on the streets away from adult supervision. Here he is to a large degree at the mercy of his own impulses with reward or punishment following immediately on his actions. Rewards here may be in terms of motor activity, physical gratification, etc. The parents are at work or are usually unaware of what he is doing." (p. 591).

For such reasons, the repression or suppression of strong emotion and the use of reason have, for the lower-class child, little familiarity or appeal. In his way of life, intellectualization and planning may actually be maladaptive.

6. The sixth middle-class value, socially acceptable expression of aggression, makes equally little sense to the lower-class child. He has not seen people, his parents or his peers, behave in such a fashion. For him, gossip is thin gruel; and sarcasm is likely to result in a beating.

7. Nor is it fashionable for the lower-class child to repress sex. As has been reported by Kinsey (1948, 1953), persons from the lower social classes are freer and more social in their expression of sex than are those from the middle class. This freedom undoubtedly includes talking about as well as indulging in sex. Lower-class children, partly because of their living arrangements, live openly with sex to a degree that is inconceivable in a middle-class family. Many children live together with their parents and other adult relatives in crowded quarters; several people sleep in the same bedroom; and uninhibited lovers are forced to do their courting on streets, in doorways, and in alleys. In one fatherless family of the author's acquaintance, the mother carried on her business of prostitution in the room in which her seven- and nine-year-old sons slept. MacKinlay Kantor, in *Andersonville,* gives a graphic account of the public nature of sex in a Civil War lower-lower class rural family. The present author has known many children of migrant farm laborers whose sexual sophistication was a source of amazement to him and a constant source of scandal to his middle-class parents.

What is sacred and taboo for the middle-class teacher in the area of sex may be a matter of indulgence and free expression for the lower-class child. Hence, the child may pose a distinct threat to the controlled and perhaps inhibited teacher.

8. The lower-class child shares little, if any, of the middle-class teacher's horror of filthy talk, "impure" accents, and messy grammar. He talks bluntly, in the argot he has learned in his particular portion of the wrong side of the tracks, and is interested only in communication, not in form. The speech of the child from the New York City or Detroit slums may be almost incomprehensible to the midwestern professional worker or to the graduate of one of the "good" eastern colleges.

9. Nor is overindulgence in alcohol regarded with the same disdain by the lower-class child as by his middle-class peer or teacher. To people from the lower class, alcohol and sex often afford the only available, albeit transitory, escapes from an all too grim reality. The not uncommon case of the worker squandering his weekly pay in the saloon on the way home, leaving

the family larder unstocked, provided powerful ammunition for those who worked to usher in the national era of prohibition. Almost the only way for a middle-class person to understand the role of drink in lower-class society is to spend a Saturday night in a bar in the wrong part of town, listening and observing. The function of alcohol and drunkenness as an escape becomes tragically obvious. Such a learning experience may be a little risky, is more open to middle-class males than to females, and is perhaps rather distasteful, but it provides an important insight concerning lower-class children. From babyhood and early childhood (when they cannot be left home alone), these children frequently accompany their parents on periodic excursions to the neighborhood drinking spot, which also serves as a neighborhood social club. Open sexuality and violent aggression typically accompany and follow evenings on the town, and the child is exposed to these manifestations as frequently and as early as to drinking itself.

10. It is probable that lower-class children and their parents endorse honesty as strongly as the middle class does. It takes a brave child, however, not to lie when the truth will be followed by a beating. It is easier to return a lost five-dollar bill when another one is available than it is to give it up when it is the only one you have ever had—and, perhaps, are likely to have in the foreseeable future. If you are well fed and have an amply stocked toy chest, it is easy not to snitch from the bakery stall or the notions counter; but if your stomach is growling, or you have never in your life owned a doll, the drive to do a little shoplifting is substantial. Therefore, although the two classes may not be so far apart in endorsing honesty as they are in endorsing other values, there are genuine differences in drive, and probably in practice.

Dishonesty in the form of shoplifting, pilfering "souvenirs" from restaurants, lying, and other forms of deceit is, however, also characteristic of middle-class children, both during and prior to adolescence. It has been pointed out that, with reference to such things as hotel towels, their elders set them an example little better than that provided by lower-class parents. It is also probable that hypocrisy—"Do as I say, not as I do"—with its attendant disillusionment, is as frequent among the middle class as among the lower class.

11. The lower-class child has little reason to believe that hard work and self-discipline result in success. Middle-class fathers do not put in eight hours of brutal labor swinging a pick. Such labor is hard; it is done in the heat and the cold; it is dirty; and it obtains relatively few of the world's goods. Nor is the unskilled and uneducated father likely to win conspicuous advancement by his diligence. He remains a day laborer—secure, indeed, from being fired as long as times are good; but at the mercy of his boss, the times, and the weather. He does not get ahead. All he has to look forward to is more of the same. The relatively well-educated and well-trained middle-class father, on the other hand, can, given any breaks at all, demonstrate clearly to his child the advantages of diligence, night work, thinking about

the job over the weekend, and so on. He gets a raise; he achieves a promotion; his self-esteem and his family's economic well-being are enhanced.

In other words, our society is not organized to demonstrate to the lower-lower class child the virtues of hard work and self-discipline; but his failure to appreciate these virtues leaves him, psychologically, far removed from his middle-class teacher.

12. The same type of argument holds for the twelfth middle-class value. The lower-class child's learning does not include convincing illustrations that doing one's duty and living up to the expectations of others pays off. If doing one's duty is rewarded only by being allowed to keep on working at the same dirty job, why do one's duty? If the expectation of others is that the old man will get drunk on Saturday night and beat up the old lady, and this state of affairs does, indeed, occur, wherein lies its virtue?

13. Finally, what is there in his life to teach the lower-class child that learning for the sake of learning is good? He grows up in a home where there are few, if any, books, magazines, or newspapers. His parents have probably done poorly in school and avoid rather than court culture because their memories of their own school days are bitter. Life is hard; intellectual satisfactions do not fill an empty stomach nor a pressing sexual urge; higher education, which might prepare the child for an "easy" job, is out of the question for practical reasons (no money; no family backing, either practical or psychological; and, all too often, not enough ability). The pleasures of the lower-class child are therefore likely to be those that are immediately available to the flesh, rather than those that delight the mind or result in advancement through education.

One cannot escape the conclusion that the gap in values between middle-class teachers and lower-class children is enormous. Of the thirteen values and beliefs that have been examined, almost complete divergence exists for eleven. Although there is agreement in principle on the other two (religion and honesty), the style of implementing them—the actual practice—differs sharply from the middle to the lower class.

Shared values facilitate communication; disparate values estrange people from each other. The unreasoning bitterness between Israelis and citizens of the United Arab Republic has its roots in different values (including different economic interests), and precludes even the effort toward, let alone the effectiveness of, communication. We tend to condemn, reject, and exclude those whose values differ from ours; this tragic state of affairs quite generally characterizes relations between lower-class children and middle-class teachers. The failure of teachers to understand such youngsters probably retards the education of at least one fourth of a nation, and is certainly related to one of our most serious educational problems.

There are, of course, middle-class teachers who are very successful in reaching lower-class children. Such flexible, creative, and sensitive teachers succeed in bridging the values chasm and provide models for many youngsters in their classes. This sort of child-teacher relationship has probably played a role in the lives of most young people who have successfully escaped from the lower class. In such cases, however, the identification of the child with his teacher and her values often partially estranges him from his family.

Social Class and Social Acceptance

It has been indicated earlier in this chapter that lower-class children are less well accepted by their peers than middle-class children. Research supporting this point of view is provided by such papers as that of Grossman and Wrighter (1948), who found that social class was related to social acceptance among a group of 117 sixth-graders. The higher the level of the father's occupation, the more popular the child. The better-accepted children in this study were also better adjusted, according to a pencil-and-paper test of adjustment. A negative relation between popularity and poor adjustment has been found in a number of studies: McCandless and his colleagues (1956), for example, obtained a correlation of —.32 between anxiety and popularity for public-school fourth-, fifth-, and sixth-graders. Thorpe (1955) reports similar although lower correlations between neuroticism and popularity for British children, as does Trent (1957) for institutionalized delinquent boys. Holding the influence of rejections constant (delinquent boys tend to form gangs, so that members of one gang may, for loyalty's sake, reject the most popular boy in another gang or clique), anxiety and popularity in Trent's population correlated —.29, a figure remarkably similar to that obtained by McCandless *et al.*

Sewell and Haller (1956, 1959) have explored in some detail the relations between children's adjustment and their social class, and find indications that low social status is associated with poor personal adjustment (as measured by the California Test of Personality) of a type that seems likely to hinder social acceptance. In a study of 1,462 fourth- to eighth-grade children (1959), they found that lower-class children, when compared with those from higher social classes, showed more concern with their families' social status, worried more about how others rate their ability and achievement ("My classmates don't think I'm bright"), rejected their homes and parents ("I often wish I had some other parents"), and confessed to neurotic symptoms, such as stomach upsets, lack of appetite, dizzy spells, and so on. Sewell and Haller theorize that lower-class children adopt their parents' values during the years before they enter school, then find high-prestige people (teachers) endorsing standards and holding goals that are sharply different from those they have learned at home. The conflict engendered by this situation leads to anxiety, parental rejection, uncertainty, and confusion.

Brown and Bond (1955) provide some interesting suggestions that social class may be of greater importance in the social acceptance of girls than of boys, at least in the rather unusual (impoverished southern) community they studied. Their rural sixth-grade group was made up of 30 girls and 20 boys, all Negro, who came mostly from the lower-lower class. The correlation between social status and popularity for girls was an amazing $+.82$, whereas it was negligible for boys. The status factor that seemed most important for the boys was their proficiency at baseball and basketball —skills that cut across social-status lines. Davis (1957) reports similar results for 97 public school eighth-grade boys in a "northeastern" city of about 23,000. McGuire, Lanmon, and White (1953), and McGuire, White, and Novak (1954) find, for high-school populations, that social-class discriminations are not made against lower-class children who accept the middle-class value of continuing into high school (into eleventh and twelfth grades) but that, for younger children, social-class bias exists.

In general, we may say that the peer relations of lower-class youngsters do nothing to enhance their enjoyment of school; both teachers and classmates seem to reject them.

THE MIDDLE-CLASS TEACHER
AND THE MIDDLE- AND UPPER-CLASS CHILD

No problem of unshared values plagues relations between teachers and middle-class children. Such children begin to absorb "appropriate" values and beliefs with their mothers' milk; and these are deeply, although not always consistently, ingrained by the time they are ready for kindergarten or first grade. If the child is assigned homework, his parents see that he gets it done. If his report card shows poor conduct marks and subject deficiencies, firm pressure is placed on him to better the conduct and remedy the deficiencies. Ordinarily, disciplinary emergencies in the school find the parent ranked solidly behind the teacher rather than the child. If the child does well as far as the teacher is concerned—that is, gets good marks and receives general approval—the parents reward him richly for it.

In earlier sections of this book, we have presented evidence indicating that the middle-class child (and probably the upper-class child) identifies more strongly with his parents, and consequently with the general standards of school and society, than the lower-class child does. He may have been toilet-trained and weaned more strictly and earlier than the experts judge advisable; but, at the same time, he has been more consistently loved and guided, and his major wants have been attended to. Hence his transfer of identification to the teacher is ordinarily quick and automatic, and meets with his parents' approval. This identification results in his respecting his teachers, conforming to their wishes, and adopting their goals. Consequently, the middle-class child is generally a docile, conforming, and respectable classroom citizen. Such behavior, and the achievement that ordinarily accompanies it, are in turn rewarding to teachers—a sign that they are doing well, are succeeding. Consequently, teachers give even more reward to middle-class children. Although often a disproportionate share of the teacher's total attention is of necessity directed toward the relatively recalcitrant and slow-learning lower-class children, this attention is, on the whole, more negative than that given to middle-class youngsters.

Although somewhat fewer teachers than in former years (Beilin, 1959) regard nonconforming and aggressive behavior as "the most serious behavior problem a child can have," they still view with jaundiced eye any child or episode that interferes with the orderly conduct of classes. Hence, lower-class children, because they are relatively nonconforming and aggressive, probably receive more than their share of teacher disapproval.

Hollingshead (1949), in his original data, and Opstad (1957), in a reworking of these data, show that lower-class youngsters are relatively slow-learning (a condition not to teachers' liking); and that, as a group, they receive a substantially greater number of low and failing grades than would be predicted even from their relatively low intellectual status.

In sharp contrast to his lower-class peer, the typical middle-class child conforms, is less aggressive, is brighter, and works harder. For these reasons, he reaps more academic rewards of all sorts. There are, of course, many middle-class children who are *not* conforming, who *are* aggressive, and who *do* underachieve. But, in general, their social class has taught them the attitudes and motives most conducive to success in the United States classroom.

It may be that there is an important distinction to be made within the middle class. The upper-middle class does not always solidly support teachers. Its members are often critical of teachers' methods and of the curriculum, although they agree on common goals. The very mobile parent of the upper middle class often pushes the child beyond his capacities. Not to take note of this distinction is to ignore the common neurotic patterns shown by this group.

Nevertheless, the broad general principles that have been developed for the middle class probably hold for those upper-class children who attend public schools. According to some (e.g., MacArthur, 1955), the upper-class child (and adult), when compared with the middle-class child (and adult), is interested rather in making himself a "good" person than in achieving an objective success; is oriented more to the present and the past, and less to the future (toward which the middle class is primarily oriented); is more selflessly interested in his fellow-man; and is more strictly disciplined. If it is true that upper-class children have such attributes, they should fit even more easily than middle-class children into schools as they are now operated.

THE SCHOOL SITUATION OF THE LOWER-CLASS CHILD

Early Childhood in the Lower Class

It is difficult to reconstruct the infantile experiences of lower-class children. It has been assumed that such children are treated more casually

—in a more relaxed fashion—than middle-class children, although Bronfenbrenner (1959) suggests that this assumption may no longer be correct. Until fairly recently, however, the lower-class child is more likely to have been breast-fed on demand, weaned relatively late, toilet-trained later and less urgently, and given more freedom (not confined to a playpen). He may also have had more total contact with adults.

But, by the time he is physically mobile, it is likely that a new brother or sister will have come along. At that point, observation suggests that he is likely to be abruptly "dropped" by his mother. Lower-class fathers seldom give their children the attention provided by middle-class fathers. Casual observations made in slum areas suggest that children from the ages of 2 or 3 years enjoy partial freedom from supervision, playing unguarded on streets and sidewalks. What supervision they receive comes from an older sister or brother (who resents being tied down, and whose supervision is something less than charitable).

As has been mentioned previously, the result of these practices may well be the production of a personality in the lower-class child which is moderately secure—secure enough so that he functions without social or emotional breakdown—but which includes an incomplete identification with adults (although, as we have seen, he is likely to sex-type—adopt masculine or feminine behavior—earlier than the middle-class child). He needs other people and will manifest a certain regard for their rights, but this social hunger, perhaps because of his obscure feelings of having been let down and deserted by adults, is likely to be satisfied through strong identification with peer groups rather than adult figures and standards. Indeed, there may be strong hostility toward adults.

Teacher-Child Perceptions of Each Other

As a result the teacher, with all of his or her proper middle-class values, is likely to face a class whose members share few of these values and, indeed, disagree sharply with the majority of them. In addition, lower-class children as a group, are rather distrustful of adults in general, particularly those in authority positions.

The teacher sees sullen and indifferent, or actually defiant, children who are on the whole less bright, less clean, more aggressive, more overtly sexual, and less book-and-study oriented than the middle-class members of the group. The teacher needs his satisfactions, just as the child does. Because such children provide few rewards, they are rejected. Himmelweit (1955) has shown that similar biases in favor of the middle class exist in Britain.

For their part, the children see a hostile foreigner, making new and (to them) unreasonable demands. Some psychological research indicates that one will conform to the values of groups in which he sees a possibility of being accepted, whereas he will reject (at least privately) the values of groups which he sees as rejecting him (Dittes and Kelley, 1956). Many, and perhaps most, lower-class children see little possibility of acceptance by middle-class groups. They are therefore unlikely to make any great effort to conform or accede to demands for such changes in their way of life as are typically made by teachers.

What, then, do lower-class children do in middle-class dominated classrooms? This depends greatly on the power of the teacher. If the teacher is weak—a poor disciplinarian—the child and his buddies will run wild, using all their energy destructively. With a strong teacher (and the typical middle-class teacher is by no means weak), the children will become passive. Their striking back will take the form of apathy and nonlearning, feats they can manage very efficiently.

There are differences, of course, in classroom atmosphere between urban and small-town or rural classrooms. The almost automatic discrimination against lower-class children probably operates less strongly and automatically in urban areas. In cities, housing and school segregation by social class as well as ethnic group exists. Hence, teachers in a given school—particularly an elementary school—may be confronted by a class relatively homogeneous in social status. In such a situation children may be perceived more as individuals and less as representatives of an "inferior" or a "superior" social class. But in areas of less population density, classes will be more heterogeneous, and the conditions for discrimination by social class may be maximized.

Lower-Class Parents and the School

Teachers, in their struggle to control, motivate, and possibly inspire the lower-class children in their rooms, do not have recourse to the support of the children's parents, as they do with both normal and problem middle-class children. Lower-class parents have themselves had educational experiences similar to those their children are going through. They distrust the middle class in general, have had unhappy experiences with teachers in their youth, are likely to have dropped out of school well before the end of their senior high-school year and, in general, are not reinforcing to or supportive of public education. They do not see (and perhaps they have some justification) that education has done them much good, nor do they regard it as an important goal for their children.

One index of this attitude is provided by attendance at PTA meetings. Middle-class parents may complain that these are anesthetic experiences, and the stereotype of mother dragging father off to PTA has provided the basis for much cartoon and joke humor. But the fact remains that middle-class mothers and fathers attempt to work with the school, whether by policing junior's homework, attending PTA meetings, or backing the school bond issue. Only rarely do lower-class parents, particularly those of the lower-lower class, give even such token support of the school as is represented by PTA attendance.

Stendler (1951) interviewed 250 mothers of first-graders and analyzed her interviews in terms of attitudes toward school. In four of the five areas of analysis she found social-class differences, most of them indicating less school support by lower-class mothers. Lower-class children were less likely than middle-class children to have attended preschool (almost 100 percent of the upper- and upper-middle class parents had sent their children to preschool, but only 14 percent of the lower-lower class parents had done so). There was, in the interview, little difference by class in the open criticism leveled against the school (this is not surprising; since the interviewers were middle-class, academic people, open criticism was not likely to be voiced). But the lower-class families had received their child's first report card with indifference; few of them had gone to school for a parent-teacher conference when this was substituted for a written card. Upper-class families were more likely to accept the report card with reservations, and to hold up higher standards for their children. More of the upper- and upper-middle class families had taught their children the alphabet, nursery rhymes, and writing or reading before they entered first grade, although all of the lower-class parents had at least taught their children to count to 10 before starting school. As one went down the social-class ladder, parents held progressively lower educational aspirations for their children, although half of the lower-class mothers reported that they hoped their children would finish high school.

SOCIAL CLASS AND THE SECONDARY SCHOOL

Previous sections of this chapter have concerned themselves more with elementary- than with junior and senior high-school populations. How do lower-class children fare in the public secondary schools of our nation?

Opstad (1957) has written a critical review of the literature dealing with this problem, and concludes that much evidence exists to indicate that the lower classes do not profit from secondary education to any degree comparable with other classes. He points out that the major studies he has reviewed contain methodological weaknesses, use different criteria of social class, and vary widely in area, size of city, nature of city, and so on; but he finds the agreement among the studies striking evidence of bias against lower-class youngsters. In other words, bias continues beyond the lower grades. Opstad believes that the well-documented social-class difference in IQ (with the lower class being, on the average, less intelligent) explains only a part of the discrepancy between the success of lower- and middle- or upper-class children. Factors of motivation and general class bias, he believes, are at least as important in this discrepancy as intelligence. He states:

It would appear that the schools could attack this problem by aiding teachers to overcome their ignorance of and bias toward the lower classes, and by making the curriculum and the extra-curricular program more meaningful to these students. However, there is much that is beyond the school's immediate power to control. So long as the children in the grades make life miserable for the students in the lower classes, and so long as occupational biases exist, the problem will still be with us. (pp. 16–17)

Extracurricular Activities

Much of the social life of adolescents revolves around their school and extracurricular activities. To the extent that children take part in such activities, they are a part of the group; to the extent that they do not take part, they are fringers or outsiders.

Hollingshead (1949) has summarized the percentages of high-school youth in a midwestern city who take part in *any* extracurricular activity (Table 14.2). He distinguishes five social classes, class I being the highest, class V the lowest.

TABLE 14.2: EXTRACURRICULAR ACTIVITIES AND SOCIAL CLASS IN HIGH SCHOOL.

Class	Percentage Participating in at Least One Extracurricular Activity
I + II	100
III	75
IV	57
V	27

Adapted with permission of John Wiley and Sons, and A. B. Hollingshead, from Hollingshead, A. B.: *Elmtown's Youth.* New York: John Wiley and Sons, 1949.

These figures and their implications are so clear that they need little discussion. For social and economic reasons, lower-class children take little part in extracurricular activities. These play an important part in one's attitude toward high school, and failure to participate probably plays a part in the decision of many lower-class children to leave school.

Smith (1945), reporting on tenth-, eleventh-, and twelfth-grade students in a large midwestern high school, found significant socioeconomic differences between the general high-school population and those who participated in sororities, academic clubs (such as language and dramatics), Quill Club, band and orchestra, glee club, publications, and leadership of school classes. Each of these organizations and activities tended to be patronized more by youth who were relatively well to do. However, participation in sports, the girls' athletic association, and the ROTC student officers' club did not differentiate the members from the average of the high-school population.

Since the tendency to drop out of secondary school before graduation is greatest among lower-class youth, many are not enrolled long enough to take part in extracurricular activities (which enlist mostly junior and senior students). It might also be asked, however, to what extent lower class students drop out *because* they are not included in the social life of the school.

School Dropouts

Table 14.3, based on Hollingshead's study (1949) of a midwestern community of 6,200, gives the number and percentage, by social class, of students of high-school age not enrolled in school.

TABLE 14.3: NUMBER AND PERCENTAGE OF YOUTH OF HIGH-SCHOOL AGE NOT ATTENDING SCHOOL.

Social Class	Number not in School	Percentage not in School
I	0	0
II	0	0
III	12	7.6
IV	129	41.3
V	204	88.7
Total	345	46.9

Adapted with permission of John Wiley and Sons, and A. B. Hollingshead, from Hollingshead, A. B.: *Elmtown's Youth.* New York: John Wiley and Sons, 1949.

Tables 14.4 and 14.5 demonstrate the effects of social class on school attendance in still a different fashion. These tables show the percentage of the total community population as well as the percentage of the high-school population in each class.

TABLE 14.4: PERCENTAGE OF HIGH-SCHOOL YOUTH AND PERCENTAGE OF TOTAL POPULATION IN EACH SOCIAL CLASS.

Social Class	Percentage of High-School Population in Each Class	Percentage of Community Population in Each Class
Upper-upper	0.00	1.44
Lower-upper	0.67	1.56
Upper-middle	9.52	10.22
Lower-middle	36.23	28.12
Upper-lower	40.91	32.60
Lower-lower	12.69	25.22

Adapted with permission of the Yale University Press and W. L. Warner, from Warner, W. L. *The Social Life of a Modern Community.* New Haven: Yale University Press, 1941.

Table 14.4, based on a study of a moderate-sized town, illustrates several of the things that have been mentioned earlier in this chapter. First is the tendency for upper-class parents to send their children to private schools. Although 3 percent of Warner's "Yankee City" population is upper-class, upper-class adolescents make up only two thirds of one percent of the high-school population actually enrolled in school. Second is the under-representation of lower-lower class children in the secondary schools. War-ner's figures bear out the earlier extrapolation from United States census figures, indicating that at least 25 percent of the population is lower-lower class (with the likelihood that, because of the lower-class tendency toward large families, the percentage of lower-lower class children in elementary schools is actually greater than 25 percent). But by high school many of these children, for reasons that have been listed, drop out of school. War-ner's figures indicate that one half or more of them have done so.

The last of this series of tables again presents figures from Hollings-head's study of "Elmtown." This table includes the percentage of *adolescents* in each social class.

TABLE 14.5: PERCENTAGE OF HIGH-SCHOOL POPULATION, PERCENTAGE OF ADOLESCENT POPULATION, AND PERCENTAGE OF TOTAL POPULATION IN EACH SOCIAL CLASS.

Social Class	Percentage of High-School Population in Each Class	Percentage of Adolescent Population in Each Class	Percentage of Community Population in Each Class
I + II	9	5	6
III	37	22	24
IV	47	42	44
V	7	31	26

Adapted with permission of John Wiley and Sons, and A. B. Hollingshead, from Hollingshead, A. B.: *Elmtown's Youth.* New York: John Wiley and Sons, 1949.

Hollingshead's figures, taken from a small midwestern town, conform closely to those of Warner.

Hollingshead also reported that 64 percent of his class IV (roughly equivalent to upper-lower) adolescents had left school before their sixteenth birthday and that 75 percent of his class V (lower-lower) youngsters had dropped out of school before this age. More boys than girls left school early. Socially, the class V youngsters were ranked by their peers as part of the "grubby gang," 85 percent of them receiving such a rating. None achieved the ranking of "elite."

In general, then, the evidence is that those lower-class children who persist into high school fare little better than they did in elementary school, and that for the most part they drop out of school without receiving a diploma, many of them before they have attained the legal age for leaving school. Some do, however, stay on. A study done in the Southwest by Mc-Guire, Lanmon, and White (1953) showed that a large group of lower-class students dropped out of high school before the twelfth grade. Against the lower-class adolescent able to tough it out into the twelfth grade, how-ever, discrimination was no longer strongly shown.

Kahl (1953) has reported on a rather small sample of boys whose fathers were in the lower middle level of the social-status range. Of this group, 12 planned to go to college, 12 did not. All were of sufficiently high IQ to manage college if they had wished. (In a part of his larger study, incidentally, it was found that, with the effect of IQ ruled out, a significantly larger percentage of boys from upper than from lower occupational classes planned to go to college.)

The parents of 11 of the 12 boys who did not plan to go to college indicated in interviews that they were primarily concerned with the present, and believed that their children should enjoy themselves while they were young. They did not consider college a goal for their children, both because it was expensive and because they harbored doubts about its over-all worth. For these parents, the steady job was the important thing. They had no ambitions for their children to be better off than they themselves were. Only 4 of the parents of boys planning to attend college responded like this. The others believed in "getting ahead," were sensitive to social hierarchies, and had themselves felt keenly the disadvantages of lack of formal education. They saw the world as one where the choice occupations went to the well-educated, and although they themselves had not availed themselves of the educational ladder, they intended that their sons should take advantage of it.

Kahl's study points up the fact that, within any social class, there will be parents who *do not,* and parents who *do,* push their children. There will be fewer of the former in the middle classes, and fewer of the latter in the lower classes—but there will be some of both types in each social class.

IMPROVING RELATIONS
BETWEEN TEACHERS AND LOWER-CLASS CHILDREN

The task of improving relations between teachers and lower-class children has received the scantiest possible research attention, although forward-looking educators have done considerable thinking, talking, and writing about this problem. The present section is based on clinical experience rather than research data.

Appreciation of and Respect for the Individual

The first step toward improving relations between lower-class children and their teachers requires that teachers, either "naturally" or as a result of their training, have a sincere respect for human beings. Psychotherapists speak of the impossibility of doing constructive therapy if the therapist does not possess a deep respect and regard for the worth and essential integrity of the patient's personality. Such an attitude is also fundamental to many religions, and the teachings of Christ, for example, are quite explicit on this point. Such an attitude does not necessitate abandoning one's own values, but it demands willingness to listen to and understand the different value systems of others. This chapter has so far had a certain "snob" over-tone—the middle class is better controlled, intellectually superior, more achievement-oriented, and so on. Snobbishness was not intended. How-ever, for a stable society in which people cooperate and postpone their own immediate gratification for the good of others, standards similar to those of the middle class (although perhaps less harsh, less rejecting, and more flexible) seem to be necessary.

Knowledge of Children's Personal and Family Lives

If the psychological schism between teachers and lower-class children (and all children, for that matter) is to be closed, teachers must know in more detail, and regard with more sympathy, the circumstances of their charges' personal lives. For lower-class children, these circumstances are frequently tragic indeed. Biographies like those of the brother and sister discussed below are typical rather than exceptional.

CASE HISTORIES OF A LOWER-LOWER CLASS BROTHER AND SISTER

Elsie and Ronald Beal have been known to the author for many years. Their biographies as given here differ from their true life stories only to the extent of a change in name.

Elsie and Ronald were sequential in a family that eventually in-cluded fourteen children and depended, for its income, on the earn-ings of the father, a ranch laborer or hired man. Elsie was the sixth, Ronald the seventh child in the family, and their birthdays were separated by fifteen months. It was rumored in the community, and the physical appearance of the children gave the rumor an aspect of truth, that at least three of the children who preceded them in the family were the product of a temporary union between the mother and a man other than Elsie's and Ronald's father. The mother, a huge woman, had at least some ethnic characteristics of a group that, in the section of the United States in which these children lived, had attrib-uted to it inferior status.

At no time during their childhood did the children live in a house of more than four rooms, and much of their life was spent in two-room shacks. Never, until late adolescence, did they encounter running water, a flush toilet, or electric light—except possibly, on an occa-sional Saturday visit to the conglomeration of frame stores and small houses that constituted the shopping and recreation center for the area.

Since part of their father's "hire" consisted of free eggs and milk, these rural lower-lower class children did not experience the malnutri-tion that might have been their lot in an urban slum. Consequently, they grew normally and, as elementary-school children, were sturdy and healthy. Elsie, beneath the dirt that caked her, was a beautiful, exotic-looking child. Ronald was a big, strapping boy whose appearance, while not handsome, was completely acceptable, particularly in the summer when he was able to go swimming occasionally to remove the dirt.

Elsie was bright and, in early elementary school, learned to read with ease, competing well with the "respectable" children of the men and women who owned the ranches on which her father and other fathers like him earned a meager living. Ronald was at best of dull-normal intelligence and repeated grades consistently, spending an average of about two years per grade until he dropped out of school at 13, when he refused to return to spend a second year in the fifth grade. At 13, being an early-maturing boy and having inherited his mother's impressive build, he was as big as the average man, and was able to work for nearly man's wages on the neighboring ranches.

These children were never accepted by other youngsters in the rural one-room school they attended. At noon they, with their numerous brothers and sisters, shared poorly balanced lunches from a common paper bag (metal lunch boxes were at that time *de rigeur*). The "respectable" children laughed at them, and were prevented from more open aggression only by the fact that Ronald was a big, strong boy with a violent temper; and he and Elsie, along with their brothers and sisters, were well able to defend themselves and join in common defense against anyone who got too much out of line. Although Ronald (and his brothers) were well enough coordinated, they were never invited to play the boys' games of football and basketball. The rationale of their more prosperous schoolmates, had they been asked to express one, would perhaps have been: "They have none of the gear. Why should they play?" But a rationale was never solicited, either by the tribe of Beals or by any teacher. It was simply accepted by the Beals, by other children of their social class, by the middle-class children, and by the teachers that the Beals and "their like" were one group, and the children of the landholders another. The middle-class children as well as the teachers exercised constant vigilance over lunch baskets, desks, and cloakrooms, because everyone "knew" that, given half a chance, the Beals would raid lunch boxes for goodies and desks for pencils, erasers, compasses, and the like. Whenever anything disappeared, accusations were first leveled against the Beals and their group. This practice was never questioned, even though the possessions were usually found where their careless owners had left them.

Elsie was the brightest of the Beals, Ronald's academic performance being more typical of the family. But her brightness earned her little more praise and acceptance than Ronald received. She completed the eighth grade, as much alone socially as when she had begun the first. At this time she was 13, and (as the community realized shortly thereafter) pregnant. The father of the child was never identified, although there were many rumors about who he was. Her baby, when born, became simply one more Beal. Elsie, strikingly beautiful in her early maturity, found a "respectable" husband in spite of her illegitimate baby, and moved from the Beal hovel to a respectable farm home. However, no women's group, no church group, gave recognition to her new status. Following her marriage, she made a few somewhat flaunting but pathetic appearances at Sunday services, but since she was never greeted or talked to, she soon dropped the whole idea. Within two years of her marriage, her husband found her in bed with one of his hired hands and sued for, and was granted, a divorce and custody of the child that had been born to him and Elsie. She was not allowed visiting privileges, nor support.

Unable to face return to the Beal household, Elsie removed herself to the nearest good-sized city, entered prostitution (having had the way paved for her by one of her older sisters, who was already in the business), and was later arrested for defending with a gun a current boy friend who was being sought by the police for armed robbery. By the time she was 30, she had been through three marriages, was a professional prostitute, and had spent about six years in jails, reformatories, and prisons. She was also racked with venereal disease and had given birth to a total of four children, none of whom remained with her.

Ronald, after leaving school at 13 — a year after Elsie was graduated from eighth grade — worked on the ranches for a year or so; then joined the Beal migration to the "big city," where he too soon ran afoul of the law because of a clumsily executed burglary. Released from the reformatory because of good behavior, he married at 18 and settled down to steady work as a manual laborer. He managed to go straight for eight years, during which time he and his wife became the parents of five children. At that time he, along with some of his blood kin and some of his in-laws, was sent to the penitentiary for bootlegging.

Neither Elsie's nor Ronald's life has changed substantially in subsequent years. Both are now middle-aged minor criminals, and several of their children are following in their footsteps. Elsie's and Ronald's lives have been very similar to the lives of their older and their younger brothers and sisters. The community costs have, of course, been enormous in terms of social-work efforts, foster homes for the children, aid to dependent children, police workups, court trials, and incarceration.

But the Beals, as children, had possibilities. They were healthy, not unduly stupid, and, in Elsie's case, actually quite bright. Several, including Elsie, were strikingly handsome. Society, however, never did anything *for* them — and, eventually they did something *to* society (and, of course, themselves).

In terms of family circumstances, Elsie and Ronald certainly had at least two strikes against them. But, had teachers really thought about the lives these youngsters lived and stressed the positive characteristics they had instead of dwelling on the negative ones, something different might have happened to them. Had the members of the church congregation supported Elsie, as the tenets of their faith directed them to, in her tentative (although self-centered) moves toward respectability following her marriage, instead of concentrating on "putting her in her place," her life might have taken on a new look and a new purpose. But neither this nor much of anything else benign occurred, and Elsie and Ronald continue to live out their lives in a fashion destructive to themselves and society.

Control Techniques of Warmth plus Strength

The lower-class child, like the delinquent, approaches middle-class authority figures with suspicion. If authorities show weakness, the lower-class child will ride over them, in subtle or not so subtle ways. But if they show coldness, rejection, or unfairness, they only confirm him in his belief that he will "never get a square shake from a teacher." Hence, as has been said before, an initial (and experimental) attitude on the part of the teacher should combine warmth, fairness, and strength. Democracy in the lower-class schoolroom is a luxury that must wait until rapport has been built with the children and they have started along the road to self-control— a road along which, as a group, they have not traveled far.

Realistic Evaluation and Appreciation of Needs

The statement, "To guide the child, we must know and appreciate his needs," has been made so often in the past twenty-odd years that it has become rather shopworn. It has often been made by intelligent people, but it is made equally often by those who truly believe that to understand is necessarily to condone and forgive.

The point taken here is not that to understand the need of a delinquent is to condone his behavior, but rather that to understand his needs, in a knowledgeable way, is to be able to guide him more effectively. Guidance may involve counseling, toughness, affection, remedial teaching. No technique should be arbitrarily ruled out, and all techniques should be regarded as tentative and exploratory. Certainly, love is not enough. Strictness and punishment, by themselves, seldom seem to work much good, except to relieve the feelings of the punisher. Counseling alone does not help the adolescent who cannot read above the first-grade level; on the other hand, remedial reading doesn't seem to accomplish much if it is not accompanied by warmth and understanding (even a modified therapeutic atmosphere).

To be genuinely successful with lower-class children, middle-class teachers must face frankly the issues that have been discussed earlier in this chapter. Abstractions and social niceties have little meaning for children who may not have had enough to eat before they arrive at school in the morning. These children will learn things they see as related to their goals (and their goals are much more immediate than their teacher's), but if the subject matter presented to them has no discernible bearing on what they want out of life, they will not learn it.

Such children *can* learn to relate certain academic skills to their way of life. The author has seen child after child leave an institution for high-grade mentally defective and predelinquent children without a smattering of reading, even though they may have received regular and remedial reading instruction for ten or more years; and he has seen them return to the institution a year or two later for a visit, reading comfortably at the fifth- or sixth-grade level even though they have not had a minute's formal instruction in the meantime. The following experience is typical:

> All the teachers ever did was yell at me. I was the dumbest kid in the class. I just didn't care. I didn't know that reading could actually help me. But when I went out on parole, I got a job in the plant. I felt like a fool. All the other guys could read the paper. I couldn't hardly even write my name, let alone read. But I must of learned something all those years in school, because when I figured I had to read to get ahead in my job and keep from making a fool of myself in front of the other guys, why pretty soon I learned to read. It was dumb not to of a long time ago.

Why did these boys learn to read? Simply because they found that their needs were intimately and obviously connected with the skill of reading. Could this not have been accomplished earlier in their school career? The writer believes that it could have been. What is needed is, first, a teacher who is interested, warm, alert; who appreciates them as persons, and who can thus function as an identification model for whose approval and understanding they are "willing" to learn to read. Secondly, teachers must have sufficient insight into the problems of these children to be able to link reading (and numbers) convincingly with their later life: "Look, you're going to be working in the plant. How can you figure out the way to the men's room—the way to operate the spray gun—the menu at the company cafeteria—the deductions from your pay check—the union contract—if you don't know how to read? OK, don't be a jerk! Let's get this show on the road!"

Unusual terminology for the elementary-school classroom, yes—but more effective than most of the methods typically used.

Textbook Changes

Another educational practice that would help lower-class youngsters is the use of reading texts that relate to their life experiences. In United States classrooms the standard introduction to reading is a bland diet indeed. The main characters are likely to be well-scrubbed, curled, and attractive children who almost invariably come three to a family: a handsome boy of 6 or 7, a winsome girl of 5 or 6, and an omnipresent, amusing, and cuddly "baby" of somewhere between 18 and 24 months. The parents of these children range in coloring from blond to very light brunet. They are youthful in appearance, lissome (or lithe) in figure, well dressed, and endowed with a limitless amount of patience, pleasantness, and time for stories. Important activities include birthday parties and excursions from their pleasant suburban house to the country, where (often) grandma lives in an attractive frame house equipped with enough twin-bedded bedrooms to sleep the whole family. In the "farmhouse" there is running water, at least a bath and a half, electric light, and central heating. Grandma's conformance to "country" ways is likely to be limited to a pony that may be hitched to a freshly painted cart for the amusement of the grandchildren. She may also have a cow that the neighbor or hired man comes in to milk.

When the children in the family need a new blue coat, the matter is simple—their mother simply takes them to the store to buy it. The family almost always has pets, who share the large pleasant lawn with the children. These pets run to cocker spaniels and fluffy kittens with endearing ways.

It is possible for the lower-class child to share emotionally in the experiences of such a family to about the degree that he shares emotionally in the experiences of a family in central Afghanistan. His is a world of cold-water flats and not enough to eat at breakfast, of a rugged, adult-independent existence among the teeming life of sunbaked or ice-covered pavements. There should be some sort of story material—less harsh, admittedly, than his life actually is—that relates more directly to these experiences. Such stories would also, one suspects, add spice and zest to the reading experiences of the middle-class child, besides being more honest in their acknowledgment of what life is really like. Six-year-olds are reasonably sophisticated individuals. They have known people who are divorced. They have experienced anger from adults. They have seen or known of automobile accidents and death. They need not be fed a diet of lukewarm sugar water. Even the bland, positive relation between husband and wife and parents and children, as it is represented in typical readers, fails to catch the depth and intensity of true-life love and family relations.

The source books for arithmetic are less vulnerable to the criticism of complete separation from life; but they too leave something to be desired in their relation to the problems faced by lower-class children. For example, a study by Marshall and Magruder (1960) demonstrates that knowledge of money, and skill in personal expenditure of money, depend on how much money a child has had to spend. Regardless of the type of parental guidance he has received, a child will tend to be ignorant and foolish about money if he has had none to spend but relatively well-informed and sensible about financial matters if he has handled money of his own. It seems to make little difference in his practices whether his money has come via an allowance or has been handed out to him as he needed it. The lower-class child almost never has an allowance, and seldom does he have any money at all to spend. How, then, is the school to help him with monetary concepts and practices?

No ready answers appear, but some effective approach to this vital problem might be found if capable educational minds would get to work on it.

Examination of Personal Values

Realistic evaluation and appreciation of the needs and goals of lower-class children does not mean accepting them as ideal for the children, nor does it mean that they should be accepted by the middle-class teacher or social worker. However, such knowledge makes possible communication with the children to a degree not now present; and where *communication,* both emotional and intellectual, is possible, *change* is possible. Some recent social research indicates, for example, that reformed criminals make more effective "social" workers than the conventional middle-class social and probation worker. Understanding and communication seem to be the relevant factors here.

Realistic evaluation and appreciation of the values of another group, and ability to face these without shock or rejection, involves honest examination of one's own value system. The middle-class teacher who comes honestly to grips with what he believes and holds valuable, who understands how he has come to be the way he is, and who has reasoned through the advantages and disadvantages of his value system, should be much better able to work with children of all social classes than the teacher who has made no such attempt at self-understanding. A certain prod toward understanding and tolerance of those of other social classes (or faiths) is to realize how strictly culture determines one's own value system, and by what a relatively circumscribed group similar values are held.

To conclude this section, it should be said—and urgently—that, in the interests of a genuine democracy, a lowered delinquency rate, a reduction in the intolerably large mental-hospital population, and the introduction of more reason and less adrenalin into the conduct of our social affairs, we need to employ our best brains and our greatest ingenuity in the education of our lower-lower class youngsters.

Although the emphasis in these last sections has been on improving communication with lower-class children, the principles and practices advocated would improve the education of all children. Too often, for bright children of the middle or upper class, the teacher and the texts remain dull, and generally unrewarding. It may be that the gifted are handicapped in their education for many of the same general reasons that hold back typical lower-class children.

SUMMARY

The United States population is often stratified according to social class by sociologists, educators, and psychologists. The most common division is into (1) upper class (relatively aristocratic, well-established people);

(2) middle class (the great body of professional and white-collar workers); and (3) lower class, the upper-lower class being made up of skilled workers, the lower-lower class of unskilled workers. Research information, particularly about family practices, is for the most part based on studies of the middle and upper-lower classes. Research workers have been timid in approaching upper- and lower-lower class parents, although children of the latter have often been studied in public schools and residential treatment centers for delinquent, mentally retarded, and emotionally disturbed children. Upper-class children are relatively unavailable for research, since they often attend private schools.

Almost all teachers are members of the middle class, but perhaps two thirds of their students (particularly during elementary-school years) come from working-class homes, and about one fourth or more of them come from the lower-lower class. The values of the middle and the lower-lower class differ sharply, even dramatically. Middle-class people in general espouse hard work, ambition, cleanliness, and self-control (although their behavior is not always in line with their values); They tend to be inhibited in sexual and aggressive behavior. Lower-class individuals on the other hand, tend to be more open and uninhibited and, as a group, are inclined toward immediate gratification of needs and impulses.

Major differences in values result in serious communication difficulties between middle-class and lower-class people; these are particularly troubling to the relations between teachers and lower-class children. Because of their failure to understand each other's behavior, standards, and goals, mutual distrust—even hostility—may result. The implications of this situation for the education of lower-class children are grave, and are made even more serious because lower-class parents typically do not support the schools' educational efforts. Middle-class parents, on the other hand, offer strong support to the schools; and teachers present about the same image to middle-class children as their parents do.

This picture is little more favorable for older lower-class students— those in high school—than for elementary-school youngsters, although some evidence indicates that lower-class youngsters who have persisted into the last years of high school are appraised on their merits rather than automatically rejected because of their social class.

Lower-class children appear to be less well accepted by their peers (as well as by their teachers) than middle-class children are. Boys may be more fortunate in this respect than girls, since they may be able to break the class barrier by means of athletic proficiency. For both boys and girls, social acceptance seems to be positively (although only moderately) related to good personal adjustment; middle-class youngsters appear to be better adjusted than those of lower social status.

Lower-class children seem to respond well to teacher techniques that combine fairness and warmth with strength. Their education might also be furthered by providing them with textbooks (particularly early in their school career) that have more in common with their way of life than the rather pallid reading fare ordinarily offered them.

Appreciation and respect for the individual can help bridge the gap between teachers and lower-class children. Specifically, teachers should strive to know these children and their families better, and to develop a more realistic understanding of their needs and standards. Developing attitudes of objectivity and acceptance toward others means that teachers must examine and justify—and, where necessary, modify—their own system of values. Such steps as these, thoughtfully and sincerely taken, can go far toward improving the education of lower-class children, and of all other youngsters as well.

REFERENCES

Adams, Abby Bonime. Choice of infant feeding technique as a function of maternal personality. *J. consult. Psychol.*, 1959, 23, 143–146.

Adorno, T. W., Frenkel-Brunswik, Else, Levinson, D. J., and Sanford, R. N. *The authoritarian personality.* New York: Harper and Brothers, 1950.

Albee, G. W. Patterns of aggression in psychopathology. *J. consult. Psychol.*, 1950, 14, 465–468.

Albers, Mary Elizabeth, and Seagoe, May V. Enrichment for superior students in algebra classes. *J. educ. Res.*, 1947, 40, 481–495.

Aldrich, C. A., and Hewitt, Edith W. A self-regulating feeding program for infants. *J. Amer. med. Assn.*, 1947, 135, 340–342.

Aldrich, C. A., Sung, C., and Knop, C. The crying of newly born babies: III. The early period at home. *J. Pediatrics*, 1945, 27, 428–435.

Aldrich, C. A., Norval, M. A., Knop, C., and Venegas, F. The crying of newly born babies: IV. Follow-up study after additional nursing care had been provided. *J. Pediatrics*, 1946, 28, 665–670.

Alexander, A. M. Teacher judgment of pupil intelligence and achievement is not enough. *Elem. Sch. J.*, 1953, 53, 396–401.

Allport, G. W., and Pettigrew, T. F. Cultural influence on the perception of movement: the trapezoidal illusion among Zulus. *J. abnorm. soc. Psychol.*, 1957, 55, 104–113.

Altus, Grace T. Some correlates of the Davis-Eells tests. *J. consult. Psychol.*, 1956, 20, 227–232.

Ames, R. Physical maturing among boys as related to adult social behavior : a longitudinal study. *Calif. J. educ. Res.*, 1957, 8, 69–75.

Ammons, R. B., and Ammons, H. S. Parent preferences in young children's doll-play interviews. *J. abnorm. soc. Psychol.*, 1949, 44, 490–505.

Anastasi, Anne, and Foley, J. P., Jr. A proposed reorientation in one heredity environment controversy. *Psychol. Rev.*, 1948, 55, 239–249.

Anderson, L. D. A longitudinal study of the effects of nursery-school training on successive intelligence-test ratings. *Natl. Soc. Study Educ.*, 39th Yearbook, 1940, Part II. Pp. 3–10.

Angelino, H., Dollins, J., and Mech, E. V. Trends in the "fears and worries" of school children as related to socioeconomic status and age. *J. genet. Psychol.*, 1956, 89, 263–277.

Angelino, H., and Mech, E. V. "Fears and worries" concerning physical changes: a preliminary survey of 32 females. *J. Psychol.*, 1955, 39, 195–198.

Angelino, H., and Shedd, C. L. An initial report of a validation study of the Davis-Eells tests of general intelligence or problem-solving ability. *J. Psychol.*, 1955, 40, 35–38.

Appel, M. H. Aggressive behavior of nursery-school children and adult procedures in dealing with such behavior. *J. exp. Educ.*, 1942, 11, 185–199.

Atkinson, J. W. Motivational determinants of risk-taking behavior. *Psychol. Rev.*, 1957, 64, 359–372.

Atkinson, J. W., Bastian, J. R., Earl, R. W., and Litwin, G. H. The achievement motive, goal setting, and probability preferences. *J. abnorm. soc. Psychol.*, 1960, 60, 27–36.

Atkinson, J. W., and Litwin, G. H. Achievement motive and test anxiety conceived as motive to approach success and motive to avoid failure.

J. abnorm. soc. Psychol., 1960, *60,* 52–63.

Ausubel, D. P. Prestige motivation of gifted children. *Genet. Psychol. Monogr.,* 1951, *43,* 53–117.

Ausubel, D. P., Balthazar, E. E., Rosenthal, Irene, Blackman, L. S., Schpoont, S. H., and Welkowitz, Joan. Perceived parent attitudes as determinants of children's ego structure. *Child Develpm.,* 1954, *25,* 173–183.

Avey, L. D. *Developmental anatomy.* Philadelphia: W. B. Saunders Co., 1954.

Bach, G. R. Father-fantasies and father-typing in father-separated children. *Child Develpm.,* 1946, *17,* 63–80.

Baldwin, A. L., Kalborn, Joan, and Breese, Fay H. Patterns of parent behavior. *Psychol. Monogr.,* 1945, *58,* No. 3.

Barrett, Helen Elizabeth, and Koch, Helen Lois. The effect of nursery-school training upon the mental-test performance of a group of orphanage children. *Ped. Sem. and J. genet. Psychol.,* 1930, *37,* 102–122.

Barry, H., III, Bacon, Margaret K., and Child, I. L. A cross-cultural survey of some sex differences in socialization. *J. abnorm. soc. Psychol.,* 1957, *55,* 327–332.

Bartlett, F. C. *Remembering: A study in experimental and social psychology.* Cambridge, England: Cambridge University Press, 1932.

Bass, B. Authoritarianism or acquiescence? *J. abnorm. soc. Psychol.,* 1955, *51,* 616–623.

Bayley, Nancy. Consistency and variability in the growth of intelligence from birth to eighteen years. *J. genet. Psychol.,* 1949, *75,* 165–196.

Bayley, Nancy. On the growth of intelligence. *Amer. Psychologist,* 1955, *10,* 805–818.

Bayley, Nancy, and Oden, Melita H. The maintenance of intellectual ability in gifted children. *J. Gerontology,* 1955, *10,* 91–107.

Beach, F. A., and Jaynes, J. Effects of early experience upon the behavior of animals. *Psychol. Bull.,* 1954, *51,* 239–263.

Becker, W. C., Peterson, D. R., Hellmer, L. A., Shoemaker, D. J., and Quay, H. C. Factors in parental behavior and personality as related to problem behavior in children. *J. consult. Psychol.,* 1959, *23,* 107–118.

Beilin, H. Teachers' and clinicians' attitudes toward the behavior problems of children: a reappraisal. *Child Develpm.,* 1959, *30,* 9–26.

Belcher, J. C. Evaluation and re-standardization of Sewell's socioeconomic scale. *Rural Sociol.,* 1951, *16,* 246–255.

Benedict, Ruth. *Patterns of culture.* New York: New American Library of World Literature, 1953.

Beres, D., and Obers, S. J. The effects of extreme deprivation in infancy on psychic structure in adolescence: a study in ego development. In *The psychoanalytic study of the child,* Vol. V. New York: International Universities Press, 1950.

Berger, E. M. The relation between expressed acceptance of self and expressed acceptance of others. *J. abnorm. soc. Psychol.,* 1951, *47,* 778–782.

Bergmann, G. The logic of psychological concepts. *Phil. Sci.,* 1951, *18,* 93–110.

Berkowitz, L. Anti-Semitism and the displacement of aggression. *J. abnorm. soc. Psychol.,* 1959, *59,* 182–187.

Bernard, J., and Sontag, L. W. Fetal reactivity to tonal stimulation: a preliminary report. *J. genet. Psychol.,* 1947, *70,* 205–210.

Bernstein, L. A note on Christie's "Experimental naivete and experiential naivete." *Psychol. Bull.,* 1952, *49,* 38–40.

Bexton, W. H., Heron, W., and Scott, T. H. Effects of decreased variation in the sensory environment. *Canad. J. Psychol.,* 1954, *8,* 70–76.

Bijou, S. W. Patterns of reinforcement and resistance to extinction in young children. *Child Develpm.*, 1957, 28, 47–54.

Bijou, S. W., Ainsworth, Mildred H., and Stockey, M. R. The social adjustment of mentally retarded girls paroled from the Wayne County Training School. *Amer. J. ment. Defic.*, 1943, 47, 422–428.

Bills, R. R. Self-concepts and Rorschach signs of depression. *J. consult. Psychol.*, 1954, 18, 135–137.

Bingham, W. E., and Griffiths, W. J., Jr. The effect of different environments during infancy on adult behavior in the rat. *J. comp. physiol. Psychol.*, 1952, 45, 307–312.

Bird, Grace E. The effect of nursery-school attendance upon mental growth of children. *Natl. Soc. Study Educ.*, 39th Yearbook, 1940, Part II, 81–84.

Blau, T. H., and Blau, Lili R. The sucking reflex: the effects of long feeding vs. short feeding on the behavior of a human infant. *J. abnorm. soc. Psychol.*, 1955, 51, 123–125.

Block, J. Personality characteristics associated with fathers' attitudes toward child-rearing. *Child Develpm.*, 1955, 26, 41–48.

Block, J., and Thomas, H. Is satisfaction with self a measure of adjustment? *J. abnorm. soc. Psychol.*, 1955, 51, 254–259.

Bloom, B. S. The 1955 normative study of the tests of general educational development. *Sch. Rev.*, 1956, 64, 110–124.

Bonsall, Marcella R. Reactions of gifted high-school pupils to elementary education. *Calif. J. educ. Res.*, 1955, 6, 107–109.

Bostock, J. Enuresis and toilet training. *Med. J. Aust.*, 1951, 2, 110–113.

Bowlby, J. *Maternal care and mental health.* Geneva, Switzerland: World Health Organization, Monogr. Ser., 1952.

Bowlby, J., Ainsworth, Mary, Boston, Mary, and Rosenbluth, Dina. The effects of mother-child separation:

a follow-up study. *Brit. J. med. Psychol.*, 1956, 29, 211–247.

Bradway, Katherine P. An experimental study of factors associated with Stanford-Binet IQ changes from the preschool to the junior high school level. *J. genet, Psychol.*, 1945, 66, 107–128.

Brazelton, T. B. Sucking in infancy. *Pediatrics*, 1956, 17, 400–404.

Brehm, J. W. Increasing cognitive dissonance by a *fait accompli*. *J. abnorm. soc. Psychol.*, 1959, 58, 379–382.

Brehm, J. W., and Cohen, A. R. Reevaluation of choice alternatives as a function of their number of qualitative similarity. *J. abnorm. soc. Psychol.*, 1959, 58, 373–378.

Brill, A. A., tr. and ed. *The basic writings of Sigmund Freud*, New York: Modern Library, 1938.

Brim, O. G., Jr. Some basic research problems in parent education with implications for the field of child development. *Monogr. Soc. Res. Child Develpm.*, 1959 (in press).

Brim, O. G., Jr., and Forer, R. A note on the relation of values and social structure to life planning. *Sociometry*, 1956, 19, 54–60.

Brodbeck, A. J. The effects of three feeding variables on the nonnutritive sucking of newborn infants. *Amer. Psychologist*, 1950, 5, 292–293.

Brodsky, C. M. *A study of norms for body form-behavior relationships.* Washington, D. C.: Catholic University of America Press, 1954.

Brody, Sylvia. *Patterns of mothering: maternal influence during infancy.* New York: International Universities Press, 1956.

Bronfenbrenner, Urie. Socialization and social class through time and space. In Maccoby, Eleanor E., Newcomb, T. H., and Hartley, E. L. (eds.), *Readings in social psychology*, 3d ed. New York: Holt, Rinehart and Winston, 1958.

Bronson, Wanda C. Dimensions of ego and infantile identification. *J. Pers.*, 1959, 27, 532–545.

Bronson, Wanda C., Katten, Edith S.,

and Livson, N. Patterns of authority and affection in two generations. *J. abnorm. soc. Psychol.*, 1959, *58*, 143–152.

Brown, D. G. Sex-role development in a changing culture. *Psychol. Bull.*, 1958, *55*, 232–242.

Brown, D. G. Masculinity-femininity development in children. *J. consult. Psychol.*, 1957, *21*, 197–202.

Brown, D. R., and Datta, Lois-Ellen. Authoritarianism, verbal ability, and response set. *J. abnorm. soc. Psychol.*, 1959, *58*, 131–133.

Brown, J. S. Pleasure-seeking behavior and the drive-reduction hypothesis. *Psychol. Rev.*, 1955, *62*, 169–179.

Brown, J. S., and Farber, I. E. Emotions conceptualized as intervening variables—with suggestions toward a theory of frustration. *Psychol. Bull.*, 1951, *48*, 465–504.

Brown, W. H., and Bond, Lucille B. Social stratification in a sixth-grade class. *J. educ. Res.*, 1955, *48*, 530–543.

Bruce, P. Relationship of self-acceptance to other variables with sixth-grade children oriented in self-understanding. *J. educ. Psychol.*, 1958, *49*, 229–238.

Brunswik, E. The probability point of view. In Marx, M. H. (ed.), *Psychological theory*. New York: The Macmillan Co., 1951.

Buros, O. K. (ed.) *The fifth mental measurements yearbook*. Highland Park, N. J.: The Gryphon Press, 1960.

Calvin, A. D., and Holtzman, W. H. Adjustment and the discrepancy between self-concept and inferred self. *J. consult. Psychol.*, 1953, *17*, 39–44.

Campbell, W. J. The influence of sociocultural environment on the progress of children at the secondary-school level. *Aust. J. Psychol.*, 1955, *7*, 140–146.

Carlson, Edith Fox. Problems in educating the highly endowed. *J. except. Child.*, 1947, *13*, 201–204.

Carmichael, L. (ed.). *Manual of child psychology*, 2d ed. New York: John Wiley and Sons, 1954.

Cass, Loretta K. An investigation of some important variables in the parent-child relationship. Data from unpublished Ph.D. dissertation, The Ohio State University, 1950.

Cass, Loretta K. An investigation of parent-child relationships in terms of awareness, identification, projection, and control. *Amer. J. Orthopsychiat.*, 1952a, *22*, 305–313.

Cass, Loretta K. Parent-child relationships and delinquency. *J. abnorm. soc. Psychol.*, 1952b, *47*, 101–104.

Castaneda, A., McCandless, B. R., and Palermo, D. S. The children's form of the manifest anxiety scale. *Child Develpm.*, 1956, *27*, 317–326.

Castaneda, A., Palermo, D. S., and McCandless, B. R. Complex learning and performance as a function of anxiety in children and task difficulty. *Child Develpm.*, 1956, *27*, 327–332.

Catalano, F. L., and McCarthy, Dorothea. Infant speech as a possible predictor of later intelligence. *J. Psychol.*, 1954, *38*, 203–209.

Cattell, Psyche. *The measurement of intelligence of infants and young children.* New York: Psychological Corp. 1940.

Cavanaugh, Maxine C., Cohen, I., Dunphy, D., Ringwall, E. A., and Goldberg, I. D. Prediction from the Cattell Infant Intelligence Scale. *J. consult. Psychol.*, 1957, *21*, 33–37.

Centers, R. Social-class identifications of American youth. *J. Pers.*, 1950, *18*, 290–302.

Centers, R. Toward an articulation of two approaches to social-class phenomena: II. The index of status characteristics and class identification. *Int. J. Opin. Attitude Res.* 1951, *5*, 159–178.

Chapman, L. J., and Campbell, D. T. Response set in the F-scale. *J. abnorm. soc. Psychol.*, 1957, *54*, 129–132.

Charles, D. C. Ability and accomplishment of persons earlier judged mentally deficient. *Genet. Psychol. Monogr.*, 1953, 47, 3–71.

Chase, W. P. Color vision in infants. *J. exp. Psychol.*, 1937, 20, 203–222.

Child, I. L. The relation of somatotype to self-ratings on Sheldon's temperamental traits. *J. Pers.*, 1950, 18, 440–453.

Child, I. L., Frank, Kitty F., and Storm, T. Self-ratings and TAT: their relation to each other and to childhood background. *J. Pers.*, 1956, 25, 96–114.

Child, I. L., and Waterhouse, I. K. Frustration and the quality of performance: I. A critique of the Barker, Dembo, and Lewin experiment. *Psychol. Rev.*, 1952, 59, 351–362.

Chittenden, Gertrude E. An experimental study in measuring and modifying assertive behavior in young children. *Monogr. Soc. Res. Child Develpm.*, 1942, 7, No. 1.

Chodorkoff, B. Adjustment and the discrepancy between the perceived and ideal self. *J. clin. Psychol.*, 1954a, 10, 266–268.

Chodorkoff, B. Self-perception, perceptual defense, and adjustment. *J. abnorm. soc. Psychol.*, 1954b, 49, 508–512.

Christie, R., and Garcia, J. Subcultural variation in authoritarian personality. *J. abnorm. soc. Psychol.*, 1951, 46, 457–469.

Christie, R., Havel, Joan, and Seidenberg, B. Is the F-scale irreversible? *J. abnorm. soc. Psychol.*, 1958, 56, 143–159.

Cohen, A. R., Terry, H. I., and Jones, C. B. Attitudinal effects of choice in exposure to counterpropaganda. *J. abnorm. soc. Psychol.*, 1959, 58, 388–391.

Cohn, T. S., and Carsch, H. Administration of the F-scale to a sample of Germans. *J. abnorm. soc. Psychol.*, 1954, 49, 471.

Colley, T. The nature and origins of psychological sexual identity. *Psychol. Rev.*, 1959, 66, 165–177.

Coopersmith, S. A method for determining types of self-esteem. *J. educ. Psychol.*, 1959, 59, 87–94.

Cowen, E. L., Heilizer, F., and Axelrod, H. S. Self-concept conflict indicators and learning. *J. abnorm. soc. Psychol.*, 1955, 51, 242–245.

Cowen, E. L., Landes, J., and Schaet, D. E. The effects of mild frustration on the expression of prejudiced attitudes. *J. abnorm. soc. Psychol.*, 1959, 58, 33–39.

Crandall, V. J., and Bellugi, Ursula. Some relationships of interpersonal and intrapersonal conceptualizations to personal-social adjustment. *J. Pers.*, 1954, 23, 224–232.

Crandall, V. J., and Preston, Anne. Patterns and levels of maternal behavior. *Child Develpm.*, 1955, 26, 267–278.

Crandall, V. J., Preston, Anne, and Rabson, Alice. Maternal reactions and the development of independence and achievement behavior in young children. *Child Develpm.*, 1960, 31, 243–251.

Crum, Janet, Brown, W. L., and Bitterman, M. E. The effect of partial and delayed reinforcement on resistance to extinction. *Amer. J. Psychol.*, 1951, 64, 228–237.

Crutchfield, R. S. Conformity and character. *Amer. Psychologist*, 1955, 10, 191–198.

Curran, F. J. Specialized techniques in the treatment of juvenile delinquency. *J. Amer. med. Assn.*, 1955, 175, 108–113.

Davids, A., and Eriksen, C. W. Some social and cultural factors determining relations between authoritarianism and measures of neuroticism. *J. consult. Psychol.*, 1957, 21, 155–159.

Davis, Allison, and Dollard, J. *Children of bondage.* Washington, D. C.: American Council on Education, 1940.

Davis, A., and Havighurst, R. J. Social class and color differences in child-rearing. *Amer. sociol. Rev.*, 1946, 11, 698–710.

Davis, Clara M. Results of the self-selection of diets by young children. *Canad. med. Assn. J.*, 1939, *41*, 256–261.

Davis, H. V., Sears, R. R., Miller, H. C., and Brodbeck, A. J. Effects of cup, bottle and breast feeding on oral activities of newborn infants. *Pediatrics*, 1948, *3*, 549–558.

Davis, J. A. Correlates of sociometric status among peers. *J. educ. Res.*, 1957, *50*, 561–569.

Davis, W. A., and Havighurst, R. J. *Father of the man: how your child gets his personality.* Boston: Houghton Mifflin Co., 1947.

Dawe, Helen C. A study of the effect of an educational program upon language development and related mental functions in young children. *J. exp. Educ.*, 1942, *11*, 200–209.

Dennis, W. Are Hopi children non-competitive? *J. abnorm. soc. Psychol.*, 1955, *50*, 99–100.

Dennis, W. Does culture appreciably affect patterns of infant behavior? *J. soc. Psychol.*, 1940, *12*, 305–317.

Dennis, W. A further analysis of reports of wild children. *Child Develpm.*, 1951, *22*, 153–158.

Disher, D. R. The reactions of newborn infants to chemical stimuli administered nasally. Ohio State University Studies: *Contr. Psychol.*, 1934, *12*, 1–52.

Dittes, J. E. Attractiveness of group as function of self-esteem and acceptance by group. *J. abnorm. soc. Psychol.*, 1959, *59*, 77–82.

Dittes, J. E., and Kelley, H. H. Effects of different conditions of acceptance upon conformity to group norms. *J. abnorm. soc. Psychol.*, 1956, *53*, 100–107.

Dollard, J., Doob, L. W., Miller, N. E., Mowrer, O. H., and Sears, R. R. *Frustration and aggression.* New Haven: Yale University Press, 1939.

Dollard, J., and Miller, N. E. *Personality and psychotherapy.* New York: McGraw-Hill Book Co., 1950.

Douvan, Elizabeth. Social status and success strivings. *J. abnorm. soc. Psychol.*, 1956, *52*, 219–223.

Douvan, Elizabeth, and Adelson, J. The psychodynamics of social mobility in adolescent boys. *J. abnorm. soc. Psychol.*, 1958, *56*, 31–44.

Duncan, O. D., and Artis, J. W. Social stratification in a Pennsylvania rural community. State College, Pa.: *Penn. agric. Sta. Bull.*, 1951.

Ebbs, J. H., Tisdall, F. F., and Scott, W. A. The influence of prenatal diet on the mother and child. *The Milbank Memorial Fund Quarterly*, 1942, *20*, 35–36.

Eells, K., Davis, A., Havighurst, R. J., Herrick, V. E., and Tyler, R. *Intelligence and cultural differences.* Chicago: The University of Chicago Press, 1951.

Empey, L. T. Social class and occupational aspiration: a comparison of absolute and relative measurement. *Amer. sociol. Rev.*, 1956, *21*, 703–709.

Engel, Mary. The stability of the self-concept in adolescence. *J. abnorm. soc. Psychol.*, 1959, *58*, 211–215.

Erikson, E. H. Childhood and tradition in two American Indian tribes. *Psychoanalytic stud. Child.*, 1945, *1*, 319–350.

Erikson, E. H. The problem of ego identity. *J. Amer. psychoanal. Assn.*, 1956, *4*, 56–121.

Escalona, Sibylle K. An appraisal of some psychological factors in relation to rooming-in and self-demand schedules. In Senn, M. J. E., *Problems of early infancy.* New York: The Josiah Macy, Jr. Foundation, 1947. Pp. 58–62.

Escalona, Sibylle K. Feeding disturbances in very young children. *Amer. J. Orthopsychiat.*, 1945, *15*, 76–80.

Estes, W. K. An experimental study of punishment. *Psychol. Monogr.*, 1944, *57*, 1–40.

Farber, I. E. The role of motivation in verbal learning and performance. *Psychol. Bull.*, 1955, *52*, 311–327.

Ferguson, G. A. On learning and

human ability. *Canad. J. Psychol.,* 1954, *8,* 95–112.

Ferguson, G. A. On transfer and the abilities of man. *Canad. J. Psychol.,* 1956, *10,* 121–131.

Feshbach, S. The catharsis hypothesis and some consequences of interaction with aggressive and neutral play objects. *J. Pers.,* 1956, *24,* 449–462.

Festinger, L. *Theory of cognitive dissonance.* Evanston, Ill.: Row, Peterson and Co., 1957.

Festinger, L., and Carlsmith, J. M. Cognitive consequences of forced compliance. *J. abnorm. soc. Psychol.,* 1959, *58,* 203–210.

Fey, W. F. Acceptance by others and its relation to acceptance of self and others. A revaluation. *J. abnorm. soc. Psychol.,* 1955, *50,* 274–276.

Findley, D. C., and McGuire, C. Social status and abstract behavior. *J. abnorm. soc. Psychol.,* 1957, *54,* 135–137.

Forgus, R. H. Advantage of early over late perceptual experience in improving form discrimination. *Can. J. Psychol.,* 1956, *10,* 147–155.

Forgus, R. H. The effect of early perceptual learning on the behavioral organization of adult rats. *J. comp. physiol. Psychol.,* 1954, *47,* 331–336.

Forgus, R. H. Early visual and motor experience as determiners of complex maze-learning ability under rich and reduced stimulation. *J. comp. physiol. Psychol.,* 1955a, 48, 215–220.

Forgus, R. H. Influence of early experience on maze-learning with and without visual cues. *Can. J. Psychol.,* 1955b, *9,* 207–214.

Fouls, Lydia B., and Smith, W. D. Sex-role learning of five-year-olds. *J. genet. Psychol.,* 1956, *53,* 105–116.

Frandsen, Arden, and Barlow, Frances P. Influence of the nursery school on mental growth. *Natl. Soc. Study Educ.,* 39th Yearbook, 1940, Part II. Pp. 143–148.

Fredeen, R. C. Cup feeding of newborn infants. *Pediatrics,* 1948, *2,* 544–548.

Frenkel-Brunswik, Else. Further explorations by a contributor to "The authoritarian personality." In R. Christie and Marie Jahoda (eds.), *Studies in the scope and method of "The authoritarian personality."* Glencoe, Ill.: Free Press, 1954a. Pp. 226–275.

Frenkel-Brunswik, Else. Patterns of social and cognitive outlooks in children and parents. *Amer. J. Orthopsychiat.,* 1951, *21,* 543–558.

Frenkel-Brunswik, Else. Social research and the problem of values: A reply. *J. abnorm. soc. Psychol.,* 1954b, *49,* 466–470.

Frenkel-Brunswik, Else. A study of prejudice in children. *Hum. Relat.,* 1948, *1,* 295–306.

Frenkel-Brunswik, Else, and Havel, Joan. Prejudice in the interviews of children: I. Attitudes toward minority groups. *J. genet. Psychol.,* 1953, *82,* 91–136.

Freud, S. *New introductory lectures on psycho-analysis.* New York: W. W. Norton and Co., 1933.

Friedman, I. Phenomenal, ideal, and projected conceptions of self. *J. abnorm. soc. Psychol.,* 1955, *51,* 611–615.

Gage, N. L., Leavitt, G. S., and Stone, G. C. The psychological meaning of acquiescence set for authoritarianism. *J. abnorm. soc. Psychol.,* 1957, *55,* 98–103.

Gallagher, J. J. Authoritarianism and attitudes toward children. *J. soc. Psychol.,* 1957, *45,* 107–111.

Gallagher, J. J. Clinical judgment and the Cattell Infant Intelligence Scale. *J. consult. Psychol.,* 1953, *17,* 303–305.

Garn, S. M., and Clark, L. C., Jr. The sex difference in the basal metabolic rate. *Child Develpm.,* 1953, *24,* 215–224.

Gesell, A. *The mental growth of the preschool child.* New York: The Macmillan Co., 1925.

Gesell, A. The ontogenesis of infant

behavior. In L. Carmichael (ed.), *Manual of child psychology,* 2d ed. New York: John Wiley and Sons, 1954. Pp. 335–373.

Gesell, A., and Amatruda, C. S. *Developmental diagnosis: normal and abnormal child development.* New York: Paul B. Hoeber, 1941.

Gesell, A., Halverson, H. M., Thompson, Helen, Ilg, F. L., Costner, B. M., Ames, L. B., and Amatruda, C. S. *The first five years of life: a guide to the study of the preschool child.* New York: Harper & Brothers, 1940.

Gesell, A., and Thompson, Helen. *Infant behavior.* New York: McGraw-Hill Book Co., 1934.

Gesell, A., and Thompson, Helen. Learning and growth in identical twins: an experimental study by the method of co-twin control. *Genet. Psychol. Monogr.,* 1929, *6,* 1–123.

Gesell, A., and Thompson, Helen. Twins T and C from infancy to adolescence: a biogenetic study of individual differences by the method of co-twin control. *Genet. Psychol. Monogr.,* 1941, *24,* 3–121.

Gibson, Eleanor J., and Walk, R. D. The effect of prolonged exposure to visually presented patterns on learning to discriminate them. *J. comp. physiol. Psychol.,* 1956, *49,* 239–242.

Gilliland, A. R. *Tests for infants 4–12 weeks old.* Boston: Houghton Mifflin Co., 1949.

Glanzer, M. Curiosity, exploratory drive, and stimulus satiation. *Psychol. Bull.,* 1958, *55,* 302–315.

Goddard, H. H. *The Kallikak family.* New York: The Macmillan Co., 1912.

Goff, Regina M. *Problems and emotional difficulties of Negro children.* Contr. Educ., No. 960. New York: Bureau of Publications, Teachers College, Columbia University, 1949.

Goldfarb, W. Effects of psychological deprivation in infancy and subsequent stimulation. *Amer. J. Psychiat.,* 1945, *102,* 18–33.

Goldfarb, W. Infant-rearing as a factor in foster home placement. *Amer. J. Orthopsychiat.,* 1944, *14,* 162–167.

Goldman, Frieda. Breast-feeding and character-formation. *J. Pers.,* 1948, *17,* 83–103.

Goldman-Eisler, Frieda. The problem of "orality" and of its origin in early childhood. *J. ment. Sci.,* 1951, *97,* 765–782.

Goodenough, Florence L., and Maurer, Katharine M. The mental development of nursery-school children compared with that of nonnursery-school children. *Natl. Soc. Study Educ.,* 39th Yearbook, 1940, Part II. Pp. 161–178.

Goodenough, Florence L., and Maurer, Katharine M. *The mental growth of children from age 2 to 14 years.* Minneapolis: University of Minnesota Press, 1942.

Goodlad, J. I. Some effects of promotion and nonpromotion upon the social and personal adjustment of children. *J. exp. Educ.,* 1954, *22,* 301–328.

Gough, H. G. Studies of social intolerance: I. Some psychological and sociological correlates of anti-Semitism. *J. soc. Psychol.,* 1951*a,* *33,* 237–246.

Gough, H. G. Studies of social intolerance: II. A personality scale for anti-Semitism. *J. soc. Psychol.,* 1951*b,* *33,* 247–255.

Gough, H. G. Studies of social intolerance: III. Relationship of the Pr scale to other variables. *J. soc. Psychol.,* 1951*c,* *33,* 257–262.

Gough, H. G. Studies of social intolerance: IV. Related social attitudes. *J. soc. Psychol.,* 1951*d,* *33,* 263–269.

Gough, H. G., Harris, D. B., Martin, W. E., and Edwards, Marcia. Children's ethnic attitudes: I. Relationship to certain personality factors. *Child Develpm.,* 1950, *21,* 83–91.

Gray, P. H. Theory and evidence of imprinting in human infants. *Student Res. Univ. Chicago,* 1957, *1,* 19–40.

Gray, Susan W. Perceived similarity to parents and adjustment. *Child Develpm.*, 1959, 30, 91–107.

Greenfield, N. S. The relationship between recalled forms of childhood discipline and psychopathology. *J. consult. Psychol.*, 1959, 23, 139–142.

Greulich, W. W. A comparison of the physical growth and development of American-born and native Japanese children. *Amer. J. phys. Anthrop.*, 1957, 15, 489–515.

Griffiths, W. *Behavior difficulties of children as perceived and judged by parents, teachers, and children themselves.* Minneapolis: University of Minnesota Press, 1952.

Grossman, Beverly, and Wrighter, Joyce. The relationship between selection-rejection and intelligence, social status, and personality among sixth-grade children. *Sociometry*, 1948, 11, 346–355.

Gurvitz, M. S. On the decline of performance on intelligence tests with age. *Amer. Psychologist*, 1951, 6, 295 (abstract).

Haggard, E. A. Social status and intelligence: and experimental study of certain cultural determinants of measured intelligence. *Genet. Psychol. Monogr.*, 1954, 49, 141–186.

Hake, H. W., Grant, D. A., and Hornseth, J. P. Resistance to extinction and the pattern of reinforcement: III. The effect of trial patterning in verbal "conditioning." *J. exp. Psychol.*, 1951, 41, 221–225.

Haller, M. W. The reactions of infants to changes in the intensity and pitch of pure tone. *J. genet. Psychol.*, 1932, 40, 162–180.

Halperin, S. L. Human heredity and mental deficiency. *Amer. J. ment. Defic.*, 1946, 51, 153–163.

Hammond, W. H. The status of physical types. *Hum. Biol.*, 1957, 29, 223–241.

Hanlon, T. E., Hofstaetter, P. R., and O'Connor, J. P. Congruence of self and ideal self in relation to personality adjustment. *J. consult. Psychol.*, 1954, 18, 215–218.

Harlow, H. F. The formation of learning sets. *Psychol. Rev.*, 1949, 56, 51–65.

Harlow, R. G. Masculine inadequacy and compensatory development of physique. *J. Pers.*, 1951, 19, 312–323.

Harms, Irene E. Development of intelligence in infancy. State University of Iowa, Iowa Child Welfare Research Station, 1957. Unpublished ms.

Harms, Irene E., and Spiker, C. C. Factors associated with the performance of young children on intelligence scales and tests of speech development. *J. genet. Psychol.*, 1959, 94, 3–22.

Harris, D. B., Gough, H. G., and Martin, W. E. Children's ethnic attitudes: II. Relationship to parental beliefs. *Child Develpm.*, 1950, 21, 169–182.

Hart, I. Maternal child-rearing practices and authoritarian ideology. *J. abnorm. soc. Psychol.*, 1957, 55, 232–237.

Hartup, W. W. Nurturance and nurturance-withdrawal in relation to the dependency behavior of preschool children. *Child Develpm.*, 1958, 29, 191–201.

Hartup, W. W., and Zook, Elsie A. Sex-role preference in three- and four-year-old children. *J. consult. Psychol.*, 1960 (in press).

Havighurst, R. J., and Hilkevitch, Rhea R. The intelligence of Indian children as measured by a performance scale. *J. abnorm. soc. Psychol.*, 1944, 39, 419–433.

Havighurst, R. J., Stivers, E., and De Haan, R. F. A survey of the education of gifted children. *Suppl. educ. Monogr.*, 1955, 83, 114.

Hayward, S. C. Modification of sexual behavior of the male albino rat. *J. comp. physiol, Psychol.*, 1957, 50, 70–73.

Heathers, G. Emotional dependence and independence in nursery-school play. *J. genet. Psychol.*, 1955, 87, 37–57.

Hebb, D. O. Drives and the C.N.S. (conceptual nervous system). *Psychol. Rev.*, 1955, 62, 243–254.

Hebb, D. O. *The organization of behavior: A neuropsychological theory.* New York: John Wiley and Sons, 1949.

Helper, M. M. Learning theory and the self-concept. *J. abnorm. soc. Psychol.*, 1955, 51, 184–194.

Heron, W., Doane, B. K., and Scott, T. H. Visual disturbances after prolonged perceptual isolation. *Canad. J. Psychol.*, 1956, 10, 13–18.

Hetzer, H., and Tudor-Hart, B. H. Die frühesten reactionen auf die menschliche stimme. *Quellen und Stud.*, 1927, 5, 103–124.

Hieronymus, A. N. A study of social-class motivation: relationships between anxiety for education and certain socioeconomic and intellectual variables. *J. educ. Psychol.*, 1951, 42, 193–205.

Hilgard, Josephine R. Learning and maturation in preschool children. *J. genet. Psychol.*, 1932, 41, 36–56.

Himmelweit, Hilde T. Socioeconomic background and personality. *Int. soc. Sci. Bull.*, 1955, 7, 29–35.

Hobson, J. R. Scholastic standing and activity participation of underage high school pupils originally admitted to kindergarten on the basis of physical and psychological examinations. *News Letter,* Division of School Psychologists, APA, 1956.

Hoefer, Carolyn, and Hardy, Mattie C. Later development of breast-fed and artificially fed infants. *J. Amer. med Assn.*, 1929, 92, 615–619.

Hofstaetter, P. R. The changing composition of "intelligence": a study in T-technique. *J. genet. Psychol.*, 1954, 85, 159–164.

Holland, J. G. The influence of previous experience and residual effects of deprivation on hoarding in the rat. *J. comp. physiol. Psychol.*, 1954, 47, 244–247.

Hollingshead, A. de B. *Elmtown's youth: the impact of social classes on youth.* New York: John Wiley and Sons, 1949.

Holway, Amy R. Early self-regulation of infants and later behavior in play interviews. *Amer. J. Orthopsychiat.*, 1949, 19, 612–623.

Homans, G. C. Group factors in worker productivity. In Maccoby, Eleanor E., Newcomb, T. M., and Hartley, E. L. (eds.), *Readings in social psychology.* New York: Holt, Rinehart and Winston, 1958.

Honzik, Marjorie P. Developmental studies in parent-child resemblance in intelligence. *Child Develpm.*, 1957, 28, 215–228.

Honzik, Marjorie P. A developmental study of thumb-sucking. Institute of Human Development, University of California, 1947. Unpublished ms.

Honzik, Marjorie P., Macfarlane, Jean W., and Allen, L. The stability of mental test performance between 2 and 18 years. *J. exp. Educ.*, 1948, 17, 309–324.

Hopper, H. E., and Pinneau, S. R. Frequency of regurgitation in infancy as related to amount of stimulation received from the mother. *Child Develpm.*, 1957, 28, 229–237.

Howard, K. I. Concept of self vs. real self: discrepancy. *Student Res. Univ. Chicago*, 1957, 1, 41–45.

Howe, Louisa, French, Fern, Bierman, Jessie, Connor, Angie, and Kemp, Dorothy. Longitudinal studies of pregnancy on the Island of Kauai, Territory of Hawaii. Paper presented before the American Public Health Association, November, 1956.

Hsu, E. H. On the application of Viennese Infant Scale to Peiping babies. *J. genet. Psychol.*, 1946, 69, 217–220.

Hull, C. L. *A behavior system.* New Haven: Yale University Press, 1952.

Humphreys, L. G. Characteristics of type concepts with special reference to Sheldon's typology. *Psychol. Bull.*, 1957, *54*, 218–228.

Hurlock, Elizabeth B. *Developmental psychology.* New York: McGraw-Hill Book Co., 1959.

Irwin, O. C. Infant speech: the effect of family occupational status and of age on use of sound types. *J. Speech Hear. Dis.*, 1948, *13*, 224–226.

Irwin, O. C. Speech development and added verbal stimulation. State University of Iowa, Iowa Child Welfare Res. Sta., 1960. Unpublished ms.

Jack, Lois M. An experimental study of ascendant behavior in preschool children. *Univ. Iowa Stud. Child Welfare*, 1934, *9*, 7–65.

Jackson, D. N., and Messick, S. J. Content and style in personality assessment. *Psychol. Bull.*, 1958, *55*, 243–252.

Jackson, D. N., and Messick, S. J. A note on "ethnocentrism" and acquiescent response sets. *J. abnorm. soc. Psychol.*, 1957, *54*, 132–134.

Jackson, D. N., Messick, S. J., and Solley, C. M. How "rigid" is the "authoritarian"? *J. abnorm. soc. Psychol.*, 1957, *54*, 137–140.

Jakubczak, F., and Walters, R. H. Suggestibility as dependency behavior. *J. abnorm. soc. Psychol.*, 1959, *59*, 102–107.

Janoff, Irma Z., Beck, L. H., and Child, I. L. The relation of somatotype to reaction time, resistance to pain, and expressive movement. *J. Pers.*, 1950, *18*, 454–460.

Jaynes, J. Imprinting: The interaction of learned and innate behavior: I. Development and generalization. *J. comp. physiol. Psychol.*, 1956, *49*, 201–206.

Jaynes, J. Imprinting: The interaction of learned and innate behavior: II. The critical period. *J. comp. physiol. Psychol.*, 1957, *50*, 6–10.

Jeffrey, W. E. The effects of verbal and nonverbal responses in mediating an instrumental act. *J. exp. Psychol.*, 1953, *45*, 327–333.

Jenkins, W. O., and Stanley, J. C., Jr.

Partial reinforcement: a review and critique. *Psychol. Bull.*, 1950, *47*, 193–234.

Jensen, A. R. Authoritarian attitudes and personality maladjustment. *J. abnorm. soc. Psychol.*, 1957, *54*, 303–311.

Jersild, A. T. *Child psychology.* Englewood Cliffs, N. J.: Prentice-Hall, 1954.

Jersild, A. T., and Holmes, Florence B. *Children's fears.* New York: Bureau of Publications, Teachers College, Columbia University, 1935. Part III, pp. 167–296.

Johnson, G. O. A study of the social position of mentally handicapped children in the regular grades. *Amer. J. ment. Def.*, 1950, *55*, 60–89.

Johnson, Laverne C. Body cathexis as a factor in somatic complaints. *J. consult. Psychol.*, 1956, *20*, 145–149.

Johnson, L. R. The status of thumbsucking and finger-sucking. *J. Amer. dent. Assn.*, 1939, *26*, 1245–1254.

Jones, H. E. Adolescence in our society. In *The family in a democratic society*, anniversary papers of the Community Service Society of New York. New York: Columbia University Press, 1949. Pp. 70–82.

Jones, H. E. The environment and mental development. In L. Carmichael (ed.), *Manual of child psychology*, 2d ed. New York: John Wiley and Sons, 1954. Ch. 10, pp. 631–696.

Jones, H. E., and Conrad, H. S. Mental development in adolescence. *Natl. Soc. Study Educ.*, 43d Yearbook, 1944, Part I. Pp. 146–163.

Jones, H. E., and Jorgensen, Ada P. Mental growth as related to nursery-school attendance. *Natl. Soc. Study Educ.*, 39th Yearbook, 1940, Part II. Pp. 207–222.

Jones, Mary C. The later careers of boys who were early- or late-maturing. *Child Develpm.*, 1957, *28*, 113–128.

Jones, Mary C., and Bayley, Nancy.

Physical maturing among boys as related to behavior. *J. educ. Psychol.,* 1950, *41,* 129–148.

Jones, Mary C., and Mussen, P. H. Self-conceptions, motivations, and interpersonal attitudes of early- and late-maturing girls. *Child Develpm.,* 1958, *29,* 491–501.

Kagan, J., and Beach, F. A. Effects of early experience on mating behavior of male rats. *J. comp. physiol. Psychol.,* 1953, *46,* 204–208.

Kagan, J., and Moss, H. A. Parental correlates of child's IQ and height: a cross-validation of the Berkeley Growth Study results. *Child Develpm.,* 1959, *30,* 325–332.

Kagan, J., and Moss, H. A. The stability of passive and dependent behavior from childhood through adulthood. *Child Develpm.,* 1960, *31,* 577–591.

Kahl, J. A. Educational and occupational aspirations of "common man" boys. *Harvard educ. Rev.,* 1953, *23,* 186–203.

Kahn, M. W. The effect of severe defeat at various age levels on the aggressive behavior of mice. *J. genet. Psychol.,* 1951, *79,* 117–130.

Kantor, M. *Andersonville.* Cleveland: World Publishing Co., 1955.

Kates, S. L., and Diab, L. N. Authoritarian ideology and attitudes on parent-child relationships. *J. abnorm. soc. Psychol.,* 1955, *51,* 13–16.

Kaufman, H. F. *Defining prestige in a rural community.* Sociometry Monogr. No. 10. New York: Beacon House, 1946.

Kaufman, H. F. Prestige classes in a New York rural community. Ithaca, N. Y.: *Cornell agric. exp. Sta. Memoir,* 1944, No. 260.

Keister, Mary E. The behavior of young children in failure: an experimental attempt to discover and to modify undesirable responses of preschool children to failure. *Univ. Iowa Stud. Child Welfare,* 1937, *14,* 27–82.

Kendig, Isabelle, and Richmond, Wini-

fred V. *Psychological studies in dementia praecox.* Ann Arbor, Mich.: Edwards Brothers, 1940.

Kent, Norma, and Davis, D. R. Discipline in the home and intellectual development. *Brit. J. med. Psychol.,* 1957, *30,* 27–33.

Kephart, N. C. Influencing the rate of mental growth in retarded children through environmental stimulation. *Natl. Soc. Study Educ.,* 39th Yearbook, 1940, Part II. Pp. 223–230.

Kephart, N. C., and Ainsworth, Mildred H. A preliminary study of the community adjustment of parolees of the Wayne County Training School. *Amer. Assn. ment. Defic.,* 1938, *43,* 161–166.

Kephart, N. C., and Strauss, A. A. A clinical factor influencing variations in IQ. *Amer. J. Orthopsychiat.,* 1940, *10,* 343–350.

Ketcham, W. A. Growth patterns of gifted children. *Merrill-Palmer Quart.,* 1957, *3,* 188–197.

Kimble, G. A. *Principles of general psychology.* New York: The Ronald Press Co., 1956.

King, J. A., and Gurney, Nancy L. Effect of early social experience on adult aggressive behavior in C57BL/10 mice. *J. comp. physiol. Psychol.,* 1954, *47,* 326–330.

Kinsey, A. C., Pomeroy, W. B., and Martin, C. E. *Sexual behavior in the human male.* Philadelphia: W. B. Saunders Co., 1948.

Kinsey, A. C., Pomeroy, W. B., Martin, C. E., and Gebhard, P. H. *Sexual behavior in the human female.* Philadelphia: W. B. Saunders Co., 1953.

Klackenberg, G. Thumb-sucking: frequency and etiology. *Pediatrics,* 1949, *4,* 418–424.

Klatskin, Ethelyn H., Lethin, A. G., and Jackson, Edith B. Choice of rooming-in or newborn nursery. *Pediatrics,* 1950, *6,* 878–889.

Klineberg, O. *Negro intelligence and selective migration.* New York: Columbia University Press, 1935.

Knief, Lotus M., and Stroud, J. B.

Intercorrelations among various intelligence, achievement, and social class scores. *J. educ. Psychol.*, 1959, 50, 117–120.

Knobloch, Hilda, and Pasamanick, B. Exogenous factors in infant intelligence. *Pediatrics*, 1960 (in press).

Kretschmer, E. *Körperbau und character*, 2d. rev. ed. Trans. by W. J. H. Sprott as *Physique and character*. London: Routledge and Kegan Paul, Ltd., 1925.

Kuenne, Margaret R. Experimental investigation of the relation of language to transposition behavior in young children. *J. exp. Psychol.*, 1946, 36, 417–490.

Kuhlmann, F. *Tests of mental development: A complete scale for individual examination.* Minneapolis: Educational Test Bureau, 1939.

Kunst, Mary S. A study of thumb- and finger-sucking in infants. *Psychol. Monogr.*, 1948, 3.

Kutner, B. Patterns of mental functioning associated with prejudice in children. *Psychol. Monogr.*, 1958, 72.

Lakin, M. Personality factors in mothers of excessively crying (colicky) infants. *Monogr. soc. Res. Child Develpm.*, 1957, 22, Ser. 64, No. 1.

Landis, J. T., and Landis, Mary G. *Youth and marriage.* Englewood Cliffs, N. J.: Prentice-Hall, 1957.

Lantz, Beatrice. Some dynamic aspects of success and failure. *Psychol. Monogr.*, 1945, 59.

Lauer, D. W., and Estes, W. K. Successive acquisitions and extinctions of a jumping habit in relation to schedule of reinforcement. *J. comp. physiol. Psychol.*, 1955, 48, 8–13.

Lazowick, L. M. On the nature of identification. *J. abnorm. soc. Psychol.*, 1955, 51, 175–183.

Leahy, Alice M. Nature-nurture and intelligence. *Genet. Psychol. Monogr.*, 1935, 17, 235–308.

Lee, E. S. Negro intelligence and selective migration: a Philadelphia test of the Klineberg hypothesis. *Amer. sociol. Rev.*, 1951, 16, 227–233.

LeShan, L. L. Time orientation and social class. *J. abnorm. soc. Psychol.*, 1952, 47, 589–592.

Lesser, G. S. Extrapunitiveness and ethnic attitude. *J. abnorm. soc. Psychol.*, 1958, 56, 281–282.

Lesser, G. S. The relationships between various forms of aggression and popularity among lower-class children. *J. educ. Psychol.*, 1959, 50, 20–25.

Levanway, R. W. The effect of stress on expressed attitudes toward self and others. *J. abnorm. soc. Psychol.*, 1955, 50, 225–226.

Levin, H., and Sears, R. R. Identification with parents as a determinant of doll-play aggression. *Child Develpm.*, 1956, 27, 135–155.

Levine, S. A further study of infantile handling and adult avoidance learning. *J. Pers.*, 1956, 25, 96–114.

Levine, S., and Otis, L. S. The effects of handling before and after weaning on the resistance of albino rats to later deprivation. *Canad. J. Psychol.*, 1958, 12, 103–106.

Levitt, E. E. The water-jar Einstellung test as a measure of rigidity. *Psychol. Bull.*, 1956, 53, 347–370.

Levy, D. M. Experiments on the sucking reflex and social behavior in dogs. *Amer. J. Orthopsychiat.*, 1934, 4, 203–224.

Levy, D. M. Release therapy. *Amer. J. Orthopsychiat.*, 1939, 9, 713–736.

Levy, L. H. The meaning and generality of perceived actual-ideal discrepancies. *J. consult. Psychol.*, 1956, 20, 396–398.

Levy, L., and McCandless, B. R. Expectancy of punishment as a function of type of differentiation in original learning. *J. abnorm. soc. Psychol.*, 1952, 47, 520–525.

Levy, Ruth J. Effects of institutional vs. boarding-home care on a group of infants. *J. Pers.*, 1947, 15, 233–241.

Lewin, K. *A dynamic theory of per-*

sonality. New York: McGraw-Hill Book Co., 1935.

Lewin, K., Dembo, Tamara, Festinger, L., and Sears, Pauline S. Level of aspiration. In J. McV. Hunt (ed.), *Personality and the behavior disorders.* New York: The Ronald Press Co., 1944. Pp. 333–378.

Lewin, K., Lippitt, R., and White, R. K. Patterns of aggressive behavior in experimentally created "social climates." *J. soc. Psychol.,* 1939, *10,* 271–299.

Lewis, Hilda. *Deprived children: The Mersham experiment—a social and clinical study.* London: Oxford University Press, 1954.

Lewis, S. J. Thumb-sucking: a cause of malocclusion in the deciduous teeth. *J. Amer. dent. Assn.,* 1930, *17,* 1060–1072.

Lewis, S. J. Undesirable habits influencing the deciduous dentition. *J. Amer. dent. Assn.,* 1931, *18,* 1766–1778.

Lindzey, G. Thematic Apperception Test: interpretative assumptions and related empirical evidence. *Psychol. Bull.,* 1952, *49,* 1–25.

Lindzey, G., and Herman, P. S. Thematic Apperception Test: a note on reliability and situational validity. *J. proj. Tech.,* 1955, *19,* 36–42.

Lindzey, G., and Kalnins, D. Thematic Apperception Test: some evidence bearing on the "hero assumption." *J. abnorm. soc. Psychol.,* 1958, *57,* 76–83.

Lindzey, G., and Tejessy, Charlotte. Thematic Apperception Test: indices of aggression in relation to measures of overt and covert behavior. *Amer. J. Orthopsychiat.,* 1956, *26,* 567–576.

Lindzey, G., Tejessy, Charlotte, and Zamansky, H. S. Thematic Apperception Test: an empirical examination of some indices of homosexuality. *J. abnorm. soc. Psychol.,* 1958, *57,* 67–75.

Lipsitt, L. P. A self-concept scale for children and its relationship to the Children's Form of the Manifest Anxiety Scale. *Child Develpm.,* 1958, *29,* 463–472.

Little, Sue W., and Cohen, L. D. Goal-setting behavior of asthmatic children and of their mothers for them. *J. Pers.,* 1951, *19,* 376–389.

Liverant, S. MMPI differences between parents of disturbed and nondisturbed children. *J. consult. Psychol.,* 1959, *23,* 256–260.

Loevinger, Jane. Intelligence as related to socioeconomic factors. *Natl. Soc. Study Educ.,* 39th Yearbook, 1940, Part II. Pp. 159–211.

Love, Mary I., and Beach, Sylvia. Performance of children on the Davis-Eells Games and other measures of ability. *J. consult. Psychol.,* 1957, *21,* 29–32.

Lowrey, L. G. Personality distortion and early institutional care. *Amer. J. Orthopsychiat.,* 1940, *10,* 576–585.

Luchins, A. S., and Forgus, R. H. The effect of differential postweaning environments on the rigidity of an animal's behavior. *J. genet. Psychol.,* 1955, *86,* 51–58.

Luckey, Eleanore B. Marital satisfaction and parent concepts. *J. consult. Psychol.* (in press, 1960).

Lyle, W. H., Jr., and Levitt, E. E. Punitiveness, authoritarianism, and parental discipline of grade-school children. *J. abnorm. soc. Psychol.,* 1955, *51,* 42–46.

Lynch, Elizabeth I., and Mertz, Alice E. Adoptive placement of infants directly from the hospital. *Soc. Casework,* 1955, *36,* 451–457.

Lynn, D. B. Sex differences in masculine and feminine identification. *Psychol. Rev.,* 1959, *66,* 126–135.

Lynn, D. B., and Sawrey, W. L. The effects of father-absence on Norwegian boys and girls. *J. abnorm. soc. Psychol.,* 1959, *59,* 258–262.

Maas, H. S. Some social-class differences in the family systems and group relations of pre- and early adolescents. *Child Develpm.,* 1951, *22,* 145–152.

McArthur, C. Personality differences

between middle and upper classes. *J. abnorm. soc. Psychol.*, 1955, *50*, 247–254.

McArthur, C., and Stevens, Lucia. The validation of expressed interests as compared with inventoried interests: a fourteen-year follow-up. *J. appl. Psychol.*, 1955, *39*, 184–189.

McCandless, B. R. Changing relationships between dominance and social acceptability during group democratization. *Amer. J. Orthopsychiat.*, 1942, *12*, 529–536.

McCandless, B. R. Environment and intelligence. *Amer. J. ment. Def.*, 1952, *56*, 674–691.

McCandless, B. R. Should a bright child start to school before he's five? *Educ.*, 1957, *77*, 1–6.

McCandless, B. R., Balsbaugh, Carolyn, and Bennett, Hannah L. Preschool-age socialization and maternal control techniques. *Amer. Psychologist*, 1958, *13*, 320 (abstract).

McCandless, B. R., Bilous, Carolyn B., and Bennett, Hannah L. The relation between peer-popularity and dependence on adults in preschool-age socialization. *Child Develpm.*, 1960 (in press).

McCandless, B. R., and Castaneda, A. Anxiety in children, school achievement, and intelligence. *Child Develpm.*, 1956, *27*, 379–382.

McCandless, B. R., Castaneda, A., and Palermo, D. S. Anxiety in children and social status. *Child Develpm.*, 1956, *27*, 385–392.

McCandless, B. R., and Heye, Helene. The relationship of certain maternal attitudes, dependency, and nervous habits in preschool-aged children. *Amer. Psychologist*, 1949, *4*, 249 (abstract).

McCandless, B. R., and Holloway, H. D. Race prejudice and intolerance of ambiguity in children. *J. abnorm. soc. Psychol.*, 1955, *51*, 692–693.

McCandless, B. R., and Marshall, Helen R. A picture sociometric technique for preschool children and its relation to teacher judgments of friendship. *Child Develpm.*, 1957, *28*, 139–147.

McCandless, Elinore O. School achievement of newly institutionalized high-grade mentally retarded children. Wayne County Training School, Northville, Mich., 1943. Unpublished ms.

McClelland, D. C. Risk-taking in children with high and low need for achievement. In Atkinson, J. W. (ed.), *Motives in fantasy, action, and society*. Princeton: Van Nostrand, 1958.

McClelland, W. J. Differential handling and weight gain in the albino rat. *Can. J. Psychol.*, 1956, *10*, 19–22.

Maccoby, Eleanor E., Gibbs, P. K., and Staff. Methods of child-rearing in two social classes. In W. E. Martin and Celia B. Stendler (eds.), *Readings in child development*. New York: Harcourt, Brace & World, Inc., 1954. Pp. 380–396.

McGehee, W., and Lewis, W. D. The socioeconomic status of homes of mentally superior and retarded children and the occupational rank of their parents. *J. genet. Psychol.*, 1942, *60*, 375–380.

McGeoch, J. A. *The psychology of human learning*, 2d ed. Rev. by Arthur L. Irion. New York: Longmans, Green, 1952.

McGinnis, J. M. Eye movements and optic nystagmus in early infancy. *Genet. Psychol. Monogr.*, 1930, *8*, 321–430.

McGraw, Myrtle B. *Growth: A study of Johnny and Jimmy*. New York: Appleton-Century, 1935.

McGuire, C., Lanmon, M., and White, G. D. Adolescent peer acceptance and valuations of role behavior. *Amer. Psychologist*, 1953, *8*, 397 (abstract).

McGuire, C., White, G. D., and Novak, E. Adolescent role behavior and age-mate acceptance. Paper read at Southwestern Social Science Association, Dallas, Texas, April 1954.

McIntyre, C. J. Acceptance by others and its relation to acceptance of self and others. *J. abnorm. soc. Psychol.*, 1952, 47, 624–625.

McKee, J. P., and Leader, Florence B. The relationship of socioeconomic status and aggression to the competitive behavior of preschool children. *Child Develpm.*, 1955, 26, 135–142.

McKelvey, R. K., and Marx, M. H. Effects of infantile food and water deprivation on adult hoarding in the rat. *J. comp. physiol. Psychol.*, 1951, 44, 423–430.

McNemar, Q. A critical examination of the University of Iowa studies of environmental influences upon the IQ. *Psychol. Bull.*, 1940, 37, 63–92.

Maier, N. R. F. Frustration theory: restatement and extension. *Psychol. Rev.*, 1956, 63, 370–388.

Malzberg, B. Some statistical aspects of mongolism. *Amer. J. ment. Defic.*, 1950, 54, 226–281.

Marshall, Helen R., and McCandless, B. R. Relationship between dependence on adults and social acceptance by peers. *Child Develpm.*, 1957, 28, 421–425.

Marshall, Helen R., and Magruder, Lucille. Relations between parent money-education practices and children's knowledge and use of money. *Child Develpm.*, 1960, 31, 253–284.

Martire, J. G. Relationships between the self-concept and differences in the strength and generality of achievement motivation. *J. Pers.*, 1956, 24, 364–375.

Masling, J. M. How neurotic is the authoritarian? *J. abnorm. soc. Psychol.*, 1954, 49, 316–318.

Maslow, A. H. The instinctoid nature of basic needs. *J. Pers.*, 1954, 22, 326–347.

Maslow, A. H., and Sakoda, J. Marie Volunteer-error in the Kinsey study. *J. abnorm. soc. Psychol.*, 1952, 47, 259–262.

Maslow, A. H., and Szilagyi-Kessler, I. Security and breast feeding. *J. ab-norm. soc. Psychol.*, 1946, 41, 83–85.

Mednick, S. A., and Lehtinen, Laura E. Stimulus generalization as a function of age in children. *J. exp. Psychol.*, 1957, 53, 180–183.

Melton, A. W. Learning. In W. S. Monroe (ed.), *Encyclopedia of educational research*, 2d ed. New York: The Macmillan Co., 1950. Pp. 668–690.

Melzack, R. Irrational fears in the dog. *Can. J. Psychol.*, 1952, 6, 141–147.

Melzack, R. The genesis of emotional behavior: an experimental study of the dog. *J. comp. physiol. Psychol.*, 1954, 47, 166–168.

Melzack, R., and Scott, T. H. The effects of early experience on the response to pain. *J. comp. physiol. Psychol.*, 1957, 50, 155–161.

Melzack, R., and Thompson, W. R. Effects of early experience on social behavior. *Can. J. Psychol.*, 1956, 10, 82–90.

Meredith, H. V. Comments on "The varieties of human physique." *Child Develpm.*, 1940, 11, 301–309.

Meredith, H. V. A descriptive concept of physical development. In Harris, D. B., (ed.) *The concept of development*. Minneapolis: University of Minnesota Press, 1957. Pp. 109–122.

Meredith, H. V. Physical growth. In *Encyclopedia Americana*, 1959, 13, 499–502 b.

Meredith, H. V. Status of Massachusetts children of North European and Italian ancestry. *Amer. J. phys. Anthrop.*, 1939, 24, 301–346.

Miles, Catherine C., and Miles, W. R. The correlation of intelligence scores and chronological age from early to late maturity. *Amer. J. Psychol.*, 1932, 44, 44–78.

Miller, D. R., and Swanson, G. E. *Inner Conflict and Defense*. New York: Holt, Rinehart and Winston Co., 1960.

Miller, N. E. Comments on theoretical models illustrated by the development of a theory of conflict behavior. *J. Pers.*, 1951, 20, 82–100.

Miller, N. E. Theory and experiment relating psychoanalytic displacement to stimulus-response generalization. *J. abnorm. soc. Psychol.*, 1948, 43, 155–178.

Milner, Esther. A study of the relationship between reading readiness in grade-one school children and patterns of parent-child interaction. *Child Develpm.*, 1951, 22, 95–112.

Milton, G. A. A factor analytic study of child-rearing behaviors. *Child Develpm.*, 1958, 29, 381–392.

Mischel, W. Preference for delayed reinforcement: an experimental study of a cultural observation. *J. abnorm. soc. Psychol.*, 1958, 56, 57–61.

Mitchell, J. V., Jr. Goal-setting behavior as a function of self-acceptance, over- and underachievement, and related personality variables. *J. educ. Psychol.*, 1959, 50, 93–104.

Montagu, M. F. A. *Adolescent sterility*. Springfield, Ill.: Charles C Thomas, 1946.

Montgomery, K. C. The relation between fear induced by novel stimulation and exploratory behavior. *J. comp. physiol. Psychol.*, 1955, 48, 254–260.

Montgomery, K. C., and Segall, M. Discrimination learning based upon the exploratory drive. *J. comp. physiol. Psychol.*, 1955, 48, 225–228.

Morgenson, G. J., McMurray, G. A., and Jaques, L. B. Effects of stress and administration of cortisone on weight gain in gentled rats. *Can. J. Psychol.*, 1957, 11, 123–127.

Mullahy, P. *Oedipus—myth and complex: a review of psychoanalytic theory*. New York: Hermitage Press, 1948.

Mundy, Lydia. Environmental influence on intellectual function as measured by intelligence tests. *Brit. J. med. Psychol.*, 1957, 30, 194–201.

Munn, N. L. Learning in children. In Carmichael, L. (ed.), *Manual of Child Psychology*, 2d ed. New York: John Wiley and Sons, 1954. Pp. 374–458.

Munn, N. L. *Psychological development*. Boston: Houghton Mifflin Co., 1938.

Murphy, D. P. *Congenital malformation*, 2d ed. Philadelphia: University of Pennsylvania Press, 1947.

Murphy, D. P. The outcome of 625 pregnancies in women subjected to pelvic radium roentgen irradiation. *Amer. J. Obst. Gynec.*, 1929, 18, 179–187.

Murphy, C., Murphy, Lois B., and Newcomb, T. M. *Experimental social psychology*, rev. ed. New York: Harper & Brothers, 1937.

Murray, E. J., and Berkun, M. M. Displacement as a function of conflict. *J. abnorm. soc. Psychol.*, 1955, 51, 47–56.

Mussen, P. H. Some personality and social factors related to changes in children's attitudes toward Negroes. *J. abnorm. soc. Psychol.*, 1950, 45, 423–441.

Mussen, P. H., and Conger, J. *Child development and personality*. New York: Harper & Brothers, 1956.

Mussen, P. H., and Distler, L. Masculinity, identification, and father-son relationships. *J. abnorm. soc. Psychol.*, 1959, 59, 350–356.

Mussen, P. H., and Jones, Mary C. Self-conceptions, motivations, and interpersonal attitudes of late- and early-maturing boys. *Child Develpm.*, 1957, 28, 242–256.

Mussen, P. H., and Kagan, J. Group conformity and perception of parents. *Child Develpm.*, 1958, 29, 57–60.

Mussen, P. H., and Naylor, H. K. The relationships between overt and fantasy aggression. *J. abnorm. soc. Psychol.*, 1954, 49, 235–240.

Mussen, P. H., and Porter, L. W. Personal motivations and self-conceptions associated with effectiveness and ineffectiveness in emergent groups. *J. abnorm. soc. Psychol.*, 1959, 59, 23–27.

Nadler, E. B. Yielding, authoritarianism, and authoritarian ideology regarding groups. *J. abnorm. soc. Psychol.*, 1959, 58, 408–410.

Nakamura, C. Y. The relationship between children's expressions of hostility and methods of discipline exercised by dominant overprotective parents. *Child Develpm.*, 1959, 30, 109–118.

Neel, Ann F. The relationship of authoritarian personality to learning: F-scale scores compared to classroom performance. *J. educ. Psychol.*, 1959, 50, 195–199.

Newman, H. F., Freeman, F. N., and Holzinger, K. J. *Twins: a study of heredity and environment.* Chicago: The University of Chicago Press, 1937.

Newton, N. R., and Newton, M. Relationship of ability to breast feed and maternal attitudes toward breast feeding. *Pediatrics*, 1950, 5, 869–875.

O'Connor, Patricia. Ethnocentrism, "intolerance of ambiguity," and abstract reasoning ability. *J. abnorm. soc. Psychol.*, 1952, 47, 526–530.

Omwake, Katharine T. The relation between acceptance of self and acceptance of others shown by three personality inventories. *J. consult. Psychol.*, 1954, 18, 443–446.

Opstad, P. Effects of social class in American secondary-school education. University of Iowa, Iowa Child Welfare Res. Sta., 1957. Unpublished ms.

O'Reilly, C. T., and O'Reilly, E. J. Religious beliefs of Catholic college students and their attitudes toward minorities. *J. abnorm. soc. Psychol.*, 1954, 49, 378–380.

Orgel, S. Z. Personality distortion and early institutional care. *Amer. J. Orthopsychiat.*, 1941, 11, 371–373.

Orlansky, H. Infant care and personality. *Psychol. Bull.*, 1949, 46, 1–48.

Otis, Nancy B., and McCandless, B. R. Responses to repeated frustrations of young children differentiated according to need area. *J.*

abnorm. soc. Psychol., 1955, 50, 349–353.

Owens, W. A., Jr. Age and mental abilities: a longitudinal study. *Genet. Psychol. Monogr.*, 1953, 48, 3–54.

Page, Marjorie L. The modification of ascendant behavior in preschool children. *Univ. Iowa Stud. Child Welfare*, 1936, 12, 1–69.

Palermo, D. S. Racial comparisons and additional normative data on the Children's Manifest Anxiety Scale. *Child Develpm.*, 1959, 30, 53–58.

Palermo, D. S., Castaneda, A., and McCandless, B. R. The relationship of anxiety in children to performance in a complex learning task. *Child Develpm.*, 1956, 27, 333–338.

Pasamanick, B. A comparative study of the behavioral development of Negro infants. *J. genet. Psychol.*, 1946, 69, 3–44.

Payne, D. E., and Mussen, P. H. Parent-child relations and father identification among adolescent boys. *J. abnorm. soc. Psychol.*, 1956, 52, 358–362.

Peterson, C. H., and Spano, F. L. Breast feeding, maternal rejection, and child personality. *Charact. and Pers.*, 1941, 10, 62–66.

Parsons, T. Family structure and the socialization of the child. In T. Parsons and R. F. Bales (eds.). *Family, Socialization, and Interaction Process.* Glencoe, Ill.: The Free Press, 1955.

Peterson, D. R., Becker, W. C., Hellmer, L. A., Shoemaker, D. J., and Quay, H. C. Parental attitudes and child adjustment. *Child Develpm.*, 1959, 30, 119–130.

Pettigrew, T. F. Regional differences in anti-Negro prejudice. *J. abnorm. soc. Psychol.*, 1959, 59, 28–36.

Phillips, E. L. Attitudes toward self and others: a brief questionnaire report. *J. consult. Psychol.*, 1951, 15, 79–81.

Pinneau, S. R. The infantile disorders of hospitalism and anaclitic depression. *Psychol. Bull.*, 1955, 52, 429–452.

Pinneau, S. R. Reply to Dr. Spitz. *Psychol. Bull.*, 1955, 52, 459–462.

Pinneau, S. R., and Jones, H. E. Mental development in infancy and childhood and mental abilities in adult life. *Rev. educ. Res.*, 1955, 25, 415–437.

Pratt, K. C. The Neonate. In L. Carmichael (ed.), *Manual of Child Psychology*, 2d ed. New York: John Wiley and Sons, 1954. Pp. 215–291.

Pratt, K. C., Nelson, Amalie K., and Sun, K. H. *The behavior of the newborn infant.* Columbus: The Ohio State University Press, 1930.

Purcell, K. The TAT and antisocial behavior. *J. consult. Psychol.*, 1956, 20, 449–456.

Rabban, M. Sex-role identification in young children in two diverse social groups. *Genet. Psychol. Monogr.*, 1950, 42, 81–158.

Radke, Marian J. Relation of parental authority to children's behavior and attitudes. *Univ. Minn. Inst. Child Welfare Monogr.*, 1946, No. 22.

Rank, O. *The trauma of birth.* New York: Harcourt, Brace, & World, Inc., 1929.

Reymert, M. L., and Hinton, R. T., Jr. The effect of a change to a relatively superior environment upon the IQ's of one hundred children. *Natl. Soc. Study Educ.*, 39th Yearbook, 1940, Part II. Pp. 255–268.

Rheingold, Harriet L. The modification of social responsiveness in institutional babies. *Monogr. Soc. Res. Child Develpm.*, 1956, 21, 3–48.

Rheingold, Harriet L., Gewirtz, J. L., and Ross, Helen W. Social conditioning of vocalizations in the infant. *J. comp. physiol. Psychol.*, 1959, 52, 68–73.

Ribble, Margaret. *The rights of infants.* New York: Columbia University Press, 1943.

Riss, W., and Goy, R. W. Modification of sex drive and O_2 consump-

tion by isolating and grouping male guinea pigs. *J. comp. physiol. Psychol.*, 1957, 50, 150–154.

Ritchie, B. F., Aeschliman, B., and Pierce, P. Studies in spatial learning: VIII. Place performance and the acquisition of place dispositions. *J. comp. physiol. Psychol.*, 1950, 43, 73–85.

Rogers, C. R. *Client-centered therapy.* Boston: Houghton Mifflin Co., 1951.

Rogers, C. R. A coordinated research in psychotherapy: A nonobjective introduction. *J. consult. Psychol.*, 1949, 13, 169–175.

Rogers, C. R., and Dymond, Rosalind F. (eds.). *Psychotherapy and personality change.* Chicago: The University of Chicago Press, 1954.

Rogerson, B. C. F., and Rogerson, C. H. Feeding in infancy and subsequent psychological difficulties. *J. ment. Sci.*, 1939, 85, 1163–1182.

Rosen, B. The achievement syndrome: a psychocultural dimension of social stratification. *Amer. sociol. Rev.*, 1956, 21, 203–211.

Rosenblum, S. The effects of differential reinforcement and motivation on prediction responses of children. *Child Develpm.*, 1956, 27, 99–108.

Rosenblum, S., Keller, J. E., and Papania, N. Davis-Eells ("Culture Fair") test performance of lower-class retarded children. *J. consult. Psychol.*, 1955, 19, 51–54.

Rosenzweig, S. Frustration as an experimental problem: The significance of frustration as a problem of research. *Charact. and Pers.*, 1938, 7, 126–128.

Rosenzweig, S. Need-persistive and ego-defensive reactions to frustration as demonstrated by an experiment on repression. *Psychol. Rev.*, 1941, 48, 347–349.

Rosenzweig, S. An outline of frustration theory. In Hunt, J. McV. (ed.). *Personality and the behavior disorders*, Vol. I. New York: The

Ronald Press Co., 1944. Ch. II, pp. 379–388.

Rosenzweig, S. Revised norms for the adult form of the Rosenzweig Picture-Frustration Study. *J. Pers.*, 1950, *18*, 344–346.

Rotter, J. B. *Social learning and clinical psychology.* Englewood Cliffs, N. J.: Prentice-Hall, 1954.

Ruja, H. J. The relation between neonate crying and length of labor. *J. genet. Psychol.*, 1948, *73*, 53–55.

Rynerson, Mary N. The relationship between scores on the Children's Manifest Anxiety Scale and clinical judgments of anxiety. Unpublished M.A. thesis, The University of Chicago, 1957.

Sandin, A. A. *Social and emotional adjustments of regularly promoted and nonpromoted pupils.* New York: Bureau of Publications, Teachers College, Columbia University, 1944.

Sarason, S. B. *Psychological problems in mental deficiency.* New York: Harper & Brothers, 1953.

Schonfeld, W. A. Inadequate masculine physique as a factor in personality development of adolescent boys. *Psychosom. Med.*, 1950, *12*, 49–54.

Scott, J. H. Some effects at maturity of gentling, ignoring, or shocking rats during infancy. *J. abnorm. soc. Psychol.*, 1955, *51*, 412–414.

Scott, T. H., Bexton, W. H., Heron, W., and Doane, B. K. Cognitive effects of perceptual isolation. *Can. J. Psychol.*, 1959, *13*, 200–209.

Sears, Pauline S. Child-rearing factors related to playing of sex-typed roles. *Amer. Psychologist*, 1953, *8*, 431 (abstract).

Sears, Pauline S. Doll-play aggression in normal young children: influence of sex, age, sibling status, father's absence. *Psychol. Monogr.*, 1951, *65*, Whole No. 323, No. 6.

Sears, R. R. A theoretical framework for personality and social behavior. *Amer. Psychologist*, 1951, *6*, 476–483.

Sears, R. R., Maccoby, Eleanor E., and Levin, H. *Patterns of childrearing.* Evanston, Ill.: Row, Peterson and Co., 1957.

Sears, R. R., and Wise, G. W. Relation of cup feeding in infancy to thumb-sucking and the oral drive. *Amer. J. Orthopsychiat.*, 1950, *20*, 123–138.

Secord, P. F., and Jourard, S. M. The appraisal of body-cathexis: body cathexis and the self. *J. consult. Psychol.*, 1953, *17*, 343–347.

Seitz, P. F. D. The effects of infantile experiences upon adult behavior in animal subjects: I. Effects of litter size during infancy upon adult behavior in the rat. *Amer. J. Psychiat.*, 1954, *110*, 916–927.

Sewell, W. H. The construction and standardization of a scale for the measurement of the socioeconomic status of Oklahoma farm families. Stillwater, Okla.: *Okla. agric. exp. Sta. tech. Bull.*, 1940, No. 9.

Sewell, W. H. Infant training and the personality of the child. *Amer. J. Sociol.*, 1952, *58*, 150–159.

Sewell, W. H. Short form of the farm family socioeconomic scale. *Rural Sociol.*, 1943, *8*, 161–170.

Sewell, W. H., and Haller, A. O. Factors in the relationship between social status and the personality adjustment of the child. *Amer. sociol. Rev.*, 1959, *24*, 511–520.

Sewell, W. H., and Haller, A. O. Social status and the personality adjustment of the child. *Sociometry*, 1956, *19*, 114–125.

Sewell, W. H., and Mussen, P. H. The effects of feeding, weaning, and scheduling procedures on childhood adjustment and the formation of oral symptoms. *Child Develpm.*, 1952, *23*, 185–191.

Sewell, W. H., Mussen, P. H., and Harris, C. W. Relationships among child-training practices. *Amer. sociol. Rev.*, 1955, *20*, 137–148.

Sheldon, W. H. *The varieties of human physique.* New York: Harper & Brothers, 1940.

Sheldon, W. H. *The varieties of temperament.* New York: Harper & Brothers, 1942.

Sheldon, W. H., Hartl, E. M., and McDermott, E. *Varieties of delinquent youth.* New York: Harper & Brothers, 1949.

Sherman, M., and Sherman, I. C. Sensori-motor responses in infants. *J. comp. Psychol.,* 1925, *5,* 53–68.

Shirley, Mary M. The sequential method for the study of maturing behavior patterns. *Psychol. Rev.,* 1931, *38,* 507–528.

Shuttleworth, F. K. The adolescent period: a pictorial atlas. *Monogr. Soc. Res. Child Develpm.,* 1949, *14.*

Siegel, Alberta A., and Kohn, Lynette G. Permissiveness, permission, and aggression: the effect of adult presence or absence on aggression in children's play. *Child Develpm.,* 1959, *30,* 131–141.

Siegel, S. M. The relationship of hostility to authoritarianism. *J. abnorm. soc. Psychol.,* 1956, *52,* 368–372.

Simpson, M. S. *Parent preferences of young children.* Contr. Educ. No. 652. New York: Bureau of Publications, Teachers College, Columbia University, 1935.

Simsarian, F. P., and McLendon, P. A. Further records of the self-demand schedule in infant feeding. *J. Pediatrics,* 1945, *27,* 109–114.

Singer, J. L. Projected familial attitudes as a function of socioeconomic status and psychopathology. *J. consult. Psychol.,* 1954, *18,* 99–104.

Singer, J. L., and Opler, M. K. Contrasting patterns of fantasy and motility in Irish and Italian schizophrenics. *J. abnorm. soc. Psychol.,* 1956, *53,* 42–47.

Singer, J. L., Wilensky, H., and McCraven, Vivian G. Delaying capacity, fantasy, and planning ability: a factorial study of some basic ego functions. *J. consult. Psychol.,* 1956, *20,* 375–383.

Skeels, H. M., and Harms, Irene E. Children with inferior social histories: their mental development in adoptive homes. *J. genet. Psychol.,* 1948, *72,* 283–294.

Skeels, H. M., Updegraff, Ruth, Wellman, Beth L., and Williams, H. M. A study of environmental stimulation: an orphanage preschool project. *Univ. Iowa Stud. Child Welfare,* 1938, *15,* No. 4.

Skodak, Marie, and Skeels, H. M. A final follow-up study of one hundred adopted children. *J. genet. Psychol.,* 1949, *75,* 85–125.

Smith, Betty. *A tree grows in Brooklyn.* New York: Harper & Brothers, 1943.

Smith, C. U., and Prothro, J. W. Ethnic differences in authoritarian personality. *Soc. Forces,* 1957, *35,* 334–338.

Smith, H. P. A study in the selective character of American secondary education: Participation in school activities as conditioned by socioeconomic status and other factors. *J. educ. Psychol.,* 1945, *36,* 229–246.

Smith, J. M. The relative brightness values of three hues for newborn infants. *Univ. Iowa Stud. Child Welfare,* 1936, *12,* 91–140.

Smith, J. R., and Coleman, J. C. The relationship between manifestations of hostility in projective tests and overt behavior. *J. proj. Tech.,* 1956, *20,* 326–334.

Snygg, D. The relation between the intelligence of mothers and of their children living in foster homes. *J. genet. Psychol.,* 1938, *52,* 401–406.

Sontag, L. W. The significance of fetal environmental differences. *Amer. J. Obst. Gynec.,* 1941, *42,* 996–1003.

Sontag, L. W., and Richards, T. W. Studies in fetal behavior: I. Fetal heart rate as a behavioral indicator. *Child Develpm. Monogr.,* 1938, *3,* No. 4.

Sontag, L. W., and Wallace, R. F. The effect of cigarette-smoking during pregnancy upon the fetal heart rate. *Amer. J. Obst. Gynec.,* 1935, *29,* 3–8.

Spearman, C. *The abilities of man.* New York: The Macmillan Co., 1927.

Spector, A. J. Expectations, fulfillment, and morale. *J. abnorm. soc. Psychol.,* 1956, 52, 51–56.

Speer, G. S. The mental development of children of feeble-minded and normal mothers. *Natl. Soc. Study Educ.,* 39th Yearbook, 1940, Part II. Pp. 309–314.

Spence, K. W. The differential response in animals to stimuli varying within a single stimulus dimension. *Psychol. Rev.,* 1937, 44, 430–444.

Spence, K. W. The nature of discrimination learning in animals. *Psychol. Rev.,* 1936, 43, 427–449.

Spence, K. W. The nature of the response in discrimination learning. *Psychol. Rev.,* 1952, 59, 89–93.

Spiker, C. C. Stimulus pretraining and subsequent performance in the delayed reaction experiment. *J. exp. Psychol.,* 1956, 52, 107–111.

Spiker, C. C., Gerjuoy, Irma R., and Shepard, Winifred O. Children's concept of middle-sizedness and performance on the intermediate size problem. *J. comp. physiol. Psychol.,* 1956, 49, 416–419.

Spiker, C. C., and McCandless, B. R. The concept of intelligence and the philosophy of science. *Psychol. Rev.,* 1954, 61, 255–266.

Spiker, C. C., and Terrell, G., Jr. Factors associated with transposition behavior of preschool children. *J. genet. Psychol.,* 1955, 86, 143–158.

Spitz, R. A. Hospitalism: An inquiry into the genesis of psychiatric conditions in early childhood. In O. Fenichel *et al.* (eds.), *The psychoanalytic study of the child,* Vol. I. New York: International Universities Press, 1945. Pp. 53–74.

Spitz, R. A. Hospitalism: A follow-up report on investigation described in Vol. I, 1945. In O. Fenichel, *et al.* (eds.), *The psychoanalytic study of the child,* Vol. II. New York: International Universities Press, 1946. Pp. 113–117.

Spitz, R. A. Reply to Dr. Pinneau. *Psychol. Bull.,* 1955, 52, 453–458.

Spitz, R. A. The role of ecological factors in emotional development in infancy. *Child Develpm.,* 1949, 20, 145–155.

Spock, B. *The pocket book of baby and child care.* New York: Pocket Books, 1950.

Starkweather, Elizabeth K., and Roberts, Katherine E. IQ changes occurring during nursery-school attendance at the Merrill-Palmer School. *Natl. Soc. Study Educ.,* 39th Yearbook, 1940, Part II. Pp. 315–335.

Steckler, G. A. Authoritarian ideology in Negro college students. *J. abnorm. soc. Psychol.,* 1957, 54, 396–399.

Stendler, Celia B. Sixty years of child-training practices. *J. Pediatrics,* 1950, 36, 122–134.

Stendler, Celia B. Social-class differences in parental attitudes toward school at grade-1 level. *Child Develpm.,* 1951, 22, 36–46.

Stern, C. Hereditary factors affecting adoption. In Schapiro, M. (ed.), *A study of adoption practice.* New York: Child Welfare League of America, 1956. Vol. II, pp. 47–58.

Stern, G. G., and Cope, A. H. Differences in educability between stereopaths, nonstereopaths, and rationals. Paper read at 1956 APA convention, Chicago.

Stevenson, H. W., and Stewart, E. C. A developmental study of racial awareness in young children. *Child Develpm.,* 1958, 29, 399–409.

Stewart, Ann H., Weiland, I. H., Leider, A. R., Mangham, C. A., Holmes, T. H., and Ripley, H. S. Excessive infant crying (colic) in relation to parent behavior. *Amer. J. Psychiat.,* 1954, 110, 687–694.

Stiles, Frances S. Developing an understanding of human behavior at the elementary school level. *J. educ. Res.,* 1950, 43, 516–524.

Stippich, Mary E. The mental development of children of feeble-minded mothers: a preliminary report. *Natl.*

Soc. Study Educ., 39th Yearbook, 1940, Part II. Pp. 337–350.

Stolz, H. R., and Stolz, Lois M. Somatic development of adolescent boys. New York: The Macmillan Co., 1951.

Stolz, Lois M., et al. Father relations of war-born children. Stanford, Calif.: Stanford University Press, 1954.

Stubbs, E. M. The effect of the factors of duration, intensity, and pitch of sound stimuli on the responses of newborn infants. Univ. Iowa Stud. Child Welfare, 1934, 9, No. 4.

Sullivan, H. S. Conceptions of modern psychiatry. Washington, D. C.: William Alanson White Psychiatric Foundation, 1947.

Sullivan, H. S. The interpersonal theory of psychiatry. Washington, D. C.: William Alanson White Psychiatric Foundation, 1953.

Sutton-Smith, B., and Rosenberg, B. G. Manifest anxiety and game preference in children. Child Develpm., 1960, 31, 307–311.

Taylor, C., and Combs, A. W. Self-acceptance and adjustment. J. consult. Psychol., 1952, 16, 89–91.

Terman, L. M., et al. Genetic studies of genius: I. Mental and physical traits of a thousand gifted children. Stanford, Calif.: Stanford University Press, 1925.

Terman, L. M., and Merrill, Maude A. Measuring intelligence: a guide to the administration of the New Revised Stanford-Binet Tests. Boston: Houghton Mifflin Co., 1937.

Terman, L. M., and Oden, Mehta H. Genetic studies of genius: IV. The gifted child grows up. Stanford, Calif.: Stanford University Press, 1947.

Thompson, G. G. Child psychology. Boston: Houghton Mifflin Co., 1952.

Thompson, W. R. The heredity-environment problem. Bull. Marit. Psychol. Assn., Spring 1955, 30–40.

Thompson, W. R., and Heron, W. The effects of restricting early experience on the problem-solving ca-

pacity of dogs. Can. J. Psychol., 1954, 8, 17–31.

Thorndike, E. L., et al. The measurement of intelligence. New York: Bureau of Publications, Teachers College, Columbia University, 1926.

Thorpe, J. G. An investigation into some correlates of sociometric status within school classes. Sociometry, 1955, 18, 49–61.

Thurston, J. R., and Mussen, P. H. Infant feeding gratification and adult personality. J. Pers., 1951, 19, 449–458.

Thurstone, L. L., and Thurstone, Thelma G. Primary mental abilities scales: Primary, elementary, and intermediate. Chicago: Science Research Associates, 1950.

Titus, H. E., and Hollander, E. P. The California F Scale in psychological research: 1950–1955. Psychol. Bull., 1957, 54, 47–64.

Tolman, E. C. Purposive behavior in animals and men. New York: Appleton-Century-Crofts, 1932.

Trainham, G., Pilafian, G. J., and Kraft, R. M. Case history of twins fed on a self-demand regime. J. Pediatrics, 1945, 27, 97–108.

Tredgold, A. F. A textbook of mental deficiency. Baltimore: The Williams and Wilkins Co., 1947.

Trent, R. D. The relationship of anxiety to popularity and rejection among institutionalized delinquent boys. Child Develpm., 1957, 28, 379–384.

Truax, C. B. Factors affecting intelligence change associated with preschool attendance. Manuscript in preparation, 1960.

Tuddenham, R. D. Correlates of yielding to distorted group norm. J. Pers., 1959, 27, 272–284.

Tuddenham, R. D., and McBride, P. D. The yielding experiment from the subject's point of view. J. Pers., 1959, 27, 259–271.

Valenstein, E. S., Riss, W., and Young, W. C. Experiential and genetic factors in the organization of sexual behavior in male guinea pigs. *J. comp. physiol. Psychol.*, 1955, 48, 397–403.

Vincent, C. E. Trends in infant care ideas. *Child Develpm.*, 1951, 22, 199–209.

Voas, W. H. Does attendance at the Winnetka Nursery School tend to raise the IQ? *Natl. Soc. Study Educ.*, 39th Yearbook, 1940, Part II. Pp. 363–376.

Walsh, Ann M. *Self-concepts of bright boys with learning difficulties.* New York: Bureau of Publications, Teachers College, Columbia University, 1956.

Warner, W. L. *Social life of a modern community.* New Haven, Conn.: Yale University Press, 1941.

Warner, W. L., Meeker, M., and Eells, K. *Social class in America.* Chicago: Science Research Associates, 1949.

Watson, J. B. *Psychological care of infant and child.* New York: W. W. Norton and Co., 1928.

Watson, J. B. *Psychology from the standpoint of a behaviorist.* Philadelphia: J. B. Lippincott Co., 1924.

Wechsler, D. *The measurement of adult intelligence.* Baltimore: The Williams and Wilkins Co., 1944.

Weininger, O. The effects of early experience on behavior and growth characteristics. *J. comp. physiol. Psychol.*, 1956, 49, 1–9.

Weininger, O. Mortality of albino rats under stress as a function of early handling. *Can. J. Psychol.*, 1953, 7, 111–114.

Weininger, O., McClelland, W. J., and Arima, R. K. Gentling and weight gain in the albino rat. *Can. J. Psychol.*, 1954, 8, 147–151.

Weiss, L. A. Differential variations in the amount of activity of newborn infants under continuous light and sound stimulation. *Univ. Iowa Stud. Child Welfare*, 1934, 9, 9–74.

Wellman, Beth L. Iowa studies on the effects of schooling. *Natl. Soc. Study Educ.*, 39th Yearbook, 1940, Part II. Pp. 377–399.

Wellman, Beth L. IQ changes of preschool and nonpreschool groups during the preschool years: a summary of the literature. *J. Psychol.*, 1945, 20, 347–368.

Wellman, Beth L., and Pegram, Edna, L. Binet IQ changes of orphanage preschool children: a re-analysis. *J. genet. Psychol.*, 1944, 65, 239–263.

Wells, W. D., Weinert, G., and Rubel, Marilyn. Conformity pressure and authoritarian personality. *J. Psychol.*, 1956, 42, 133–136.

Wheeler, L. R. A comparative study of the intelligence of East Tennessee mountain children. *J. educ. Psychol.*, 1942, 33, 321–334.

Whiting, J. W. M. Sorcery, sin, and the superego: a cross-cultural study of some mechanisms of social control. In R. Jones, ed., Nebraska Symposium on Motivation. Lincoln: University of Nebraska Press, 1959, pp. 174–197.

Whiting, J. W. M., and Child, I. L. *Child training and personality.* New Haven, Conn.: Yale University Press, 1953.

Williams, Judith R., and Scott, R. B. Growth and development of Negro infants: IV. Motor development and its relationship to child-rearing practices in two groups of Negro infants. *Child Develpm.*, 1953, 24, 103–121.

Winch, R. F. The relation between the loss of a parent and progress in courtship. *J. soc. Psychol.*, 1949, 29, 51–56.

Winch, R. F. Some data bearing on the Oedipus hypothesis. *J. abnorm. soc. Psychol.*, 1950, 45, 481–489.

Wolfenstein, Martha. Trends in infant care. *Amer. J. Orthopsychiat.*, 1953, 23, 120–130.

Wooley, Helen T. The validity of standards of mental measurement in young childhood. *Sch. and Soc.*, 1925, 21, 476–482.

Worbois, G. M. Changes in Stanford-Binet IQ for rural consolidated and rural one-room school children. *J. exp. Educ.*, 1942, 11, 210–214.

Worcester, D. A. Acceleration: good or bad? American Psychological Association, Division of School Psychologists, Midwestern Psychological Association Meetings, 1959. Mimeographed, 31 p.

Yarrow, L. J. The relationship between nutritive sucking experiences in infancy and non-nutritive sucking in childhood. *J. genet. Psychol.*, 1954, *84*, 149–162.

Young, R. K., Benson, W. M., and Holtzman, W. H. Change in attitudes toward the Negro in a southern university. *J. abnorm. soc. Psychol.*, 1960, *60*, 131–133.

Zelen, S. L. The relationship of peer acceptance, acceptance of others and self-acceptance. Iowa Acad. Sci., *Proc.*, 1954, *61*, 446–449.

Zetterstrom, B. The clinical electroretinogram: IV. The electroretinogram in children during the first year of life. *Acta ophthal.*, 1951, *29*, 295–304.

Zook, Elsie. Sex role preferences in three- and four-year-old children. Unpublished M.A. thesis, State University of Iowa, Iowa Child Welfare Res. Sta., 1959.

Zubek, J. P., and Solberg, Patricia A. *Human development.* New York: McGraw-Hill Book Co., 1954.

Zuckerman, M., Ribback, Beatrice B., Monashkin, I., and Norton, J. A., Jr. Normative data and factor analysis on the parental attitude research instrument. *J. consult. Psychol.*, 1958, *22*, 165–171.

acceleration, for gifted children, 229, 231
acceptance, group, 181–182
and self-acceptance, 196–197, 204
achievement motivation, 418–422, 446
and concrete rewards, 433–434
vs. fear of failure, 422–425
see also level of aspiration
achievement orientation, and dependency, 328
Adams, A. B., 72
Adelson, J., 414–417
adequacy, see self-concept
adjustment
and authoritarianism, 382
and prejudice, 374
and self-concept, 181, 186–187, 193
and self-depreciation, 194–195, 204
admission phenomenon, 182–183
adolescence, 54, 58, 284
definition of, 59
identity diffusion in, 318
proportions in, 288
see also physical growth and physical maturity
adolescents, 198, 308–309
intelligence tests for, 219–221
prejudice in, 372, 373
adopted children, 273
and hereditary factors, 242
intelligence of, 243–245
Adorno, T. W., 359, 360, 361
adulthood, 58
affection, 63
age, and intelligence, 225–228
aggression, 274, 332, 455–456
and early experience, 271–272
and frustration, 426–428
in lower-lower class, 461–463

aggression training, 97–101, 114
aggressiveness, 61
Ainsworth, M., 435
alcohol, use of, 456, 464–465
alcoholism, 153, 165, 168
Alexander, A. M., 222
Allport, G. W., 4
amaurotic idiocy, 239
ambiguity, fear of, 358, 359
ambivalence, 360
amentia, 240
Ames, R., 298–299, 300
Ames window, 4, 5
anal stage, 53, 317, 359, 362
animals, use of, in research, 145, 261–262, 273
anti-Semitism, 358, 359, 372
see also prejudice
anxiety, 28, 56, 57, 154–155, 397
over achievement, 418–422, 446–447
chronic, 419–420
initial, 82
and self-concept, 180–181, 182–183, 193, 204
and sex-role identification, 343
socialization, 82, 89
Appel, M. H., 98–99
approach-avoidance gradients, 158–159, 168
aspiration, see level of aspiration
Atkinson, J. W., 423
attitudes
change of, 198–200
social, 357, 403
audition, 15, 20–21, 31
Australian Bush tribes, 8
authoritarianism
and child-rearing practices, 386–389, 396–398, 402–403
development of, 395–401
in groups, 436–438